EMPLOYMENT LAW

AUSTRALIA
LBC Information Services
Sydney

CANADA and USA
Carswell
Toronto

HONG KONG
Sweet & Maxwell Asia

NEW ZEALAND
Brooker's
Auckland

SINGAPORE and MALAYSIA
Sweet & Maxwell Asia
Singapore and Kuala Lumpur

EMPLOYMENT LAW

By

GWYNETH PITT, LL.B.

*Professor of Law and Dean of the Faculty of Business
at Kingston University*

Published in 2004 by
Sweet & Maxwell Limited of
100 Avenue Road, London NW3 3PF
(http://www.sweetandmaxwell.co.uk)
Typeset by J.P. Price, Chilcompton, Somerset
Printed by Ashford Colour Press, Gosport, Hants

First edition	1992
Second edition	1995
Reprinted	1995
Third edition	1997
Fourth edition	2000
Fifth edition	2004

**A catalogue reference for this book is available
from the British Library**

ISBN 0–421–799–404

To Dorothy and Walter Pitt,
and to the memory of
Stanley William Pitt

Preface

Once again the pace of change in the three years since the last edition of this book has been terrific, with massively important developments in legislation and case law.

When this book was originally published, it was probably the only employment law textbook to include sections on age discrimination, religious discrimination and sexual orientation discrimination in employment alongside discrimination on grounds of sex, race and disability. This approach has now been vindicated, and it is a great pleasure in this edition to be discussing the new sets of Employment Equality Regulations dealing with religion and sexual orientation, as well as the consultation paper on age discrimination. It is unfortunate, however, that the Government's chosen mode of implementing the EU Employment and Race Directives has left us with no fewer than three distinct regimes of discrimination law, depending on what is at stake.

The Employment Act 2002 was called "the stealth Act" by some. It arrived without fanfare (it was not previewed in the Queen's Speech) and it was what one MP called "an empty shell", as it has few substantive provisions and consists mainly of sections empowering the making of regulations. However, the areas dealt with in the Act are fundamental – important new rights for working parents and the most significant changes in the structure of unfair dismissal law since its introduction 30 years ago. It remains to be seen whether the "family-friendly" rights will translate into new patterns of working and the statutory procedures for disciplinary decisions, dismissals and grievances have yet to be finalised, but there is potential for major change.

As well as legislative developments, important decisions have been handed down, not only from British courts but also the European Court of Justice and the European Court of Human Rights, resulting in over 80 new cases being dealt with in this edition. I am grateful to the publishers for allowing me some additional space to deal with these developments, while concealing the extra length to some extent in a larger, more user-friendly format.

It is, of course, axiomatic that a book on employment law will be out of date the moment the "send" button is pressed. As this edition goes to print, the Government has announced its intention to set up a single equality commission, to be called the Commission for Equality and Human Rights, and a new Employment Bill is promised for the forthcoming session of Parliament. For these and other developments, readers should refer to the website accompanying this book: *www.sweetandmaxwell.co.uk/academic*.

Gwyneth Pitt

Contents

Table of Cases

Table of Statutes

Table of Statutory Instruments

Table of European Material

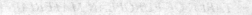

Table of Abbreviations

Acas	Advisory, Concilation and Arbitration Service
ASRS	Amalgamated Society of Railway Servants
AUEW	Amalgamated Union of Engineering Workers
CAC	Central Arbitration Committee
CLJ	Cambridge Law Journal
CLP	Current Legal Problems
COET	Central Office of Employment Tribunals
CRE	Commission for Racial Equality
Crim. L.R.	Criminal Law Review
DDA	Disability Discrimination Act 1995
DPA	Data Protection Act 1998
DRC	Disability Rights Commission
DRCA	Disability Rights Commission Act 1999
EAT	Employment Appeal Tribunal
EC	European Community
ECHR	European Convention on Human Rights
ECJ	European Court of Justice
EEPTU	Electrical, Electronic, Telecommunication and Plumbing Union
EOC	Equal Opportunities Commission
EPA	Employment Protection Act 1975
EPCA	Employment Protection (Consolidation) Act 1978
EqPA	Equal Pay Act 1970
ERA	Employment Rights Act 1996
EU	European Union
HSC	Health and Safety Commission
HSE	Health and Safety Executive
HSWA	Health and Safety at Work, etc., Act 1974
I.L.J.	Industrial Law Journal
ILO	International Labour Organisation
IPCS	Institute of Professional Civil Servants
ITA	Industrial Tribunals Act 1996
ITF	International Transport Workers's Federation
L.Q.R.	Law Quarterly Review
M.L.R.	Modern Law Review
NDC	National Disability Council

NIRC	National Industrial Relations Court
NSFU	National Sailors' and Fireman's Union
NUJ	National Union of Journalists
NUM	National Union Miners
NUR	National Union of Railwaymen
NUS	National Union of Seamen
NUT	National Union of Teachers
NUVB	National Union of Vehicle Builders
O.J.L.S.	Oxford Journal of Legal Studies
PAYE	Pay as you earn
POEU	Post Office Engineering Union
RMT	Rail Maritime and Transport Union
ROET	Regional Office of Employment Tribunals
RRA	Race Relations Act 1976
SDA	Sex Discrimination Act 1975
SMP	Statutory maternity pay
SSP	Statutory sick pay
TICE	Transnational Information and Consultation of Employees Regulations 1999
TUC	Trades Union Congress
TULRA	Trade Union and Labour Relations Act 1974
TULRCA	Trade Union and Labour Relations (Consolidation) Act 1992
TUPE	Transfer of Undertakings (Protection of Employment) Regulations 1981 (S.I. 1981 No. 1794)
TURERA	Trade Union Reform and Employment Rights Act 1993
UCW	Union of Communication Workers
UPOW	Union of Post Office Workers

Further Reading

Chapter 1 – Further Reading

Labour Market Trends (formerly *Employment Gazette*), published by the Office for National Statistics supplies statistics and useful analyses of the British labour market.

Acas, the Certification Officer, the CAC, CRE, DRC and EOC all issue Annual Reports, which are an invaluable source of information about their work and their perceptions of it.

Many institutions also have useful information on their websites:

Acas	www.acas.org.uk
CAC	www.cac.gov.uk
Certification Officer	www.certoff.org
CRE	www.cre.gov.uk
DRC	www.drc.gov.uk
EOC	www.eoc.org.uk
EAT	www.employmentappeals.gov.uk
EU	www.europa.eu.int
ILO	www.ilo.org
Low Pay Commission	www.lowpay.gov.uk

On the changing role of the EAT, see the articles by its Presidents:
Browne-Wilkinson J., "The Role of the Employment Appeal Tribunal in the 1980s" (1982) 11 I.L.J. 69.
Phillips J., "Some Notes on the Employment Appeal Tribunal" (1978) 7 I.L.J. 137.

Popplewell J., "Random Thoughts from the President's Chair" (1987) 16 I.L.J. 209.
Waite J., "Lawyers and Laymen as Judges in Industry" (1986) 15 I.L.J. 32.
Wood J., "The Employment Appeal Tribunal as it enters the 1990s" (1990) 19 I.L.J. 133.

and on employment tribunals:

J.K. MacMillan, "Employment tribunals: philosophies and practicalities" (1999) 28 I.L.J. 33.
Resolving Employment Rights Disputes, Cm. 2707 (1994).

On the influence of the EU see:

B. Bercusson, "The Dynamic of European Labour Law after Maastricht" (1994) 23 I.L.J. 1.
B. Hepple, "The Implementation of the Community Charter of Fundamental Social Rights" (1990) 53 M.L.R. 643.
R. Nielsen and E. Szyszczak, *The Social Dimension of the European Union,* Copenhagen Business School, 1997.
Lord Wedderburn, *The Social Charter, European company and employment rights,* (Institute of Employment Rights, 1990).

The monthly journal *European Industrial Relations Review* is a useful source of current EU developments in employment law.
Eds B Towers and W Brown, *Employee Relations in Britain: 25 Years of ACAS,* Blackwell, 2000.
S. Palmer, "Human rights: implications for labour law", [2000] C.L.J. 168.
R. Nielsen, *European Labour Law*, Copenhagen, DJO/F Publishing, 2000.
R. Rideout, "What shall we do with the CAC?", 31 I.L.J. 1 (2002).

Chapter 2 – Further Reading

There is an enormous literature on this area. In addition to the books and articles mentioned, an invaluable source of references is the bi-monthly journal *Equal Opportunities Review* (Industrial Relations Services).

N. Addison and T. Lawson-Cruttenden, *Harassment Law and Practice,* (Blackstone Press, 1998).
C. Barnard. *E.C. Employment Law,* (OUP, 2nd ed., 2000).
Mark Bell, *Anti-Discrimination Law and the European Union*, OUP, 2002.
B. Bercusson, *European Labour Law,* (Butterworths, 2nd ed., 2003).
G. Clayton and G. Pitt, "Dress Codes and Freedom of Expression" (1997) 1 *European Human Rights Law Review* 52.
H. Collins, "Discrimination, equality and social inclusion", 66 M.L.R. 16 (2003).
J. Dine and B. Watt (ed.) *Discrimination Law: Limits and Justifications* (Longmans, 1996).

B. Doyle, *Disability, Discrimination – law and practice* (Jordans, 4th ed., 2003).
E. Ellis, *EC Sex Equality Law*, 2nd ed., Clarendon Press, 1998.
Sandra Fredman, *Discrimination Law*, OUP, 2002.
S. Fredman, *Women and the Law*, (Clarendon Press, 1997).
B. Hepple and E. Szyszczak (ed.), *Discrimination: the Limits of Law* (Mansell, 1992).
C. Docksey, "The Principle of Equality between Women and Men as a Fundamental Right under Community Law" (1991) 20 I.L.J. 258.
B. Doyle, "Disabled Workers' Rights, the Disability Discrimination Act and the UN Standard Rules" (1996) 25 I.L.J. 1.
S. Fredman, "Reversing discrimination" (1997) 113 L.Q.R. 575–600.
C. McCrudden, "Institutional Discrimination" (1982) 2 O.J.L.S. 303.
C. McCrudden, "Merit principles" (1998) 18 OJLS 543–579.
G. Moon and R. Allen, "Substantive rights and equal treatment in respect of religion and belief: towards a better understanding of rights and their implications", [2000] E.H.R.L.R. 580.
R. Wintemute, "Recognising new kinds of sex discrimination: transsexualism, sexual orientation and dress codes" (1997) 60 M.L.R. 334-359.

Chapter 3 – Further Reading

H. Collins, "Independent Contractors and the Challenge of Vertical Disintegration to Employment Protection Law" (1990) 10 O.J.L.S. 353.
L. Dickens, *Whose Flexibility? Discrimination and equality issues in atypical work* (Institute of Employment Rights, 1992).
M. Freedland, *The Personal Employment Contract*, OUP, 2003.
J. Kenner, "Statement or contract? – Some reflections on the EC Employee Information (Contract or Employment Relationship) Directive after *Kampelmann*", (1999) 28 I.L.J. 205.
G. Pitt, "Law, Fact and Casual Workers" (1985) 101 L.Q.R. 217.
E. Szyszczak, *Partial Unemployment: the Regulation of Short-Time Working in Britain* (Mansell, 1990).

Chapter 4 – Further Reading

D. Brodie, "Beyond exchange: the new contract of employment", (1998) 27 I.L.J. 79.
D. Brodie, "Legal coherence and the employment revolution", 117 L.Q.R. 604 (2001).
J. Craig, *Privacy and Employment Law*, Hart Publishing, 1999.
Y. Cripps, *The Legal Implications of Disclosure in the Public Interest* (ESC Publishing, 2nd ed., 1995).
M. Ford, "Two conceptions of worker privacy", 31 I.L.J. 135 (2002).
M. Freedland, *The Personal Employment Contract*, OUP, 2003.
J. Gobert and M. Punch, "Whistleblowers, the public interest and the Public Interest Disclosure Act 1998" (2000) 63 M.L.R. 25–54.

B. Hepple, "A Right to Work?" (1981) 10 I.L.J. 65.

Lindsay J., "The implied term of trust and confidence", 30 I.L.J. 1 (2001).

H. Oliver, "Email and Internet Monitoring in the Workplace: information privacy and contracting-out", 31 I.L.J. 321 (2002).

G. Pitt, "Rights and Employee Rights: the case of free speech" in *Understanding Human Rights,* eds C. Gearty and A. Tomkins, (Mansell, 1995).

L. Vickers, *Freedom of Speech and Employment*, OUP, 2002.

Chapter 5 – Further Reading

B. Bercusson, "Collective Bargaining and the Protection of Social Rights in Europe", in eds K. Ewing, C. Gearty and B. Hepple, *Human Rights and Labour law* (Mansell, 1994).

B. Bercusson, "The European social model comes to Britain", 31 I.L.J. 209, (2002).

M. Carley and M. Hall, "The implementation of the European Works Councils Directive", (2000) 29 I.L.J. 103.

P. Davies and M. Freedland, *Kahn-Freund's Labour and the Law* (Stevens, 3rd ed., 1983) Chaps 3, 5 and 6.

H. Gospel and G. Lockwood, "Disclosure of information for collective bargaining: the CAC approach revisited", (1999) 28 I.L.J. 233.

M. Hall, "Beyond Recognition? Employee Representation and E.U. Law" (1996) 25 I.L.J. 15.

B. Simpson, "Trade union recognition and the law, a new approach" (2000) 29 I.L.J. 193.

Lord Wedderburn, "Collective bargaining or legal enactment: the 1999 Act and union recognition", (2000) 29 I.L.J. 1.

Lord Wedderburn, "Collective bargaining or legal enactment: the 1999 Act and union recognition", 29 I.L.J. 1, (2000).

Lord Wedderburn, "Consultation and collective bargaining in Europe: success or ideology?, (1997) 26 I.L.J. 1.

A. Wilson, "Contract and Prerogative: a Reconsideration of the Legal Enforcement of Collective Agreements" (1984) 13 I.L.J. 1.

Chapter 6 – Further Reading

S. Evans and R. Lewis, "Anti-Union Discrimination: Practice, Law and Policy" (1987) 16 I.L.J. 88.

M. Gray, "A recalcitrant partner: the UK reaction to the Working Time Directive", 17 Yearbook of European Law 323.

A. McColgan, "Family friendly frolics? The Maternity and Parental Leave etc Regulations 1999", (2000) 29 I.L.J. 125.

S. McRae, *Maternity Rights in Britain* (Policy Studies Institute, 1991).

G. Pitt and J. Fairhurst, *Blackstone's Guide to Working Time*, (Blackstone Press, 1998).

Chapter 7 – Further Reading

On equal pay see: S. Fredman, "The Poverty of Equality: Pensions and the ECJ" (1996) 25 I.L.J. 91.

A. Lester and D. Rose, "Equal Value Claims and Sex Bias in Collective Bargaining" (1991) 20 I.L.J. 163.

A. McColgan, *Just Wages for Women*, (Clarendon Press, 1997).

C. McCrudden, "Third Time Lucky? The Pensions Act 1995 and Equal Treatment in Occupational Pensions" (1996) 25 I.L.J. 28.

On protection for low-paid workers, see:

S. Deakin and F. Wilkinson, *Labour Law, Social Security and Economic Inequality* (Institute of Employment Rights, 1989).

S. Deakin and F. Wilkinson, "Rights v Efficiency? The Economic Case for Transnational Labour Standards" (1994) 23 I.L.J. 289.

T. Goriely, "Arbitrary deductions from pay and the proposed repeal of the Truck Acts" (1983) 12 I.L.J. 236 (an authoritative account of the abuses which prompted the special provision for retail workers).

S. Keevash, "Wages Councils: an Examination of Trade Union and Conservative Government Misconceptions about the effect of Statutory Wage-Fixing" (1985) 14 I.L.J. 217.

C. Pond, *The Great Pay Robbery* (Low Pay Unit, 1988).

B. Simpson, "Implementing the National Minimum Wage – the 1999 regulations", (1999) 28 I.L.J. 171.

Chapter 8 – Further Reading

H. Collins, *Justice in Dismissal: the Law of Termination of Employment* (Clarendon Press, 1992).

D. Brodie, "Specific performance and employment contracts" (note), (1998) 27 I.L.J. 37.

H. Collins, "The Meaning of Job Security" (1992) 20 I.L.J. 227.

L. Dickens, M. Jones, B. Weekes, M. Hart, *Dismissed* (Basil Blackwell, 1985).

P. Elias, "Fairness in Unfair Dismissal: Trends and Tensions" (1981) 10 I.L.J. 201.

K. Ewing and A. Grubb, "The Emergence of a New Labour Injunction?" (1987) 16 I.L.J. 145.

K. Ewing, "Job Security and the Contract of Employment" (1989) 18 I.L.J. 217.

M. Freedland, *The Personal Employment Contract*, OUP, 2003.

P. Goulding, "Injunctions and Contracts of Employment: the Evening Standard Doctrine" (1990) 19 I.L.J. 98.

G. Pitt, "Dismissal at Common Law: the Relevance in Britain of American Developments" (1989) 52 M.L.R. 22.

G. Pitt, "Justice in Dismissal: a Reply to Hugh Collins" (1993) 22 I.L.J. 251.

Chapter 9 – Further Reading

A. Garde, "Recent developments in the law relating to transfers of undertakings", 39 C.M.L.Rev. 523.

C. Grunfeld, *The Law of Redundancy* (Sweet & Maxwell, 3rd ed., 1989).

Ed. J. McMullen, *Redundancy: the Law and Practice*, Sweet & Maxwell, 2000.

John McMullen, *Business Transfers and Employee Rights* (Butterworths, looseleaf).

C. de Groot, "The Council Directive on the safeguarding of employees' rights in the event of transfers of undertakings: an overview of recent case law" 35 C.M.L.R. 707.

B. Napier, *CCT, Market Testing and Employment Rights* (Institute of Employment Rights, 1993).

M. Sargeant, "New Transfer Regulations", 31 I.L.J. 35 (2002).

Chapter 10 – Further Reading

S. Corby, "Limitations on Freedom of Association in the Civil Service and the ILO's response" (1986) 15 I.L.J. 161.

B. Creighton, "The ILO and Protection of Freedom of Association in the United Kingdom" in eds K. Ewing, C. Gearty and B. Hepple, *Human Rights and Labour Law* (Mansell, 1994).

P. Davies and M. Freedland, *Kahn-Freund's Labour and the Law* (Stevens, 3rd ed., 1983), Chap. 7 (very out of date on the law, but still worth reading for the arguments).

S. Dunn and J. Gennard, *The Closed Shop in British Industry* (Macmillan, 1984).

P. Elias and K. Ewing, *Trade Union Democracy, Members' Rights and the Law* (Mansell, 1987) Chaps 1, 3, 5.

K. Ewing, *Britain and the ILO* (Institute of Employment Rights, 2nd ed., 1994).

K. Ewing, "The implications of *Wilson and Palmer*", 32 I.L.J. 1 (2003).

M. Forde, "The 'Closed Shop' Case" (1982) 11 I.L.J. 1.

W. McCarthy, *The Closed Shop in Britain* (Basil Blackwell, 1964) (this is the clasic study; Dunn and Gennard present an updated survey).

G. Morris, "Freedom of Association and the Interests of the State" in eds K. Ewing, C. Gearty and B. Hepple, *Human Rights and Labour Law* (Mansell, 1994).

G. Morris and T. Archer, *Collective Labour Law,* (Hart Publishing, 2000).

T. Novitz, "Freedom of association and *Fairness at Work*: an assessment of the impact and relevance of ILO Convention No 87 on its fiftieth anniversary", (1998) 27 I.L.J. 169.

T. Novitz, "International promises and domestic pragamatism: to what extent will the Employment Relations Act 1999 implement international labour standards relating to freedom of association?", 63 M.L.R. 379 (2000).

H. Pelling, *A History of British Trade Unionism* (Macmillan, 4th ed., 1987).

F. von Prondzynski, *Freedom of Association and Industrial Relations* (Mansell, 1987).

B. Simpson, "Individualism versus Collectivism" (1993) 22 I.L.J. 181.

Lord Wedderburn, "Freedom of Association and Philosophies of Labour Law" (1989) 18 I.L.J. 1.

Lord Wedderburn, "Freedom of Association or Right to Organise? The Commons Law and International Sources" in Wedderburn, *Employment Rights in Britain and Europe* (Lawrence and Wishart, 1991).

For the Conservative Government's arguments on the closed shop during the 1980s, see:

Removing Barriers to Employment, Cm. 655 (1989) Chap. 2;

Trade Unions and Their Members, Cm. 95 (1987) Chap. 4;

Working Paper for Consultations on Proposed Industrial Relations Legislation – Closed Shop (Department of Employment, July 1979).

Chapter 11 – Further Reading

J. Bowers and S. Auerbach, *The Employment Act 1988* (Blackstone Press, 1988) Chaps 3, 4, 6, 7.

P. Elias and K. Ewing, *Trade Union Democracy, Members' Rights and the Law* (Mansell, 1987) Chaps 2, 4–8.

K. Ewing, "The Strike, the Courts and the Rule-Books" (1985) 14 I.L.J. 160 (on the litigation in the miners' strike 1984–1985).

K. Ewing, *Trade Unions, the Labour Party and the Law* (Edinburgh University Press, 1982) (but note that this is pre the 1984 amendments).

R. Kidner, "Trade Union Democracy: Election of Trade Unions Officers" (1984) 13 I.L.J. 193 (on the Trade Union Act 1984).

The thinking of the Conservative Government over the 1980s on this area may be followed through its Green Papers preceding trade union law reform:

Democracy in Trade Unions, Cmnd. 8778 (1983);

Industrial Relations in the 1990s, Cm. 1602 (1991) Chaps 1, 2, 5, 6, 7;

Removing Barriers to Employment, Cm. 655 (1989);

Trade Unions and Their Members, Cm. 95 (1987).

Chapters 12 – Further Reading

R. Benedictus, "The Use of the Law of Tort in the Miners' Dispute" (1985) 14 I.L.J. 176.

H. Carty, *An Analysis of the Economic Torts*, OUP, 2001.

P. Elias and K. Ewing, "Economic Torts and Labour Law: old principles and new liabilities" (1982) C.L.J. 321.

P. Elias, "The Strike and Breach of Contract: a Reassessment" in eds K. Ewing, C. Gearty and B. Hepple, *Human Rights and Labour Law* (Mansell, 1994).

K. Ewing, *The Right to Strike* (Clarendon Press, 1991).

K. Miller and C. Woolfson, "Timex, Industrial Relations and the Use of the Law in the 1990s" (1994) 23 I.L.J. 209.

B. Napier, "Strikes and the Individual Worker" (1987) C.L.J. 287.

G. Pitt, *The Limits of Industrial Action* (I.E.R., 1995).

R. Rideout, "Industrial Relations: the empire strikes back," [1997] C.L.P. 361.

M. Sterling, "Actions for Duress, Seafarers and Industrial Disputes" (1982) 11 I.L.J. 156.

Chapter 13 – Further Reading

S. Auerbach, "Injunction Procedure in the Seafarers' Dispute" (1988) 17 I.L.J. 227.

S. Auerbach, "Legal Restraint of Picketing: New Trends; New Tensions" (1987) 16 I.L.J. 227.

S. Auerbach, *Legislating for Conflict* (Clarendon Press, 1990).

H. Carty, "The Public Order Act 1986: Police Powers and the Picket Line" (1987) 16 I.L.J. 146.

K. Ewing and B. Napier, "The Wapping Dispute and Labour Law" [1986] C.L.J. 285.

A. Goodhart, "The Legality of the General Strike" (1926) 36 Yale Law Journal 464 (reprinted in Goodhart, *Essays in Jurisprudence and the Common Law*).

G. Lightman, "A Trade Union in Chains: Scargill Unbound—the Legal Constraints of Receivership and Sequestration" (1987) 40 C.L.P. 25.

G. Morris, "Industrial Action in Essential Services: the New Law" (1991) 20 I.L.J. 89.

G. Morris, "Industrial Action: Public and Private Interests" (1993) 22 I.L.J. 194.

"The Public Order Act 1986" [1987] Crim. L.R. 156, especially P. Wallington "(3) Some Implications for the Policing of Industrial Disputes" at p. 180.

G. Morris, *Strikes in Essential Services* (Mansell, 1986).

P. Wallington, "Injunctions and the Right to Demonstrate [1986] C.L.J. 86.

P. Wallington, "Policing the Miners' Strike" (1985) 14 I.L.J. 145.

The Department of Education and Employment's monthly *Labour Market Trends* publishes annual statistics about strikes.

The thinking of the Conservative Government over the 1980s on this area may be followed through its papers preceding trade union law reform:

Democracy in Trade Unions, Cmnd. 8778 (1983), Chap. 3;
Industrial Relations in the 1990s, Cm. 1602 (1991) Chaps 1–4;
Removing Barriers to Employment, Cm. 655 (1989), Chap. 3;
Review of Public Order Law, Cmnd. 9510 (1985);
Trade Union Immunities, Cmnd. 8128 (1981);
Unofficial Action and the Law, Cm. 821 (1989);

Working Paper for Consultations on Proposed Industrial Relations Legislation—Picketing (Department of Employment, July 1979);
Working Paper on Secondary Industrial Action (Department of Employment, February 1980).

Chapter 14 – Further Reading

B. Barrett, "Harassment at work: a matter of health and safety" [2000] J.B.L. 214.

B. Barrett and P. James, "Safe Systems: Past, Present—and Future?" (1988) 17 I.L.J. 26.

S. Dawson, P. William, A. Clinton and M. Bamford, *Safety at Work: the limits of self-regulation* (Cambridge University Press, 1988).

P. James, *The European Community: a positive force for U.K. health and safety law?* (Institute of Employment Rights, 1993).

P. James and D. Walters "Non-union rights of involvement: the case of health and safety at work", (1997) 26 I.L.J. 35.

C. Miller, *Health and Safety at Work*, (Sweet & Maxwell, 2nd ed., 2000).

K. Miller, "Piper Alpha and the Cullen Report" (1991) 20 I.L.J. 176.

R. Moore, *The Price of Safety* (Institute of Employment Rights, 1991).

G. Shannon, *Health and Safety: Law and Practice*, Round Hall, 2002.

Other useful websites for Employment Law

www.incomesdata.co.uk	Incomes Data Services website
www.hmso.gov.uk	HMSO – for legislation, etc.
www.courtservice.gov.uk/judgments	Judgments
www.tuc.org.uk	TUC website
www.bailii.org	British and Irish Legal Information Institute website – general legislation and case law
www.dti.gov.uk	Department of Trade and Industry
www.dwp.gov.uk	Department for Work and Pensions

1. Introduction

In the mid-fourteenth century about half of the adult working population **1–001** was wiped out by the Black Death. The workers who were left found that they were suddenly a scarce commodity and could command a high price for their services, to the chagrin of the powerful landowners who employed them. The Statutes of Labourers 1349 and 1351 were soon passed, fixing wages at the pre-plague rates and making it a criminal offence for workers to leave employment without their employers' consent. In Tudor times this was transformed into a system where justices of the peace fixed wage rates for different sorts of jobs in their localities, a jurisdiction which was only abolished in the nineteenth century, although it had fallen into disuse some time earlier.

There was no free market in labour then, and there is no free market now. Today the employment relationship is characterised by an enormous amount of statutory regulation aimed at achieving a proper balance between the interests of the parties. However, it remains the case that the central relationship between employer and worker is one of contract, on which the statutory requirements operate. Common law contract principles remain important in interpreting the statutes, although some would argue that they operate as a negative force.

Contract law has always been predicated on the notion that the parties are assumed to enter freely into agreements on the basis of roughly equal bargaining power. The role of the law is seen as facilitating the process of agreement and then supporting observance of the agreement, but not intervening to control the substance of it: the parties are free to agree pretty well what they want. Today it is generally acknowledged that equal bargaining power rarely exists, even between businesses, let alone between businesses and individuals. Hence in the post-war period we have seen legislation intervening on behalf of the weaker party to prevent undue exploitation, a trend of which the Unfair Contract Terms Act 1977 is a good example.

In the employment sphere particularly, the bargaining power of the **1–002** parties is inherently unequal. The employer usually holds all the trumps; but for a few exceptionally talented people most of us are in greater need of an employer than the employer is in need of us. The would-be worker is rarely in a position to negotiate about terms. The only choice is to take it or leave it.

1

But employees can equalise the situation if they all act together. Individually they are weak, but an employer cannot ignore them if they combine and act in concert. This is the *raison d'être* and principal justification for trade unions. "Men who have no property except their manual skill and strength ought to be allowed to confer together, if they think fit, for the purpose of determining at what rate they will sell their property", as Sir Robert Peel put it in the debates on the Combination Acts 1824 and 1825.

The history of employment law in the nineteenth century is very much the story of trade unions' struggle to shake off criminal liability for their activities and then to achieve legal status in the eyes of the civil law. By 1906, when the Trade Disputes Act was passed, trade unions had attained a legally recognised status and were able to take industrial action in pursuit of their objectives with impunity most of the time. The attitude of the law was fairly laissez-faire; unions and employers should get on with reaching their own agreements, and if unable to do so, unions were free to take industrial action to press their demands and employers were free to dismiss workers and to try to find more amenable employees.

1–003 This historical development leads to a feature of British industrial relations which is wholly unlike most of our industrialised partners: the agreements (collective bargains) made between employers and trade unions almost never have the status of binding contracts. They are informal understandings, binding in honour only. One of the problems that the law has faced is explaining how it is that these agreements have any effect as between the worker and the employer (see below, Chapter 5). This is a facet of a wider issue: the law is structured on the whole to deal with disputes between two individual parties and vindicating the rights of one or the other. In practice for many workers in the United Kingdom the work relationship is tripartite: they are represented for negotiating purposes by a trade union. The union, as the collective voice of the employees, may at times be at odds with individual members, but the traditions of the common law and the experience of judges and counsel militate against an understanding of collective interests. This tension is frequently visible in the operation of the law as it relates to trade union affairs in particular and has led some commentators to call for the replacement of common law principles by a Labour Code which would be tailored to the realities of the situation, as has happened in other countries (compare the National Labor Relations Act in the United States). The closest we have got to a Labour Code, however, during 1971–74 when the Industrial Relations Act 1971 was in force, was not a happy experience for trade unions or employers. It was ostensibly modelled on the United States code, but in fact adopted many of the control measures in that legislation without the *quid pro quo* of union rights and safeguards; nevertheless, it dampened the enthusiasm for a code among many involved in industrial relations.

The laissez-faire, non-interventionist stance from the beginning of the twentieth century until the 1960s meant that the focus in industrial relations was on the collective bargaining process. There was a consensus that this was the best way to conduct industrial relations and that the role of the law should be to support the process. During the last 40 years of the twentieth century, however, the picture changed in a number of important respects.

In 1963 the Contracts of Employment Act was passed, the first of what became a flood of statutes offering protection to employees, and in 1964 industrial (later called employment) tribunals were set up, with jurisdiction over statutory claims. The pace of legislation was leisurely in the 1960s but exploded in the 1970s when the action for unfair dismissal was introduced and the principal anti-discrimination statutes applying to employment were passed. Far from undermining the role of trade unions, protective legislation operated for strong unions as a minimum starting point, a springboard to better terms and conditions for their members. Furthermore, trade unions had an essential part to play in helping members to enforce their rights. As legal aid is generally not available for employment tribunal claims, trade unions were needed to fill the gap.

In 1979 the Conservative administration of Margaret Thatcher was **1–004** returned to power with a mission, among other things, to break trade union power and to move away from collective negotiation of terms and conditions of employment. This was assisted by moves to privatise the nationalised industries, to reduce the size of the public sector and to introduce the market-driven philosophy of the private sector into the remaining public services. From the Employment Act 1980 to the Trade Union Reform and Employment Rights Act 1993 (TURERA) substantial new pieces of legislation were introduced on a biennial and sometimes annual basis. The most visible effects of these were in the field of industrial action, where it became more and more difficult to organise lawful strikes, but other important changes outlawed all manifestations of the closed shop and intervened substantially in the internal affairs of trade unions, prescribing their relationships with their members. It was during this time that the previous hostility of many trade unions to the European Union began to melt away, for it was only via EU directives and decisions of the European Court of Justice (ECJ) that there was any advance in legal protection for workers.

In May 1997 the 18-year Conservative administration was replaced by a Labour Government whose watchwords were social justice and social inclusion. However, the new Government was anxious to keep the goodwill of the business community and to avoid any suggestion of a return to what were perceived as the days of too much union power and too many strikes. In its first term of office the new Labour Government planned only one major piece of employment legislation, the Employment Relations Act 1999, although this took the major steps of re-introducing compulsory recognition of unions by employers (see Chapter 5) and improving protection for individuals taking part in industrial action (see Chapter 12). However, two other government initiatives proved to be of almost equal importance in the employment law field. First, at the Treaty of Amsterdam negotiations in 1997 the United Kingdom agreed to be bound by the Social Chapter protocol which had been agreed by all the other Member States of the EC at the Treaty of Maastricht in 1993. That meant that a number of social policy directives, such as those on transnational consultation, part-time work and parental leave, became applicable at once and the way was opened for future developments in relation to such topics as fixed-term contracts and the extension of anti-discrimination legislation. Secondly, the Human Rights Act 1998 was passed, allowing the provisions of the

European Convention on Human Rights to be enforced in British law, which brought rights into the workplace in a wholly novel way.

In its second term of office (from June 2001) the Government's focus for employment law became the work-life balance and, in particular, the implementation of "family-friendly" policies – improved maternity rights, new rights to paternity leave and parental leave and a right to request flexible working (see Chapter 6). At the same time European Union law reform proceeded apace, with particular emphasis on extending workers' protection, both through wider anti-discrimination provisions (see Chapter 2) and through inclusion of marginalised groups of workers such as fixed-term and agency workers (see Chapter 3).

1–005 Although compulsory recognition may lead to an upturn in the extent of collective bargaining, reversing the wane of the last 20 years, it is likely that this will continue alongside an increasing focus on a rights-based structure. The language of treaties such as the European Convention on Human Rights and the Conventions of the International Labour Organization (ILO) is the language of rights. The Treaty of Rome speaks to Member States in mandatory terms, but the ECJ permits individuals to sue their own states on the basis of a failure to comply, which is also a process of vindication of rights. Directives in the employment field have been implemented by giving new statutory employment protection rights to workers. As the rights culture develops, rights discourse will be more and more important in the workplace.

The rest of this chapter will outline some of the major institutions in British employment law. This part may be used as a reference section to be consulted when unfamiliar organisations are mentioned.

Institutions of Employment Law

Advisory, Conciliation and Arbitration Service (Acas)

1–006 The Advisory, Conciliation and Arbitration Service (Acas) was set up in 1974. Its existence as a statutory independent body with a wide remit in industrial relations was established by the Employment Protection Act 1975 (EPA); the relevant law is now to be found in the Trade Union and Labour Relations (Consolidation) Act 1992 (TULRCA). Under s.209 it is charged with the general duty of promoting improvement in industrial relations. Originally the Acas mission specifically included a duty to encourage the extension of collective bargaining, reflecting the former political commitment to voluntary collective bargaining as the appropriate means of regulating industrial relations mentioned above. However, a Department of Employment quinquennial review of Acas in 1992 recommended that this be deleted because of the decline in importance of collective bargaining (on which, see Chapter 5). Its terms of reference were altered in 1993 by TURERA, deleting the reference to collective bargaining and adding that its duty should be carried out "in particular by exercising its functions in relation to the settlement of trade disputes". This new emphasis did not make a real difference in practice to the functions of Acas, but in so far as it could be regarded as restrictive, the repeal of those words by the Employment Relations Act 1999 was welcome.

The constitution of Acas is set out in TULRCA, ss.247–253. It is governed by a council chaired by an appointee of the Secretary of State (who may be appointed on a part-time basis since 1993) and has nine members, three representing employers, three representing trade unions and three independents. This kind of tripartite structure has been traditional in all sorts of industrial relations organisations from the ILO to employment tribunals. While the funding for Acas is provided by the government, its independence from government interference is specifically guaranteed by s.247(3). TURERA, s.251A granted the Secretary of State power to require Acas to charge for some services, but this has been limited to some of its publications and conferences. The success of Acas is largely conditional on its being perceived as independent and its reputation for independence and impartiality would be damaged if it were seen to be profiting from its services.

Advice

As its name suggests, Acas has a variety of functions, which are carried out **1–007** by over 800 staff, principally based at 11 regional centres. In practice, advice is an important function, with some 750,000 inquiries a year being dealt with by telephone helplines. Anyone may telephone with employment queries and receive free advice. Since 2001 there has been a dedicated helpline, Equality Direct, to advise employers on equality issues. Advice is also given through the medium of seminars, training events and advisory handbooks on many aspects of employment relations. These advisory handbooks must be distinguished from the Codes of Practice also issued by Acas: the latter, but not the former, have a certain legal status.

Conciliation

Conciliation may be defined as bringing disputing parties together with a **1–008** view to facilitating them reaching agreement by themselves without further legal process. Acas's main activity is providing individual conciliation in situations where employees are in dispute with their employer, for example where they claim to have been unfairly dismissed. This is because virtually all applications to employment tribunals are referred to an Acas officer for conciliation, to see if there is any possibility of settlement without going through with a tribunal hearing. This is a huge workload. In 2001–2002 there were over 100,000 references to Acas, more than double the 52,000 in 1989–1990 and nearly four times the caseload in 1983.

Since legal aid is not available for employment tribunal hearings, it is often only when talking to an Acas officer that the applicant begins to appreciate whether or not she has a good claim; sometimes this is true of employers also. Usually about three-quarters of all tribunal applications are either settled or withdrawn following Acas conciliation. Thus the conciliation procedure seems to act as a successful filter to tribunal hearings.

Acas also offers conciliation services in collective disputes. It is a voluntary process, although many collective agreements make provision for Acas conciliation in the event of deadlock on a particular issue. The idea is that an independent but knowledgeable third party acting as go-between may be able to take some of the heat out of a dispute and may sometimes be able to help the parties see a way forward. Under TULRCA, s.210, Acas need not wait to be asked by one side before offering its services, but the parties are not bound to accept. It seems to be an effective part of the organisation's activities: in 2001–2002 Acas reported 1,371 requests for collective conciliation and assessed it as unsuccessful in only 104 cases. About a quarter of Acas's collective conciliation caseload is now concerned with union recognition, since the introduction of the statutory procedure (see para. 5–015 below).

Acas has found that disputes triggering a request for conciliation often stem from deeper underlying problems, frequently precipitated by the wholesale, rapid organisational changes which typify private and public sector organisations today. To tackle these in a preventive manner, it has developed techniques of advisory mediation. Mediators have more discretion than conciliators in initiating possible courses of action, and more flexibility than arbitrators, in that they are not limited to deciding between the claims of the parties. The preferred way of working is for senior Acas staff to set up and chair joint working groups of management and employee representatives to deal with each issue. Again, the system is successful and Acas aims to carry out about 500 advisory mediation projects each year.

Arbitration

1–009 Arbitration does mean making a decision between the parties. Under TULRCA, s.212, where a trade dispute exists or appears to be imminent Acas may offer arbitration where requested by one party to a dispute, but only as long as all parties agree. Thus the process is again voluntary; furthermore, the arbitrator's decision is not legally binding, although in practice it will be followed. If the parties are prepared to refer the matter to arbitration, they are fairly certain to accept the result. Before setting up an arbitration, Acas should consider whether an agreement can be reached through conciliation and negotiation and should try this route first. If arbitration is inevitable, it is not provided by Acas personnel but either through the Central Arbitration Committee (CAC) or by an arbitrator selected from a panel maintained by Acas. The virtue of arbitration has traditionally been that it is not committed to an outright win for one side or the other; compromises may be ordered where appropriate. In 2001–2002 only 68 references were made to Acas for arbitration, the majority of which were to deal with one-off issues, typically about pay and conditions of employment, but including 22 dismissal cases.

In the 1990s the extension of arbitration to a wider range of individual employment matters was mooted, partly as a response to the ever-increasing workload of tribunals and partly in acknowledgment that tribunal proceedings are often much more legalistic than was ever intended, meaning that they are frequently not speedy, cheap or informal. The length of time that therefore elapses between the cause of the dispute and the tribunal hearing and the increasing use of legal representation means that it is in practice unlikely that the applicant will be re-employed at the end of any proceedings. It was therefore decided that an arbitration procedure should be set up as an alternative to tribunal proceedings. The Employment Rights (Dispute Resolution) Act 1998 inserted a new TULRCA, s.212A empowering Acas to draw up an arbitration scheme for certain individual disputes. Although it was originally intended to introduce this in 1999, it was not until May 2001 that it finally came into force. The Acas Arbitration Scheme applies only to unfair dismissal cases where the sole question is whether or not the dismissal was unfair. If there are other issues (such as whether the worker is qualified to claim or whether there was a dismissal at all) then the case cannot be dealt with by an arbitrator but must go to a tribunal. The Scheme is voluntary and will apply only where the parties agree in writing that they wish the case to be handled in this way and are prepared to waive their rights to have the case heard by a tribunal. The arbitration is carried out by an independent arbitrator appointed by Acas who is enjoined to "have regard to general principles of fairness and good conduct in employment relations" (including relevant Acas Codes of Practice) instead of applying legal tests – although he must apply any relevant EU law. This is one of the great uncertainties of the Scheme: if arbitrators do not follow legal principle, how are fairness and consistency to be ensured? Given that the arbitrator's decision cannot be appealed, there must be doubt as to whether parties will be willing to take the risk of submitting themselves to this process – a doubt borne out by the fact that in the first 10 months of the Scheme only 13 cases went to arbitration. Acas believes that this is because of parties' ignorance of the potential benefits of arbitration. What are these? First, it should be very quick – cases are meant to be heard within two months of the matter being referred for arbitration. It should be cheap. Cases are heard at a neutral venue, such as an Acas office or an hotel room and are expected to last only half a day. There is no cross-examination of witnesses – any questioning is done by the arbitrator. Parties can have representation, including legal representation, but will not be able to recover any costs for this. Perhaps the main advantage for an employer is the avoidance of publicity, as hearings are held in private. The main advantage for an employee is that there is much more chance of being re-employed at the end of the proceedings. However, it seems that it may take some while for individual arbitration to catch on.

Codes of practice

The power of Acas to issue codes of practice "containing such practical **1–010** guidance as the Service thinks fit for the purpose of promoting the improvement of industrial relations" (TULRCA, s.199) is extremely important. These codes of practice are not legally binding, in that failure to follow the requirements of the code will not of itself attract liability, but they are to be taken into account whenever relevant by employment tribunals (s.207).

Any code must be produced in draft first for consultation among interested parties. It must then be approved by the Secretary of State and laid before Parliament; in the absence of positive disapprobation it will then be brought into force by statutory instrument. The first Acas Code of Practice, on Disciplinary Practices and Procedures in Employment, was issued in 1977 and had a huge influence on employers' disciplinary procedures. However, it was quite short and therefore limited in scope. A revised and extended version was rejected by the Secretary of State in 1987 but was issued instead as an Advisory Handbook, *Discipline at Work*. However, in the light of the new right for individuals to be accompanied during disciplinary and grievance proceedings and in a climate more favourable to employment protection, Acas issued a revised Code of Practice on Disciplinary and Grievance Procedures in 2000. In the new Code the opportunity was taken to expand advice on a range of matters in the light of developing case law and theory in relation to discipline and dismissal, as well as to include two new sections on grievance procedures and the statutory right to be accompanied. These matters are discussed further in Chapter 8 (below, para. 8–070). Other Acas codes cover *Disclosure of Information to Trade Unions for Collective Bargaining Purposes* (revised 1997), and *Time Off for Trade Union Duties and Activities* (revised 2003).

Acas is not the only body with the power to issue codes of practice. The Health and Safety Commission, CRE, DRC and EOC may also issue codes and more controversially, since 1980 so may the Secretary of State (by virtue of TULRCA, s.203). The Secretary of State's power was largely introduced because Acas was reluctant to risk its reputation for independence and lack of bias by publishing codes of practice on such sensitive issues as picketing and the closed shop. Those codes were drawn up by the Secretary of State, as was the code on trade union ballots. These codes have come in for substantial criticism as attempting to legislate by the back door by introducing requirements for which there is no warrant in the legislation. It is important, therefore, to distinguish them from the Acas codes which have met with general approval.

Central Arbitration Committee (CAC)

1–011 The Central Arbitration Committee (CAC) was established by the Employment Protection Act 1975 and took over the functions of the former Industrial Arbitration Board as well as new duties under that statute. The chair, deputy chairs and members are appointed by the Secretary of State and include people with expertise in the field of industrial relations as well as representatives of both sides of industry. Provisions relating to it are now to be found in TULRCA, ss.259–265. Originally the chief function of the CAC was to conduct arbitrations in collective employment disputes. When it was first set up it had statutory powers to decide disputes where an employer refused to recognise a trade union and also where it was claimed that an employer was not affording employees terms and conditions up to the industry or local standard. Both jurisdictions were abolished by the Employment Act 1980 as one of the Conservative Government's first reforms of industrial relations law. This meant that from 1980 to 2000 the only situation where the CAC had compulsory arbitration powers was in relation to disputes over disclosure of information to recognised trade unions for the purposes of collective bargaining (discussed below, para. 5–022), although it could also be called upon to act where parties voluntarily approached Acas seeking arbitration, as described above. This jurisdiction was fairly limited in its effects. The CAC had an average of only 21 complaints a year about disclosure of information referred to it in the 1990s and in 1998 there were only six references about disclosure of information and no other arbitration issues at all.

The picture has changed considerably since the Employment Relations Act 1999 introduced a new procedure for the compulsory recognition of trade unions (below, para. 5–015) as it is the CAC which has the duty of deciding on applications for recognition. Between June 2000, when the procedure came into force, and March 2003 trade unions made 255 applications to the CAC for recognition. After an initial flood, the number of applications has dropped, but there were no fewer than 80 claims in 2002–2003. The CAC's caseload for disclosure of information and its other jurisdictions remains tiny.

Certification Officer

When trade unions were first recognised as legal bodies under the Trade **1–012** Union Act 1871 they had to register with the Registrar of Friendly Societies to qualify for certain advantages in relation to tax and the holding of property through trustees. While the process was not compulsory, most unions registered. Under the Industrial Relations Act 1971, however, registration took on a different complexion, and non-registration became the rallying call for trade union opposition to that Act.

The Industrial Relations Act was repealed by TULRA 1974, by which time the terms "register" and "registrar" had attracted such opprobrium that although the wish was to return substantially to the pre-1971 position, it was felt that these terms could not be used. For a while the Registrar of Friendly Societies was brought back into service, but in 1975 a new office, that of the Certification Officer, was instituted (see now TULRCA, s.254).

The principal function of the Certification Officer was originally to maintain a list (not a register, note) of independent trade unions and to issue certificates of independence (TULRCA, s.2). As will be seen, (below, para. 10–032) the status of independence is of some importance, and it is the Certification Officer who decides whether a trade union meets the criteria. However, from 1979 onwards the Conservative administration pursued a policy of increased intervention in the internal affairs of trade unions and the Certification Officer became a key player in its implementation.

The Certification Officer is now responsible for keeping records of the **1–013** annual financial and membership returns of trade unions, copies of union rules and the other documents which trade unions are now required to file – a list which grew considerably in the 1980s. Additionally he has jurisdiction over complaints relating to the elections of trade union officials; ballots to set up political funds in trade unions; complaints over political expenditure and the amalgamation of trade unions. In 1993 TURERA extended the Certification Officer's powers considerably by introducing a wide authority for him to investigate the financial affairs of trade unions on his own initiative, including a right to demand production of documents and to appoint an inspector where fraud or misfeasance is suspected (TULRCA, ss.37A–E).

The Certification Officer's functions, therefore, are a mixture of administrative and judicial duties. In relation to some matters, such as complaints about elections, the political fund rules or industrial action ballots, union members had a choice of taking their claims to the Certification Officer or to the court. The advantage of a complaint to the Certification Officer was that the procedure would be cheaper and quicker; the disadvantage was that his powers were limited to making a declaration. If the union did not comply with the declaration the member would then have to invoke court proceedings. The Employment Relations Act 1999, as part of the general policy of encouraging disputes to be settled away from courts where possible, made a number of amendments to TULRCA which basically extend the Certification Officer's powers of adjudication to some areas where he had no jurisdiction before (such as dealing with complaints of refusal of access to the union's accounts) and give him powers to enforce his orders. In future, members will have to choose to complain either to the Certification Officer or to the court, but will not be able to do both. A new right of appeal from a decision of the Certification Officer to the Employment Appeal Tribunal (EAT) on a point of law is contained in TULRCA, s.108C.

The Equality Commissions

1–014 The first anti-discrimination legislation passed in the 1970s (the Sex Discrimination Act 1975 and the Race Relations Act 1976) set up two separate Commissions to promote equality and work towards the elimination of discrimination on grounds of sex and race respectively. Although having similar powers and remit, the two Commissions developed different emphases and ways of working. When legislation against disability discrimination was passed in 1995 there was a strong argument for a further Commission, which was finally set up in 1999.

Even before the establishment of the Disability Rights Commission in 1999, however, there were calls for a single commission to promote equality on the grounds that this would be more effective (and economical) than three separate commissions. The argument became stronger when the European Union adopted the Employment Directive (2000/78/EC) which extends protection against discrimination to discrimination on grounds of age, religion and sexual orientation. Either there would have to be a proliferation of commissions or there would have to be an amalgamation of some kind. In its 2002 consultation document, *Equality and Diversity: making it happen*, the Government indicated a strong preference for a single equality body, although not for a single over-arching Equality Act. However, a further complication arose as a result of the Human Rights Act 1998, for many influential commentators argued that a Human Rights Commission was needed to ensure that the Act was effective and properly understood and applied. This raised the question of whether it should subsume the proposed Single Equality Body or whether they should be separate and distinct.

The matter was considered by the Joint Parliamentary Committee on Human Rights which reported in March 2003 after a two-year inquiry. Its recommendation was that there should be a single integrated body combining a Human Rights Commission and the Single Equality Body. At the time of writing, no proposals have been published, so for the time being, the three existing Commissions continue.

Commission for Racial Equality (CRE) and Equal Opportunities Commission (EOC)

The Commission for Racial Equality (CRE) and the Equal Opportunities **1–015** Commission (EOC) were established by the Race Relations Act 1976 (RRA), s.43 and Sex Discrimination Act 1975 (SDA), s.53 respectively. The two anti-discrimination statutes operate on the same lines so that the powers and responsibilities of the two Commissions are similar, although the Commission for Racial Equality replaced an older body, the Race Relations Board and so has a wider remit in non-employment aspects. There are between eight and 15 Commissioners appointed by the Secretary of State on a full-time or part-time basis, and they have general duties to work towards the elimination of discrimination, to promote equality of opportunity and to keep under review the working of the legislation (discrimination law is discussed generally in Chapter 2, below).

As part of this remit, the Commissions have powers to undertake research and educational activities, and like Acas may issue codes of practice. The CRE Code of Practice on discrimination in employment came into force in 1984. The EOC Code on discrimination in employment came into force in 1985. In 1993 the EOC was given power to issue a Code of Practice on Equal Pay, which came into force in March 1997. In addition both Commissions have issued advisory pamphlets on particular issues. The Commissions may give assistance with proceedings brought under the anti-discrimination legislation, usually where there is a question of principle. Some of the legislation is so complex (such as that governing equal pay) that legal assistance is essential and many cases could not be brought without the Commissions' assistance.

Discriminatory advertisements

To publish discriminatory advertisements is unlawful (SDA, s.38; RRA, **1–016** s.29) and if done knowingly or recklessly both the publisher and the person who placed the advertisement are liable to prosecution. Only the Commissions, however, may take action on discriminatory advertisements, but cases are relatively few.

Investigations

The Commissioners have extensive powers to conduct investigations where **1–017** "they think fit" (SDA, s.57; RRA, s.48). The situations where investigations may be conducted were cut down, however, by the restrictive interpretation of the House of Lords in *Prestige Group plc, Re* (1984) where it was held that the Commission could not embark on a formal investigation unless it had at least some suspicion that unlawful acts were taking place.

The reason that the Commissions have these powers is because sex and race discrimination are by definition about worse treatment for groups, so normal enforcement procedures via individual action are unlikely to have much impact on the problem. However, it is also of the nature of discrimination that it can be very difficult to pin down acts of discrimination, although results are fairly clear. The requirement for definite evidence before the investigation is thus an inhibiting factor. Additionally it should be noted that the Commissions must draw up appropriate terms of reference before commencing an investigation, and may not afterwards exceed those terms.

In the course of an investigation the Commission has powers to ask for information and to require the production of documents. Failure to comply is an offence. At the end of the investigation the Commission must prepare a report, which must at least be available for consultation. Where appropriate, the Commissions may make recommendations for changes in the procedures or policies of the organisation. If in the course of the investigation the Commission becomes satisfied that breaches of the legislation are taking place, it may issue a non-discrimination notice, requiring that the recipient does not commit unlawful acts and, where changes to practice are needed to achieve this, requiring the recipient to inform the Commission when the notice has been complied with. An appeal against a non-discrimination notice lies to an employment tribunal, but if it is considered that the Commission has exceeded its powers (as in *Re Prestige Group plc* (1984)) the employer can instead apply for judicial review to have the notice quashed.

The experience of the Commissions with formal investigations has not been entirely happy, in that their procedures have been successfully attacked on a number of occasions. Commentators have criticised what they see as inadequate use being made of their powers under this head by the Commissions.

Disability Rights Commission

1–018 One of the major criticisms of the Disability Discrimination Act 1995 (DDA) as originally passed was that no Commission comparable to the CRE and EOC was created. Instead of an independent body committed to maximising the effectiveness of the legislation, the DDA created a National Disability Council (NDC) which, in striking contrast to the CRE and EOC, had no enforcement or investigatory powers. Its function was purely to give advice on matters relating to disability discrimination and the operation of the legislation (DDA, s.50). It could propose codes of practice, but only when asked to do so by the Secretary of State, and indeed the first code of practice made under the Act preceded the establishment of the Council.

The Labour Government made good its manifesto promise to remedy this situation by issuing a consultation paper on the establishment of a Disability Rights Commission (DRC) soon after coming to power in May

1997. This was implemented by the Disability Rights Commission Act 1999 (DRCA) which abolished the NDC and established the new Commission, which came into operation in April 2000.

The DRC consists of 10–15 members, the majority of whom must be people with disabilities. Its duties are to work towards the elimination of discrimination against people with disabilities; to promote equal opportunities for people with disabilities; to keep the DDA under review, and to encourage good practice in the treatment of people with disabilities (DRCA, s.2). Like the CRE and EOC it can now give advice to the Government and other public authorities without waiting to be asked and it has similar powers to conduct investigations and to issue non-discrimination notices. There are some novelties in relation to enforcement, however: under DRCA, s.5, the DRC has an express power to agree to hold back from enforcement action provided that the discriminator enters a legally binding agreement to take specified remedial action. Furthermore, if a non-discrimination notice is issued, it may specify that the discriminator produce an action plan which, once it is approved by the DRC, becomes binding and enforceable through legal proceedings. As with the other Commissions, the DRC has power to give assistance to individuals bringing proceedings and to prepare codes of practice (DDA, s.53A). Unlike them, it has no specific powers in relation to discriminatory advertisements. This is because a regime for individual claims was provided in the DDA, given the limited powers of the NDC at that time.

Employment tribunals

Employment tribunals were originally set up with a limited jurisdiction **1–019** under the Industrial Training Act 1964. From such humble beginnings they have become fundamental institutions in present employment law. In 1965 they were given an important jurisdiction under the Redundancy Payments Act, but it was the introduction of the action for unfair dismissal in 1972 which really led to their workload taking off: they now hear over 27,000 cases a year.

Employment tribunals are usually composed of three members. They are chaired by a solicitor or barrister of seven years' standing and then have two lay members, drawn from each side of industry. In making any decision, the lay members have an equal vote, and can thus outvote the legal chairperson. The tripartite composition is so that the lay members can bring their knowledge and experience of practical industrial relations to bear on the issues before them, hence they have often been referred to as "industrial juries".

Jurisdiction

Until 1994 the jurisdiction of employment tribunals was entirely statutory. **1–020** Although provision for the Secretary of State to extend their jurisdiction to contractual matters had existed since 1975, it was not exercised until the Employment Tribunals Extension of Jurisdiction Order 1994. The fact that the Secretary of State's power had not been exercised was a constant cause for criticism. When an employee is dismissed, she may well have a claim for breach of the contract of employment as well as a claim for unfair dismissal and it seemed absurd that the two claims could not both be brought in the same court. The problem was highlighted when the Wages Act 1986 was passed and apparently provided an avenue for bringing contract claims in employment tribunals; the number of applications under the Wages Act rocketed, indicating the need for such a mechanism.

Following TURERA amendments, the Employment Tribunals Extension of Jurisdiction Order 1994 was made, permitting contract claims which arise or are outstanding on the termination of the employee's employment to be taken to employment tribunals, provided that the claim does not relate to: personal injuries; a term requiring the employer to provide living accommodation; intellectual property; breach of confidence or restrictive covenants. A further limitation is that the maximum that can be claimed in a contract claim (or a number of different claims relating to the same contract) is £25,000 (an amount which has remained unchanged since 1994). It is worth noting that there is no requirement that the employee should be bringing a statutory claim at the same time. However, the usual limitation period for statutory claims of three months applies. The employer may counter-claim on grounds of the employee's breach of contract within six weeks of receiving the originating application.

It is perhaps unfortunate that it was not decided to extend contract jurisdiction generally. For example, in *Sunderland Polytechnic v Evans* (1993), an employee disputed the amount of pay her employer had deducted after a half-day strike. It seems odd that the assembled expertise of the tribunal could still not be used in a situation like that just because there had been no termination of the contract.

Procedure

1–021 Like other tribunals, employment tribunals are meant to be cheap, speedy and informal. The first is particularly necessary, given that legal aid is not available for employment tribunal proceedings. However, while applicants are in theory encouraged to appear in person, the issues heard by tribunals are often complex and it is the case that it is certainly advantageous to have legal representation. In some areas, especially discrimination and equal value claims, it must be almost impossible for an unaided litigant to present her case adequately. Some applicants can get representation through their trade union, but not all unions have the resources to fund this. To prevent the disadvantage where one side is represented while the other (usually the employee) is not, it is submitted that it is time that legal aid was extended to employment tribunal proceedings. After all, loss of your job is one of the most serious events that can befall you.

Employment tribunals at first succeeded in their aim of being speedy, but their caseload has increased substantially without a corresponding increase in personnel. Claims to employment tribunals peaked at over 130,000 in 2000–2001 and there were 112,277 claims in 2001–2002. Not all cases result in tribunal hearings; many are withdrawn or settled before that stage. Nonetheless, in 2001–2002 tribunals actually heard over 27,300 cases. The

14

result of the overload is that less than 70 per cent were heard within six months of application. In an attempt to deal with this problem, TURERA 1993 introduced a power for a tribunal chairperson to sit alone on certain types of case and the categories were extended again by the Employment Rights (Dispute Resolution) Act 1998. At any time the chair may decide that a full tribunal is necessary and before sitting alone, she should in any case consider the views of the parties and also whether a dispute on the facts is likely so that the case would be better heard by a full tribunal. These provisions have drawn a lot of criticism because they undermine the basic concept of employment tribunals as tripartite bodies with an important lay industrial element, although in practice it appeared that chairs were careful in not abusing this discretion.

Further efforts to expedite tribunal proceedings were made in the revised Employment Tribunals (Constitution and Rules of Procedure) Regulations 2001 (SI 2001/1171), which made some changes aimed at giving tribunals greater powers to manage proceedings. Thus Regulation 10 states that the tribunal's overriding objective is to deal with cases justly, which includes saving expense, dealing with them proportionately in relation to the complexity of the issues involved and dealing with them expeditiously. Rule 4 is entitled "Case Management" and gives the tribunal power to make directions about witnesses, evidence and time-limits of its own motion as well as on the application of a party. This is in line with the Woolf reforms to civil procedure, which are generally designed to promote proactive case management by the courts.

As to informality, anyone going to an employment tribunal expecting a cosy chat can think again, despite the injunction in the regulations that tribunals should seek to avoid formality. In general tribunals follow a procedure which is akin to the procedure of ordinary civil courts, although if either party is unrepresented the tribunal chairperson often takes a more inquisitorial role. The usual procedure followed is outlined below (there are special rules for equal value claims, which are discussed below, para. 7–008).

Before the hearing

All claims to an employment tribunal must be submitted to the Central **1–022** Office of Employment Tribunals (COET) within the statutory time-limit for the claim in question (usually three months) or to a Regional Office of Employment Tribunals (ROET). Applicants are encouraged to use a Form IT1 for the claims, but this is not mandatory: any written document will suffice as long as it contains the relevant information. The basic essentials are the names and addresses of applicant and respondent and the grounds on which the claim is being made. A copy of the claim is then sent to the respondent employer together with a Form IT3 requesting its response to the claim, and the matter is also referred to Acas. An Acas individual conciliation officer will investigate each claim and talk to the parties with a view to seeing if the matter can be settled without a hearing. As noted above, this conciliation service has generally been successful.

If the respondent wishes to contest the claim, the notice of appearance (Form IT3) originally had to be returned within 14 days, although in striking contrast to the rigid rules on limitation periods for applications, it was easy for the respondent to gain extensions of that period. Amendments were made in 1996 in an attempt to tighten this up: the respondent now has 21 days in which to respond, but an extension will only be granted if the respondent has given reasons for the delay, and there is a risk of a costs award if it was reasonably practicable to reply in time. It has always been possible for parties to request further particulars and order discovery and inspection of documents from the other side, with the possibility of seeking an order from the tribunal in case of non-compliance; however, the revised rules now permit the tribunal of its own motion to ask for further particulars, order discovery or inspection and also to require either party to furnish written answers to any question, if this will clarify issues or enable progress to be made.

Because of the relative ease with which tribunal proceedings may be commenced, and especially because it is rare to order one party to pay the costs of the other, employers complained that they sometimes had to go to the expense and trouble of defending claims which were hopeless from the outset. A pre-hearing assessment procedure was therefore introduced, intended to filter out the hopeless cases, but it was not regarded as successful and it was replaced by a new procedure for a pre-hearing review. A tribunal may order a pre-hearing review either on the application of one party (usually the employer) or of its own motion where it appears that some contention (of either party, but most likely to be the applicant) is unlikely to succeed. Unlike the previous pre-hearing assessment, pre-hearing reviews may be conducted by the chairperson alone. The parties may make written or oral representations, but no witnesses are heard nor documents (other than the application and notice of appearance) considered. If the tribunal considers that the contention is unlikely to succeed, it can require the party to pay a deposit of up to £500 within 21 days as a condition of continuing the proceedings, although in making this order it must take into account the party's ability to pay. The deposit order will record the contention thought to be untenable and the reasons for that view and the party is warned that persistence in the face of the order could lead to an order of costs and thus forfeiture of the deposit. No one who has been involved in the pre-hearing review can chair or be a member of the tribunal which ultimately hears the case; however, if the party against whom a deposit order was made loses on that issue, the tribunal must specifically consider whether or not costs should be awarded against him. If so, the deposit will be used towards defraying the costs.

The hearing

1–023 Tribunals have the right to regulate their own procedure, as long as they act within the regulations, and the regulations instruct them to seek to avoid formality; however, they usually follow something like ordinary civil court procedure. The party with the burden of proof starts: in an unfair dismissal case, for example, this will be the employer, if dismissal is admitted, because the employer has the burden of proving the reason for the dismissal. If, however, the employer denies that the employee was dismissed, the employee has the burden of proving it, and would begin

16

instead. Witnesses, who are invited to give evidence on oath, are examined in chief and then cross-examined by the other side; tribunals are usually reluctant to accept hearsay evidence or to permit leading questions in examination in chief even though they are not bound by the rules of evidence.

After both sides have presented their cases and called their witnesses, they sum up and the tribunal retires to consider its decision. Where possible, tribunals try to deliver decisions orally on the day, with written reasons being sent later. In an attempt to streamline procedure, it was provided in 1985 that tribunals should give reasons in summary form only, except in discrimination and equal pay cases. However, parties may request full reasons in writing to be given either at the hearing or within 21 days of the summary reasons being sent out; alternatively, the tribunal may decide to give full reasons if the decision is such that a summary would give an insufficient explanation.

Costs are not normally awarded against the unsuccessful party. Originally costs were only awarded against a party who had acted frivolously, vexatiously or otherwise unreasonably; but the power was extended in 1993 to include abusive or disruptive conduct of proceedings. This was extended again by Rule 14 of the 2001 Regulations, which allowed costs to be awarded against an applicant for his or her representative's unreasonable behaviour, and raised to £10,000 the maximum costs order which can be made without going through a detailed assessment. In 2001–2002 costs were awarded against applicants in 467 cases but against respondents in only 169. The average costs award was nearly £1,000.

After the hearing

Tribunals may review their decisions either of their own motion or on **1–024** application of a party made within 14 days of the decision being sent out. However, the grounds for review are limited and their scope interpreted strictly. The five grounds are: that the decision was wrong because of an error by tribunal staff; that one party did not receive notice of the proceedings leading to the hearing; that the decision was made in the absence of one party; that new evidence has become available which could not reasonably have been known about or foreseen at the time of the hearing; or that the interests of justice require such a review. The last two are the widest, but it must be stressed that new evidence will not be a ground if its non-availability at the hearing was merely because its relevance had not been appreciated or because of insufficient preparation, and that the interests of justice ground is far from being a *carte blanche* for challenges and an alternative to a right of appeal.

Parties have a right to appeal to the EAT within six weeks of the decision being sent out, but only on a point of law. There is no appeal on questions of fact. This has led to much debate over what is a question of fact and what is a question of law, an issue taken up elsewhere in this book (below, paras 3–013, 8–033). Suffice it for present purposes to say that the question is really a policy issue rather than a question of legal theory. With over 27,000 cases a year being heard by employment tribunals, if there were many appeals the EAT would be swamped. Hence there is a clear trend to limit situations in which appeal will be possible.

Employment Appeal Tribunal (EAT)

1–025 The Employment Appeal Tribunal (EAT) was set up by the EPA 1975 and is governed now by ETA, Pt II and regulations thereunder. It has the same tripartite structure as an employment tribunal, save that this time it is chaired by a High Court judge (and the lay members tend to be more senior citizens than in local employment tribunals). Following TURERA reforms, the EAT may be composed of just the chairperson when hearing appeals from a single person employment tribunal and can be constituted of just the judge and one lay member where both parties to the case agree. As with employment tribunals, the judge can be outvoted by the lay members (*e.g. Nethermere v Gardiner* (1984)).

The EAT is a court of record and its decisions should be followed by inferior courts, especially employment tribunals. Different divisions of the EAT are not obliged to follow their own earlier decisions and occasionally different streams of authority can appear, which makes more difficult the task of employment tribunals. In the mid-1970s, when tribunals were coping with a sharp increase in the number of unfair dismissal cases and a host of new claims under the Employment Protection Act, the EAT saw its duty very much as setting guidelines on the meaning and application of the law. Unfortunately the guidelines began to be treated as if they were statutory requirements, attracting the wrath of the Court of Appeal, which mounted a counter-attack stressing the importance of the words of the statute and the limited situations in which there could be an appeal from an employment tribunal (see below, para. 8–033). This development was understandable, perhaps, but given the huge number of tribunal decisions being handed down each year, there is a danger of lack of uniformity if this approach is taken too literally, a danger clearly spelt out by Lord Browne-Wilkinson when he was President of the EAT.

From the EAT appeals lie to the Court of Appeal – on questions of law – and thence to the House of Lords.

The European Community (EC) and European Union (EU)

1–026 The United Kingdom joined the then European Economic Communities (EEC) on January 1, 1973 by accession to the Treaty of Rome, the fundamental treaty underpinning the organisation. This was given effect in British law by the European Communities Act 1972. British membership has transformed the employment law scene as will be apparent throughout this book. While the initial treaties constituting the EEC were aimed at economic goals, it was always the intention of the founders that the ultimate objective should be a closer political union between the Member States with aspirations to more than economic co-operation. A major step towards this was taken by the Single European Act agreed by the Member States in 1986 and implemented in the United Kingdom by the European Communities (Amendment) Act 1986. This extended the areas in which the

EEC could legislate to social policy (including employment) and also increased the use of qualified majority voting by allowing the process to be used for measures designed to harmonise the functioning of the internal market (Art. 95). In employment law this was particularly important because, while unanimity was still required for general employment law matters, majority voting could be used for health and safety measures. In the face of a Conservative administration in the United Kingdom during the 1980s and up to 1997, which opposed almost every improvement to working life proposed by the European Commission, it was only by an extended interpretation of what amounted to health and safety legislation (*e.g.* the Pregnant Workers Directive 1992, below, para. 6–005 and the Working Time Directive 1993, below, para. 6–038) that any progress was possible.

The next stage was the Treaty on European Union (the Treaty of Maastricht) in 1992, under which the EEC became the European Community (EC) and the European Union (EU) was set up. From the point of view of employment law the main importance of the negotiations leading to the Treaty on European Union was the promulgation of an annexed Protocol containing the Agreement on Social Policy. In 1989 all Member States, with the notable exception of the United Kingdom, agreed upon a Community Charter of the Fundamental Social Rights of Workers. The Social Charter, as it became known, had no legal status as such, but was a very clear indication of the way that most Member States wanted to see social policy developing and a potential source for directives and other EC instruments. At the Maastricht negotiations, proposals to include the Charter within the Treaty of Rome were blocked by the veto of the United Kingdom, with the result that the other members added the Protocol to the Treaty on European Union stating their intention to implement it if necessary by directives applying only to those signatories (this happened with the European Works Councils Directive, below, para. 5–024).

The Treaty on European Union made provision for a further Inter-Governmental Conference to take place to consider amendments to the Treaty of Rome. By the time of the final negotiations in the summer of 1997 the Conservative administration had been replaced by the new Labour Government which had committed itself to accepting the Social Charter. So the Treaty of Amsterdam in 1997 revoked the United Kingdom opt-out and included the terms of the Agreement on Social Policy in the Treaty of Rome. In 2001 the Treaty on European Union and the Treaty of Rome were merged by the Treaty of Nice, which came into force in February 2003.

Membership of the EU carries with it the obligations to implement in **1–027** British law the requirements of the Treaties and directives and to submit to the jurisdiction of the European Court of Justice (ECJ) as final arbiter on the interpretation of EU law. Member States cannot always be relied upon to implement directives promptly or properly and so quite early on the ECJ developed the doctrine of direct effect, meaning that Community legislation can in some circumstances have immediate effect in Member States even if implementing legislation has not been passed or is incorrect. In *Van Gend en Loos* (1963) the ECJ held that Treaty Articles would have direct effect provided that they were clear, unconditional and did not require further implementation. Most importantly for sex discrimination law, in *Defrenne v Sabena* (1976) it was held that Article 141 stipulating equal pay for men and women for equal work had direct effect (see below, Chapter 2). The first cases on direct effect involved what is called vertical direct effect, meaning that Treaty Articles could be relied upon in actions involving the State, since it would be wrong to allow the State to benefit from its own failure to implement EU law. However, in *Defrenne v Sabena* it was held that Article 141 also had horizontal direct effect, meaning that a claimant could rely on it as against another private citizen.

In *Van Duyn v Home Office* (1974) the ECJ extended the doctrine of direct effect to directives, again subject to their being sufficiently precise and unconditional and not requiring further implementation: this can be relied on by individuals once the deadline for implementing the directive has passed. Although *Marshall v Southampton and South West Hampshire AHA* (1986) (another sex discrimination case) made it clear that this was limited to vertical, not horizontal, direct effect it also indicated that the concept of "the State" should be construed widely for the purposes of vertical direct effect, to include the State as employer as well as governing authority, and extended to embrace "emanations of the State". Thus, in that case, a health authority responsible for managing hospitals and employing hospital staff was held to be an emanation of the State and the claimant was able to rely directly on the Equal Treatment Directive (76/207/EEC) against it. In *Foster v British Gas* (1990) (also concerned with sex discrimination) the ECJ defined an emanation of the State as including:

> "a body, whatever its legal form, which has been made responsible, pursuant to a measure adopted by the state, for providing a public service under the control of the state and has for that purpose special powers beyond those which result from the normal rules applicable in relations between individuals".

On that basis the House of Lords held that British Gas was an emanation of the State (*Foster v British Gas* (1991)).

What happens if there is a conflict between British law and EU law and the claimant cannot rely on direct effect of the EU law? Since EU law is supreme, in *Von Colson v Land Nordrhein Westfalen* (1984) the ECJ set out the duty of national courts to take EU law into account in interpreting national laws and to interpret them in accordance with EU law so far as possible. In *Marleasing SA v La Comercial Internacional de Alimentacion* (1990) it was made clear that this applied to national laws which preceded the relevant EU measure as well as those made after it (which could be assumed to have been intended to implement it). In this way, EU legislation can have indirect effects even if it cannot be used directly. The possibility of British legislation being subject to judicial review to check its compliance with Community law was accepted in *R. v Secretary of State for Employment ex p. EOC* (1995) where the House of Lords granted a declaration that a statutory provision excluding part-time workers from employment protection rights contravened Article 141, the Equal Pay Directive (75/117/EEC) and the Equal Treatment Directive (76/207/EEC).

Where there is doubt as to whether or not EU law is applicable to a case **1–028** arising in British courts, or there is doubt as to the meaning of EU law, the court or tribunal hearing the case can refer it to the ECJ. This can be done at any level, from employment tribunal to the House of Lords. The ECJ will answer the questions put by the national court and the case then returns to the original forum for decision in the light of the ECJ's advice.

Where British law is clearly not in accordance with directly effective EU law and it is not possible for the British court to interpret its way out of the difficulty, then the British law must be set aside, even if it was passed by Parliament after the Community law was made (*R. v Secretary of State for Transport ex p. Factortame* (1990)). If a directive cannot be relied on by the claimant because it would involve giving it horizontal effect against a private party, then an individual may have an action against the state for any losses caused (*Francovich v Italian Republic* (1992)) provided that the directive was intended to confer rights on individuals.

The first and greatest impact of European Union law in employment was in the field of sex discrimination and equal pay, but it has subsequently pervaded nearly every aspect of the employment relationship. Since the Treaty of European Union there has been a procedure whereby directives in the employment field can be adopted on the joint recommendation of representatives of workers and employers ("the social partners") and, as has been seen, alterations to the Treaty of Rome have greatly extended the areas in which the European Community is competent to legislate. It is therefore to be expected that EU law will continue to be an important source of new developments for British employment law in years to come.

The International Labour Organization (ILO)

The International Labour Organization (ILO) was established in 1919 by **1–029** the Treaty of Versailles as an organ of the League of Nations. However, to indicate its independence from the League of Nations, that part of the treaty was detached and reformed as the separate Constitution of the ILO. Since the Second World War it has been a separate agency with a special relationship with the United Nations. It has a tripartite structure with representatives of employers, workers and governments.

The mission of the ILO is to promote fair working conditions in all countries. Its main method of doing this is by the adoption of Conventions and Recommendations. ILO Conventions are treaties on particular issues (such as freedom of association, non-discrimination, minimum wage protection) which, once agreed by the ILO, are opened for signature by Member States. Once a state has ratified a treaty, it has the usual obligations under international law to abide by the treaty – which may mean that it has a duty to change municipal law to give effect to it. There is, however, no body comparable to the ECJ to enforce compliance.

Since states are under no legal compulsion to accede to treaties in the first place, they can be expected to abide by the obligations which they voluntarily undertake. Should a state change its mind, it must withdraw from (denounce) the treaty, usually after giving a stipulated period of notice. Generally a change in the political complexion of the Government in the United Kingdom has not led to a change in policy on these international obligations. However, in the 1980s legislation of the Conservative Government was held by the ILO to be in breach of accepted conventions on more than one occasion and a number of conventions were denounced.

Low Pay Commission

1–030 The Labour Government originally set up the Low Pay Commission in 1997 to assist it in implementing its manifesto commitment to legislating for a national minimum wage. At that stage it had no legal status, but under the National Minimum Wage Act 1998 (ss.5–8 and Sch.1) it was put on a statutory footing. The Low Pay Commission consists of a chair and eight members appointed by the Secretary of State and having an appropriate balance of members with trade union and employer association experience as well as independent members. The Government largely followed the Commission's advice in setting the initial national minimum wage in April 1999 (see below, para. 7–035) and has continued on the whole to do so since.

2. Discrimination Law

Freedom of contract is the basic principle where contracts of employment **2–001** are considered, just as it is for any other kind of contract. This means, so far as recruitment is concerned, that in general employers may select their workforce according to any principle they like, or according to none. The trouble with this, however, is that it is perfectly clear that if there is no constraint, certain groups are prevented from competing equally in the labour market because of unfounded prejudices. The problem is sufficiently serious for the law to intervene and to prohibit discrimination on certain grounds which are regarded as irrelevant to someone's ability to do a job. The effect is that employers may not refuse to enter contracts of employment on these grounds.

This is an important restriction on the principle of freedom of contract, because it affects not only the terms of contracts, but the very question of with whom one may make a contract. It is justified, however, by the greater importance of the principle of equal opportunity. The first legal instruments enshrining this principle were international treaties. The Universal Declaration of Human Rights 1948, Article 2, stated:

> "Everyone is entitled to all the rights and freedoms set forth in this Declaration without distinction of any kind, such as race, colour, sex, language, religion, political or other opinion, national or social origin, property, birth or other status."

(See also the International Covenant on Economic, Social and Cultural Rights 1966, Arts 2.2, 3, 6–8.) The International Labour Organization's Conventions of 1958, 1965 and 1980 were aimed at the elimination of sex and race discrimination, but in the absence of effective enforcement procedures, the language of such treaties may seem purely aspirational. However, this is very definitely not the case where the European obligations of the United Kingdom are concerned.

British membership of the European Union has been without doubt the most important positive influence on discrimination law. Originally this was only in the field of sex discrimination and it resulted from Article 141 of the Treaty of Rome, which provides that Member States must maintain "the principle that men and women should receive equal pay for equal work". This article may seem to be mainly relevant with regard to achieving parity

23

in terms and conditions once people are actually employed, but it acted as the springboard for the Equal Treatment Directive of 1976 (76/207/EEC) which required implementation of the principle of equal treatment for men and women not only in relation to terms and conditions of employment but also recruitment, training, promotion and dismissal. Article 141 was held to have direct horizontal and vertical effect in *Defrenne v Sabena* (1976), meaning that litigants have the right to rely on it to found claims in any British court or tribunal even if it has not been fully implemented by national legislation (see above, para. 1–027). The importance of directly effective Community law is dramatically illustrated by *Marshall v Southampton & S.W. Hants AHA* (1986), where a female dietician claimed that the health authority's policy of requiring women to retire at 60 while men retired at 65 was in breach of the Equal Treatment Directive. Under British legislation this difference was permissible and it was thought to be consistent with EU law, which allowed some exceptions in relation to death or retirement. However, the ECJ held that a contractual term about retirement ages was a term about dismissal, which meant that it was subject to the requirement of equal treatment in the Equal Treatment Directive. While the ECJ held that the Equal Treatment Directive had only vertical, not horizontal, direct effect, this was enough for the claimant, as her employer was considered to be an "emanation of the State". The result was that the Government had to act swiftly to equalise retirement ages for women and men through the Sex Discrimination Act 1986.

2–002   While British membership of the EU has had a dramatic impact in combating sex discrimination it had no direct impact on discrimination on other grounds until recently. This was because there was no legislative base in the Treaty of Rome to allow the EU to act on other forms of discrimination. However, in 1997 the Treaty of Amsterdam amended the Treaty of Rome by introducing Article 13, empowering the EU to take action against discrimination "based on sex, racial or ethnic origin, religion or belief, disability, age or sexual orientation". This was swiftly followed by two directives based on Article 13. The Employment Directive (2000/78/EC) requires Member States to legislate against discrimination in employment on grounds of racial or ethnic origin, religion or belief, disability, age or sexual orientation: that is, all the grounds stipulated in Article 13 except sex, which is adequately dealt with by existing measures. Member States have until the end of 2006 to implement the provisions relating to disability and age discrimination, but the rest must be in place in 2003. The Race Directive (2000/43/EC) covers all discrimination on grounds of racial or ethnic origin, including not only employment but also discrimination in spheres such as social security, education and the supply of goods and services. It was implemented by the Race Relations Act 1976 (Amendment) Regulations 2003.

Discrimination is also referred to in the European Convention on Human Rights (ECHR). This treaty emanates from the Council of Europe, a society of 40 European democracies. This Council of Europe is not to be confused with the European Council, which is the main law-making body of the European Community. Article 14 of the ECHR states that the rights given by the Convention are guaranteed:

"without distinction on any grounds such as sex, race, colour, language, religion, political or other opinion, national or social origin, association with a national minority, property, birth or other status".

Until the Human Rights Act 1998 this Convention was enforceable only by individual action in the European Court of Human Rights, but the Act provides for the enforcement of Convention rights in two ways. Firstly, section 3 articulates a general duty to interpret all legislation consistently with the Convention so far as possible. If an interpretation consistent with the Convention is not possible, the court has no power to set aside legislation, but when the case reaches the level of the High Court, Court of Appeal or House of Lords a declaration of incompatibility can be made, which leads to a "fast-track" procedure for government review of the law. Secondly, section 6 imposes a duty on public authorities to ensure that their actions are compatible with Convention rights.

Section 6 means that employees of public authorities can enforce Convention rights directly against their employers. It is as yet unclear whether people employed by bodies with mixed public and private functions (*e.g.* British Telecom) will be in a similar position, but anyone employed by a private employer does not enjoy such rights. There is some parallel here with the concepts of vertical and horizontal direct effect in EC law, where a worker employed by an emanation of the State may be able to rely on the terms of a directive while a private sector worker cannot. It would seem likely that if a public worker succeeds in a claim that some facet of employment law is inconsistent with Convention rights there would be political pressure to reform the law generally. In addition, since courts and tribunals have a duty to interpret the law in accordance with Convention rights, private sector workers may gain the indirect protection of Convention rights provided that they can frame a claim based on a separate cause of action. So far as discrimination law is concerned, Article 14 promises more than it delivers, because it is not a freestanding Convention right but only prohibits discrimination in relation to the enjoyment of the other rights and freedoms in the Convention.

While British legislation has prohibited sex and race discrimination in **2–003** employment since 1975 and 1968 respectively, disability discrimination was not made unlawful in Britain until 1995. Of the other grounds stipulated in the Employment Directive (2000/78/EC), sexual orientation was only partially covered as a result of EU case law, and discrimination on grounds of age and religion was not dealt with by legislation at all (although both ageism and religious discrimination may sometimes be covered indirectly under existing rules). This is set to change as a result of the Employment Directive, as will be seen.

Sex and Race Discrimination

The first legislative attempt to address the question of sex discrimination **2–004** was the Sex Disqualification (Removal) Act 1919. This limited measure, however, merely removed existing bars on women entering certain professions. It did not prohibit discrimination in training or selection for these professions. Thus after 1919, a woman could become a solicitor, but a university did not have to treat her application equally with one from a man, and employers could refuse to employ her just because she was a woman. That remained the position until the passage of the Sex Discrimination Act 1975.

The first Race Relations Act was passed in 1965, but it made no attempt to outlaw discrimination in the employment field. It did set up the Race Relations Board with powers of investigation and conciliation: this was quite important as it was the precursor of the present Commission for Racial Equality and the Equal Opportunities Commission. The 1968 Race Relations Act prohibited racial discrimination in employment, but was not very effective. It was felt that conciliation, education and persuasion would be more likely to produce results than a series of legal proceedings. Thus complaints of discrimination had to be made to the Race Relations Board, which alone could take proceedings, and would do so only if all else failed. In the end, this screening process was a serious deterrent to claims and came to be seen as a major defect of the Act.

Building on this, and on American experience, the Sex Discrimination Act was passed in 1975. In 1976 a new Race Relations Act was passed with parallel provisions, modified as necessary. These form the basis of the law today. Since then, the Sex Discrimination Act has been modified as a result of rulings by the European Court, for example, by the Sex Discrimination Act 1986, the Sex Discrimination and Equal Pay (Remedies) Regulations 1993, the Sex Discrimination and Equal Pay (Miscellaneous Amendments) Regulations 1996, the Sex Discrimination (Gender Reassignment) Regulations 1999 and the Sex Discrimination (Indirect Discrimination and Burden of Proof) Regulations 2001. However, reforms to the Race Relations Act have not always proceeded in parallel.

Scope of the legislation

2–005 The Sex Discrimination Act covers not only discrimination on grounds of sex, but also discrimination against married people on the grounds of their marital status (SDA, ss.1, 3). This suggests that discrimination against single people in employment on grounds of their marital status is not unlawful, but it should be noted that Article 2(1) of the Equal Treatment Directive prohibits discrimination on grounds of "marital or family status", so such discrimination would be actionable in EU law.

The Race Relations Act, s.3 forbids discrimination on grounds of "colour, race, nationality and ethnic or national origin". None of these terms is defined by the Act. In *BBC v Souster* (2001) an English journalist who had presented *Rugby Special* for BBC Scotland claimed that the BBC replaced him with a Scotswoman because he was English. The Court of Session held that this was capable of constituting discrimination on grounds of "national origin" and also that "nationality" need not be defined exclusively in terms of citizenship. Therefore although the English, Scots and Welsh have common nationality as citizens of the United Kingdom, they can be regarded as having different national origins (see also *Northern Joint Police Board v Power* (1997)).

The inclusion of "ethnic origin" was clearly to cover groups such as Jews who do not constitute a separate race or nationality, yet whose group identity is based on more than just religious adherence. In the leading case, *Mandla v Dowell Lee* (1983), the House of Lords had to consider whether Sikhs constituted an ethnic group. The claimant was an orthodox Sikh boy, required by the custom of his religion to grow his hair. He was refused admission to a private school unless he would give up wearing his turban and have his hair cut to the regulation length. Lord Fraser quoted with approval the definition of ethnic group given in a New Zealand case (*King-Ansell v Police* (1979)):

". . . a group is identifiable in terms of its ethnic origins if it is a segment of the population distinguished from others by a sufficient combination of shared customs, beliefs, traditions and characteristics derived from a common or presumed common past, even if not drawn from what in biological terms is a common racial stock. It is that combination which gives them a historically determined social identity in their own eyes and in the eyes of those outside the group. They have a distinct social identity based not simply on group cohesion and solidarity but also on their belief as to their historical antecedents."

On this basis, Sikhs, Jews (*Seide v Gillette Industries* (1980)) and gypsies (*CRE v Dutton* (1989)) have naturally been held to constitute ethnic groups, although Rastafarians have not (*Dawkins v Department of the Environment* (1993)). In *Walker v Hussain* (1996) it was assumed that Muslims did not constitute a distinct ethnic group although the point was not argued. The reason would seem to be that Islam, like Christianity, is so widespread that it is not possible to identify any common characteristic among its adherents beyond their religious faith. Also, like Christianity, it is a proselytising religion.

Unlike the Race Relations Act 1976, the Race Directive (2000/43/EC) **2–006** only applies to discrimination on grounds of race or ethnic or national origin – *i.e.* it does not cover discrimination on grounds of colour or nationality. It has been implemented in the United Kingdom by the Race Relations Act 1976 (Amendment) Regulations 2003 made under the authority of the European Communities Act 1972. This is unfortunate, because it means that the regulations can go no further than is absolutely necessary in order to implement the directive. Therefore, the amendments which it makes (in the spheres of harassment, burden of proof and indirect discrimination) do not apply to discrimination on grounds of colour or nationality. As a matter of principle, these improvements ought to apply across the board. It will also cause problems to have different regimes of race discrimination law applying according to which ground of race discrimination is invoked.

The SDA and RRA provide protection not only for employees (*i.e.* those working under a contract of service: see below, Chapter 3) but also to anyone who works or applies for "a contract personally to execute any work or labour" (SDA, s.82; RRA, s.78). In *Mirror Group v Gunning* (1986) the

Court of Appeal held that the test for this was whether the dominant purpose of the contract involved a personal obligation to perform work. In this case the respondent had applied for the distributorship of the appellant's newspapers which had become vacant on the retirement of her father. She claimed that she had been rejected on grounds of sex. The Court of Appeal held that the dominant purpose of the distributorship contract was the efficient distribution of newspapers rather than a requirement to perform work; also that even if the contract required work, it was largely irrelevant who did the work, and so it could not be said to require a personal obligation to work.

Agency workers are also covered by the law: it is unlawful both for employment agencies to discriminate (SDA, s.15; RRA, s.14) and for the clients of employment agencies (the principals) to do so (SDA, s.9; RRA, s.7). These provisions have been interpreted liberally: in *Harrods Ltd v Remick* (1997) it was held that the store could be liable under RRA, s.7 for race discrimination in refusing store accreditation for certain employees of firms operating franchises inside Harrods. The store's argument that they did not "work for" Harrods but for the franchisees was rejected. In *BP Chemicals Ltd v Gillick* (1995) an agency worker was able to sue the principal for sex discrimination when she was not allowed to return to work for them following maternity leave (see also *Patefield v Belfast City Council* (2000)).

2–007   While the focus at present is on recruitment, it should be noted that the legislation prohibits discrimination at all stages of employment – in arrangements as to who should be offered employment (*e.g.* advertising, interviewing and appointment procedures); the terms on which employment is offered; access to training, benefits and promotion; and in relation to dismissal or any other detriment. However, in relation to sex discrimination only, any disparity in the actual terms and conditions of the contract of employment fall under the Equal Pay Act 1970 rather than the Sex Discrimination Act (see below, Chapter 7). Thus to offer a female applicant a lower salary than would be offered to a male applicant contravenes the Sex Discrimination Act; to pay a female employee less than a male employee contravenes the Equal Pay Act.

Definition of discrimination

2–008 What is actually meant by "discrimination"? There are four types of unlawful discrimination, called for convenience "direct", "harassment", "indirect" and "discrimination by way of victimisation". Direct discrimination embodies the concept of adverse treatment because of one's race or sex, including, but not limited to, intentional and overt discrimination. Indirect discrimination embodies the notion of adverse impact, where an apparently neutral condition has a greater effect on one group rather than another. A major difference between them is that it is possible to defend indirect discrimination as justified in the circumstances. No such defence is available for direct discrimination. Discrimination by victimisation attempts to protect those who suffer adverse treatment as a result of their involvement in other discrimination proceedings. Harassment used to be regarded only as a form of direct discrimination but has become an independent ground as a result of EU directives.

Direct discrimination

Direct discrimination consists of less favourable treatment on one of the **2–009** prohibited grounds. The Sex Discrimination Act, s.1(1)(a) defines direct discrimination as less favourable treatment of a woman (or a man) "on the ground of *her* sex" (my emphasis). The Race Relations Act, s.1(1)(a) defines it as less favourable treatment "on racial grounds". The difference in wording is important. In *Showboat v Owens* (1984), a white man employed as manager of an amusement arcade was dismissed for refusing to obey an instruction not to admit young blacks to the arcade. It was held that this was direct race discrimination: he had been treated less favourably (by being dismissed) on racial grounds – it did not matter that his own race was not the reason (see also *Weathersfield v Sargent* (1998)).

In a most important decision, *James v Eastleigh BC* (1990), the House of Lords considered the meaning of the words "on the ground of her sex". Mr and Mrs James were both aged 61. She was allowed free admission to the municipal swimming pool, but he was not, because free admission was only allowed to those who had reached state pension age – that is, 60 for women, but 65 for men. The Council clearly had no intention to discriminate on grounds of sex: it was following the common policy of giving concessions to pensioners. The House of Lords held first, that the test of whether an action is done on the ground of sex is objective not subjective. That means, if the action causes less favourable treatment of one sex, or the less favourable treatment would not have occurred but for the complainant's sex, it is direct discrimination. Intention, motive or purpose of the discriminator are irrelevant to the issue of liability. Secondly, they held that to use a criterion which is itself discriminatory on grounds of sex (like state pensionable age) must inevitably involve direct discrimination. Thus, the Council was liable for direct discrimination.

The importance of holding that this was direct discrimination rather than indirect (which is what the Court of Appeal thought it was) was twofold: first, as noted already, the Council could not avail itself of the defence of justification; secondly, at that time compensation was only payable for indirect discrimination if it was intentional, whereas an award can always be made for direct discrimination. The case also established that use of a criterion which is itself discriminatory is direct discrimination. The relevance of this in relation to pregnancy dismissals is considered below.

Less favourable treatment cannot be justified by the employer providing **2–010** its own compensation mechanism. In *Ministry of Defence v Jeremiah* (1979) only men were required to work in the shop producing colour-bursting shells. The work was dirty and workers had to shower at the end of the day, and as Lord Denning explained, "A woman's hair is her crowning glory, so it is said. She does not like it disturbed: especially when she has just had a 'hair-do'. The women at an ordnance factory in Wales are no exception. They do not want to work in part of the factory – called a 'shop' – which ruins their hair-do". The men were paid extra "obnoxious" pay for this work, but nonetheless claimed that they were being discriminated against on grounds of sex. Despite the extra money – you cannot buy the right to discriminate – the Court of Appeal held that it was direct discrimination. The chivalrous motive of the employer did not excuse this. The court took the opportunity to contradict its earlier decision to the contrary on this point (*Peake v Automotive Products* (1977), now only supportable on the grounds that allowing women to leave the factory five minutes earlier than men came within the maxim *de minimis non curat lex*).

In the United States it was at one time held that "separate but equal" provision for blacks and whites was not racially discriminatory. Leaving aside the fact that such provision is rarely equal, segregation on racial grounds seems inherently wrong, and section 1(2) of the Race Relations Act puts the point beyond argument by declaring that it constitutes less favourable treatment. This is an issue which an employer must approach with some sensitivity, since it is possible that members of minority racial groups, particularly if their first language is not English, may manifest an associational preference for others of the same group, not least because this makes them feel less of a minority. If the employer, hoping to achieve a proper racial mix, moves people about, it would be likely to amount to less favourable treatment on racial grounds. But if departments or shifts are staffed entirely by members of one racial group there is the possibility of running foul of the segregation provision. This very problem arose in *FTATU v Modgill* (1980) where a particular shift in a furniture factory was staffed entirely by workers of Asian origin. Their shift worked 42½ hours per week as against the 40 worked by other shifts. They claimed that the segregation provision had been contravened. It was found that the all-Asian shift had arisen from the preferences of the workers rather than being imposed by the employer; also that the extra time worked was because it was that particular shift rather than because of their racial origin. In the circumstances the EAT found that there had been no direct discrimination.

2–011   Two particular problems arise in relation to direct discrimination. First, the Acts do not speak of *unfavourable* treatment on grounds of sex or race, but of *less favourable* treatment. This means that there has to be some sort of comparison and in the sex discrimination field in particular, it can be difficult to make such comparisons between men and women – the effect of pregnancy is a good example, and this is discussed below (para. 2–012). The second problem is that to make direct sex or race discrimination in employment actionable, there has to be a further condition: the complainant must show that she has suffered some sort of adverse consequence, such as discrimination in promotion, training, access to other benefits, or in dismissing her or "subjecting her to any other detriment" (SDA, s.6(2)(b); *cf.* RRA, s.4(2)(c)). What amounts to a detriment? The question has arisen frequently in harassment cases where the complaint is essentially that the harassment itself constitutes the detriment. Is being offended or upset or humiliated by insulting behaviour enough to found an action? In *Ministry of Defence v Jeremiah* (1980) and *De Souza v AA* (1986) the Court of Appeal postulated a test of whether or not a reasonable worker would take the view that he or she had been put at a disadvantage. This begged the question, however: what are the characteristics of the reasonable worker? Surely account has to be taken of the sex, race, age and experience of the complainant? In recent years this has been recognised and a more liberal approach is evident. The leading authority is now the decision of the House of Lords in *Shamoon v Chief Constable of the Royal Ulster Constabulary* (2003) where the issue was whether a police inspector suffered a detriment by having the duty of conducting annual appraisals of junior officers taken away from her following complaints about her manner. The House of Lords restated the "reasonable worker" test and denied that there needed to be any adverse physical or economic consequence to demonstrate detriment. While an "unjustified sense of grievance" would be insufficient, Lord Scott indicated that detriment should be considered from the victim's point of view.

Pregnancy

It may seem obvious that discrimination on grounds of pregnancy is sex **2–012** discrimination, since pregnancy is something which only happens to women, but in fact the development of the law has not been so straightforward. As noted already, the Sex Discrimination Act outlaws *less* favourable treatment on grounds of sex, not *un*favourable treatment. The use of the word "less" implies that a comparison needs to be made and accordingly, SDA, s.5(3) requires that in making the comparison, "the relevant circumstances in the one case are the same, or not materially different, in the other" (*cf.* RRA, s.3(4)). It is not necessary to show that there is an actual comparator who has been treated differently; it is enough if a hypothetical comparator of the opposite sex who had relevantly similar characteristics would have been treated differently. The necessity for comparison has caused particular problems in pregnancy discrimination cases. If a woman is dismissed because she is pregnant then under ERA, s.99 the dismissal is automatically unfair. However, to rely on this an employee used to have to have been employed for two years. In *Turley v Allders* (1980) the applicant did not have the requisite period of continuous employment and so she claimed under the Sex Discrimination Act instead, since it has no minimum qualifying period of employment. The action failed, because the EAT held that there was no male equivalent to a pregnant woman. However, in *Hayes v Malleable WMC* (1985) the EAT held that a comparison could be made between a pregnant woman and a man with a long-term health problem; it would thus be sex discrimination if a woman was dismissed on grounds of pregnancy if a man would not be dismissed if needing the same amount of absence because of illness. This analogy, it is submitted, was misplaced: pregnancy is not an illness and is frequently planned; it is not really comparable to an unexpected absence caused by illness or accident. An alternative line of reasoning in cases such as *Hayes* or *Turley* could have been as follows: by dismissing a woman for becoming pregnant, the employer is effectively making it a condition of employment for women, but not for men, that they should not become parents. This is applying an extra condition to the continued employment of women and is thus obviously less favourable treatment of them. However, in a later decision, with a

31

five-member tribunal especially assembled to deal with the point, the EAT reiterated the *Hayes* approach and it was confirmed by the Court of Appeal (*Webb v EMO Cargo* (1990), (1991)).

2–013   Meanwhile, the ECJ decided in *Dekker v VJV Centrum* (1991) that a woman who was not appointed to a post for which she had been adjudged the best candidate because she was pregnant at the time of the interview had been the victim of direct discrimination. However, at the same time the ECJ also held, in *Hertz v Aldi Marked* (1991), that dismissal for sickness absence resulting from a difficult pregnancy did not involve unlawful discrimination where the employee had had her full maternity leave and a man needing a similar amount of sickness absence would have been dismissed. In the view of the House of Lords, this left some doubt as to how far, if at all, comparison with a sick man could be relied on and *Webb v EMO* was referred to the ECJ, which made its decision in 1994.

Webb v EMO concerned a small air freight company with 16 employees. One of the import clerks, S, discovered that she was pregnant in June 1987, so she would need maternity leave early in the following year. W was taken on in July to be trained by S to take over her job during S's maternity leave; importantly, however, the firm expected to keep W on after S returned to work. Two weeks later, W discovered that she was pregnant as well and would need maternity leave around the same time as S. Because she would not be able to cover for the critical period, W was dismissed. The ECJ held that dismissal in these circumstances constituted direct discrimination. The court considered that the fact that the employer would have dismissed a man who was similarly absent, for illness or other reason, at the critical time was nothing to do with the issue: the dismissal was on grounds of pregnancy, which affects only women, and comparison with sickness was inappropriate. It is notable, however, that both the Advocate-General's opinion in the case and the judgment of the court laid emphasis on the fact that this was a contract for an indefinite period – thus her unavailability applied only to a relatively small portion of her expected employment, even though an important time from the employer's point of view. This was seized on by the House of Lords when the case returned to them for consideration (*Webb v EMO (No.2)* (1995)). While holding that W had been the victim of direct discrimination, Lord Keith, giving the opinion of the House, indicated that the answer might be different if the pregnant employee had been taken on for a fixed-term. It was argued that this exception was applicable in *Caruana v Manchester Airport* (1996), where the applicant had been employed under two consecutive fixed-term contracts which she reasonably expected to be renewed. The employer declined to renew the contract because she was pregnant and would be unavailable at the beginning of the next fixed term. The EAT held that this was sex discrimination and that the so-called exception did not apply, as she would not be absent on maternity leave for the whole of the fixed term. In reaching this decision, EAT showed itself sensitive to the risk that too ready an acceptance of an "exception" would risk opening the door to widespread abuse of fixed-term contracts.

Most of the heat went out of the issue in relation to pregnancy and **2–014** discrimination following the implementation of the Pregnant Workers Directive (92/85/EEC), which renders all dismissals on grounds of pregnancy automatically unfair regardless of length of service or whether the contract is indefinite or for a fixed-term (ERA, s.99; see below, para. 6–016). The logical conclusion was spelt out by the ECJ in *Tele Danmark v Brandt-Nielsen* (2001) (see also *Jimenez Melgar v Ayuntamiento de Los Barrios* (2001)), where the ECJ held that it was unlawful sex discrimination and contrary to the Pregnant Workers Directive to dismiss an employee who disclosed that she was pregnant one month after she commenced a six-month fixed-term contract. The baby was due in the fifth month of the contract and she had known that she was pregnant when she got the job but did not tell them, but the ECJ held that these facts made no difference.

Having first applauded the apparent demise of the "sick man" comparison as a result of the ECJ's decision in *Webb v EMO* (1994), some commentators began to have second thoughts. Did this mean that "benign" use of the sick man comparison, in favour of a pregnant woman, was also ruled out? For example, if employees on sick leave are entitled under their contracts to full pay for the first six months, does this mean that a woman absent because of pregnancy or childbirth should get full pay for six months? If so, this would be more generous than their statutory entitlements (see below, para. 6–005).

A number of cases were referred to the ECJ in the wake of *Webb v EMO* to test the position. The final resolution may be regarded as strong on pragmatism but short on logic. The general approach of the ECJ has been to treat pregnancy as a "special case": gender-based, so that unfavourable treatment for this reason will constitute sex discrimination, but a unique situation, so that different treatment of maternity rights and sickness rights will not necessarily do so. Thus dismissing a woman following a disciplinary hearing which she was unable to attend because of her pregnancy was sex discrimination (*Abbey National v Formoso* (1999)), as was the failure to allow a woman the opportunity to have an annual performance review (and thus a chance of a pay increase) because her maternity leave meant that she had not been at work for sufficient time during the relevant year (*Caisse Nationale v Thibault* (1998)). However, in *Gillespie v Northern Health and Social Services Board* (1996) the ECJ held that women were not entitled to full pay during maternity leave even though men and women on sick leave would get full pay. The court held that women on maternity leave were in a special situation which could not be compared with men or women on sick leave. On the same principle, it held in *Boyle v EOC* (1998) that a condition that women return to work for a certain period after maternity leave to qualify for enhanced pay was not sex discrimination even though employees on sick leave did not have to comply with this condition to qualify for full sick pay.

These cases illustrate how easily the concept of comparison can be **2–015** manipulated (through deciding what circumstances are relevant for comparison purposes). This is highlighted by the fact that the ECJ has not abandoned its decision in *Hertz v Aldi Marked* (1991) that sickness absence arising from pregnancy or childbirth *can* be compared with other kinds of sickness absence (thus not treating pregnancy and maternity leave as a special case in these circumstances). The ECJ's final position as laid out in *Brown v Rentokil* (1998) is that it will be sex discrimination to dismiss a woman for any reason related to pregnancy or childbirth during a "protected period" comprising pregnancy and such period of maternity leave as is provided for under national law. This includes dismissal for an illness related to pregnancy and childbirth. However, after the period of maternity leave has ended, if a woman is still absent through illness, she can be dismissed if a man would have been dismissed for a similar amount of absence, even if her illness is related to pregnancy or childbirth. But in making this comparison, the absence during the "protected period" of pregnancy and maternity leave must not be taken into account.

Since comparison between a pregnant woman and a man is not really possible, it may seem sensible for there to be a special regime to deal with this situation, which is effectively what has resulted both from European legislation (the Pregnant Workers Directive (92/85/EEC)) and from the case law of the ECJ. However, the danger of this approach is that unfavourable treatment of women in this situation may not always be protected, as the cases on maternity pay indicate (see also below, para. 6–005).

Dress codes

2–016 The concept of comparison in SDA, s.5(3) causes difficulties not only in relation to pregnancy but also in relation to dress codes. Unlike pregnancy, a dress code can apply to both men and women; however, as conventions relating to male and female dress are different, the rules as to dress may be different for each sex. The approach of courts and tribunals to dress codes demonstrates the high degree of discretion which they have in deciding what are the relevant circumstances for comparison. In *Schmidt v Austicks Bookshops* (1978) it was held that it was not direct discrimination to forbid women to wear trousers where men had to wear jackets and ties. The decision was approved by the Court of Appeal in *Smith v Safeway* (1996), who stated the principle as follows:

> "Rules concerning appearance will not be discriminatory because their content is different for men and women if they enforce a common principle of smartness or conventionality, and taken as a whole and not garment by garment or item by item, neither gender is treated less favourably in enforcing that principle."

In *Smith v Safeway* a male delicatessen assistant who wore his long hair in a ponytail had been dismissed for refusing to have it cut short. Female assistants were permitted to have long hair, provided it was tied back, but men were not. On this basis, the EAT held that there was a direct comparison between the treatment of a man and a woman and the man had clearly been treated less favourably. However, the Court of Appeal held that this was not the appropriate comparison, preferring to consider whether or not there were rules applying to men and women in general. The rejection of a straight comparison and the choice to frame the comparison of dress code rules in terms of their overall impact rather than considering whether some elements were equally applicable to men and women is a clear exercise of discretion based on value judgments which has nothing to do with the principle of equality embodied in the Act. (Compare *McConomy v Croft Inns* (1992), where the Northern Ireland High Court considered that it was no longer unconventional for a man to wear earrings, and a dress code which forbade this to men but not women resulted in men being treated less favourably.)

Problems of proof

One of the biggest problems in direct discrimination cases is proving that **2–017** discrimination has taken place. This is particularly so when it is alleged at the recruitment stage. Frequently an applicant knows only that he or she has been rejected; not why, nor who was appointed instead. Even if you know the identity of the successful candidate, you may well not know whether his or her qualifications for the job were superior to your own. Even if you know that your qualifications were better, in many jobs personality and character matter a great deal too – a factor which tends to increase with the status of the job in question. The question, who was the best candidate, may not have an obvious answer. For the same reasons, discrimination may be occurring unconsciously. It is a fact that we all tend to prefer people like ourselves. If a board of interviewers composed predominantly of white males is thinking about who will "fit in" best with the organisation, they are apt to think it will be a white male.

The difficulties of proving discrimination when the relevant information is peculiarly within the knowledge of the employer led some commentators (and the CRE and EOC) to argue that the burden of proof should be on the employer to disprove discrimination, even though this would be contrary to the general principle of law which requires claimants to establish their claims. For sex discrimination claims a change was made as a result of the Sex Discrimination (Indirect Discrimination and Burden of Proof) Regulations 2001, implementing the Burden of Proof Directive (97/80/EC). The Regulations inserted a new section 63A into the SDA, providing that if the complainant proves facts from which the tribunal could conclude, in the absence of an adequate explanation by the employer, that an act of discrimination had occurred for which the employer would be responsible, then the complaint will be upheld unless the employer proves that he did not commit, or can otherwise avoid responsibility for, that act. This is broadly in line with the position the Court of Appeal had already reached in *King v Great Britain-China Centre* (1991). Similar changes to the burden of proof for race discrimination are contained in the Race Relations Act 1976 (Amendment) Regulations 2003 – although, as noted already, these do not apply to discrimination on grounds of colour or nationality. In practice, however, it can still be difficult to persuade a tribunal to draw an inference of discrimination, especially as more respondents are running the "lousy employer" defence, explained by the House of Lords in *Zafar v Glasgow City Council* (1998). In that case an employee who had been dismissed for sexual harassment claimed that he had been the victim of race discrimination. The tribunal found that the Council's conduct of the disciplinary and dismissal proceedings fell far below the standards of a reasonable employer: there was unreasonable delay in dealing with the matter and some allegations were not properly investigated. The House of Lords held that the fact that the employer had acted *unreasonably* in relation to this employee did not mean that he had been treated *less favourably* than anyone else would have been: the employer might have acted just as unreasonably towards other employees.

2–018   In an attempt to help with the proof of discrimination, a questionnaire procedure is provided for by statutory regulations (SDA, s.74; RRA, s.65). The applicant fills in a questionnaire stating the occasion on which she thinks the discrimination occurred, and the reasons for thinking there was discrimination. The employer is asked whether or not it did discriminate. One cannot help but think that there are few replies of "yes" to this question! If the employer denies discrimination, then further information by way of reply to the claimant's questions must be supplied. Adverse inferences may be drawn if the employer fails to reply promptly, is evasive or equivocal, or attempts to give a different story in front of an employment tribunal (*cf. King v Great Britain-China Centre* (1991)).

How far is it possible to discover whether or not you were better qualified than the other candidates? Relevant information is usually sought by way of an order for the discovery of documents. But much of the information which is relevant may be confidential – for example, references. Guidelines on this problem were given by the House of Lords in *Nassé v Science Research Council* (1979). Confidentiality of the documents is not *per se* a reason to refuse discovery. The test is whether the proceedings can be fairly disposed of without this information. In order to make this decision, it may well be appropriate for the judge or the tribunal chair to look at the documents first. In exercising its discretion over discovery the court must take into account the interests of third parties. Thus disclosure may be ordered subject to certain conditions; for example, excising information that would allow individuals to be identified, or covering up confidential parts. Thus it is possible, though difficult, to get this information. Usually other evidence giving rise to at least some question about the appointment will have to be available first. The court will not order discovery for a "fishing expedition".

2–019   Is it relevant to proof of discrimination to point out that the employer has a workforce composed almost entirely of men, or of whites? Possibly not: it could be that they are the only ones qualified for the job in question. However, if the workforce is composed mostly of workers drawn from the local area, which has a 40 per cent non-white population, but the business employs only 5 per cent non-whites, this would seem to raise a question to be answered.

In an early case the EAT took the view that evidence of this kind was not relevant, for even if it disclosed past discrimination, that would not prove that discrimination had taken place on this particular occasion. The Court of Appeal took a more realistic view in *West Midlands PTE v Singh* (1988). Singh, of Indian origin, was employed as an inspector on the buses and sought promotion to chief inspector. To support his claim that he had been discriminated against in being refused promotion he wanted statistics going back four or five years relating to the ethnic origins of those applying for promotion both for the post of chief inspector and posts of a similar grade, and the ethnic origins of those who were successful. The Court of Appeal ruled that this evidence was relevant. Balcombe L.J. pointed out that ethnic monitoring was recommended by the CRE Code of Practice, presumably for this sort of purpose, and that employers frequently point to the presence of women or ethnic minorities in their workforce in order to *dis*prove discrimination. Thus statistics can cut both ways: they can be used to support or to rebut a claim of discrimination.

Sexual and racial harassment

The concept of harassment did not originally appear in the anti- **2–020** discrimination legislation. However, once again American jurisprudence and legal theory were influential. The American Equal Employment Opportunities Commission defined sexual harassment as being of two main kinds: first, unwelcome sexual advances and other verbal or physical conduct of a sexual nature where submission or rejection of the conduct would affect the recipient's employment; and secondly, conduct having either the purpose or effect of creating an intimidating, hostile or offensive working environment. In British law, this concept of harassment became accepted as a form of direct sex or race discrimination, on the basis that it amounted to treating someone less favourably on grounds of sex or race (*Porcelli v Strathclyde Regional Council* (1984); *De Souza v AA* (1986)).

British law was in turn influential when the EU turned its attention to harassment and the two-pronged definition of harassment was largely adopted for all forms of harassment – in the Race Directive (2000/43/EC) for race discrimination, in the Equal Treatment Amendment Directive (2002/73/EC) for sex discrimination and in the Employment Directive (2000/78/EC) for discrimination on other grounds. However, until all the directives are implemented there will be two separate regimes for harassment. The Equal Treatment Amendment Directive is not due for implementation until 2005, so for the time being sexual harassment will be actionable only if it amounts to direct sex discrimination. The Race Directive had to be implemented by July 2003 and so the Race Relations Act 1976 (Amendment) Regulations 2003 provided a new definition of harassment as a separate head of discrimination, which came into force in July 2003. It is therefore necessary to consider sexual and racial harassment separately.

Sexual harassment

As sexual harassment is a form of direct discrimination, it is necessary for **2–021** the claimant to show that she has been less favourably treated on grounds of her sex. Thus in *Porcelli v Strathclyde Regional Council* (1984) the employee was driven from her job as a school laboratory technician by a concerted campaign of vindictive unpleasantness by her two male co-workers. It was argued that she had not suffered less favourable treatment on the ground of her sex because a disliked male colleague would also have faced a campaign to get rid of him. However, the Court of Session held that the means adopted to make her life unpleasant were used because she was a woman and would not have been used against a man, so direct sex discrimination was established.

As noted already, harassment as direct discrimination is only actionable if it amounts to a "detriment" to the worker: but it is clear that what is detrimental is to be judged from the recipient's point of view (*Shamoon v Chief Constable of the Royal Ulster Constabulary* (2003) above, para. 2–011), although it is likely that an extreme and wholly unreasonable reaction would not be considered as a detriment. The converse may also hold true: if the recipient is not upset by the harasser's conduct then she will not have suffered a detriment (*Snowball v Gardner Merchant* (1987)). But conduct cannot be judged in the abstract: as Popplewell J. said in *Wileman v Minilec Engineering* (1988), "A person may be quite happy to accept the remarks of A or B in a sexual context, and wholly upset by similar remarks by C".

It is clear that the motive of the perpetrator is not relevant: it is no defence to say that no offence was intended if the words or conduct were offensive and either the recipient had indicated as much or any reasonable person would have realised that this was the case (*Insitu v Heads* (1995); *Reed and Bull Information Systems Ltd v Stedman* (1999)).

Racial harassment

2–022 The Race Relations Act 1976 (Amendment) Regulations 2003 introduce a concept of harassment as a freestanding head of discrimination in a new section 3A(1) of the RRA. Harassment is there defined as "unwanted conduct which has the purpose or effect of (a) violating [a] person's dignity, or (b) creating an intimidating, hostile, degrading or offensive environment for him". This applies to harassment on grounds of race or ethnic or national origin. Harassment on grounds of colour or nationality will be actionable only if it amounts to direct race discrimination. However, harassment which *is* covered by the new definition will not be actionable as direct discrimination because a new definition of "detriment" in RRA, s.78 excludes it.

The new definition makes it clear that harassment is to be judged from the recipient's point of view and also removes the need for the recipient to show that there have been detrimental consequences for him or her. However, it is qualified by the introduction (in RRA, s.3A(2)) of an explicitly objective standard for judging whether conduct will amount to harassment: words or conduct are only to be regarded as having the harassing effect "if, having regard to all the circumstances, including in particular the perception of that other person, it should reasonably be considered as having that effect". This may end up being a greater stumbling block than showing detriment, since the widening of the latter concept in *Shamoon*.

Employers' liability

2–023 Sexual and racial harassment are activities which could well be carried out not by the employer but by an employee, or even by the employer's customers or clients. This raises the general question of the employer's responsibility for the discriminatory acts of other people. The Sex Discrimination Act, s.41 and the Race Relations Act, s.32 provide that an employer is liable for the acts of employees done in the course of their employment, whether or not done with the employer's knowledge or approval. Whether or not employees' actions were "in the course of their employment" was originally interpreted as being the same as the common law test for vicarious liability in tort. However, in *Jones v Tower Boot Co Ltd* (1997) the Court of Appeal held that there were important differences between the statutory formulation and the common law test (for example, the defence available under the statute has no common law counterpart) so that it was not appropriate to treat them as identical. In *Jones v Tower Boot* a 16-year-old apprentice of mixed race had been subjected by two fellow employees not only to verbal racial abuse but also to serious physical attacks. The EAT took the view that this was so far removed from what they were employed to do that it could not possibly be said to be in the course of employment for the purposes of vicarious liability. The Court of Appeal, recognising that it would be anomalous if the employer was more likely to escape liability the more serious the harassment was, and taking account of the purpose of the legislation, held that the words "in the course of employment" in the statute should be given their normal meaning, not the technical meaning used in relation to vicarious liability. On this basis the boy's attackers could be said to have been acting in the course of employment and the employer was liable.

In *Chief Constable of Lincolnshire Police v Stubbs* (1999) the EAT held that the employer could be liable for harassment taking place outside working hours where it took place during social events which could be regarded as "extensions of work" (a leaving party and the regular team drink after work). However, in *Sidhu v Aerospace Composite Technology Ltd* (2000) racial harassment happening during a day's outing to a theme park organised by the employer for workers and their families was held by a tribunal to be outside the course of employment, and this was upheld by the Court of Appeal, even though the employer had used its disciplinary procedure in relation to those involved, which seemed to indicate that the employer at least considered it as an extension of employment! The case illustrates the difficulty of attacking tribunal decisions, as long as the tribunal has applied the correct legal test.

Where the employer is held liable under the statute, the actual perpetrator will also be liable and so could be ordered to pay compensation (SDA, s.42; RRA, s.33). However, if the action is held not to be in the course of employment, so that the employer escapes, the perpetrator does too, since the legislation only prohibits discrimination by employers, not fellow employees or customers of the employer. This again illustrates the importance of the Court of Appeal's decision in *Jones v Tower Boot*, for if the original decision had stood, the employees who carried out the attacks would not have been liable under the Race Relations Act (although they could have been liable to prosecution for criminal offences or to being sued for assault and battery).

In *Burton v De Vere Hotels* (1996) the EAT held that an employer could **2–024** also be directly liable for discrimination consisting of the acts of third parties: not only employees, but also customers, clients and others. The action was brought against a hotel which had been booked for a club dinner, attended by 400 men. They had invited as after-dinner speaker a comedian notorious for sexually explicit and racial jokes. Two young Afro-Caribbean waitresses clearing tables at the end of the dinner attracted his attention and in the course of a speech containing many offensive words and jokes he made insulting comments directed at them too. The EAT held that although the hotel could not be vicariously liable for the actions of third parties, it was directly responsible for discrimination in these circumstances because as employers, they had control of the situation in which the harassment took place. Members of the hotel management were present to supervise the event. They could at least have minimised the effects of the harassment by withdrawing the waitresses as soon as the comedian became offensive. Failure to do so meant that the employer had directly subjected them to a detriment, namely the racial harassment.

Burton v De Vere Hotels was relied on in numerous cases over the next six or seven years, but was then disapproved by the House of Lords in *Pearce v Governing Body of Mayfield School* (2003). The case involved a lesbian teacher forced out of her job by homophobic abuse by pupils at the school and the central issue was whether gender-specific abuse (*e.g.* calling her a "dyke") was sex discrimination even though it was clear that a male homosexual teacher would have been subjected to similar abuse. The House of Lords held that this did not constitute direct sex discrimination because a male homosexual would have been treated just as badly as the female homosexual applicant had been. However, even though it was not essential to their decision, the Law Lords went on to hold that even if it had been discrimination, the school would not have been liable for the actions of the pupils. The school's liability was argued to reside in its failure to protect her. Only if it could be shown that this was itself an omission to act on grounds of her sex would the school be liable. Although the House of Lords' comments are strictly *obiter*, it is inconceivable that *Burton v De Vere Hotels* can be regarded as good law in future and so, unfortunately, an important spur for employers to ensure that the workplace is harassment-free has been removed.

An employer has a defence to a claim of direct discrimination if it has taken reasonable practicable steps to prevent discriminatory acts. In *Balgobin v Tower Hamlets* (1987) two cleaners employed by the Council at a hostel complained of sexual harassment by a chef working in the same place. The Council relied on the fact that it had a clear equal opportunities policy promulgated to employees, and that there was proper and adequate supervision of employees at work. In these circumstances the EAT held that the employer had established the defence, rejecting the applicants' claims that all reasonably practicable steps had not been taken because sexual harassment was not a specific disciplinary offence and because the chef was not moved from his post after a disciplinary hearing (*cf.* also *Canniffe v East Riding of Yorkshire Council* (2000)).

Indirect discrimination

2–025 In the White Paper preceding the Sex Discrimination Act, the Government envisaged only that intentional discrimination should be unlawful. Motive would be what mattered, not impact. However, the then Home Secretary,

Roy Jenkins, was convinced by a visit to the United States during the summer recess that of far more importance in achieving equality of opportunity was preventing the effect of apparently neutral practices and policies which in fact excluded women or ethnic minorities. The Supreme Court decision in *Griggs v Duke Power Company* (1971) laid the foundation for the concept of indirect discrimination in the British statutes. In *Griggs* the company administered an aptitude test to all job applicants. It was shown that significantly fewer blacks than whites passed the test, and that the skills examined by the test were not particularly relevant to the jobs applied for. In these circumstances, it was held that the test was discriminatory.

This concept of "adverse impact discrimination" was given statutory form in the United Kingdom as indirect discrimination (SDA, s.1(1)(b); RRA, s.1(1)(b)). Its potential to catch apparently innocuous requirements and thus to begin to address systemic discrimination was demonstrated at an early stage. For example, in *Price v Civil Service Commission* (1978) applicants for the post of Executive Officer had to be aged between $17\frac{1}{2}$ and 28. The applicant, aged 32, successfully argued that this was indirect discrimination against women, since between these ages many women are likely to be out of the labour market bringing up small children. However, the original definition of indirect discrimination required applicants to identify a "requirement or condition" which had the effect of screening them out. The problem with this was that in *Perera v Civil Service Commission (No.2)* (1983) the Court of Appeal held that a criterion for recruitment should not be regarded as a requirement or condition unless it constituted an absolute bar to appointment if one did not meet it. This was followed with some reluctance in *Meer v Tower Hamlets* (1988) where the point was made that this could drive a coach and horses through the protection given by the legislation, in that it allowed discriminatory preferences free rein, as long as they were not expressed as absolute requirements. In that case there was a preference for a candidate who had previous experience working for the local authority, which would tend to screen out non-British workers, although this was not an absolute requirement for the job.

In accordance with the Burden of Proof Directive (97/80/EC), the Sex Discrimination (Indirect Discrimination and Burden of Proof) Regulations 2001 introduced a new definition of indirect discrimination, which only applies in the employment field. Under SDA, s.1(2)(b) it is now sufficient if there is a "provision, criterion or practice" which "would be to the detriment of a considerably larger proportion of women than men". The Race Directive required a similar change for indirect discrimination on grounds of race and national or ethnic origin (but not colour or nationality) – see the new RRA, s.1A introduced by the Race Relations Act 1976 (Amendment) Regulations 2003. It is to be hoped that this is wide enough to encompass the kind of second-order preferences which were at issue in *Perera v Civil Service Commission (No.2)*.

Having identified the provision, criterion or practice which is alleged to **2–026** be having the exclusionary effect, the next stage is to demonstrate adverse impact. The SDA and RRA originally said that there would be adverse impact if the proportion of women, or married people, or members of a particular racial group who could comply with it was "considerably smaller" than the proportion of the comparator group who could comply. The new definitions (which only apply to discrimination in employment and, in the case of the RRA, not to discrimination on grounds of colour or nationality) are different from each other, raising the unwelcome complication of no fewer than three separate definitions of adverse impact to be considered. In the case of indirect sex discrimination in the employment field, adverse impact is shown if the provision "would be to the detriment of a considerably larger proportion of women than men" (SDA, s.1(2)(b)). It is not clear whether this is different in practice from the original definition. In the RRA, s.1A, it is enough if it puts people of one racial group "at a particular disadvantage" compared with other people – *i.e.* there is no mention of proportions at all. It is a pity that this formulation was not used in the SDA, especially as tribunals and courts have struggled with statistical evidence in the past (see, *e.g. Kidd v DRG* (1985), *Jones v University of Manchester* (1993) and *R. v Secretary of State ex p. Seymour-Smith and Perez* (1999)).

The question of what degree of adverse impact needed to be shown was specifically referred to the ECJ in *R. v Secretary of State ex p. Seymour-Smith and Perez* (1999), where two women dismissed with 15 months' service challenged the then law that no claim for unfair dismissal could be brought unless the applicant had two years' service. Their argument, that this continuity requirement tended to screen out women, succeeded in the Court of Appeal, where it was noted that between 1985 (when the continuity requirement was extended from one year to two) and 1991 (when they were dismissed), for every 100 men who could comply with this condition, only between 88.5 and 90.5 women could do so (although the evidence also showed that the gap seemed to be narrowing). The House of Lords referred the case to the ECJ but, disappointingly, the ECJ did not answer the question directly. The ECJ did indicate that a smaller disparity could be regarded as sufficiently exclusionary if it persisted relatively unchanged over a long period and when the case returned to the House of Lords (*R. v Secretary of State ex p. Seymour-Smith and Perez (No.2)* (2000)) it was held by a majority that the persistent and relatively stable disparity between 1985 and 1991 did indicate that the two-year requirement had a considerably greater adverse impact on women. This indicated indirect sex discrimination, but it was also held that the Secretary of State could rely on the defence of justification.

2–027   Even if a condition does tend to rule out women, in indirect sex discrimination the employer has a defence if it is justifiable to impose it. What does "justifiable" mean here? Although in the early case, *Steel v UPOW* (1977) it was held that the employer would have to show the condition was "necessary", the standard became easier to satisfy, until in *Ojutiku v Manpower Services Commission* (1982) the Court of Appeal held that it was justifiable if the requirement "would seem sound and tolerable to right-thinking people". However, in *Bilka-Kaufhaus v Weber von Hartz* (1986) the ECJ, construing Article 141 of the Treaty of Rome, held that an employer would have to show "objectively justified" grounds to make out the defence. This involves three elements: the employer's objective for the rule having an adverse impact must (a) correspond to a real need on the part of the undertaking, (b) be appropriate to that end and (c) necessary to that end. This sounds like a stricter test than that propounded in *Ojutiku*, but in *Hampson v DES* (1989) the Court of Appeal considered that there was no significant difference between them, a decision later approved by the House of Lords.

The test for a government justifying legislation with a discriminatory impact appears to be set at a lower level: in *R. v Secretary of State for Employment ex p. Seymour-Smith* (1999) the ECJ held that it would be sufficient if the rule reflected a legitimate aim of social policy; if that aim was unrelated to sex discrimination; and the government could reasonably consider that the means chosen were suitable for attaining that aim. Applying this test, the House of Lords held in *R. v Secretary of State for Employment ex p. Seymour-Smith and Perez (No.2)* (2000) that the only question was over the third element. The purported aim of the extension of the qualifying period to two years was to encourage job creation by reducing one of the risks associated with taking on employees. While there was little hard evidence to support this, the House of Lords considered that it was more than a mere generalised assumption on the part of the Secretary of State and that to hold that an impact analysis should have been undertaken first would be unreasonably burdensome. In these circumstances, it was held that the defence of justification was made out.

The defence in indirect race discrimination cases is now expressed **2–028** differently: as a result of the 2003 amendments the employer will have a defence if it can show that the provision having adverse impact was "a proportionate means of achieving a legitimate aim" (RRA, s.1(1A)(b)). This appears broadly to embody the ECJ test from *Bilka-Kaufhaus v Weber von Hartz*.

Finally, for indirect sex discrimination, the requirement or condition must be to the detriment of the applicant because he or she cannot comply with it. The House of Lords made clear in *Mandla v Dowell Lee* (1983) that the question whether someone "can comply" must be judged not according to whether it is theoretically possible for them to comply, but whether they can reasonably be expected to do so. It was theoretically possible for the Sikh boy to comply with the requirement to have a short back and sides, but not reasonable to expect him to do so. Under the RRA, s.1(1A)(a) the test for race discrimination is now easier in any case: the issue is only whether the applicant has been "put at a disadvantage".

Discrimination by victimisation

Discrimination by victimisation may be defined as less favourable treatment **2–029** of someone on the grounds that he or she has done a protected act – broadly, these are bringing proceedings or assisting in the bringing of proceedings or making a complaint under the Acts (SDA, s.4; RRA, s.2). The object of the provisions is to prevent people from being discouraged from making complaints because of fear of repercussions at work. Indeed, it could be argued that there is a need for such anti-victimisation provisions on a wider scale, for example, in unfair dismissal cases.

Although the purpose of the provisions is straightforward, their interpretation has caused problems. The Court of Appeal held in *Aziz v Trinity*

Street Taxis (1988) that in order to succeed in a victimisation claim the applicant had to show not only that he had been treated less favourably for doing a protected act, but also that the motive of the employer was connected to the race discrimination legislation. This meant that the victimisation provisions could rarely be relied on, since that extra motive would be difficult to show. In *Aziz* itself, the protected act was making secret recordings of conversations with colleagues in the taxi association which the applicant planned to use in discrimination proceedings. The Court of Appeal accepted the association's argument that it would have expelled anyone guilty of such a breach of trust, whatever the reason behind it. The decision also meant that the interpretation of the victimisation provisions was out of line with the similarly worded provision on direct discrimination, where it is necessary only to show less favourable treatment on grounds of race or sex and the need for a discriminatory motive has been specifically denied (*James v Eastleigh BC* (1990) above, para. 2–009).

The House of Lords considered the issue in *Nagarajan v London Regional Transport* (1999). In this case, a tribunal found that members of an interview panel that rejected the claimant were at least subconsciously influenced by the fact that he had made several claims of race discrimination against the company in the past (protected acts for the purposes of the victimisation claim). The House of Lords held that if the protected act was a "substantial reason" or an "important factor" leading to the less favourable treatment, a claim for victimisation would succeed. Note that the protected act need not be the only or even the main reason. This seemed to mean that the test for victimisation was now the same as for direct discrimination: whether the claimant would not have been treated less favourably but for doing the protected act. Unfortunately, almost at once the House of Lords had second thoughts.

In *Chief Constable of West Yorks Police v Khan* (2001) a police sergeant of Indian origin sued for race discrimination when he failed on several occasions to gain promotion. While these proceedings were ongoing he applied for an inspector's post in a different force. The West Yorkshire Police refused to give him a reference in case it prejudiced the case. The sergeant therefore added a claim for victimisation. The Court of Appeal held that if he had not brought the discrimination proceedings he would have been given a reference and that his victimisation claim therefore succeeded. In adopting this "but-for" test the Court of Appeal was following its understanding of the House of Lords' decision in *Nagarajan v London Regional Transport*. The House of Lords reversed, holding that the treatment complained of had to be "by reason of" the protected act and that this required more than causation (but for the protected act the less favourable treatment would not have occurred): it also required some level of mental connection between the two facts by the employer – some degree of motivation. And, in a display of semantic nicety, they also held that it was the *existence* of the other proceedings, rather than the fact that the applicant had *brought* them, which was the relevant reason here. The applicant's victimisation claim was therefore rejected. It is frankly hard to square this with *Nagarajan*. It seems that the Law Lords' sympathy for the practical dilemma for an employer in these circumstances has led to a most unfortunate development in this area of law. We are back at a situation where employers will only be liable if conscious or unconscious desire to discriminate is established – which is notoriously difficult. This was well recognised by the House of Lords when it rejected a test of motivation and adopted a but-for test for direct discrimination in *James v Eastleigh BC*. It is difficult to see any justification for a different test in relation to victimisation.

In *Coote v Granada Hospitality* (1999) the applicant left the company **2–030** after making an allegation of sex discrimination against it. That claim was settled, but thereafter the employer refused to supply her with a reference, which made it very difficult for her to find another job. She claimed that she was being victimised because of her earlier discrimination claim, and that the employer was "subjecting her to a detriment" within the meaning of SDA, s.6(2). However, this section only applies to a "woman employed" by the employer and in *Adekeye v Post Office (No.2)* (1997) the Court of Appeal had held that the parallel provision in RRA, s.4(2) could not be invoked once the employment had terminated. The EAT was bound to adopt the same interpretation for SDA, s.6(2), but it referred to the ECJ the question of whether this was compatible with Article 6 of the Equal Treatment Directive (76/207/EEC) which requires that there must be effective remedies for breach of the Directive. The ECJ held that the principle requiring effective remedies would be infringed if employers could take retaliatory steps affecting the employee after the employment had ended and that someone in the applicant's position should be protected by the law. When the case came back to the EAT it was able to construe "a woman employed" as covering someone who used to be employed as well as someone currently employed and so her claim for victimisation was upheld (*Coote v Granada Hospitality (No.2)* (1999)). *Adekeye v Post Office (No.2)* was distinguished on the grounds that it was a decision under the RRA rather than the SDA. However, the House of Lords considered the whole question of discrimination arising after employment had terminated in *Relaxion Group plc v Rhys-Harper* (2003) and *D'Souza v Lambeth LBC* (2003). It held that both the SDA and the RRA could be interpreted as covering post-employment discrimination, provided that the connection between the post-employment discriminatory act and the employment could be proved. For sex discrimination law, this was probably unnecessary, as the Sex Discrimination Act 1975 (Amendment) Regulations 2003 had already inserted a new SDA, s.20A to cover post-termination discrimination. A similar amendment was made to the RRA by the Race Relations Act 1976 (Amendment) Regulations 2003, but this only applies to the grounds of race and ethnic or national origin, so *D'Souza v Lambeth LBC* could continue to be of importance.

Exceptions to the legislation

Genuine occupational qualifications

There are certain exceptional situations where being of one sex or a **2–031** particular racial group is a genuine occupational qualification so that job offers (only) may be restricted to that group. In relation to sex discrimination the list of exceptions was narrowed following adverse findings by the

ECJ in *Commission of the EC v UK* (1984). Under SDA, s.7 as amended, sex is an occupational qualification where physiological authenticity requires a man (*e.g.* a dramatic performance); to preserve decency and privacy; where the work is in a private home and involves close physical or social contact with the employer (a Jeeves, but not a gardener); where the job requires living in, and there are only facilities for one sex; where the job is at an all-male institution such as a hospital or prison; where the job involves provision of personal services to individuals promoting their welfare or education and the services can best be provided by a man; where the law prohibits the employment of women; where the job is in another country whose laws or customs preclude its being done by a woman; or where the job is one of two to be held by a married couple. Strength is specifically excluded from being a genuine occupational qualification; thus where a degree of strength is genuinely required, the employer must consider whether each applicant, male or female, can cope; if it is not genuinely required, it would be indirect discrimination on grounds of sex. In general these exceptions are construed fairly narrowly. In *Wylie v Dee* (1978) it was claimed that being a man was a genuine occupational qualification to work in the menswear department of a shop because the job could involve taking inside leg measurements. It was held that there was no real likelihood of customers objecting to a woman doing this, and even if there were, there were plenty of male assistants available who could be called on.

The list of genuine occupational qualifications under RRA, s.5 was always shorter. Physiological authenticity is included here also (not that this has led to many black Othellos) and is extended to restaurants (so that it is lawful, for example, to have only Indian waiters in an Indian restaurant); the only other exception is where personal services promoting welfare or education are being provided to members of a particular racial group and can most effectively be provided by someone of the same racial group. This has been interpreted restrictively. In *Lambeth v CRE* (1990) the Council advertised the posts of group manager and assistant head of housing benefits in their housing benefits department as available only for Asian or Afro-Caribbean applicants. The Council pointed out that over half of the tenants with whom the department dealt were of Afro-Caribbean or Asian origin, and they relied on the provision of welfare services exception, arguing that it was important that the department should be sensitive to the needs and experiences of black people. The Court of Appeal, implicitly adopting the view that the employer's judgment is open to review, upheld the tribunal's decision that the exception did not apply because the holders of these particular posts would have little or no contact with the public and therefore could not be said to be providing personal services. By contrast, in *Tottenham Green Under Fives' Centre v Marshall* (1991) the EAT accepted that caring for children did involve the provision of personal services and that the employer could rely on race as a genuine occupational qualification where 84 per cent of the children in the nursery were of Afro-Caribbean origin and the tribunal had found as a fact that someone of Afro-Caribbean or African origin could talk or read to them in West Indian dialect.

In accordance with the Race Directive (2000/43/EC) the 2003 Regulations have introduced a new exception which is capable in theory of applying to all employers. Under RRA, s.4A it applies where the nature or the context of the employment in which it is carried out makes being of a particular race, ethnic or national origins a genuine and determining occupational requirement, provided also that the exception meets a proportionality test.

Other exceptions

The SDA makes special provision for a number of occupations: police, prison officers, ministers of religion, midwives and mineworkers. There are also exceptions in relation to death or retirement, which are dealt with in the discussion of equal pay (below, para. 7–024). The only special occupation exception in the Race Relations Act relates to seamen recruited abroad and it has been narrowed as a result of the Race Directive (2000/43/EC). It remains lawful to pay them less than their British counterparts, on grounds of nationality. 2–032

Positive discrimination and positive action

To a very limited extent, the Acts permit positive or reverse discrimination – that is, allowing preferential treatment of one group at the expense of another. This is only in relation to training. Employers or training bodies may offer training to one sex only, or to one racial group only in order to equip them for a job if no one, or very few, of that sex or group have been doing that work in the previous 12 months (SDA, ss.47–48; RRA, ss.37–38). As one of the major problems in sex discrimination is the *de facto* separation of "men's work" and "women's work", this has considerable potential: however, since training courses cost money, it is likely that an employer would only take advantage of this *in extremis*. 2–033

Under British law any other positive discrimination is unlawful, since discrimination in favour of women or one racial group is simply discrimination against men or other racial groups, who are equally protected under the legislation. Thus it was held unlawful for the Labour Party to insist upon all-women shortlists (*Jepson v Labour Party* (1996); however, since then the Sex Discrimination (Election Candidates) Act 2002 has been passed to permit this). However, the position is different in relation to sex discrimination under EC law. Article 2(4) of the Equal Treatment Directive 1976 permits measures designed to remove existing inequalities which affect women's opportunities, but it was held in *Kalanke v Bremen* (1995) that this did not cover a situation where a state law provided for a female candidate automatically to be preferred over an equally qualified male candidate whenever women were under-represented (*i.e.* there were fewer than 50 per cent) in the particular employment grade. This decision caused a political uproar as other Member States had similar laws and the European Commission itself operated a similar policy! In consequence, when faced with almost the same issue in *Marschall v Land Nordrhein-Westfalen* (1998) the ECJ managed to distinguish *Kalanke*. In *Marschall*, the law preferring women was the same as in *Kalanke* except that it contained a proviso that the preference would not apply "if reasons specific to another candidate predominate". This allowed some flexibility to appoint a better male candidate even where he and the female candidate had equal qualifications. Meanwhile, in 1997 the effect of *Kalanke* was largely nullified when the Treaty of Amsterdam amended the Treaty of Rome to add a new sub-paragraph, Article 141(4), stating that:

> "the principle of equal treatment shall not prevent any Member State from maintaining or adopting measures providing for specific advantages in order to make it easier for the under-represented sex to pursue a vocational activity or to prevent or compensate for disadvantages in professional careers".

This is, of course, permissive rather than mandatory, and it is unlikely that it will lead to a change to British law in the near future.

2–034 Positive discrimination must be distinguished from positive action. Whereas positive discrimination postulates taking a less well-qualified candidate in order to have a woman or someone from a minority group, positive action does not preclude taking the best candidate available. Positive action is designed to get more of the under-represented groups into a position where they will be the best candidates. Thus the placing of advertisements in publications which are more likely to reach minorities, and statements that applications from them are particularly welcome may improve the application rate and thus the chances of minority candidates being appointed. In the case of women, allowing flexitime working, job-sharing and the provision of child-care facilities increases the chances of many to work. Special career counselling for members of under-represented groups may assist them to achieve promotion, and so on. These kinds of activities, which are among the suggestions made in the Codes of Practice issued by the EOC and the CRE, are not contrary to the legislation, nor are they required by it, but they are an important next stage if there is to be a real change in the white male dominated world of employment.

Remedies

2–035 If finding a complaint of discrimination proved, a tribunal has power (a) to make an order declaring the rights of the parties; (b) to require the employer to pay compensation, and (c) to recommend the employer to take action within a specified period to obviate or reduce the adverse effect of the discrimination. The latter remedy in particular has attracted criticism as being inadequate.

Compensation

2–036 Discrimination is a statutory tort and in principle damages should be assessed as for any other tort with the aim of compensating the claimant so that she is in the position in which she would have been but for the unlawful conduct (*Ministry of Defence v Wheeler*, 1998)). Unusually, however, it is expressly provided that claimants can be compensated for injury to feelings (SDA, s.66(4); RRA, s.57(4)). This may be particularly important in harassment cases where the victim may not suffer any quantifiable financial loss.

The position in relation to compensation for discrimination was transformed as a result of *Marshall v Southampton & S.W. Hants AHA (No.2)*. In 1989 an employment tribunal awarded Ms Marshall a sum nearly double the maximum allowed under English law (including a sum for interest on the award) on the basis that Community legislation requires remedies to be adequate. The case was referred to the ECJ, which held in 1993 that the statutory limits on compensation were in breach of Article 6 of the Equal Treatment Directive, as was the ban on allowing interest. As a result the Sex Discrimination and Equal Pay (Remedies) Regulations 1993 were passed to remove the ceiling on compensation. While the ECJ decision did not require any change to the limits of compensation in race discrimination cases, it was recognised that it would be arbitrary and invidious for there to be such a major distinction between the two claims. Thus the Race Relations (Remedies) Act 1994 abolished the upper limit on compensation in race discrimination cases and the Race Relations (Interest on Awards) Regulations 1994 made provision for the payment of interest parallel to the sex discrimination regulations.

One group who benefited greatly from the removal of the limit on **2–037** compensation were women dismissed from the armed forces on grounds of pregnancy, which the Ministry of Defence conceded in 1991 was a breach of the Equal Treatment Directive, although it had been permitted under the SDA. In *Ministry of Defence v Cannock* (1994) the EAT held that the correct approach to future loss of earnings was to ask what the chances were of the woman staying in the employment. In the case of the armed forces, women and men usually sign up and stay for fixed terms of many years and so the figures awarded under this heading were often high. It is less likely to be the case in ordinary employment, although in *Vento v Chief Constable of West Yorkshire Police (No.2)* (2003) the Court of Appeal, endorsing the approach of *MoD v Cannock*, stressed that this was a question of fact for the tribunal.

Vento v Chief Constable of West Yorkshire Police (No.2) (2003) also contains useful guidance on the award of compensation for injury to feelings. The Court of Appeal reiterated the guidance given in *Alexander v Home Office* (1988) and *Armitage v Johnson* (1997). First, the objective of the award is restitution. It should not be minimal, for this trivialises and diminishes respect for the public policy behind the Act; but excessive awards could have the same effect. Secondly, awards should bear "some broad, general similarity" to awards in personal injury cases – but the overall value in everyday life of the award contemplated should also be borne in mind. The Court of Appeal ruled that compensation for injury to feelings should fall into three broad categories. For the most serious cases, such as a lengthy period of sustained sexual or racial harassment, as in *Armitage*, compensation should normally be between £15,000–£25,000. The middle band, for serious cases not falling in the top band, it should be £5,000–£15,000; and for "less serious" cases – such as an isolated incident without major consequences, the band should be £500–£5,000. The Court of Appeal thought that awards below £500 should be avoided as tending to trivialise the gravity of injury to feelings.

49

Finally, it should be noted that compensation for discrimination is not confined to pecuniary loss, and sometimes aggravated damages may be appropriate.

Recommendations

2–038 The main question in relation to the power to make recommendations is, can the employer be compelled to give the next available post to the applicant? In *North West Thames RHA v Noone* (1988) the Court of Appeal held that a health authority found to have discriminated directly against the applicant on grounds of race could not be ordered to offer the next available vacancy to the applicant because statutory procedures require such posts to be advertised. However, it did say that if she applied again, a future interview board should be apprised of the previous history. In *British Gas v Sharma* (1991) the EAT relied on this decision to hold that a tribunal did not have the power to recommend that the applicant should be promoted to the next available vacancy in a particular clerical grade. This seems to go further than warranted by the Court of Appeal's decision. The EAT held also that this would be tantamount to positive discrimination, and that it also failed because no time-limit was specified. Only the last ground seems supportable. To give the victim of discrimination the next post is not to discriminate in her favour but merely to ensure that she has the most appropriate form of compensation for the wrong done to her. Indeed, if this remedy is to be seen as at all effective, it is essential that such orders should be able to be made.

Disability Discrimination

2–039 Laws to prevent discrimination against people with disabilities were originally introduced in many countries, including the United Kingdom, to provide some protection in employment for soldiers returning from war. The original British legislation, the Disabled Persons (Employment) Act, was passed in 1944 and imposed a quota requirement related to the proportion of disabled people thought to be in the workforce. At least 3 per cent of the workforce of employers with 20 or more employees were meant to be people registered as disabled. This legislation was widely recognised to be ineffective, but there was little impetus for reform until campaigning began in 1993, inspired by the American experience. The comprehensive and ambitious Americans with Disabilities Act 1992 was predicated on the philosophy that a society which excludes people with disabilities from social institutions, including the workplace, is denying them their civil rights. This provided both a powerful argument for reform and a single banner under which groups representing people with different disabilities could unite. The Civil Rights (Disabled Persons) Bill, heavily influenced by the American Act, was introduced as a private member's Bill and almost became law in 1994. It was defeated by the filibustering of a few Conservative MPs, in circumstances which caused a public outcry. This led the Government to bring forward its own proposals, finally passed as the Disability Discrimination Act 1995. In fact, the, Act was not brought into force until December 1996, when supporting regulations, guidance and a code of practice had been prepared. The Statutory Guidance on the meaning of disability and the Code of Practice for the elimination of discrimination in employment drawn up by the Secretary of State are to be taken into account by courts and tribunals in any proceedings where they are relevant (DDA, ss.3, 51, 53) and so must also be considered as part of the overall picture. While weaker than the reformers had proposed and wished for, the Disability Discrimination Act was nonetheless a great improvement on the former position.

Since then the Disability Rights Task Force (a non-statutory body set up by the Government in 1999) and the Disability Rights Commission have been active in pressing for improvements to the DDA. In addition, disability was one of the grounds included in the Employment Directive (2000/78/EC), which made some reform to the DDA essential, but did not need to be implemented until 2006. In fact the Disability Discrimination Act 1995 (Amendment) Regulations 2003 have already been made, although they will not come into force until October 1, 2004.

Scope of the legislation

The DDA adopts the extended definition of employment used in the SDA **2–040** and RRA, thus including anyone employed under a contract personally to perform work and apprentices as well as employees. Originally employers with fewer than 20 employees were exempt, an exception which was reckoned to remove protection from a large proportion of workers with disabilities, who are generally more likely to work for small employers. In 1998 the exemption limit was reduced to 15 employees, which brought a further 750,000 employees within the scope of the Act, according to government estimates, although disability groups reckon that this still leaves 92½ per cent of employers outside it. However, this exemption will be abolished from October 1, 2004 as a result of the DDA (Amendment) Regulations 2003.

Definition of disability

A disabled person is defined by DDA, s.1 as someone having "a physical or **2–041** mental impairment which has a substantial and long-term adverse effect on his ability to carry out normal day-to-day activities". The definition is expanded in Schedule 1 to the Act, the Disability Discrimination (Meaning of Disability) Regulations 1996 and the Statutory Guidance on the definition of disability. Mental impairment covers mental illness as well as learning disabilities, but only mental illnesses which are "clinically well-recognised". This could include depression, if the effects are severe enough (*Kapadia v Lambeth LBC* (2000)). The Regulations provide that psychopathic or anti-social disorders such as kleptomania or paedophilia are excluded. Addiction to alcohol, tobacco or drugs does not count as a disability, although physical manifestations of such dependency (such as liver or heart disease) are capable of doing so.

As the reference to "clinically well-recognised" mental illnesses indicates, the DDA largely adopts a "medical model" of disability, meaning that the question of who is disabled is one which is essentially to be answered by medical experts. This presumably is thought to have the advantage that the test depends on objective facts and that a fair degree of precision may be obtained. In practice it has turned out to have the disadvantage that in any case where the issue of disability is contested it is virtually essential for both parties to call expert medical evidence, adding substantially to the cost of the proceedings. In *Kapadia v Lambeth LBC* (2000) the employer argued that the employee was not disabled by his depression, given that he had successfully applied for promotion while receiving treatment. But since the employer had not produced any medical evidence, preference had to be given to the uncontradicted evidence of the employee's psychologist and doctor to the effect that he was.

2–042   More fundamentally, however, disability rights activists argue that the biggest problem facing people with disabilities is the blinkered attitude of the rest of the community, who frequently perceive them as having greater limitations than is in fact the case or who exhibit irrational prejudices. They therefore argue that a "social model" of disability would be more appropriate, which would treat people as disabled if they are liable to be perceived as disabled or to suffer from prejudice against people with disabilities. There are some elements in the DDA which do adopt the social model, so that certain conditions which are perceived as disabilities are included, even though they would not in reality affect someone's performance (such as severe disfigurement or past disability). Others, such as being believed to have a disability, or association with someone who has a disability, are not covered.

According to the Code of Practice and Statutory Guidance, "substantial" means "more than 'minor' or 'trivial' ", and factors such as the time taken to do something, or the manner of doing it are among the things to be taken into account in deciding how substantial an effect is. At the beginning tribunals were inclined to interpret "substantial" as meaning "very large". In *Goodwin v Patent Office* (1999) the employee suffered from paranoid schizophrenia. At a time when he was not on proper medication his behaviour towards his colleagues was bizarre, leading to complaints and his eventual dismissal. Despite this, an employment tribunal held that the effects of his mental illness were not substantial, since he was able to live alone and look after himself and carry out his work to a satisfactory standard. The EAT held that the tribunal had misdirected itself on the meaning of "substantial" and substituted a finding that he was disabled, reminding tribunals that people with disabilities usually develop effective "coping strategies" to enable them to function in an often hostile environment and warning that this should not be allowed to obscure the actual degree of impairment. Because of evidence that blind and partially sighted people were failing to convince tribunals that they were disabled, so effective were their coping strategies, the Disability Discrimination (Blind and Partially Sighted Persons) Regulations 2003 had to be passed. They provide that anyone who is certified as blind or partially sighted by a registered ophthalmologist will automatically count as "disabled" under the DDA.

In the case of progressive illnesses (such as multiple sclerosis, muscular **2–043** dystrophy or infection with HIV, all of which are specifically mentioned in the Act), the effects may not at first be substantial, or there may be periods of remission. People with such disabilities will nevertheless receive the protection of the Act as soon as the illness manifests itself in any adverse effect on their normal day-to-day activities (DDA, Sch.1, para.8). The Disability Rights Commission has pressed for people with progressive conditions to be covered from the point of diagnosis, since it is from this point that they may suffer discrimination. In view of the restrictive approach taken to this provision, this would be a good idea. In *Mowat-Brown v University of Surrey* (2002) the EAT held that it was not enough for an applicant (with multiple sclerosis) to show that he had *some* impairment if he could not go on to show that the impairment was likely to become substantial. In *Kirton v Tetrosyl Ltd* (2003) the Court of Appeal held that a cancer patient was covered by the DDA where his non-substantial impairment resulted not from the cancer but from the surgery he had had for it. It was relevant that the surgical procedure was the standard treatment for this cancer and that the impairment was a common side-effect of it. However, the applicant had lost his case in the lower courts.

An impairment which would have a substantial effect if it were not being treated or corrected is to be treated as if it actually has that effect (DDA, Sch.1, para.6). This makes sense, since an employer may be unwilling to believe in the effectiveness of the treatment and might discriminate against someone with a disability even though it causes no adverse effect in practice: epilepsy controlled by medication might be an example. In *Goodwin v Patent Office* (1999) the EAT described this situation as "deduced effects" of the disability. This important point was overlooked by the employment tribunal in *Kapadia v Lambeth LBC* (2000) which decided that the effects of the applicant's depression were not substantial. This finding could not stand in the face of medical evidence to the effect that without regular counselling sessions from his psychologist he would have had a complete mental breakdown. A sight impairment which would be substantial but is corrected by wearing spectacles or contact lenses is not to be treated as substantial (DDA, Sch.1, para.6(3)).

A long-term effect is defined in DDA, Schedule 1 as one which is capable **2–044** of lasting for a year or more, or the rest of the applicant's life, although its severity may vary over time. An impairment which ceases, but which is more likely than not to recur, will be taken to have a long-term effect (although hay fever is specifically excluded by regulation).

The final condition is that the disability must affect the worker's capacity to undertake "normal day-to-day activities" (not the work in question, it should be noted). Normal day-to-day activities are exhaustively defined as involving mobility; manual dexterity; physical co-ordination; continence; ability to lift, carry or move everyday objects; speech, hearing and eyesight; memory or ability to learn, concentrate or understand; or perception of the risk of personal danger (DDA, Sch.1, para.4).

In addition to people with current disabilities the Act also treats as a **2–045** disabled person someone who has had a disability in the past, even though it may now no longer have any effect. This again is in recognition that an employer might not be prepared to accept that there is no risk of recurrence and could still discriminate because of a past condition. This may especially be the case with mental illness. In *Greenwood v British Airways* (1999) an employee was refused promotion because he was regarded as unreliable by reason of his previous absence record caused by depression. The employment tribunal held that he was not disabled because he was not suffering from depression when he applied for promotion. The EAT held that he had established that the depression constituted a past disability and so he should have been treated as a disabled person for the purposes of the Act: it was not necessary to show that he continued to suffer from the effects of depression.

The DDA abolished the old registration system for disabled people, but those who were registered as disabled under the old law were treated without more as having a disability for the purposes of the DDA for three years after it came into effect; since then they are treated as people who have had a disability.

The meaning of discrimination

2-046 Under section 5 of the DDA there are two forms of unlawful discrimination. It is unlawful to treat a disabled person less favourably, for a reason which relates to her disability, than someone without that disability is or would be treated, unless the employer can justify the less favourable treatment. This sounds rather like the formulation of direct discrimination under the SDA and RRA, but it is different in significant respects. Firstly, the less favourable treatment need only be for a reason related to the disability, rather than being "on grounds of" it, which is the formulation used in the other Acts: arguably, this is an easier connection to establish. Secondly, and most importantly, the DDA gives the employer the possibility of justifying direct discrimination, breaching the important principle in sex and race discrimination that there is no defence for direct discrimination. This will change when the DDA Amendment Regulations come into force, as the Employment Directive (2000/78/EC) does not allow justification of direct discrimination. Thirdly, it should be noted that only less favourable treatment of someone with a disability is prohibited, not less favourable treatment of someone without a disability by comparison with a disabled worker. This means that, unlike sex and race discrimination legislation, disability discrimination legislation is not symmetrical. It is possible for an employer to engage in positive discrimination in favour of disabled workers. Unfortunately, this does not apply to one of the only groups of employers which would have been likely to make use of this facility, namely local authorities, because of the provision in the Local Government and Housing Act 1989, s.7 that all appointments to local government service must be made on merit.

As with sex and race discrimination, the question of the appropriate standard of comparison for less favourable treatment has given rise to initial problems. Section 5(1) says that an employer discriminates if, for a reason relating to her disability, it treats the disabled person less favourably than someone to whom that reason does not apply. In *Clark v Novacold* (1999) the employee was dismissed for long-term absence resulting from a back injury. The EAT held that the comparison should be made with someone to whom the reason of disability did not apply but who had been similarly absent for some other reason. Not surprisingly, they thought that the employer would have dismissed such a person too. The Court of Appeal held that this was the wrong comparison. The reason relating to his disability for which the applicant had been dismissed was his absence from work. The comparison should have been with someone to whom that reason – absence – did not apply. On this basis, it was clear that the applicant had been treated less favourably. In *Heinz v Kenrick* (2000) the EAT held that an employer could treat a person less favourably for a reason related to his disability even if the employer was not aware that he had a disability. The EAT considered that the reference to the employer's "reason" required an objective test of whether the treatment was related to the disability, not the subjective reason which operated on the employee's mind.

The second situation identified as unlawful discrimination is where the **2–047** employer fails to make reasonable adjustments, as required by section 6, and cannot justify that failure (DDA, s.5(2)). The section 6 duty to make adjustments is at the heart of this legislation. It is a duty to take such steps as it is reasonable in all the circumstances of the case to take in order to prevent any arrangements made by the employer, or any physical feature of premises occupied by the employer, placing the disabled person at a substantial disadvantage by comparison with non-disabled workers. A number of examples of reasonable adjustments are given in section 6(3) and amplified in the Code of Practice, including making adjustments to premises (*e.g.* wheelchair ramps); reallocation of some duties (*e.g.* occasional driving duties could be reassigned where a disability prevents a worker from driving); transferring someone who becomes disabled to an existing vacancy elsewhere in the organisation; altering working hours (*e.g.* allowing flexitime or even part-time working: failure to consider allowing an employee recovering from ME to work at home was a breach of the duty in *Hillingdon LBC v Morgan* (1999)); assigning someone to a different (and more accessible or suitable) workplace; allowing time off work for treatment; giving special training; acquiring or modifying equipment (*e.g.* a talking computer for someone with a visual impairment, or a modified telephone for someone with a hearing deficiency); providing a reader or interpreter, and providing special supervision. This last does not extend to a duty to provide personal assistance to an employee to enable him to work (*Kenny v Hampshire Constabulary* (1999)).

When does this duty arise? Employers are not obliged under the Act to make their employment arrangements and premises "disability-proof". Apart from anything else, disabilities vary so greatly in nature and degree that it would be quite impossible to do so. The duty is owed to individuals with disabilities, and the question of reasonable adjustment is to be related to that individual's position. Furthermore, section 6(6) specifically provides that the duty arises only if the employer knows of the disability. Thus in the case of job applicants who could be disadvantaged by the employer's usual recruitment practices, the onus will be on them to make known the existence of their disability and their needs in order for the employer to have a duty to accommodate them (*Ridout v T C Group* (1998)). This may

55

put the disabled person in a dilemma, for she may fear that premature disclosure of her disability may lead to her application being screened out at an early stage, ostensibly for other reasons. However, if special arrangements are going to be needed, then it is inevitable that this disclosure will have to be made. In the case of existing employees, if their disability is not apparent, it will require their being prepared to disclose it appropriately, or else the employer will have no obligation to make a reasonable adjustment.

2–048   The cost of making reasonable adjustments is a concern for many employers. Despite its scaremongering over possible costs when the Civil Rights (Disabled Persons) Bill 1994 was before Parliament, when the DDA was going through, the Conservative Government's assessment of the cost of making reasonable adjustments was an average of around £200 per adjustment. The Act allows for regulations to be made which would place a limit on the cost of any adjustment, but it is not presently intended to use this power. Instead section 6(4) lists factors to be considered in assessing reasonableness: the efficacy of the adjustment; its practicability for the employer; the cost to the employer; how disruptive it would be; the employer's financial and other resources and the availability of financial or other assistance from other sources (*e.g.* government grants). The Code of Practice suggests as one rule of thumb that it would be reasonable to expect an employer to spend at least as much as it would cost to recruit and train a replacement for the job.

A major difference between disability discrimination law and sex and race discrimination is that the same conduct can give rise to alternative claims under the DDA, whereas this would be very unlikely under the SDA and RRA. Sex or race discrimination is usually direct or indirect, but cannot be both at the same time. However, it is possible for disability discrimination to be both less favourable treatment under DDA, s.5(1) *and* a breach of the duty to make reasonable adjustments under DDA, s.5(2). The claims are clearly alternative and success under one head has no inevitable implications for a claim under the other. It is important, however, to work through the conditions (and possible defence) for each claim separately.

Harassment on grounds of disability was not covered expressly in the DDA, although as with sex and race discrimination, it would come within the definition of less favourable treatment. However, when the 2003 amendments come into force in October 2004 there will be a separate claim for harassment along the lines of that in the RRA (above, para. 2–022). In *Jones v 3M Healthcare* (2003) the House of Lords held that the DDA could be construed to cover discrimination occurring after employment had terminated, as long as it was sufficiently connected to the employment. The DDA Amendment Regulations 2003 make this clear.

Justification

2–049   An employer has a potential defence of justification both for less favourable treatment for a reason related to disability and for failure to make a reasonable adjustment. The defence will only succeed if the reason put forward is "both material to the circumstances of the particular case and substantial" (DDA, s.5(3), (4)). The justification defence was always the potential Achilles' heel of the legislation and so it has proved. It took a little while for employers and their advisers to wake up to it, but in *Heinz v Kenrick* (2000) the EAT confirmed that "substantial" in this context too only meant "more than trivial or minor". In other words, provided that the employer can put forward a relevant reason which is more than trivial, discrimination against disabled people is all right. Furthermore, in *Jones v Post Office* (2001) the Court of Appeal held that in judging the employer's action the tribunal should only consider whether it had a material and substantial reason and should not substitute their own judgment, likening the process to the "band of reasonable responses" test in unfair dismissal (see below, para. 8–032).

Justification is discussed extensively, with supporting examples, in the Code of Practice. This makes it clear that a generalised assumption about the capacities of people with a particular kind of disability will not constitute a justification, nor will the fear of adverse reaction by customers or other employees. In relation to the thorny problem of sickness absence, it suggests that if the disability causes an absence level very little more than is regarded as acceptable for other employees, it is unlikely to be regarded as a justification for less favourable treatment. However, this must be read in the light of the case law discussed above and the Code will have to be revised by October 2004.

In order to comply with the Employment Directive (2000/78/EC) the **2–050** DDA Amendment Regulations make three main changes to the DDA, which will come into force on October 1, 2004. First of all, an employer will not be able to justify discrimination which is purely by reason of the applicant's disability, rather than any consideration of his abilities. In effect, this is intended to mean that direct discrimination on grounds of disability cannot be justified, to make it the same as for race and sex discrimination. Secondly, the justification defence will be removed for failure to make reasonable adjustments. It has been argued with some force that if the employer's duty is only to do what is reasonable, it cannot make sense for there to be a defence that it was justified in not acting reasonably. Thirdly, for the employment field, the familiar concept of indirect discrimination will be introduced.

Finally, it should be noted that there are some statutory justifications. With Disability Discrimination (Employment) Regulations 1996 it is provided that paying a disabled worker less as a result of a generally applicable performance-related pay system will be justified and also that discrimination in pension schemes both in eligibility conditions and amount of benefits is to be regarded as justified if the reason for it is that the cost of providing the benefit is projected to be "substantially greater" than it would be for a comparable person without the disability (reg.4). These exceptions will also be modified from October 2004.

It was made clear in *Morse v Wiltshire CC* (1998) that the question of justification is to be judged by an objective standard: that is, it is insufficient that the employer believed that there were no reasonable adjustments which could be made. The tribunal should make its own decision on the evidence as to whether or not this was the case. If no reasonable adjustment was possible, there is no breach of the duty and the question of justification does not arise. But if the tribunal considers that there were adjustments which could reasonably have been carried out, it must then consider if the employer is justified in not doing so.

Pre-employment medical checks are not prohibited by the legislation. However, if applied only to applicants with disabilities, they would very likely be discriminatory and would need to be justified. The Code points out that a blanket exclusion of people with a particular kind of disability for a particular job will usually discriminate unlawfully, as it fails to take account of the circumstances of the individual applicant.

Victimisation

2–051 As with the SDA and RRA, discrimination by way of victimisation is also unlawful. This is dealt with by DDA, s.55, which is in similar terms to the parallel provisions on sex and race discrimination. Protected activities are: bringing proceedings under the Act; giving evidence or information in relation to proceedings brought under the Act; doing anything else with reference to the Act; and alleging (in good faith) that another person has contravened the Act.

Enforcement and remedies

2–052 Since the National Disability Council (NDC) originally set up by the DDA had no enforcement powers, enforcement of the DDA in its early years has been largely through individual action. The Disability Rights Commission, set up by the Disability Rights Commission Act 1999 to replace the NDC, has powers more like the CRE and EOC (above, para. 1–015). For individual claims, as with most employment protection rights, including race and sex discrimination, claims must be submitted to an employment tribunal within three months of the discriminatory act. The remedies of declaration, recommendation and compensation are available. Compensation is to be assessed according to the principles for damages in tort and is unlimited in amount. In one of the first cases on compensation, *British Sugar v Kirker* (1998), an award of £103,146 to a visually impaired chemist aged 40 was upheld. The major element in the award was for loss of earnings because the tribunal considered it very likely that he would never obtain a comparable job. Given very high levels of unemployment among people with disabilities, it is possible that this could be a regular feature of awards for discriminatory dismissals on grounds of disability.

Sexual Orientation

2–053 Sexual orientation was not originally a protected ground in the legislation and so it was thought that discrimination against homosexuals and transsexuals would only be unlawful if an employer treated male homosexuals or transsexuals differently from female homosexuals or transsexuals. This position, however, required radical review following the ECJ's decision in *P v S and Cornwall CC* (1996).

The applicant in this case was dismissed from his post because he proposed to undergo gender reassignment surgery and to live thereafter as a woman. She claimed that this was sex discrimination. The employment tribunal considered that the claim was not sustainable within the terms of the Sex Discrimination Act, but referred to the ECJ the question of whether this was inconsistent with the Equal Treatment Directive. Could this be said to be discrimination "on grounds of sex"? The United Kingdom argued that it could not, as the employer would clearly have treated a female-to-male transsexual in the same (unfavourable) way.

The ECJ held that this was discrimination on grounds of sex, for two main reasons. First, the Court described the Equal Treatment Directive as giving expression to the principle of equality, which it stated was a fundamental principle of Community law. Secondly, the fact that the person concerned would be treated less favourably by comparison with persons of his or her former sex showed that the discrimination was on grounds of sex. This entailed a change in the law which was carried out by the Sex Discrimination (Gender Reassignment) Regulations 1999. They added a new section 2A to the SDA providing that less favourable treatment of a person is unlawful if it is on the ground that she or he "intends to undergo, is undergoing, or has undergone gender reassignment". Gender reassignment is defined as a process undertaken with medical supervision, presumably in order to ensure that that there can be some precision in deciding whether a particular person is in that situation or not. At the same time, the definition implicitly recognises that the process does not necessarily entail medical intervention.

In establishing transsexual discrimination it is specifically provided that less favourable treatment of someone undergoing gender reassignment compared with someone absent for sickness or injury constitutes discrimination, as does less favourable treatment compared with someone absent for a different reason, unless this is reasonable in the circumstances. It is perhaps surprising that the government opted for a policy of minimum compliance in making these Regulations, so that indirect discrimination against transsexuals is not covered.

It was thought by many that the reasoning in *P v S and Cornwall CC* **2–054** would mean that discrimination against homosexuals on grounds of their sexuality would also constitute sex discrimination. In *Grant v South West Trains* (1998) the employing company gave travel concessions to the spouses or live-in partners of their employees but refused to extend the concession to Ms Grant's lesbian partner. *Grant v South West Trains* was referred to the ECJ and the Advocate-General duly opined that the case was indistinguishable from *P v S and Cornwall CC*. Not so the ECJ, which accepted the argument of the United Kingdom government that if the employer would have treated a male homosexual in the same (unfair) way as it treated female homosexuals, there was no sex discrimination. This, of course, was precisely the comparison which it had rejected in *P v S and Cornwall CC*. References to the fundamental principle of equality in EU law, so vaunted in that case, were conspicuous by their absence in *Grant v South West Trains*. It follows that the SDA only offers protection to homosexuals in circumstances where male and female homosexuals are treated differently (*Pearce v Governing Body of Mayfield School* (2003)).

However, sexual orientation was included in the Employment Directive (2000/78/EC) as one of the grounds on which employment discrimination should be made unlawful and as a result the Employment Equality (Sexual Orientation) Regulations 2003 were passed, to come into force on December 2, 2003. The Regulations make it unlawful for employers to discriminate on grounds of "a sexual orientation towards persons of the same sex; persons of the opposite sex; or persons of the same sex and of the opposite sex". Thus discrimination against homosexuals, heterosexuals and bisexual people is covered. It may seem surprising that heterosexuals are included, but at least in America a heterosexual working in a theatre alleged that she was discriminated against because of her sexual orientation by the predominantly gay management.

The Regulations make direct and indirect discrimination, harassment and victimisation on grounds of sexual orientation unlawful. These terms are defined in the same way as the new definitions for race discrimination, discussed above. It is worth noting that the Regulations cover discrimination "on grounds of sexual orientation" rather than on the grounds of *the applicant's* sexual orientation. This wider definition means that a heterosexual who suffers discrimination for having gay friends or for refusing to discriminate against gay people would be covered (*cf. Showboat v Owens* (1984) above, para. 2–009). Importantly, it also means that someone who is discriminated against because their employer *believes* that they are gay (whether or not they are in fact) would be protected – and that they can preserve their privacy by not needing to reveal their sexuality to a tribunal. It is enough if they show they suffered discrimination because of the employer's belief.

2–055   As with the new race discrimination regime, there are exceptions to the Regulations for jobs where having a particular sexual orientation is a genuine and determining requirement and it is proportionate to apply it (reg.7). Because of lobbying from religious groups a specific genuine occupational requirement for employment exists for the purposes of an organised religion, either to comply with the doctrine of the religion or to "avoid conflicting with the strongly held religious convictions of a significant number of the religion's followers" (reg.7(3)). The key question here is what will count as employment for the purposes of an organised religion. It was suggested in Parliamentary debate that this would essentially apply to priests (rather amusingly, since they are usually considered as not being employed: see below, para. 3–028). However, the NUT is concerned that it could be used to discriminate against gay teachers in faith schools and has indicated its intention to challenge its compatibility with the Directive. Another controversial exception (reg.25) states that employers may still make access to benefits, such as survivors' pensions, dependent on marital status.

In unfair dismissal law, before the Employment Equality (Sexual Orientation) Regulations 2003 were passed tribunals generally stated that homosexuality alone was not a good reason for dismissal, but in practice seemed to require little else before holding that a particular decision to dismiss was reasonable. A notorious example is *Saunders v Scottish National*

Camps (1981) where the applicant, dismissed on the grounds of homosexuality, was employed as a maintenance handyman at a boys' camp. His duties did not specifically bring him into contact with the children; nevertheless his dismissal was held to be fair on the basis that many other employers would have responded in the same way (*cf.* also *Boychuk v Symons* (1977)). It is not yet clear what impact, if any, the new law will have on this.

Religious Discrimination

The Fair Employment (Northern Ireland) Acts 1976 and 1989 outlawed **2–056** religious discrimination in Northern Ireland but it was not perceived as a problem in the rest of the United Kingdom and was not originally included in the anti-discrimination legislation. However, Sikhs and Jews did gain protection under the RRA because they met the other tests of being an ethnic group (*Mandla v Dowell Lee* (1983), above, para. 2–005; *Singh v Rowntree Mackintosh* (1979); *Seide v Gillette Industries* (1980)). Rastafarians were held not to be an ethnic group in *CRE v Dutton* (1989). There was no clear ruling on whether Muslims constituted an ethnic group: the Muslim community in Britain originates from a number of different countries, and therefore may not necessarily be regarded as having the same level of group cohesion as Sikhs, for example. On the other hand, the same could be said of the Jewish community. Given that most Muslims are non-white, it must at least be the case that discrimination against them is indirectly discrimination on grounds of race, and cases concerning Muslims seem to have proceeded on that basis without discussion of the point (*e.g. Walker v Hussain* (1996)).

The Employment Directive (2000/78/EC) required Member States to legislate against discrimination on grounds of religion in the employment field and so the Employment Equality (Religion and Belief) Regulations 2003 were passed, coming into force on December 2, 2003. The general structure follows the new scheme for race discrimination and sexual orientation discrimination: *i.e.* direct and indirect discrimination, harassment and victimisation in the employment field are unlawful. One of the most difficult issues for this form of discrimination is deciding what amounts to "religion or belief". The Regulations largely duck this issue, instead leaving it to employment tribunals to decide (presumably as a question of mixed fact and law). Thus regulation 2(1) simply defines religion or belief as, "any religion, religious belief, or similar philosophical belief". Explanatory notes to the Regulations (which have no legal standing) suggest that factors such as collective worship, clear belief system or a profound belief affecting way of life or view of the world may be relevant to tribunals or courts making this decision. As discrimination is "on grounds of religion or belief" rather than on grounds of *the applicant's* religion or belief, an employer would be liable for discriminating on what was assumed to be the applicant's religion or belief, whether or not that belief was accurate.

2–057   As with sexual orientation, there is an exception where having a particular religion or belief is a genuine and determining occupational requirement and it is proportionate in the circumstances to apply it (reg.7(2)). Unlike the genuine occupational qualifications of the SDA and RRA, these are not specified further and could apply to any employer. It is to be expected that they will be construed strictly. Regulation 7(3) adds a particular exception for an employer who "has an ethos based on religion or belief". In these circumstances the employer may require someone of a particular religion or belief if it is a genuine occupational requirement (even if not a determining or decisive one), having regard to the nature of the employment and the test of proportionality. This does not affect current special exemptions such as that for Sikhs working on construction sites under the Employment Act 1989 who do not have to wear safety helmets.

When the Sunday Trading Act 1994 allowed shops to open on Sundays, special protection was provided for those who did not wish to work on Sundays, whether for religious or other reasons (see below, para. 6–037). However, in *Ahmad v ILEA* (1978), the plaintiff teacher, a Muslim, required an extra three-quarters of an hour on his Friday lunch break in order to attend the nearest mosque for prayer. The education authority allowed all its employees leave with pay for days of religious obligation where, by religious custom they could not work, but drew the line at this. Eventually they offered him a four-and-a-half day working week, but he refused and left, claiming unfair dismissal. The Court of Appeal, by a majority, held that the dismissal was fair. He could not claim the right to rewrite his contract of employment.

2–058   Article 9 of the European Convention on Human Rights guarantees freedom of thought, conscience and religion, including the freedom to manifest one's religion or beliefs. The Court of Appeal in *Ahmad v ILEA* (1978) considered that there was no breach of Article 9 given the proviso in Article 9(2) that the freedom is subject to, among other things, the rights and freedoms of others. This decision was later upheld by the European Commission on Human Rights: *Ahmad v UK* (1982). It will be interesting to see how issues like this are dealt with under the legislation. It seems likely that they will be treated only as indirect discrimination (since it is not the religion of the applicant which is the reason for disadvantage, but rather a blanket requirement of full-time work which has an adverse impact on members of one religious group. If so, the employer will be able to use a defence of justification and much will depend on how tribunals interpret the defence of "proportionate means of achieving a legitimate aim" (reg.3(1)(b)). In the USA employers must make a "reasonable accommodation" of employees' religious beliefs: it may be that the new regime will fall short of that.

Age Discrimination

2–059   The belief that anyone over 40 is past it is common among employers as well as among students, and causes enormous problems for anyone unfortunate enough to be made redundant after that age. Yet until Article

13 of the Treaty of Rome was introduced, age discrimination was not mentioned in most international instruments, such as the ECHR or the ILO Convention No.111 on Discrimination in Employment. To a limited extent age discrimination could amount to sex discrimination, as in *Price v Civil Service Commission* (1978) (above, para. 2–025) or even race discrimination. In *Perera v Civil Service Commission (No.2)* (1982) the EAT held that an age limit could work against immigrants, who might be older than a British citizen by the time they gained relevant qualifications.

The Employment Directive (2000/78/EC) also requires Member States to legislate against age discrimination in employment, although they have until 2006 to do so. Age discrimination is seen as particularly problematic because it can be on grounds of being too young as well as too old. Thus younger workers can lawfully be paid a lower wage than older workers for the same job (see below, para. 7–035) and workers over retirement age lose their rights to claim unfair dismissal and redundancy (below, para. 8–016). It is also a difficult area because age discrimination of different kinds is so entrenched in widely-used systems not only for pay and conditions but also retirement, pensions and state benefits. For example, it is common for employers to have incremental pay scales which reward longer service – but this would obviously have an adverse impact on younger workers. Should the practice continue to be allowed?

In 2003 the Government issued a consultation paper (Age Consultation 2003, DTi) setting out initial proposals. It is likely that the general scheme will follow the new regime for discrimination on other grounds, discussed above, but that there will be a number of special provisions to deal with issues such as employment protection rights after retirement age, and pay and non-pay benefits based on length of service. Proposals for legislation are likely to be brought forward in 2004.

3. Employment Status

The relationship between an employer and a worker is governed principally **3–001**
by contract. It is true that for many workers – especially those classified as
employees – the contract is overlaid by a mass of statutory regulation of
great importance. However, much of the legislation (for example, the law of
unfair dismissal and redundancy) is predicated on the background of
contractual principles and thus requires an understanding of the contractual
position before it can be applied. This is a two-way process: interpretation
of the legislation has had an effect on the development of contract law
applied to the contract of employment. Of course, for much of the time the
relationship between the employer and worker will carry on without
reference to the contract, and it may also be affected by informal
understandings and arrangements that are without contractual effect. While
everything goes smoothly, law is forgotten. However, when the chips are
down, if there is a problem, it will ultimately be resolved by reference to the
contractual arrangements. The contract of employment is therefore central
to the relationship of the employer and the worker.

We saw in Chapter 2 that the law against disability, sex and race
discrimination applies in the employment field to all those with a contract
personally to execute any work or labour. It is now necessary to divide up
that category more precisely: we must distinguish between those personally
providing work under a contract of employment; those personally providing
work on a self-employed basis who count as "workers" for statutory
purposes; other self-employed workers, and the few personally providing
work but not falling into either of the two major subdivisions.

There are five reasons for making these distinctions. Firstly, the statutory
overlay of protection rights already referred to is usually only available to
those having a contract of employment, not to the self-employed. Secondly,
at common law, certain terms are implied into every contract of employment, but not into other kinds of relationship. Thirdly, liability for tax and
National Insurance contributions varies according to the status of being an
employee or self-employed. Fourthly and relatedly, entitlement to many
social security benefits is reserved to employees. Finally, an employer's duty
of care towards, and responsibility for the acts of, employees is much
greater than the duty to, and responsibility for, self-employed workers. In
this and the following chapters, it is the position of employees which will be
the central concern.

Employees and Independent Contractors

3–002 The worker who has a contract of employment is called an employee. In times past this area of the law was known as the law of master and servant and it is not wholly unknown for these terms to be used even today, though they are rather archaic. But the contract of employment is very commonly referred to as a contract of service, as a convenient way of distinguishing it from a contract for services, which is the kind of contract under which the self-employed person works. In law, the self-employed worker is most likely to be referred to as an independent contractor. The term highlights the fact that the worker supplies work under a contract, but is not in the same state of dependence on the employer for work as the employee is. The intermediate category of "worker", used for certain statutory purposes, is examined later (below, para. 3–009).

Who is an employee?

3–003 How is an employee to be distinguished from an independent contractor? The definition in ERA, s.230(1) is not very helpful, as it defines an employee as someone with a contract of employment, itself defined as a contract of service or a contract of apprenticeship. So the answer has to be found in the common law.

In the nineteenth century (when the issue usually arose in the context of establishing the employer's responsibility for acts of, or towards, its employees) the test was said to be one of control. "A servant is a person subject to the command of his master as to the manner in which he shall do his work" (Bramwell L.J., *Yewens v Noakes* (1880)). It was soon realised that control over the manner of working might be exercised by the employer of domestic servants or unskilled manual workers, but was hardly appropriate where the worker was taken on precisely as the possessor of a needed skill, or where she would be expected to exercise a degree of discretion in performance of the work. Not only brain surgeons but even football players are not really subject to the control of their employer as to the manner in which they do their work – a fact apparently regretted by football managers at least. So, in a case concerning an injured football player claiming for an industrial injury (*Walker v Crystal Palace F.C.* (1910)), the Court of Appeal gave the test a different slant by focusing instead on whether the employer had the right to control the background arrangements for the work – when and where it was done, holiday entitlements and so on. Given that the football club's control here extended even to requiring that the player should not reside in a public house, the court had no difficulty in deciding that the contract was a contract of employment.

This emphasis on the context of the work was developed into the so-called "organisation" or "integration" test, classically propounded by Lord Denning in *Stevenson Jordan and Harrison v MacDonald & Evans* (1952):

". . . under a contract of service, a man is employed as part of the business and his work is done as an integral part of the business; whereas under a contract for services, his work, although done for the business, is not integrated into it but is only accessory to it."

However, while this test may have been useful in establishing the employee status of hospital consultants and other highly-skilled professionals, it is increasingly inappropriate to the modern labour market, with its emphasis on flexible employment and the need to match supply and demand ever more closely. Increasingly businesses have stripped down to a core of permanent, full-time workers, usually with indispensable professional skills, who receive the security elements traditionally associated with employment: pension and sickness schemes, structured career advancement and severance payments. These are supplemented by supply workers, taken on for particular tasks but having no permanent relationship with the organisation, and "flexible workers", who are generally available because in the locality in which they live they have no other outlet to work under the conditions they need (*e.g.* to work part-time or at home), and who can thus be safely called on only when needed, for whatever hours suit the firm, and, of course, need only be paid for those hours.

One might describe this situation as referring to different classes of **3–004** worker rather than neutrally to different kinds. However, the point to make for the present discussion is that the workers in the two last categories may or may not be employees of the firm. Often it is part of their attraction to the employer that they are not employees, because it reduces the administrative and other overheads and the employer's responsibility for them. But it is clear that the work they do is an integral part of the work of the business. Thus it is suggested that the integration test is less and less likely to be useful in the future. Take, for example, the task of cleaning a hospital. In the past, hospitals employed cleaners to do the work and supervisors to see that they did it properly. The work is clearly essential to the successful running of the organisation. Since the 1980s it has become common for hospitals to outsource their cleaning needs: that is, they buy in the services of cleaners under a contract entered into with another organisation, or indeed with representatives of the former employees as a group. It is clear in this case that the cleaners are no longer employees of the hospital; yet it is equally obvious that the task of cleaning remains as integral as ever it was to the running of the hospital.

The inadequacies of these tests have led courts and tribunals to adopt a multi-factor approach: they take into account all the possible relevant factors and weigh them against each other to reach their decision. A most useful survey of the authorities is to be found in the judgment of Cooke J. in *Market Investigations v Minister of Social Security* (1969). He distilled the following factors: whether or not the worker provides personal service; control, which "will no doubt always have to be considered, although it can no longer be regarded as the sole determining factor"; whether the employer or the worker provides the tools and equipment; whether the worker hires his own helpers; what degree of financial risk the worker takes, if any; what responsibility for investment and management the worker has, if any; and how far the worker profits directly from good work. Cooke J. summarised the position in this test: "Is the person who has engaged himself to perform these services performing them in business on his own account?"

3–005   Cooke J.'s test concentrates on whether the worker can really be regarded as an individual entrepreneur and has the advantage of emphasising the economic realities of the situation. Another case using the multifactor approach provides a different emphasis. In *Ready Mixed Concrete v Minister of Pensions and National Insurance* (1968) the company instituted a scheme whereby delivery of its concrete to customers would be carried out by a team of "owner-drivers". The issue was whether the owner-drivers were employees of the company: if so, the company was liable to pay National Insurance contributions in respect of them. It was the company's position that they were self-employed – and so they were described in their extensive written contracts. The case highlights the difficulties of the multifactor approach, as almost every factor was equivocal.

Firstly, the drivers were the owners of the lorries and had to keep them maintained at their own expense. However, they were buying the lorries on hire-purchase from a subsidiary of the company; they had to paint them in the company colours, and the company could instruct them to carry out repair work and specify where it should be done. Furthermore, they could not use the lorries for work for anyone but Ready Mixed Concrete. Secondly, as regards personal service, the drivers could delegate the work to another competent driver – but the company had the right to insist on the driver himself performing. Thirdly, control: the drivers had no fixed hours of work and could choose their own routes. But they had to be available when required and to obey reasonable orders "as if . . . an employee". What about the risk of profit and loss? Essentially they were paid by results: typical of the self-employed worker, but also common among employees, such as the piece-worker or the sales representative remunerated by commission calculated as a percentage of sales. And in any case, they received a guaranteed annual minimum wage.

MacKenna J. held that there were three conditions for a contract of service: firstly, that the employee undertakes to provide his or her own work or skill to the employer in return for a wage or other payment; secondly, that the employee agrees to be subject to the employer's control to a sufficient degree "to make that other the master" (a somewhat circular test!); and thirdly, that the other provisions of the contract are consistent with its being a contract of service. In the end the judge found that there was nothing here inconsistent with the contention that the drivers were independently running their own small businesses, as the company had argued. However, as many have pointed out, if the judge had framed the question in the opposite way, asking if there was anything inconsistent with its being a contract of service, he would probably have found nothing inconsistent with that either. True, the driver could delegate, and so the fundamental requirement of personal service might seem to be missing. But in reality the terms of the drivers' contracts were in some respects internally inconsistent. The right to delegate was to a large extent theoretical, given that the company had the right to demand personal service.

This decision illustrates the important point that there is no definitive list **3–006** of necessary and sufficient conditions for the identification of a contract of employment. Nor is it clear how many have to be present before one would conclude that the contract exists. The contract of employment is a cluster concept. If one conceives of the factors as a list A–E, one contract might have A, B and C, but not D and E; another might have D and E or A and C but not the others. All could be capable of being contracts of employment.

The decisions in *Market Investigations v Minister of Social Security* and *Ready Mixed Concrete v MPNI*, although only High Court decisions, have both been frequently cited over the years as indicating the correct approach to the distinction between employees and independent contractors. However, it is arguable that they actually pull in different directions and are not entirely consistent with each other, as *Express & Echo v Tanton* (1999) shows. The applicant in this case had been employed as a delivery driver for the newspaper company until being made redundant in 1995. Thereafter, he was taken on by the company again as a delivery driver, but on a self-employed basis. It was the clear intention of the parties that he should *not* be an employee of the company, although it is not clear how much choice he had in the matter. His job was exactly as it had been before: he drove the company's van on the route laid down by the company, conformed in all respects to instructions given to him and was paid a fixed fee decided on by the company. However, the contract also contained a "substitution clause" to the effect that if the applicant was unwilling or unable to drive, he should find another driver at his own expense. This clause had been invoked for a lengthy period when the applicant was ill. Despite this the EAT upheld the employment tribunal's decision that this was in substance a contract of employment. The Court of Appeal reversed: relying on the decision in *Ready Mixed Concrete* they held that personal service was essential for a contract of employment and that this factor was lacking because of the substitution clause. However, had the court applied the "in business on his own account" test from *Market Investigations* it seems highly unlikely that they could have held that the applicant was an independent contractor. The danger of the decision in *Express & Echo v Tanton* is that it hands unscrupulous employers an easy way of avoiding the responsibilities inherent in the relationship of employer-employee, with the added advantage of passing some of the risks to the worker! (There was some mitigation of this position in *MacFarlane v Glasgow City Council* (2001) where gym instructors employed by the Council had to organise their own replacement if they were ill or otherwise unable to take a class. The substitutes had to be from the Council's own list and were paid by the Council. The EAT held that this was distinguishable from *Express & Echo v Tanton* and that the instructors were employees.)

Express & Echo v Tanton and *Ready Mixed Concrete v MPNI* also indicate **3–007** the relevance of another factor as yet unmentioned: the name given to the relationship by the parties. MacKenna J. framed his question in the way he did in *Ready Mixed Concrete* because the parties themselves alleged that it was a contract of employment. In some ways it may seem strange that the parties' opinions should matter. After all, if I persuade you to commit a breach of contract, it will hardly be a defence that neither of us thought it was a breach. Thus the courts have frequently said, in this and other contexts, that they will decide according to the substance of the contract, not according to the label given to it by the parties.

This approach is exemplified in *Ferguson v John Dawson* (1976). The plaintiff was injured when he fell off a roof at the defendants' construction site. Contrary to regulations, there was no guard rail on the roof. If the plaintiff had been an independent contractor, he would have been responsible for his own safety and unable to sue the company. As was not uncommon in the construction industry, he was working on "the lump" – where workers contracted as a gang for the job and were paid without deductions for tax and National Insurance, on the basis that they were self-employed and responsible for their own deductions. However, the plaintiff was employed as an unskilled labourer, and was clearly subject to the control of the site agent. Where tools were required, the company provided them. He was paid an hourly wage. In the circumstances the Court of Appeal held that, despite the label apparently given by the parties to the relationship, the substance was a contract of employment.

3–008   It seems, however, that the label given by the parties can be a relevant factor, but only if other factors do not dictate a different answer and if the label is the product of genuine agreement between the parties. Here Ferguson had no choice but to be employed on these terms, and probably little appreciation of any other than the fiscal consequences of the difference. This was not the case in *Massey v Crown Life Insurance* (1978). Massey, the branch manager of one of the insurance company's offices, asked to change his status from employee to independent contractor because it would be economically advantageous to do so. The company agreed and repaid his pension contributions. He registered himself as "John Massey and Associates," and that organisation (Massey under another name) was appointed manager of the branch. His duties were effectively unchanged. Then he was dismissed on one month's notice and sought to claim unfair dismissal.

The Court of Appeal held that the new agreement represented a genuine change in status, rather than an attempt to deprive the Inland Revenue of tax (which would have been illegal), and was consequently binding on both parties. While reaffirming the general principle that a different label could not alter the substance of the relationship, the court held that if the contract were capable of being either a contract of service or one for services, then the explicit agreement of the parties was relevant in resolving the ambiguity. They distinguished *Ferguson* on the basis that no such explicit agreement existed in that case.

It may be felt, looking at the last two cases in particular, that the decisions of courts are sometimes swayed by what is at stake, and that they are more likely to hold that the plaintiff is an employee where health and safety are at issue. Indeed, this is explicitly recognised in the Court of Appeal's decision in *Lane v Shire Roofing Ltd* (1995). The plaintiff here had been in business on his own as a builder, but as work was scarce, he hired himself out to the defendant company. The company was anxious not to incur liability to employees and recruited workers for particular jobs, paying them a daily rate. Lane was offered an all-in fee to re-tile the porch at a house and was injured when he fell from his ladder while doing the job. He argued that the company was negligent in not providing scaffolding to give him a safe place from which to work. The company argued that he was not an employee. Giving the main judgment in the Court of Appeal, Henry L.J. drew attention to the differences in the employment background in the mid-1990s from what pertained in the 1960s: more temporary and casual jobs, more self-employment and more flexible working arrangements, making it more difficult to apply the traditional tests. He also remarked that "when it comes to the question of safety at work, there is a real public interest in recognising the employer/employee relationship when it exists . . .". This set the tone for the court's decision. Although Lane had his own business, was paying tax on a self-employed basis, worked without supervision and had been taken on for the particular job only, it was held that he was not an independent contractor. These factors, in the court's view, could as well apply where someone was working under a short-term contract of employment. The question asked by the court was, whose business was being carried out on this occasion? The answer was that it was the company's, and it therefore owed Lane a duty of care as an employee.

The realistic approach of the court is to be welcomed and may assist in bolstering the position of casual workers, to be considered shortly. However, one can take issue with the implication that recognition of the reality of the situation is more important in health and safety cases than anywhere else. It may be that the factor of control rightly has more weight where this is the question, but it is submitted that it is equally important to ensure that employees are recognised as such for all employment protection purposes, and that it would be undesirable if different tests were to develop for identifying contracts of employment according to what was at stake.

"Workers"

In Chapter 2 we saw that anti-discrimination legislation applies not only to **3–009** employees but to anyone with a contract personally to execute any work or labour (above, para. 2–006). This is similar to the definition of "worker" contained in ERA, s.230(3) as being someone employed under a contract of employment or any other contract "whereby the individual undertakes to do or perform personally any work or services for another party" except where the other party is a professional client or customer. This clearly includes some independent contractors, although the boundary between the self-employed who count as "workers" and other independent contractors is not wholly clear.

The category of "worker" was once important in relation to employers' liability for health and safety and the payment of wages without deductions. It had virtually ceased to have much practical importance until the government indicated in its White Paper, *Fairness at Work*, (Cm.3968, 1998) that it wanted to encourage the flexible labour market, but not at the expense of fair minimum standards of protection for those employed on non-standard work contracts. The first steps with this policy were taken with the Public Interest Disclosure Act 1998 (now ERA 1996, ss.43A–43L), the Working Time Regulations 1998 and the National Minimum Wage Act 1998, all of which were applicable to "workers" (defined as per ERA, s.230(3)) rather than just to employees. The Employment Relations Act 1999, s.23 went further, giving the Secretary of State power to extend all employment protection rights to individuals other than employees. Should this power be exercised, one option would be to extend rights generally to "workers". Following a consultation exercise in 2002, proposals to use the section 23 power are still awaited.

More recent extensions of employment protection have been mixed. The statutory right to be accompanied in disciplinary and grievance proceedings (ERelA 1999, s.10) and the Part-time Workers (Prevention of Less Favourable Treatment) Regulations 2000 apply to workers, but protection for those on fixed-term contracts and new rights to leave for family reasons are limited to employees. It is worth noting that extending employment protection rights to "workers" would not help someone like the applicant in *Express & Echo v Tanton* (1999) because the definition of "worker" also emphasises the need for personal service.

Casual workers

3–010 With the advent of the flexible workforce, tribunals and courts have faced new problems in deciding the nature of the relationship between parties where the worker regularly performs certain tasks for the employer but is not continuously employed. Examples include seasonal workers, many homeworkers and some catering workers. The difficulty here is that while the work is done regularly, and there is an expectation that it will continue to be offered to and performed by the same people in the future, there is no binding legal obligation either on the employer to offer it or on the workers to perform it in the future. A more recent variant, the so-called "zero hours contract" differs from the usual casual work arrangement in that it frequently purports to place an obligation on the worker to accept work when offered, although the employer has a discretion whether to offer work or not. Other casual work arrangements may be described as "on call" or "stand by" contracts. The question with all of them is whether mutuality of obligation is a necessary factor for the existence of a contract of employment.

This was the main issue in *O'Kelly v Trusthouse Forte* (1984). At one of its hotels in London the company dealt with a lot of functions. This meant it had a fluctuating need for staff, and it relied heavily on casual workers. Of these, some were used a great deal and were given priority when work was available. They were termed, accurately if paradoxically, as "regular casuals". In addition to about 100 regular casuals, there were another 200–300 "casual casuals". In practice there was enough work so that the regular casuals were employed full time and had no other jobs. Further, there were special grievance and disciplinary procedures applicable to them and they received a kind of holiday pay. The company provided their uniforms; while on duty they were subject to the control of the function supervisors; they were paid according to the hours actually worked; tax was deducted and social security contributions made as if they were employees. What of mutual obligation?

Work was assigned by the employer preparing a roster showing who was needed to work the following week. A worker could decline any particular shift – but to do so jeopardised future offers and could lead to someone being removed from the list of regulars. In these circumstances the employment tribunal held that there was no legal mutual obligation, although the economic power of the employer and corresponding weakness of the workers meant that in practice the workers were obliged to accept work when it was offered. The EAT reversed, holding that the tribunal had failed to distinguish between two separate questions: firstly, what was the relationship of the workers and the company when they were actually carrying out work having accepted an offer for a specific engagement; and secondly, what was the nature of the overall relationship (or "general engagement")? In the view of the EAT, when they had accepted a specific engagement, the casual workers were under a legal obligation to work and the employer had a legal obligation to allow them to work, so they were employed on a contract of employment. On the facts of the case, there was no need to consider the general engagement.

The EAT's decision was in turn reversed by the Court of Appeal, **3–011** essentially because it considered that this was a question of mixed fact and law on which the EAT should not have interfered with the decision of the employment tribunal. Nonetheless, the EAT's identification of two separate issues in relation to the specific engagement and the general engagement has been widely accepted since. Thus in *Clark v Oxfordshire HA* (1998) the applicant had been employed as a "bank nurse", meaning that she was on call to be offered employment as and when the health authority needed her. Except that her contract specifically stated that there was no guarantee of work being available, her terms and conditions were the same as for other nurses. The Court of Appeal held that in the absence of mutual legal obligation there could be no overall or "umbrella" contract of employment in relation to the general engagement, but as the employment tribunal had not considered the separate question of the nature of the specific engagement the case was remitted on that point.

As very many employment protection rights are dependent on accumulating a certain period of continuous employment, finding that a specific engagement is a contract of employment will not assist many casual workers: for example, they cannot claim unfair dismissal unless they have one year's continuous employment. But there are employment protection issues where continuity is not required, such as common law implied terms of the contract and payment of tax and National Insurance (remember that *Market Investigations v Minister of Social Security* (1969) was itself a case about a casual worker, yet the issue of mutual obligation posed no problems there). Furthermore, there are now several grounds on which dismissal will be automatically unfair, and for these a finding of a specific engagement will be sufficient. The employer's duty of care to employees, which is one of the most important incidents of a contract of employment, does not depend on continuity and, as noted above, following *Lane v Shire Roofing* (1995) it seems inconceivable that a court would find that a casual worker was not an employee for this purpose except in very special circumstances. This is borne out also by the Privy Council decision in *Lee v Chung* (1990).

3–012   Are there any circumstances in which the general engagement between a casual worker and an employer can be regarded as a contract of employment? One possibility is where the arrangement has gone on for some time, so that what started out as a casual relationship can be said to have hardened into a situation where there is a legal obligation to provide work and to accept work. This occurred in *Nethermere v Gardiner* (1984) The applicants were homeworkers who worked as machinists, putting pockets in trousers. They had no fixed hours of work, and were paid according to the number of garments processed. The first applicant usually worked 5–6 hours a day. She got daily deliveries of work and the sewing machines were provided by the employer. There was, however, no obligation on the employer to provide work, nor on the applicant and the other homeworkers to accept. The arrangement continued for about four years until terminated by the employer. The Court of Appeal held that there had to be "an irreducible minimum of obligation" on each side to create a contract but that on the facts the employment tribunal was entitled to find that such mutual obligation did exist in this case. Stephenson L.J. commented, "I cannot see why well founded expectations of continuing homework should not be hardened or refined into enforceable contracts by regular giving and taking of work over periods of a year or more" (see also *Airfix Footwear v Cope* (1978)).

While these cases may be seen as an attempt to take account of the realities of the situation, there has been a return to a harder line in recent cases, which may yet require *Nethermere v Gardiner* and *Airfix v Cope* to be reconsidered. In *Carmichael v National Power plc* (2000) the Court of Appeal held that a letter of appointment which required tour guides at a nuclear installation to work "on a casual as required basis" could be construed as importing sufficient mutual obligation to amount to an overall contract of employment: on the part of the employer, to offer them a reasonable share of such work as it had to offer, and on the part of the workers, to accept a reasonable amount of such work as was offered. However, this was reversed by the House of Lords, which reverted to the traditional interpretation that there was no mutual obligation between the parties in these circumstances. The letter of appointment simply set up a framework within which a series of ad hoc, specific contracts (which might or might not be contracts of employment) took place. The application of these principles in *Stevedoring & Haulage Services Ltd v Fuller* (2001) raises concern about whether the development of mutual obligation over time will remain a tenable argument. The case concerned dockers with permanent contracts of employment who were made redundant and then re-employed at once as casual workers. They were required to sign a letter which expressly stated that they were not employees, that they did not have to accept work when offered and that the company was not under any obligation to offer them work. It also spelt out that they had no sick pay, holiday entitlement, etc. and that although they would be taxed as employees, this was for administrative convenience. They then worked on a regular basis for the company for a further three years. The employment tribunal held that the original agreement in the letter was subject to an implied term that they would be offered a reasonable amount of work and that they must accept a reasonable amount – rather like the Court of Appeal's analysis in *Carmichael*. This was roundly rejected by the Court of Appeal: if the express terms of the agreement was that there was *no* mutual obligation, it was not possible to imply a term saying exactly the opposite. The case was not argued on the basis that there was a variation of the agreement over time, as in *Airfix* or *Nethermere*, but if it had been, the answer might well have been that there had been no alteration in conduct during the three years and so no variation could be identified. It is also worth noting that the case could be criticised as giving undue weight to the label given by the parties (or in reality, unilaterally given by the employer) to the relationship. However, what weighed with the court was the express negation of mutual obligation in the written agreement. If this cannot be re-examined, it shows a relatively easy way in which an employer can avoid a contract of employment arising.

Law and fact

The history of *O'Kelly v Trusthouse Forte* (1984) illustrates an important **3–013** point. So far as statutory jurisdiction is concerned, appeals lie from employment tribunals to the EAT (and above) only on questions of law, not on questions of fact. This means that provided that the tribunal directs itself correctly on the law, that there is evidence on which it could have reached its decision, and that its decision is not perverse on the evidence, it cannot be disturbed by a higher court on the ground that the higher court would have reached a different decision from the tribunal.

There are good reasons for this rule: after all, it is the tribunal which hears the witnesses, and thus has the best opportunity for judging their truthfulness and accuracy. It would make no sense to allow another court to study a transcript of evidence (even if one existed, which in a tribunal would not be the case) and to make different findings of fact. But the difficulty is that the issues which have been held to be questions of fact are rather wider than what one would usually understand to be factual. You might think that a question of fact is one which is capable of objective verification – that is, you can say whether the answer is true or false. That is not what it means in this context. There is little doubt that the Court of Appeal has extended the category of issues which count as questions of fact as a matter of policy, in order to cut down the number of appeals to higher courts.

Now, it may be the case that reasonable people, fully instructed in the relevant law, could still disagree as to whether a particular dismissal was fair or unfair, which is why the tribunal's decision is to be treated as a question of fact and not disturbed on appeal. But it seems surprising that a question about the correct categorisation of a contract should be treated as one of fact. It seems to be a question of law *par excellence*, requiring as it does a detailed knowledge of contract law to answer it. Nevertheless, in *O'Kelly v Trusthouse Forte* the Court of Appeal held that the question of whether or not someone was an employee was a mixed question of fact and law, and therefore the employment tribunal's decision should not be disturbed unless there was a misdirection on the law. This decision has been criticised, but received the approval of the Privy Council in *Lee v Chung* (1990). The Privy Council emphasised that the determination has to depend on an investigation and evaluation of the factual circumstances in which the work is performed: and this should be regarded as a question of fact (although it is worth noting that in that case the Privy Council held that the decision of the original court was perverse and substituted its own view!). The only, limited exception to this comes as a result of the House of Lords' decision in *Davies v Presbyterian Church of Wales* (1986) (concerning the status of a minister of the church, which has often given rise to problems as to the identity of the employer), where it was held that if the contract were wholly in writing, its construction would be a matter of law.

Part-time workers

3–014 Until the historic decision of the House of Lords in *R. v Secretary of State ex p. EOC* (1994), a week only counted for continuity purposes if it involved 16 hours of employment. Part-timers who worked between eight and 16 hours per week could count those weeks as part of a qualifying period of continuous employment, but only if they had worked for five years or more. What this meant in practice was that part-timers who worked for fewer than eight hours a week never qualified for things like unfair dismissal protection and redundancy pay, and part-timers working between eight and 16 hours a week had to work five years to qualify as against two years for other workers.

As we saw in Chapter 2, less favourable treatment of part-time workers is unlawful sex discrimination unless it can be justified objectively. This appeared to be limited to provisions in contracts of employment until the ECJ decided in *Rinner-Kühn v FWW Spezial-Gebäudereinigung Gmbh* (1989) that German legislation excluding part-time workers from the right to receive sick pay required objective justification. The EOC therefore commenced proceedings for judicial review in 1990, seeking a declaration that the threshold provisions in EPCA, Sch.13 were in breach of Article 141, the Equal Pay Directive 1975 and the Equal Treatment Directive 1976 in relation to the right not to be unfairly dismissed, to receive compensation for unfair dismissal and to receive redundancy pay.

Given that the discriminatory effect of the hours requirement was established, the main issue in the House of Lords was whether or not it could be objectively justified. The then Conservative Government's argument was that the rules meant that there were more part-time jobs available than there would be if employers were exposed to these liabilities. Whereas naked assertion of this "fact" had sufficed for that government in the political arena, the House of Lords required some proof. This was not forthcoming; indeed, the evidence was that in other EU countries where part-timers received the same protection as other workers, the number of part-time jobs had actually increased. The EOC was therefore granted its declaration that the hours requirement for redundancy pay was a breach of Article 141 and the Equal Pay Directive, and the conditions for unfair dismissal claims were at least a breach of the Equal Treatment Directive, if not also of Article141. The House of Lords did not pronounce on whether unfair dismissal compensation could be regarded as "pay" for the purposes of Article 141 and it was not until the ECJ decision in *R. v Secretary of State ex p. Seymour-Smith* (2000) that it was definitively settled that it was. However, the Government responded to the House of Lords' decision in *R. v Secretary of State ex p. EOC* by promulgating the Employment Protection (Part-time Employees) Regulations 1995. The regulations abolished all hours requirements so that there is no longer a minimum threshhold for protection and periods of qualifying service are equalised (see now ERA, s.212).

Meanwhile, the position of part-time workers was being addressed at EU **3–015** level in accordance with the Social Charter aspiration of improving employment conditions for various forms of "atypical" work relationships, including part-time work. The subject was referred to the "social partners" (*i.e.* UNICE, CEEP and ETUC as representatives of management and labour) in accordance with Article 139 of the Treaty of Rome, who reached a Framework Agreement in June 1997. This was implemented by the Directive on Part-time Work (97/81/EC), which had to be brought into force in 2000. Power to make regulations and issue a code of practice on part-time work was included in the Employment Relations Act 1999, ss.19–21 and the resulting regulations, the Part-time Workers (Prevention of Less Favourable Treatment) Regulations 2000, came into force in July 2000.

Under regulation 5 a part-time worker has a right not to be less favourably treated on grounds of working part-time than a comparable full-time worker, unless that treatment can be objectively justified. In judging whether or not there is less favourable treatment the *pro rata* principle is to be used, meaning that the part-timer's treatment should be proportionately the same as the full-timer's unless there are objectively justified grounds for any difference. Workers who were full-time and then change to part-time work, whether or not after a period of absence such as maternity leave, have a right not to be treated less favourably than they were before going part-time. Under regulation 6 a part-time worker who believes that she has been treated less favourably may request a written statement of the reasons for this, which must be provided within 21 days. Part-time workers who believe that they have been treated less favourably may make a complaint to an employment tribunal which can make a declaration, award compensation and recommend that the employer takes action to remedy the adverse effects on the complainant of the less favourable treatment. They also receive protection from detriment for exercising their rights under the Regulations and dismissal on this ground is automatically unfair (reg.7).

Since less favourable treatment of part-time workers without justification is already likely to constitute indirect sex discrimination, what difference do these Regulations make? The main effect is that they remove the need to show adverse impact on grounds of sex, making successful claims possible even where the majority of full-time workers as well as part-timers are women so that adverse impact on grounds of sex cannot be established (*cf. Staffordshire CC v Black* (1995)). By the same token, claims by male part-time workers will be easier to mount.

3–016   However, a major constraint on the effectiveness of the Regulations is likely to result from the condition that less favourable treatment can only be established by comparison with an actual full-time comparator (under the SDA a hypothetical comparison with how a man would be treated is allowed). This means that a part-timer will have no claim under the Regulations unless there is a "comparable full-time worker", defined as someone employed by the same employer under the same type of contract and engaged on broadly similar work (and, where relevant, having a similar level of qualification, skills and experience) (reg.2(4)). As a result of the Fixed-term Employees (Prevention of Less Favourable Treatment) Regulations 2002 the fact that the contract of either the part-timer or the full-timer is for a fixed term will not prevent them from being regarded as comparable.

While the Part-time Work Directive seeks to encourage enhanced opportunities for part-time work, this is not expressed as a binding obligation and it is not addressed in the Regulations. The Secretary of State deliberately chose not to promulgate a code of practice on part-time work and instead guidance on compliance was issued. The guidance does make reference to increasing part-time opportunities, but as it has no legal status employers are free to ignore it.

Fixed-term contracts

3–017   While no one really expects that a contract of employment will go on forever, it is nonetheless usual to enter them on a permanent basis. The vast majority of contracts of employment are therefore of indefinite duration, although they may be terminated by either party giving notice (see below, para. 8–004). However, sometimes an employer may have a genuinely short-term need for workers and in these circumstances will wish to employ the worker for that specific period only. Examples might be catering staff to work during Wimbledon fortnight, fruit pickers to bring in the harvest, someone to cover another employee's maternity leave or a builder to work on a construction project.

It can be seen that some of these sorts of employment have something in common with casual work. It obviously makes sense for employers to be able to make use of fixed-term contracts when there is a genuine short-term need. However, the form is capable of abuse, for example where the employee has a succession of fixed-term contracts, with all the attendant insecurity, but the employers will not make the position permanent because they want to avoid incurring the responsibilities which they would have to a permanent employee.

The possibility of abuse of fixed-term contracts was always recognised in relation to redundancy and unfair dismissal law. At common law, at the end of the defined term, a fixed-term contract would terminate automatically. However, under ERA ss.95 and 136, for the purposes of unfair dismissal and redundancy claims this situation is designated as a dismissal, because otherwise employers could indirectly evade the operation of unfair dismissal legislation, in the following way. The employer could put all staff on fixed-term contracts of, say, six months or one year's duration, renewable.

At the end of every fixed period, the employer could review the situation and decide whether or not she wished to retain the employee. If she decided against renewal, the employee would have no redress, because there would have been no dismissal (see further below, para. 8–018). It is true that if the employer dismissed the employee during the currency of the fixed term, the employee would have the usual right to claim. But provided that the fixed term was not for too long a period, it would not be much of a hardship for the employer to wait until the end of the period and then let the employee go.

It was to prevent such abuses that the definition of dismissal was framed so as to include the expiry of a fixed-term contract without renewal. The fact that the employee has the right to claim does not, of course, mean that he will succeed. Thus the employer who genuinely needed someone for a specific period only should have no fear of an adverse claim, in theory at least. However, many employers did not think this satisfactory: they could be faced with unmeritorious claims, and would still spend time and money defending them, which would probably not be recouped even if they won. To take account of this, then, an exception was included which allowed the employee to waive the right to claim unfair dismissal on expiry of a fixed-term contract. Unfortunately, this opened the way for precisely the abuse which the original provision was intended to prevent. There was no mechanism for ensuring that employers only used this exception when they had a genuine short-term need, and so it was possible for employers to have a pool of second class employees on fixed-term contracts whose dismissal did not expose the employer to any kind of financial liability. The Employment Relations Act 1999 dealt with this abuse by abolishing the possibility of waivers of unfair dismissal rights in fixed-term contracts, but made no change in relation to redundancy.

At about the same time, however, changes occurred at EU level as part **3–018** of the programme to improve employment protection for atypical workers. As with the Part-time Work Directive (97/81/EC), the matter was referred to the social partners, whose agreement became the Fixed-term Work Directive (99/70/EC), mainly implemented in the United Kingdom by the Fixed-term Employees (Prevention of Less Favourable Treatment) Regulations 2002, in force from October 2002.

The Fixed-term Work Directive had two main aims: to prevent discrimination against workers on fixed-term contracts by comparison with those on permanent contracts, and to limit the abuse inherent in allowing employers to keep people on a series of successive fixed-term contracts. The Directive also made it necessary to introduce a new, wider definition of what would count as a fixed-term contract. In *Wiltshire CC v NATFHE and Guy* (1980), Court of Appeal had held that a fixed-term contract meant one with a defined beginning and end: in effect, that the dates should be known at the outset. Thus in *Ryan v Shipboard Maintenance* (1980), where a skilled ship repair worker was taken on by the company for the duration of specific projects, and carried out 31 different jobs over five years, it was held that these were not fixed-term contracts. This was because it was not known in advance precisely when each job would end. This had the unfortunate result that employees on "task" or "purpose" contracts had no unfair dismissal or redundancy rights because the termination of their contracts did not amount to a dismissal in law.

Regulation 1(2) of the Fixed-term Employees (Prevention of Less Favourable Treatment) Regulations 2002 now defines a fixed-term contract as including not only one which terminates on expiry of a specific term, but also one which terminates on completion of a specific task or on the happening of a specific event (other than the employee reaching retirement age). This means that in a case like *Ryan v Shipboard Maintenance* the only question now would be whether or not continuity was preserved between the successive contracts (see below, para. 3–023). However, it is not clear whether this definition covers casual workers working "as and when required" on a zero-hours contract.

Under regulation 3, fixed-term employees have the right not to be treated less favourably than comparable permanent employees, unless the treatment can be objectively justified. Following the model of the Part-time Workers (Prevention of Less Favourable Treatment) Regulations 2000 (and the Equal Pay Act 1970, below, para. 7–011) comparison has to be made with an actual comparator and the *pro rata* principle applies. Unlike the Equal Pay Act, it is possible for an employer to argue justification on the basis that the job package for the fixed-term employee is as favourable as that of the permanent employee, taken as a whole, rather than on a term-by-term basis. The Regulations also repeal the redundancy waiver for all fixed-term contracts entered into, renewed or extended after July 2002.

3–019   The issue of successive contracts is more difficult to deal with. The idea of setting an upper ceiling, whether in number or length of time, sounds sensible – but not if it results in the employer replacing the fixed-term employee with another fixed-term employee when she approaches the limit, rather than making her permanent. That would result in the employee's rights being reduced rather than enhanced. Regulation 8 deals with this by instituting an upper limit for successive fixed-term contracts of four years, but allowing the possibility of this being modified by a collective agreement or workforce agreement. Where this limit is exceeded, the contractual term relating to the duration has no effect and the employee is treated thereafter as a permanent employee. There are exceptions to this position. Firstly, an initial fixed-term contract can be for any period: it is only if there is a renewal which takes the whole period beyond four years that regulation 8 kicks in. Secondly, the four-year period can be exceeded if the employer can show objective justification for continuing it as a fixed-term contract. Finally, the Regulations apply only to employment under a fixed-term contract from July 10, 2002 onwards. It should also be noted that regulation 8 may be of less importance than it seems. Now that it has become impossible for employers to insist that fixed-term employees should waive their rights to claim unfair dismissal and redundancy, the distinction between permanent and fixed-term employees becomes of limited importance for most practical purposes.

As with the Part-time Workers (Prevention of Less Favourable Treatment) Regulations 2000, fixed-term employees can ask for written statements, apply to a tribunal and receive protection from detriment or dismissal in connection with their rights. There is one major difference, however. As the title indicates, the Fixed-term Employees (Prevention of

Less Favourable Treatment) Regulations 2002 apply only to "employees" not to "workers". This is an unfortunate departure from the more inclusive trend of recent legislation. Agency workers, apprentices and members of the armed forces are also expressly excluded.

Agency workers

The number of workers employed on temporary work through an employ- **3–020** ment agency has increased substantially in recent years and temporary employees are now reckoned to constitute some 7 per cent of the entire workforce. Temporary workers sign on with an agency which undertakes to try to place them in suitable employment for temporary periods. They are in some respects like other casual workers in that the agency does not have an obligation to find work for them, and they do not have an obligation to accept work when it is offered. However, as argued above, mutuality of obligation should not be regarded as decisive in determining their status. They may or may not be fixed-term workers: sometimes the contract period will be clearly defined at the outset and sometimes it is indefinite. However, as noted above, agency workers are excluded from the ambit of the Fixed-term Employees (Prevention of Less Favourable Treatment) Regulations 2002.

Statutory regulations made under the Employment Agencies Act 1973 require agencies to give temporary workers written statements of the terms and conditions of employment, to deduct tax and National Insurance contributions from their pay as for employees and to state whether they are employees of the agency or self-employed. This might be thought to go some way towards resolving their ambiguous status, but was held not so in *Wickens v Champion Employment* (1984), where despite the fact that the written statement described the temporary workers as having a contract of service with the agency, the EAT held that they were not employees. The factors which the EAT focused on in deciding that the contract could not be one of employment were the lack of control over their work, the lack of mutual obligation, the fact that each engagement was treated as a separate contract and that the temporary workers were stated to be responsible for their own safety.

But if not employees, temporary workers do not look much like self-employed workers in business on their own account either. In *Ironmonger v Movefield Ltd* (1988) the EAT held that an employment tribunal had fallen into error precisely because it reasoned that since the agency worker was not self-employed, he must be an employee, and if he was not the employee of the hiring firm then he must be the employee of the agency. The EAT held that there were other possibilities besides the division of employee or self-employed – although unfortunately declining to enlighten us further on the nature of such a contract, other than saying it was *sui generis*!

There had been a tendency to assume that *Wickens v Champion* **3–021** *Employment* had settled the status of temporary workers, but this was denied by the Court of Appeal in *McMeechan v Secretary of State* (1995). In this case, an employment agency became insolvent while owing wages to the applicant. In these circumstances, an employee can claim unpaid wages from the Secretary of State instead, and this is what the applicant did. The employment tribunal thought that it was bound by *Wickens* to hold that he was not an employee. The Court of Appeal held that there was no rule to this effect and cases would depend on their own facts. As in the casual work cases, the court drew a distinction between the "general" and the "specific" engagements, and held that in this case the applicant could be regarded as an employee of the agency when actually working on his last specific engagement (for which the wages were owed). The court did not consider the nature of the overall relationship, because it was not necessary for their decision.

While *McMeechan* is welcome as at least opening the door to greater protection for agency workers, it still leaves them in something of a limbo, as the Court of Appeal recognised in *Montgomery v Johnson Underwood Ltd* (2001). The applicant in this case had been placed by the agency with a client for whom she had worked for well over two years. When the arrangement was suddenly terminated, she sued the agency for unfair dismissal. Although this, too, was a specific engagement, the Court of Appeal on this occasion rejected the argument that the agency could be her employer, because of their lack of control over her day-to-day work. If this is an absolute requirement, it is strange that it was not decisive in *McMeechan*.

Since *Montgomery v Johnson Underwood Ltd* (2001) a number of inconsistent decisions have been reported, as is to be expected when tribunals are given *carte blanche* to decide on the facts of the particular case. Perhaps the most startling is the Court of Appeal's decision in *Franks v Reuters Ltd* (2003) that an employment tribunal had erred in not considering whether or not there was an implied contract of service between the agency worker and the client. If this is a possible explanation of the legal relationship, it is surprising that no one had thought of it before!

3–022   It is clear that the law relating to agency workers is in an unsatisfactory state. In some cases they may genuinely be skilled entrepreneurs hiring out their services on an independent basis, but it is contrary to reality to regard the large numbers of temporary secretarial and clerical staff in that light. At present the chances are usually against them being able to establish their status as employees and so to access employment protection rights. The Working Time Regulations 1998, reg.36 and the National Minimum Wage Act 1998, s.36 both make special provision for agency workers by stating that they are to be treated as if they have a worker's contract with either the agency or the principal, according to which has the responsibility for paying the agency worker. This is an approach which could usefully be adopted more widely in legislation.

Once again, it is likely that the EU will be the catalyst for change. The issue of working conditions for temporary workers was referred to the social partners by the EC Commission in 1996, along with the issue of fixed-term workers. However, the social partners were unable to agree and so temporary workers were left out of the agreement which became the Fixed-term Work Directive (99/70/EC). The EC Commission therefore produced its own draft Directive, amended in December 2002 after it had been considered by the European Parliament, and it is likely that a directive in substantially this form will be adopted fairly soon, with Member States then having two years within which to implement it. As with the Part-time Work Directive (97/81/EC) and the Fixed-term Work Directive (99/70/EC), the central requirement is to end discrimination against temporary workers and to improve their access to permanent employment if they want it. The biggest issue for the United Kingdom, however, will be determining who comes within the scope of the directive and who should take responsibility as employer of the temporary worker.

Continuity of Employment

As has been seen already, casual workers may face problems in establishing **3–023** that they count as employees, because the employer has no definite legal obligation to offer them work, and they have no legal obligation to accept it. Thus there would seem to be three possibilities for casual workers: (i) they are not employees; (ii) they are employees, but they work under a series of separate contracts of employment; (iii) they have ceased to be casual, because it has come to pass that their series of contracts takes place in the context of a "global" or "umbrella" contract (as discussed above, para. 3–012). Even when they have been classified as employees, both casual and other temporary workers will face another hurdle in terms of legal protection. This is that many employment protection rights require a certain period of continuous employment before the employee qualifies for the right in question. For example, it is necessary to have been employed for one year in order to be able to claim for unfair dismissal and additional maternity leave, and for two years to qualify for redundancy payments.

The qualification period for unfair dismissal used to be two years. This was challenged in *R. v Secretary of State ex p. Seymour-Smith* (2000) on the grounds that the two-year requirement indirectly discriminated on grounds of sex in that women are generally more likely to have an interrupted pattern of employment to take account of family commitments and thus less likely than men to be able to comply with it. The House of Lords referred the issue to the ECJ in 1997 on the question of what constituted a "considerably smaller proportion" of one sex, and at what point this should be measured: when the law was made or when it was applied to the particular case? In 1999 the ECJ held that what was a "considerably smaller proportion" was essentially a question of fact for the national tribunal, although it also indicated that this should be tested at the time of its application as well as at the time of its adoption. In the light of this, the House of Lords held by a majority in *R. v Secretary of State ex p. Seymour-Smith (No.2)* (2000) that a ratio around 90:100 of women and men able to comply with the two-year requirement, which had remained fairly constant for a number of years, did indicate that the rule had a sufficiently adverse impact on women to amount to indirect discrimination. However, the House of Lords also held that the Government had established the defence of justification, so the claims failed and the two-year limit was upheld. In the meantime, however, the practical effects of this had become somewhat less important because in June 1999 the qualifying period for unfair dismissal was reduced to one year. It is still necessary to have two years of continuous employment to qualify for redundancy payments.

Continuity has two aspects. Firstly, continuity must not be broken. Secondly, certain periods of continuity must be built up for the different employment protection rights. If continuity is broken in any week, the counting must start afresh. Usually any week in which continuity is not broken also counts towards the overall period. However, there is a notable exception in relation to industrial action, where ERA, s.216 provides that any week in which the employee is taking part in a strike or is locked out does not count towards the period of continuous employment, but also that it does not break continuity. Subject to these points, a week in which the employee has no contract breaks continuity. However, ERA, s.212(3) provides for three exceptional cases where weeks in which no contract is in existence will not only not break continuity but will also count towards the period of continuous employment. The three cases are as follows:

- absence through sickness or injury;
- temporary cessation of work;
- absence by arrangement or custom.

Absence through sickness or injury

3–024 Generally the contract of employment continues to exist while an employee is off work because of sickness or injury – nor does this depend on whether or not sick pay is payable. In such a situation there is no problem about continuity because the employee continues to be employed under a contract of employment. This exception goes further and provides that even if the contract has been terminated because of the employee's sickness, the employee can still be continuously employed, and count in the weeks of absence, provided that the employee recommences work with the employer within 26 weeks of the termination.

This makes sense. In general, sickness arrangements are more generous for higher status jobs than for those of lower status. One employer might keep someone employed and continue to pay them throughout a long illness; another employer might keep the contract alive, but not pay salary, or at least not after a certain length of time; a third might terminate the contract altogether. Where sick pay is not payable, it may be almost a matter of chance whether the employer keeps the contract alive or terminates it formally. If the latter, it seems reasonable that the worker's continuity should be preserved if he recovers sufficiently to return. If that return is within six months, it is likely to be referable to the previous period of employment.

Temporary cessation of work

3–025 Some difficulty has arisen in interpreting the exception which preserves continuity where the employee is absent through a temporary cessation of work, an exception frequently relied on by casual workers trying to link together a series of contracts. There is no upper time-limit on the length of the cessation. In *Ford v Warwickshire CC* (1983) the House of Lords held that the temporariness or otherwise of an absence should be judged with hindsight, looking back over the whole duration of the relationship to decide whether the absence was temporary in relation to the whole time worked. On the facts of the case they were thus able to hold that where a teacher had worked on eight fixed-term contracts from September to July each year, the absences between contracts were temporary, and she had continuous employment.

Absence by arrangement or custom

The third exception is a situation where, although absent, the employee is **3–026** to be regarded as still employed "by arrangement or custom" for all or any purposes. As the wording suggests, this is capable of covering *ad hoc* personal arrangements (*e.g.* unpaid leave to tend a dying relative) as well as generally recognised occurrences. In *Lloyds Bank v Secretary of State for Employment* (1979) it was held to cover a bank clerk who worked a one-week-on, one-week-off arrangement, although there was no contract for the week off. This might seem a surprising analysis, though the justice of the result is unquestionable.

Unfortunately a much stricter approach was taken in *Curr v Marks & Spencer plc* (2003) where a female manager with 17 years' service was encouraged to take advantage of a new child break scheme at the end of her maternity leave. The scheme allowed her to return to an equivalent level post after four years, but spelt out that she would have to resign at the end of her maternity leave. During the absence, the arrangement required her to work for the company for at least two weeks a year. In fact, she worked for five separate periods amounting to over one year in total. Five years after she returned to work full-time she was made redundant and the company argued that the four-year child break had broken her continuity of employment.

The Court of Appeal reluctantly rejected her argument that this was an absence by arrangement during which she was regarded by both parties as continuing in employment, essentially because it was so clear that it was a resignation followed by a re-engagement. However, the decision does rather beg the question of how an employee can be regarded as continuing in employment by reference to a contract of employment when by definition, ERA, s.212(3) only applies in situations where there is no contract of employment!

Special Types of Work Relationship

Company directors

In business although not in law there is a well-recognised distinction **3–027** between executive directors, who are involved in the day-to-day running of the company, and non-executive directors, who are expected to attend board meetings but whose main duty is to advise on broad policy issues (or sometimes, to lend their title or fame to the company).

Non-executive directors are most unlikely to be employees of the company. So far as executive directors are concerned, the position is not clear-cut. It depends entirely on the nature of the contract which they have with the company. In *Parsons v Albert J. Parsons & Sons Ltd* (1979), although the director worked full-time in the family business, he had no express service contract, and directors were paid such sums as were voted to them at the general meeting each year as "directors' emoluments". It was held that he was not an employee. Contrast *Morley v C. T. Morley* (1985) where the family butcher's business had been incorporated by a father and his two sons who worked full time for it. They all claimed redundancy payments when the business folded and were treated without discussion as employees by the EAT. It is likely that in this case they drew salaries from the company as employees, and in practice it seems that the method of payment may be important (*cf. Eaton v Robert Eaton Ltd* (1988)).

In *Buchan v Secretary of State* (1997) the EAT suggested a general principle that a director who was the controlling shareholder of a company, in effect a self-employed businessman carrying on his business through the medium of a company, should not be regarded as an employee for the purposes of employment protection legislation, whatever the contractual arrangements, on the grounds that it would be undesirable if the person able to decide whether or not the company went into liquidation were able to claim from the Secretary of State for unpaid wages. However, in *Secretary of State for Trade and Industry v Bottrill* (1999) the Court of Appeal held that there could be no such general rule, commenting acidly that it was difficult to see how the possession of a controlling shareholding could turn a contract of employment into something different. It is open to tribunals to examine whether or not the contract of employment of such a director is genuine or not (if entered into just when the company got into trouble, it might not be), and to consider its nature according to the usual tests (see also *Sellars Arenascene Ltd v Connolly* (2001)).

Where directors do have an express contract of service the Companies Act 1985 provides that it may not be for more than five years without the agreement of a general meeting, and copies must be open to inspection by the shareholders. This is intended to reduce the amount of compensation that the company might have to pay if it removes a director from office, and to ensure that members have the information on which to make an accurate assessment of the costs.

Office holders

3–028 Office holders have traditionally been regarded as a separate kind of worker from employees and independent contractors. The distinguishing factor about an office holder is that the office has some sort of public status and exists independently of the person holding it for the time being. An example might be the Archbishop of Canterbury.

Historically the relevance in employment law of finding that someone was an office holder was that he was entitled to public law remedies: *i.e.* the rules of natural justice had to be observed before any disciplinary or dismissal decision and such a decision was subject to judicial review (para. 8–014, below). Essentially this meant that such workers had employment protection before the statutory rules were developed.

Today, ironically, the question is most likely to arise where someone is claiming statutory protection available only to employees (such as unfair dismissal) and it is alleged that she is not qualified through being an office holder rather than an employee. However, in *102 Social Club v Bickerton* (1977) it was pointed out that, for the purposes of the legislation, some office holders may be held to be employees as well as office holders, although some may not. In *Lincolnshire CC v Hopper* (2003) it was argued that a registrar of births, deaths and marriages, who was clearly an office holder, could also be regarded as having a contract of employment with the local authority which was responsible for appointing her, paying her and to whose disciplinary procedure she was subject. This was rejected, however, by the EAT on the grounds that only the Registrar General had power to remove her from office. The EAT held that it was an essential characteristic of a contract of employment that the employer should have the power to dismiss. This left the unfortunate registrar in the position of being subject to the local authority's disciplinary procedure but having no reciprocal right to take action against the authority!

It is clearly anomalous that office holders should not have the usual rights of employees. Another class of office holder who have usually been denied employment protection rights are ministers of religion. While priests in the Church of England may be regarded as office holders because of the church's established status, this is not automatically the case in relation to ministers of other denominations or religions. In *President of the Methodist Conference v Parfitt* (1983) and *Davies v Presbyterian Church of Wales* (1986) the Court of Appeal and House of Lords respectively held that ministers did not have a contract of employment, but held back from deciding whether or not they were office holders.

Crown servants

Crown servants hold office at the pleasure of the Crown at common law, **3–029** and thus in theory would enjoy no security of tenure. However, most employment protection legislation is specifically extended to them, although with some exceptions (ERA, s.191). It remains debatable whether or not Crown servants, or some of them, can be regarded as having contracts of employment. For this reason the Employment Act 1988 provided that if their terms did not amount to a contract of employment, they would nonetheless be treated as doing so for the purposes of the law of industrial action (now TULRCA, s.245). What this means is that anyone organising a strike among civil servants is at the same risk of liability for interference with contracts as any other union organiser.

Police

3–030 All police officers are office holders (*Ridge v Baldwin* (1964)). Thus they qualify for public law remedies, but not for most employment protection rights. Under ERA, s.200, they are excluded from all rights except to receive a written statement of terms, a minimum period of notice and redundancy payments. Under the Police Act 1964, s.17, the Chief Constable or police authority is treated as their employer for the purposes of vicarious liability.

4.   The Contract of Employment

Chapter 3 dealt with the definition of the contract of employment. In this **4–001** chapter we will examine how contracts of employment come into being and their content. In practice parties will usually enter a contract after the stages of advertisement, interview, offer and acceptance. The offer may be made and accepted at the interview, or may be made later by a letter of appointment. While a limited amount of negotiation may be possible, perhaps over the starting date or the starting salary, most prospective employees need the position more than the employer needs their particular individual qualities, and so the contract tends to be entered on the employer's terms. This does not, however, mean that it will be totally one-sided. Very many employers, especially large organisations, recognise trade unions and bargain with one or more trade unions about the principal terms and conditions of different groups of workers; a new employee will be taken on within the framework of the collectively agreed terms. Further, at common law, judges have developed the concept of terms which are to be regarded as implied into every contract of employment simply by virtue of the employment relationship; these implied terms are sometimes expressed as the common law duties of employer and employee. Finally, the inherent inequality in the bargaining relationship (particularly where there is no recognised trade union) has been recognised with the result that certain protective measures for employees have been introduced by statute. Most of these statutory protection rights are not incorporated into the contract of employment; rather, they exist alongside and supplement contractual rights, although they will override any less favourable inconsistent contractual term. Some, such as the equality clause derived from the Equal Pay Act 1970, are implied into the contract of employment.

The result is that where there is a question about the respective rights and liabilities of the employer and worker, the answer may require a fairly complex analysis of a variety of different sources, to establish first what the parties actually agreed, and secondly, whether there are other constraints affecting the position.

Formation

4–002 In general no special formalities are required for entry into a contract of employment: as with other contracts, the agreement may be purely oral. There are some exceptions, of which the most notable are the contracts of merchant seafarers and contracts of apprenticeship, which have to be in writing. However, there are fewer formal apprenticeships these days.

References

4–003 Employers have no general obligation to provide references in respect of employees seeking alternative employment, although most are willing to do so. To have any value, a reference must be entirely frank, and so employers have traditionally been unwilling to provide them except on a confidential basis. Under the Data Protection Act 1998, employees do not have a right to see a reference which their employer sends to a prospective employer. Although this is "personal data" within the meaning of DPA, s.1, there is a specific exception covering it in DPA, Sch.7, para.1. However, it is open to an employee to ask their new employer for a copy of a reference supplied by a previous employer and the Information Commissioner's Employment Practices Data Protection Code, Pt 2 recommends that this should be made available. Under DPA, s.7(4), access should not be given to information which identifies a third party unless the third party consents or it is reasonable to go ahead without their consent. The Information Commissioner's Code recommends that employers should make it clear to referees that their references may be shown to the employee concerned and comments that referees should not expect their references to be confidential in all circumstances. It is quite difficult to strike a balance here between the referee's right to privacy and the employee's right to know what information is held about him or her. Some employers now deal with this by seeking the referee's consent to disclosure, but if the referee refuses, it will be difficult in practice to edit the reference in such a way as to protect the referee's identity and so an employer would probably be justified in refusing disclosure.

Note, however, that since the request for disclosure can only be made to your own employer, not to the employer who provided the reference, unsuccessful job applicants are unlikely to get to know what their references said, although they may draw inferences from a continuing failure to get other work. But can anything be done about an unfavourable reference (short of changing your referee)?

4–004 If the reference contains defamatory matter, it is protected by qualified privilege, which means that the employer will not be liable unless she acted maliciously. In *Lawton v BOC Transhield* (1987), Tudor Evans J. was prepared to accept that an employer owed a duty of care to an employee in preparing a reference, although finding that there had been no breach on the facts of that case. The decision was subsequently criticised as inconsistent with the law of defamation. It was argued that to allow an employee a right of action where the employer had prepared a reference negligently was to permit the defence of qualified privilege to be defeated by carelessness rather than only by malice.

The issue came before the House of Lords in *Spring v Guardian Assurance* (1994). The plaintiff had worked for an insurance firm as an authorised representative selling Guardian Assurance policies. He left to set up his own business selling policies for a different insurance company. As required by the rules of the relevant regulatory authority, LAUTRO, the second insurance company approached Guardian Assurance for a reference regarding him. The reference impugned the plaintiff's honesty as well as his competence and was aptly described as "the kiss of death" to his career in the insurance industry. It was found that the referee had acted honestly but negligently in drawing it up.

By a majority, the House of Lords held that an employer owed a duty to the subject of a reference to take reasonable care in drawing it up. This did not mean that the employer would be taken to warrant that facts relied on or stated were true, but only that the employer had taken reasonable care in assembling the facts and verifying them. The main policy reason against imposing a duty of care in these circumstances was said to be that employers might be deterred from giving frank references. This did not seem a very real or serious risk to the majority, especially when balanced against the serious consequences for the employee. As they pointed out, liability for negligently prepared references has existed since *Hedley Byrne v Heller* (1964), the only difference being that the duty in that case was owed to the recipient rather than the subject. In *Hedley Byrne* the referee had included a disclaimer of liability, which is one way an employer could protect itself, although it should be remembered that this would have to pass the reasonableness test imposed by the Unfair Contract Terms Act 1977, s.2.

Two other points of interest arise from *Spring v Guardian Assurance*. **4–005** Firstly, it was not finally decided whether the plaintiff's contract was one of employment or for services; however, in the view of the House of Lords, the employer's duty was the same in either case. Secondly, while holding the claim to be made out in tort, the majority also considered that a comparable implied duty could exist in some circumstances in contract. Lord Woolf thought that in a case like this, where employment would be impossible without a reference from the former employer, there would be a duty on the employer to provide a reference.

It is possible that *Spring v Guardian Assurance* deterred some employers from giving references; others reacted by confining themselves to purely factual statements. However, such a policy will not necessarily absolve them from liability. In *Bartholomew v Hackney LBC* (1999) a reference stated truthfully that disciplinary proceedings for gross misconduct had been commenced against the claimant at the time when he took voluntary severance from the council. By analogy with the law of defamation the Court of Appeal held that accurate statements could give an unfair impression and accepted that the employer had a duty not to give an unfair or misleading impresssion overall, even if each individual statement in the reference was correct. In *TSB Bank plc v Harris* (2000) the employer was also entirely accurate in telling a prospective employer of the applicant that she had had 17 complaints made against her by customers, of which four had been upheld and eight were still outstanding. The trouble was, the bank had not told her about 15 of these, so this information came as a shock to her as well as to the prospective employer (who withdrew the job offer). She had never had the chance to offer any comments or explanation in relation to them. In these circumstances the EAT held that the bank had committed a fundamental breach of the implied contractual duty to maintain mutual trust and confidence.

Under the Rehabilitation of Offenders Act 1974, s.4(2), where a reference is sought in relation to someone who has a "spent" conviction, the referee has a duty not to mention the conviction or the ancillary circumstances. In such a case, the referee is protected from any legal liability. However, there are by regulation various exceptional situations where this does not apply.

Conditional offers

4–006 Some employers require employees to pass a medical examination before taking up employment. In that case, the offer of employment will be conditional on a satisfactory report. Today it is not uncommon to find employers who only take up references once they have decided to offer someone a job. This seems odd, since the whole point of the reference is to help assess the candidate's suitability, and it should thus be taken into account as part of the selection process. In *Wishart v NACAB* (1990), the plaintiff was offered a job "subject to receipt of satisfactory written references". The references indicated that he had had quite a lot of sick leave, and the employer therefore decided to withdraw the offer. The plaintiff claimed that the references would have been regarded as satisfactory by a reasonable employer, and that an objective standard was the appropriate test to use. The Court of Appeal thought this was just about arguable, but tended to the view that the correct test is whether or not the references are seen as satisfactory by the employer in question. It is submitted that this is the better view, and that the test here must be subjective.

If an offer is unconditional and has been accepted, then of course, neither party has the right to vary or withdraw from it. In *Sarker v South Tees Acute Hospitals NHS Trust* (1997) the EAT held that withdrawal of an accepted offer before the date on which the employment was due to start was a termination of employment in breach of contract, giving the applicant a cause of action in an employment tribunal.

Written Particulars of Terms

4–007 The variety of sources from which the terms of the contract may be drawn can result in confusion as to what has been agreed, and therefore to unnecessary disputes. Thus the very first provision of all the protective legislation was the requirement, introduced by the Contracts of Employment Act 1963, that employees should receive a statement in writing of the principal terms and conditions of the contract. This now appears, in amplified form, in ERA Pt I. Substantial changes were effected by TURERA 1993 in order to comply with the 1991 EU Directive on the Proof of the Employment Relationship (91/533/EEC), and the Employment Act 2002 also makes amendments.

Under ERA, ss.1 and 198, employees with one month's service are entitled to a written statement of their main terms and conditions, although the employer has two months in which to provide it. The particulars may be provided in instalments, provided that one of them ("the principal instalment") includes all of the following: the identity of the parties; the date of commencement; whether any previous period of employment counts as part of the employee's continuous employment; any terms about holidays; job title or job description; and place of work or mobility clause. The other matters to be included are: pay, or the method of calculating it; intervals at which wages are paid; hours of work, including any rules on overtime; sick pay and pension arrangements, if any; the length of notice to be given on either side; and details of any collective agreements affecting the contract. If the employment is not expected to be permanent, the particulars should state the period for which it is expected to continue, or the finishing date in the case of a fixed-term contract. If there are no terms on any of these matters, this must be expressly stated. Job title can be important: a "till operator" probably cannot be transferred to duties in the store room; however, an "unskilled worker Grade 1" can be asked to do any type of unskilled work, and would have no legitimate complaint if taken off what she has come to regard as "her" job. From an employer's point of view, there are obvious advantages in flexibility and it may seem like a good policy not to use job descriptions and to draw job titles widely so that staff can be used in whatever way seems best at the time. However, that policy backfired in *Nelson v BBC* (1977) where the employee was a Grade 3 producer who had always worked in the Caribbean Service. When that service was closed down, he successfully resisted the employer's argument that he was redundant, because his contract merely described him as an employee in that particular grade, and this was backed up by an express mobility clause elsewhere in the contract.

The requirement to stipulate the place of work, or alternatively that the **4–008** employee may be required to work at different places was introduced by TURERA and should have reduced the number of disputes over whether an employee can be moved to a different location without her agreement (which often arises in relation to redundancy: see below, Chapter 9).

It has long been the case that the written statement should include details of any disciplinary rules applicable to the employee, although there was an exemption for employers with fewer than 20 employees (ERA, s.3). However, the Employment Act 2002 introduces statutory disciplinary and grievance procedures as a compulsory part of all contracts of employment (see further below, Chapter 8). When this comes into force (October 2004), section 3 will be amended to require details of the statutory disciplinary procedure to be included and to abolish the small employer exemption. It is obviously sensible for employees to know what the disciplinary rules and procedures are and so it makes sense for this information to be included in the written statement. The small employer exemption never applied to grievances and it remains mandatory for the statement to say to whom the employee should complain if he has a grievance. In *Goold (Pearmak) Ltd v McConnell* (1995) failure to provide a grievance procedure was held to be a fundamental breach of contract by the employer.

Employers used to be able to avoid providing lengthy documents to every employee by referring them to some other document which was reasonably accessible. However, individual notification is now required of everything except sickness and pension arrangements and disciplinary and grievance procedures.

Not every employee qualifies for the right to receive written particulars. Employees must work for at least a month, although part-timers are now included on the same footing as full-timers, and certain seafarers and share fishermen are excluded.

Status of the written statement

4–009 The written statement is not the same thing as a written contract of employment. A contract creates the rights and duties of the parties; the written statement merely declares what they are after they have been agreed, and it follows that it is therefore capable of being inaccurate. This distinction may be easy enough for a lawyer to grasp, but may not be so obvious to ordinary employers and employees, especially given the special veneration that lay people reserve for things in writing. It is an important distinction, for if a document is held to be a written contract, it will be presumed that it accurately records the terms agreed by the parties and it will be very difficult to persuade a court that the terms are otherwise. If it is a statement, then it has no special legal status and could be a mistaken record of what was agreed. Indeed, as was pointed out in *System Floors v Daniel* (1981), a written statement supplied to meet the employer's statutory obligation is not an agreed document: it represents only the employer's unilateral view of the agreement.

That said, it remains the case that the written statement will usually be the best evidence, and sometimes the only evidence, of the agreement; also that it seems unlikely in many cases that the decision to give a written contract rather than a written statement is made consciously. In *System Floors v Daniel* the document was headed "Written statement" and the employee's signature was merely to indicate receipt; in *Gascol Conversions v Mercer* (1974) the employee signed a document headed "Non-staff employees' contract of employment": this was held to be a written contract. One may perhaps doubt whether the parties realised that the difference in wording would have the result that the former employee, but not the latter, would be able to claim his terms were different.

Enforcing the obligation

4–010 What happens if an employer fails to provide the written statement? When the requirement was originally introduced, failure to comply was a criminal offence! This was overkill perhaps, but the present "sanction", that the employee may apply to an employment tribunal for a declaration of what should have been included (ERA, s.11), is not entirely satisfactory either: it is hardly a way to endear oneself to one's employer, and it is thus unlikely that the employee will take such action unless some more serious problem has arisen. Previous editions of this book suggested that a more effective sanction would be to require an employer to pay two weeks' pay to an employee if it failed to provide a written statement, by analogy with the sanction under ERA, s.93 where an employer fails to provide a written statement of reasons for dismissal. It is encouraging to see a move in this direction. Under the Employment Act 2002, s.38, tribunals must award an employee who successfully brings proceedings under some other jurisdiction (such as unfair dismissal or discrimination) an extra two to four weeks' pay if it transpires that the employer was in breach of its duty to provide a written statement. Unfortunately, this claim is not freestanding and no award will be made if the employee is unsuccessful. It is difficult to see the rationale for these restrictions, since the wrong to the employee is the same in all cases and should be independent of any other claim.

Another problem arising under section 11 concerns the jurisdiction of the tribunal, and comes about because of the continuing rule that tribunals do not have complete jurisdiction over purely contractual issues. If the statement is not given, is incomplete, or is said to be inaccurate, does it not mean that the tribunal will have to find out what the terms of the contract are, in order to make a declaration of what particulars the employee should have been given? But if so, does this not mean that the tribunal is exercising jurisdiction over contractual matters while the contract is still ongoing? The issue received detailed consideration from the Court of Appeal in *Mears v Safecar Security* (1982). The Court concluded that the tribunal clearly had the right and the duty to correct a statement which was incorrect as well as to state the terms where no statement had been given. In doing so, it should investigate what the actual agreement of the parties was. So far, so good; however, Stephenson L.J. went even further than this and held that where there was no evidence of what the parties had agreed on a matter which should have been contained in the written statement, then the tribunal should nonetheless determine what they should have agreed, in effect inventing the term which would best fit in the circumstances. This was doubted by another Court of Appeal in *Eagland v British Telecom* (1992). Pointing out that Stephenson L.J.'s remarks were *obiter*, Parker L.J. drew a distinction between mandatory terms (necessary incidents for the contract of employment to exist) and non-mandatory terms (*e.g.* disciplinary rules and terms about pensions, sickness or holidays). If non-mandatory terms were not reflected in the written statement then tribunals should not invent them. In the case of mandatory terms, tribunals would have power to declare an agreement if one were discoverable, but if not, he doubted the tribunal's power to impose terms which had not been agreed. As the Court of Appeal in *Eagland* recognised, this guidance was also *obiter*; however, as it is the product of further reflection on the matter and accords better with general principle, it is undoubtedly to be preferred. Finally, it remains the case that the tribunal has no power to interpret what a term which has been stated actually means (*Construction Industry Training Board v Leighton* (1978)).

Variation of the contract

4–011 Under ERA, s.4, the employer has a further obligation to inform employees of any changes in their terms and conditions within a month of the change. This is to ensure that the statement is kept up to date. It must be noted, however, that this does not confer on the employer any right to make such changes: any variation must be agreed between the parties, as with any other contract. Should the employer insist on unilateral variation, it will be a breach of contract, usually a fundamental breach. This is not to say that the employee will always be able to insist on her right to continue on the old terms; if the employer pushes the issue to the point of dismissing those who will not consent to a change, it does not follow that the dismissal will be unfair, even though there is a breach of contract (see below, para. 8–057). What happens if the employee continues to work but expressly states that she does not accept the change? In *Burdett-Coutts v Herts CC* (1984) the Council wrote to employees purportedly changing their conditions in a way which resulted in an overall reduction in pay. They continued to work under protest, and then brought an action claiming arrears of pay. They were successful, as the variation had not been agreed. However, this cannot go on indefinitely. In *Henry v London General Transport Services Ltd* (2002) the Court of Appeal held that employees who had worked a new rota system for two years, albeit having made their opposition clear, had to be taken to have agreed the revised terms.

In *Jones v Associated Tunnelling* (1981) the employee was issued with a new written statement which included a mobility clause. He made no protest until some four years later when the employer tried to move him from the place where he had been employed. The EAT held that agreement could not be implied solely from his failure to protest at a time when the variation had no immediate practical effect on him, for he might well have no wish to precipitate a confrontation with the employer. It would be different for a change, such as a reduction of pay, which does have immediate effect. There, a continuation to work without protesting would probably be held to amount to agreement to the variation. This reasoning was applied in *Aparau v Iceland Frozen Foods* (1996). The applicant had been employed as a cashier by Bejams, which was taken over by Iceland. Following the takeover, Iceland issued all staff with new written terms and conditions of employment, which included a mobility clause. Iceland relied on the employee's failure to object to this term to show that it was now part of the contract. As the term had no effect on the employment relationship until the day when they asked the cashier to move, the EAT held that mere continuance of employment without objection could not be taken to indicate acceptance.

Other Documents

4–012 Employers may use all sorts of papers to communicate with their employees. Lots of employers have staff handbooks, or works rules books;

the noticeboard is an important means of communication in many work-places, large employers often have an in-house journal and today there may also be a company intranet. Some enlightened companies now give their employees a version of the annual report that they must give to their shareholders and this is recognised as good practice. The purpose of these documents varies; some are designed to be acted on by the workers; others are merely for information and others still are a public relations exercise designed to build a corporate image and to develop a positive feeling among the workforce towards their employer. Not only does the function vary from company to company, but it may well be that the same document carries out more than one function. For example, a staff handbook may well contain general information about the history and structure of an organisation as well as details of holiday entitlements, disciplinary and grievance procedures, and so on.

Whether or not other documents have any contractual status will depend on the intention of the parties and whether or not they have been incorporated into the contract of employment. As this will be a question of fact in each case, it is not possible to make generalisations about particular classes of document. Express incorporation of a document, where a letter of appointment, the contract or even the written statement expressly refers to it, is unlikely to cause too many problems, unless the document fulfils more than one function, where it may be difficult to know whether a particular section is intended to have contractual effect.

Implied incorporation will most usually depend on whether the parties have acted in the past as if this kind of document is part of the contract, as well as a consideration of whether the kind of thing it covers is appropriately viewed as a contract term. In *Trusthouse Forte v Adonis* (1984) a notice was posted saying, "Last warning. Anyone smoking in non-smoking areas will be dismissed for gross misconduct". Two days later the employers issued an updated written statement to employees which included smoking in prohibited places under the category of ordinary misconduct for which a final warning would be given. Six months later the employee was dismissed for smoking in a non-smoking area. The EAT clearly treated the notice as capable of having contractual effect, although on the facts it was negated by the inconsistent written statement, which had been issued later. Had the sequence of events been reversed, the dismissal would probably have been fair. In *Taylor v Secretary of State for Scotland* (2000) it was held that an equal opportunities policy which had been notified to prison officers by circular was incorporated into their contracts of employment in the light of evidence that other changes to contracts had been implemented in the same manner. However, in *Grant v South West Trains* (1998) the High Court declined to find that an equal opportunities policy was incorporated on the strength of a contractual statement that employees should act in the spirit of it. The policy was in "very general, even idealistic" terms and the manner of its agreement indicated that the parties did not intend it to be binding.

Mixed messages were a problem in *Crédit Suisse Asset Management v* **4–013** *Armstrong* (1996), where the company sought to rely on a restrictive covenant contained in a staff handbook. The handbook had been issued in 1994 with a covering memorandum which described it as "largely an update of existing terms" but urged staff to "try to find time to read it". The memorandum also said that the new handbook superseded previous documentation and that it contained "important contractual rights and obligations". The employees argued that they were not bound by this because the memorandum had misrepresented the contents, by describing it as "largely an update . . .", and if it was meant to be contractual, it was strange that the memorandum only said, "try and find time to read it". However, the Court of Appeal pointed out that the index at the front of the handbook had a footnote stating that the provisions of the handbook were contractual; furthermore, the employees were highly paid investment fund managers: "men of experience and sophistication", in the court's estimation, who were used to dealing with complex documents. In these circumstances, the handbook could be taken to be incorporated. It is possible that this could be regarded as a gloss on the principle laid down in *Jones v Associated Tunnelling*, where the employee had a sufficient degree of knowledge and experience to realise the significance of a variation introduced in this way.

One of the most important reasons for knowing whether or not a particular document has contractual effect is to know whether it is binding on the employer as well as the employee. The point is famously illustrated by *Secretary of State v ASLEF (No.2)* (1972). In the course of an industrial dispute, the rail workers instituted a work-to-rule. This involved their zealous adherence to all the instructions in their enormous rule-book, and had the desired effect of causing havoc on the railways. The beauty of the tactic, as they saw it, was that they were not acting in breach of their contracts of employment; they were carrying out its terms to the letter! The argument, not surprisingly, did not commend itself to the Court of Appeal, which found against them on a number of points. One reason was that the court denied that the rule-book was a part of the contract. Rather, it contained the employer's standing instructions on how the work was to be done. The implication of this finding was that the rule-book provisions were within the unilateral discretion of the employer and could thus be changed without the prior agreement of the workers. Thus by insisting on following the rules when the employer wanted them to be disregarded, the employees were in breach of contract.

Another example of the discretion which this kind of interpretation vests in the employer is *Dryden v Greater Glasgow Health Board* (1992). Dryden was an auxiliary nurse, who smoked 30 cigarettes a day. Until 1991 the Health Board provided smoking areas within the hospital, but then it decided that it should implement a complete no-smoking policy. Consultation took place from 1990; staff were given plenty of warning and offers of help to give up. A few days after the policy was finally implemented, Dryden resigned because she could not cope with the ban. She claimed unfair dismissal, so the tribunal had to decide whether introducing the ban on smoking was a breach of contract by the employer. The Scottish EAT held that it was not. This concerned the employer's rules governing behaviour in the workplace, and they were not contractual terms. In the view of the EAT, making rules for the conduct of employees was within the employer's discretion as part of the right to give reasonable orders. If the employer is entitled to make rules, it is also entitled to change them.

Custom and Practice

The phrase "custom and practice" is widely used in industrial relations, but **4–014** its meaning in law is opaque. As Davies and Freedland point out, it is necessary to consider whose custom and practice we are talking about: is it a cloak for managerial prerogative, so that if the workforce acquiesces for long enough, they will be bound by it? Or does it mean that where the workers do things "their way" without objection, then they have a right to do it that way? Or does it refer to some sort of joint regulation? There is no clear answer to these questions, although it is true to say that on the whole the courts lean towards the managerial prerogative. In the Part-time Workers (Prevention of Less Favourable Treatment) Regulations 2000 there is a very unusual legislative reference to custom and practice as the test for determining whether a worker is full-time or part-time. It seems likely that it is managerial practice which will be decisive here.

For a custom to be regarded as part of the contract, it seems it must pass similar tests to customary law: *i.e.*, that it is reasonable, notorious (meaning very well-known in this context) and has existed for a very long time. In *Sagar v Ridehalgh* (1931) the employer claimed the customary right to make deductions from a weaver's wages for bad work, either on the basis that this had been the practice in their factory for more than 30 years or on the basis that it was customary in the whole Lancashire cotton weaving trade. The Court of Appeal found both grounds established, and held that it was immaterial if the weaver did not know of the practice.

Now that written statements must be given, the scope for there to be customary terms in the contract is likely to be limited. In times of rapid technological change, to claim a customary right to work in the way to which one has been accustomed is unlikely to be received with judicial sympathy. In *Cresswell v Board of Inland Revenue* (1984) employees feared that computerisation of all tax records would ultimately lead to job losses. Failing to get the assurances they sought on the subject, they refused to co-operate in using the computers and claimed a customary right to do the work manually as before. This latter-day Luddism received short shrift from Walton J., who held that the employer could properly require them to do what was the same job albeit done by different methods.

Does this indicate that while it may be difficult for employees to argue **4–015** for contractual rights based on custom, it may be easier for the employer? This potential one-sidedness was recognised by the EAT in *Duke v Reliance Systems* (1982) where Browne-Wilkinson J. said that for a unilateral management policy to become a term of employees' contracts on the basis of custom and practice, there were at least two conditions: firstly, that it had been drawn to the attention of employees, and secondly, that it had been acted on without exception over a substantial period of time.

This was applied, although not to the advantage of the employees in question, in *Quinn v Calder* (1996). In the mid-1980s the management of the company had decided, as a matter of policy, to give enhanced redundancy payments to smooth the path of compulsory redundancies. The arrangements were contained in a management policy document and had not been the subject of negotiation with the recognised trade unions, although they were generally known to the union and the workforce, and had been applied on all four occasions when there had been redundancies between 1986 and 1994. However, in summer 1994 the applicants were made redundant and were not given the enhanced payments. They claimed that it was an implied term of their contracts that they should receive the enhanced payments. Using the test in *Duke v Reliance Systems*, the EAT held that they were not entitled to the payments. This was a unilateral management policy (not a collectively agreed term) and, although it was known to employees, it had not been brought to their attention in any official or systematic way. The conditions were not therefore fulfilled.

Implied Terms

4–016 Contracts of employment differ from many other kinds of contract in that they are usually intended to be indefinite. It would be impossible, in making the contract at the outset, to cover absolutely every eventuality. It follows that there will frequently be situations where the parties just have not reached agreement on a particular point. In these circumstances, it may be appropriate to fill the gaps by implying terms into the contract.

Terms may certainly be implied according to the usual contract law tests: *i.e.* when it is necessary to give "business efficacy" to the contract (*The Moorcock* (1889)) or according to the "officious bystander" test (*Southern Foundries v Shirlaw* (1940)): where something is so obvious that it goes without saying, and if there had been someone standing by listening to the parties make the agreement who had suggested that they express the term, they would have silenced him with a testy "Of course!". In *Liverpool CC v Irwin* (1977) the House of Lords continued with the orthodox view that courts cannot imply terms into contracts just because the term would be a reasonable one for the parties to have agreed. However, they suggested that terms could be implied when the nature of the contract indicated that there was a need for such a term, as in the situation where there was an ongoing contractual relationship such as employer and employee and the contract as agreed was incomplete in some crucial respect.

An example of this could be *Courtaulds Northern Spinning Ltd v Sibson* (1988). The employee, an HGV driver, had left his trade union after a dispute, causing bad feeling among the other employees who were all members. To avoid trouble, the employer proposed to move him to a different depot a mile away. He argued that this was a breach of contract as there was no express mobility clause in his contract. The Court of Appeal held that there must be some term about place in his contract: he had to work somewhere. Thus if there was no express term, one would have to be implied, because of the nature of the relationship, to complete the contract. But not every contract of employment would have the same term on place implied into it, unlike, *e.g.* an implied term such as mutual respect, which is the same for all contracts of employment. In the event, as he was a driver and therefore did not work always in the same place anyway, they held that it would be reasonable to expect him to work from a depot a mile away and held that it was an implied term of the contract that he could be so moved.

This is subject to the *caveat* that the term may not be essential in this sense and the gap may have been left deliberately. In *Ali v Christian Salvesen* (1997) the employee was employed under an annualised hours contract which meant that he only became entitled to overtime after having worked 1,824 hours in a year. This had been agreed through collective bargaining. Ali was made redundant after five months during which time he had regularly worked more than 40 hours a week, but had not received any overtime. He argued for an implied term that he should be entitled to *pro rata* overtime in these circumstances; the employer argued for a literal interpretation of the contract. The Court of Appeal considered that this was not an example of an incomplete contract: the terms had been settled through free collective bargaining and in the circumstances, an omission of a term on this point was more likely to have been deliberate. In consequence, no term as to overtime should be implied.

It has been argued that while the courts are reluctant to imply terms into **4–017** the contract when it amounts almost to inventing them for the parties, they are more prepared to imply terms to control the employer's express powers under the contract. Thus in *United Bank v Akhtar* (1989) the bank included an express mobility clause giving it the right to move employees to any branch in the United Kingdom and a discretion as to whether or not it would give relocation allowances. The applicant, a bank clerk in the lowest grade, was given less than a week's notice to move permanently from the Leeds branch where he worked to the Birmingham branch. His request for three months' notice to sort out a move (he had a house to sell and his wife was ill) was rejected, the bank relying on the mobility clause. The EAT held that although an implied term could not contradict an express term, it could control its exercise. In this case, they implied a term that the bank should give reasonable notice of exercise of the mobility clause, so as not to make it impossible for him to comply with his contractual obligation to move.

Similarly, in *Johnstone v Bloomsbury HA* (1991) a junior hospital doctor worked under a contract which provided for a basic 40-hour week, but also for unlimited overtime (although it should not average out at more than an extra 48 hours per week!). He argued that to be required to work an average 88 hours per week and sometimes to work over 100 hours per week would damage his health. By a majority, the Court of Appeal agreed that the express term which allowed this extraordinary amount of overtime was subject to the control of an implied term, although one judge held that it was subject to an implied term that the power to demand overtime would be exercised reasonably and the other, to the implied term that an employer must take reasonable care to ensure the health and safety of employees.

These cases lead us to a consideration of another kind of implied term in **4–018** employment contracts. Certain types of contract are so prevalent that they receive repeated judicial scrutiny, and in the end develop their own special rules. Contracts of employment are in such a category. There are certain terms which are held to be implied into every contract of employment just because it is a contract of employment. These implied terms are frequently expressed as being duties of the employer and employee respectively.

Two major duties of the employer are the subject of separate chapters. The duty to pay wages is the most fundamental duty of the employer, furnishing as it does the basic consideration for the contract. It is now subject to considerable legislative control and is dealt with below, Chapter 7. The employer's duty of care to its employees is a large subject and greatly amplified by statutes on health and safety at work; these matters are dealt with in Chapter 14. There remain three other duties of an employer which must be considered: the duty to provide work for the employee; the possible duty to respect the employee's privacy; and the duty to maintain mutual trust and confidence, an implied duty of recent vintage.

Duty to provide work?

4–019 Does the employer have a duty simply to pay wages, or is there also a duty to supply the employee with work? It may seem odd that the question ever arises, but in fact there are situations where an employee may not be content to remain at home with pay but without work, not least because this is hardly going to be a permanent situation.

The classic view is that there is no duty to provide work: "Provided I pay my cook her wages regularly, she cannot complain if I choose to take any or all of my meals out." (*per* Asquith J. in *Collier v Sunday Referee* (1940)). However, there have always been two well-recognised exceptions to this. Where wages depend on commission for the work actually done, or the worker is paid by the piece, it is recognised that an employer has a duty to provide work to give the employee a chance to earn his wages. Thus in *Devonald v Rosser* (1906) a rollerman at a tinplate factory was given six weeks' notice. He argued that the employer had a duty to provide him with work for those six weeks. The court held it was a necessary implication from the terms of the contract (which provided for payment by the piece) that the employer would find him a reasonable amount of work to do and his damages were assessed by reference to his average earnings over the previous six weeks. Similarly, in *Turner v Goldsmith* (1891) it was held to be an implied term in the contract of a salesman paid by commission that he would be sent a reasonable supply of samples to sell.

Secondly, where the refusal of work denies the employee a chance of enhancing her reputation, there is a duty to provide work. In *Clayton & Waller v Oliver* (1930) Oliver was to be employed in one of the three leading roles in a musical called *Hit the Deck*. The employer then reneged. Oliver was entitled to damages for the loss of the opportunity to enhance his reputation. In addition to performers, this exception could extend also to writers such as journalists.

4–020 Beyond these two exceptions, it is generally thought that there is no right to work at common law. In a few cases (*e.g. Nagle v Feilden* (1966); *Edwards v SOGAT* (1971)) Lord Denning attempted to establish such a right. One of the notable examples of this was *Langston v AUEW* (1974) where he quoted several of his own judgments as well as Longfellow's "Village Blacksmith" in support of this contention. This line of authority ceased on Lord Denning's retirement.

As long ago as *Turner v Sawdon* (1901) the Court of Appeal rejected the argument that a failure to provide work would mean that the employee's skills would deteriorate, denying that the employer had a duty to keep the employee in service in such a manner as to enable him to become *au fait* with his work. However, that argument has been treated more sympathetically in recent cases dealing with "garden leave". It has become common for firms to insist on lengthy periods of notice for their senior executives, and, if they resign, to refuse either to have them at work or to release them to a new employer before the notice period is up. They may spend months with nothing to do but the garden. The reason for this phenomenon is that companies are worried about their confidential information reaching a competitor – and this seems a safer method of dealing with the problem than a restraint of trade clause. By the time the executive moves to her new employer, her information will be out of date. In *Provident Financial v Hayward* (1989), the fact that the skills of an accountant would not atrophy in the period under consideration was treated as a relevant consideration by the Court of Appeal (*cf.* also *Breach v Epsylon Industries* (1976)), but *William Hill v Tucker* (1998) went a good deal further in using the right to work argument in this context. The employee was a senior dealer who had been specifically charged with developing spread betting, a relatively novel and risky form of betting. When his employer tried to hold him to a six-month garden leave period he claimed that it was a breach of his right to work. The Court of Appeal agreed, mainly because of their construction of this particular contract. The employee held a unique position and maintenance of his skills in this developing area did require frequent practice. Furthermore, references in the contract to the employee having to work such hours as were necessary for the proper performance of his duties, to the employer's commitment to developing employees' skills and to an express right to suspend in disciplinary cases were held to be inconsistent with the notion that the contract allowed for the employee to be remunerated without the opportunity to work. While the first grounds for the decision would limit it to special classes of employment, the terms in the contract itself that were relied on as indicating a right to work are very common and would therefore suggest that very many employees could argue that they had a right to work even if they could not show any risk of their skills atrophying. However, as it is an implied term of the contract of employment it is open to an employer to negative it by express provision.

Duty to respect the employee's privacy?

Privacy issues are increasingly dealt with by legislation and the whole area **4–021** is affected by Article 8 of the ECHR, which guarantees individuals' rights to respect for their private life (subject to the provisos in Article 8(2)). It may be that an implied obligation on the employer to respect the employee's privacy should be recognised as providing a coherent conceptual framework for these developments and as enabling courts and tribunals to fill any gaps. There are three main aspects to privacy in employment. The first aspect concerns the employee's right to know what information is held about her: this has been considered above in relation to references (see para. 4–003). The second aspect concerns the privacy of information about the employee; and the third is about non-intrusion into the employee's private life.

An obligation not to disclose information about an employee was recognised in *Dalgleish v Lothian and Borders Police Board* (1991), where the local council wanted to discover which council employees had not paid their poll tax (community charge) and asked the Police Board to disclose this information. By analogy with the cases establishing the employee's duty to the employer in relation to confidential information, the court granted an injunction to prevent this on the grounds that it would be in breach of the employer's duty of confidentiality. This is now reinforced by statute. Under the Data Protection Act 1998 employers have a duty to ensure that personal data is only obtained for specified, lawful purposes and is used only for those purposes. The information kept must be accurate, up-to-date, relevant and not excessive – suggesting that personnel records should be regularly culled of old and irrelevant information. The Act contains strict limitations on the processing of such information, which includes its disclosure, and further guidance is given by the Information Commissioner's Employment Practices Data Protection Code, Part 2 on Records Management (August 2002).

4–022   Surveillance and monitoring of employees' activities and communications has become particularly sensitive with the advent of increasingly sophisticated and relatively inexpensive technology to enable it to happen. There is a divergence of view between those who feel that employees should not leave their human rights behind at the office door and those who think that an employer is entitled to know what goes on in its time and on its premises. The vulnerability of an employer if employees misuse the firm's e-mail, for example, also provides a good reason for employers to wish to monitor. In *Halford v UK* (1997) the applicant, who was Assistant Chief Constable of the Merseyside force, claimed that there was an invasion of privacy contrary to Article 8 of the ECHR where her office telephone had been tapped to get information about sex discrimination proceedings which she had instituted against the force. The European Court of Human Rights rejected the Government's argument that employees should have no general expectation of privacy for their telephone calls at work and that an employer should be able to monitor calls without the employee's knowledge, and held that there was a breach of Article 8. However, the case was unusual in that she had been provided with a phone specifically for her private use. Furthermore, the Court seemed to accept the argument that the proper test was "reasonable expectation", suggesting that an employer could avoid liability provided employees were informed that they would be subject to monitoring.

While Article 8 and the Human Rights Act may offer limited protection, EU developments may be of more use. The Regulation of Investigatory Powers Act 2000, passed to implement the Telecommunications Data Protection Directive (97/66/EC) and to take account of the Human Rights Act 1998 creates a civil wrong of intercepting communications on private as well as public systems, which is actionable by either the sender or the recipient (s.1(3)). Unfortunately, the thrust of the Act was watered down considerably by the Telecommunications (Lawful Business Practice) (Interception of Communications) Regulations 2000 which allows exceptions for legitimate business purposes. These include ensuring compliance with internal regulatory procedures, monitoring quality and investigating unauthorised use – which appears to give employers pretty much *carte blanche* to monitor widely, provided it takes reasonable steps to bring this to employees' attention. However, employers have to comply with the Data Protection Act 1998 (itself passed to implement the EC Directive on Data Protection (95/46/EC)) and any monitoring which involves the collection of information (*i.e.* recording the results of observation) must comply with that Act. Where communications are intercepted, employers must comply with both the Data Protection Act 1998 and the Lawful Business Practice Regulations 2000. The approach of the Information Commissioner's Employment Practices Data Protection Code, Part 3 on Monitoring at Work (June 2003) is far more worker-orientated than the Lawful Business Practice Regulations and firmly discourages routine surveillance and monitoring. It emphasises the need to balance the adverse impact on employees with the benefits to the employer and tends to take a stronger view of what constitutes adverse impact.

Another form of invasion of privacy which was held to be a breach of **4–023** Article 8 by the European Court of Human Rights was the intrusive questioning of members of the armed forces about their sexuality and relationships in *Smith and Grady v UK* (1999) and *Lustig-Prean and Beckett v UK* (2000). While employees of public authorities may now rely on Article 8 directly by virtue of the Human Rights Act 1998, other employees can only do so indirectly, for example in the context of a constructive dismissal claim. These examples show why an implied duty on employers to respect privacy may be desirable in addition to the statutory protection. An alternative view is that this may develop anyway as an aspect of the pervasive duty to maintain mutual trust and confidence, discussed next.

Duty to maintain mutual trust and confidence

In recent years it has become established that it is an implied term of the **4–024** contract that neither side should act in such a way as to damage the mutual trust and confidence which ought to subsist between them in order for the contract to be carried out properly. This developed at first in the context of unfair dismissal where in order to establish constructive dismissal the employee would have to show that the employer had committed a fundamental breach of contract. For example, in *Robinson v Crompton Parkinson* (1978) an employee of many years' standing and good character was accused of theft. He was acquitted and asked for an apology. It was refused and he left, claiming unfair dismissal. The EAT stated that there was a duty of mutual trust and confidence which could be breached in these sorts of circumstances, although not in this particular case. However, there was a breach in *Courtaulds v Andrew* (1979) where a manager had a row with a foreman of 18 years' service which ended with the manager saying, "You can't do the bloody job anyway". In *Gardner v Beresford* (1978) it was held that an arbitrary or capricious refusal to give a wage rise to one employee when everyone else got one could be a breach of this term, although it was not on the facts of the case; and in *Post Office v Roberts* (1980), where without adequate grounds a senior officer described an employee as wholly unsuitable for promotion, such a breach was found.

These were all EAT cases, and there are several others to like effect. The duty to maintain mutual trust and confidence was accepted as an implied term in employment contracts by the Court of Appeal in *Woods v W M Car Services* (1982) and *Lewis v Motorworld* (1985). In 1997 it was recognised by the House of Lords in *Malik v BCCI* and its parameters were explored. In that case, which arose out of the collapse of the Bank of Credit and Commerce International after years of fraudulent dealing came to light (see below, para. 8–021) the House of Lords stated the duty (in so far as it related to an employer) in the following terms:

". . . the employer shall not, without reasonable and proper cause, conduct itself in a manner calculated or likely to destroy or seriously damage the relationship of confidence and trust between employer and employee" (*per* Lord Steyn).

The Law Lords held that whether or not the term had been breached was to be judged objectively, meaning that it was not necessary to show that the employee had actually lost confidence in his employer (although that could be relevant to the question of remedies) but whether the employer's conduct was likely to bring about such a result, whether the employer intended it or not. It followed that it was not necessary to show that the employer's breach was aimed directly at the employee, nor that the employee knew of the breach before his employment terminated.

4–025 *Malik v BCCI* was a landmark because not only was it the House of Lords' endorsement of the implied duty to maintain mutual trust and confidence but it also sanctioned the possibility of a claim for damages for the loss caused (although the claim by BCCI employees subsequently failed: *BCCI v Ali (No.2)* (2002). Predictably, this led to a flood of damages claims and equally predictably, this led to some retreat by the courts. The most important manifestation of this is the House of Lords' decision in *Johnson v Unisys Ltd* (2001) to the effect that the term does not apply to a decision to dismiss the employee (see further below, para. 8–009). While most claims for damages for breach of the implied term have been unsuccessful, it is worth mentioning two which did succeed. In *French v Barclays Bank* (1998) the Court of Appeal held it was a breach of the implied term of mutual trust and confidence when the employer changed to the employee's detriment the terms of a bridging loan which they had granted to assist him in moving house when they relocated him. In *Gogay v Herts CC* (2000) the employer was found to be in breach by suspending the employee without reasonable grounds to do so and the Court of Appeal upheld an award of £26,000 damages for psychiatric injury caused by the breach.

It is to be noted that the duty to maintain mutual trust and confidence applies to both employers and employees although, as was pointed out in *Malik v BCCI*, it has more impact on employers in that employees have always been subject to fairly stringent duties of good faith under the contract. It clearly has considerable potential for control of the managerial prerogative, if tribunals and courts wish to use it in that fashion, since all sorts of conduct may be held to fall within the scope of the duty: Lord Nicholls described it as a "portmanteau, general obligation" in *Malik v*

BCCI. Indeed, some commentators suggest that it may in time subsume all the other specific duties, in that it may be conceptualised as their underlying rationale. However, there are some advantages in breaking down the implied terms into more specific obligations, as discussed here.

Duty to obey reasonable and lawful orders

The most fundamental duty of the employee is to obey the employer's **4–026** orders: working as instructed is the employee's basic consideration under the contract, as providing remuneration is the basic consideration of the employer. Breach of this duty is invariably regarded as a fundamental breach of contract which at common law entitles the employer to dismiss the employee without notice. It is for this reason that a strike is certain to be a breach of contract at common law, for the employees are not prepared to accept instructions to work. The classic modern statement of the duty is found in the judgment of Lord Evershed M.R. in *Laws v London Chronicle* (1959):

> "wilful disobedience of a lawful and reasonable order shows a disregard – a complete disregard – of a condition essential to the contract of service, namely the condition that the servant must obey the proper orders of the master, and that unless he does so the relationship is, so to speak, struck at fundamentally".

The duty as stated does not require unquestioning obedience to every instruction – although the employee who justifiably refuses may find that she is dismissed just the same. In *Morrish v Henlys* (1973) the employee, a van driver, used to take fuel from the company's pump and fill in the amounts in a book. He noticed that the amounts were being altered; when he protested to the manager he was told not to worry, it was just to make the figures balance. He was unwilling to go along with this, and was eventually dismissed for refusing to leave the entry in its changed condition. He successfully claimed that the dismissal was unfair. Even if it was common practice, as the employer alleged, it could not be a reasonable order "to connive at the falsification of one of his employer's records", as the NIRC put it.

While an order to do something unlawful clearly need not be obeyed, it is more difficult to decide what is an unreasonable order. Many disputes arise over whether a duty is within the employee's job description. Presumably a "machine operator" cannot reasonably be instructed to clean the factory floor instead – but what if it is just a temporary expedient so that she has something to do while her machine is being mended? The answer is not clear-cut. No doubt it will depend on the circumstances: whether a similar level of skill is required, the status of the different work, how temporary it is, and perhaps on the state of the job market altogether. Subject to the rules on redundancy (see below, Chapter 9) an employment tribunal might well be persuaded that an employee was unreasonable in not accepting instructions to do work outside the strict confines of the contract, particularly if the business was under pressure. This shades into the next issue to be examined: does the employee have a duty to co-operate with the employer?

Duty to co-operate

4–027 There is now considerable judicial support for the idea that the employee owes an implied duty to perform the contract in a co-operative manner. The starting point is *Secretary of State v ASLEF (No.2)* (1972), considered above in relation to whether the rule-book was a contractual document (para. 4–013). The Court of Appeal held that the work-to-rule was a breach of an implied term, expressed by Lord Denning as a duty not to wilfully obstruct the employer's business, or by Roskill L.J. as a duty not to obey instructions in a wholly unreasonable way which has the effect of disrupting the business. Buckley L.J. expressed the idea as an aspect of the duty of fidelity, a duty to promote the employer's commercial interests, an idea which was developed further in *Ticehurst v British Telecom* (1992) (discussed below, para. 12–006). In general, while accepting that no one has an obligation to do more than she has contracted to do, the court seemed to suggest that employees had a duty to be co-operative.

This conclusion has been criticised as inconsistent. It is clear that employees have a duty to obey reasonable orders and to observe the terms of the contract – and equally clear that they cannot be expected to do more. Therefore, it is argued, there is no scope for this implied duty: if the employee ignores contractual requirements or refuses to obey reasonable orders, he is in breach of contract; in any other case he is acting perfectly legitimately. While this seems a powerful argument, it cannot be denied that the notion of an implied duty of co-operation is becoming established – and that it may be used to require employees to do more than the contract requires. For example, in *Sim v Rotherham BC* (1986), one of the cases arising from the teachers' dispute in 1985, the Council deducted from a teacher's wages a sum representing a 35-minute period during which she refused to cover for an absent colleague. She sued for her full wages, claiming that it was no part of her contract to cover. Scott J. held that as members of a profession the contractual obligations of teachers were more likely to be defined by the nature of their profession than detailed specifically. These professional obligations included a duty to co-operate in the running of schools in accordance with the reasonable instructions of the head teacher. The decision in *Cresswell v Board of Inland Revenue* (1984) that employees could not refuse to take part in the computerisation of their work may be seen as an aspect of the same trend.

Perhaps the correct conclusion is that for professional workers, who enjoy a high degree of discretion and self-direction in the arrangement of their work, it may be necessary to read in a limitation in terms of a duty of overall co-operation with the employer's undertaking; this seems to be the message from *Ticehurst v British Telecom* (1992). However, for other workers it is submitted that the combination of contractual undertakings and the duty to obey reasonable orders is the beginning and end of their contractual obligations, and that there is no room for further demands to be made on the employee via this alleged implied duty.

Duty of fidelity

It has long been recognised that the employment relationship is one of **4–028** those involving duties of good faith, sometimes expressed as a duty of fidelity, or a duty to give good and faithful service. The duties are extrapolated to a large extent from the law of agency, and may be subdivided into a number of more specific duties.

Secret profits

An employee is under an obligation not to make a secret profit from the **4–029** employment relationship, for example by taking bribes from a supplier to ensure that orders are placed with that supplier rather than another. It is clear that this is a fundamental breach of contract (*Boston Deep Sea Fishing v Ansell* (1888); *Devis v Atkins* (1977); *Neary v Dean of Westminster* (1999)).

Disclosure of misconduct

In *Bell v Lever Bros* (1932) the House of Lords held that an employee is not **4–030** under a duty to disclose her own wrongdoing to the employer: the contract of employment imposes a duty of good faith, but it is not a contract of the utmost good faith (*uberrimae fidei*). This position was narrowed by *Sybron v Rochem* (1983), where the employee was manager of the European operations of the company. Shortly after he took a generously compensated early retirement, it was found that in conspiracy with several other employees he had been systematically defrauding the company for years by diverting business opportunities to a rival company which he had set up. The Court of Appeal held that he was in breach of a duty to disclose the wrongdoing of his subordinates even though that would inevitably have led to his own misconduct being revealed. *Bell v Lever Bros* was distinguished on the grounds that the employees in that case were innocent of fraud, which was not the case here, and that the issue in that case had been whether there was a duty to disclose one's own wrongdoing, not that of another.

The duty to disclose the misconduct of others was not said to be an implied term of every employment contract, but existed here because of the employee's position in the hierarchy: he was a senior executive, the manager of the European operation. However, a number of questions remain: does a senior executive have a duty to report the misconduct of her peers and superiors as well as inferiors, and does anyone in a position of superiority have a duty to report her subordinates' misconduct, even if she is not very senior?

In *Neary v Dean of Westminster* (1999), Lord Jauncey, acting as a special commissioner appointed by the Queen as Visitor to Westminster Abbey, had to decide whether the Abbey organist-choirmaster had been guilty of gross misconduct over fees which he had received for performances by the choir outside the Abbey. The judge was critical of the petitioner's failure to disclose information about this to the Abbey authorities, but rather than finding that this constituted a breach of contract in its own right, he held that first, it undermined mutual trust and confidence so that there was a breach of that implied term, and secondly, that the petitioner's profits were therefore secret profits, so that he was in breach of that aspect of the good faith duty. In *Nottingham University v Fishel* (2000) a senior embryologist employed by the university who used other university staff to assist his private work abroad was held to have committed a breach of contract because he had not obtained his employer's consent for either his work or theirs. However, it was held that he had no duty to disclose his own misconduct, nor that of the staff who assisted him, since on the facts, unlike *Sybron v Rochem*, he did not appreciate that their actions were in breach of contract.

Competition

4–031   In *Sybron v Rochem* (1983) the misconduct consisted in setting up a competing company and expropriating business which should have gone to the employer. However, so far as directors of companies are concerned, it is only the latter activity which is a breach of the implied duty of good faith. In the absence of express agreement, competition *per se* is not objectionable, provided that the director can keep on the right side of the nearly invisible barrier between that and a conflict of interests.

If the law is relaxed so far as senior executives such as directors are concerned, one would expect it to be at least as relaxed as regards ordinary employees. However, in *Hivac v Park Royal Scientific Instruments* (1946) the employer of employees engaged in very specialised work making parts for hearing aids was granted an injunction to prevent a rival company from employing them on the same work in their spare time. While it is accepted that what the employee does in his own time is his own business, it seems that this is subject to a limitation if it can be shown to damage the employer's business. In *Nottingham University v Fishel* (2000) it was held that the work which the embryologist did for clinics abroad was not in competition with his employer, although using other employees of the university in this work did raise a conflict of interest and duty which was a breach of his fiduciary duty to the employer.

The mere fact that the employee is intending to leave and set up in competition involves no breach of the good faith duty, even though many employers may regard it as disloyal. In *Laughton v Bapp Supplies* (1986) two young men working in the supplies department in a fairly junior capacity wrote to suppliers of their employer outlining their intention to set up on their own and asking for details of products and prices. When their employer heard of it, he immediately dismissed them. It was held to be unfair: they were not in breach of the duty of good faith by intending to compete. It would have been otherwise if they had been accumulating confidential information or trying to steal the employer's customers, but that was not the case. By way of contrast, in *Lancashire Fires v S. A. Lyons* (1997) a senior employee of the plaintiff company (in fact, the founder's brother) used his spare time to acquire and renovate business premises and equipment with a view to setting up his own competing business, making use of contacts acquired during his employment as well as his thorough knowledge of the company's processes. It was held that this was a clear breach of his duty of fidelity, and the Court of Appeal suggested that: "any employee with technical knowledge and experience can expect to have his spare time activities in the field in which his employers operate carefully scrutinised in this context". Once the employee has left employment, there is of course no implied term that she may not compete. However, employers frequently try to limit possible competition from former employees by inserting restraint of trade clauses into contracts of employment. The validity of these is considered below.

Confidential information

While competition in the employee's own time is all right in itself, such **4–032** activity carries a high risk that confidential information belonging to the employer will be used, and this will most certainly be a breach of the duty of good faith. Misuse of confidential information is a major concern for employers not only in relation to existing employees but also those who have left. The leading modern authority on how far the employer can protect information is *Faccenda Chicken v Fowler* (1986), where the Court of Appeal held that there were two types of confidential information. The first kind consists of trade secrets or information of such a highly confidential nature that it should be treated as if it were a trade secret: the employee can be restrained from using this even after leaving employment. The second is information which is confidential, in that it would be a breach of the duty of good faith for the employee to use it for her own purposes, or to disclose it to someone else while employed, but which she would be entitled to use after leaving. Both kinds are to be distinguished from the employee's ordinary skill and knowledge, albeit gained from the employment, which the employee must be free to use subsequently.

The difficulty arises in trying to classify different types of information as being one kind or the other. Clearly secret formulae or processes will be trade secrets, but what about policies and strategies? The attitude of the employer towards the information, for example, whether its availability was restricted, whether its confidentiality was impressed on the employee, may be relevant, although the employer cannot turn non-confidential matter into confidential information by treating it as secret. In *Faccenda* the ex-employee had used a package of sales information: the list of customers, the delivery routes, the customers' usual requirements, the times of deliveries and pricing policy. The Court of Appeal held that this package fell into the second category: it would no doubt have been a breach of duty for the employee to disclose this information while still employed, but after employment he was free to use it, in the absence of any valid restraint of trade clause. This must be read subject to the *caveat* that had the employee deliberately memorised the information (or worse, copied out the information) while employed with a view to using it later, there would be a breach of the duty of good faith (*Robb v Green* (1895)). In *Lancashire Fires v S. A. Lyons* the employee argued that a particular process unique to the company was not subject to a duty of confidence because it had never been stressed to him that it was a secret, and it had become part of his skill and knowledge. The Court of Appeal did not accept that the employer must point out to an employee the precise limits of what is to be regarded as confidential and held that on the facts, the employee must have known that he was using confidential information. An injunction was granted to prevent a further breach of the obligation of confidence.

Whistleblowing

4-033 The general duty that confidential information must not be disclosed has always been subject to an important common law exception, that disclosure may be justified where it is in the public interest. Thus in *Initial Services v Putterill* (1968) a former employee revealed to the *Daily Mail* that the company was involved with others in a price-fixing scheme contrary to the Restrictive Practices Act, and in *Lion Laboratories v Evans* (1985) another ex-employee blew the whistle on a breathalyser machine widely used by police forces but whose accuracy was in doubt. In both cases injunctions to prevent disclosure were refused to the former employers on the grounds that what was revealed was in the public interest.

A number of highly-publicised cases either of whistleblowers being victimised for their actions or, worse, of disasters occurring from failure to heed their warnings, created the climate for the passage of the Public Interest Disclosure Act 1998, which attempts to clarify the parameters of public interest disclosures and to create a framework where employees can blow the whistle responsibly and remain in their jobs without fear of reprisal. The Act works by introducing new sections 43A–43L into the Employment Rights Act 1996, making it automatically unfair to dismiss workers or subject them to any detriment where they have made a protected disclosure. A disclosure of information is only protected where the worker honestly believes on reasonable grounds that it tends to show one of the following: commission of a criminal offence; failure to comply with a legal obligation; miscarriage of justice; danger to health or safety; damage to the environment; or the deliberate concealment of any of these (ERA, s.43B). In *Parkins v Sodexho Ltd* (2002) the EAT held that failure to comply with a legal obligation could cover a situation where an employee claimed that he had been dismissed for complaining to the employer that the employer was in breach of contract. This means that there can be a huge overlap between ERA, s.43B and other claims, especially the statutory protection rights to which remedies for detriment and dismissal are attached.

4-034 The protection applies only if the worker makes the disclosure to a proper person. Disclosure is protected if it is made to the employer or to the third party who is actually responsible for the problem; to a legal adviser; where the employer is a public body, to the relevant Minister, or to a person prescribed by regulations (ERA, ss.43C–43F). Under the Public Interest Disclosure (Prescribed Persons) Order 1999 regulatory bodies such as the Audit Commission, Data Protection Commissioner, Health and Safety Executive and many more are so prescribed.

Under ERA, s.43G disclosure to anyone else *can* be protected, but only if the worker has reasonable grounds to believe that she will be victimised or that evidence will be destroyed or concealed if she goes to the employer and there is no prescribed regulator to go to instead. This protection is further qualified by the requirements that the worker must be acting in good faith, making no personal gain from the disclosure and acting reasonably in the circumstances. In deciding whether the worker acted reasonably tribunals are expressly told to consider the identity of the recipient of the information, the seriousness of the failure and the likelihood of recurrence and whether or not the worker has complied with the employer's own procedure. It is thus unlikely that disclosure to the media will be regarded as reasonable except in the most extreme cases.

Workers have a right not to be subjected to a detriment for making a protected disclosure (ERA, s.43B) and dismissal or selection for redundancy on these grounds is automatically unfair. As with other automatic unfair dismissal situations, there is no qualifying period of employment for this, and it is also provided that there will be no limit on the compensatory award in these cases.

Restrictive covenants

As Lord Denning pointed out in *Littlewoods v Harris* (1978), there may be **4–035** situations where the identification of the confidential information which the employee may not use even after termination of her employment is so difficult that the employer may seek to resolve the problem by getting the employee to agree not to work for a rival firm after leaving, or not to set up in competition on her own account.

Such a contract is in restraint of trade, in that it inhibits the employee's right to earn a living by any legal means, which is bad for her and not in the public interest either. Originally all covenants in restraint of trade were regarded as void for these reasons. However, around the turn of the nineteenth century, the House of Lords developed the law to its present position which is, essentially, that a covenant in restraint of trade is *prima facie* void, but may be upheld if it complies with two conditions: first, that it is reasonable as between the parties, and secondly, that it is reasonable having regard to the public interest (*Nordenfelt v Maxim Nordenfelt Guns and Ammunition* (1894)).

In the case of employees, the courts are aware that the parties are unlikely to be in an equal bargaining position and that restrictive covenants should therefore be scrutinised more severely than, for example, restrictive covenants entered into by the seller of a business who promises not to compete with her successor. Thus in *Herbert Morris v Saxelby* (1916) the House of Lords held that a restraint would be void unless it was protecting some genuine proprietary interest on the part of the employer, "whether in the nature of trade connection or in the nature of trade secrets" (*per* Lord Parker); it would be void if it was only directed at avoiding competition or prevented the employee using the personal skill and knowledge acquired during employment.

Thus the restrictive covenant must not be too wide in its subject-matter and it must also not be too wide in terms of the geographical and temporal limits placed on the employee's activities. This will be a question of fact: in

Nordenfelt v Maxim Nordenfelt Guns and Ammunition (1894) a worldwide restraint lasting 25 years was upheld on an inventor of weapons, but in view of his key position, the large payment he received to agree to it, the worldwide nature of the trade and, it would seem, the fact that this restraint kept the business in England (public interest having a parochial nature), it was reasonable. But in *Mason v Provident Clothing* (1913) a restriction on trading within 25 miles of London for three years after termination was held to be void in relation to a sales representative who had worked entirely in Islington.

4–036   Where a clause is too wide, the court may sever the unreasonable part and enforce the rest, but only if this can be done by leaving something intelligible after striking out the offending part (the "blue pencil rule"). The court will not rewrite the contract for the parties. Furthermore, severance will only be carried out of a separate, unenforceable promise; if the court construes the covenant as being one indivisible promise, it will stand or fall as a whole even though it might have been upheld if some words had not been present. Thus in *Attwood v Lamont* (1920) the employee had been the manager of the tailoring department of a store carrying on business as a general outfitter, draper, tailor and haberdasher. The covenant which the employer sought to enforce prohibited him from carrying on the trades of tailor, dressmaker, general draper, milliner, hatter, haberdasher or outfitter. Only a restriction on the first activity would have been legitimate, but although it would be possible to strike out the other words, the Court of Appeal refused to do so on the grounds that this was a single, indivisible agreement and the doctrine of severance permitted only separate promises to be removed.

In *General Billposting v Atkinson* (1909) the House of Lords laid down the important principle that a restrictive covenant would not apply if a contract of employment was wrongfully terminated by the employer. In *Briggs v Oates* (1990) this principle was applied where a five-year fixed-term contract was terminated one year before its expiry by the dissolution of a partnership. Although the restrictive covenant in the employee's contract expressly said that it applied to termination "for whatever reason", Scott J. held that it could not apply where the termination was caused by the employer's repudiatory breach. He went on to hold that, if the covenant could be interpreted as meaning exactly what it said and thus survive a wrongful termination, it would be an unreasonable restraint of trade, and unenforceable on that ground. This led to a number of cases where covenants which purported to apply regardless of how the contract was terminated (even, in one case, where it expressly stated "whether lawfully or unlawfully") were attacked on the grounds that they were unreasonable restraints and thus void *ab initio*. If correct, this meant that the employee could escape from the restrictive covenant even if the contract had in fact been terminated lawfully. A conflict of authorities was resolved by the Court of Appeal in *Rock Refrigeration v Jones* (1996). Pointing out that prior to *Briggs v Oates* such clauses had frequently been construed by the higher courts without any attack on this particular ground, the court held that the argument was founded on an assumption which was erroneous, namely that a restrictive covenant could survive a wrongful termination of the contract by the employer. It could not, because of the principle in

General Billposting v Atkinson. It did not follow that the clause was void from the start. Thus, if the contract were terminated unlawfully by the employer, the covenant would not apply; if it were terminated lawfully, it would depend on its terms whether or not it was an unreasonable restraint of trade according to the usual tests. The court did not accept that there were any stronger arguments here for striking down the clause on the grounds that employees might be inhibited through thinking that it gave the employer greater protection than applies generally to clauses which are ultimately found to be too wide.

In *Kores v Kolok* (1959) the Court of Appeal refused to enforce a **4–037** contract between two competing employers that neither would employ the former employees of the other for a period of five years after termination. It is clear that, had a restriction of that kind against working for a competitor been included in the employees' contracts, it would not have been enforceable, and it would be strange if this could be circumvented by such an agreement between employers. However, this leaves open the question of whether a restrictive covenant aiming to stop an employee poaching other employees can be valid. In *Hanover Insurance Brokers Ltd v Schapiro* (1994) the Court of Appeal held that such a covenant was unenforceable on similar principles to *Kores v Kolok*. This was not followed in a subsequent, unreported Court of Appeal decision (*Ingham v ABC Contract Services* (1993)). In *Dawnay, Day & Co. v De Braconier* (1997) the High Court followed the latter decision.

If the employer is prepared to pay a salary, it may be possible to achieve the same effect as a restrictive covenant through a garden leave provision. Instead of obtaining a promise that the employee will not work for a rival for a certain time after leaving, the contract contains a provision for a long period of notice to be given. If the employee tries to leave, the employer insists that the employee is held to the notice period, but not required to work (thus allowing the employee's contacts and knowledge of the inside workings of the business to go stale and out of date). This is clearly more beneficial to the employee, as at least he will be paid; thus an injunction to stop an employee working for a competitor during a year-long notice period was granted in *Evening Standard v Henderson* (1987). However, garden leave provisions are also capable of abuse and have restrictive tendencies. Thus in *Provident Group v Hayward* (1989) the Court of Appeal suggested that these terms also would be subject to scrutiny and not enforced if wider than necessary, and in *William Hill v Tucker* (1998) it went so far as to say that they should be judged by the same standards as restrictive covenants. In *GFI Group Inc. v Eaglestone* (1994) the notice period of a highly-paid options broker was reduced from 20 weeks to 13, which the court thought was all that was necessary to protect the employer's business.

5. Collective Bargaining

Collective Bargaining

Collective agreements between trade unions and employers were tradi- **5–001** tionally the major source of terms and conditions of employment for the majority of workers in this country. In entering a contract of employment the bargaining power of the potential employee is much less than that of the employer: the worker needs the job more than the employer needs the particular individual. The main purpose of trade unions is to redress this balance by harnessing the collective power of all the employees. The employer may be able to resist the demands of one individual, but will have to pay attention to a body representing the whole workforce.

Unfortunately in real life this redress of the balance through trade unions does not mean that a perfect equilibrium is obtained. Some employers will always have the upper hand, perhaps because work in their industries is so desirable that it is easy to find replacements for a recalcitrant workforce, perhaps because of high unemployment. Employers also have the upper hand where unions are weak, as in industries where there is a high turnover of staff, or where the workers are in small groups and therefore have difficulty in invoking the power of numbers. The hotel and catering industry is a prime example of both factors. Better publicised are those situations where the union has had the upper hand, such as transport or traditional heavy industries, where there are long traditions of high union membership and of loyalty to union instructions.

Nonetheless, in the period from the end of the Second World War to the end of the 1970s, the prevailing orthodoxy was that voluntary collective bargaining was the appropriate method of regulating industrial relations. This policy manifested itself in a number of ways. Under the Fair Wages Resolution of 1946 government contractors were required to implement terms and conditions no less favourable than those resulting from collective bargaining in their industry in their region. This scheme was taken further under Schedule 11 to the Employment Protection Act 1975 which allowed unions or employers' associations to refer a case to Acas where a particular employer was alleged to be providing terms and conditions less good than those recognised within the trade or industry or than the general level prevailing in the trade or industry. These provisions prevented employers who did engage in collective bargaining from being undercut by those who did not and gave an incentive for the latter to engage in collective bargaining, since if they could have collectively agreed terms imposed on them willy-nilly, they might as well have a say in them.

Other examples of the law's support for collective bargaining were found in the fact that Acas was originally set up with the purpose, among other things, of promoting collective bargaining; the provision of a legal mechanism to force employers to recognise trade unions in the Employment Protection Act 1975 and to disclose information to them; and the wages councils system, which was designed to foster the development of collective bargaining in poorly paid industries with weak unionisation.

5–002 From 1980–1997 there was a very clear shift away from this position, fuelled at least in part by the Conservative Government's general antipathy towards trade unions. The Employment Act 1980 abolished the Schedule 11 procedure and statutory recognition for unions; the Wages Act 1986 drastically curtailed the powers of wages councils and TURERA 1993 finally abolished them altogether along with Acas's duty to promote collective bargaining. In the view of that Government, as expressed in its Green Paper *Industrial Relations in the 1990s* (Cm.1602) and White Paper, *People, Jobs and Opportunity* (Cm.1810), collective bargaining hampered flexibility – presumably because changes could only be made after negotiation – and was also in opposition to concepts of profit-related and merit-related pay, which it believed should be encouraged. As an employer itself, the Conservative Government showed a clear preference for bargaining to be carried out at local levels rather than at national level. This may partly have been because industrial action – the union's traditional final sanction if collective bargaining is not successful – is easier to deal with if it affects only one workplace rather than the whole country, as well as making less of a splash in the media. It will be seen when the law relating to industrial action is examined (see below, Chapters 12 and 13) that the trend of reform there was to reduce lawful industrial action to bite-sized chunks which offered more chance of successful resistance. This is largely unaffected by the Employment Relations Act 1999.

While the policy of the British Government from 1979 to 1997 was away from collective bargaining, the thrust at European level was in the opposite direction. The so-called "social dialogue" between representatives of management and labour began at an informal level in the 1980s but was given formal status through the addition of a new Article 138 to the Treaty of Rome by the Single European Act in 1986. This instructs the EU Commission to endeavour to develop the social dialogue, and makes an interesting parallel with the former duty of Acas to promote collective bargaining, which was abolished in 1993 and was not restored by the Employment Relations Act 1999. The Protocol on Social Policy, finally acceded to by the United Kingdom in 1997, also encourages collective negotiation as a central means of dealing with employment issues and its provisions have now been included in the revised Treaty of Rome. Article 138(2) instructs the Commission to consult management and labour before submitting proposals on social policy for Community action and Article 139 enables the implementation of directives via agreements between management and labour. This procedure was used for the Part-time Work Directive (97/81/EC) (above, para. 3–015) and the Parental Leave Directive (97/75/EC) (below, para. 6–018).

The advent of the new Labour administration of 1997 signalled a new **5–003** approach to collective bargaining. Central to the Employment Relations Act 1999, the single piece of legislation that it was prepared to pass during its first term, was the implementation of its longstanding commitment to reintroduce a statutory recognition procedure where this was the wish of the majority of the relevant workers. This took some time to implement. The proposals outlined in the Government's White Paper, *Fairness at Work* (Cm.3968) (which itself was not published until one year after the Government had taken office) were subject to considerable lobbying and behind-the-scenes negotiation between the CBI, the TUC and the Government. The Employment Relations Act finally reached the statute book in July 1999, but the new statutory recognition procedure was not brought into force until June 2000. It remains to be seen whether it will mean that proportion of the workforce covered by collective bargaining will increase. In the run-up to the introduction of the statutory procedure a large number of new voluntary agreements for recognition were agreed and in the first three years of its operation, the Central Arbitration Committee (CAC) reports that it has ordered recognition for collective bargaining in respect of some 10,000 workers. However, this is a very small percentage of the working population. In autumn 2001 it was estimated that about 36 per cent of all workers were covered by collective agreements: 22 per cent in the private sector and 73 per cent in the public sector.

Collective bargaining is carried on at a variety of levels in this country, **5–004** and the picture can therefore be confusing. It may be industry-wide, at national level, or it may be at company level, or plant level or a combination of these. It may be that some matters are settled at national level and others at local level (as has traditionally been the case in most kinds of public employment) or it may be that national agreements provide a baseline on which local agreements are built (as in *Gascol v Mercer* (1974)). The preference for local bargaining evinced by the Conservative Government has been mentioned already. An additional advantage, in their view, was that it allowed account to be taken of local circumstances. However, it should be remembered that collective bargaining takes time and, to be effective, it requires the participation of people of sufficient seniority to be able to give undertakings for one side or the other. Where bargaining is devolved to plant level, it is necessary to consider whether the benefits of flexibility, if any, are worth the extra costs in terms of staff time and the additional pressure on local industrial relations. Furthermore, to take local circumstances into account risks producing even greater regional stratification of the job market than presently exists, reducing opportunities for movement and thus reducing one kind of flexibility.

Where collective bargaining does take place, the workforce is usually treated in a number of separate groupings, or bargaining units, reflecting different kinds of terms and conditions. Sometimes different unions represent the different groups, sometimes one union represents them all, and sometimes different unions represent the same group – which tends to make the process very fragmented. Even though some employees may not be members of the union, where the union is recognised for their grade, it will bargain on their behalf as well, as an employer would be reluctant to have the administrative chaos that would result from treating non-members separately from members.

Collective agreements depend on the union being recognised by the employer for the purposes of collective bargaining. If the employer does recognise the union, then there will be procedure agreements to regulate their relationship. These are agreements which lay down what topics may be the subject of negotiation, how often the two sides meet, who chairs the meeting, how many representatives they have and so on. The procedure agreement may also make provision for industrial action, perhaps stipulating that conciliation must be tried first, or that a certain period of notice shall be given. Procedural collective agreements, then, provide the framework within which bargaining about substantive issues such as pay and other terms and conditions of employment takes place. The resulting agreements on these matters may be termed substantive agreements. How is either kind to be enforced?

Legal Enforceability of Collective Agreements

Union and employer

5–005 There are two major problems to be overcome before collective agreements can be legally enforced. One is the legal doctrine of privity of contract, under which the only people who can enforce a contract are those who are party to it. Therefore, even if the contract is made for the benefit of a third party (such as the union member/employee), that third party has no standing to enforce it. Under the Contracts (Rights of Third Parties) Act 1999 this position is modified if the contract expressly provides for enforcement by the third party or if it confers a benefit on him or her and does not otherwise indicate an intention that the third party should not be able to enforce it. However, that brings us to the other, most important reason why collective agreements cannot legally be enforced, which is that almost invariably collective agreements are not contracts between employers and unions at all. This is a feature of British industrial relations which is almost unique in the industrialised world and certainly among our EU partners. As a result there are sometimes problems in fitting EU directives into British law.

The original reasons for the non-enforceability of collective agreements as between the employer and the union are historical. Collective bargaining was an important force before trade unions were recognised as being bodies able to enter contracts at all; also, until 1971, if the agreement was between a union and an employers' association as opposed to an individual employer, it was probably unenforceable by virtue of the Trade Union Act 1871 which prohibited the legal enforcement of contracts between trade

120

unions: by a curious quirk, employers' associations used to fall within the definition of trade unions.

By the 1960s this position had become entrenched, with neither management nor unions expecting or seeking legal recognition of their agreements. By that time Otto Kahn-Freund had provided a satisfactory theoretical underpinning for this position: collective agreements, he said, were not contracts because neither side had the requisite intention to create legal relations. This explanation of the legal position was accepted by the Donovan Commission, of which Kahn-Freund was a member, and in the only case where the matter was considered, *Ford v AUEFW* (1969). The position was essentially satisfactory to both sides of industry. If a union or employer did not deliver on their promises, they would have no credibility for the future. This was a more effective sanction than suing for breach of contract. And it was recognised that if agreements were to be legally enforceable, they would need to be couched in language that would withstand judicial scrutiny – which would no doubt involve considerable legal expense coupled with a decrease in comprehensibility.

The Industrial Relations Act 1971 attempted to reverse the position by **5–006** introducing a presumption that all written collective agreements were legally enforceable contracts in the hope that this would facilitate greater control over industrial relations. The attempt failed, as it was bound to do, because you cannot force parties to enter contracts if they do not want to do so. The Act had to allow employers and unions who did not want to enter legally binding contracts to insert a clause to that effect. In practice virtually all agreements after the Act included this exemption clause, known by the acronym TINA LEA (This Is Not A Legally Enforceable Agreement).

When the Industrial Relations Act 1971 was repealed by the Trade Union and Labour Relations Act 1974 it was thought necessary to put the previous understanding on a statutory footing. Thus it provided that a collective agreement is conclusively presumed *not* to be legally binding unless it is in writing and contains a specific provision, however worded, that it is intended to be legally enforceable (see now TULRCA, s.179). The Conservative Government wanted to change this position, largely in the hope of making unions liable should they break agreements about procedures to be followed before taking industrial action, or seek better terms and conditions before the current agreement has run its course. Change was mooted in the 1981 Green Paper, *Trade Union Immunities* (Cmnd.8128), noting the prevalence of enforceable agreements among Britain's industrial competitors; however, the idea was rejected reluctantly, recognising that change depended on employers and unions being willing to change. After all, as TULRCA, s.179 makes clear, it has always been open to employers and unions to enter binding agreements if they want to.

It is now clear that where the legal enforceability of a collective agreement is at issue, then the only question is whether or not there is a section 179 statement: other questions about the intentions of the parties are irrelevant (*Monterosso v ITF* (1982)). There are possible ambiguities, however, in the reference in that section to a "... provision (however expressed) ...". *National Coal Board v NUM* (1986) arose out of the attempt by the NUM to prevent the NCB from entering negotiations with the newly formed Union of Democratic Miners as well as themselves. Under the 1946 Agreement between the NCB and the NUM, made shortly after the nationalisation of the coal industry, the NUM had exclusive negotiating rights for miners. The NCB purported to terminate that agreement preparatory to entering a new arrangement with both unions. The NUM argued that the agreement was legally binding and that it would be a breach of contract for the NCB to terminate it, because of the use of the terms "binding" and "being bound" in the agreement. This argument was rejected by Scott J., who regarded the terms as equivocal. In the circumstances, he did not believe that they were meant to mean "legally bound". In the context, this judgment was no doubt correct; however, the case indicates a potential source of difficulty.

Single union deals

5–007 Since employees can belong to whatever union they want, and since in the United Kingdom there is no tradition of one union per industry, it is possible for employers to discover that a whole range of unions represent different groups among their employees. The report of *Ford v AUEFW* (1969) reveals that Ford's workers at that time belonged to at least 19 different unions, and in 1985 Austin Rover was negotiating with eight unions in respect of its workforce (*cf. Austin Rover v AUEW (TASS)* (1985)). While an employer may not be obliged to recognise all, or indeed any, of these unions, in practice if employers recognise one union they frequently accept all those which have a significant representation in the workforce. However, getting agreement from a number of different unions with different policies can be time-consuming and difficult. Thus during the 1980s it became common for companies setting up new plants to seek to control this proliferation by offering exclusive negotiating rights to just one union, representing everyone from unskilled manual workers to senior management. This was a particular trend with foreign investors, who were used to dealing with single unions and having binding collective agreements. The company would require a *quid pro quo* in return for promising exclusive recognition: usually this meant that the union had to agree to employees being totally flexible about their duties (no demarcation disputes) and to binding arbitration in the event of a dispute. Sometimes the employer would wish to go as far as a no-strike deal.

So far as the law is concerned, employees cannot be restricted to joining only one union, for it would be a breach of their right to freedom of association (see below, Chapter 10). However, if the employer will only recognise one union, that provides a powerful incentive for the workforce to join that union in preference to any other. As between the employer and the union, the undertaking to recognise the union exclusively is not enforceable unless the parties intend the collective agreement to be binding between them, and comply with TULRCA, s.179 to make it so. Many of the single union deals which were concluded in the early 1990s were binding contracts.

Union as agent

If a collective agreement has no legal effect as between the employer and **5–008** the union, how can it have any effect on the relationship between the employer and the individual worker? A superficially attractive idea, to a lawyer at least, is an explanation in terms of agency. This would seem to accord with reality: the union is after all negotiating on behalf of its members. It also has the advantage of being a relationship familiar to lawyers: where an agent negotiates on behalf of a principal with a third party, the result is an enforceable contract between the principal and the third party with the agent dropping out of the picture. If this analysis is adopted, then an individual employee could enforce the terms of the collective agreement with the employer and vice versa. (The agreement would not fall foul of TULRCA, s.179, because that refers to agreements made between unions and employers.)

But the difficulties of the agency approach are quickly obvious. First, an agent must act for defined principals. So how could such an agreement apply to employees taken on after the agreement had been made? And how would it apply to non-members? The agency of the union would have to be derived from the fact of membership, so it could not possibly be regarded as the agent of non-members; yet collective agreements invariably apply to all the workers in the relevant bargaining unit, not just the union members. Secondly, it would mean that if the member who did not like a particular agreement left the union, or otherwise withdrew her authority for the union to act, she would not be bound by the collective agreements, which would be highly inconvenient to say the least. Finally, trade union members would probably be rather surprised to learn that simply by joining a union they had invested it with authority to make all sorts of decisions on their behalf.

It is submitted that the position in relation to agency is correctly stated in the EAT decision in *Burton Group v Smith* (1977) where Arnold J. said:

> "There is no reason at all why, in a particular case, union representatives should not be the agents of an employee to make a contract, or to receive a notice, or otherwise effect a binding transaction on his behalf. But that agency so to do does not stem from the mere fact that they are union representatives and that he is a member; it must be supported in the particular case by the creation of some specific agency, and that can arise only if the evidence supports the conclusion that there was such an agency."

This test was applied in *Harris v Richard Lawson Autologistics Ltd* (2003) where the collective agreement gave the shop steward authority to negotiate with the employer. The Court of Appeal held that it was within the ostensible authority of the steward to make an agreement on holiday pay on behalf of the employees which was binding on them. Similarly, in *Edwards v Skyways* (1964), where the union negotiated *ex gratia* payments for a group of pilots who were being made redundant, it was held that the pilot could enforce the agreement when the company tried to renege. However, where membership alone is relied on to establish the relationship of principal and agent, it has usually been rejected (*cf. Holland v London Society of Compositors* (1924), and *NUGSAT v Albury Bros* (1979), on the effect of membership of an employers' association).

The agency approach could also lead to strange results in the field of industrial action. If the union instigated strike action in breach of the law, would individual members become liable as principals? The idea may seem improbable, yet in *Chappell v Times Newspapers* (1975) newspaper proprietors responded to the union's statement of its intention to continue industrial action by stating that they regarded all union members as having repudiated their contracts of employment. Two union members sought an injunction to stop their employer from treating them as dismissed: they had not said or done anything. Lord Denning said that they must be taken to have authorised what the union had done on their behalf! The statement was *obiter*, but it indicates dangers inherent in the agency approach (*cf.* also *Boxfoldia v NGA (1982)* (1988), below, para. 12–004).

Incorporation into individual contracts

5–009   If the agency argument is rejected, as authority and reason suggest it should be, then the question remains: how are collective agreements to have effect at the individual level? The answer is, they have effect if and in so far as they become incorporated into the individual's own contract of employment. If a term of a collective agreement is imported into the individual employee's contract then it may be enforced by the individual in the same way as any other term of the contract. Note that this means it is being enforced because it is a term of the contract of employment, not because it is a term of the collective agreement.

Express incorporation

5–010   How does incorporation take place? The most straightforward situation is where the contract of employment expressly refers to the collective agreement and incorporates its terms, as in *National Coal Board v Galley* (1958) and *Marley v Forward Trust* (1986). Yet even with express incorporation there can be confusion if it is not clear exactly what is incorporated. In *Gascol v Mercer* (1974) the national collective agreement for gas fitters specified a 40-hour basic working week. The local collective agreement specified a 54-hour week, and this is what Mercer had in fact been working. When he was made redundant, he claimed a payment based on his earnings over a 54-hour week. Since he had signed a written contract which referred to the national agreement, it was held that this was binding on him, regardless of what had happened in practice.

Where the collective agreement is not a binding contract between the employer and the union, either side can withdraw at any time without penalty. What effect does that have if the agreement has been incorporated in an individual's contract? In *Robertson v British Gas* (1983), the plaintiff's contract as a meter reader was to be found in part from his 1970 letter of appointment which said, "bonus conditions will apply". The bonus scheme had been laid down in a collective agreement, subsequently updated.

However, in 1981 British Gas terminated the agreement, and argued that since there was no agreement, there was no bonus scheme. The Court of Appeal disagreed. The letter of appointment expressly incorporated the collectively agreed bonus scheme and the plaintiff was therefore entitled to bonus under his contract. The demise of the collective agreement could not affect this entitlement. He could therefore claim bonus on the basis of the last existing agreement.

This case illustrates how important the precise form of the incorporation can be. From an employer's point of view, there is a lot to be said for a contract which incorporates "the collective agreement in force for the time being", since it avoids the need constantly to update individual contracts or written statements. It may also mean that if the employer withdraws from the agreement, the employee loses any benefits previously incorporated. This would not apply in a case like *Robertson v British Gas* because there a contractual document (the letter of appointment) categorically stated that bonus conditions would apply, and so a scheme had to be found from somewhere. But if the letter had simply said that workers were employed according to the terms of the collective agreement in force for the time being, it would seem that withdrawal from the agreement would mean that there were no longer any terms in the employee's contract on the matters previously covered by the agreement. Support for this view is found in *Cadoux v Central Regional Council* (1986) where rules drawn up by the employer were held to be expressly incorporated into the contract of employment; yet because as employer's rules they were subject to unilateral change, the Court of Session further held that benefits under the rules could be removed by the employer's unilateral act (see also *Airlie v City of Edinburgh DC* (1996)). The case starkly illustrates the potential disadvantages for employees in agreeing to be bound by "the agreement in force for the time being": in effect they sign a blank cheque and may find themselves bound in the future by rules not at all to their taste.

Implied incorporation

Where express incorporation of a collective agreement has not taken place **5–011** it may yet be found that the agreement has been impliedly incorporated into individual contracts. If the facts indicate that both employer and employee intended that the agreement should be part of the contract then the way will be clear for holding that it has been impliedly incorporated. The clearest evidence of such an intention will usually be that the parties have consistently acted as if the agreement were part of the contract: *e.g.* if wage rates, holidays, overtime, etc. have always been fixed by reference to the collective agreement. In *Alexander v Standard Telephones and Cables (No.2)* (1991) the plaintiffs argued that a redundancy selection procedure was impliedly incorporated into their contracts. Hobhouse J. distinguished between matters of day-to-day relevance such as pay and hours of work where it would be fairly clear from the course of conduct what the parties' intentions were, and matters which arose only occasionally such as the need to make redundancies. The evidence here was that although the collective agreement had been in existence for some time it had never actually been used in a redundancy situation because in the past there had always been enough volunteers, and it had not been necessary to declare compulsory redundancies. In these circumstances, the judge held that there was insufficient evidence from the conduct of the parties to support the argument that they intended impliedly to incorporate the collective agreement on redundancy selection into individual contracts of employment.

In *Henry v London General Transport Services Ltd* (2002) it was accepted that a collective agreement could be impliedly incorporated on the basis of custom and practice. The applicants, who argued that they were not bound by a collective agreement, conceded that it was custom and practice in the trade for all relevant employees to be bound by collective agreements made between their union, the TGWU, and the employer, but only if the agreement had been approved by a majority in a ballot first. They contended that this had not taken place. The Court of Appeal remitted the case to the tribunal on the question of whether employees were bound by the collective agreement even though there had been no ballot. The case raises interesting questions about unions' authority to act on behalf of their members in collective bargaining, which is rarely dealt with expressly in union rules (see below, Chapter 11).

Which terms are incorporated?

5–012 It is fairly clear that not all parts of all collective agreements are appropriate for incorporation into the bargain between the individual employee and the employer. Earlier the distinction between procedural and substantive collective agreements was mentioned. Procedural matters are hardly likely to be regarded as apt for incorporation. Thus in *National Coal Board v NUM* (1986), where the NUM was attempting to enforce the old collective agreement and stop the recognition of the UDM, the NUM also argued that the entire 1947 Agreement was incorporated into the contracts of the individual miners. The argument was rejected on the grounds that the procedural agreement was inappropriate for incorporation into individual contracts.

However, the distinction between what is procedural and what is substantive is not always clear-cut. What about a redundancy selection procedure? In one sense, this is procedural, because it will cover timetables for consultation, and the criteria for selection; but, on the other hand, it is an aspect of the collective agreement which is of the first importance to individuals and more likely to affect them than many matters which may be clearly incorporated. In *Young v Canadian Northern Railway* (1931), the Privy Council held that a collective agreement providing for "last in, first out" in a redundancy situation was not apt for incorporation into individual contracts and an employee dismissed in contravention of the policy had no claim. However, the opinion seems to take an over-strict view of the process of incorporation. In *Marley v Forward Trust* (1986), the Court of Appeal held that a collective agreement which provided for a six-month trial period for workers redeployed in a redundancy situation could be relied on by an employee, although *Young* was not cited to the court and this particular point was not discussed. In *Alexander v Standard Telephones and Cables (No.2)* (1991) Hobhouse J. reviewed the authorities and held that the selection procedure (last in, first out) was not apt for incorporation, although other parts of the agreement dealing with redundancy (such as enhanced rates of pay for redeployed workers) were. Similarly, in *Lee v GEC Plessey* (1993) it was held that the terms of a collective agreement providing for enhanced severance payments were appropriate for incorporation in individual contracts. It seems unreasonable to distinguish between different elements of a redundancy procedure, holding that while some parts are enforceable, the selection procedure itself is not. In *Airlie v City of Edinburgh DC* (1996) it was held that express incorporation of a collective agreement meant exactly what it said: incorporation of the whole collective agreement. Thus the employees were bound by a term as to the right of the employer and the union to give each other notice of termination of an incentive bonus scheme. If such a term was considered suitable for incorporation, it is difficult to see why a redundancy selection procedure should not be.

No-strike clauses

While employees may find themselves bound by the terms of changing **5–013** collective agreements over which they have only limited control, they are provided with one important protection by TULRCA, s.180. This states that any collectively agreed term which has the effect of restricting or prohibiting the right of workers to take industrial action will not become part of the individual's contract of employment unless the collective agreement is made by an independent trade union and is in writing, expressly states that such terms may be incorporated into contracts of employment and is reasonably accessible for workers to consult during working hours. It is also required, of course, that the worker's contract should actually incorporate the term, either expressly or impliedly.

By implication, it would appear that a term requiring notice to be given of strike action would be regarded as something binding on an individual rather than as a matter of procedure (*cf. Alexander v Standard Telephones and Cables (No.2)* above).

Recognition of Trade Unions

It is of the first importance for a trade union to be recognised by an **5–014** employer as the bargaining agent for its employees. There is little point in workers belonging to a trade union unless that union has power to negotiate on their behalf. Collective bargaining is the basic reason for the existence of the trade union, but it can only take place if the employer will recognise the union for this purpose.

When collective bargaining was seen as the best way of running industrial relations – which includes the whole of the period from the Second World War up to the advent of the Conservative Government in 1979 – the law supported and encouraged the extension of collective bargaining in various ways. In 1975 the Employment Protection Act introduced a scheme whereby an independent trade union could refer a recognition dispute to Acas for investigation. Acas could recommend recognition, and failure by an employer to comply could lead ultimately to the sanction of the employer being compelled to accept an unbargained betterment to the employees' terms and conditions of employment. The 1975 procedure foundered on two rocks: first, Acas was not given the requisite powers to carry out investigations. This was dramatically illustrated in the bitter Grunwick dispute shortly after the legislation came into force, where the employer was able to undermine completely an Acas investigation into the wishes of the workforce by the simple expedient of refusing Acas access to the workplace, as he was quite entitled to do (see *Grunwick v ACAS* (1978)). Secondly, there was no consensus, even among trade unionists, as to what level of support there should be before recognition should be granted. While Acas decisions were ultimately upheld by the House of Lords, by then the damage had been done and there was a general lack of confidence in the scheme. Its abolition by the Employment Act 1980 was not seriously opposed. This left a situation, persisting for 20 years, where recognition was at the discretion of the employer, meaning also that the employer could derecognise a union at any time without being required to follow any procedure for consulting the workforce first. If the trade union was recognised by the employer, it was entitled to certain rights: to disclosure of information for collective bargaining purposes (see below); to consultation over redundancies, transfers of undertakings and health and safety (below, paras 9–041 and 9–043) and to time off for trade union duties and activities for its members and officials (below, para. 6–029). But if the employer did not wish to disclose information or give time off, it could simply cease to recognise the union. This position was changed dramatically as a result of the new statutory recognition scheme introduced by the Employment Relations Act 1999. It works by introducing a new Schedule A1 into TULRCA.

The statutory recognition procedure

5–015   In striking contrast to the scheme in the Employment Protection Act 1975, the new scheme is extremely detailed, running to no fewer than 172 paragraphs. The general thrust is aimed at giving the parties the opportunity to agree at each stage, with reference to the CAC for decision where that is not possible. The statutory scheme applies only to employers who have at least 21 workers (not including professionals: see *R v CAC ex p. BBC* (2003)) and affords the right to apply for recognition only to independent trade unions (see below, para. 10–032). The process is triggered by the union (or unions) making a written request for recognition to the employer which identifies the group of workers (the "bargaining unit") in respect of whom recognition is sought. To avoid undue procrastination, the employer is required to respond within 10 working days, although it can request time to negotiate in which case the period for response is extended by 20 days.

Under TULRCA, s.178(1) collective bargaining is defined as negotiations connected with a long list of matters: terms and conditions of employment; recruitment and dismissal; allocation of work; discipline; trade union membership or non-membership; facilities for union officials; and machinery for negotiation about any of these, including issues around recognition. However, where recognition results from the statutory recognition procedure, the range of matters on which the employer will have to negotiate is much more limited: it is confined to pay, hours and holidays, unless the parties agree to extend it further.

Compulsory recognition

If the employer is not prepared to agree, the union may apply to the CAC, **5–016** whose first step is to decide whether the application meets the general validity criteria. No application will be accepted if any of the workers in the proposed bargaining unit are already covered by a recognition agreement, even if it is with a non-independent union (see below, para. 10–032). Also, if an unsuccessful application has already been made, there is a moratorium of three years before another application can be made in relation to substantially the same group of workers. Most importantly, the union must show a sufficient degree of prior support: under TULRCA, Sch.A1, para.36 this is defined by two conditions: 10 per cent of the members of the bargaining unit must be union members, and a majority of workers must be in favour of recognition. To date most applications (150 out of 171) have successfully passed this stage.

The second step is to decide whether the bargaining unit is appropriate. Once an application has been accepted the parties are again invited to try and reach their own agreement on this, but in the absence of that, the CAC panel must decide, and is instructed above all to consider whether the unit is compatible with effective management. As far as possible it should also take into account existing national and local bargaining arrangements, the desirability of avoiding small, fragmented units and the characteristics and location of the workers as well as the views of the employer and union (para.18). In *R. v CAC ex p. Kwik-Fit (GB) Ltd* (2002) the Court of Appeal held that the CAC acted correctly in limiting its consideration to the bargaining unit proposed by the union. Any counter-proposal made by the employer should be considered in making that decision, but the CAC's job is not to decide whether the bargaining unit suggested by the employer is better than that proposed by the union.

Having identified the bargaining unit, there are two possible routes to **5–017** recognition. Automatic recognition may be awarded where the majority of workers in the bargaining unit are already members of the relevant union or unions (para.22). According to the Government's original proposal, recognition would always have followed automatically where the union already had a majority. However, this was a topic on which the CBI lobbied intensively and ultimately successfully, in that this is now subject to the qualification that the CAC should order a ballot even in these circumstances if any one of three conditions is fulfilled. These are: (i) that it would be in the interests of good industrial relations to hold a ballot; (ii) that a "significant number" of members within the unit tell the CAC that they do not wish the union to represent them (one wonders why they would belong in these circumstances); or (iii) that other evidence is produced (presumably by the employer) which leads the CAC to that conclusion. Concerns that this would lead to a situation where balloting would become the norm are not borne out by the statistics. In the first three years of the procedure in practice, ballots were ordered in 58 cases and recognition without a ballot was ordered in 23.

The CAC may order a workplace or postal ballot (in contrast to other ballots, which have to be fully postal) but does not conduct it itself: a "qualified independent person" is appointed by the CAC to carry it out. To deal with the problem which arose in *Grunwick v ACAS* (1978), paragraph 26 stipulates that an employer has a duty to co-operate generally with the ballot and specific duties to provide the CAC with names and addresses of workers in the bargaining unit and to allow the union reasonable access to the workforce to enable it to put across its case for recognition. Guidance is given in the Secretary of State's Code of Practice on Access to Workers during Recognition and Derecognition Ballots. Should the employer fail in any of these duties, the CAC may order recognition without a ballot. Costs of the ballot are borne equally by the employer and the union. Unlike other ballots, gaining a majority in its favour will not necessarily be enough for the union to gain recognition: it is further necessary that the union must additionally be supported by at least 40 per cent of the workers in the bargaining unit. This means that a high level of participation in the ballot will be necessary and that any abstention in effect counts as a vote against. This may account for the fact that in 58 ballots, unions have not succeeded in 23, although participation rates have averaged 75 per cent. If the requisite majority is achieved the CAC will make a declaration that the union should be recognised. A declaration in favour of recognition will usually last for three years, in that an employer may not apply to derecognise the union within three years of a CAC declaration (para.97).

At this point the union will become entitled to the rights of recognised unions outlined above (para. 5–014). However, the declaration would not on its own mean that collective bargaining would actually take place. Thus following a declaration in favour of recognition the parties have 30 days in which to agree a "method of collective bargaining" – in effect, a procedural collective agreement dealing with the scope of negotiations, how meetings will take place and what is to happen if agreement cannot be reached. Again, the structure of the Schedule gives the parties every opportunity to reach their own agreement on this, but in the end, if they cannot agree, the CAC will impose a method. In the first three years of the procedure's operation the parties reached their own agreement in 35 cases and the CAC only had to make an order in 6 cases.

TULRCA, Sch.A1 stops short of imposing a requirement on an employer to bargain in good faith (as is required in the United States) or stipulating for arbitration to follow if agreement fails. The Government's reasoning for this was that there are no such requirements for voluntary collective bargaining and that this procedure is intended to put unions for whom recognition has been ordered in the same position as unions engaging in voluntary collective bargaining, not in a stronger position. This rather overlooks the important difference that the employer who is involved in voluntary collective bargaining is already prepared to engage in negotiation, which will not be the case with an employer who has been forced to recognise a union. There are limited sanctions for an employer who fails to comply with the method of collective bargaining imposed by the CAC (it will count as a legally enforceable contract and the union may apply for specific performance of it), but if the employer is prepared to go through with the charade without giving any ground, it is difficult to see what can be done about it.

Voluntary recognition

In keeping with the general policy of encouraging the parties to reach their **5–018** own agreements in so far as possible, Schedule A1 makes provision for "agreements for recognition" in Part II which is headed, perhaps mis-leadingly, "Voluntary recognition". An agreement for recognition arises where the union has made a formal request for recognition under Part I of Schedule A1 but then exits from the procedure for one of a variety of reasons laid out in paragraph 52 in circumstances where the employer has agreed to recognise the union. Such an agreement will also last for three years. However, this situation should be distinguished from genuine voluntary recognition, which was the kind of recognition which preceded the statutory procedure. Where unions and employers are prepared to engage in voluntary collective bargaining the statutory procedure will have no effect. However, if an employer engaged in genuinely voluntary collective bargaining should derecognise the union, the union will have the option of making an application under the statutory procedure.

Derecognition

Employers who wish to end collective bargaining arrangements no longer **5–019** have the option of instant derecognition, at least where the union is recognised in accordance with the statutory procedures. First of all, the employer can always apply for this if the number of workers employed falls below 21. Otherwise, the CAC will not entertain applications for a union to be derecognised for three years after a declaration of recognition has been granted. Thereafter, the procedure mirrors the recognition procedure. The employer must first make a written request to the union to end recognition arrangements, making an application to the CAC if the union does not agree. If the original declaration resulted from a ballot, the CAC must then apply the 10 per cent rule in reverse, deciding whether 10 per cent of the workers definitely favour ending bargaining arrangements and whether the majority would be likely to do so. Even if the employer makes no application, it is possible for the workers themselves to seek derecognition by the same route. The CAC then orders another ballot, with the same requirements as for recognition. If the original declaration was automatic, the employer's application must state that fewer than half of the workers in the bargaining unit now belong to the union. If this is so, derecognition is not ordered automatically; rather, if the CAC decides that this is the case, it will order a ballot.

Finally, Part VI of Schedule A1 makes special provision for workers to apply for the derecognition of a non-independent trade union. This may be done at any time by application to the CAC, which will apply the usual admissibility tests. If the application is admissible, a ballot will be ordered.

Since the 1980s union membership levels and the percentages of workers covered by collective bargaining have been in freefall. The new statutory recognition procedure offers trade unions a chance to reverse the trend and it will be interesting whether this happens. Figures for 2002–2003 show a continuing decline in union membership, although at a much slower rate. However, it is probably still too soon to pass judgment on this.

Information and Consultation

5–020 Having accurate and up-to-date information about the employer's business is obviously critical for successful bargaining by trade unions. However, the need for information goes beyond this. People like to know what is going on and if they are kept in the dark they often feel insecure, anxious and resentful. This is as true in the workplace as outside it. There is a view that workers are entitled to more than just information about what is going on: a view that their voice should be heard in the policy-making process and that they should be represented in important decisions affecting the business. This philosophy finds expression in countries such as Germany with the system of employee representation through works councils and worker-directors who sit on the boards of companies. This was briefly considered in the United Kingdom with the Bullock Committee's Report on Industrial Democracy 1977 (Cmnd. 6706) but was never close to becoming reality, given that there was a fair degree of scepticism on the part of trade unions as well as employers. The United Kingdom remains firmly wedded to the notion that the purpose of business is to enhance value for shareholders. Although lip service is frequently paid to stakeholder theory, which would certainly identify the workforce as key players, this tends to manifest itself as an expression of the need to keep the workforce on board with whatever the business wants to do rather than as a reason for genuinely taking workers' interests into account. Thus many companies now give employees an annual report which contains the same sort of information that they give to their shareholders – which is after all in the public domain. The Employment Act 1982 introduced amendments to the Companies Act so that the directors' report in companies employing more than 250 people must contain a statement describing what action has been taken to introduce, maintain or develop the systematic dissemination of relevant information to employees; consultation with employees on matters likely to affect them; encouraging their involvement with the company through employee share schemes and similar arrangements and achieving employee awareness of the financial and economic factors affecting its performance (Companies Act 1985, Sch.7, para.11). Although this provision falls short of requiring companies to do these things, it does indicate support for them as a matter of general policy. Similarly, section 309 of the Companies Act 1985 requires companies to have regard to the interests of their employees as well as their shareholders – but as employees have no standing to enforce it, it is pretty much a dead letter.

The divergence of view between the "social model" of business and the **5–021** "enterprise model" also created tensions at EU level. Ever since the 1970s there have been proposals for directives which would require employee participation in decision-making in the enterprise: the so-called "Vredeling directive" and the draft fifth directive on harmonisation of company law. Both were controversial and failed to progress because of the need for unanimous agreement. In 1994, however, the European Works Council Directive (94/45/EC) was agreed as a tangible result of the Protocol on Social Policy. Its passage was no doubt aided by the fact that the United Kingdom at that time had opted out of the Protocol and was thus in no position to oppose it. The EU Commission realised that this could be the way to break the log-jam of stalled social policy measures. History showed that measures giving workers consultation and information rights were fairly uncontroversial, but that there was no consensus on measures designed to involve them in decision-making. Hence the Commission decided that the best way forward was to produce a single new directive requiring businesses at national level to inform and consult their work-forces, complementing the European Works Councils Directive on trans-national information and consultation. Despite opposition from a few countries (led by the United Kingdom, which had by now signed up to the Protocol on Social Policy), the Information and Consultation Directive (2002/14/EC) was agreed in March 2002.

Hence, in British law, employers who recognise trade unions had had a duty to disclose relevant information to them since as long ago as 1975. While recognition was genuinely voluntary, this was neither controversial nor onerous and it fell well short of requiring employers to involve workers in decision-making. As a result of EU policy, there are now two further situations in which employers will be required to give information to and consult with the workforce, regardless of whether a trade union is recognised. Each of these three information obligations will be examined in turn.

Disclosure of information under TULRCA

Unions which are recognised (whether voluntarily or under the statutory **5–022** procedure) are entitled to disclosure of information according to TULRCA, ss.181–185 (introduced in 1975). Section 181 imposes a duty on employers who recognise unions to disclose to the union all information which the union requests, which is both information without which the union representatives would be impeded to a material extent in carrying out collective bargaining, and information which it is in accordance with good industrial relations practice to disclose.

The major limitation on the right is that it only applies in relation to those matters for which the union is recognised for collective bargaining. Thus in *R. v CAC ex p. BTP Oxide Ltd* (1982) the company negotiated with the union on some matters, such as salaries, but had carried out a job evaluation scheme without involving the union. It did give the union the right to represent workers dissatisfied with their new gradings. The union sought disclosure of information about the job evaluation scheme. It was held that it was not entitled to the information since it did not have negotiating rights on this topic. This is particularly relevant to recognition under the statutory procedure since it covers only bargaining about pay, hours and holidays.

Even if the union is recognised for collective bargaining, the right to disclosure is limited to the topics listed within the statutory definition of collective bargaining, *i.e.* negotiation about the matters listed in TULRCA, s.178. Thus even if the employer recognised the union for the purpose of bargaining about its investment strategy, for example, it is unlikely that the union would have a right to seek information about it, because it would be outside the statutory definition of collective bargaining.

5–023   The Acas Code of Practice on Disclosure of Information to Trade Unions for Collective Bargaining Purposes (Acas Code No.2, 1977, updated 1997) aims to give guidance on the kind of information which it is good industrial relations practice to disclose. Its examples of the kind of information which could be relevant to collective bargaining are: pay and benefits, including job evaluation schemes, breakdown of earnings by grade, sex, etc.; conditions of service, including policies on recruitment, redundancy, promotion, health and safety; analysis of staff make-up, including staffing plans and investment plans; data on performance, such as productivity, efficiency, the state of the order book; and financial, including cost structures, gross and net profits, assets and liabilities (para.11).

This list, which the Code stresses is not exhaustive, is wide-ranging. However, there are further restrictions on the right to disclosure in section 182, which lists a number of exceptions. Disclosure is not required if it would be against the interests of national security; if it would be a contravention of statute; if the information had been communicated in confidence; if it relates specifically to an individual, unless he has consented to its disclosure; if it would cause substantial damage to the employer's undertaking; and if it was obtained for the purpose of legal proceedings. It is clear that any forward-looking planning information could be useful to the employer's competitors, and so might come within the exception where there is a risk of substantial damage to the undertaking. As the Code points out, cost information on individual products, detailed analysis of proposed investment, marketing or pricing policies and the make-up of tender prices could be used by a competitor to the serious detriment of the undertaking. Unfortunately, this is just the information likely to be of most use to a trade union.

A less defensible restriction is found in section 182(2) which provides that the employer need not produce originals of the information for the union, but may draw up a document especially for the purpose of disclosure. This means that there can be an editing, filtering process, which may affect the way the material is understood, given the importance of presentation in these matters. Furthermore, the employer is not required to assemble any information if its compilation would involve an amount of work or expenditure out of reasonable proportion to its collective bargaining value. Presumably the union could circumvent this if it were prepared to bear the cost.

The Acas Code recommends that employers and unions should agree a procedure for requests for disclosure of information (covering such matters as length of time for a response) and that where possible, they should agree those items of information that the union should be supplied with on a regular basis (*e.g.* an annual analysis of the workforce by gender and ethnic background). Where an employer refuses to disclose information which has been requested, the union's remedy is to complain to the CAC. If the CAC thinks it is capable of being settled by conciliation, it will refer the question to Acas. If this is not the case, or if conciliation fails, then the CAC will conduct a hearing and make a declaration specifying the information which should have been disclosed (if any) and a timetable within which it should be made available (s.183). If the employer still fails to comply, the union must again complain to the CAC and this time may present a claim for improved terms and conditions for employees. The CAC's ultimate sanction, therefore, is not to order the employer to disclose the information, but to make an award of terms and conditions to employees. It does not seem a particularly appropriate remedy for the kind of breach involved. In practice, the disclosure of information provisions appear to work satisfactorily, in that there are very few applications to the CAC under this jurisdiction.

European Works Councils

The European Works Council Directive (94/45/EC) was an initiative **5–024** resulting from the Protocol on Social Policy and was adopted by all Member States except the United Kingdom in September 1994. It came into force in September 1996. Following the United Kingdom's agreement to the Protocol, it was extended to the United Kingdom with effect from December 1999 and was implemented by the Transnational Information and Consultation of Employees Regulations 1999 (TICE). Even before this it was reckoned that 100–300 British companies carrying on business in other Member States were already affected by the Directive.

The purpose of the Directive is to encourage consultation with employees and the sharing of information among all the employees of multinationals at the European Community level through the creation of a European Works Council. It applies to businesses with at least 1,000 employees in the Community and with at least 150 employees in two different Member States. Such businesses must set up a European Works Council if requested by at least 100 employees or their representatives from at least two different establishments in at least two Member States. The onus is on management to set up negotiations in the form of the Works Council with a "special negotiating body" consisting of between three and 17 members elected or appointed from the workforce. If the special negotiating body cannot reach agreement on how the European Works Council should be set up, the fall-back arrangements set out in the

Schedule of TICE will come into play. These state that the Council will be composed of between three and 30 members elected or appointed by the employees' representatives or, if there are no such representatives, elected by the workforce. There must be at least one member from each Member State where the business operates, and additional members should be in proportion to the numbers of employees in each state. It should receive information about and be consulted on matters affecting the business at the European level, or affecting plants in at least two different states and should meet at least once a year. It may invoke expert assistance, and all costs are to be borne by the business.

During the period between the Directive being passed and coming into force, the derogation in Article 13 assumed great importance: provided multinational enterprises had an information and consultation agreement in place, covering the whole workforce, before the deadline for implementation of the Directive, it would not apply to them. This led to tremendous activity between 1994 and 1996 as affected companies hurriedly put together such arrangements in the hope of avoiding the more stringent measures in the Directive. This was a major reason for British multinationals adopting works councils, for although the Directive did not apply to them when it came into force, there was a good chance that it would at some time in the near future, as indeed proved to be the case. But as that would be after the September 1996 deadline, the companies would be stuck with the procedures laid down in the Directive. Rather than risk this, a number of large British companies decided instead to set up information and consultation agreements before September 1996. In practice the operation of European Works Councils has not been controversial. Only one application has ever been made to the CAC under this jurisdiction and it was withdrawn without adjudication.

National consultation

5–025 Building on the European Works Council Directive and the longstanding EU requirements to consult workers over redundancies and transfers of undertakings (below, para. 9–039) the EU Commission first proposed a general information and consultation directive in 1998. The basic idea was to promote social dialogue between management and workers in accordance with Article 136 of the Treaty of Rome. Even though the business case for improved communication was emphasised, the directive was opposed by representatives of employers and was blocked for some years by a coalition of four Member States led by the United Kingdom. In 2001 the other three countries dropped their objections and the United Kingdom reluctantly followed suit. The Information and Consultation Directive (2002/14/EC) was agreed in March 2002 for implementation by March 2005. The final version, however, has dropped the most controversial provision which would have rendered void any decision taken by management without consultation complying with the directive.

In summer 2003 the Government began consultation over draft regulations to implement the directive. The structure has quite a lot in common with the TICE Regulations, with a dash of the statutory recognition procedure thrown in. It is intended that the statutory system should not impede voluntary arrangements for information and consultation and this is reflected in the draft regulations. Thus if there are no pre-existing arrangements for information and consultation, the statutory scheme will be triggered by a request in writing from 10 per cent of the workforce (subject to a minimum of at least 15 employees). However, if arrangements already exist, the employer will be able to ballot employees on whether to retain these. Only if 40 per cent or more of all employees vote in favour of new arrangements will the employer be obliged to negotiate a new agreement. This is a very high percentage: as with the statutory recognition procedure, an abstention counts as a vote against. Where a new agreement is needed, the employer will have six months in which to negotiate it with employee representatives, elected by the workforce (surprisingly, this will be the case even if there is a recognised trade union). It is only if no agreement can be reached that the fall-back procedure will come into play, which will involve setting up an information and consultation committee consisting of one representative per 50 employees up to a maximum of 25. The CAC will be largely responsible for enforcement of the regulations.

Where voluntary agreement is reached, the parties can decide on the scope of the information to be provided and the extent of consultation. If not, the fall-back arrangement states that information must be provided on three areas: the development of the undertaking's activities and its economic situation; the state of employment in the undertaking and measures anticipated if there is a threat to employment; and any decisions likely to lead to substantial changes in work organisation (including redundancies and transfers). The employer will also have to consult about these three areas – and in the case of the last (decisions affecting work organisation), the consultation must be with a view to reaching agreement. It is this aspect which makes employers particularly nervous because they fear that it will draw them into collective bargaining even where they have not recognised a trade union.

When introduced in March 2005 the regulations will only apply to undertakings with at least 150 employees (counting all employees in the United Kingdom for this purpose). In March 2007 the system will be extended to undertakings with 100 employees or more and in March 2008, to those with 50 or more.

6. Statutory Employment Protection Rights

In the mid-1970s the Labour Government and trade unions entered an **6–001** informal "Social Contract" which was essentially to the effect that unions would show restraint in wage claims in return for favourable legislation. The Government kept its side of the bargain by passing the Employment Protection Act 1975 which introduced a range of new rights for trade unions and workers. The trade union rights, such as the right to be recognised, to disclosure of information for collective bargaining purposes and to protection for their members from discrimination are discussed elsewhere (see paras 5–014, 5–022, 10–004). The positive rights for employees have since been greatly extended, partly as a result of EU directives and partly as a result of the present Labour Government's commitment to "family-friendly" policies. These positive rights are the subject of this chapter.

Until the Employment Protection Act 1975 statutory protection for employees had been negative, in the sense that it merely gave some protection from dismissal, or more probably a right to compensation for certain kinds of dismissal. This Act addressed the ongoing relationship between employer and employee rather than its termination and gave employees maternity rights, rights to time off for specified activities and certain kinds of pay protection. Some trade unionists regarded this development with a degree of suspicion because these kinds of matters had traditionally been the subject of collective bargaining. If they were dealt with by statute, it could undermine the position of trade unions: why bother to belong to a union if it is not negotiating for you? However, others regarded the statutory advances as providing a minimum benchmark and measured their success according to how far they could persuade employers to offer terms which were better than the statutory minimum, accepting that for weak or non-unionised workers there was a need for a statutory safety-net.

The positive rights given by the Employment Protection Act are now to be found in the Employment Rights Act 1996. Strictly they are not a source of contract terms, for (unlike the equality clause under the Equal Pay Act, for example) they do not operate by way of implication into the contract of employment but rather exist alongside it and override inconsistent contractual provisions. Some are subject to a minimum qualifying period of employment, usually one year, although this restriction does not operate for most of the rights introduced in accordance with EU Directives. The employee who is denied her entitlement under the statute has a right of recourse to an employment tribunal.

Family Rights

6–002 There is much talk today of the "work-life balance". In the country with the longest working hours in Europe, how far can the law intervene to ensure that workers are able to allocate sufficient time to family life? In its second term the Labour Government has placed a lot of emphasis on measures to assist those in the workplace with family responsibilities, building on the maternity rights introduced in 1975 and the requirements of EU directives in the 1990s. These mainly take the form of increased entitlements to paid and unpaid leave to allow parents more time to care for their children, but it would be fair to say that they have transformed the basic legal entitlements of working parents. Whether the law will have a real impact on existing working practices remains to be seen. There are four categories of family rights: maternity rights; parental rights; paternity rights; and leave for dependants.

Maternity rights

6–003 Women are accorded four basic rights in connection with pregnancy and childbirth: a right to time off for ante-natal care; a right to maternity pay; a right to maternity leave; and a right not to suffer detriment or dismissal on grounds of pregnancy and childbirth.

Time off for ante-natal care

6–004 The right to time off for ante-natal care set out in ERA, s.55 was actually introduced by the Employment Act 1980 as a response to figures showing that the United Kingdom had one of the worst records for perinatal deaths among industrialised countries. There is no qualifying period of service for this right.

A woman has a right to paid time off in order to attend an ante-natal appointment advised by her doctor, midwife or health visitor. The employer is entitled to ask for written proof of the appointment – a letter or appointment card – and indeed, of the pregnancy. It is not an absolute right: the employer's duty is not to refuse the time off unreasonably. Thus an employer would presumably be entitled to ask that the woman should go in her own time so far as possible. However, the employer is not entitled to ask her to make the time up on another occasion: that is not time off.

Where time off is unreasonably refused, the woman may apply to an employment tribunal for a declaration to that effect. The tribunal can also award her a sum equal to what she should have been paid for the time off.

If the employer subjects an employee to a detriment or dismisses her for exercising her right to paid ante-natal leave she will have a remedy for detriment or dismissal connected with pregnancy or childbirth, which is discussed further below, para. 6–016. It will also constitute sex discrimination.

Maternity pay

Until 1987 women were entitled to a state maternity allowance (provided **6–005** that they met National Insurance contribution requirements), and after 1975, to six weeks' maternity pay from their employer (provided that they met the service qualification). The Social Security Act 1986 changed this position in so far as it placed the duty to provide state maternity pay on the employer, largely to avoid the overlap inherent in the employer and the State both administering a maternity pay system. The reform followed the philosophy which had already been implemented in relation to sick pay (discussed below, para. 7–028).

The picture was radically changed by the Pregnant Workers Directive (92/85/EEC). The health and safety argument underpinning the Directive was that women could endanger their own health and that of the child through continuing to work because of anxiety over keeping their jobs if they did not have rights to maternity leave. Hence the Directive introduced a right to leave and also to maternity pay, on the basis that a leave right would be of little use if the woman could not afford to avail herself of it. Member States were therefore required to establish a right to maternity pay for at least 14 weeks; they could stipulate a qualifying period of service for this of not more than one year. In *Gillespie v Northern Health and Social Services Board* (1996) the ECJ was asked whether it was contrary to Community law not to grant full pay during maternity leave. The argument was that maternity pay should be regarded as "pay" within the meaning of Article 141. Therefore, since discrimination on grounds of pregnancy is sex discrimination (*Dekker v VJV Centrum* (1991) and *Webb v EMO* (1994), above, para. 2–013), and since maternity pay is a consequence of pregnancy, it was unlawful discrimination if full pay was not given during maternity leave. It will be noted that if this argument had been successful, it would have gone much further than what was required by the Pregnant Workers Directive, which merely stipulated that the equivalent of statutory sick pay should be given during a 14-week period.

While agreeing that maternity pay was covered by Article 141 and the Equal Pay Directive, the ECJ managed to avoid the decision that full pay should therefore be given by holding that the situation of women on maternity leave was unique and could not be compared with the position of either men or women who were at work. Thus they were not entitled to full pay, but they were entitled to have any backdated pay increase taken into account in assessing the income-related component of their maternity pay. This part of the decision was implemented by the Statutory Maternity Pay (General) Amendment Regulations 1996.

The ECJ's reasoning is hardly convincing, relying as it does on the **6–006** manipulation of the concept of comparing like with like. If women on maternity leave are not to be compared with men and women at work, why was it a breach of Community law not to give them the benefit of any backdated pay increase? However, for the time being, Member States are not required to do anything more than what is required by the Pregnant Workers Directive. *Gillespie* left open the question of whether a woman on maternity leave could claim full pay if a man taking a comparable amount of sick leave would get full pay: in *Todd v Eastern Health and Social Services Board* (1997) the Northern Ireland Court of Appeal held that this too was not a breach of Community law. The point did not arise directly in *Boyle v EOC* (1998), for the civil service maternity pay scheme provided that women should get full pay during maternity leave, as they would for sick leave. However, in the case of maternity leave, the entitlement to full pay was dependent on the women returning to work after maternity leave for at least one month. No such condition applied to sick pay entitlement. Nonetheless, the ECJ held that there was no breach of the equal pay principle: following *Gillespie*, it held that pay during maternity leave and pay during sick leave were not comparable.

Apart from any contractual entitlement to maternity pay, most working women are entitled either to Statutory Maternity Pay or to maternity allowance.

Statutory Maternity Pay (SMP)

6–007 Women who have 26 weeks of continuous employment by the fifteenth week before the expected week of childbirth and whose average earnings are at or above the lower earnings limit for the payment of National Insurance are entitled to SMP from their employer for a period of 26 weeks. It is paid at the rate of 90 per cent of their usual pay for the first six weeks ("the higher rate") and then at a rate equivalent to Statutory Sick Pay (SSP) for the remaining 20 weeks ("the lower rate"; £100 in 2003). This is more beneficial than the previous system in that the qualifying period used to be two years and after the first six weeks the rate of pay was equivalent to lower rate SSP (at that time there were two rates of SSP).

Employers are entitled to a rebate on their SMP payments, which they may set off against the National Insurance contributions which they transmit to the Inland Revenue in respect of the workforce. However, whereas the rebate used to be set at 104 per cent of the cost (the extra amount reflecting the additional administrative burden for the employer) it was reduced in 1994 to 92 per cent, except for small employers (those paying less than £40,000 in National Insurance contributions annually, who currently get a 104.5 per cent rebate).

The right to SMP is independent of the question of whether the employee has a statutory right to maternity leave and SMP is payable even if she has no intention of returning to work. However, the position is complicated in that many employers are prepared to pay more than the statutory requirement (*e.g.* 100 per cent of earnings, and for a longer period than six weeks) but only on condition that the employee returns to work for a certain time. As a matter of contract there is nothing to prevent this, and the employer would be entitled to claim back the extra if the employee did not in fact return.

To qualify for SMP a woman must give her employer 28 days' notice (in writing, if so requested) of the day it should start, but this can be combined with notice of maternity leave.

Maternity allowance (MA)

Women who do not qualify for maternity pay from their employer may yet **6–008** qualify for maternity allowance as a state contributory benefit. They have to have worked and made National Insurance contributions for 26 weeks out of the 66 weeks before the expected week of childbirth, and be employed during the fifteenth week before the expected week of childbirth. Maternity allowance is equivalent to SMP at the lower rate and to SSP (£100 in 2003) and is paid for 26 weeks. Note that for this benefit the woman need not have been employed by the same employer, or even have been an employee at all: she could have made contributions as a self-employed person.

Maternity leave

The Employment Protection Act 1975 introduced the original right for an **6–009** employee to return to work up to six months after the birth of her child, in effect providing for a period of statutory maternity leave. However, this was only available to women with two years' continuous service. The Pregnant Workers Directive required that all women workers should have at least 14 weeks' leave, and should be compelled to take at least two weeks at the time of childbirth. The right to 14 weeks' leave regardless of length of service was implemented in 1994.

In pursuance of its "family-friendly" work policies the current Labour Government has improved these entitlements through the Maternity and Parental Leave, etc. Regulations 1999 and the Maternity and Parental Leave (Amendment) Regulations 2002, applying in respect of babies born on or after April 6, 2003.

Ordinary maternity leave

The basic right to maternity leave which is not dependent on a qualifying **6–010** period of employment is now known as "ordinary maternity leave" and is dealt with in ERA, s.71 as substituted by the Employment Relations Act 1999, the Maternity and Parental Leave, etc., Regulations 1999 and the MPL (Amendment) Regulations 2002. Going beyond the requirements of the Pregnant Workers Directive, ordinary maternity leave has been extended to 26 weeks, which has the advantage of coinciding with the period during which SMP or maternity allowance is payable.

The notice provisions for qualifying for maternity leave used to be horrendously complicated and the penalty for a false step was loss of entitlement. The position is now much improved. Although a woman will still lose her right to leave if she fails to give the proper notice, the notice requirements have been reduced and simplified. By a deadline of the fifteenth week before the expected week of childbirth the woman must inform her employer (a) that she is pregnant; (b) what the expected date of birth is (by medical certificate, if requested), and (c) when she expects her maternity leave to start. She need only put this in writing if requested by the employer and she can change her mind about the start date – as long as she still has time to give at least 28 days' notice of the new date. A request for SMP may be incorporated in this notice. On receipt of the notice the employer must then give the woman notice of the date on which her maternity leave will end, which will be at the end of the additional maternity leave period if she is entitled to that as well. There are considerable advantages in this: it is the employer, not the woman herself, who must now do the calculation and both parties will know at the outset what the date is. This should reduce the number of cases where women lose their rights because of some miscalculation. If the employer fails to notify her of this date then she is protected from detriment or dismissal if she does not return on that date. Furthermore, she has the right to return before that date without giving notice.

6–011   In two situations the start of maternity leave is automatically brought forward. The first is if the birth occurs before the notified date. In this case, maternity leave will start at the date of birth and the employee must give notice to the employer as soon as is reasonably practicable thereafter. The second is if the employee is absent for a pregnancy-related reason at any time after the fourth week before birth is due. Again, this triggers the maternity leave period automatically. This is to stop employees taking sick leave rather than maternity leave at this stage, which they might wish to do if the employer pays for sick leave at the normal contractual rate. The rule has been criticised as inflexible, however, because a woman who intended to work until closer to the birth could lose her right to do so just for one day's absence, even if she were fit to return the following day.

ERA, s.71 provides expressly that the contract of employment continues during ordinary maternity leave by stating that all terms and conditions of employment apply as if she were not absent, with the important exception of any terms and conditions about "remuneration". The reason for the exception is that pay is dealt with by the maternity pay provisions, above. The word "pay" was not used because of the very wide meaning it has been given in EC case law on the scope of Article 141 of the Treaty of Rome (see below, para. 7–024). However, there was confusion also about the scope of "remuneration". In consequence, regulation 9 now states that "only sums payable to an employee by way of wages or salary are to be treated as remuneration". This means that employees remain entitled to other benefits (such as use of a company car or private medical insurance) during ordinary maternity leave and that annual leave entitlement continues to accrue. By virtue of the Social Security Act 1989, Sch.5, ordinary maternity leave is treated as pensionable employment and the employer is liable to continue to pay full contributions on the employee's behalf (see also *Boyle v EOC* (1998)). Continuation of the contract also means that the employee remains bound by its terms, in particular by the obligation of good faith and the duty to maintain mutual trust and confidence.

6–012   At the end of ordinary maternity leave the employee is entitled to return to work without giving further notice. If she wishes to return before the end of that period she must give 28 days' notice of her return date to the employer. Only if she gives less than 28 days' notice is the employer entitled to postpone her return, and then only so far as is necessary to comply with the statutory notice requirement (reg.11). She has a right to return to her original job on the terms she would have had if she not been absent (ERA, s.71(4), (7)). This is subject to an exception where the employee becomes redundant while on ordinary or additional maternity leave. In this situation she is entitled to be offered a suitable alternative vacancy if one exists (reg.10). This means that she may actually be better off than other employees in a similar situation, who should be considered for alternative posts or else their dismissals may be unfair, but who do not have any entitlements and who will therefore be considered after any employee on maternity leave.

Failure to allow the employee to return after maternity leave will otherwise constitute automatically unfair dismissal (reg.20), unless the employer can show that it was not reasonably practicable on grounds other than redundancy to allow her to return to a suitable and appropriate job and she has unreasonably refused an offer of such a job with an associated employer. In these circumstances the dismissal will not be automatically unfair, but the employee could claim unfair dismissal on general principles if she had one year's employment, or possibly for sex discrimination. It should be noted that where maternity leave is brought to an end by dismissal, the employer must provide the employee with a written statement of the reasons for the dismissal without her having to ask for it (ERA, s.92(4)).

Where an employee has a contractual right to maternity leave as well as her statutory right, she can exercise the rights together as a composite right, taking advantage of whichever has the most favourable terms in any respect (reg.21).

Additional maternity leave

The right to a longer period of leave, originally introduced in 1975 as a **6–013** "right to return to work", is now contained in ERA, s.73 as modified by the Employment Relations Act 1999 and the Maternity and Parental Leave, etc., Regulations 1999. It is now styled "additional maternity leave", and in order to qualify it is now only necessary for the employee to have been continuously employed for 26 weeks by the fourteenth week before the expected week of childbirth. Additional maternity leave is subject to the same requirements for notice and conditions for commencement of leave and return afterwards as ordinary maternity leave, and it is no longer necessary for an employee to give notice of her intention to take the longer period: the presumption is that she will take it. Furthermore, the employer no longer has the right to require her to reaffirm her intention to return while she is taking additional maternity leave. Additional maternity leave is now fixed at 26 weeks, meaning that altogether a woman can take a whole year off (and may also exercise other parental leave rights as well). In practice, since only 26 weeks of maternity leave are paid most women opt to work nearly up to the birth, in order to maximise their right to paid leave once the baby is born. A curiously paternalistic provision in the Pregnant Workers Directive requires that employed women should have a compulsory period of at least two weeks' leave before and/or after birth: under ERA, s.72 and reg.8, this is a two-week period starting with the date of birth. The employee may not work for the employer during those two weeks and it is a criminal offence on the part of the employer to contravene this.

The former right to return which has been replaced by additional maternity leave gave rise to two main problems. First, it was not clear whether or not the contract of employment continued during the employee's absence. What, then, was the position if she lost her right to return (perhaps through not giving requisite notice) and her employer refused to take her back? The answer depended on whether the tribunal or court construed the available evidence as indicating that the contract continued. If so, the contract was terminated by dismissal and she could claim under the ordinary unfair dismissal rules. If not, she had no claim.

This problem has now been dealt with by reg.17 which provides that during additional maternity leave the contract continues to the extent that the employer remains under the implied obligation of trust and confidence towards the employee and must continue to comply with contractual terms relating to disciplinary and grievance procedures, notice of dismissal and redundancy compensation. The employee remains bound by the contractual term relating to notice, her implied obligation of good faith and any specific terms about disclosure of information, acceptance of gifts or other benefits and competition. Other terms and conditions are apparently suspended, subject to any contractual provision to the contrary. Thus, while additional maternity leave will not affect continuity of employment, it will not count for the purposes of rights which accrue such as annual leave and pensionable employment unless the contract says otherwise.

6–014   The second problem with the old formulation arose because of the use of the phrase "right to return". Conflicting decisions were made as to whether the employee needed physically to return to work on the due date, or whether the right to return was exercised simply by giving notice even if, for example, the employee was too unwell at that stage to come back to work. This problem no longer arises since there is no longer any obligation on the employee to give notice of her return from additional maternity leave unless she wishes to return early (when she must give 28 days' notice, as with ordinary maternity leave, above). If an employee is ill and unable to return to work at the end of either ordinary or additional maternity leave she is entitled to be treated like any other sick employee and has the corresponding obligation to comply with the usual contractual arrangements for notifying sickness absence. In deciding whether or not to dismiss her on grounds of incapability the employer must ignore all absence during pregnancy or maternity leave: it will be unlawful sex discrimination if this is taken into account (*Brown v Rentokil* (1998) above, para. 2–015).

The success of the right to return provisions is dependent on how far they actually guarantee the employee a return to her former position as if she had never been away. If the employer is allowed to slot her in anywhere then she is disadvantaged through taking the leave and equality of opportunity is denied. While the right to return was originally formulated in 1975 as a right to return to her former job as if she had never been away, it was watered down in 1980 in two ways. First, the employee lost her right to claim unfair dismissal if the employer could show that it was not reasonably practicable to give her her old job back for a reason other than redundancy but that she was offered suitable alternative employment which she unreasonably refused (see now reg.20(7)). This was a major attack on the fundamental principle that women should not be disadvantaged by comparison with men because of child-bearing. It meant in effect that a woman's career could be marginalised in the interests of the employer. The second exception went even further: an employer with five or less employees did not have to offer her any job at all if it was not reasonably practicable to do so (see now reg.20(6)).

This remains the position for an employee exercising the right to **6–015** additional maternity leave. However, the right to what is now ordinary maternity leave, introduced to implement the Pregnant Workers Directive, was originally an unconditional right for the employee to return to her former job exactly as if she had not been away, with an exception only where the post genuinely became redundant during the employee's maternity leave. It is therefore surprising to find that under the Maternity and Parental Leave, etc., Regulations 1999 the right to return from ordinary maternity leave has been reduced. Regulation 20(7), which gives a defence to automatic unfair dismissal if the employer can establish that it was not reasonably practicable for a reason other than redundancy to allow her to return to a suitable and appropriate post, now applies to both ordinary and additional maternity leave. The reason for this is not clear and it may constitute a breach of the Pregnant Workers Directive.

The same rules as for ordinary maternity leave apply where the employee becomes redundant while on additional maternity leave. She has the same right to written notification of the reason for dismissal and to composite any contractual right to leave with her statutory right to additional maternity leave.

Where the employer takes on a temporary replacement for an employee on maternity leave, ERA, s.106 provides that if the replacement employee is given notice in writing at the outset that his employment is only temporary because it is as a replacement for an employee on maternity leave, and if the ultimate dismissal is to make room for the returner, the dismissal of the replacement will count as being for "some other substantial reason". This means that it can be justified as a fair dismissal, although it does not follow that it will be.

No detriment or dismissal on grounds of pregnancy

The Employment Protection Act 1975 made it automatically unfair to **6–016** dismiss a woman for pregnancy, but this applied only to women with two years of continuous service. It was also subject to two major exceptions: if the employee was incapable of doing her work or it became unlawful to employ her as a result of her pregnancy, she could be fairly dismissed if there was no other suitable alternative work available. This no doubt appeared to strike a fair balance between the interests of employers and employees at that time. However, it fell a long way short of giving women real job protection in case of pregnancy, which is essential if they are to be equal in the workplace.

As pregnancy is a condition related only to one sex, it was inevitable that pregnant workers would seek assistance under the Sex Discrimination Act, a campaign which was ultimately successful (see *Webb v EMO* (1994) above, para. 2–013). But greater assistance was forthcoming from Europe, not only in the form of the ECJ but by directive. The Pregnant Workers Directive (92/85/EEC) was adopted in October 1992. It was opposed by the United Kingdom Government, but because it had been proposed as a health and safety measure, it could be approved by the qualified majority voting procedure and the United Kingdom had no right of veto. Implementation was required by October 1994 and was carried out in the United Kingdom principally by TURERA. Further amendment followed in the Employment Relations Act 1999. By virtue of ERA, s.99 as amended by the Maternity and Parental Leave, etc., Regulations 1999, dismissal is automatically unfair if the reason or principal reason for it is connected with: pregnancy; childbirth; suspension on maternity grounds in accordance with ERA, s.66, and taking or seeking to take ordinary or additional maternity leave, parental leave or time off for ante-natal care. If there is a genuine redundancy situation while she is on maternity leave, the employee must be given a suitable alternative vacancy if there is one available, or the dismissal will be automatically unfair. Finally, the two former exceptions have now been abolished. A dismissal because the employee has become incapable of work would be for a reason connected with her pregnancy and thus unfair. In these circumstances she will be entitled to sick leave on her usual contractual terms, or maternity leave in appropriate circumstances. If it would be contrary to any enactment or Code of Practice for the employee to continue in her employment while pregnant, dismissal will be automatically unfair; she has a right instead to be offered any suitable alternative employment or to be suspended on maternity grounds (ERA, s.66). The suspension will be on full pay unless she has unreasonably refused alternative work, in which case she need not be paid. To complete the dismissal protection, selection for redundancy on any of these grounds is also automatically unfair. Further assistance is provided by ERA, s.92(4), which stipulates that an employer who dismisses an employee while she is pregnant or on maternity leave must give her a written statement of the reasons for her dismissal regardless of her length of service or whether she actually asks for one. It is important to notice that there is no longer any continuity or hours requirement for this protection: every woman worker has it from day one.

6–017   Until 1999, only dismissal for reasons connected with pregnancy and childbirth was expressly dealt with by statute. If an employee suffered detriment short of dismissal on these grounds she would have had to bring a claim under the Sex Discrimination Act. That remains possible, but in the Employment Relations Act 1999 the opportunity was taken to rationalise remedies for leave for family reasons, among other things by extending the right not to suffer detriment to detriment on grounds of pregnancy or childbirth. This is now contained in ERA, s.47C and reg.19: the specific situations protected mirror exactly the provisions for automatic unfair dismissal.

Thus the protection for women workers is now much more extensive. If *Webb v EMO* (1994) were to arise today, there is no doubt but that the dismissal would be unfair, even if the new employee had been taken on just to cover the maternity leave period. Presumably, however, it will still be necessary to establish a causal link between the pregnancy-related reason and the dismissal. Thus an employer who dismisses a woman for an unacceptable rate of absence without knowing that she is pregnant could perhaps be taken to have acted fairly even though her pregnancy could account for some of it: this puts a premium on a woman giving early notice to her employer.

In *Berrisford v Woodard Schools* (1991), a case brought under the SDA, an unmarried matron at a church boarding school for girls was dismissed when she announced her pregnancy and that she had no intention of getting married. The EAT held that this was a dismissal on grounds of morality rather than pregnancy and that no discrimination had occurred because there was evidence that a male teacher who lived with a woman had been instructed to marry her or leave, so both sexes were treated the same in comparable circumstances. The reasoning would not work now, because in these circumstances, the matron would have been dismissed for a reason connected with her pregnancy, and it would be automatically unfair (see also *O'Neill v Governors of St Thomas More School* (1996)).

Parental rights

Parental leave

While there are good reasons for making special provision for women in **6–018** relation to childbirth it is not as clear that any extended period of leave should be limited to mothers, for this simply reinforces stereotyped views on who should carry out family responsibilities. At the same time strong arguments can be put forward for allowing a period of paternity leave at the time of birth.

The majority of EU countries have had some kind of provision for paid or unpaid parental leave for some time and the EU Commission was pushing for a directive on parental leave from as long ago as 1983, but proposals were always blocked by the United Kingdom. In 1994 it was decided to deal with the issue under the procedure stipulated in the Protocol on Social Policy annexed to the Treaty of European Union, the agreement whereby the other Member States could take forward social policy matters without the United Kingdom. Under that procedure there has to be consultation with representatives of management and labour ("the social partners") before proposals on social policy can be put forward (see now Treaty of Rome, Art.138). Under Article 139 of the Treaty of Rome, representatives of management and labour can themselves reach agreement on these issues and ask the Council to implement their agreement. This is what happened in relation to the Parental Leave Directive. Agreement on a framework directive on parental leave was reached in December 1995 and then implemented by the Council in June 1996 (96/34/EC). Following the Labour Government's acceptance of the

Agreement on Social Policy, the Parental Leave Directive was extended to the United Kingdom (97/75/EC), and implementation was carried out by the Maternity and Parental Leave, etc. Regulations 1999, which came into force on December 15, 1999.

Essentially parental leave is an entitlement to up to 13 weeks of unpaid leave per child, to be taken between birth and the child reaching five years of age. Both parents are entitled to such leave and it cannot be transferred from one to the other. This is an attempt to counteract social stereotyping which tends to place responsibility on the mother alone to take time off to look after children. However, the fact that the leave is unpaid means that very many employees, especially men, will be unwilling or unable to take advantage of it, and the Government's own estimate is that only two per cent of fathers and 35 per cent of mothers are likely to invoke their parental leave entitlements. Employees will not qualify for parental leave until they have one year's continuous employment. If an employee changes jobs during the first five years of a child's life he will have to serve one year with the new employer before being entitled to take any leave remaining to him. Where a child is adopted, leave can be taken in the five years following the placement for adoption or up to the child's eighteenth birthday, whichever is earlier. There is also more flexibility for children with disabilities: in this case, the parents can exercise their right to leave at any time up to the child's eighteenth birthday, although since the total entitlement is 13 weeks it is difficult to imagine anyone being able to eke it out over so long a time!

6–019 One of the most controversial aspects of the implementation of the Parental Leave Directive was the Government's decision to restrict the right to parents of children born or adopted on or after December 15, 1999, the date when the Directive and the Regulations came into force in the United Kingdom. The TUC argued that this was in breach of the Parental Leave Directive and that the rights should be available to the parents of all children aged under 5 at that date. The Irish Confederation of Trade Unions had previously made a similar challenge to the Irish Parental Leave Act 1998 and their case was upheld before a reference from the British High Court could be heard. The Government therefore capitulated without further ado and the Maternity and Parental Leave (Amendment) Regulations 2001 extended the right to all parents whose children were aged under five on December 15, 1999.

As with additional maternity leave, regulation 17 provides that the contract of employment continues during parental leave, but with most obligations suspended. The employee remains bound by terms as to notice, confidential information, acceptance of gifts or other benefits, competition and the implied term of good faith. The employer is bound by the implied term of mutual trust and confidence and any terms relating to notice, disciplinary and grievance procedures and compensation for redundancy. If the employee takes parental leave of four weeks or less, either independently or adding it on to ordinary maternity leave, she has the right to return to the job she was doing before the absence. However, if the employee takes parental leave of more than four weeks (or adds any parental leave on at the end of additional maternity leave) the employer may instead reassign her to a different job, if it is not reasonably practicable to allow her to return to her former job and provided that the alternative is suitable and appropriate (reg.18).

Within these parameters the Maternity and Parental Leave, etc., Regu- **6–020** lations 1999 leave it to employers and employees to make their own arrangements on how to implement parental leave, by individual, collective or workforce agreement. If no such agreement is reached, however, the default scheme set out in Schedule 2 to the Regulations will apply. The default scheme states that leave has to be taken in minimum periods of one week and that the employee can only take a maximum of four weeks in any one year. This has been criticised because a parent who wished to take one day's leave in order to take a child to a dental appointment, for example, would lose a whole week's leave. However, the answer would seem to be to make an individual agreement to override the default scheme. The default scheme requires the employee to give at least 21 days' notice of leave. A father wishing to take leave at the time a child is born must give 21 days' notice of the expected week of childbirth and adoptive parents should give 21 days' notice of the date of placement. In these two situations the employer must allow the leave, but in other circumstances the default scheme allows the employer to postpone it for up to six months if "the employer considers that the operation of his business would be unduly disrupted" by the proposed leave. The employee has a right to complain to an employment tribunal within three months that the postponement is unreasonable, in which case the tribunal can award such compensation as it considers to be just and equitable (ERA, s.80). Regulations 19 and 20 extend the protection of ERA, ss.47C and 99 (protection against detriment and dismissal) to an employee who is dismissed or subjected to a detriment for taking or seeking to take parental leave.

Symbolically at any rate, the parental leave provisions are an important step forward in assisting employees to achieve an appropriate balance between work and family responsibilities, and, indeed, in recognising that men have families too. It remains to be seen whether in practice there is any great change in who takes responsibility for children.

Flexible working

At a relatively late stage of the passage of the Employment Act 2002 **6–021** through the House of Commons, a new and controversial provision was added allowing the Secretary of State to make regulations to allow parents to seek changes to their contracts of employment to facilitate their child-care responsibilities. The right for employees with children aged under 6, or disabled children aged under 18, to request flexible working patterns is contained in two statutory instruments: the Flexible Working (Procedural Requirements) Regulations 2002 and the Flexible Working (Eligibility, Complaints and Remedies) Regulations 2002. To be qualified to ask for flexible working the employee must be the parent, adoptive parent, foster parent or guardian of a child, or the spouse or partner of such a person who expects to have responsibility for the child's upbringing. There is also a 26-week qualifying period.

An application for flexible working must be made in writing and on receipt the employer must either agree or hold a meeting to discuss the proposal within 28 days. Strict time-limits apply to all stages of the procedure. The employee will be entitled to be accompanied by a co-worker at the meeting to discuss the application and to receive the employer's decision within 14 days of the meeting. If it is unfavourable, the employee may appeal within 14 days and an appeal meeting must be held within 14 days of the appeal being lodged. The employer can only reject a request for flexible working on "business grounds" – such as additional costs, detrimental effect on company performance, etc.

The most severe limitation on the right to flexible working is that the employee can only bring a claim in a tribunal if the employer has failed to follow the procedure or has reached a decision on incorrect facts. That means that there is no opportunity for the tribunal to review the substance of an employer's decision, provided that the employer has gone through the procedural hoops. Many commentators have expressed concern that this will lead to employers merely "going through the motions". The remedy is also limited – even if a claim is successful, the maximum a tribunal can award is eight weeks' pay (*i.e.* £2,080).

Paternity rights

6–022 While parental leave was introduced in part in the hope of encouraging fathers as well as mothers to take their share in combining childcare with work, there were no specific provisions for fathers. Many firms had introduced a scheme for paternity leave which permitted fathers two weeks off at the time of a child's birth and this pattern has now found its way into the legislation. The Secretary of State was given power to make regulations for paternity leave and pay by the Employment Act 2002 and the Paternity and Adoption Leave Regulations 2002 came into force in December 2002. Paternity leave is available to the father of the child or the mother's partner (who could be a same-sex partner or a close relative) provided that he or she is likely to take major responsibility for bringing up the child. They must have been employed for 26 weeks by the 14th week before the expected week of childbirth. Paternity leave lasts for a maximum of two weeks and must be taken within eight weeks of the child's birth. It is paid at the rate of lower rate SMP and SSP, which was £100 per week in 2003, or 90 per cent of actual earnings if lower.

Adoption leave

6–023 There was a degree of doubt about whether maternity rights could be claimed by mothers who were adopting children. When the Employment Act 2002 introduced a range of other family-friendly rights the opportunity was taken to regularise the position. Effectively the Paternity and Adoption Leave Regulations 2002 give adoptive parents equivalent rights to natural parents: one parent may take ordinary and additional adoption leave, mirroring maternity leave, and partners can take the equivalent of paternity leave.

Leave for dependants' care

The Parental Leave Directive (96/34/EC) also required Member States to **6–024** give workers the right to take time off for urgent family reasons such as sickness or accident. In the original draft of the Employment Relations Act 1999, this was going to be time off for domestic incidents, raising interesting questions as to whether malfunction of a washing machine or sickness of the family pet would be regarded as sufficiently disruptive to count as a justification for time off. However, the Government stepped back from the brink and the final version of this new right was framed as being for the care of (human) dependants. Schedule 4 to the Employment Relations Act 1999 introduces a new section 57A into the Employment Rights Act (ERA) 1996 giving employees a right to "reasonable" time off (not necessarily paid) to take action that is necessary in the following circumstances: to assist when a dependant is ill, giving birth or has been injured or assaulted; to arrange care for an ill or injured dependant; because of the death of a dependant; because of unexpected disruption to care arrangements for a dependant; or to deal with an unexpected incident concerning the employee's child during school hours.

"Dependant" is defined in section 57A(3)–(5) to mean the spouse, child or parent of the employee, or someone who lives in the same household who is not an employee, lodger, tenant or boarder. This is apt to include unmarried partners, including same-sex couples, and more remote relatives or friends, provided that they live in the empoyee's household. In relation to situations where a dependant is ill, injured or assaulted the definition of dependant is extended to include "any person who reasonably relies on the employee" for assistance in these circumstances. This could include relatives or friends who do not live with the employee, or a neighbour.

Time off for dependant care is intended to cover unforeseen occurrences: **6–025** if the employee wants time off to deal with a situation which she knows is coming up, such as moving house or taking a child to a new school, she should arrange to take annual leave or parental leave, if appropriate. Although it is therefore in the nature of things unlikely that the employee will seek permission in advance to take the time off, if she does, and it is unreasonably refused, she has a right to complain to a tribunal within three months. The tribunal will make a declaration and can award such compensation as it considers to be just and equitable having regard to the seriousness of the employer's fault and any loss to the employee (ERA, s.57B). By the same token, the employee will frequently be unable to give notice prior to taking the time off. ERA, s.57A(2) therefore stipulates that the employee should notify the employer as soon as reasonably practicable of the reason for his absence and how long it is likely to last. The Act envisages that the employee may sometimes only be able to notify the employer after he has returned to work. This means that an employer faced with an employee who is absent without explanation may need to review disciplinary procedures for dealing with unauthorised absences. Absence from work without permission would normally be a fundamental breach of contract justifying summary dismissal (*cf. Hanley v Pease* (1915)). An employer who made no inquiries and did not give an employee an opportunity to explain the situation before dismissing him would no doubt be liable for unfair dismissal on general principles (see below, para. 8–043) but this would not apply to anyone with less than one year's service. However, if the employee was entitled to take the time off by virtue of section 57A, any such dismissal will be automatically unfair under ERA, s.99. As with rights to maternity and parental leave, there is no continuous service requirement for the right to time off for dependant care. In addition, employees may bring an action under ERA, s.47C if they are subjected to a detriment for exercising their time off rights. Again, as with other time off rights, the employer is not entitled to ask the employee to make up the time later and any insistence that the employee should do so would amount to a detriment under section 47C.

For the time being there is likely to be considerable uncertainty as to what precisely is covered by the right to time off for dependant care. It is probable that tribunals as well as employers will rely on the statutory guidance produced by the DTI, although it must be borne in mind that this guidance has no legal status at all. In practice, it may be that this new time off right will have little effect. Most employers deal with these situations formally or informally by allowing employees to take paid time off.

Guarantee Payments

6–026 The object of the provisions on guarantee payments in ERA, ss.28–35 is to provide employees with a minimum payment where they are laid off work through no fault of their own. Two points should be noted at the outset. Firstly, no employer has the right to lay workers off without pay unless that right is embodied in the contract of employment. If there is no contractual right, the employer would be committing a fundamental breach which would entitle the employee to leave and claim that she had been constructively dismissed (see below, para. 8–021). Secondly, if the lay-off lasts for four weeks or more the employee may be entitled to leave and claim a redundancy payment (see below, para. 9–016).

The qualifying period of service for this right is only one month (s.29). The employee is entitled to guarantee pay if laid off for one of two reasons: a diminution in the requirements of the employer's business for work of the kind that the employee is employed to do (s.28(1); compare the definition of redundancy below, para. 9–004); or because of any other occurrence affecting the normal working of the business in relation to work of the kind that the employee is employed to do.

The employer has a defence if she offers the employee suitable alternative work for the day which he unreasonably refuses – a defence which is again modelled on the redundancy provisions (s.29(4)). Rather more significantly, the employee is not entitled to payment if the reason for the lay-off is a strike, lock-out or other industrial action involving the employer or any other company in the same group (s.29(3)). So if supplies dry up because there is a strike in a different part of the enterprise, the employees will not get guarantee payments even if they are not involved in any industrial action themselves. This may seem harsh, but can be justified on the ground that such an exclusion was found in most of the collective agreements which made provision for guarantee payments before the Act was passed, and it has a parallel also in that social security benefits are not normally payable in those circumstances. Incidentally, if there is a collective agreement covering these matters, the parties can opt out of the statutory scheme provided that the contractual scheme is at least as advantageous, and there are a number of opted-out agreements. Even if an agreement is not opted out, any contractual right to pay during a lay-off would reduce the employer's liability under sections 28–35.

It may perhaps be doubted whether the right is worth this amount of legislative effort. Broadly, the amount payable is the employee's gross daily rate of pay subject to a maximum which has always been ridiculously low. In 2003 it stood at only £17.30 per day. Further, guarantee pay can only be claimed for a maximum of five days in any three-month period. Not only are the sums involved very small, but the overall effect of this is simply to stave off by a few days the payment of other benefits. But for the guarantee payment, a worker would be entitled to jobseeker's allowance after three workless days. Therefore the worker who receives a guarantee payment (worth roughly the same as jobseeker's allowance) gets paid for the first three days, and the employer has to pay for the next two instead of the State. If the worker is still laid off after that, she will have to wait for three days, and will then qualify for jobseeker's allowance.

If an employer refuses to pay guarantee pay, the employee has a right of recourse to the employment tribunal.

Suspension on Medical Grounds

Under health and safety regulations a business may sometimes be required **6–027** to shut down its operations. In such a situation, employees remain entitled to their regular pay even if they cannot work, unless the employer has a contractual right to suspend them. If the employer has a right to suspend them in these circumstances and the shut-down was required under regulations listed in ERA, s.64 (Control of Lead at Work Regulations 1980; Ionising Radiation Regulations 1985; COSHH Regulations 1999), then ERA, s.64(1) provides that the employees are entitled to a week's pay for every week of shut-down up to a maximum of 26 weeks.

An employee need only be employed for one month in order to receive this protection (s.65(1)) and if the employee is dismissed because of the shut-down in these circumstances, the qualifying period for unfair dismissal is also reduced to one month (s.108(2)). However, the employer has a defence where the employee unreasonably refuses suitable alternative employment during the suspension period (s.65(4)) and the employee has no entitlement if she is unfit to work through illness during that time. As usual, the employee's remedy is to apply to an employment tribunal, which can order the employer to pay the requisite amount.

Time Off Rights

6–028 The Employment Protection Act 1975 introduced a range of rights to time off work in certain circumstances, which are now found in the ERA and TULRCA. Since 1975 further time off rights have been introduced: the right to paid time off for ante-natal care and the right to time off for dependant care, discussed above (paras 6–004, 6–024) and rights to time off for employee representatives. The rights to time off for trade union duties and activities; for employee representatives; and for public duties are discussed here; time off to look for work in a redundancy situation is discussed in Chapter 9 (below, para. 2–019) and time off for safety representatives in Chapter 14 (below, para. 14–026).

Time off for trade union duties and activities

6–029 Two very important rights to time off for trade unionists are contained in TULRCA, ss.168–170. Guidance on their application is contained in the Acas Code of Practice on Time off for Trade Union Duties and Activities, a new edition of which was issued in 2003. While there is no service qualification for the exercise of these rights, they are limited to the officials and members of recognised trade unions (see above, para. 5–014).

Paid time off

6–030 Officials of recognised trade unions are entitled to paid time off for two purposes: to carry out their duties, and to receive relevant training. Two kinds of duty qualify for paid time off under section 168(1): negotiations with the employer or performing functions on behalf of employees. However, not all such duties qualify. The right to paid time off is limited to duties which fulfil the conditions of being related to matters listed in TULRCA, s.178 (issues which can be the subject of collective bargaining) and, in the case of negotiations, matters on which the employer recognises the union for bargaining purposes. In the case of other functions on behalf of employees, the employer must have agreed to their performance by the union.

The formulation of duties for which paid time off is allowed was narrowed by the Employment Act 1989 effectively to reverse a Court of Appeal holding that an official's duties could relate to matters other than those on which the employer was prepared to negotiate with them (*Beal v Beecham Group* (1982)). In *Adlington v British Bakeries* (1989) the Court of Appeal held that preparatory work was included within the definition of duties. Thus officials of the Bakers' Union were entitled to paid time off to attend a one-day workshop on the implications of the repeal of the statute regulating hours of work in the industry. The question to be asked is whether any particular preparation or advisory meeting is sufficiently proximate to the negotiations with the employer – a question of fact where a tribunal's decision should not normally be overturned. The decision remains valid after the amendment, although it must now be read as applying to a more restricted range of duties (*cf. London Ambulance Service v Charlton* (1992)). This makes sense, as the Code of Practice indicates that preparation for meetings and reporting back to members are included (para.12). Meetings with other union officials and interviews with constituents who have grievances are still included within an official's duties, provided that they relate to matters for which there is recognition; and if an official can represent a member in disciplinary proceedings, she should also have paid time off to represent the member against the employer in an employment tribunal, even though this is not spelt out in the Code.

Paid time off for training is now limited in the same way to duties relating to matters in respect of which the union is recognised by the employer; additionally it must be approved by the employee's own union or by the TUC (s.168(2)). There may need to be agreements over how many officials can be away at any one time.

Paragraph 15 of the Code of Practice draws attention to the fact that the statute does not require payment for time when the official would not otherwise be at work. This causes problems for shift workers and part-timers. What if a night shift worker misses a shift to get some sleep so as to be able to attend a day-time meeting? In *Ryford Ltd v Drinkwater* (1996) it seemed to be accepted that this was time off to which the official was entitled, although the point was not argued. But in *Hairsine v Hull CC* (1991), where the employee worked an evening shift and took time off from that in lieu of time he had spent at a training course during the day, it was held that he was not entitled to be paid for it. The first situation should clearly attract a right to time off, since otherwise the employee cannot exercise the right meaningfully. However, the second case is more difficult. On the one hand, it would be unfortunate if some employees were deterred from taking office because the time involved would always be over and above their working hours commitment; on the other hand, employees who do become union officials must expect to give up some of their free time for that purpose.

Similar issues arise in relation to part-time workers. If part-time workers **6–031** go on a full-time training course for trade union duties, for example, should they get their normal pay, or should it be grossed up to full-time pay? In *Arbeiterwohlfahrt der Stadt Berlin v Bötel* (1992) the ECJ held that it would be indirect sex discrimination contrary to Article 141 of the Treaty of Rome to pay a part-time worker receiving full-time training to be a staff council representative in Germany less than full-timers on the same course. This case was distinguished by the EAT in *Manor Bakeries v Nazir* (1996), where a part-timer had claimed equal pay for full-time attendance at a union conference on the basis that conference attendance was not "work" – something that could only be said by someone who had never done it. Subsequently, in *Kuratorium für Dialyse v Lewark* (1996), on facts similar to *Bötel*, the ECJ reiterated that "pay" in the context of Article 141 includes anything received by the employee from the employer which is referable to the contract of employment, even if only indirectly. This reinforced the view that *Manor Bakeries v Nazir* was wrongly decided, and that was the conclusion of another EAT in *Davies v Neath Port Talbot County BC* (1999), holding that a part-time worker who was elected as a union safety representative was entitled to pay at the full-time rate for her attendance at a full-time training course. In so far as TULRCA, s.169 was inconsistent with this, the EAT held it should be set aside. However, since the claim proceeds on the basis of indirect discrimination, there is the possibility of the employer being able to justify paying less to the part-timer. In *Lewark* the ECJ indicated that it thought the justification put forward for the inequality (that the independence of the staff council might be jeopardised if councillors got more for being members than they would from their ordinary work) might be sufficient, although this should be balanced against the fact that part-timers might be reluctant to take on such posts if they had to do much more of the work in their own time than full-timers did.

This issue is not addressed directly in the Part-time Workers (Prevention of Less Favourable Treatment) Regulations 2000, with DTi guidance confined to recommending that training should be scheduled in such a way that part-timers can attend so far as possible. It is probable that paying a part-time official less than a full-timer on full-time training would constitute less favourable treatment, but objective justification is permitted by these Regulations also. However, they would make it easier for a male part-timer to claim and the necessity of proving adverse impact on grounds of sex would be removed.

6–032   Two other rights to paid time off should be mentioned. First, a lay union official who accompanies a worker to a disciplinary, dismissal or grievance hearing in accordance with ERelA 1999, s.10, is entitled to paid time off for this purpose (see further below, para. 8–070). Secondly, the Employment Act 2002 put the role of the Union Learning Representatives on a statutory footing and gave them an entitlement to reasonable paid time off. Union Learning Representatives are union officials whose role is to promote learning in the workplace among their co-workers. They may not necessarily have any other official union capacity. Union Learning Representatives are entitled to a reasonable amount of paid time off to carry out their functions, which include identifying learning needs, arranging for needs to be met, providing advice to workers and consulting with the employer about these matters. Some practical advice is given by the Acas Code of Practice.

Where a complaint that paid time off was wrongfully refused is upheld, the tribunal must make a declaration to that effect and award the employee the pay that he should have received. It was held in *Ryford Ltd v Drinkwater* (1996) that there is no liability for refusing to agree to a request for time off where the employer is not aware of the request. This reinforces the advice given in the Code of Practice that employers and unions should agree effective procedures for making and processing requests.

Unpaid time off

6–033 As well as paid time off for officials, members of recognised trade unions are entitled to unpaid time off during working hours for trade union activities (s.170). Acting as a representative of the union is stated to be an activity, and would cover things like being a member of the national executive of the union, or a representative at branch, area or regional meetings or at the annual conference of the TUC. Taking part in industrial action is specifically stated not to be a trade union activity, which is hardly surprising; however, the Code of Practice, para.49, suggests that an official representing members who are on strike could be carrying out her duties and thus entitled to paid time off under section 168. Further examples of trade union activities given by the Code are taking part in union elections and attending meetings to discuss or vote on the outcome of negotiations. In practice, in some situations where paid time off is not available to officials under section 168, they may be entitled to unpaid time off under section 170.

In *Luce v Bexley LBC* (1990) the NUT sought permission from local authorities for teachers who were union officials to have time off in 1988 to attend a lobby of Parliament over the Education Reform Bill (later Act). The lobby involved all teaching unions and had been organised by the TUC. Considering that it was essentially an expression of political and ideological objection to the legislation, an employment tribunal held that the employer was entitled to refuse time off on the ground that this was not a trade union activity. The EAT upheld the decision, but warned that it would be too sweeping to turn down all lobbying. Lobbying, said the EAT: "is the presentation of arguments intended to persuade a member of Parliament to vote in a particular way on a particular issue. It is to be contrasted with an approach which is in essence based upon mere protest". Thus if it could be shown that the lobbying was of the persuasive kind rather than the protest kind, and that the issue was relevant to the employment of the members, it could count as a trade union activity. This might have been possible on the facts here, but the applicant did not help himself by failing to give evidence or call any witnesses!

Where unpaid time off is wrongly refused, the tribunal again makes a declaration and can award just and equitable compensation, taking account of the degree of blame attaching to the employer and the loss to the employee (s.172).

How much time off?

The Act does not stipulate how much paid and unpaid time off officials and **6–034** members should get: it is such amount as is reasonable. The Code of Practice is not much more specific, recommending that the parties should try to reach advance agreement taking into account the size of the organisation and the number of workers; the production process; the need to maintain a service to the public; and the need for safety and security. Where workplace meetings are held, it is suggested that they could be held at the end of a shift or before or after meal breaks to minimise disruption. It is pointed out that it may be in the interests of employers to be flexible about workplace meetings in order to ensure a representative turnout.

In practice a certain amount of flexibility is almost certain to be necessary in the interests of both sides, but the right to time off is not unlimited. In *Wignall v British Gas* (1984) a NALGO official employed as a meter reader by British Gas had for many years been an active trade unionist and was vice-chair of his district committee and a member of 22 committees. As a result he was getting 12 weeks' leave a year from the employer, some paid and some unpaid. He asked for a further 10 days' unpaid leave in order to edit a magazine for members; it was held that the employers acted reasonably in refusing this.

To date, the provisions for time off for trade union duties and activities have not caused great dispute between employers and workers, no doubt because they have been limited to members of recognised trade unions and recognition used to be a voluntary process. An employer who did not wish to allow employees time off for these matters could simply refuse to recognise a union. Now that compulsory trade union recognition has been introduced it is possible that time off rights may become more contentious.

Time off for employee representatives

6–035 In *EC Commission v UK* (1994) the ECJ held that United Kingdom law on consultation with the workforce over redundancies and transfers of undertakings did not properly implement the relevant EC directives because it only provided for consultation with recognised trade unions. This meant that non-unionised workforces, or those where the employer refused to recognise a union, had no rights to be consulted. As a result the law had to be changed in order to allow for consultation with employee representatives (see further below, para. 9–039). It was further necessary to make provision for employee representatives in other areas where EC law provided for consultation or negotiation, such as health and safety and working time. In general such employee representatives receive the same protection as trade union representatives while they are carrying out their duties, but their rights to time off are not always the same. Under ERA, s.61 employees who are representatives for the purposes of redundancy and transfers consultation are entitled to reasonable time off for their duties and for training for their duties (although the training provision was only introduced in 1999). Employee health and safety representatives are also entitled to time off for their duties and training (see below, para. 14–026) as are employee trustees of occupational pension schemes (ERA, s.58). Curiously, however, employee representatives for purposes of the Working Time Regulations 1998 have no express statutory rights to time off. There are also no codes of practice covering time off for employee representatives, even though it might be felt that this is an area where guidance is especially needed.

Time off for public duties

6–036 Many public institutions, most notably the criminal courts, are heavily dependent on the work of volunteers. It is important that lay magistrates, school governors and so on should represent a wide cross-section of society and not become the preserve of the middle classes or the retired. Hence the formalisation in ERA, s.50 of what already was the practice of many employers, a right to time off for certain kinds of public duties. There is no service qualification for this. An employee is entitled to time off under section 50 if she is: a magistrate; a member of a local authority, health service body or education body; a member of a prison visiting committee; a member of a statutory tribunal or a member of the Environment Agency. Activities for which time off should be allowed include attendance at meetings and sub-committee meetings and other things approved by the body (*e.g.* visits or inspections). There is no provision in the Act for pay, and employers vary as to their practice on this.

The allowance once again is for reasonable time off, as to which section 50(4) states that regard should be had to: how much time off is needed to carry out the duties (*e.g.* magistrates are required to be available for a certain number of sittings and training sessions); how much time the employee has already had for other public duties or for trade union duties and activities; and the circumstances of the employer's business and the role of the employee in the business. Clearly it will be more difficult for a key employee to take much time off.

A tribunal which upholds a complaint must make a declaration that time off should have been allowed and may order compensation (s.51). It does not have power to stipulate how much time off should be given, or that it should be paid: however, it may make recommendations on the amount of time off, which may be expected to carry weight with the employer (*Corner v Bucks CC* (1978)).

Sunday Working

After several years of false starts at reform, the Sunday Trading Act 1994 **6–037** came into force at the end of August 1994, permitting shops to do what many of them had already been doing for some time. In the debate over whether Sunday trading should be permitted, a major consideration was the position of shop workers and a concern to protect them from being compelled to work on Sundays.

Protection for shop workers is now provided by Part IV of the Employment Rights Act 1996 and it is important to notice that it applies to all shop workers except for those employed to work only on Sundays. "Shop worker" is defined as anyone who is or may be required under their contract of employment to do shop work, which is work in or about a shop at a time when it is open to customers. It will be interesting to see whether work "about a shop" is construed as including making deliveries to it.

Shop workers who were already employed on August 25, 1994 (when the Sunday Trading Act came into force) have the status of "protected shop workers". This means that they cannot be required to work on Sundays, that dismissal or selection for redundancy for such refusal is automatically unfair and they must not be subjected to any detriment short of dismissal either. Similar protection is afforded to "opted-out shop workers", who are any other shop workers except those employed exclusively for Sundays. To gain the protection, however, these workers must serve the employer with written notice of their wish to opt out of Sunday working, which only becomes effective three months later. While receiving protection from dismissal or other retaliatory action on grounds of having given the notice during that time, such an employee can be required to work on Sundays until the three months are up.

These provisions override anything in the contract of employment and protection is not dependent on any qualifying period of continuous employment. In other words, while there is nothing to stop an employer discriminating in recruitment and only taking those who express willingness to work on a Sunday, once in the job an employee will be entitled to change her mind. The employer must give new employees a statement of their rights to opt out within two months of their starting work. Both protected shop workers and opted-out shop workers will lose their protection if they opt in to Sunday working, by giving written notice to this effect and then agreeing with the employer actually to work on Sunday, although there is nothing to stop them opting out again at a later stage.

There is no requirement that workers should receive premium rates for Sunday working, although this was included in the Code of Practice agreed between USDAW and the Shopping Hours Reform Council (SHRC), representing major retailers. Equally, financial inducements to workers to persuade them to work Sundays is not a detriment to those who do not. Nor is it an actionable detriment if the employer does not give additional weekday hours to an employee who opts out to make up for hours formerly worked on Sunday.

While the protection for shop workers looks complete, concerns have been expressed that individuals can actually find it quite difficult in practice to stand on their rights, especially as payment systems can be manipulated to render Sunday working an economic, if not a legal, necessity. Historically shop workers have been a low paid and fairly vulnerable group of workers and the protection given against compulsion to work on Sundays must be seen in the context of other developments which reduce their protection. These are first, the abolition of the wages council applicable to the industry in 1993, which used to set minimum hourly rates; and secondly the Deregulation and Contracting Out Act 1994, which removed all restrictions on weekday opening hours for shops.

Limits on Working Time

6–038 Traditionally in the United Kingdom there has been little statutory control over working hours, largely because it was thought to be adequately dealt with by voluntary collective bargaining. In the nineteenth century the Factories Acts introduced limits on the working hours of women and young workers, but they did not apply to men or to employment outside their scope. Despite being instrumental in the framing of ILO Convention No.1 on Hours of Work (1919), which provided for a maximum eight-hour day and 48-hour working week, the United Kingdom declined to ratify it. Thus it was not until the Working Time Regulations 1998 came into force on October 1, 1998 that there was any general regulation of working hours in this country.

The Regulations were passed in order to implement the 1993 Working Time Directive (93/104/EC). The Directive, which should have been brought into force by November 23, 1996, was passed as a health and safety

162

measure under Article 137 of the Treaty of Rome, which meant that it did not require unanimous agreement. The legal basis of the Directive was challenged by the United Kingdom, which claimed that it was really an employment measure, requiring unanimity. However, in *United Kingdom v Council of the European Union* (1997) the ECJ held that it was primarily a health and safety measure and properly passed under Article 137. Implementation finally took place in 1998, nearly two years late.

Scope of the Working Time Regulations

In line with the current Government's general policy of extending the scope **6–039** of employment protection rights, the Working Time Regulations cover "workers", defined as including employees and those working under contracts to perform personally any work or services (reg.2). Trainees and agency workers are expressly included and there is no qualifying period of employment.

The Working Time Directive (93/104/EC) originally allowed the exclusion of workers in all forms of the transport industry, because of the difficulties caused by their unusual working patterns. Curiously, however, this extended even to non-mobile workers such as office staff (*Bowden v Tuffnells Parcels* (2002)). Another important group excluded, at the behest of the United Kingdom, were doctors in training. However, it was never intended that these exclusions should be permanent and in May 1999 agreement with the EU social partners was reached on the Horizontal Amending Directive (2000/34/EC) (HAD) to extend the Directive generally, and specific directives were passed to deal with mobile workers in the following industries: seafarers, road transport, and aviation.

The HAD was implemented in the United Kingdom by the Working Time (Amendment) Regulations 2003. The result is that the Working Time Regulations now apply in full to all non-mobile workers in these industries and to mobile and non-mobile workers in the rail industry. The position for road transport is more complicated, because the Road Transport Directive (2002/15/EC) only applies to those workers who are covered by the EC Drivers' Hours Regulation – broadly, long-distance lorry drivers. Other mobile road transport workers (such as taxi drivers or motorcycle couriers) are covered by the amended Working Time Regulations, but do not have the usual entitlements to rest breaks. Junior hospital doctors are now covered by the Regulations – but only from August 1, 2004. Even then, their working hours need only be reduced to an average of 58 per week until July 2007, and then 56 per week from August 1, 2007 to July 31, 2009.

Another contentious exclusion in the Regulations was the "unmeasured **6–040** working time" category. Article 17 of the Directive allowed Member States a derogation:

> "when, on account of the specific characteristics of the activity concerned, the duration of the working time is not measured and/or predetermined or can be determined by the workers themselves . . ."

This wording was reproduced almost exactly in the Regulations along with the non-exhaustive list of examples, which includes "managing executives or other persons with autonomous decision-taking powers". On one view this would take out almost all professional workers who have a large amount of autonomy as to how they organise their time and whose work time tends to be defined in terms of the tasks to be performed rather than in terms of set hours. However, given that the Directive is a health and safety measure, it seems hardly likely that such a large group should be excluded and the better view is that very few workers would actually fall into this category. This alarmed the business community which balked at the prospect of having to get written agreements of their professional workers to work beyond the limit and of having to keep records of how much work was being done. Their lobbying proved so successful that even before the Regulations had been in force for a year the Government proposed an amendment which was carried through at the end of 1999. Regulation 20 now provides that workers whose work is partly predetermined and partly unmeasured can choose voluntarily to work beyond the limit on hours and that the Regulations will not apply to this voluntary extra time. The danger of this, of course, is that for large numbers of workers "voluntary" extra time will be compulsory in practice and that the Regulations will have little impact on the long hours culture which is a striking feature of the British employment scene.

The 48-hour week

6–041   The basic rule in regulation 4 is that average working time for each seven-day period should not exceed 48 hours, including overtime. However, this is a limit on *average* working hours, taken over a standard reference period of 17 weeks (or longer, in certain circumstances). In practice, this should mean that workers can do well above 48 hours for quite sustained periods without going over the limit and should give sufficient flexibility to meet most employers' surges in demand or unforeseen shortages of staff. "Working time" is defined as any time when the worker is working, at the employer's disposal and carrying out his duties. Are these requirements separate or cumulative? For example, is it part of working time when a worker is "on call" at home even though she may not need to do any work if she is not called out? In *SIMAP v Conselliera de Sanidad y Consumo de la Generalidad Valenciana* (2000) the ECJ held that time when the employee was on call and at the employer's premises would count as working time, but not if they were on call at home.

Individual workers can opt out of the 48-hour limit (reg.5). This derogation was controversially included in the Directive, but only for seven years. It is due to be reviewed by November 2003 and the EU Commission was consulting on this at the time of writing. Those who argued against it were concerned that financial or other pressures could mean that workers effectively had to opt out of the protection and that the limit would become a dead letter. A worker who opts out can change his mind on giving seven days' notice, unless he has agreed to a longer period (which cannot be more than three months). Regulation 5 originally required any opt-out agreement to be in writing and that employers should keep records of its terms plus the actual number of hours worked by the opted-out worker. Again, pressure from business led the Government to water down this requirement in an amendment to the Working Time Regulations in 1999. It is no longer necessary for the agreement to be in writing and the employer need only keep a general record. This is bad news for workers, as the potential for argument about what was agreed and whether the agreement is being adhered to is greatly increased.

Subject to the exceptions noted, the limit on working time is mandatory and an employer who fails to take all reasonable steps to ensure compliance is guilty of a criminal offence. Workers who are penalised or dismissed for insisting on their rights under the Regulations are protected from detriment and dismissal under ERA, ss.45A and 101A. In addition, in *Barber v RJB Mining* (1999) the High Court held that the 48-hour limit was contractual, and workers were entitled to a declaration that they were not contractually bound to work until their average hours dropped below the limit.

There are further restrictions for night workers, defined as workers who **6–042** as a normal course, work at least three hours of their daily working time during the night. In *R. v Att.-Gen. (Northern Ireland) ex p. Burns* (1999) the High Court in Northern Ireland confirmed that someone who worked nights one week in every three was a "night worker": the test was whether she regularly worked nights, not whether the majority of her working time was at night. Under regulation 6, the normal working hours of night workers should not exceed eight in any 24-hour period, averaged over 17 weeks. As with the 48-hour limit, this is mandatory and enforcement is similar.

Rest breaks

The Working Time Regulations also make provision for daily rest, weekly **6–043** rest and rest breaks during the working day. Under regulation 10, adult workers are entitled to 11 hours' rest and young workers to 12 hours' rest in each 24-hour period. In the case of shift workers changing shift, this does not apply, although they should get an "equivalent period of compensatory rest". There is an exception also for workers whose working day is split (*e.g.* cleaners). Adult workers are entitled to a 24-hour rest period in every seven days (although this can be averaged as 48 hours in every 14 days (reg.11)). Young workers should get 24 hours a week. This is in addition to daily rest. So far as rest breaks during the working day are concerned, it may be surprising to find that break entitlement only arises when the working day is longer than six hours (reg.12). The conditions for this (length, location, etc.) can be laid down in a collective or workforce agreement, but in the absence of agreement, the worker's entitlement is only to a 20-minute break, spent away from the workstation. In general, while there may be some advantages in having specific provision about rest breaks, the minimum entitlements under the Regulations are really very limited and it seems unlikely that many workers will need to avail themselves of these rights.

Annual leave

6–044 In practical terms probably the most important provision in the Working Time Regulations is regulation 13 which introduced the entitlement to paid annual leave. This is a right to four weeks' paid leave a year, although until November 23, 1999 it was only three weeks, in accordance with a derogation permitted in the Directive. The Government's own estimate was that 0.7 million full-time and 1.8 million part-time workers got less than three weeks' paid leave, and 1.1 million full-time and 2 million part-time workers got less than four weeks' paid leave before this right was introduced.

One of the problems for employers in relation to annual leave is whether they can stop workers taking paid leave before they have "earned" it: many employers have treated leave as accruing proportionately during the year and refuse to let employees take more paid leave than is accrued. In part concession to employers' fears on this score, the Working Time Regulations originally stipulated a 13-week qualifying period for the right to annual leave, but this was successfully challenged by BECTU as contrary to the Directive (*R. v Secretary of State ex p. BECTU* (2001)). The Regulations were amended to remove this requirement in October 2001. The fact that an employer can reach agreement with an employee to claw back pay if the employee leaves before the end of a leave year having used up more than her proportionate entitlement suggests that the employer should not be able to insist upon accrual.

Another major issue has been to decide whether it is acceptable for the employer to designate part of the worker's regular pay as "holiday pay" so as to avoid having to pay the worker when they actually take leave. This kind of "rolled-up" payment is used in particular by employers of casual or temporary workers. In *Blackburn v Gridquest* (2002) the Court of Appeal held that this could not be done in respect of a worker who had never been notified that his pay was meant to include an element of holiday pay, but declined to make a more general ruling. However, in *MPB Structure Ltd v Munro* (2003) the Scottish Court of Session held that the practice was impermissible as contrary to the Directive. Their view was that workers would be deterred from exercising their right to annual leave unless they actually got the payment at the time of the holiday.

7. Pay

While the duty to pay remuneration is far from being the employer's only **7–001**
duty under the contract of employment, it is certainly the central element of
the consideration given by the employer. In this chapter the most important
statutory measures on the protection of wages will be considered: the right
of men and women not to be discriminated against in the terms on which
they work; wages during sickness; deductions from wages and protection for
the lowest-paid workers.

Equal Pay

At one time the idea of a woman's rate for the job which was less than the **7–002**
man's rate for exactly the same job was considered perfectly acceptable. No
doubt this was to a large extent bound up with the stereotypical assumption
that men work as breadwinners for the family, whereas the woman's wage
was merely "pin-money" – a top-up for the extras rather than an essential
component in the family budget. Today vestiges of such outdated ideas
remain, although no one would seriously deny that anyone doing a job
ought to have a right to the rate for that job regardless of personal
characteristics irrelevant to its performance.

   The right to equal pay – which actually means equal terms and conditions
of employment, not just pay – is enshrined in the Equal Pay Act 1970 (in
force December 29, 1975). Relevant to its passage was not only ILO
Convention No.100 (1951), which requires equal remuneration for work of
equal value, but also that it was necessary for British entry to the EU.
Article 141 of the Treaty of Rome stipulates adherence to the principle that
"men and women should receive equal pay for equal work". This was
inserted in the Treaty in the first place not so much because of philosophical notions about the equality and dignity of human beings but because
some of the original six EC members had equality laws and others did not;
it was felt by those who did that businesses in their countries would be at a
competitive disadvantage with those who could get away with using women
as a cheap source of labour. Since then, however, the institutions of the EU
have shown a genuine commitment to furthering the cause of equality for
women by imaginative extrapolation from the bare statement in Article 141.

One reason that it took over five years to bring the Equal Pay Act into force is that on its own it would have probably had a bad effect on women's job prospects. In the absence of any law prohibiting discrimination at the point of job entry, a law which required terms offered to be the same for men and women could simply have made it more difficult for women to get jobs. Thus the Equal Pay Act had to wait for the Sex Discrimination Act 1975 and both were brought into force together. It was always intended that there should be a lengthy period before the Act was brought into force so that employers would have plenty of notice of what was expected of them and would have time to clean up their act without the need for wholesale disruption of established pay and grading systems.

7–003   Since equal pay for men and women is an aspect of sex discrimination it follows that this is an area where EU law has an enormous impact. Indeed, the Article in the Treaty of Rome which provides the legal basis for Community sex discrimination law, Article 141, actually begins by saying that "men and women should receive equal pay for equal work". This is amplified by the Equal Pay Directive 1975 (75/117/EEC). As noted already, Article 141 has been held to have direct effect (above, para. 2–001) and in *Jenkins v Kingsgate* the ECJ held that Article 1 of the Equal Pay Directive does not go further than Article 141, but only deals with its application. Thus, in any action based on Article 141 in a domestic court or tribunal it is possible to rely on the Equal Pay Directive to assist in interpreting the Treaty article. In considering equality of terms and conditions the Equal Treatment Directive 1976 (76/207/EEC) is also relevant in some circumstances, although the ECJ has made it clear that the Equal Pay Directive and Equal Treatment Directive are mutually exclusive: they cannot both apply in the same situation (*Gillespie v Northern Health and Social Services Board* (1996)).

Under the Equal Pay Act, women and men can claim equal terms with someone of the opposite sex employed by the same or an associated employer in three situations: like work, work rated as equivalent, and work of equal value.

Like work

7–004   If a woman is doing work which is "of the same or a broadly similar nature" to that of a man, and the "differences (if any) between the things that she does and the things that they do are not of practical importance" then she is entitled to equal terms and conditions with him (EqPA, s.1(4)).

On the whole a fairly liberal approach has been taken to what is like work, the keynote being established in the first case to reach the EAT on its interpretation, *Capper Pass v Lawton* (1977). In that case, a woman who worked as the sole cook in the directors' dining room, preparing lunch for 10 to 20 people a day, claimed that she should get the same hourly rate as two male assistant chefs who worked under the head chef preparing 350 meals a day in six sittings, two for breakfast, lunch and tea in the works canteen. Although there were obvious differences between what they did, the EAT held that they were not of practical importance, and that this was like work.

Where it is alleged that there are differences between what the woman and the man do, the tribunal must consider whether in practice this is the case. In *Shields v Coomes* (1978) male counter staff in a betting shop got a higher hourly rate than female counter staff. When challenged, the employer claimed that these shops were at risk of robbery and that a man was employed at each for security reasons. There had been no incidents at the applicant's shop in the three years that she had worked there, and the men received no training for their security role. The Court of Appeal held that the existence of the claimed difference consisting in the men's security role could not be established. It was based purely on stereotypical assumptions about sex rather than on any extra duties which the men had to perform in practice. In this case Bridge L.J. recommended a two-stage approach to the question, deciding first whether the jobs are broadly similar, and then if so, moving on to consider whether any differences which do exist are of practical importance.

It is possible that the Court of Appeal's approach in *Shields v Coomes* (1978) is more stringent than the position in EU law. In *Angestellten-betriebsrat der Wiener Gebietskrankenkasse v Wiener Gebietskrankenkasse* (1999) graduate psychologists and medical doctors were all engaged in providing psychotherapy services as employees of the Vienna Area Health Fund. The graduate psychologists, predominantly women, earned substantially less than the doctors and claimed that as they were doing the same work they should receive the same pay. The employer argued that this was not the same work because the psychologists and doctors had entirely different training and skills, and although ostensibly both groups were providing the same services, inevitably they drew on different knowledge and expertise derived from their separate disciplines. Furthermore, the doctors could be called on to perform other medical duties for which the psychologists would not be qualified (although there was no evidence as to whether this happened in practice or, if so, how often). The ECJ held that in these circumstances the two groups were not engaged in the same work, mainly because of their different training and qualifications, but the court also adverted to the fact that the doctors could be called on to do different things. The result in this specific case may seem supportable, although if it were true that psychotherapeutic services as performed by the two groups were qualitatively different it might be expected that there would be evidence of different kinds of patients being referred to each, or at least some assessment of which kind of practitioner would be most appropriate for each patient. If any such system was in place, no evidence of it appeared in the decision of the ECJ.

It is possible for different qualifications and skills to result in unequal **7–005** terms for employees engaged on like work, but this is normally done by accepting that the work is the same but that there are other factors specific to the employees justifying the difference (*cf. Glasgow City Council v Marshall* (2000)). The fact that that approach was not taken in this case seems to allow some weakening of the equal pay principle. There is no reason why British equal pay law should not be more demanding than EU law and it is to be hoped that British courts will stand by the principle in *Shields v Coomes* that the possibility of extra duties for the man which he is not called upon to perform in practice does not prevent his work being like work with that of the woman.

In *Dugdale v Kraft Foods* (1977) the EAT held that differences in the time at which work was done did not justify a difference in basic rates of pay. Where employees work unsocial hours, the appropriate recompense is a premium for those shifts rather than a difference in basic terms. This should not be used as a device to pay men more: in *NCB v Sherwin* (1978) the EAT held that the employer had no defence to a like work claim where the premium paid was well above usual uplift for night work (which they said was about 20 per cent). It might be justifiable to pay a different basic rate for night work if the fact of doing it at night makes it different in nature, because there is no supervision and there are frequently emergencies to cope with (see *Thomas v NCB* (1987)).

As well as differences in the actual tasks performed, it was held by the EAT in *Eaton v Nuttall* (1977) that differences in responsibility could constitute differences of practical importance. In that case, both the man and the woman were employed as production schedulers, but she was dealing with much less valuable items, so a mistake on her part would have nothing like as serious consequences as a mistake by him. His higher pay was therefore justifiable.

Work rated as equivalent

7–006 On its own, the provision for equal pay when men and women are employed on like work would have little effect, for despite the Sex Discrimination Act there is *de facto* segregation in the job market. Some work is still done predominantly by women and some by men. There are still very few male secretaries and female mechanics; in textiles men tend to have the (skilled) tailoring work and women the (less skilled) machinists' jobs. In manual work in particular it is not at all uncommon to have a plant which is all male or all female (although in the latter case, there will often be male managers).

Hence the need for a mechanism which will permit a comparison to be made between totally different jobs. This is what was provided under EqPA, s.1(5). If the jobs of the woman and the man have been rated as having equivalent value under a job evaluation study, then she is entitled to equal pay. The converse is also true: if the jobs have been rated as unequal, the woman cannot try to claim that they are of equal value.

What is a job evaluation study? It is an attempt to measure the worth of jobs and may be used by management essentially as a way of trying to demonstrate to the workforce that differentials are justified. Some job evaluation studies have been very crude: drawing up a list of jobs from most valuable to least valuable on a "felt fair" basis is inherently subjective, and "pairing", where every job in the organisation is compared with every other and scored 2 for a win, 0 for a loss and 1 for a draw, a bit like the Football League, is not much better. In *Bromley v Quick* (1988) the Court of Appeal held that for the purposes of section 1(5), only analytical job evaluation studies would be acceptable. This means that the comparison must be done on an objective basis. First, there must be an accurate description of what each job involves. Then criteria must be selected against which the demands of the job can be measured and scored. The EqPA lists effort, skill and decision-making as examples of suitable criteria, but clearly these are not mandatory and others could be used as well or instead. The criteria must be objectively justifiable, although the ECJ held that this does not mean that factors which tend to favour one sex (such as strength) may not be taken into account (*Rummler v Dato-Druck* (1987)). What would be important is that the study should not give undue weight to such criteria.

Inevitably job evaluation is not an exact science, and there will be value judgments involved both in deciding how jobs rank under the criteria and even more in how the criteria should rank against each other. For this reason, although employers are not required to involve recognised trade unions in carrying out a job evaluation study, as a matter of good industrial relations it is certainly wise to do so. A woman who believes that the study itself is discriminatory may attack its validity, but a tribunal has no power to substitute its own judgment of relative worth and it cannot compel an employer to carry out a new study (*England v Bromley LBC* (1978)). This has been the greatest drawback of section 1(5) in that it is dependent on the employer being willing to institute a study. Thus it is not surprising to find that only a minority of employers did so, and that very few equal pay claims were brought under this head.

Work of equal value

In 1982 the EC Commission sued the United Kingdom before the ECJ on **7–007** the grounds that it had not implemented the Equal Pay Directive 1975 properly. The essence of the complaint, which was upheld, was that there was no means by which an employee could initiate a claim where her work was dissimilar to a man's but where she thought it was as valuable (*Commission of the EC v UK* (1982)). Hence in 1983 the Equal Pay (Amendment) Regulations were passed to amend the EqPA by introducing a third situation where equal pay could be awarded: where it is claimed that the woman's work is of equal value to that of a man.

EqPA, s.1(2)(c) provides that a woman is entitled to equal pay where the work, in terms of the demands that it makes on her under such headings as effort, skill and decision-making, is of equal value to that of a man. However, there is an important qualification to this: a claim may only be brought under this heading if it is not work to which section 1(2)(a) (*i.e.* like work) or section 1(2)(b) (*i.e.* work rated equivalent) applies.

In *Pickstone v Freemans* (1987) female warehouse operatives got the same rate of pay as a male warehouse operative, but claimed that their work was of equal value to that of a male warehouse checker. The employer argued that as there was a man employed on the same work as them who got the same pay as them, this was a situation to which the "like work" paragraph applied and they could not avoid it by choosing to compare themselves with a different man. If this argument were correct, it would blow a huge hole in the equal value protection because it would mean that provided an employer always employed a "token man" on the same work as the women, they would never be able to claim under the equal value heading. However, on a literal reading of the section, this is what it seemed to mean.

The House of Lords declined to interpret the Act in a way which would be so subversive of what was intended when the amendment was introduced, stressing the importance of interpreting national law in accordance with EU law whenever possible. Thus they held that a woman would only be unable to claim equal value if it were held that the actual comparator she had chosen was employed on like work, or was employed on work rated as equivalent.

The prohibition on an equal value claim if the woman's job and the man's job have already been compared under a valid job evaluation scheme and rated differently was taken a step further in *Dibro Ltd v Hore* (1990). In that case the job evaluation study was only instituted after the equal value claims had been lodged, yet it was held that this barred the equal value claims. In other words, an employer can instigate a job evaluation study as a way of heading off an equal value claim. Another way of looking at it is to say that a woman (or her union) can persuade an employer to carry out a job evaluation study by a few strategic equal value applications.

Procedure for bringing an equal value claim

7–008   The procedure for bringing an equal value claim is complex. It is contained in section 2A of the EqPA together with the Complementary Rules of Procedure in Schedule 3 to the Employment Tribunal (Constitution and Rules of Procedure) Regulations 2001. At the initial stage the tribunal may invite the parties to try to settle, with the assistance of Acas. This must usually be a forlorn hope, as Acas will already have been involved when the application was first made, as with all employment tribunal cases.

As originally formulated, the tribunal had a choice at the initial hearing of dismissing the claim if it had no hope of success or of appointing an independent expert to investigate the claim. However, equal value claims were very slow in moving from application to decision, with 30 months being the average time taken. The main reason for this was because of the time it took to get an independent expert's report. Thus, the Sex Discrimination and Equal Pay (Miscellaneous Amendments) Regulations 1996 amended section 2A so that the tribunal could, if it wished, proceed directly to determine the case itself. It was thought that this meant that there were now three options for the tribunal: to listen to the evidence and determine the case itself; to dismiss the claim on the basis that there were no reasonable grounds for claiming that the work was of equal value or to appoint an independent expert to prepare a report. However, doubt was thrown on this by *Wood v William Ball Ltd* (1999), where the employment tribunal had dismissed the applicants' claims as hopeless and declined to refer the issue to an independent expert. The EAT concluded that the real meaning of the new wording was that if the tribunal decided not to order an independent expert's report it should not dispose of the case itself without giving the parties the opportunity to adduce evidence – which could, of course, include experts' reports commissioned by one or both parties! If this is correct, it means that the amendments are actually likely to lead to more delays, since the tribunal no longer has power to dismiss hopeless claims.

The statute provides for one situation where the tribunal can conclude that there is no reasonable prospect of the claim succeeding and can dismiss it without more: where the jobs have already been rated differently under a valid job evaluation scheme (EqPA, s.2A(2)). The employer may also at this initial stage raise the material factor defence: *i.e.* that there is a genuine material difference, other than sex, between the man and the woman which justifies any inequality in terms (discussed below, para. 7–014). However, this will involve the employer in a difficult decision, for the genuine material factor defence may only be used once. It used to be the case that the employer had two opportunities to raise the genuine material factor defence: at this initial stage and, if failing there, by way of defence if the jobs were found to be *prima facie* of equal value. However, in an attempt to expedite these cases, the rules were changed in 1994 so as to remove the second opportunity. Thus the employer has only one chance to use this argument.

Originally, where an independent expert was appointed, the report was **7–009** meant to be submitted within six weeks, but in practice this deadline was rarely met. This was the greatest contributory factor to the inordinate delays in equal value cases. Reforms were made in 1994 and 1996 in an attempt to speed things up by giving tribunals the power to be more proactive in managing the process. The procedure now is for the tribunal to stipulate a date by which the report must be submitted at the same time as appointing the independent expert and also intervals at which a progress report should be submitted. The expert has a duty to inform the tribunal if she considers that she will be unable to meet the deadline and the tribunal can finally replace the expert if to do so would be in the interests of justice (reg.10A). If either of the parties is responsible for the delay, they are at risk of being ordered to pay the expert's fees or having the application or notice of appearance struck out. Unfortunately, this reform, carried out in 1996, has not had a great deal of effect and delays are as bad as ever: it is not unusual for many months to pass after the appointment of an independent expert before the next hearing can be held. Since it is also standard practice for parties to commission their own expert reports, the process is also very costly.

The independent expert's report can be attacked even before it has been admitted into evidence if it does not comply with the rules in the Regulations, if it reaches a perverse conclusion or is unsatisfactory for some other reason. However, in *Aldridge v British Telecom* (1990) the EAT allowed acceptance of an expert's report even though the rules had not been strictly complied with: given the delay already inherent in using this procedure, it would have been unsatisfactory to add to it by commissioning a new report.

The expert should send a summary of the information supplied and any representations of the parties to them for their comments before finalising the report. On receiving the report, the tribunal sends it to the parties and reconvenes the hearing. The report will usually include a conclusion as to whether the jobs compared are of equal value, but it is clear from the decision of the Northern Ireland Court of Appeal in *Tennants Textile Colours v Todd* (1989) that accepting the expert's report into evidence does not imply acceptance of that conclusion. The tribunal could reach a different conclusion – although this is probably an unlikely contingency.

While regulation 11(2C) states that the findings of fact in the expert's report may not be challenged, this is subject to major exceptions. Firstly, they can be challenged where a party is arguing that the report should not be admitted in the first place; secondly, the expert may be called to give evidence and may be cross-examined on these findings; thirdly, the parties may each have one expert of their own, who may attempt to contradict the independent expert; finally, factual matters can be reopened when they are relevant to a genuine material factor defence. Note that the parties' own experts do not have the same powers as the independent expert appointed by the tribunal: this was illustrated in *Lloyds Bank v Fox* (1989) where the EAT confirmed that employees did not have to be interviewed by the employer's expert if they did not want to be. Once all the evidence has been heard, the tribunal makes its decision in the usual way.

7–010   Clearly the procedure for equal value claims is defective. It is enormously cumbersome and long-winded. The first case under the provisions, where the EOC gave assistance, took over four years from start to finish (*Hayward v Cammell Laird* (1988)). Given the delays which have developed in practice, and the numerous pitfalls in the way of a successful claim, it would not be surprising if perfectly valid claims were deterred. Given the complexity of the actual claim as well as of the procedure, it must be nearly impossible to pursue such a claim without expert representation – yet legal aid is not available. The EOC assists in some cases, but because of limited resources can only assist in cases of importance – perhaps because a new point is at issue. In 1993 the EOC requested the EU Commission to consider infringement proceedings on the grounds that the statutory procedure was so defective that it constituted a breach of Article 2 of the Equal Treatment Directive. This was backed up by further evidence in 1994, but the EU Commission declined to take action. The EOC, trade unions and others have continued to campaign on this issue and in 2001 the Government suggested that an independent assessor system might be introduced to replace the use of experts (including parties' experts) in order to make the system simpler and faster – but to date nothing further has happened on this front.

Choice of comparator

7–011 An important difference between a claim under the EqPA and a claim under the SDA is that for equal pay claims an *actual* comparator has to be identified by the claimant. It is not enough for a woman to adduce evidence that if a man were employed, he would enjoy better terms and conditions than her. In *Macarthys v Smith* (1980) the ECJ held that this was in accordance with Article 141. Comparison under the EqPA is dealt with in section 1(6) which stipulates that a woman may only claim equal pay with a man who is in the "same employment", which means employed by the same or any associated employer either at the same establishment, or at a different establishment which shares common terms and conditions with hers for relevant categories of staff.

A liberal view of what constitutes "common terms and conditions" was taken by the House of Lords in *Leverton v Clwyd CC* (1989). A nursery nurse claimed parity with clerical staff employed by the council at a different establishment. The council, which had hundreds of staff, had concluded a comprehensive collective agreement with NALGO covering all staff and recorded in "the Purple Book", containing six separate pay scales. The House of Lords construed this as a situation where there were common terms and conditions for all the employees covered, rejecting the argument that common terms and conditions had to be in some sense similar. In *British Coal v Smith* (1996), 1,286 women employed as canteen workers and cleaners by British Coal at 47 different establishments claimed equal pay with 150 male surface mineworkers and clerical staff employed at 14 different establishments. The employer argued that "common terms and conditions" did not apply across the establishments because, while national bargaining dealt with most matters, some terms and conditions were negotiated at area or even plant level. In particular, entitlement to concessionary coal was dealt with at area level, and incentive bonuses at plant level, meaning that surface mineworkers and clerical staff at different pits did not have exactly the same terms and conditions. Despite these differences the House of Lords held that there were common terms and conditions for the purposes of section 1(6). It was enough if their terms and conditions were broadly similar: they did not have to be exactly the same.

Provided that she chooses a man in the same employment, the woman may choose whoever she wants to compare with and may choose more than one comparator. However, she must be realistic. In *Leverton* the applicant identified 11 male comparators doing clerical work, some of whom were on Scale 3 and some on Scale 4. Could she really be claiming that her work was of equal value with both of these when it was widely accepted that they were not of equal value with each other? The House of Lords warned that in such circumstances the woman risks having her claim, or at least part of it, not treated seriously.

The wording of the Act seems to suggest that the woman and the man must be employed at the same time. This was the subject of an early reference to the ECJ in *Macarthys Ltd v Smith* (1979), where a woman taken on as the stockroom manager discovered that she was being paid considerably less than her male predecessor. The ECJ held that Article 141 did not require speculative comparisons with what a hypothetical male might have got for the same work, but also that the principle of equal pay should not be limited by a requirement of contemporaneity. Thus in the absence of any good reason for the difference, she was entitled to equal pay. In *Diocese of Hallam v Connaughton* (1996) the EAT confirmed that comparison with a successor was also possible.

One problem that a woman will encounter in identifying a suitable comparator is that if her male colleagues do not choose to reveal details of their terms and conditions, she has no right to obtain such information. Secrecy about pay is quite common and a surprising number of employers actually prohibit employees from disclosing their details of their own pay to their colleagues. A trade union may help in getting general information about terms, although not about specific individuals (see above, para. 5–023). Of course, once a claim has been lodged with a tribunal it is possible to request further and better particulars and discovery of documents, but at that stage it would be a bit late to discover that she had selected the wrong man. In April 2003 an equal pay questionnaire procedure was introduced, along the same lines as that for sex discrimination (see above, para. 2–018). This should assist greatly in equal pay cases, although an inhibiting factor is that an employer may refuse to disclose confidential information relating to another worker without that worker's consent.

7–012　It is clear that EqPA, s.1(6) is more restrictive than Article 141 in relation to the choice of comparator. In *Defrenne v Sabena* (1976) the ECJ said that the principle of equal pay could be relied on when unequal pay is received for equal work "which is carried out in the same establishment or service, whether private or public". This suggested that workers should be able to compare themselves with employees of another employer in the same establishment (*e.g.* where sub-contractors have workers on the same site as the main employer) or with employees of another employer in a different place, provided that they are engaged in the same service (*e.g.* teachers working for different education authorities at different schools).

The question was referred to the ECJ by the Court of Appeal in *Lawrence v Regent Office Care Ltd* (2002). The applicants were women employed in catering and cleaning by contractors who provided these services for North Yorkshire County Council. Most had previously done exactly the same work as employees of the Council, but as a result of compulsory competitive tendering (CCT) contracts for much of the catering and cleaning function were won by outside contractors to whom the employees were transferred by virtue of TUPE (see below, para. 9–023). The Council had rated their jobs as having equal value to those of male manual workers, but the contractors paid them at a lower rate. Thus, although the private contractors were separate legal entities and independent of the Council, they argued that they were still employed in the same undertaking and should be allowed to compare themselves with the Council's male manual workers. In its decision the ECJ expressly stated that comparisons under Article 141 are not limited to men and women working for the same employer. However, it held that differences in terms had to be attributable to a single source – such as a collective agreement or a legislative provision. In this case, following the TUPE transfer, the women and their former colleagues were employed by two different employers with different arrangements for negotiating terms and conditions. Comparisons in this situation were not allowable.

The decision suggests that an earlier EAT case, *Scullard v Knowles* (1996), where a cross-employer comparison was allowed in relation to employees of separate regional education councils across the United Kingdom which were all funded by the Department of Employment, was correctly decided. Similarly, the Court of Session in Scotland must have been right in holding (in a decision made after the Advocate-General's opinion in *Lawrence v Regent Office Care*) that teachers employed by one education authority could compare with those employed by other education authorities (*South Ayrshire Council v Morton* (2002)). Since a single collective agreement applied across a number of different employers the Court of Session considered that comparisons could be made across the boundaries of the education authorities implementing it. It is also clear that the Equal Pay Act should be amended to allow for cross-employer comparisons in these circumstances.

In 2001 the Court of Appeal referred *Allonby v Accrington & Rossendale College* to the ECJ on similar issues. The applicant was employed as a part-time lecturer at the college on a series of fixed-term contracts between 1990 and 1996. To avoid having to give part-time staff equivalent benefits to full-time staff, the college decided to cease employing part-timers directly and instead to contract with an agency for their services. This resulted in a substantial reduction in pay for the part-timers as well as loss of access to benefits such as sick pay. The applicant, now a self-employed worker contracted to the employment agency, sought to compare herself with a male lecturer employed directly by the college. The Advocate-General's opinion in 2003 indicated that this was indistinguishable from *Lawrence v Regent Office Care* (2002), but noted the problem for equality law if employers could so easily flout the principle of the legislation.

Less favourable terms

Having established that her work is the same as or of equal value to that of **7–013** an appropriate comparator of the opposite sex, a claimant is in a position to invoke the equality clause. This is explained in EqPA, s.1(2) as being a provision which has the effect of modifying the contract so that any less favourable term is made equal and any term in the man's contract which is missing from the woman's is inserted.

The reference to "less favourable" terms again brings in a notion of comparison which provides an opportunity for value judgments with the potential to limit the ambit of the equality principle (*cf.* above, para. 2–016). In *Stadt Legerich v Helmig* (1995) overtime rates for all workers were only paid on completion of the normal hours for full-time workers. Part-time workers claimed that this was less favourable treatment because, unlike full-time staff, they were not paid overtime for hours in excess of their contracted hours. However, the ECJ held that there was no difference in the treatment of full-time and part-time workers here, as both groups had to work the same number of hours in order to get overtime rates. Discrimination has been defined by the ECJ on a number of occasions as treating like cases differently or in treating unlike cases in the same way (*e.g. Gillespie v Northern Health and Social Services Board* (1996)). In effect in this case the claimants were arguing that they were the same in relevant respects to the full-timers, but treated in a different manner. The ECJ, however, denied that this was different treatment by choosing to treat as relevant only the fact that they received the same pay for the same number of hours as full-timers and choosing to treat contracted hours as not relevant. Another way of looking at the facts would have been to say that these were unlike cases (part-timers and full-timers) being treated the same, in that all had to work more than 38 hours a week to get overtime rates.

If *prima facie* discrimination had been established in *Stadt Lengerich v Helmig* (1995) it would have been indirect sex discrimination rather than direct, on the grounds that most part-timers are women. Thus it would have been open to the employer to make out the defence of justification, which would probably have succeeded on these facts. The significance of the

ECJ's holding that the part-timers' terms were not less favourable is that this line of inquiry is closed off.

The same approach was taken by the House of Lords in *Barry v Midland Bank* (1999), another striking example of the scope for judicial choice inherent in the concept of comparison. The applicant had worked full-time for the bank for 11 years but returned to work part-time after maternity leave, taking voluntary redundancy two years after that. The bank's severance pay scheme was based purely on final salary and number of years' service, so her severance payment thus took no account of the fact that she had been full-time during most of her time with the bank. She claimed that the scheme had an adverse impact on part-timers who had previously worked full-time – nearly all of whom were women.

The applicant's complaint in this case was that the employer was treating different groups (full-timers and part-timers) in the same way although they were relevantly different. The majority of the House of Lords held that the purposes of the scheme had to be taken into account in deciding whether or not the part-timers were in a relevantly different situation from the full-timers. These were twofold: compensating employees for loss of income and rewarding past service. The House of Lords held that the part-timers and full-timers were the same in these respects: their severance payments were based on actual income, which is what they were losing, and their past years of service. Since the claimant had not got over the first hurdle of showing *prima facie* discrimination, the question of justification did not arise. Once again, the appropriate field of inquiry was closed off.

The "genuine material factor" defence

7–014 The employer will have a defence if it can show that the reason for the different terms is genuinely due to a material factor, other than sex, which constitutes a material difference between the case of the claimant and her comparator (EqPA, s.1(3)). What sorts of factors will justify differences of pay for work which is the same or of equal value? The central situation which this is aimed at is a difference in the personal equation. Thus differences in length of service, levels of performance, merit and qualifications are capable of being material factors which will justify differences in terms and conditions. In *Clay Cross v Fletcher* (1978) the Court of Appeal indicated that only matters relevant to the personal characteristics of the workers being compared could count as a material difference, ruling out external factors such as shortage of applicants which might result in higher pay being offered. However, as the House of Lords made clear in *Rainey v Greater Glasgow Health Board* (1987), it is now clear that material factors are not confined to personal differences but may involve external factors. While some of the more common factors are discussed below, it should be noted that no exhaustive list can be given. All that is required is that the employer's reason is genuine (in the sense of not being "a sham or a pretence" as the House of Lords put it in *Strathclyde Regional Council v Wallace* (1998)), that it is material, and not a difference of sex.

The requirement of materiality has led to debate as to whether or not the reason has to be objectively justified. In *Jenkins v Kingsgate* (1981) the ECJ held that a factor other than sex which predominantly affected women (in that case, part-time working) would be contrary to Article 141 unless its use could be justified. This was strengthened in *Bilka-Kaufhaus v Weber von Hartz* (1986) (another case involving part-timers) where the ECJ held that the employer would have to show that any factors having a disparate impact on men and women "correspond to a real need on the part of the undertaking, are appropriate with a view to achieving the objectives pursued and are necessary to that end". The issue was whether this requirement of objective justification applied whenever the genuine material factor defence was raised, or only where the factor was tainted with sex discrimination, in that it had a disproportionate effect on women. For example, in *Yorkshire Blood Transfusion Service v Plaskitt* (1994) the factor relied on by the employer was that it had made a mistake in putting the man on a higher grade. In terms of the *Bilka* test, this would clearly not constitute objective justification. However, it was a genuine reason, and it was not related to sex. In those circumstances, the EAT held that the employer had established the defence: the EqPA is not about achieving fair wages but about eliminating sex discrimination (see also *Tyldesley v TML Plastics* (1996)). This approach was endorsed by the House of Lords in *Strathclyde Regional Council v Wallace* (1998) and *Glasgow City Council v Marshall* (2000). Provided that the employer's reason is genuine, and material in the sense of being "significant and relevant" (*per* Lord Keith in *Rainey v Greater Glasgow Health Board* (1987)), the employer will not have to prove further that it is a good reason, from the point of view of a reasonable observer, unless it is a factor which affects women disproportionately.

There is a danger in requiring only that the employer's reason is genuine without also requiring that it should be reasonable, in that it could permit prejudice to creep in by the back door. For example, in *Tyldesley v TML Plastics* the employer was paying a newly appointed man one-third more than a woman doing the same job, because he was perceived to have more knowledge and experience of total quality management systems. The tribunal considered that there was no objective evidence supporting this perception. Is it unduly sceptical to fear that unfounded but genuine perceptions about relative worth of employees will usually work to the benefit of men?

Market forces

The ECJ formulation in *Bilka* was adopted by the House of Lords in **7–015** considering whether market forces could count as a genuine material factor justifying a difference in pay in *Rainey v Greater Glasgow Health Board* (1987). In the earlier case, *Clay Cross v Fletcher* (1978), a male clerk was taken on at a higher salary than the two female clerks because he was already earning that much in his present job. The fact that he would not come for less was rejected by the Court of Appeal as a material difference. The Court accepted the argument that market forces tend to undervalue work done by women – this was a prime reason for unequal pay.

This approach was overruled by the House of Lords in *Rainey*. In that case female prosthetists working in the National Health Service claimed equal pay with male prosthetists who had been recruited from the private sector at a higher rate of pay which reflected the fact that they already earned rather more than Health Service rates. There was no plan to phase out these differential rates over time. Rejecting the *Clay Cross* dictum that only the personal equation rather than extrinsic forces could constitute a genuine material difference, the House of Lords held that their different routes of entry to the employment were attributable to sound, objectively justified reasons and that the difference in pay was therefore justified.

The extent of the market forces defence received welcome clarification in the important decision of the ECJ in *Enderby v Frenchay HA* (1993). In that case, senior speech therapists employed by the health authority claimed that their work was of equal value with that of male principal pharmacists and male clinical psychologists, whose salaries exceeded theirs by up to 60 per cent. The employees pointed out that speech therapists were predominantly female whereas the comparator professions were predominantly male. This, they alleged, was the real reason that speech therapists were paid less. One of the employer's justifications for the difference in pay with the pharmacists was that an overall shortage of applicants for those jobs meant that higher starting salaries had to be offered. It was accepted, however, that this would not account for the whole of the difference. While accepting that market forces could constitute a genuine material difference, the ECJ indicated that the defence would only hold good for such part of the difference as could be attributed to that reason. Thus, if a proportion of the difference could not be accounted for in this way, there would be no objective justification in respect of it.

7–016   Both *Rainey* and *Enderby* proceeded on the basis that the condition for higher pay (route of entry to the profession in *Rainey*, *de facto* sex segregation in *Enderby*) had an adverse impact on women and therefore indirectly discriminated on grounds of sex. Thus the factor put forward as a defence had to be objectively justifiable. However, in *Ratcliffe v North Yorkshire CC* (1995) the House of Lords went a step further and upheld an employment tribunal's finding that in that case, market forces were directly discriminatory. The work of the applicant catering assistants, all women, had been rated as equivalent to that of male manual workers employed by the Council in 1987, so they got equal pay. But when compulsory competitive tendering for certain services was introduced, the Council's own direct service organisation lost one of its contracts because it was undercut by a private company which paid its all-female workforce less than the Council did. To be sure of getting the remaining contracts, the Council made the women redundant and then took them back on lower rates of pay. The employment tribunal held that the women's pay had been reduced by market forces, which was a "material difference"; however, they considered that it was a material difference based on sex. Crucially, the tribunal found as a fact that catering work was low-paid precisely because it was done almost exclusively by women, and the lack of available part-time work where they lived meant that women would accept work on poor terms.

In giving the opinion of the House of Lords upholding the tribunal's decision, Lord Slynn argued that the EqPA should be interpreted without importing the distinction between direct and indirect discrimination found in the SDA. However, this seems inconsistent with the pronouncements of the ECJ in *Jenkins v Kingsgate* (1981) and *Enderby* (1993). Given the impact of Community law, where this distinction is used, on equal pay, it seems that it is inevitable that tribunals must consider whether reasons put forward in the context of the genuine material factor defence have discriminatory impact.

Market forces can work in another way to depress pay: limited budgets **7–017** may lead to employers paying less than the recognised rate for the job. In *Strathclyde Regional Council v Wallace* (1998) the applicants were women teachers who were "acting up" as principal teachers, but not being promoted or paid at the principal's rate. They claimed parity with male principal teachers, who were admittedly doing like work. The tribunal found that the reason for the difference was financial constraints on the council, coupled with its particular promotion rules. The House of Lords held that this was a material factor and, as it was not based on sex, they were not entitled to equal pay. The difference between this and the other cases is that here there was no evidence of the factor affecting women more than men. In fact, of 134 unpromoted teachers who claimed to be acting as principals, 81 were men and 53 were women. A gloss is put on this by *Benveniste v University of Southampton* (1989), where it was found that financial constraints which had led to a woman lecturer being taken on at a lower rate than normal in 1981 had eased a year later (surely the only university in the country where this was the case!). It was held that the university could no longer use the financial situation as a defence to her claim for equal pay.

Collective bargaining

In *Enderby v Frenchay HA* (1993), the main argument for the employer was **7–018** that, as the pay structures in each case resulted from free collective bargaining which was not affected by sex discrimination, this constituted sufficient justification (a genuine material factor) for the difference. Existing authority had been to the effect that if the difference between the woman's and the man's pay was because they had been graded differently (perhaps on merit) or because they belonged to different unions who bargained with the employer separately (as in *Reed Packaging v Boozer* (1988)), then this would constitute a genuine material difference.

The ECJ held that this was not an acceptable reason on its own for unequal pay where the result of the process adversely affected one sex. Separate collective bargaining could explain the differences, but would not on its own justify them. Thus in *British Coal Corp. v Smith* (1996) separate bargaining had led to jobs being done by male ancillary workers (such as gardeners) being assimilated to the better-paid "surface mineworker" grade, whereas this had not happened with ancillary work done by women (such as catering). Such an adverse impact required further justification beyond simply pointing to separate bargaining structures, and in the absence of any explanation the House of Lords held that the women were entitled to equal pay. This case, like *Enderby*, involved a group composed almost exclusively of women; however, in *British Road Services v Loughran* (1997) the Northern Ireland Court of Appeal held that this was not an essential requirement. The relevance of the proportion of women in the lower-paid work is that it identifies it as work being done predominantly by women and therefore at risk of being rated lower on that account. Thus the number of women in the bargaining unit is certainly pertinent, in that it indicates whether or not there is adverse impact which requires objective justification. Where separate collective bargaining structures, untainted by discrimination, result in unequal pay for different groups of workers but do not indicate an adverse impact on women, the genuine material factor defence can be relied on (*Glasgow City Council v Marshall* (2000)).

Performance-related pay

7–019 Giving additional "merit" payments for some staff over and above what others receive for the same job because of particularly good performance has long been a standard management practice. In the 1980s its newer incarnation, performance-related pay, was seen by some management gurus, and especially by the then Government, as the prime way of producing keen, highly motivated workers. In general, the idea is that targets are set for employees and their final salary in any particular year will contain a retrospective element reflecting how far they do or do not meet their targets. It would be cynical to suggest that for those in the lower echelons of management this policy worked to depress basic salary levels while for higher management, especially in newly privatised industries, it was a green light for massive hikes in pay levels.

The danger with any kind of merit payment or performance-related pay is that the judgments about who is deserving may be very subjective; if subjective, there is every chance that prejudice and discrimination may seep in, even unconsciously. The point was well taken by the ECJ in the *Danfoss* case (*Handels-og Kontorfunktionaerernes Forbund i Danmark v Dansk Arbejdsgiverforening (acting for Danfoss)* (1991)), where minimum rates of pay were set for each grade, but differentials were permitted according to merit. It was alleged that the system resulted in women generally being at the bottom of each grade earning less on average than the men. The ECJ held that, given the resulting disparity in pay and given that the criteria on which decisions were made were "lacking in transparency" (in that the employees did not know what the criteria were and how they were implemented) there was a potential breach of the Equal Pay Directive. The burden was therefore on the employer to prove that the differences in pay were not discriminatory. Specifically considering criteria which have a discriminatory impact, the ECJ held that reference to length of service was acceptable, but that reference to flexibility (in hours and place of work) or training must be justified by the employer showing their importance in relation to the work to be done, because they would tend to screen out women. This emphasis on openness requires employers operating merit payment schemes to ensure that clear criteria are adopted and applied objectively; to consider whether any criteria have a discriminatory impact, and if so, whether they are justifiable on objective grounds and to monitor the practice in relation to performance-related pay and other discretionary or merit pay systems.

The same considerations apply in relation to piecework. In the *Royal Copenhagen* case the ECJ held that Article 141 applied to piecework systems so that if a particular system had the consequence that the average piecework earnings of women (here employed as blue pattern painters on Royal Copenhagen china) were lower than the average earnings of men (employed as automatic machine operators) doing work of equal value, the difference would require justification by the employer. One difficulty here is that on a piecework system, differences in pay may well result purely from different work rates: this is, of course, the difference which the payment system is trying to take account of. However, provided that there are sufficiently large groups of workers to compare (so as to iron out any fortuitous or short-term differences) and all are included in establishing the average rate, the ECJ considered that appropriate comparisons could be made.

Red-circling

One of the first kinds of genuine material difference to be accepted was the **7–020** practice of red-circling, where an employee who was once on a higher-rated job is moved to a lower-rated job, often because of ill health, or because the job has been regraded, but is still paid at the higher rate. Workers of the opposite sex in the lower job cannot claim equal pay: the fact that he (as it usually is) has been red-circled in the list for special treatment can constitute a genuine material difference between their cases.

This is subject to the important qualification that if the reason for the higher pay is past discrimination, the defence will not apply. In *Snoxell v Vauxhall Motors* (1977) the company had had separate pay scales for men and women doing the same job before the EqPA. The scales were integrated before the Act came into force and the woman's rate was fixed as the rate for the job. Thereafter all new men doing the job got the same as the women, but the men who had previously been paid on the higher rate were red-circled. As their higher rate was attributable to sex discrimination, it was held that the defence was not available and the women were entitled to equal pay. Another relevant factor was that the company had no plans to phase out the differential in the future, which may also be relevant where regrading is the reason for red-circling.

Part-time working

Is the fact that the woman is part-time and the man full-time a genuine **7–021** material difference? As about 90 per cent of all part-time workers are women, worse terms for part-timers have a tendency to disadvantage women disproportionately. However, the concept of indirect discrimination is not specifically written into the EqPA. In *Jenkins v Kingsgate* (1981) the ECJ held that worse terms for part-time workers were capable of infringing

Article 141 because of the disproportionate effect on women, and that objective economic reasons were required to justify the difference. The ECJ put the point even more strongly in *Bilka-Kaufhaus v Weber von Hartz* (1987). It was clear from these cases that an employer who, without objective justification, treated part-timers less favourably than full-timers would usually be at risk of an indirect discrimination claim under the EqPA interpreted in accordance with EU law, although it remained the case that the adverse impact on women had to be proved: it could not simply be assumed (*cf. Staffs CC v Black* (1995): see now the Part-time Workers (Prevention of Less Favourable Treatment) Regulations 2000, above, para. 3–015).

Building on this the ECJ then moved to hold that state policies discriminating against part-time workers could also be in breach of EC law, holding in *Rinner-Kühn v FWW Spezial-Gebäudereinigung GmbH* (1989) that disqualifying German part-time workers from sickness benefits was discriminatory and in *Kowalska v Freie und Hansestadt Hamburg* (1990), that a redundancy scheme which excluded part-timers was unlawful: they should have received payments on a *pro rata* basis.

These decisions prompted the EOC to attack the rules requiring part-timers who worked between eight and 16 hours a week to have worked for more than five years before they qualify for employment protection rights. That claim was ultimately upheld by the House of Lords in *R. v Secretary of State for Employment ex p. EOC* (1994), as discussed in Chapter 3 (above, para. 3–014).

Other genuine material factors

7–022 Geographical differences have been held to justify different working conditions (*e.g. NAAFI v Varley* (1977)) and would permit employers to give "London weightings", for example. Differences in qualifications or experience may also constitute a genuine material factor, although in *Angestelltenbetriebsrat der Wiener Gebietskrankenkasse v Wiener Gebietskrankenkasse* (1999) the ECJ held that the different qualifications and training background of graduate psychologists and medical doctors meant that they were not employed on like work. It would seem from *North Yorks CC v Ratcliffe* (1996) that compulsory competitive tendering is capable of being a genuine material factor, provided there is no taint of sex discrimination. A final area of difficulty is whether radical differences in the job packages of the employees can count as a material difference. In *Leverton v Clwyd CC* (1988) a nursery nurse employed by the Council claimed equal pay with clerical staff. Her annual salary was considerably less than theirs, but on the other hand, she worked a 32½ hour week to their 37 hours and had 70 days' holiday a year to their 20 days. Taking these things into account, their hourly rates for the times they actually worked were in fact very similar. Although there was no evidence to show that the packages had been constructed so that more and less favourable terms in one were set off against the other, the House of Lords held that there was a genuine material difference between the two cases. However, it is difficult to reconcile this with their earlier decision in *Hayward v Cammell Laird* (1988) and the ECJ decision in *Barber v Guardian Royal Exchange* (1990), discussed next.

What is equalised?

If an equal pay claim succeeds, the woman's contract is deemed to include **7–023** an equality clause which has the effect that any term of the contract which is less favourable is modified to become as favourable as the man's (EqPA, s.1).

In *Hayward v Cammell Laird* (1988), a canteen cook claimed that her work was of equal value to that of three men employed by the same employer: a painter, a thermal insulation engineer and a joiner. While they were training they had all received the same rate of pay. But on completion, her pay was raised to £92 per week, while they got £117 per week. They also got a higher overtime rate. In 1984 an employment tribunal decided in her favour. The employers then tried to argue that there was a genuine material difference between her job and theirs: that although her pay rate was less, other terms and conditions were more favourable to her than to them. She got free meals and a paid meal break: they did not. She got two more days of paid holiday than them. Sickness arrangements were more beneficial for her than for them. Indeed, according to the employer's calculations, far from being £25 a week worse off than them, if you compared the whole job package she was actually £11 better off!

The House of Lords rejected the employer's contention that overall job packages were to be compared, holding that the Act required each separate provision to be looked at. Thus, if the jobs are of equal value, each term must be brought up to the best possible standard – for, of course, the men can claim parity with her for those terms of hers which are more beneficial.

Employers were most unhappy about the "leap-frogging" that would be allowed by this decision; however, the House of Lords indicated that the genuine material factor defence might be available in such a case, although it would be necessary for them to show that the more favourable term was designed to compensate for the less favourable one. In *Barber v Guardian Royal Exchange* (1990) the ECJ made it clear that the term-by-term approach was the correct one under European law, although it was unclear whether they would accept this qualification. This decision throws some doubt on the decision in *Leverton* on this point.

The meaning of "pay" in Article 141

While the Equal Pay Act was always clear that it applied to all terms of the **7–024** contract, not just pay, it did originally contain a number of exclusions relating to death or retirement benefits, as did the Sex Discrimination Act 1975. It was thought that these exceptions were permitted under EU law, a view apparently shared by EU administrators, who had issued directives which would eventually lead to equalisation on such matters, but not in the immediate future.

185

This was to reckon without the ECJ, which in a string of epoch-making decisions largely brought about total equality through its interpretation of the word "pay" in Article 141 as amplified by the Equal Pay Directive (76/207/EEC), which states that pay includes "all aspects and conditions of remuneration" (Art.1(2)). This has been interpreted to include: travel concessions on retirement for British Rail workers (*Garland v British Rail* (1983)); access to occupational pension schemes (*Bilka-Kaufhaus v Weber von Hartz* (1986)); sick pay (*Rinner-Kühn v FWW Spezial-Gebäudereinigung* (1989)); pension ages (*Barber v Guardian Royal Exchange* (1990)); pension benefits (*Barber*); statutory or contractual severance payments (*Barber*) and unfair dismissal compensation (*R. v Secretary of State ex p. Seymour-Smith* (1999)).

In *Barber v Guardian Royal Exchange* the ECJ stated that its judgment would not apply retrospectively, because they recognised how disruptive this could be, but did not make it clear what this meant in practice. It was clear that retirement ages and accrual of benefits would have to be equal from May 17, 1990 (the date on which the decision was handed down), but not whether benefits paid after that date but referring to service before it should be equalised, nor whether retirement ages could be equalised upwards, to the detriment of women with retiring ages lower than men's. Most of the issues were clarified following a series of references to the ECJ in subsequent years.

In *Ten Oever* (1993) it was made clear that equal occupational pension benefits were payable only in respect of employment subsequent to May 17, 1990. This was the narrowest possible interpretation of *Barber*; however, it accorded with the agreement made by EU Member States and recorded as the second Protocol to the Treaty of Maastricht. The decision also makes it clear that survivors' benefits are within the principle of equality. With regard to retirement ages, in *Smith v Avdel* (1994) and *Van den Akker v Stichting Shell* (1994) the ECJ held that retirement ages could be equalised upwards without infringing Article 141; however, they could not be levelled up retrospectively and in the period between May 17, 1990 and the implementation of a common retirement age, both sexes were entitled to the best conditions for either. Emphasising the nature of the equality principle as a fundamental right, the ECJ also held that transitional provisions which would inevitably perpetuate discrimination, albeit for a limited period, could not be condoned. In *Bird's Eye Walls Ltd v Roberts* (1994) the employer deducted an amount equivalent to state pension from occupational pension payments to women aged between 60 and 65, since otherwise they would be getting more than male pensioners, who would not qualify for a state pension until 65. It meant, of course, that the employer was actually paying women a lower rate than men. The Advocate-General's opinion was that this was sex discrimination, but that it was objectively justified and thus not a breach of Article 141. This could have opened the door to justification of direct discrimination, and was therefore castigated by commentators. Fortunately, the approach of the ECJ was different: in holding that the deduction was not a breach of Article 141 the ECJ held that the equality principle presupposed men and women in identical positions. This was not the case here because of the impact of the state pension scheme. However, while the outcome of the case may seem just, and while the ECJ avoided saying that direct discrimination could be justified, the reasoning in the judgment is not very convincing.

The final raft of issues concerned the rights of part-timers in relation to 7–025 pension schemes. It had already been decided in *Bilka-Kaufhaus v Weber von Hartz* (1986) that refusal of access was capable of constituting a breach of Article 141. In *Vroege v NCIV Institut voor Volkshuisvesting* (1994) and *Fisscher v Voorhuis Hengelo* (1994) the ECJ further decided that this applied to all part-timers, regardless of how many hours they worked and that there was no reason for the decision not to be applied retrospectively to 1976 – the date when it was held in *Defrenne v Sabena* (1976) that Article 141 had direct effect. Unlike the situation in *Barber*, the ECJ considered that there were no grounds for employers reasonably to have thought that the position was otherwise. However, employees wishing to claim had to be prepared to pay the relevant employee contributions.

Time limits

The extension of rights resulting from the *Barber* litigation caused a huge 7–026 number of retrospective claims to be lodged at tribunals by part-timers claiming that their employers had refused them access to occupational pension schemes, often in respect of periods of service which had finished many years earlier. The applicants faced two problems: first, under EqPA, s.2(4) claims for equal pay had to be lodged within six months of the claim arising. Thus, while the refusal to deny membership could be regarded as ongoing throughout the employment relationship, the applicant would have to present any claim within six months of the employment being terminated. Secondly, EqPA, s.2(5) stated that claims for equal pay could only be backdated to two years before the claim was made. In *Preston v Wolverhampton Healthcare Trust* (2000) the ECJ held that the six-month limitation period did not make the exercise of rights under EU law too difficult and was therefore compatible with EU law. The two-year limit on backdating claims was held to breach the EC law requirement for effective remedies. This was in line with the ECJ's earlier decision in *Levez v Jennings* (1999). When that case returned to the EAT (*Levez v Jennings (No.2)* (1999)) it held that the limit should be six years, as for other claims for breach of contract.

An extension to the limit on backdated claims to six years was eventually enacted by the Equal Pay Act 1970 (Amendment) Regulations 2003. The Regulations also provide that if an employer has deliberately concealed information about inequality from the employee (*e.g.* details of other people's earnings) then there is no limit to how far back a claim can go and the six-month time-limit for bringing claims is extended to six months from the date on which the employee could reasonably be expected to have become aware of the relevant information.

Relationship with the Sex Discrimination Act

The Equal Pay Act and the Sex Discrimination Act are intended to be 7–027 mutually exclusive, in that a claim ought to fall under one or the other but not both. The major benchmark is whether the complaint has anything to do with the contract of employment: if so then only the Equal Pay Act should apply. An offer of discriminatory terms, however, would come under the Sex Discrimination Act only.

Not only can there be traps for the unwary in this, it is also possible for some claims to fall through the gaps which are inevitably revealed where there is more than one Act to look at. Until the decision of the ECJ in *Jenkins v Kingsgate* (1981) it was not clear that the concept of indirect discrimination could be used in relation to an equal pay claim, and there are still doubts about how far decisions on one Act are relevant to the other. The distinction is rendered even more opaque by the flood of decisions on EC law where there is no such divide. For several years the EOC has advocated replacing the two principal Acts with a single code and it would be a welcome clarification if this were done.

Sick Pay

7–028   Under ERA, s.1(4)(d), details of any terms or conditions of employment relating to sickness or injury, including sick pay, should be given in the written statement of particulars of employment. Therefore there should always be an express term of the contract covering this, although this does not mean that the employer is bound to pay sick pay. However, there may still be situations where no express term covers the case, as where no written statement is given to the employee or where the employee wishes to argue that the statement is inaccurate. In such a case the court may have to decide whether there is an implied term of the contract that the employee should receive pay while off sick.

In older cases it was held that, in the absence of an express term, there was an implied term that sick pay should be paid. If the employer did not wish to pay, the remedy was either to put in an express term to that effect, or simply to dismiss the employee. Since the introduction of claims for redundancy and unfair dismissal, this reasoning is harder to justify. In any case, any presumption in favour of sick pay was cut down considerably in the leading decision of the Court of Appeal in *Mears v Safecar Security* (1982). Here there was no express term about sick pay, but it was well known that the employer's practice was not to provide it. The employee knew this – significantly, he made no attempt to claim sick pay until some time after he had left the employment altogether. It was held that the issue could not be solved simply by the application of a presumption. The tribunal or court should look at all the facts of the case and determine the correct inference in the light of all the circumstances (thus here nothing was payable). The presumption in favour of sick pay would only have effect if there was absolutely no other evidence to go on – which must be a very rare case.

7–029   Employees who are off work sick are usually entitled to state benefits – this is one of the things for which National Insurance is paid. Many employers take this entitlement into account when deciding on their own sick pay schemes. The most common provision is that the employer will top up the state benefit to the worker's usual level of wages. In 1983 the Government introduced the Statutory Sick Pay Scheme (now governed by the Social Security Contributions and Benefits Act 1992). The effect of the scheme was to shift the administrative burden of paying sickness benefits from the State to the employer. Instead of the employee putting in a claim to the Benefits Agency, the employee is now paid Statutory Sick Pay (SSP) by the employer, who, under the original scheme, deducted that amount from the National Insurance contributions it would normally have forwarded to the State. As employers pointed out, they received no allowance for the extra administrative burden of this scheme, but otherwise there was no cost to them.

The rationale behind this was that if the employer paid sick pay on a topping-up scheme, then the employer already had the administrative burden of making wage adjustments; also most employees are off work for a relatively short period of time. If the employer was already making adjustments, then it was a needless reduplication of effort for a government department to do the same thing. It also had the effect of making such benefits taxable in the hands of employees (because paid by the employer), whereas state benefits are not!

When introduced, the employer's obligation was relatively short term: the employer was responsible for paying SSP in respect of any individual employee for eight weeks in any one year. However, this was significantly extended by the Social Security Act 1985: the employer is now responsible for up to 28 weeks in any three-year period. To the fury of employers, the Statutory Sick Pay Act 1991 then reduced to 80 per cent the amount that they could set off against National Insurance contributions, except for small employers. This was estimated to cost industry over £250 million in its first year of operation. Not entirely unexpectedly, the Statutory Sick Pay Act 1994 removed the right to any reimbursement for employers, except small employers. The latest amendment removes the distinction between small and large employers. Any employer is now entitled to recover any amount by which their SSP payments exceed 13 per cent of their liability for National Insurance contributions in the same month (Statutory Sick Pay Percentage Threshold Order 1995 (SI 1995/12). Thus most of the time the entire burden of SSP falls on the employer, unless or until the employee qualifies for long-term incapacity benefit.

The fact that the employer is now responsible for paying state sickness benefit has no effect on the contractual position. If an employer does not have a contractual obligation to pay sick pay, this remains the case, even though the employer must pay SSP. If under the contract the employer is bound to pay sick pay, then this must be given in addition to SSP. Generally speaking, courts have been unwilling to allow employers to defeat employee expectations under contractual sickness or long-term incapacity schemes by moving the goalposts. In *Aspden v Webbs Poultry* (1996) it was held that the employer was not entitled to terminate the employee's employment so as to deprive him of benefits under a generous permanent health insurance scheme once he had qualified for them. Although there was an express term of the contract permitting termination on three months' notice, the High Court held that this was subject to an implied term prohibiting termination in these circumstances, except for good cause (see also *Adin v*

Sedco Forex (1997)). However, termination for good cause unrelated to the employee's illness will be allowed (*Hill v General Accident* (1998)).

Deductions from Wages

7–030   In the nineteenth century it was common for employers to abuse their dominant position by paying workers in kind instead of in cash (a "truck" or barter system), or by giving them vouchers which were only exchangeable in shops belonging to the employer ("tommy-shops"). The abuse lay in the fact that the goods given were not of the claimed value and the prices in the tommy-shops were artificially inflated. Protection against this exploitation began with the first Truck Act in 1831, which stipulated that workers must be paid in coin of the realm. In 1896 another Truck Act gave protection against another commonly abused power of an employer: the power to make deductions from wages as a disciplinary measure or for bad work. Such deductions had to be agreed in writing, and to be fair and reasonable.

The Truck Acts did not apply to all employees, but only to manual workers. In the post-war period the requirement to pay wages in coin of the realm became more onerous to employers, understandably concerned about security when large amounts of cash were needed, often on a weekly basis. The Payment of Wages Act 1960 allowed manual workers to be paid by cheque or by transfer to a bank account if they requested it in writing, but they could not be compelled to do so. The desire to facilitate the move towards "cashless pay" was the mainspring behind the reform of the Truck Acts by the Wages Act 1986 which repealed the Truck Acts 1831–1940, thus permitting employers to pay all employees by cheque or money transfer rather than by cash.

The replacement of the Truck Acts by the Wages Act 1986 (now ERA, Pt II) led to significant reforms in the law relating to the employer's right to make deductions from wages. The scope of the protection is considerably greater, in that it applies to all workers, defined as including not only employees but anyone rendering personal service under a contract other than as a professional or someone carrying on a business (ERA, s.230(3)). However, the protection given is narrower, in that there is no requirement that deductions must be fair and reasonable. Claims under ERA, Pt II are now within the jurisdiction of employment tribunals (s.23) – a point of some significance, as will be seen.

When are deductions allowed?

7–031   A deduction is unlawful unless it is authorised in one of three ways (s.13(1)). Firstly, it may be authorised by statute. Clearly there is nothing wrong with deducting PAYE contributions and the like. Secondly, it may be authorised by a term of the contract, provided that either the contract is in writing or the term is notified in writing to the worker before the deduction is made (s.13(2)). Finally, it may be authorised by specific consent of the worker, signified in writing. To ensure fairness to the employee, the Act gives no effect to a "consent" or to an "agreement" to a term allowing the deduction given after the events leading to it. But provided the consent or agreement is given before the event, it is valid even if the notification in writing is given later, provided it is notified before the deduction is made (see *York City & District Travel v Smith* (1990)).

All of this is subject to basic contractual principles. If an employer wishes to introduce a power to make deductions, this variation will require agreement from existing employees before it will become effective. In *Kerr v Sweater Shop* (1996) the EAT in Scotland held that displaying a notice in the factory was not sufficient notification to employees of a proposed variation which would reduce the employer's obligation to pay accrued holiday pay on termination.

While section 13(1) states when an employer will be allowed to make deductions, section 14 stipulates exceptional situations where the deduction will not infringe the Act if it is otherwise lawful. These are deductions made for overpayment of wages or expenses; in consequence of disciplinary proceedings held by virtue of a statutory provision; because of a statutory requirement; where the worker has agreed in writing to a deduction being made in favour of a third party (*e.g.* union subscriptions); where the worker has taken part in industrial action; and finally where the worker has agreed for a court or tribunal order obtained against her by the employer to be satisfied in this way.

In *Home Office v Ayres* (1992) the EAT held that overpayments could only be deducted where there was power to do so at common law. However, considering a deduction in relation to industrial action in *Sunderland Polytechnic v Evans* (1993) a different EAT concluded that the earlier decision was wrong: if a deduction comes under section 14 the tribunal has no jurisdiction under the Act at all and cannot therefore consider whether it is lawful or not. This was applied by the EAT in relation to overpayments in *SIP (Industrial Products) Ltd v Swinn* (1994). Lawfulness of such a deduction is a question to be decided at common law.

The exception for deductions made in consequence of disciplinary **7–032** proceedings "if those proceedings were held by virtue of any statutory provision" (s.14(2)) seems clearly to apply only to some public employments, such as the police, where disciplinary procedures are regulated by statute. In *Chiltern House v Chambers* (1990) the EAT rejected the argument that the references to disciplinary proceedings in the EPCA (now ERA) brought them within its scope.

A tribunal only has jurisdiction under ERA, Pt II if there has been a "deduction" and the deduction is out of "wages". The definition of both terms gave rise to a lot of case law after 1986 because the extension of protection from deductions to all kinds of employees seemed to offer a back door way of getting some contractual disputes in front of employment tribunals. Before contractual jurisdiction was conferred on employment tribunals in 1994, this was important. Suppose that an employee claiming unfair dismissal also wanted to claim that she had not received outstanding holiday pay or notice money: her entitlement to the latter depended on the contract and she could find herself needing to take county court proceedings as well as making an employment tribunal claim. Hence it became common for employees to claim that failure to pay things like notice money were really deductions from wages and within the protection of wages jurisdiction of tribunals and, from forming 1.5 per cent of all claims in 1987–88, ERA, Pt II claims formed 24 per cent by 1995. Now that tribunals can hear most contractual claims arising out of termination of employment, the problem is mostly solved; however, it may remain an issue where there is no termination, as in *Sunderland Polytechnic v Evans* (1993).

The question of what would count as a deduction was definitively analysed by the House of Lords in *Delaney v Staples* (1992). The applicant was summarily dismissed but was given a cheque for £82 as payment in lieu of notice. The cheque was later stopped. She also claimed to be entitled to commission and holiday pay amounting to £55.50. She claimed at an employment tribunal that these were unlawful deductions from wages contrary to the protection of wages legislation. The employer's central argument here was that no payment at all was not a deduction from payment, that there was a distinction between a deduction from a payment recognised to be due and a total non-payment resulting from a denial of liability to pay. It was also denied that a payment in lieu of notice could be regarded as "wages", defined in ERA, s.27 as

".. . any sums payable to the worker by his employer in connection with his employment, including – (a) any fee, bonus, commission, holiday pay or other emolument referable to his employment, whether payable under his contract or otherwise".

Giving the opinion of the House, Lord Browne-Wilkinson adopted the opinion of the Court of Appeal that any deficiency counts as a deduction and that the Wages Act does not distinguish between non-payment, refusal to pay and deduction. Turning to the definition of "wages", he noted that the phrase "payment in lieu of notice" is commonly used in four separate situations. The first situation is where the employer lawfully terminates the contract with notice but does not require the employee to work during the notice period and pays the wages as a lump sum. The second and third situations are where the employer terminates the contract summarily and pays the employee a lump sum and either the contract permits termination in this manner or the employee agrees to it. In each of these cases the employer would not be acting in breach of contract. The fourth and most common situation of payment in lieu is where the employer terminates the contract summarily without the employee's agreement and offers payment in lieu of notice. Here the employer may be in breach of contract and the payment in lieu operates as a set-off, or usually an extinction, of the employee's right to claim damages.

While accepting that the term "wages" was defined widely enough to cover all such payments, the House nevertheless declined to hold that payments in lieu in the last three categories were within ERA, Pt II because of the inconsistent results which would follow.

Retail workers

Special provision is made under ERA, ss.17–22 for retail workers who are **7–033** sometimes subject to onerous contract terms requiring them to make good cash shortages or stock deficiencies out of their wages. Those involved in the supply of services (including financial services) as well as in the supply of goods are covered (s.17(2)). Any deduction from wages to cover shortages (or as a disciplinary fine) would in any case have to be lawful according to the rules already considered, but for retail workers the Act limits the amount that can be recovered on any one occasion to not more than 10 per cent of the gross wage. This is to stop the worker's entire wage or a substantial part of it from being wiped out by a claw-back, as had occurred in some notorious cases. It is also necessary for the deduction to be made within 12 months of the deficiency being discovered.

This protection has been criticised as inadequate in two main respects: firstly, the 10 per cent limit does not apply to a final payment, so the last pay packet the worker receives could still be empty; secondly, and more fundamentally, the Act does not control the substance of such clauses, which may therefore operate when the employee is in no way at fault.

The National Minimum Wage

The best protection for employees is combination in trade unions. Collec- **7–034** tive power, if not unduly limited by law, should ensure that workers' interests are reasonably protected. However, there have always been industries where organisation has been very difficult, and in these areas legislative protection is needed. Among the various strategies which can be used to this end is the minimum wage. Originally the strategy adopted in the United Kingdom was to provide for minimum terms and conditions only in certain industries where the problem of low wages was considered to be acute.

The genesis of this system was the Trade Boards Act 1909 which established boards which fixed minimum wages in the "sweated trades" – those where the exploitation of workers was most acute. They were replaced by wages councils. A wages council was composed of representatives of both sides of the industry together with an uneven number of independent members whose vote could break any deadlock. Originally wages councils could set a minimum hourly wage and terms about holidays. In 1975 the Employment Protection Act significantly extended their powers by allowing them to make orders about all terms and conditions of employment and to make these orders by their own authority rather than submitting them first to the Secretary of State. The reforms of 1975 (consolidated with earlier legislation in the Wages Councils Act 1979) were the high point for wages councils. The Conservative Government of the 1980s, firmly committed to a policy of deregulation of industry, was ideologically opposed to this kind of system; however, it remained the case that the United Kingdom was a signatory to the ILO Convention No.26, which requires the maintenance of minimum wage fixing machinery.

In June 1985 the Government gave notice to denounce (withdraw from) the ILO Convention, and the Wages Act 1986 repealed the Wages Councils Act 1979. Existing wages councils (26 of them) were retained in existence, but their powers were drastically curtailed. The final stage was reached when TURERA abolished the remaining wages councils in 1993.

During the early 1990s the Labour Party committed itself to universal minimum wage legislation as the appropriate strategy to combat the problems of low pay. Following its return to power in May 1997, consultation on a national minimum wage was one of its first tasks. The framework for the system was set up by the National Minimum Wage Act 1998 and implemented by the National Minimum Wage Regulations 1999.

Who is covered?

7–035   In keeping with its general policy of inclusive employment protection rights, entitlement to the minimum wage is extended to "workers", defined in section 54 in parallel terms to ERA, s.230(3) (see above, para. 3–009), thus including at least some workers on contracts for services. Agency workers are expressly covered by s.34 and the problem of identifying who is the employer is solved by providing that the employer for purposes of the National Minimum Wage Act is the one who is responsible for paying the worker, or who actually pays him or her. Following the practice of the wages council legislation, homeworkers are also included even if they sometimes get others to perform some of the work (s.35). Furthermore, the Secretary of State has power under section 41 to extend the legislation to "any individual of a prescribed description" who would not otherwise count as a worker.

The National Minimum Wage is usually reviewed annually in accordance with the recommendations of the Low Pay Commission. It was £4.50 an hour in October 2003. There are important differences for young workers, apprentices and trainees. The rates for younger workers have been criticised both on grounds of their complexity and because in principle it is argued not to be fair for one worker to be paid less than another where they are doing the same work. That said, however, we have seen with equal pay that experience can be a factor justifying different pay for the same work and employers have traditionally been reluctant to take on young workers on exactly the same terms as older workers. Thus, the National Minimum Wage Regulations 1999 provide that workers aged 16 and 17 are not entitled to the National Minimum Wage. Those aged between 18 and 22 were entitled to a minimum rate of only £3.80 per hour in October 2003. However, apprentices aged 18 do not qualify for this rate, and apprentices aged between 19 and 26 are not entitled to it during the first 12 months of their apprenticeship. As if this were not confusing enough, apprentices must be distinguished from other trainees. Trainees aged 22 or more can be paid a minimum rate of £3.80 per hour, but only for the first six months of their training. To guard against abuse, the Regulations provide that trainees must undergo accredited training on at least 26 days during this six-month period. In *Edmunds v Lawson* (2000) the Court of Appeal held that a pupil barrister aged over 26 was not entitled to the minimum wage, since although she was properly to be regarded as having a contract with the members of her chambers, this was neither a contract of employment nor of apprenticeship.

Calculating pay

In order to check whether there has been compliance with the obligation to **7–036** pay the National Minimum Wage there has to be a mechanism for reducing all forms of payment to a notional hourly rate. This further requires rules as to which elements of a remuneration package will and will not count in this assessment and as to the period of time over which the measurement will take place. The last of these is the most straightforward element. The "payment reference period" cannot be longer than one month (reg.10). If the worker is paid at shorter intervals (*e.g.* weekly or daily), the period is reduced accordingly.

Which payments count towards the National Minimum Wage?

Calculations are based on gross pay *less* loans from the employer; any **7–037** advance on wages; pension payments; a lump sum paid on retirement; redundancy payments; an overtime premium; and any expenses paid, allowances given or amounts deducted for expenditure required by the employer. The essential idea is that the employer should not be able to pass itself off as paying the minimum wage by including sums payable for other reasons or sums which are essentially for the employer's benefit. If, for example, a shop assistant in a clothes shop were to be given an allowance to buy clothes from the shop to wear as a kind of uniform and advertisement for the shop's products, this allowance would not count in assessing her hourly rate, since it is not money which she is free to spend as she wishes but must be spent for the employer's benefit. An overtime premium is the amount by which the overtime rate exceeds the usual hourly rate, and the reason for excluding it is the principle that the worker should not have to work overtime in order to reach the level of the National Minimum Wage. However, subject to the requirements of the Working Time Regulations (above, para. 6–038), there is nothing to stop an employer requiring workers to do a certain amount of overtime and consolidating the amount equivalent to the overtime premium into the basic hourly rate. Accommodation is the only benefit in kind which can be counted towards discharging the employer's obligation to provide the National Minimum Wage, but only to a maximum £3.50 per day.

Elements which do count towards the minimum wage include incentive payments; performance-related pay; bonuses; and tips, gratuities or service charges paid through the employer (*cf. Nerva v UK* (2002)).

The hourly rate

7–038 Having established the amount of pay which the worker received in the relevant payment reference period, the next stage is to calculate the number of hours worked during that period. The Regulations identify four kinds of work. The first is time work, which is work paid according to the time the worker works and which is not salaried hours work (reg.3). The hours need not be regular and it should be noted that this category includes piecework in situations where the worker is contracted to work for a set number of hours. To find out if time workers are being paid the National Minimum Wage, the hours worked in the payment reference period are simply divided by the pay received during that period. The second kind is salaried hours work, which is work paid for by an annual salary referable to a fixed number of basic hours per year, divided into weekly or monthly instalments (reg.4). Variations in hours worked in any week or month do not result in alteration to the weekly or monthly salary. To find out whether salaried hours workers are receiving the National Minimum Wage, their annual hours are divided by 12 or 52 (according to what is the payment reference period) and the amount of pay received in the payment reference period is divided by the resulting number of hours to get the hourly rate.

There are no great difficulties in establishing an hourly rate where hours are stipulated in this way. More problematic are the last two kinds of work. Output work is work which, but for the Act, would be paid for entirely by results – e.g. piecework where the worker has no set hours, or is paid entirely by commission (reg.5). There are two options for converting pay for output work to an hourly rate. The first is to divide the worker's pay by the actual number of hours she works in the reference period; the second is to divide the worker's pay by a "fair estimate" of hours worked in the reference period. A "fair estimate" must be agreed in writing between the parties ahead of each reference period and set out the number of hours the work is likely to take. The worker must keep a record of actual hours worked, to be passed to the employer, and there must also be a contract setting out the piece rate. In the first situation, the worker is entitled to the National Minimum Wage for every hour worked. In the second, the worker is entitled to the National Minimum Wage only for the number of hours identified in the "fair estimate".

The final category is unmeasured work, which is anything which does not fall within one of the preceding three categories (reg.6). Again, there are two options for dealing with this: either the National Minimum Wage is paid for every hour actually worked, or it is paid in accordance with a "daily average" agreement. A daily average agreement must be in writing, agreed with the worker before the start of the reference period and set out a realistic daily average number of hours.

The importance of the difference between timed work and unmeasured work is illustrated by *Walton v Independent Living Organisation* (2003), concerning a care worker whose job required her to live in for three days a week with a client who needed someone on hand at all times in case she suffered an epileptic fit. The Court of Appeal upheld a tribunal's decision that this fell into the unmeasured time category rather than the timed work category. The significance of this was that she was then only entitled to the National Minimum Wage for the estimated seven hours per day which her duties actually required rather than 24 hours a day as she claimed. It will be clear from this that the definition of working time for the purposes of the National Minimum Wage Regulations 1999 is different from that under the Working Time Regulations 1998 (above, para. 6–041).

Enforcement

Employers must keep adequate records for establishing that they are **7–039** complying with the requirements to pay the National Minimum Wage, including where appropriate training agreements, fair estimate agreements and daily average agreements. Failure to do so, or falsifying records, is a criminal offence. These records are not only for the benefit of the Inland Revenue, which is the government body responsible for enforcement of this legislation, but also for workers themselves, who have a right to inspect their own records, accompanied by someone of their choice if they wish, and to take copies of them. This is part of the policy of trying to ensure that the national minimum wage legislation is largely self-enforcing. Thus, although failure to comply with the National Minimum Wage Act is a criminal offence which is punishable with a fine of up to £5,000, the remedies open to individuals may be more important in practice.

Workers can submit a claim to an employment tribunal where they believe that they have not been paid the National Minimum Wage. In these circumstances, the normal burden of proof is reversed: the employer must prove that the claim is not well-founded. Workers may also take tribunal proceedings (under the ERA, as amended) where the employer dismisses them or subjects them to a detriment for asserting their rights to the National Minimum Wage, or because they are, or will become, eligible for it.

Critics of the minimum wage legislation argued that it would lead to higher unemployment as employers would not be able to afford to pay these rates. The contrary argument is that employers paying very low wages should not be effectively subsidised by the State through the social security system. In the first months after the National Minimum Wage Regulations 1999 came into force 3,000 complaints of non-compliance were made to the Inland Revenue and there did not appear to be an adverse impact on the availability of jobs. The legislation apppeared, therefore, to be having the desired effects.

8. Discipline and Dismissal

In a contract of indefinite duration, such as contracts of employment **8–001** usually are, it is almost inevitable that dispute will arise because one or other party is dissatisfied with some aspect of the other's performance. When the common law was all that regulated the employment relationship, virtually the only recourse for a dissatisfied party was to terminate the relationship. Clearly, this was an easier option for an employer than for an employee. Provided that the contract was terminated lawfully, usually by giving notice of a certain length, no further remedies were available. It was open to an employer to provide for disciplinary powers short of dismissal by express term (*e.g.* to make deductions from wages, above, para. 7–030 and *Sagar v Ridehalgh* (1931), above, para. 4–014). The weak bargaining position of the employee meant that there was no corresponding way of holding the employer to what was agreed.

The common law left employees in particular extremely exposed since there was no fetter on the employer's ultimate disciplinary power of dismissal and workers could be lawfully deprived of their means of livelihood for no good reason. The only time the employee would have a remedy was if the dismissal was in breach of contract, in which case it was possible to sue for wrongful dismissal, although the remedy, as we shall see, was limited.

This changed with the introduction of the Redundancy Payments Act **8–002** 1965 (now ERA 1996, Pt XI) and the statutory claim for unfair dismissal in 1972. These did not affect the common law position, but they did give employees an alternative, statutory claim, in specified circumstances. Unfair dismissal law soon began to have an impact on employers' disciplinary practices, because employers were likely to be found to have acted unfairly if they had not followed norms of good industrial practice, especially those set out in the Acas Code of Practice (No.1) on Disciplinary Practices and Procedures in Employment, issued in 1977.

In recent years, statute law has intervened more directly in relation to disciplinary and grievance procedures. First, the Employment Relations Act 1999, s.10 introduced a right for workers to be accompanied at disciplinary or grievance meetings. This triggered a wholesale revision of the Acas Code, which was republished in 2000 as the Acas Code on Disciplinary and Grievance Procedures. Secondly, the Employment Act 2002 provided the framework for statutory disciplinary and grievance procedures to be introduced as part of the contract of employment. Consultation about its implementation was ongoing in 2003 and it will commence in October 2004. This will necessitate a further revision of the Acas Code.

In the meantime, the common law relating to termination of the contract has continued to develop, both in relation to the extent of the claim for damages and in relation to the possible enforcement of the contract. The relationship between the statutory regime to the common law has given rise to difficult issues, which are increasingly being heard in employment tribunals, as tribunals were given jurisdiction over most claims for breach of contract arising on termination of the contract of employment in 1994 (see above, para. 1–020).

This chapter will first consider the common law relation to termination of the contract of employment, principally the claim for wrongful dismissal. It will then deal with the law of unfair dismissal, including the right to be accompanied and the new statutory disciplinary and grievance procedures. The claim for a redundancy payment, the third possible course of action which may be available to an employee on dismissal, will be examined in Chapter 9.

Termination at Common Law

Wrongful dismissal

8–003 Wrongful dismissal is basically an action for breach of contract, although we will see that to some extent there is a special regime for employment contracts. Like other claims for breach of contract, it may be brought in the county court or High Court, although employment tribunals now have jurisdiction also in many cases (see above, para. 1–020). There are two conditions to be fulfilled for a successful action for wrongful dismissal: first, that the employer terminated the contract without notice or with inadequate notice, and secondly, that the employer was not justified in doing so.

Notice

8–004 As noted already, contracts of employment are usually drawn up to last indefinitely. But people cannot be tied to each other forever, and at common law the rule grew up that either party could lawfully terminate the contract of employment provided that reasonable notice was given. It is interesting to contrast this with the United States, where instead the doctrine of employment-at-will developed, meaning that employment continues only so long as both parties want it to, and that either party can terminate the contract without notice. American employers frequently do just that, which makes for an entirely different perspective on the employer-worker relationship.

At common law it is still true that if reasonable notice to terminate is given, then the contract is terminated lawfully, and it follows that the employee has no claim for wrongful dismissal. It does not matter that the employer has terminated for a bad or arbitrary reason, or indeed no reason at all; nor does it matter for how long the employee has been employed, nor his record: provided that the employer has given adequate notice, or pay in lieu of notice, the employee has no claim. This is seen as the major defect of the common law position. It seems unjust that an employee can be thrown out of work without compensation when there is no good reason for the dismissal.

Since 1963 employers have been required to give employees a written statement of the notice they must give, and be given, for the contract to be terminated (see now ERA, s.1(4)(e)). Thus today in all cases this is something which should be covered by an express term of the contract. Furthermore, under ERA, s.86, there are certain minimum periods of notice: an employee with between one month and two years of continuous employment must be given at least one week's notice; an employee with between two and 12 years of continuous employment must have one week for every complete year of employment (thus 10 years' employment equals 10 weeks' notice), and employees who have served for over 12 years are entitled to a minimum of 12 weeks' notice.

The minimum notice which the employee must give is only one week. The lack of symmetry may seem surprising at first sight, but in fact is a sensible recognition of two facts: firstly, that it is usually easier for an employer to replace an employee than for an employee to get another job, hence the employee should be given more warning; secondly, that it is easier for an employer to stipulate a longer period expressly than it is for an employee. In practice most employers require employees to give the same amount of notice as they are entitled to receive.

Where the contract specifies an entitlement to notice which is greater **8–005** than the minimum statutory period, the employee is entitled to rely on the more beneficial provision, and can claim for wrongful dismissal if given less notice than stated in the contract even if the notice given satisfies the statutory requirement. It has further been held, at least once, that "reasonable notice" is capable of being longer than either the statutory or contractual period (*Hill v Parsons* (1972)). However, the facts of the case were unusual. Hill had been employed by the company as a chartered engineer for 35 years and was two years short of retirement. The employer was faced with strike action unless he was dismissed, because of his refusal to join the union. Reluctantly, the company dismissed him with a month's notice. Under statute, he should have had three months. However, the Court of Appeal held that reasonable notice in his case would be at least six months, and perhaps even 12. But two things should be noted: the employer here retained confidence in the employee and had no desire to dismiss him and, even more importantly, by extending his period of employment in this way, the Court of Appeal ensured that the termination would only take effect after the new law of unfair dismissal had come into force – under which Hill would have far more extensive remedies.

Justified summary dismissal

Even if the employer terminates the contract with no notice or with **8–006** inadequate notice, the employee will not be able to claim wrongful dismissal if the employer is justified in thus summarily dismissing him or her. When is summary dismissal justified? Essentially, in the same circumstances in which an innocent party would be entitled to terminate any other contract: that is, when the other party has committed a fundamental breach. Translated into the language of employment law, an employer is entitled to dismiss an employee summarily if the employee has committed an act of gross misconduct. The test is whether the employee has disregarded a fundamental term of the contract (*cf. Laws v London Chronicle* (1959), above para. 4–026). In that case, the employee had been faced with conflicting orders by two superiors, and should not have been dismissed for obeying the wrong one.

Generally speaking, things like disobedience, dishonesty and violence are regarded as gross misconduct, although it seems that the employer may stipulate offences as very serious which would not usually be so regarded, to take account of the firm's particular circumstances. For example, smoking in prohibited areas would be much more serious where food is being prepared or where there is a fire risk than it would be in the average solicitor's office. The EAT has held that an employee who deliberately gains unauthorised access to the company's computer system is guilty of gross misconduct, although they also recommended that employers should make their rules abundantly clear and have them available for reference near computer terminals (*Denco Ltd v Joinson* (1991); see also the Acas Code of Practice on Disciplinary and Grievance Procedures, para.5). The Acas Code of Practice on Disciplinary and Grievance Procedures is strictly relevant to unfair rather than wrongful dismissal cases, but in practice it is influential in all areas of dismissal law. It identifies the following as examples of gross misconduct: theft, fraud and deliberate falsification of records; physical violence; serious bullying or harassment; deliberate damage to property; serious insubordination; misuse of an organisation's property or name; bringing the employer into serious disrepute; serious incapability while on duty brought on by alcohol or illegal drugs; serious negligence which causes or might cause unacceptable loss, damage or injury; serious infringement of health and safety rules; and serious breach of confidence (para.7).

A congeries of minor offences may coalesce into a sufficient reason for summary dismissal, as in *Pepper v Webb* (1969), where a gardener with a history of inefficiency and insolence surpassed himself when his employer remonstrated with him by confiding, "I couldn't care less about your bloody greenhouse and your sodding garden" and walking off. Accepting that this was the last straw, the Court of Appeal held that he had not been wrongfully dismissed.

At common law, in stark contrast to the law of unfair dismissal, the employer may justify a dismissal by reference to facts only discovered after the contract has been terminated. This was established in *Boston Deep Sea Fishing v Ansell* (1888), where the managing director of a company was summarily dismissed on inadequate grounds, but was later found to have been taking bribes: a breach of his duty of good faith and thus a fundamental breach of the contract.

Suspension

Suspending an employee with or without pay is something an employer may **8–007**
wish to do either as a disciplinary measure or where there is not enough
work to occupy everyone. Suspension with pay is frequently used where
serious allegations of misconduct need to be investigated; suspension
without pay is sometimes used as a punishment in circumstances where
dismissal is thought to be too severe. It is important to note that unless the
contract of employment permits it, suspension without pay will be a
fundamental breach of contract by the employer and thus will constitute
wrongful dismissal. A good example is *Hanley v Pease* (1915) where the
employee was absent one day without permission; when he turned up the
next day, the employer suspended him without pay for the day as a
punishment. There was no power in the contract to do this, and so the
employee was entitled to sue for his day's wages – and this was despite the
fact that his absence was a breach which would have justified the employer
in dismissing him. But the employer had waived the right to do that, and
had instead committed a fundamental breach by suspending him without
pay.

The right to suspend without pay is useful to an employer, and the Acas
Code of Practice on Disciplinary and Grievance Procedures recommends
its use as a sanction, provided that it is permitted by the contract. In cases
where suspension is used because of a shortage of work, employees are
protected to some extent by being able to claim a redundancy payment if
the lay-off is for a lengthy period (see below, para. 9–016). It is possible for
there to be an implied term allowing suspension, for example, that it is
customary in the trade (*cf. Marshall v English Electric* (1945)), but it is
clearly safer to have an express term. From the point of view of employees
also, it may be to their advantage for the employer to have the power to
impose sanctions short of dismissal, since it may result in a job being
retained following misconduct where an employer without such a power
would have dismissed rather than let it go at a warning.

Suspension on full pay is not usually a breach of contract by an employer:
for the situations where it may be, see the discussion of the "right to work"
(above, para. 4–019).

Damages for wrongful dismissal

Since the basic common law position is that dismissal can take place **8–008**
lawfully at any time and for any reason, provided that adequate notice is
given, it follows that employees can only complain of wrongful dismissal
where they get no notice or short notice and no pay in lieu of notice. As a
result, the courts held that the employee's damages were limited to the
equivalent of net wages during the notice period. Since they could have
been lawfully dismissed had proper notice been given, all they have lost by
the wrongful dismissal is wages for the notice period. Considering that
many manual workers only get the minimum statutory period of notice, and
that even professional workers are unlikely to be entitled to more than six

months' notice, wrongful dismissal is not a very expensive option for the employer, and, until employment tribunals had jurisdiction over these matters, claiming damages was rarely worth the bother for the employee.

Despite many assaults on the citadel, the courts refused to extend the damages claim, because of the House of Lords' decision in *Addis v Gramophone Co Ltd* (1909), where the employee was denied damages for injured feelings and for the fact that the manner of his dismissal was likely to make it more difficult to find another job. This was relied on in *Bliss v South East Thames RHA* (1987) to prevent a claim in respect of illness said to have been brought on by the dismissal. The principle is now subject to an important qualification as a result of the House of Lords' decision in *Malik v BCCI* (1997). The Bank of Credit and Commerce International collapsed in a blaze of publicity in 1991, owing US $6 billion. It had been insolvent for five years, but this was concealed through the fraudulent dealings of about 30 very senior officers of the bank, including its president and chief executive. All 1,400 UK employees lost their jobs. The two claimants, who had been employed as branch managers in London, claimed damages for breach of contract resulting from their dismissal. Essentially, this was a claim for what came to be called "stigma" damages, on the grounds that their association with a bank which had been guilty of wrongdoing would be very harmful to their career prospects in the financial services industry.

The House of Lords allowed their claim that they should be compensated for loss resulting not so much from their dismissal but because of their employer's breach of the implied term of mutual trust and confidence (see above, para. 4–024). The House of Lords held that this did not conflict with the rule in *Addis* because their claim was not because of the manner of dismissal but because of breach of a different term of the contract, which was an issue that had not arisen in *Addis*.

8–009   Nonetheless, the decision in *Malik v BCCI* (1997) revealed a potential route for extra damages to be claimed in wrongful dismissal cases because the employee could almost always argue that the wrongful dismissal also breached the implied duty to maintain mutual trust and confidence. In the immediate aftermath of a major common law development there is usually a period of backtracking as the courts try to contain what they fear may be a flood of litigation, followed by a gradual move forward as the new approach is assimilated. This is the pattern which followed *Malik v BCCI*, most significantly with the House of Lords' decision in *Johnson v Unisys Ltd* (2001). The claimant sought damages for mental breakdown and consequent loss of earnings alleged to have been caused by the manner of his dismissal. The House of Lords held that damages were not available for a breach of mutual trust and confidence consisting of the manner of dismissal because the term did not survive the termination of the contract and because it would be wrong to circumvent the statutory protection for unfair dismissal (under which compensation is subject to a limit) by providing a common law remedy instead. The first reason is an argument of principle; the second, one of policy, and arguably easier to defend. The problem with the first reason in *Johnson v Unisys Ltd* is that it leaves it very unclear as to when damages for a breach of mutual trust and confidence will be available.

In *Gogay v Hertfordshire CC* (1999) the Court of Appeal awarded damages for breach of mutual trust and confidence when an employee was unjustifiably suspended, and this decision was not disapproved by the House of Lords in *Johnson v Unisys Ltd*. This led some judges to think that the distinction was to be drawn between cases where the contract had not been terminated (like *Gogay*), where damages for breach of mutual trust and confidence could be claimed, and cases where the contract had been terminated (like *Johnson*), where the only remedy would be the statutory claim for unfair dismissal. However, this would be an illogical distinction and would also mean that an employer could escape liability for damages for breach of the implied term by the simple expedient of sacking the employee! Hence the latest view of the Court of Appeal in *McCabe v Cornwall CC* (2003), which is that the issue is really whether or not there is identifiable damage caused by the breach of the implied term which can be seen as separate from any damage flowing from the act of dismissal. The former will be compensatable, the latter will not.

The limitation of damages in most cases to the notice period, coupled with the generally held view that a claim for damages was the only possible remedy for wrongful dismissal, explains why the common law was thought to be so inadequate a protection for employees. The only kind of worker for whom it offered much scope was the highly paid employee who was taken on for a lengthy fixed-term which could not be overridden by notice. Directors of companies and the managers of football teams are the usual beneficiaries of these kinds of terms. Hence the growing interest in methods of enforcing the contract.

Enforcement of the contract of employment

While the major drawback of the action for wrongful dismissal was that **8–010** damages were limited to the notice period, in the 1980s there was also increasing disenchantment with the law of unfair dismissal. Awards of compensation were running at very low levels and only about 40 per cent of all unfair dismissal claims before tribunals were succeeding. In 1994 employment tribunals were given jurisdiction to deal with breach of contract claims related to compensation up to the value of £25,000 and this also gave a fresh impetus to the common law claim. All these factors led to a revival of interest in the action at common law. True, damages may be limited. But what if it were possible to get an order enforcing the terms of the contract? That is, an order preventing the employer from dismissing in breach and keeping the contract alive on the terms agreed; this might be an order worth having.

The orthodox view of employment law has seen two major obstacles in the way of such developments. Firstly, orders for specific performance or injunctions are not available to enforce contracts of personal service. Secondly, it was thought that a termination by the employer must be effective even if in breach of contract and not accepted by the employee. The strength of these objections will be examined before looking at the creeping tide of enforcement orders.

Specific performance and injunctions

8–011 Because forcing someone to work for another without consent is tantamount to slavery or forced labour, it has been a general principle that specific performance of contracts of employment should not be ordered. This is one reason why the law has never reacted to strikes by ordering employees to go back to work. Also, since the contract is a contract for personal service, it has been thought similarly objectionable to compel employers to continue to employ someone they do not wish to employ. This common law position is reinforced now by TULRCA, s.236, which forbids orders for specific performance or injunction to compel anyone to work.

However, this basic position has never been entirely absolute. In *Lumley v Wagner* (1852) an opera singer was tempted into breaking her contract to sing exclusively in Lumley's theatre when offered more money by another impresario. Lumley was able to get an injunction to stop her working for the rival theatre. This did not force her to work for him, but merely stopped her entering another contract in breach of the first. (Incidentally, Lumley could also sue the other impresario for inducing her to break her contract: *Lumley v Gye* (1853), below, para. 12–025.) The process was taken a step further in *Warner Bros v Nelson* (1937), where the film star Bette Davis was proposing to break her eight-year contract with Warner Bros. The court granted an injunction to stop her making films for any other company in breach of contract. Did this not force her to work for Warner Bros, by closing off all other activity? The court held it did not: she could make her living in some other way, at least in theory.

The fact that such orders are practically equivalent to forcing the employee back to the original employer suggests that the objection to forced labour in the sense of economically forced labour is not actually as strong as it seemed at first sight. Furthermore, since 1975 employment tribunals have had the power to order employers to take back employees who have been unfairly dismissed. While it is true that in the end such an order will not be enforced against the obdurate employer (who will end up having to pay enhanced compensation, but need not take back the employee), this development nonetheless is another indication that traditional objections may have lost their strength.

As a result, in recent years there have been cases where the courts have accepted that an injunction may properly be granted against an employer to prevent a dismissal in breach of contract. One of the first was *Hill v Parsons* (1972), where an injunction was granted to prevent the employer dismissing the employee with inadequate notice. As noted above (para. 8–005), the circumstances of the case were rather special in that the employer did not really want to get rid of the employee, and the effect of the temporary injunction was to keep him in employment until the Industrial Relations Act came into force. In *Irani v Southampton & South West Hampshire AHA* (1985), where an interlocutory injunction was granted to stop a dismissal in breach of the contractual procedure, the fact that the employer retained confidence in the employee was seen as crucial to this sort of order.

The High Court actually granted a permanent injunction against an employer in *Jones v Gwent CC* (1992), although there have been no orders of specific performance as such. However, it would appear that this barrier has been lowered a great deal, even if it has not disappeared altogether.

Termination effective without acceptance

Usually, if one party to a contract commits a fundamental breach, the **8–012** innocent party may elect whether to accept it as a termination of the contract or to waive it and keep the contract alive. Traditionally it was argued that contracts of employment were an exception to this rule, so that if an employer dismissed an employee, albeit in fundamental breach, then that dismissal brought the contract to an end without the need for acceptance by the employee. One of several cases expressing this view is *Vine v National Dock Labour Board* (1957), where Lord Kilmuir said, "if the master wrongfully dismisses the servant . . . the employment is effectively terminated, albeit in breach of contract". However, at this time there was a lot of support for the view that any contract could be terminated by fundamental breach without acceptance, a view finally and firmly scotched by the House of Lords' decision in *Photo Production v Securicor* (1980).

Some of the difficulties reconciling the view that contracts of employment are different from other contracts in this regard were pointed out by Megarry V.C. in *Thomas Marshall v Guinle* (1978), where he noted that no one had ever doubted the correctness of the decisions in *Lumley v Wagner* (1852) and *Warner Bros v Nelson* (1937), yet if contracts of employment really were an exception to the general rule then the employers of these delinquent employees would have had no choice but to accept the breach and be relegated to a claim in damages. Megarry's admirable arguments were not given the attention they deserved when this issue was canvassed in front of employment tribunals in a number of cases where employers argued that by some particularly egregious misconduct the employee had "dismissed himself " – the employee's fundamental breach terminating the contract without any acceptance, (that is, dismissal) by the employer.

In unfair dismissal cases, this particular argument was finally rejected by the Court of Appeal in *LTE v Clarke* (1981) (below, para. 8–022), but even then it was argued in some quarters that this applied to unfair dismissal cases only. A final determination of the debate by the House of Lords was eagerly awaited: which makes it the more disappointing that when the opportunity to decide finally reached the House, the issue was ducked.

In *Rigby v Ferodo* (1988) the employer had reduced wages rather than make people redundant; however, they had never got the employees' agreement to this. After 18 months on reduced wages, an employee sued for back pay. The employers argued that their fundamental breach (in reducing pay without agreement) operated as a termination of the contract, and his continued employment must be construed as a new contract on new terms. The employee argued that there could be no termination in breach without his acceptance. The House of Lords effectively (and unnecessarily) drew a distinction between two kinds of fundamental breach. If, as here, the fundamental breach did not actually interrupt the employment, then they held that it did require acceptance before the contract came to an end. But they expressly declined to give an opinion on whether this was also the case if the fundamental breach took the form of a walking out by the employee (wrongful resignation), or refusal to treat the employee as employed by the employer (wrongful dismissal).

It is submitted that this distinction is without relevance and that the way is open for courts to hold that no breach terminates a contract of employment unless accepted by the innocent party. To this it may be objected that if the employer refuses to have the employee at work, then the employee has no choice but to accept the termination of the contract. However, it is fairly clear that the consideration provided by the employee under a contract of employment is being ready and willing to work, not actually performing work; as illustrated by the fact that the employer still has an obligation to pay wages even if there is no work for the employee to do. Therefore if the employer, in breach of contract, refuses to allow the employee to work, the employee may still perform her side of the bargain by remaining ready and willing to work. If this is correct, then until the employee accepts the termination (by taking another job, for example, or suing for unfair dismissal) she would remain entitled to wages, and this entitlement would not be limited to the notice period. So far there have been no successful claims for wages on this kind of argument, but it is a possible route for development. That the obstacles are not so great as once they seemed has been recognised in recent cases which will be examined next.

Limitations on the power to terminate

8–013 There are essentially two situations where it has been recognised that the contract may contain limitations on the employer's power to terminate, which the employee may be able to enforce by getting a declaration or an interim injunction to prevent dismissal. The first is where the contract lays down a procedure to be followed before dismissal and the employer purports to dismiss in breach of the procedure. One of the first cases where this was upheld was *Gunton v Richmond LBC* (1980), where a college proposed to dismiss its registrar on disciplinary grounds without following the disciplinary procedure. The Court of Appeal granted him a declaration that this was a breach of contract; on the facts he could not get an injunction because it was found that he had accepted the termination before the trial, but he got damages to represent his salary for the time it would have taken to operate the disciplinary procedure as well as his notice money (see also *Boyo v Lambeth LBC* (1994)).

In the same year, in *Jones v Lee* (1980) the Court of Appeal granted an interlocutory injunction to prevent the dismissal of a head teacher in breach of the contractual disciplinary procedure, and since then such injunctions have been granted in numerous cases (*e.g. Irani v Southampton & South West Hampshire AHA* (1985); *Dietman v Brent LBC* (1988); *Robb v Hammersmith & Fulham LBC* (1991); *cf.* also *Anderson v Pringle* (1998)). This is now a well-established exception to the alleged rule that enforcement of contracts of employment is not possible.

The second situation where the employer's power to dismiss may be limited is where there are substantive rather than procedural limitations in the contract: that is, where the contract stipulates that it may only be terminated on certain grounds. Traditionally contracts for academic staff in universities provided that they could only be dismissed for "good cause", which was seen as fundamental to the preservation of the freedom for academics to challenge received opinion. Such contractual provisions are comparatively rare, but they were recognised as limiting the power to dismiss by the House of Lords in *McClelland v NI General Health Services Board* (1957), where a declaration was granted.

Judicial review

A quite different avenue tried by some employees in recent years has been **8–014** the claim for judicial review. In *R. v BBC ex p. Lavelle* (1983) the BBC dismissed an employee when BBC property was discovered at her flat. The disciplinary procedure in her contract was not followed, and she sought the public law remedy of *certiorari* (now known as a quashing order) to get the court to review the decision. Woolf J. held that public law remedies such as an application for judicial review were inappropriate to deal with the relationship of employer and employee, which was a private law matter. A similar view was adopted by the Court of Appeal in *R. v East Berks AHA ex p. Walsh* (1984). Here the terms of the employee's contract as a senior nursing officer were subject to statutory regulation, but the court held that the enforcement of those terms was purely a private law matter for which public law remedies were not available.

Subsequent case law has confirmed that for the time being judicial review is likely to be limited in scope to a fairly small category of public employees and even then, not for all aspects of their contracts of employment.

Unfair Dismissal

The proximate reason for the introduction of the law on unfair dismissal **8–015** was the recommendation of the Donovan Commission in its 1968 Report (Ch.IX), but a consensus on the need for legislation had already developed, fuelled by similar reforms in other European countries and reflected in the United Kingdom's acceptance in 1964 of the ILO's Recommendation No.119 on Termination of Employment. This advised that contracts should be terminated only if there was a valid reason related to the conduct or capacity of the worker or the operational requirements of the business. This, broadly speaking, is the principle underlying the law of unfair dismissal, although its implementation is by no means so simple.

Qualification to claim

The ILO Recommendation accepted that certain categories of worker **8–016** could legitimately be excluded from protection against unfair dismissal, such as those taken on for a specific period rather than indefinitely, those on probation and those employed on a casual or temporary basis. Under the ERA, only employees have the right to claim unfair dismissal, and they must have completed a minimum qualifying period of continuous employment which presently stands at one year (ERA, s.108(1); see above). Trade unions have long argued that all employment protection rights, including the right to claim unfair dismissal, should be available from the first day of employment. The arguments in favour of a qualifying period are essentially pragmatic: firstly, that it is reasonable to have some sort of probation period during which the employer can decide whether or not an employee suits without having a decision to dismiss scrutinised too closely; secondly, that tribunals would be completely overwhelmed with claims if there were no qualifying period. Over the years the length of the qualifying period has fluctuated. It was two years when first introduced, then reduced to six months, then increased to one year, then (in 1985) back to two. It was reduced to one year from June 1, 1999 as a compromise between the aspirations of unions and the wishes of employers. However, the 1990s witnessed a huge extension of the categories of dismissal which are automatically unfair (see below, para. 8–061) for which there is no qualifying period of employment. It seems that employees dismissed with less than one year's service are increasingly trying to frame their claims to fall within one of these categories or else as unlawful discrimination, where again no qualifying periods apply (see above, Chapter 2). Incidentally, there is nothing to stop an employer having a longer probation period: the standard probation period for many university teachers is three years, for example. However, after one year a decision not to confirm the employee in post will at least be reviewable by an employment tribunal.

Employees who continue to work past retiring age are currently excluded from the right to claim unfair dismissal, except for the reasons which constitute automatically unfair dismissal, although the rationale for their exclusion is far from obvious. Today, retirement before the age of 65 is common, and so ERA, s.109 provides alternative upper age limits: either the normal retiring age for employees in that position or, if there is no normal retiring age, 65 (equalised for men and women by the Sex Discrimination Act 1986). In *Waite v GCHQ* (1983) the House of Lords held that normal retiring age is not necessarily the same as contractual retiring age. The presumption that the retiring age stipulated in the contract is the normal retiring age can be displaced by evidence that people in fact retire at a different age, so that the reasonable expectation of an employee would be that she would continue until this other age. If the evidence shows only that the contractual age is not the normal retiring age, and that people in fact retire at a variety of ages, then one falls back instead on the statutory retiring age of 65. The test is clear enough, but it is worth noting that in the case itself the House of Lords held that the fact that one quarter of the relevant group of employees had not retired at the contractual age was insufficient to establish that it had been displaced! Thus, it is not too fanciful to imagine circumstances where the employer might fix the retiring age at an artificially low level, so as to have the option of whether or not to retain employees, yet avoiding redundancy and unfair dismissal claims of those it chooses not to keep.

This will have to alter by 2006 when the age discrimination provisions of the Employment Directive (2000/78/EC) come into force, which will

210

prevent employers having mandatory retirement ages unless they can be objectively justified. In the DTi consultation paper (Age Consultation 2003, Ch.5), the Government proposes that employees should not be barred from claiming unfair dismissal because they are past retirement age, but that having reached a justifiable retirement age should be a potentially fair reason for dismissal. It remains to be decided whether there should be an overall cut-off at the age of 70. Legislation to implement the Employment Directive on age discrimination is due in 2004.

The other categories of employee disqualified from unfair dismissal **8–017** claims are share fishermen, the police, and Crown employees where the relevant minister has issued an excepting certificate on grounds of national security, as was done in the GCHQ trade union membership dispute (see below, Chapter 10) (ERA, ss.199, 200, 193). TURERA introduced ERA, s.192, permitting members of the armed forces to claim unfair dismissal, but not under section 100 (health and safety grounds). In general, any attempt to contract out of the unfair dismissal protection is void; however, there are two exceptions. Under section 110, a dismissals procedure voluntarily agreed between employers and independent trade unions can be designated by the Secretary of State to apply instead of the statutory regime. Such designation will be granted only if it is at least as beneficial to employees as the statutory protection. This provision is a result of the feeling among some members of the Donovan Commission that voluntary self-regulation was better than imposed regulation and could develop better systems. In fact only one such agreement was ever made and it has now terminated. The other exception is where the parties opt for arbitration, discussed above, para. 1–009.

Where there is any dispute as to whether a worker is entitled to claim unfair dismissal, the burden of proof is on the employee to establish his or her right to claim.

The meaning of dismissal

Another hurdle to getting an unfair dismissal claim started is that the **8–018** employee must have been dismissed: *i.e.* the contract must have been terminated in such a way that it falls within the threefold definition of dismissal to be found in ERA, s.95. Any other form of termination will not suffice. Again, this is for the employee to prove if it is in dispute.

Termination with or without notice

The most straightforward case of dismissal under section 95 is where the **8–019** contract is terminated by the employer with or without notice. Whereas the giving of notice of the right length is crucial to a wrongful dismissal claim, it is pretty well irrelevant to unfair dismissal, one of the differences between the statutory and the contract claim.

The only problem likely to arise in this connection is whether or not the precise form of words used meant that the employee was dismissed. Few of us would find, "You're fired!" ambiguous, and we would probably understand what was meant if we were told to get our cards and go. "On your bike" enjoyed a brief vogue in the 1980s, but is not so obvious; and being told to "go down the road" means you are dismissed in Yorkshire, but might be quite innocuous elsewhere. The difference between mere abuse and dismissal has caused a surprising number of problems: in *Futty v Brekkes* (1974) "Fuck off!" was taken to mean "Go away for the rest of the day and come back tomorrow", but clearly there are occasions when it could constitute termination (apart from possibly giving rise to a constructive dismissal claim, below). The test appears to be, what did the employer intend by the words used, and what would a reasonable employee have understood from what was said? (*Tanner v Kean* (1978)). Where words are spoken in the heat of the moment, they should not always be taken at face value: however, it should also be noted that once given, a notice of dismissal cannot be unilaterally revoked.

Expiry of a fixed term contract without renewal

8–020   The position of workers on fixed-term contracts is discussed in Chapter 3 (above, para. 3–017). Where a fixed-term contract comes to an end without renewal, it will constitute a dismissal for the purposes of unfair dismissal.

Constructive dismissal

8–021   The third situation which counts as dismissal is where:

> "the employee terminates the contract . . . with or without notice) in circumstances in which he is entitled to terminate it without notice by reason of the employer's conduct" (ERA, s.95(1)(c)).

Here a resignation by the employee will be construed as dismissal. In *Western Excavating v Sharp* (1978) the Court of Appeal adopted a strictly contractual approach to the interpretation of this phrase and held that the only circumstances where the employee would be entitled to terminate the contract without notice would be where the employer was in fundamental breach of contract. The most obvious example of such a breach would be where the employer attempts unilaterally to change the terms of the contract, perhaps by increasing hours, or changing the employee's duties where this is not permitted under the contract.

Although the Court of Appeal made it clear in *Western Excavating v Sharp* that unreasonable conduct by the employer causing an employee to leave would be insufficient for constructive dismissal unless it was also a breach of contract, to some extent notions of unreasonableness have returned by the back door through the development of the reciprocal duty of mutual trust and confidence as a fundamental term of the contract (see also above, para. 4–024). Thus if an employer is so unreasonable that the work relationship becomes impossible, the employee may resign and claim to have been constructively dismissed on the basis that the employer has destroyed the mutual trust and confidence which should subsist between them. An unreasonable accusation of theft against an employee of good character and many years standing (*Robinson v Crompton Parkinson*

(1978)), arbitrary or capricious refusal of a pay rise to one employee when everyone else got one (*Gardner v Beresford* (1978)), swearing at the employee (*Palmanor v Cedron* (1978)) and giving her a dressing down in front of other employees (*Hilton International v Protopapa* (1990)) have all been held to be acts which destroy mutual trust and confidence in the context of constructive dismissal. The standards of acceptable behaviour have risen over the years, so that there is more likelihood of bad behaviour being held to destroy mutual trust and confidence. For example, bullying behaviour amounting to sexual harassment may lead to constructive dismissal as well as a possible sex discrimination claim (*Reed v Stedman* (1999)). Bullying and harassment is increasingly recognised also as being a potential breach of another important implied term in the contract: the employer's duty to take reasonable care for the health and safety of employees at work. In *Waltons & Morse v Dorrington* (1997) failure to treat seriously an employee's complaints about being exposed to a smoky atmosphere through proximity to a heavy-smoking colleague was held to breach this implied term, enabling the employee to claim that she had been constructively dismissed.

These are all decisions of the EAT, but the concept was accepted by the House of Lords in *Malik v BCCI* (1997). In *Lewis v Motorworld* (1986) an employee was demoted and his salary package reduced. The employee did not resign but remained in employment, thus waiving the breach and affirming the contract. However, the employer persistently and unfairly criticised the employee, threatening him with dismissal, until eventually he resigned. The Court of Appeal held that a series of minor incidents taken together could destroy mutual trust and confidence and thus amount to a fundamental breach; furthermore, the employee was entitled to rely also on the unilateral demotion as evidence of the employer's breach of the implied term, even though he had waived his right to treat it as a repudiatory breach.

Resignation and termination by mutual agreement

A resignation other than in response to a fundamental breach by the **8–022** employer will not constitute dismissal. Tribunals in general show awareness that they should not too easily find that the contract was terminated by voluntary resignation or by mutual agreement, since if there is no dismissal the tribunal has no jurisdiction to inquire into the merits of the case. Thus it has been held since the earliest cases that where an employee is faced with the choice of resigning or being dismissed and chooses to resign (because it may make trying to find another job easier) then this will usually operate in fact as a dismissal (*East Sussex CC v Walker* (1972); *cf.* also *Jones v Mid-Glamorgan CC* (1997)). In *Martin v MBS Fastenings* (1983) an employee who crashed the company minibus (which he was allowed to use in his own time) after drinking seven pints of beer was told that disciplinary proceedings were likely to result in his dismissal and it would be in his interests to resign. He did so, but later claimed he had been unfairly dismissed. It was held that his resignation was genuine: he had done it in order to pre-empt the disciplinary proceedings. Again, in *Sheffield v Oxford*

Controls (1979), the director of a small private company fell out with the owner and threatened to leave. The owner asked him how much he wanted to go; they agreed on £10,000 and the director resigned. He later claimed that he had been forced to resign because he would otherwise have been dismissed. However, it was held to be a genuine resignation: it was the offer of satisfactory compensation which induced his resignation, not fear of dismissal.

Where the employer needs to declare redundancies, volunteers are often sought – a course of action preferred by trade unions and employees. But if the employees volunteer, does this mean that the contract terminates by mutual agreement rather than by dismissal? In one sense, yes. However, for a redundancy claim as with an unfair dismissal claim, it is necessary that the employee should have been dismissed. Hence the analysis usually adopted in this situation is that the employee has simply volunteered to be dismissed and that there is still a termination by the employer. But it seems that employees and their advisers should be careful of this point: in *Birch v University of Liverpool* (1985) academic staff who volunteered for early retirement under what was in effect a redundancy scheme were held to have terminated their contracts by mutual agreement with the employer and not to have been dismissed. The circumstances were slightly unusual in that the scheme provided compensation considerably in excess of a statutory payment on the understanding that the statutory payment was not payable as well, so their claims were not meritorious. But this is not meant to be the point. It is interesting further to note that the Court of Appeal treated this as a question of law and overturned the employment tribunal's decision, despite its earlier decision in *Martin v MBS Fastenings* (1983) that such issues are questions of fact.

As with termination by the employer, a resignation should not automatically be taken at face value where words are spoken in anger (*Sovereign House Security v Savage* (1989)), although again it will depend on what a reasonable employer would have understood in the circumstances. Unlike termination by the employer, it would appear that there is no room for a concept of "constructive resignation", where the employer terminates but is entitled to do so because of the employee's fundamental breach. Ingenious arguments to the contrary were finally laid to rest by the Court of Appeal in *LTE v Clarke* (1981). In general in contract law, where one party commits a fundamental breach, the contract is not terminated unless and until the innocent party accepts it as a repudiation of the contract. It is therefore the innocent party who terminates the contract. In *LTE v Clarke* the Court of Appeal held that contracts of employment were no exception to this rule. This, indeed, is why it is necessary to have statutory provision for an employee's resignation in the face of the employer's breach to count as dismissal, for at common law it would undoubtedly be a termination by the employee.

Automatic termination

8–023 Contracts sometimes provide for their own termination on the happening of a certain event. It might be stipulated that the contract is to last only for a specific period, or that it will terminate if one party becomes insolvent, and so on. At common law, if the event occurred the contract would be terminated automatically, rather than being terminated by either party. But in the employment context, this possibility is open to abuse. The employer could, for example, stipulate that the contract would terminate automatically if the employee were off ill for more than two weeks or if the employee were late three times within a two-month period. Instead of being able to try a claim for unfair dismissal, the employee might find that he fell at the first hurdle because of the form of the termination. The dangers of such abuse were recognised in relation to fixed-term contracts, as we have already seen, and it was expressly provided that expiry of a fixed-term would amount to dismissal. What about a term providing for automatic termination?

The problem actually arose when employers were faced with employees seeking lengthy periods of leave to visit family in other countries and found that they did not always return on time. Some employers started getting employees to sign statements saying variously that failure to return on time would be taken to have terminated the contract (*Midland Electrical Manufacturing Co. v Kanji* (1980)), that if they failed to return on time they would be taken to have resigned (*Tracey v Zest Equipment* (1982)) or explicitly that the contract would be terminated automatically (*Igbo v Johnson Matthey* (1986)). At EAT level, the employer who worded such a clause carefully enough was held not to have dismissed the employee. However, *Igbo v Johnson Matthey* went to the Court of Appeal, where the point was taken that the effect of such clauses was to permit avoidance of the requirements of the ERA, contrary to section 203 of that Act. Thus it was held that such provisions would be void; if the contract was terminated, it would be a termination by the employer, and a dismissal. This does not necessarily mean that the employee has been unfairly dismissed; what it does mean is that the possibility of claiming unfair dismissal has not been closed off. As was intended when the legislation was enacted, the employment tribunal will at least have the opportunity of examining the merits of the case.

Frustration

As with other sorts of contract, the contract of employment may be **8–024** terminated if it becomes impossible to perform without the fault of either party. If so, the contract is frustrated, and there is no dismissal in law. This was recognised at common law as long ago as *Poussard v Spiers & Pond* (1876), where an opera singer caught a cold and was unable to take part in a week of rehearsals and the first few performances of the opera in which she was contracted to appear. The management hired a replacement, who was only prepared to step in if she was given a month's contract. Poussard sued the management for breach of contract in not letting her return to the part once she had recovered. The court held that the illness which had prevented her from performing went to the root of the contract and discharged the defendants from further obligation to her. The circumstances were unusual, in that an absence for a matter of days would not be so crucial in most jobs; also it would have been different if the management had been able to get a temporary substitute just for the first few performances. That was not the case on the facts. Thus the contract had been frustrated.

In practice, the incapacity of the employee through illness, as in *Poussard v Spiers*, is one of the main situations where frustration is likely to be argued. Incapacity of the employer is more rare: first, the personal presence of the employer is rarely essential to the performance of the contract, and secondly, if the employer is an individual who dies, or a company which is wound up, special rules apply (below). Guidance on when the employee's incapacity will be taken to frustrate the contract was given in *Egg Stores v Leibovici* (1977), where the EAT said that the basic question was, "has the time arrived when the employer can no longer reasonably be expected to keep the absent employee's post open for him?" The following considerations are relevant: the length of previous employment (greater efforts should be made for a long-serving employee); how long the employment had been expected to continue (usually, but not always, indefinitely); the nature of the job; the nature, length and effect of the disabling event (will the employee make a full recovery? is the period of absence relatively clear-cut?); the need for the work to be done by a replacement (rather than getting other workers to cover it); the risk of acquiring unfair dismissal or redundancy obligations to a replacement; whether wages have continued to be paid (if so, it is more burdensome to hold the job open, but it indicates a belief in the contract's continuance); the acts and statements of the employer (whether there has been a dismissal or not), and whether, in all the circumstances, a reasonable employer could be expected to wait any longer before replacing the employee on a permanent basis.

8–025   This guidance, with its emphasis on reasonableness, bears a striking resemblance to the criteria which would be applied if a tribunal were deciding whether an employee had been unfairly dismissed on grounds of incapability to do the job; but if the contract is frustrated, there is no dismissal, and a tribunal will not get to consider the merits. For this reason, in *Harman v Flexible Lamps* (1980), Bristow J., giving the judgment of the EAT, said that the doctrine of frustration should hardly ever be invoked in relation to ordinary contracts of employment which are, after all, terminable on notice. If the employee is absent for a long period, the contract is not really impossible to perform, since the employer is able under its terms to issue a valid notice of termination. This would, of course, constitute dismissal, and could found an action for unfair dismissal, but it is submitted that this would be desirable given the general policy underpinning the law.

However, the Court of Appeal expressly disapproved this in *Notcutt v Universal Equipment* (1986), saying that although a contract might be terminable on short notice, the parties probably intended it to be long lasting, and that that intention could be frustrated by the employee's incapacity. The Court adopted the approach in *Egg Stores v Leibovici*, holding that a contract of employment could be terminated both by a dramatic, shattering event, and by an uncertain event such as illness or accident where a long process would be involved before it was possible to say that there had been frustration. In the case of illness, it is necessary to consider any provisions in the contract for sick pay, permanent health insurance and ill-health early retirement. In *Villella v MFI* (1999) the Court of Appeal made the point that where the employee was contractually entitled to permanent health insurance benefits which were designed to last until death or retirement age, his incapacity for three years could not be regarded as frustrating the contract, as it had made provision for this very situation.

Apart from illness or accident, the other common situation where **8–026** frustration is alleged is where the employee is sentenced to a term of imprisonment. Yet is this really a situation of impossibility without the fault of either party? It is in one sense the employee's fault, for committing the offence in the first place. But on the other hand, the employee no doubt did not commit the offence with the intention of breaking the contract, and indeed, the offence might have resulted in a different punishment, like a fine. This point was recognised early on by Lord Denning, who commented, "If a prima donna thoughtlessly sits in a draught and loses her voice, the contract may be frustrated by her illness, even though it may be said to be 'self-induced' " (*Hare v Murphy Brothers* (1974)). It may be noted that some employers do attempt to distinguish between avoidable illnesses or injuries (such as sporting injuries) and the rest, declining to top up sick pay in the former case.

A further complication in the imprisonment situation is that it is the employee who will be trying to argue that he or she was at fault and that it is a self-induced breach rather than frustration. For if it is frustration, the tribunal will have no jurisdiction to hear the case, whereas if the contract is terminated by the employer, it will. This is in contrast to the usual disputes over frustration where the claimant is claiming that the defendant was at fault and the defendant tries to defend herself by claiming she was not at fault and that the contract is frustrated. When this situation came before the Court of Appeal in *Shepherd v Jerrom* (1986), they held that it was contrary to the general principle that no one should profit from his own wrong to allow the employee to rely on his own wrongdoing to improve his position. Thus it was held that a prison sentence of between six months and two years was capable of frustrating an apprenticeship contract which had been due to last for four years.

Death or dissolution of the employer

At common law the death of an individual employer or the compulsory **8–027** liquidation of a company would probably have resulted in the frustration of the contract. Since the introduction of the law of redundancy, the matter has been dealt with by statute, which provides that in these circumstances (and in cases of voluntary liquidation or the dissolution of a partnership), the employee will be treated as having been dismissed and entitled to a redundancy payment if the business is not continued under new ownership, or if the employee's contract is not continued.

The effective date of termination

The exact date on which a contract comes to an end is vitally important for **8–028** two reasons. First, the employee must institute any claim within a comparatively short limitation period – three months for unfair dismissal and six months for a redundancy payment – and hence it is necessary to know from what date time begins to run. Secondly, the existence of employment protection rights and the calculation of unfair dismissal compensation and redundancy payments depend on the amount of continuous employment that the employee has, and thus it is necessary to know exactly when the contract ended in order to compute the overall period of continuous employment. Unfortunately the statutory provisions are less than straight-forward, and complexity is compounded by the fact that the effective date can be different according to which of these two questions is being answered.

So far as limitation periods are concerned, the effective date of termination is the date on which notice expires (where the dismissal is with notice) or the date on which termination takes effect (if the dismissal is without notice) (ERA, s.97). In general, this means that it is the last day on which the employee attends for work, and an employee who is dismissed with inadequate notice cannot treat the date as deferred until after the date on which she would have been dismissed if she had received the notice to which she was entitled.

Difficulty arises in the very common case where the employer dismisses the employee with wages in lieu of notice. This could be interpreted as a termination at once, with a sum equivalent to damages for breach of contract, or dismissal on notice, except that the employee is not required to work for the period of notice. In the second case, the effective date would be later, thus extending the limitation period. Tribunals and courts generally prefer the first view, and therefore the limitation period runs against the employee from the last day that he was at work. However, it has been held (*e.g. Leech v Preston BC* (1985)) that sometimes the true construction may be that the employee is not being required to work his notice. One would probably advise an employee given wages in lieu of notice to claim within three months of the last day worked, but if he is already too late, it might be worth arguing for the other construction, although without much hope of success unless there is other supporting evidence.

8–029 What if the employee makes an unsuccessful internal appeal against dismissal? Is the date of the original dismissal the effective date of termination, or is it the date when the appeal is turned down? This depends on whether, on a proper construction of the contract, the situation is one where the dismissal takes effect, but there is a possibility of reinstatement, in which case the effective date of termination is the date of the original dismissal (*e.g. Sainsbury v Savage* (1981)), or whether the employee is suspended (although the contract continues) until the appeal is heard, in which case the later date is the effective date of termination (*e.g. Drage v Governors of Greenford School* (2000)).

For a fixed-term contract, the effective date of termination is the date on which it expires without renewal; constructive dismissal is not dealt with expressly by the statute, but usually the effective date is the date on which the employee leaves.

For continuity purposes, the effective date is usually the same, but with one important qualification. If the employer dismisses the employee with less notice than that to which he was entitled by statute, the balance of the statutory period of notice is added on. This may be crucial in getting the employee over the one year's continuous employment hurdle or in improving his compensation rights. Note that the balance of a contractual period of notice, if longer than the statutory minimum, may not be added in.

The fair reasons for dismissal

Once the employee has established that she is qualified to claim and that **8–030** there has been a dismissal, the burden of proof shifts to the employer to show first, what was the reason for the dismissal, and secondly, that it falls under one of the categories of fair reason laid out in ERA, s.98. Neither task should cause the employer too much problem, for the categories are wide. Fair reasons are:

    (a) reasons relating to capability or qualifications;
    (b) reasons relating to conduct;
    (c) redundancy;
    (d) that continued employment would be in breach of statute;
    (e) "some other substantial reason of a kind to justify dismissal".

The existence of the last category in particular means that an employer will rarely be unable to show that the reason for the dismissal was potentially fair. Under section 92 an employee is entitled to ask for the reasons for dismissal to be stated in writing. If the employer refuses to comply (and a persistent failure to reply may be held to amount to a refusal) the employee will be awarded two weeks' pay. Such a statement may be of use to the employee in that the employer will then lack credibility if attempting to put forward some additional or alternative reason at a tribunal hearing.

Employers are not compelled to classify their reason for dismissal under just one of the fair categories. In cases of under-performance, for example, it may not be clear if the reason is that the employee simply cannot do any better (a reason relating to capability) or that he does not trouble to work well (a reason relating to conduct), so both reasons may be given in the employer's notice of appearance. Similarly, where an employee is dismissed in the course of a reorganisation, the reason may not be within the technical definition of redundancy, so "some other substantial reason" may be relied on as well. Indeed, if in doubt, it is probably wise for the employer to plead alternatives. In *Devonshire v Trico-Folberth* (1989) the employee was dismissed for poor attendance, which the employer categorised as incapability. It was held that the employer had not acted as a reasonable employer would in dismissing on this ground – although it would have been reasonable if the dismissal had been for misconduct.

Once the decision to take action against an employee has been made, **8–031** there is a temptation for the employer to gild the lily and dredge up all sorts of shortcomings in order to justify the dismissal. There are dangers in this approach, as indicated by *Smith v City of Glasgow DC* (1987). Here, the employers alleged that the employee had been dismissed for incapability, evidenced by three specific allegations of incompetence. The employment tribunal considered that one of these allegations could not be substantiated.

In these circumstances, the House of Lords held that the dismissal was unfair: the employers had not shown that the unsubstantiated allegation did not form a main part of their reason for dismissal, and it could not be reasonable to dismiss an employee for a reason which could not be supported.

Generally, establishing a potentially fair reason for dismissal is easy, and is rarely at issue between the parties. However, there is a further requirement, and it is this that in practice is the focus of just about every unfair dismissal case. It is that the employer should have acted reasonably in treating the reason as a sufficient reason for dismissal. Originally the employer bore the burden of proving that the decision to dismiss was reasonable; however, the Employment Act 1980 altered the position so that the burden of proof is neutral. Under ERA, s.98(4), it is for the employment tribunal to decide whether the employer acted reasonably or unreasonably, having regard to the circumstances including the size and administrative resources of the employer's undertaking, although in practice the employer will lead evidence about the reasonableness of the decision at the same time as evidence to show the reason for the dismissal. This means that if it is admitted that the employee has been dismissed and is otherwise qualified to claim, it will be for the employers to put their case first.

The standard of review

8–032   "We consider that the authorities establish that in law the correct approach for the [employment] tribunal to adopt in answering the question posed by [ERA, s.98(4)] is as follows: (1) the starting point should always be the words of [section 98(4)] themselves; (2) in applying the section an [employment] tribunal must consider the reasonableness of the employer's conduct, not simply whether they (the members of the [employment] tribunal) consider the dismissal to be fair; (3) in judging the reasonableness of the employer's conduct an [employment] tribunal must not substitute its decision as to what was the right course to adopt for that of the employer; (4) in many, though not all, cases there is a band of reasonable responses to the employee's conduct within which one employer might reasonably take one view, another quite reasonably take another; (5) the function of the [employment] tribunal, as an industrial jury, is to determine whether in the particular circumstances of each case the decision to dismiss the employee fell within the band of reasonable responses which a reasonable employer might have adopted". (Browne-Wilkinson J. in *Iceland Frozen Foods v Jones* (1983)).

For years this passage has been taken to summarise the duties of tribunals in deciding whether or not an employer acted reasonably in dismissing the employee. The first point is obviously uncontroversial. The second is also clearly supportable, because otherwise the tribunal would only be substituting its subjective view for that of the employer; it also indicates that the tribunal must focus on judging the employer's conduct, not necessarily on whether or not the employee was justly dismissed. Furthermore, the employer's conduct must be judged according to the facts known to the employer at the time of the decision to dismiss, not what was discovered later (*Devis v Atkins* (1977)). The last three points have recently been the subject of controversy, especially the "band of reasonable responses" test. "Frequently there is a range of responses to the conduct or capacity of an employee on the part of the employer, from and including summary dismissal downwards to a mere informal warning, which can be said to have been reasonable". (*Rolls-Royce v Walpole* (1980); *cf.* also *British Leyland v Swift* (1981)). This may be so, but it tends to limit the scope for a tribunal to find that a dismissal was unfair because even if a tribunal is sure that many other employers would have dealt with a case by some penalty other than dismissal, it may not be able to say that the employer's action is outside the band or range of reasonable responses. This is exacerbated by the fact that the so-called reasonable employer does not always act reasonably. In *Saunders v Scottish National Camps* (1981) it was held fair to dismiss a homosexual employee because of a quite unfounded concern about his coming into contact with children on the grounds that many other employers would have reacted similarly. Thus the reasonable employer is rather the average employer, with the prejudices of the general populace.

Although it has been denied that the band of reasonable responses **8–033** approach requires "that such a high degree of unreasonableness be shown . . . that nothing short of a perverse decision to dismiss" can be unfair (*Rentokil v Mackin* (1989)), it comes pretty close to it. This led to an outspoken attack by the outgoing president of the EAT, Morison J., in *Haddon v Van den Bergh Foods* (1999), who argued that the "band of reasonable responses" test was apt to lead tribunals to find dismissals unfair only if the decision to dismiss was perverse in the light of the facts known to the employer and implied that it should not be used. For good measure, he suggested that the fear of being found to have substituted their opinion for that of the employer was also likely to lead to tribunals failing properly to examine the employer's decision. The furore caused by *Haddon* swiftly resulted in a statement from the incoming president of the EAT, Lindsay J., in *Midland Bank v Madden* (2000) that the EAT was not at liberty to abandon the "band of reasonable responses" test, hallowed as it was by repeated approval in the Court of Appeal. The uncertainty caused by these decisions led the Court of Appeal to expedite the appeal in *Madden* and to restate firmly the *Iceland* approach (*HSBC v Madden* (2000)). It is probably not surprising that the Court of Appeal came down on the side of the orthodoxy which had prevailed for nearly 20 years, but it is unfortunate that the merits of the arguments in *Haddon* could not be explored. The result is that *Haddon* may be regarded as a minor, short-lived heresy and the "band of reasonable responses" test is more securely entrenched than before (see also *Sainsbury's Supermarkets Ltd v Hitt* (2003)).

This rigorous standard used for reviewing the decision of the employer is directly analogous to the standard to be used by the EAT and higher courts in reviewing the decision of an employment tribunal on appeal. Appeals lie to the EAT only on questions of law, and a decision as to whether a dismissal is unfair or not has been firmly categorised as a question of fact. It is true that tribunals hearing unfair dismissal cases day in, day out and develop a wealth of experience, and that because they see the witnesses, they are in the best position to judge the merits of the case. However, it is clear that the major reason for strictly limiting appeals is one of policy: a fear that the EAT, and in turn the Court of Appeal, would be swamped by the appeals which might otherwise be thrown up by several thousand employment tribunal decisions a year.

8–034   In *Piggott Bros v Jackson* (1991) the Court of Appeal summarised the situations in which the EAT would be entitled to interfere as falling into three categories. They are first, if there was a misdirection on the law; secondly, if there was no evidence to support a finding of fact; and thirdly, if it was perverse. The problem with perversity is that it tends to be in the eye of the beholder. The much-quoted dictum of May L.J. in *Neale v Hereford & Worcester CC* (1986) to the effect that a perverse decision can be recognised when "one can say in effect, 'My goodness, that was certainly wrong' " was thought by the Court in *Piggott Bros v Jackson* to carry the danger that it might encourage the EAT to think it was entitled to intervene in any case where it strongly felt that its own decision would be different from that of the employment tribunal. "Furthermore the more dogmatic the temperament of the judges concerned, the more likely they are to take this view", as Lord Donaldson M.R. put it. Yet the fact that the EAT would have come to a different decision from the employment tribunal is most emphatically not regarded as a sufficient reason for it to intervene. This led Lord Donaldson M.R. in *Piggott Bros v Jackson* to define perversity very restrictively, implying that it would rarely be found unless there was a misdirection on the law or a finding unsupported by the evidence. But this, of course, would be tantamount to ruling out perversity as a ground for interference as it would be subsumed in the other two categories. The EAT struck back in *East Berkshire HA v Matadeen* (1992), reasserting that perversity was a separate and distinct ground for intervention and pointing out that there would be little justification for an EAT constituted with lay representation if the only grounds for interference were misdirection or unsupported findings.

It is submitted that the power of the EAT to review tribunal decisions is already too limited, which helps to account for the fact that a browse through the reports will disclose a number of decisions which can strike the reader as distinctly odd. Cases with similar facts are therefore of limited value as precedents in this area. The lack of uniformity inevitably resulting from this approach is apparently seen as a risk worth taking to secure the benefit of a sensible workload at the appellate level but it would be regrettable if appeals were limited yet further.

Finally, the emphasis on tribunals directing themselves in terms of section 98(4) should be noted. In the latter part of the 1970s the EAT saw its role very much as providing assistance to employers on what was good industrial relations practice, and it laid down guidelines on handling various types of dismissals. These guidelines were treated almost as statutory requirements by some employment tribunals, provoking a backlash from the Court of Appeal against putting a gloss on the words of the statute (*cf.*

Hollister v National Farmers' Union (1979)). In what follows, the requirements of reasonableness in relation to the different categories of unfair
dismissal will be considered, but should be read with this warning in mind.

Capability or qualifications

Under ERA, s.98(2)(a), dismissal may be fair if it is for a reason relating to **8–035**
the employee's capability or qualifications for the job. These terms are
defined in section 98(3): capability "means . . . capability assessed by
reference to skill, aptitude, health or any other physical or mental quality"
and qualifications "means any degree, diploma or other academic, technical
or professional qualification relevant to the position which he held". There
are thus in effect two sub-categories comprised in this: dismissals for
incompetence and dismissals for sickness.

In deciding whether an employer was reasonable in dismissing for
incompetence, it may be relevant to know whether appropriate training was
given. For example, in *Davidson v Kent Meters* (1975) a woman was
dismissed for assembling 471 out of 500 components incorrectly. She
claimed that this was the way she had been shown to assemble them by the
chargehand. The chargehand denied ever having shown her how to do it.
Either way the employer was damned, for either she had been trained
wrongly, or else she had never been trained. However, if the employee is
taken on on the understanding that he has a particular skill or qualification,
the employer would not be expected to train him in things he should
already know. The question of adequate training may be particularly
apposite where the nature of jobs changes substantially because of new
technology. It may be fair to dismiss employees who cannot adapt, but only
if they have had proper opportunities to learn. Again, depending on such
things as the length of service of the employee, it may be reasonable to
expect that the employer will try to find some other work for someone who
cannot adapt.

Another relevant factor might be whether or not the employee was
warned that her performance was not satisfactory: "in the case of incapacity, the employer will normally not act reasonably unless he gives the
employee fair warning and an opportunity to mend his ways and show that
he can do the job" as Lord Bridge put it in *Polkey v Dayton Services* (1988).
While no amount of warning will increase someone's competence, the
employee may genuinely not realise that her work is not up to scratch. Also,
it is difficult to be sure whether poor performance is because of innate
inability or because of lack of effort: "many do not know they are capable
of jumping the five-barred gate until the bull is close behind them", as
Donaldson J. pointed out (*Winterhalter Gastronom v Webb* (1973)). But this
is not a hard and fast rule: in *Dunning v Jacomb* (1973) a contracts manager
was dismissed without warning because of his inability to get on with
clients, many of whom had complained about him. It was held fair: in his
responsible position he must have been aware that this lack of co-operation
placed his job in jeopardy, and it seemed likely that he could not have
changed even if he had wanted to. Usually a continuous record of
unsatisfactory performance will be relied on to justify dismissal for

223

incompetence, but a single error may warrant dismissal if it is serious enough. In *Alidair v Taylor* (1978) a pilot was dismissed for landing his plane badly in fair weather conditions, causing damage to the plane, though no injuries to passengers. His dismissal was fair, for the employer not unreasonably had lost confidence in his ability to do the job.

8–036 It is cases like these where there is a clear overlap with misconduct dismissals and many employers treat incapability as something to be dealt with under the disciplinary procedure which they use for misconduct dismissals regardless of whether the employee is deliberately at fault or doing her incompetent best. This has now assumed some importance as a result of the new right in the Employment Relations Act 1999, s.10 for workers to be accompanied by a trade union official or a co-worker at any disciplinary or grievance hearing. It would seem strange if a worker's right to a companion should depend on whether or not the employer has separate capability and conduct procedures. This is addressed in the Acas Code of Practice on Disciplinary and Grievance Procedures which tends to assume that capability and conduct issues will both be dealt with in disciplinary procedures and states that even if they are separate, the right to be accompanied will apply to a worker in any situation where the outcome could be a formal warning or other sanction. Where a warning is given, the employee should be given a reasonable time in which to show improvement before a final decision is taken.

Different considerations are relevant in judging the reasonableness of a dismissal on grounds of ill-health, and the matters to be taken into account are similar to those outlined in judging whether the contract is frustrated on this ground (*cf. Egg Stores v Leibovici* (1977) above, para. 8–024). It is first necessary for the employer to gain an informed view of the position, which will best be done by consultation with the employee (*East Lindsey DC v Daubney* (1977)). The value of consultation is not merely so that the employer is fully briefed on the medical situation, but also to keep the employee informed about the employer's thinking. If the employee knows that the employer is contemplating dismissal, she may be able to suggest some alternative herself – a sideways move, perhaps, or early retirement.

The employer may well wish to have a doctor's report on the employee's medical condition. However, the employee's doctor will not talk to the employer without the employee's permission, and the employee has a right to see any report prepared by his doctor and can veto its transmission to the employer (Access to Medical Reports Act 1988). Furthermore, an employer does not have an implied right to require employees to undergo a medical examination by a company doctor, or an independent doctor (*Bliss v South East Thames RHA* (1987)), so this is dependent to a large extent on the employee's co-operation. However, if the employee refuses to provide information to the employer, the employer may well be considered to have acted reasonably in drawing adverse inferences from this fact, and concluding that dismissal is necessary.

Once the employer has as good a grasp of the medical position as possible, it is a matter of weighing in the balance the needs of the organisation for someone else to do the job, bearing in mind the probable length of the employee's absence and the likelihood of a full recovery. In general, an employer might be expected to wait longer in the case of a long-serving employee. A further consideration for employers is the effect of the Disability Discrimination Act 1995 in this area. There has always been a risk that a dismissal on grounds of ill-health incapability could be unfair if the employer has not considered redeployment. However, if the nature of the employee's incapacity is such that she may be regarded as having a disability within the meaning of the Disability Discrimination Act 1995 (discussed above, para. 2–039) the employer will be under a positive duty to make reasonable adjustments to facilitate her continued employment (DDA, s.6). The employer who dismisses without considering this is very likely to be liable for unjustified discrimination. In *Kent CC v Mingo* (2000) the EAT warned that a dismissal which constituted discrimination contrary to the DDA should not automatically be regarded as unfair, but it upheld the finding that it was in that case and there are likely to be few cases where this is not so.

A difficulty frequently faced by management is the worker who has a **8–037** record of short absences, too short to be covered by a doctor's certificate, and perhaps involving ailments which are hard to pin down – backache, migraine, gastric attack, etc. The difficulty is knowing whether this is a genuine illness or whether the employee is malingering; even if genuine, the absences may constitute an unacceptable level of unreliability. Some employers find that a policy of self-certification, where employees are required to submit a written explanation for their absences, reduces the problem, in that people are less ready to put specious reasons in a permanent form. Others automatically investigate if absences run above a certain level, which is sometimes agreed with the trade union. The danger of this approach is that some employees treat this as an addition to their holiday entitlement, and ensure that they use all their "sick leave" each year! It is important that procedures used are suitable given that this is an area where the distinction between incapability and misconduct is blurred (*cf. Devonshire v Trico-Folberth* (1989)). In *International Sports Co. v Thompson* (1980) the EAT suggested that a quasi-disciplinary procedure, involving warnings and a chance to improve, was more appropriate to this kind of absence than the usual ill-health approach. They declined to find the dismissal unfair on the ground that the company doctor had not examined the employee because he felt it would serve no useful purpose given the transient nature and variety of complaints from which the employee suffered.

In relation to dismissals for illness it may again not always be clear whether or not the employee has a statutory right to be accompanied under the Employment Relations Act 1999, s.10. If the situation is dealt with in a quasi-disciplinary manner it is fairly clear that the right will apply, but it is not so clear for those employers who have separate ill-health procedures which might result in ill-health early retirement rather than dismissal. It would obviously be bad industrial relations practice for an employer to refuse an employee the right to be accompanied, but it is not entirely obvious that the statutory right would apply in these circumstances.

Conduct

8–038 Misconduct is by far the commonest ground put forward to justify dismissal. In judging misconduct, courts and tribunals must have regard to the revised Acas Code of Practice on Disciplinary and Grievance Procedures. Although its guidance does not have the force of law, tribunals are bound to take account of it in reaching their decisions. Thus failure to follow the recommendations of the Code will count against an employer in judging the reasonableness of a dismissal, but will not mean that the dismissal is necessarily unfair.

The Code recommends that disciplinary rules should be stated clearly, preferably in writing with a copy to every employee, and that special care should be taken to ensure that workers whose first language is not English or who have a disability affecting their ability to read can understand them. While accepting that rules will vary according to the circumstances of the workplace, the Code suggests that they should usually cover such things as misconduct; substandard performance (unless there is a separate capability procedure); harassment or victimisation; misuse of company facilities (such as e-mail and the internet); poor timekeeping and unauthorised absences. Bizarrely, the Employment Act 1989 exempted employers with fewer than 20 employees from the requirement to put information about any disciplinary rules in the employee's written particulars of terms. This exemption, justified as a reduction in the administrative burden on small employers, seemed counter-productive, since it is obviously in the employer's interest for employees to have a clear understanding of what they may and may not do. However, it is due to be repealed when the new statutory dismissal, disciplinary and grievance procedures come into force in October 2004 (see below, para. 8–071).

All employers should establish a procedure for dealing with disciplinary matters. Paragraph 9 of the revised Code now recommends that such procedures should take account of the rules of natural justice, meaning that workers should be informed in advance of any disciplinary hearing, told what the allegations are against them and be given the opportunity to challenge these allegations and any evidence against them before a decision is reached. In *Hussain v Elonex* (1999) a dismissal was held not to be unfair merely because the employee had not been provided with a copy of witness statements relied on by the employer, since he had been made aware of their substance (see also *Asda Stores Ltd v Thompson* (2002)). However, in the light of the revisions to the Code, which now specifically recommends that workers should be informed of all relevant evidence before a disciplinary hearing, where possible, this may need to be reconsidered. The other essential features for a disciplinary procedure stipulated in paragraph 9 are that it should be in writing; indicate to whom it applies; be non-discriminatory; provide for prompt disposal of issues; indicate the range of possible sanctions and who may impose them; provide the worker with the right to be accompanied and to state her case; ensure that no decision is taken before matters are properly investigated; ensure that an explanation is given for any penalty; and ensure that there is a right of appeal which is explained to the worker. In view of the worker's right under the

Employment Relations Act 1999, s.10 to be accompanied at any disciplinary hearing it becomes more necessary for employers to distinguish between what is counselling, coaching or an informal warning, where the right does not apply, and what is part of the disciplinary procedure, when it will (see below, para. 8–070).

Warnings

The Code recommends that, except for gross misconduct, no one should be **8–039** dismissed for a first breach of discipline (para.9), and this is amplified by paragraph 15, which effectively lays out a three-stage procedure: (i) an oral warning for minor misconduct or a first written warning for more serious misconduct (or a continuing record of minor offences); (ii) a final written warning in case of a further offence; and finally (iii) disciplinary action – which could be dismissal, but could also be a suspension without pay or a disciplinary transfer or demotion. In relation to these lesser penalties, it must be remembered that they may only be imposed where the employer has contractual power to do so – otherwise it would be a fundamental breach by the employer, and the employee could treat herself as constructively dismissed (*cf. Hanley v Pease* above, paa. 8–007; it could, of course, be a fair constructive dismissal).

To say that the Code suggests a three-stage procedure does not mean that all three stages must always be followed except in cases of gross misconduct, where summary dismissal may be justified without any prior warning. The meaning of gross misconduct was considered in relation to the justification of summary dismissal (above, para. 8–006), and that discussion is applicable here also. It should be noted that summary dismissal does not mean instant dismissal: the employer will still be under an obligation to investigate in order to have a reasonable belief in the employee's guilt. Even where it is not gross misconduct it may be justifiable for the employer to enter the procedure at a later stage. The Code itself envisages that serious misconduct might justify a written warning, even for a first offence and there may well be cases where an employer could properly decide to move straight to a final warning. The warning should be clear: the Code recommends that a written warning should give details of the complaint, specify what improvement or change in behaviour is necessary, give the timescale for this, specify the consequences of a further offence and notify the worker of his right to appeal. Because of the selectiveness of memory, many employers prefer to give a written confirmation even of oral warnings and the Code recommends that a note of an oral warning should be kept on file.

Should different offences be treated separately or can they be regarded as part of a pattern of misconduct? If the purpose of a warning is to improve the employee's conduct, then it could be argued that a different offence does not warrant the next stage of procedure (for the employee has improved in the sense of not repeating the first offence). On the other hand, it would be crazy to have an employee with, say, an oral warning for lateness, a written warning for failing to follow safety procedures and a final warning for insubordination! Such doubt as there was on this point seems to have been resolved in *Auguste Noel v Curtis* (1990). The employee was dismissed for abuse of two cheeses (*sic*); the employment tribunal considered that two previous warnings he had received for an altercation with other employees and for failing to keep proper worksheets were irrelevant in relation to this offence. Their decision was reversed by the EAT, who thought the employer was entitled to look at the whole picture in deciding whether the employee's conduct overall was unsatisfactory.

8–040 Warnings should not remain on the employee's file indefinitely. The Acas Code now suggests that oral warnings should be disregarded after six months and written warnings after a year (para.15). If a period is stipulated, the employer had better stick to it. In *Bevan Ashford v Malin* (1995) the employee was given a final written warning on January 29, 1992, which was to stay on his file for 12 months. On January 29, 1993 he committed a further act of misconduct and his employers, a firm of solicitors, dismissed him, taking into account that he was on a final warning. However, 12 months from January 29, 1992 expired on January 28, 1993 and it was held that the dismissal was unfair because the employer had been influenced by a "spent" warning.

Where it is clear that a warning would make no difference to an employee's conduct, it may be fair to dismiss without a warning first. In *Retarded Children's Aid Society v Day* (1978) the house-father in a home for adults with learning disabilities punished a resident in contravention of the home's rules. At a meeting to discuss this, it became clear that he thought the policy behind the rules was wrong and that what he had done was right. In these circumstances, it was fair to dismiss him at once, without a warning and a chance to improve.

Proof of misconduct

8–041 For a dismissal on grounds of misconduct to be justified, it is not necessary to show that the employee was indeed guilty of the offence. What must be established is that the employer honestly believed on reasonable grounds that the employee was guilty, at the time when the employer took the decision to dismiss (*BHS v Burchell* (1978), approved by the Court of Appeal in *Weddel v Tepper* (1980)). It follows that the two elements of honest belief and reasonable grounds for that belief depend on a third element: that the employer has "carried out as much investigation into the matter as was reasonable in all the circumstances of the case" (*per* Arnold J. in *BHS v Burchell*). While this threefold test evolved in the context of cases where the employee was suspected of theft from the employer, it is equally apt in any case where the question of whether or not the employee actually committed the misconduct is at issue. However, it was pointed out in *Boys and Girls Welfare Society v McDonald* (1996) that the threefold test is not necessarily appropriate in misconduct cases where there is no significant dispute as to the facts, and this was reiterated by the Court of Session in *Scottish Daily Record v Laird* (1996). In *Boys and Girls Welfare Society v McDonald* the EAT also stressed that in applying the *Burchell* test, tribunals should not be misled into placing the burden of proof on the employer to show reasonable grounds through reasonable investigation, etc.

BHS v Burchell was decided at a time when the employer had the burden of showing not only the reason for the dismissal, but also that it was reasonable to dismiss in the circumstances, but as noted above (para. 8–031), the burden of proof is now neutral. In *Scottish Daily Record v Laird* the employer had dismissed the employee for being involved in the publication of a free newspaper competing with the company's publications in breach of an express term in his contract. Although there was no dispute as to his involvement, the tribunal found the dismissal unfair because the company had not investigated whether or not there was significant competition. The Court of Session held that therefore this was a case where the *Burchell* test was relevant in assessing whether the employer had reasonable grounds for its belief in the reason for the dismissal. While accepting the point that the employer does not have to prove this, the Court considered that it was at least necessary for the employer to lead some evidence to indicate that the requirements of the test had been satisfied.

A reasonable investigation where facts are in dispute would involve talking to any witnesses, gathering relevant documents and, crucially, putting the charges to the employee (Acas Code, para.9). In *Weddel v Tepper* (1980) the unfairness was held to reside principally in the fact that the employer decided to dismiss without hearing first whether the employee had any explanation for the suspicious conduct. This may be difficult if the police have been called in, for they will take over the investigation, and the employee is likely to be advised by his solicitor to say nothing at all. Some employers may decide to suspend the employee on full pay pending the outcome of criminal proceedings; the problem with this is that it may take several months for the case to come to court. It has been held therefore that the employer may act reasonably in dismissing in these circumstances if, in the light of what is known to her at the time, it seems on the balance of probabilities that the employee is guilty (*Parker v Clifford Dunn* (1979); *Carr v Alexander* (1979)). Furthermore, the Court of Appeal has made it clear that the "band of reasonable responses" test also applies to the question of whether an investigation is reasonable (*Sainsbury's Supermarkets Ltd v Hitt* (2003)). However, it has been held improper for the employer effectively to wash his hands of responsibility, deciding to dismiss automatically if the employee is found guilty by a criminal court (*McLaren v NCB* (1988)).

What if the employer is certain that one or other of two employees must **8–042** be guilty, but is genuinely uncertain which it is? Perhaps surprisingly, in *Monie v Coral Racing* (1981) the Court of Appeal held that dismissal of them both was fair, and in *Parr v Whitbread* (1990) the EAT extended this to a situation where four employees were under suspicion and all dismissed. It is assumed, however, that there would be a point at which wholesale sacking would not be justified where at least one must have committed the offence.

Failure to follow procedure

As we will see, dismissal in breach of the statutory dismissal and disciplin- **8–043** ary procedure will be automatically unfair (below, para. 8–073). However, the fact that that procedure has been followed is not intended to be determinative of whether the dismissal is fair or unfair. This therefore leads to the question, what happens if the employer fails to follow the procedure laid down in the Acas Code, or in its own contracts? Will this alone lead to a finding of unfair dismissal? It is not easy to give a hard and fast answer, for it seems that it will depend on what kind of breach of procedure it is. Some points can be noted. First, if an employer has drawn up a procedure, it will normally be expected to follow it; indeed, if it is embodied in contracts of employment, the employees may be able to enforce it at common law (see above, para. 8–013). This is particularly true of large organisations with sophisticated procedures (since the size and administrative resources of the employer are to be taken into account in judging reasonableness: ERA, s.98(4)), so such employers should ensure that their procedures are not too sophisticated for their managers to understand and implement correctly. Secondly, some basic elements of fair procedure are so vital to the process whereby the employer forms a view of the facts that a failure to observe them is virtually bound to make the dismissal unfair. In this category comes the natural justice-type requirement of giving the employee an opportunity to respond before the decision is taken: "in the case of misconduct, the employer will normally not act reasonably unless he investigates the complaint of misconduct fully and fairly and hears whatever the employee wishes to say in his defence or in explanation or mitigation" (*per* Lord Bridge in *Polkey v Dayton Services* (1988); *cf.* also *Earl v Slater & Wheeler (Airlyne) Ltd* (1972) and *Devis v Atkins* (1977): this is also a crucial step in the statutory procedure). In *A v B* (2003) the EAT held that a 2½ year delay in investigating alleged misconduct made the dismissal unfair. But thirdly, there may be other procedural steps which are not so crucial and whose omission will not render the dismissal unfair. Thus in *Bailey v BP Oil* (1980) the applicant claimed to be away sick when in fact he was on holiday in Mallorca; unluckily for him, so was one of the managers, who saw him. The disciplinary procedure stated that no one would be dismissed without a full-time trade union official being present. Because they were unable to get hold of the full-time official, the procedure went ahead without his presence and the employee was dismissed. It was held that the dismissal was fair. In *Westminster City Council v Cabaj* (1996) the employee was similarly entitled under the disciplinary procedure to a three-person appeal panel. Since one member did not arrive for the hearing, his appeal went ahead with only two and was rejected. The EAT took the point that the disciplinary procedure was part of the employee's contract and thus the failure to follow it was a breach of contract. In their view, a procedural failure amounting to a breach of contract was so serious that it must make the dismissal unfair. However, the Court of Appeal held that this was not the case as a matter of law. The correct question was whether the failure of procedure prevented the employee from getting a fair hearing, and the case was remitted to the tribunal on this issue. This indicates that the courts are far from saying that all procedural failures render dismissals unfair.

Conduct outside employment

8–044 Paragraph 26 of the Acas Code of Practice recommends that conviction of a criminal offence outside employment should not automatically be treated as a reason for dismissal. "The main consideration should be whether the offence is one that makes workers unsuitable for their type of employment." Thus a section leader at a department store was properly dismissed after being convicted of shoplifting in another store: the offence was clearly relevant to her position (*Moore v C&A Modes* (1981)); on similar grounds it has been held fair to dismiss a schoolteacher for a conviction for indecent conduct, albeit with another consenting adult (*Nottinghamshire CC v Bowly* (1978); see also *X v Y* (2003)) and a school groundsman who had been convicted of indecent assault on his daughter, a pupil at the school (*P v Nottinghamshire CC* (1992)). Surprisingly, in the last case, the Court of Appeal seemed to suggest that there might be an obligation to consider alternative employment in such a case.

Trade union officials

Employees who are lay officials for trade unions, such as shop stewards, are **8–045** subject to the same disciplinary rules as anyone else. However, because of the chance that disciplinary action against a trade union official could be perceived as an attack on the union, the Code recommends that "if disciplinary action is contemplated then the case should be discussed with a senior trade union representative or full-time official" (para.26).

After-discovered conduct and appeals

What if, after the decision to dismiss has been taken, further relevant facts **8–046** come to light? The basic position was settled early on by the House of Lords in *Devis v Atkins* (1977). The employee, manager of an abattoir, was dismissed for buying animals from dealers instead of directly from farmers, in contravention of instructions given to him. These grounds for dismissal were held to be inadequate by an employment tribunal, and this was not challenged by the employer. Their point, however, was that after they dismissed him, they discovered that he had been dealing dishonestly with the stock, and they wanted this after-discovered information to be taken into account. The House of Lords pointed out that the wording of the Act focuses on the conduct of the employer ("whether . . . the employer acted reasonably or unreasonably . . . "), not on the justice or injustice to the employee, and that the question is whether the decision to dismiss was reasonable or unreasonable. That could be judged only in the light of what the employer knew at the time of dismissal, not on what was uncovered later on. As the House noted, this is directly opposite to the position at common law, where after-discovered conduct may be used to justify a summary dismissal initially carried out on inadequate grounds (*Boston Deep Sea Fishing v Ansell* (1888), above, para. 8–006). After-discovered conduct might be relevant to the remedy for unfair dismissal, but could not affect the finding on fairness.

This means also that if an employer dismissed an employee for misconduct and it was later conclusively proved that the employee did not commit the offence, the dismissal could still be fair. The issue is whether the employer had reasonable grounds for believing in the employee's guilt at the time of the decision to dismiss.

231

8–047   The next problem, however, is how this operates when the other misconduct is discovered in the course of an appeal. The Code of Practice recommends that there should be an internal procedure for appealing any disciplinary decision. However, if a dismissed employee appeals, and the appeal is turned down, the dismissal usually counts as having occurred on the date of the original decision to dismiss, not on the date of the appeal decision (*Sainsbury v Savage* (1981), approved in *West Midlands Co-operative Society v Tipton* (1986)). So in one sense, everything that happens at the appeal hearing is after the dismissal. But obviously if evidence was discovered on appeal which proved that the employee had not committed the offence, it would have to be taken into account: otherwise why have the appeal? If so, why not take into account new evidence showing that the employee did commit the offence, or that he committed some other offence? The House of Lords dealt with this in *West Midlands Co-operative Society v Tipton* (1986) by holding that the appeal process was part and parcel of the dismissal process, so that if matters came to light during the appeal which were relevant to the original decision to dismiss, they could and should be taken into account. (Thus, on the facts of the case, they found that a refusal in breach of contract to allow an appeal could itself be evidence of unfairness.) What about the discovery of different and hitherto unsuspected misconduct? Here the House approved the decision in *National Heart and Chest Hospitals v Nambiar* (1981) to the effect that the employer would not be able to use the new reason to validate the original decision to dismiss. The proper course would be for the employer to allow the appeal and then dismiss, if appropriate, for the new reason.

In general then, the constitution of the Act militates clearly against the use of hindsight. The case must be judged according to how it looked at the time of the dismissal. This has a particular importance in relation to a failure to follow procedure or to act in accordance with good industrial relations practice. Even after *Devis v Atkins* (1977), employers accused of unfairness because of some procedural failure commonly argued that this was not really relevant because even if they had gone through all the procedural hoops, it still would not have altered their decision. The argument was accepted, and tribunals regularly instructed themselves to consider, in relation to procedural failures, whether following the right procedures would have made a difference to the ultimate decision to dismiss. But this brings in precisely that use of hindsight which *Devis v Atkins* declares to be impermissible. It required another decision of the House of Lords, *Polkey v Dayton Services* (1988), to rid unfair dismissal law of this particular heresy (known as the rule in *British Labour Pump v Byrne*).

In *Polkey* the House of Lords reaffirmed the rule in *Devis v Atkins* that the reasonableness of the employer's decision to dismiss must be judged according to what the employer knew and ought to have known at the moment of making that decision. If the procedural failure affects the state of the employer's knowledge, for example, where the employer has not investigated properly, or has not given the employee an opportunity to explain, then almost certainly the employer's decision to dismiss will be unreasonable. This is because a proper investigation might have revealed that the employee was not to blame, or the employee might have had a valid explanation for apparent misconduct. The House accepted that there might be a few – a very few – cases where such procedural failures would not render the dismissal unfair. But this would only be if the employer, at the moment of making the decision to dismiss, could say to herself, "if I investigated, or heard the employee, it could not possibly make a difference to what I am going to do". (And, incidentally, that that conclusion was not because the employer was unreasonably intransigent.) This will hardly ever be the case.

Following *Polkey*, the question arose as to whether the employer must **8–048** actually have thought about whether procedural steps would make any difference to the final decision, or whether an objective test suffices (*i.e.* that if the employer had thought about it, she could reasonably have decided that following particular procedural steps would not make a difference). The Court of Appeal held in *Duffy v Yeomans* (1994) that it was not necessary that an employer should have to show an actual decision not to consult; the objective test was good enough. The worry about this is that it once again encourages tribunals to consider hypothetical considerations, and may lead them back to asking something rather like whether proper procedure would have made any difference to the decision to dismiss.

What if further investigation would have revealed that the employee certainly did commit the offence, or that he would have had not a word of explanation to give? Is it not grossly unjust to the employer to hold the dismissal unfair? The House of Lords in *Devis v Atkins* said it was not. In these circumstances the dismissal is technically unfair and the justice or otherwise of this should be taken into account at the next stage, consideration of the remedy. The employee could be refused re-employment and awarded no compensation. However, the argument has eventually been accepted and in the Employment Act 2002, s.34, a new s.98A is added to the ERA, 1996. When this is brought into force, failure to follow procedure (other than the statutory minimum procedures described below, para. 8–071) will not render a dismissal unfair if the employer can show that it would have made no difference to the final decision to dismiss – *i.e.* there will be a statutory reversal of the House of Lords' decision in *Polkey*. This has caused considerable disquiet, articulated most notably by the outgoing President of Employment Tribunals, Judge Prophet, on the grounds that it will encourage employers to become lax about procedure and will involve tribunals in undesirably speculative exercises, at odds with their primary role as fact-finding bodies.

Redundancy

It is usually fair to dismiss an employee for redundancy because in such a **8–049** case the employee will be compensated by receiving a redundancy payment (see below, Chapter 9). However, awards of compensation for unfair dismissal are higher than redundancy payments, so it is not surprising that employees will often seek to claim that the dismissal is unfair. There are three main grounds on which redundancy may be held to be unfair: where an unfair selection process is used; where there is no prior warning or consultation with the employees; and where redeployment is not considered.

Unfair selection process

8–050 Trade unions prefer employers to carry out redundancies first by seeking volunteers, and then by using LIFO (last in, first out): that is, selecting employees on the basis of length of service and keeping the more senior people. Length of service has the advantage of being an objective and demonstrable fact, and one generally recognised as giving an employee a claim on the employer. Employers, on the other hand, may have good reason to reject this method. Volunteers may not come from the right parts of the business, and may be the very people you do not want to lose. While the least senior employees get the smallest redundancy payments and are thus the cheapest to make redundant, they may be young, keen and have the most up-to-date training; they may also have lower salaries than long-serving employees. For these reasons, then, the employer may well want a selection process that takes more account of the managerial interest.

It is recognised that choice of criteria for selection is a matter for management, and, subject to the points about to be made, in general management has a wide discretion as to what sort of selection procedure should be used. Where there are more than 20 redundancies, representatives of the workforce must be consulted over the selection criteria, but the procedure does not have to be agreed with them (see below, para. 9–041). The main danger for employers is that if they wish to keep the "best" workers, they may use over-subjective methods of deciding who the best workers are. In the leading case, *Williams v Compair Maxam* (1982), managers were told to pick those to be made redundant by listing those who needed to remain in order to keep the company viable. The EAT described this as an entirely subjective criterion, subjectively applied, which allowed scope for decisions to be made on the basis of personal likes and dislikes. The selection procedure was held to be unreasonable. Managers should have objective standards against which to test who are the best workers (*e.g.* productivity, attendance, conduct, appraisal records) and there should be some mechanism for ensuring that the criteria are fairly applied. Where there is a recognised trade union, the EAT in *Williams v Compair Maxam* recommended that the employer should seek to get the union's agreement to the selection criteria and, after selection, should consider with the union whether the criteria had been properly applied. Now that consultation must take place with employee representatives even where there is no recognised union it will no doubt be recognised as good practice to involve them in the same sort of way. It should be noted, however, that consultation with trade union or other representatives does not necessarily suffice. In *King v Eaton Ltd* (1996) the Court of Session said that the test must always be whether there has been fair and proper consultation, and this will sometimes mean consultation with individuals.

8–051 In order to claim unfair dismissal on grounds of unfair application of selection criteria, it seems necessary that employees should be able to see how they have been assessed against the employer's criteria and, in order to make comparisons, that they should be able to see the assessments of comparators. But this would raise problems of confidentiality as well as potentially oppressive requests for discovery of documents and drastic increases in the length of proceedings. To keep a lid on this, the Court of Appeal held in *British Aerospace v Green* (1995) that documents relating to other employees would not be relevant in anything other than exceptional circumstances and the applicant would need to be able to make a good case for such disclosure.

While length of service is the criterion generally favoured by trade unions, it has been pointed out that the emphasis on continuous service may disproportionately disadvantage women, who are more likely than men to have a record of broken service because of child-rearing responsibilities. It was held that, even if discriminatory, it could be justified in *Brook v Haringey LBC* (1992), although selecting part-timers before full-timers was held to be indirect sex discrimination in *Clarke v Eley (IMI) Kynoch Ltd* (1983) and would now contravene the Part-time Workers (Prevention of Less Favourable Treatment) Regulations 2000 unless justified (see above, para. 3–015).

Automatically unfair redundancy

Under ERA, s.105, selection for redundancy will be automatically unfair **8–052** where the reason for selection is one for which dismissal would be automatically unfair. These are discussed below, para. 8–061. It used to be the case that selection in contravention of an agreed procedure or customary arrangement was automatically unfair, unless there were special circumstances justifying the departure. This was removed by the Deregulation and Contracting Out Act 1994. However, selection in contravention of recognised procedures could well render the dismissal unfair under the general rubric of ERA, s.98(4).

Failure to warn or consult

The Industrial Relations Code of Practice 1972, which was repealed in **8–053** 1991, recommended giving employees as much warning as possible of impending redundancies and consulting with them over how best to handle the situation. This has become entrenched as good practice and thus survives despite the repeal. In the case of multiple redundancies, it is enforced by statute (see below, Chapter 9) and in *Williams v Compair Maxam* (1982), where the EAT laid down some guidelines on how a reasonable employer should handle redundancies, the need for maximum warning and consultation were the first points made. While the warning against putting a gloss on the words of the statute may here be reiterated, the relevance of warning and consultation to fairness was emphasised by the House of Lords in *Polkey v Dayton Services* (1988). The company had four van drivers. It planned to replace them with two van salesmen and a sales representative. Having decided that three of the van drivers would not be able to cope with the sales duties as well as the driving, it was decided to make them redundant. The first Polkey knew of this was when he was called into the office out of the blue and dismissed. As a mark of consideration, the employers arranged for another driver to take Polkey home; that driver was himself made redundant on his return!

The issue which reached the House of Lords was whether the failure to give prior warning or consult with the employee could make the dismissal unfair where the employer argued that even had this been done it would have made no difference to the ultimate decision to dismiss. As noted already, the House of Lords held that the fact that, as it turned out, it would have made no difference, should not be taken into account, because the employer's reasonableness had to be judged in the light of the facts known to the employer at the time of the decision to dismiss. The House held that the manner of the dismissal could be relevant to this, and Lord Bridge said,

> "in the case of redundancy, the employer will normally not act reasonably unless he warns and consults any employees affected or their representative, adopts a fair basis on which to select for redundancy and takes such steps as may be reasonable to avoid or minimise redundancy by redeployment within his own organisation".

It should be noted that on the facts of *Polkey* it may well be that the employer could have shown that, at the time of the decision to dismiss, they could have decided that there was no point in warning or consulting with the employees affected. The House of Lords actually remitted the case to the employment tribunal to consider this point, having indicated the proper test to be applied. The case was actually settled without further litigation. However, it is clear that safety considerations, as well as common humanity, dictate that the employer should give warning and consult with employees, whether or not the statutory duty applies.

Failure to consider redeployment

8–054 The final procedural step recommended by Lord Bridge in *Polkey* is that the employer should consider redeployment; this is also one of the recommendations of the guidelines in *Williams v Compair Maxam* (1982). Obviously this will depend on the kind of work done by the employee and the size of the organisation. A very small company will not have much scope for offering alternative work. However, in *Vokes v Bear* (1974), where the works manager of the company, a middle-aged man with a company car and a company house, was made redundant, it was pointed out that the employing company was part of a group of 300 companies, at least one of which was seeking senior managers at that time. Because no thought at all had been given to whether he could be placed in another position within the group, his dismissal was held to be unfair.

Statutory prohibition

8–055 Where the continued employment of the employee in her particular job would be in breach of statute or statutory regulation, her dismissal on this account may be fair. This provision, no doubt included for the sake of completeness, is actually hardly ever relied on in practice. The most obvious example where it might apply is where someone employed as a driver is banned from driving. Even here, it does not necessarily follow that the employer would act reasonably in dismissing. The employer should consider the length of the ban, whether the employee could be redeployed for the duration, and so on.

"Some other substantial reason"

In addition to the four reasons specified in ERA, s.98(2), section 98(1)(b) **8–056** states that a dismissal may be justified if it is for "some other substantial reason of a kind such as to justify the dismissal of an employee holding the position which that employee held". This formulation has been greatly criticised, in that its circularity and vagueness means that almost any reason could qualify, subject only to the qualification that it must be "substantial" – a quality which may be in the eye of the beholder. Indeed, cases over the years have shown a bewildering variety of reasons which have been held to justify dismissal on this ground, giving extra impetus to the point that it is really very easy for an employer to establish a potentially fair reason for dismissal. Bearing in mind that nearly anything can be "some other substantial reason", two of the commonest and most striking categories of cases to emerge under this heading will be examined.

The needs of the business

Where the employee is dismissed because of a reorganisation of the **8–057** business with which he cannot or will not fit in, his dismissal may be fair. Surprisingly, such a dismissal may be justified even if what is required is a breach of the employee's contract. Thus in *RS Components v Irwin* (1973) the employer found it was losing business because its sales staff were moving to work for its competitors. The employer therefore sought to impose a unilateral variation of employees' contracts by inserting a restraint of trade clause which would prevent them working for competitors for a certain period after leaving. The dismissal of an employee who refused to agree was held to be fair. Similarly, in *Hollister v National Farmers' Union* (1979) the union reorganised its insurance business with the result that the terms of the group secretaries who sold it would be changed. One objected, not least because the new pension arrangements would not be so good. His dismissal was held to be fair: the Court of Appeal held that the tribunal should ask only, "whether the reorganisation was such that the only sensible thing to do was to terminate the employee's contract unless he would agree to a new arrangement" (*per* Lord Denning).

How far can an employer go in changing employees' conditions for the **8–058** worse and still get away with justifying it under "some other substantial reason"? A long way, it seems. In *St John of God (Care Services) Ltd v Brook* (1992) a charity-run hospital, faced with possible closure for financial reasons, offered totally new contracts of employment on inferior terms to the workforce. Thirty out of 170 employees refused to accept and were dismissed. An employment tribunal found that the reorganisation was a substantial reason for the dismissals, but that they were unfair because it was unreasonable of the employer to expect the workers to bear such cuts. The EAT reversed this decision and remitted the case, considering that dismissals even in these extreme circumstances were capable of being fair. Note that if they were held to be fair, the employees would get nothing at all. If the hospital had ceased trading because of its financial problems, they would at least have been entitled to redundancy payments. The position should also be compared with what would happen in similar circumstances but in the context of the transfer of an undertaking (see below, para. 9–033).

While tribunals pay lip service to the need for reasonableness on the part of the employer (for example, by insisting on consultation beforehand), the primacy of the managerial prerogative in this area is striking. It can be difficult to try to explain to an employee why it is that she is bound by the contract of employment, but it is not necessarily unfair when she is dismissed because of her employer's refusal to adhere to it.

Pressure from third parties

8–059　Where customers or other employees provide the pressure for the employer to dismiss, even though the employee has not done anything to warrant dismissal under one of the other headings, the dismissal may be for a substantial reason, and fair. Thus in *Treganowan v Knee* (1974) a woman who upset the other office staff by boasting about her affair with a much younger man (before this became fashionable) was fairly dismissed on that account. She was dismissed without notice, and as she had committed no fundamental breach of contract, it would have been wrongful dismissal at common law. However, this illustrates the point that whether notice is given or not is largely irrelevant to unfair dismissal cases. It should be noted that if pressure from employees takes the form of a threat to take industrial action, a tribunal should take no account of it in deciding whether or not the dismissal is fair (ERA, s.107). A concerted refusal to work with a colleague would constitute such a threat (although this seems to have been overlooked in *Buck v Letchworth Palace* (1986), where a film projectionist who was homosexual was dismissed because his two colleagues refused to work with him because of an irrational fear of contracting AIDS).

The problem about allowing third party pressure to justify a dismissal is that the third party's reason for wanting the dismissal might be one that would be unfair if it were relied on directly by the employer. It seems unjust that a reason inadequate on its own can suffice when used at one remove. For example, in *Dobie v Burns International Security Services* (1984) the company provided the security service at Liverpool Airport, and the applicant was employed as a security officer there. Following a couple of incidents which the Court of Appeal were prepared to assume were not his fault, the airport authority refused to have him working there. The only alternative work that the employers could offer him was at a lower rate of pay, and he refused it. In these circumstances, the Court of Appeal held that his dismissal was capable of being fair, although it was remitted on the facts. Yet it is fairly clear that if the employer had relied on the incidents as justifying dismissal, it would have been unfair. While appreciating the employer's dilemma in such cases, it does not seem unreasonable to expect the same standard of the employer as if the reason behind the customer's objection were the reason for dismissal.

Other cases

In *Terry v East Sussex CC* (1976) it was held that the expiry of a fixed-term **8–060** contract without renewal was capable of being a dismissal for some other substantial reason. However, the onus will be on the employer to show the reason for the non-renewal to convince the tribunal that it was substantial and that the employer acted reasonably in the circumstances.

Under the Transfer of Undertakings (Protection of Employment) Regulations 1981, dismissal in connection with a transfer which is justified as being for an economic, technical or organisational reason will constitute "some other substantial reason" for dismissal (reg.8(2)). It will therefore be subjected to the scrutiny of the tribunal to judge whether or not it was reasonable in the circumstances (see below, para. 9–033).

Automatically unfair dismissals

Certain reasons for dismissal are categorised as automatically unfair. The **8–061** range of reasons falling in this category has waxed and waned in line with government policy. They have little in common except that there is no requirement of one year's continuous employment before the employee is protected from dismissal for these reasons, nor does the protection cease once the employee has reached normal retiring age.

Some of these categories of automatically unfair dismissal are dealt with elsewhere in this book: dismissal on grounds of family rights (above, paras 6–017, 6–020, 6–025) dismissal for refusal to do shop work or betting work on a Sunday (ERA, s.101, above, para. 6–037); dismissal in connection with the Working Time Regulations 1998 (ERA, s.101A, above, para. 6–041); dismissal of an employee trustee of an occupational pension scheme (ERA, s.102); dismissal of an employee representative for consultation (ERA, s.103, below, para. 9–040); dismissal for making a protected disclosure (ERA, s.103A, above, para. 4–033); dismissal contrary to the National Minimum Wage Act 1998 or the Tax Credits Act 1999 (ERA ss. 104A, 104B, above, para. 7–039); dismissal for taking part in protected industrial action (TULRCA, s.238A, below, para. 12–015); and dismissal for union membership reasons (TULRCA, s.152, below, para. 10–005). There remain two other categories of automatically unfair dismissal, both introduced by TURERA 1993.

Dismissal on health and safety grounds

Protection for employees against retaliation for complaints about health **8–062** and safety matters was introduced as a result of the EU Framework Directive on Health and Safety (89/391/EEC). The relevant health and safety grounds, defined in ERA, s.100, are sixfold: carrying out health and safety activities as an employer-designated representative; carrying out health and safety activities as a designated workers' representative; acting as a representative for consultation purposes; drawing what is reasonably believed to be a health or safety risk to the employer's attention; leaving or refusing to return to the place of work because of what is reasonably believed to be a serious and imminent danger (*cf. Piggott Bros v Jackson* (1991)); and taking appropriate steps to protect oneself or others in circumstances of serious and imminent danger. Not only is dismissal on any of these grounds automatically unfair, but also the employee must not be subjected to any detriment during employment for any of these reasons (ERA, s.44).

Problems will arise in interpreting the scope of the last two grounds in particular. So far they have received a fairly liberal interpretation. Thus in *Harvest Press v McCaffrey* (1999) the EAT held that the source of the danger could include a fellow employee, not just dangers arising from the workplace itself, so that an employee who refused to work because he was frightened of being attacked by another employee was protected. In *Goodwin v Cabletel UK Ltd* (1997) a tribunal held that an over-enthusiastic safety representative who had been heavy-handed in dealing with one of his employer's sub-contractors, causing a dispute, had been dismissed for the way he carried out his duties rather than because of his duties. The EAT held that the manner of carrying out duties could be within the protection of s.100 and remitted the case to a fresh tribunal. In *Masiak v City Restaurants (UK) Ltd* (1999) the EAT held that the reference in section 100(1)(e) to protecting "other persons" from danger could include members of the public as well as other employees, so that a chef dismissed for refusing to cook chicken which he thought was a health risk was covered.

It is specifically provided that refusing to work, etc., in these circumstances will not constitute participation in industrial action (as it could otherwise do if there were concerted action by a group of employees) (TULRCA, ss.237, 238). In relation to this last ground, it should be noted that the employer will have a defence if the steps taken by the employee were so negligent that any reasonable employer might have responded in the same way.

There is no upper limit on compensation for dismissals held to be unfair under section 100.

Dismissal for asserting a statutory right

8–063   Under ERA, s.104 it is automatically unfair to dismiss an employee if the reason or principal reason is either that the employee brought proceedings to enforce a statutory right or that the employee asserted that the employer had infringed a statutory right. Provided that the employee acts in good faith, it is irrelevant that she is not in fact entitled to the right in question or that it has not been infringed (*Mennell v Newell & Wright* (1997)). The statutory rights to which this applies are, broadly, individual rights under the ERA and rights in connection with trade union membership or activities or subscriptions under TULRCA.

This new right was introduced on the back of the health and safety grounds described above and is a welcome innovation. However, comparison with the non-victimisation provisions in the anti-discrimination legislation reveals a glaring omission: there is no protection as such for assisting another employee in asserting her statutory right.

Remedies for unfair dismissal

Reinstatement and re-engagement

Under ERA, s.112, a tribunal which has found that an employee was **8–064** unfairly dismissed must first explain the remedies of reinstatement and re-engagement and see whether the employee wishes to be re-employed. The clear intention of the legislation is that, if at all possible, the best remedy for unfair dismissal is for the employee to get his job back.

Reinstatement in essence means that the employee is returned to her former job as if she had never been away. She is entitled to net back pay, any other benefits which would have been received (*e.g.* a Christmas bonus or annual increment) and her continuity and seniority rights are preserved intact (ERA, s.114). Re-engagement should usually be as favourable as reinstatement, but differs in that it may mean that the employee is taken back in a different (though suitable) job, or the same job but a different place, or by a new company which is in the same group as her former employer. Generally the employee should again receive back pay and other benefits (ERA, s.115).

The tribunal has a discretion as to whether to make an order for re-employment. The wishes of the employee are paramount in the sense that re-employment will never be ordered against the employee's wishes. However, if the employer offers reinstatement and the employee unreasonably turns it down, compensation may be reduced (s.122(1)). The wishes of the employer are not taken into account, which is just as well since there would otherwise be no orders for re-employment. Employers almost invariably are unwilling to take back the employee, because they fear losing face, or that it will undermine their authority. The tribunal must consider whether it is practicable for the employer to take the employee back. The fact that a replacement has been taken on does not render re-employment impracticable; but if, for example, there have been redundancies in the meantime, or if the other workers are reluctant to have the employee back, this could be a ground of impracticability. Finally, the tribunal must also consider whether it is just to make such an order where the employee was to some extent to blame for the dismissal. This could lead to the tribunal deciding to order re-engagement rather than reinstatement, in that re-engagement need not be ordered with full back pay in these circumstances.

Although reinstatement or re-engagement have always been possible remedies for unfair dismissal, until 1975 the tribunal could only recommend them. They may now be ordered, but it remains the case that if the employer flouts the order, the only sanction is to make an additional award of compensation to the employee. In *Port of London Authority v Payne* (1994) the Court of Appeal held that the issue of practicability of re-employment should be judged afresh if the employer fails to comply with an order of reinstatement or re-engagement, meaning that the appropriateness of the original order can in effect be attacked. Furthermore, the court stressed that impracticability can be proved by a lot less than proof of impossibility and, most worrying of all, that the commercial judgment of the employer (which, you may be sure, will always argue the impracticability of re-employment) is a factor which should be taken into account. It is, perhaps, hardly surprising that despite their status as the primary remedies for unfair dismissal, reinstatement and re-engagement are still only awarded in about one per cent of successful unfair dismissal cases heard by tribunals. This can partly be put down to employee reluctance to return, usually because they fear that the employer will look for the first opportunity to dismiss them, or victimise them in other ways. However, in times of high unemployment when alternative jobs are hard to find, it is difficult to believe that this is the whole explanation, and it may be that tribunals do not take seriously enough their duty to promote these orders.

Compensation

8–065 The other, and more usual, remedy is compensation. Compensation for unfair dismissal is generally made up of two elements: a basic award and a compensatory award. In some circumstances, an additional award may be payable as well.

The basic award

8–066 The basic award is calculated according to a strict arithmetical formula in almost exactly the same way as a redundancy payment. The amount of a week's gross pay is multiplied by the number of years' service and then by a multiplier of ½, or 1, 1½, according to the employee's age (s.119). A week's pay is subject to a maximum limit which stood at £260 per week in 2003. The figure used to be reviewed regularly, but under the Employment Relations Act 1999, s.34 it is now linked to the retail prices index and will be altered accordingly every September. Years of service refers to complete years of service and is subject to a maximum of 20. Finally, this figure is multiplied by 1½ for all years when the employee was aged over 41, by 1 for all years between the ages of 22 and 41, and by ½ for all years under the age of 22. It follows that the maximum is £7,800, which would be the basic award for an employee aged 61 or more with at least 20 years' service and earning at least £260 gross per week.

The basic award may be reduced by a percentage if the employee unreasonably refuses an offer of reinstatement from the employer, or if it would be just and equitable to do so on account of any conduct of the employee before the dismissal (ERA, s.122(2)). This not only allows a reduction where the employee was partly to blame for the dismissal, but also in cases like *Devis v Atkins* where the misconduct is only discovered after the dismissal. It is not wholly uncommon for 100 per cent reductions to be made. However, it is not possible to reduce the basic award on account of the employee's conduct after dismissal, as the EAT held in *Soros v Davison* (1994), where the dismissed couple, butler and housekeeper to a well-known financier, sold their story to a national newspaper. Where the employee successfully argues that his dismissal for redundancy is unfair, then the redundancy payment is set off against the basic award to prevent double compensation. If the employee was dismissed for a reason relating to trade union membership (that she was, or was not, a union member) then the basic award cannot be less than £3,400. This was originally part of a special regime of compensation for dismissal for union membership reasons which was punitive in nature and designed in effect to deter dismissals on these grounds. It has since been extended to certain dismissals on health and safety grounds, in working time cases or for acting as an employee representative (ERA, s.120).

The compensatory award

The amount of the compensatory award is to be: **8–067**

> "such amount as the tribunal considers just and equitable in all the circumstances having regard to the loss sustained by the complainant . . . in so far as that loss is attributable to action taken by the employer" (s.123(1)).

It will include expenses incurred as a result of the dismissal and benefits the employee would have expected to receive but for the dismissal, but is subject to the general rule that the employee has a duty to mitigate his loss. The compensatory award is subject to an overall limit, which was widely criticised as much too low (£11,300 until October 1999). In the White Paper, *Fairness at Work* (Cm.3968, 1998) the Government originally proposed to scrap the limit on the compensatory award altogether. It was persuaded that this might make cases more difficult to settle (since it might be harder to quantify the value of a claim) and instead it lifted the limit very substantially to £50,000. It had been raised to £53,500 by 2003.

While the statutory formulation seems to give tribunals a wide discretion, early on general principles as to the heads of recoverable loss were established in *Norton Tool Co. v Tewson* (1973). First is the immediate loss up to the time of the tribunal hearing. This will include net wages which would have been received, including such things as overtime if it is likely that the employee would have worked overtime, any benefits in kind and tips. Private health insurance, the use of a company car and any other employment perquisites may be quantified and included. The sum will be reduced by the amount of any wages earned in new employment, and in effect by the amount of any social security benefits received (although the employer will have to pay back an equivalent amount to the State). Secondly, using similar principles, the tribunal must try to quantify the employee's future loss, if the employee is still out of work by the time of the hearing or has taken lower-paid employment. This may involve the tribunal in making difficult estimates about how long the employee is likely to be out of work, or catch up the former level of earnings. Where the employee was a member of an occupational pension scheme, loss resulting from the termination of that membership should also be taken into account; finally, a small conventional sum will be awarded for loss of employment protection rights, to reflect the fact that the employee will have to build up one year of continuous employment with a new employer before being protected against unfair dismissal and two years for redundancy, etc.

8–068 Injury to feelings and general distress at the manner of the dismissal was held not to be compensatable in *Norton Tool Co v Tewson*, but in *Johnson v Unisys Ltd* (2001) (above, para. 8–009) Lord Hoffmann expressed the *obiter* view that this might be wrong. Given that the emphasis of the statute is on "just and equitable" compensation he suggested that it could be appropriate to make an award for distress, humiliation, damage to reputation or to family life. However, in *Dunnachie v Kingston-upon-Hull City Council* (2003), the first case to reach the EAT subsequently on this point, it was held that this kind of damage could not come within the compensatory award.

Like the basic award, the compensatory award may be reduced by a percentage if conduct of the employee contributed to the dismissal (s.123(6)). While conduct which was only discovered after dismissal would not be within this, the overall discretion in the tribunal to award what is just and equitable permits it to take subsequently discovered misconduct into account. In practice, tribunals work out the global figure for the basic and compensatory award and then knock a percentage off that is appropriate, rather than treating them separately.

While the maximum possible award for general unfair dismissal is £61,300, in practice most applicants never see anything like this amount. In 2002–03 the median award made by tribunals was only £3,225, which suggests that for the vast majority of applicants to tribunals, the lifting of the limit on the compensatory award may not make much difference. This is one of the reasons for dissatisfaction with the law of unfair dismissal.

The additional award

8–069 If an employer refuses to implement an order for reinstatement or re-engagement, or fails to implement it fully, the tribunal may order it to pay an additional award of compensation to the employee (s.117(3)). This will be between 26 and 52 weeks' gross pay (subject to the £260 maximum), at the tribunal's discretion.

Statutory Disciplinary and Grievance Procedures

The right to be accompanied

8–070 The right to be accompanied during disciplinary and grievance hearings was introduced by the Employment Relations Act 1999, ss.10–13. It is available to the wider category of "workers" rather than just employees and is a right to be accompanied by a fellow worker or a trade union official (who may be an official not employed by the employer). Guidance on exercise of the right is given in section 3 of the Acas Code of Practice on Disciplinary and Grievance Procedures. The companion need not act unless she is willing to do so, but if she agrees, she will be entitled to paid time off to prepare for the hearing and to attend it. According to ERelA, s.10(2)(b), the companion has a right to address the hearing on the worker's behalf, but cannot answer questions for him.

The main issue which arises in relation to the right to be accompanied is identifying which hearings it applies to. In the past employers may not have distinguished clearly between the stages of investigating misconduct, say, and then disciplining the worker for it. The Act means that these stages must be distinguished and the Code makes clear that while investigations, informal interviews and counselling sessions are not within the scope of the right, any meeting which may result in the administration or confirmation of a warning, or any other disciplinary action, attracts the right. Thus the possible outcome of the meeting seems to be the critical issue. In *London Underground Ltd v Ferenc-Batchelor* (2003) the applicant was denied a companion because the result of the meeting was what the employer called an "informal oral warning". However, it transpired that it would be recorded in writing on the employee's file and would be taken into account in any later disciplinary proceedings. In these circumstances the EAT held that this was a disciplinary hearing and the employee had been wrongly denied her right to be accompanied.

Because grievance proceedings are instigated by employees and may cover all sorts of issues from the trivial to the extremely serious, the Act limits the right to be accompanied to grievance hearings which concern a "duty by an employer in relation to a worker" (ERelA, s.13(5)). This may be a statutory duty or a contractual duty, but would not cover, for example, a request for better terms and conditions which the employer turns down.

Where an employer fails to allow a worker to be accompanied, the worker may apply to a tribunal for up to two weeks' compensation. However, in practice a stronger sanction may be the increased likelihood of a dismissal being found to have been procedurally unfair where this right has been denied to an employee.

Statutory dismissal, disciplinary and grievance procedures

The introduction of statutory minimum requirements for dismissal, disci- **8–071** plinary and grievance procedures resulted was presaged by the DTi's 2001 consultation paper, *Routes to Resolution*, and was aimed as much as anything at trying to reduce the numbers of cases going to employment tribunals. It was thought that by compelling parties to go through basic procedural steps first, more disputes would be settled without the need for tribunal hearings.

The Employment Act 2002, ss.29–33 and Sch.2 lay out the basic procedures and they are due to be supplemented by Regulations which were produced for consultation in summer 2003. The new scheme is due to come into force on October 1, 2004. There are separate procedures for dismissals and discipline and for grievances; each consists of a standard, three-step procedure and a modified, two-step procedure.

Statutory dismissal and disciplinary procedure

8–072 The standard, three-step procedure is laid out in the Employment Act 2002, Sch.2, Pt 1. The draft Regulations indicate that it is to apply to all dismissals except constructive dismissal (because that comes about as a result of the employee's initiative); dismissals with a collective aspect; dismissals such as multiple redundancies, (because there is an obligation to consult in relation to these anyway); and certain cases of gross misconduct. So far as action short of dismissal is concerned, the statutory procedure will only apply to disciplinary measures for reasons of conduct or capability and the draft Regulations propose that it should not apply before a warning is given. Step One is for the employer to set out in writing the matter which may result in disciplinary action and dismissal and to send this to the employee with an invitation to a meeting to discuss the issue. Step Two consists of the meeting, which must happen before any action (other than an investigatory suspension on full pay) is taken against the employee. General provisions require parties to act reasonably in setting the time and place of the meeting and to be able to put their sides of the story – and the employee will, of course, be entitled to be accompanied, as described above. The employee must be informed of the outcome of the meeting and of any right of appeal. Step Three (if needed) is the appeal. The employee must inform the employer that she wishes to appeal; the appeal meeting must take place and the employee must be informed of the employer's final decision.

The modified, two-step procedure (also in Sch.2, Pt 1) is envisaged for the rare situations where the employer will have been entitled to dismiss the employee without having gone through the procedure. There are two situations where this may be the case: where it would be illegal to continue to employ the employee (for example, someone working without a required work permit) or what the consultation paper describes as "a small sub-set" of gross misconduct cases, where the employer would be justified in dismissing the employee without carrying out an investigation first. It is hard to imagine where this might be the case and it is somewhat at odds with the Acas Code which is at pains to make clear that investigation is necessary, even in cases of gross misconduct (see Code, para.7). Where the modified procedure applies, all that is necessary is for the employer to inform the employee in writing of the reasons for dismissal and her right of appeal (Step One) and for the appeal procedure to be followed as Step Two.

8–073 The consequences of failing to follow the statutory procedure are severe: any dismissal in breach of the procedure will be automatically unfair and the employee must be awarded a minimum of four weeks' pay (unless this would result in "injustice to the employer"!). Furthermore, any additional compensation is to be increased by between 10 per cent and 50 per cent (although it may not go above the current maxima described above, para.

8–066). If the procedure is not carried through because of fault on the employee's part then any award for unfair dismissal will be reduced by the same percentage. There is no sanction against an employee in these circumstances whose dismissal is held to be fair.

A critical issue in this is the relationship between the statutory procedure and the norms of good industrial practice developed in the case law on unfair dismissal over the past 30 years and also embodied in the Acas Code of Practice on Disciplinary and Grievance Procedures. The consultation paper on the new Regulations is at pains to emphasise that the fairness or unfairness of a dismissal is to be decided according to the usual principles in situations where the procedure has been followed so that the dismissal is not automatically unfair. However, if employers have been through the statutory minimum procedure, even if not doing everything recommended in the Acas Code, it is likely that they will argue with force that their decision to dismiss cannot be seen as outside the band of reasonable responses.

Statutory grievance procedure

The statutory grievance procedures (standard and modified) are laid out in **8–074** the Employment Act 2002, Sch.2, Pt 2. It will not apply in all situations where an employee wishes to raise a grievance. The draft Regulations propose that it will be limited to situations where an employee is aggrieved about an action taken against him for a reason other than his conduct or capability. This is apparently an attempt to avoid too much overlap with the statutory dismissal and disciplinary procedure. It does include constructive dismissal, but other exclusions are as for the dismissal/disciplinary procedure.

Step One of the grievance procedure is for the employee to make a complaint in writing to the employer. Step Two consists of the meeting and then the employer's decision being communicated to the employee together with notification of his right of appeal. Step Three is the appeal. As with the dismissal and disciplinary procedure, the modified procedure will only apply when employment has ended and either the parties both agree in writing not to meet or it is not reasonably practicable for them to do so. In this case, Step One is for the employee to set out the nature and basis for the grievance in writing and Step Two is for the employer to send a written response.

The main thrust of the grievance procedure provisions is to prevent employees bringing tribunal proceedings without going through it. The draft Regulations provide that an employee cannot bring an action until performing Step One and then waiting 28 days (time-limits for tribunal claims are extended by three months in these situations). If the procedure is not followed properly because of the employee's fault then any tribunal award will be reduced by 10–50 per cent. If the procedure is not carried through properly because of the employer's fault, then any tribunal award will be increased by 10–50 per cent, subject to the current maximum limits.

It is possible that the Regulations in their final form may differ from the above, but it is unlikely that they will be terrifically different. The

Government has, however, indicated that it is not now intending to exercise the power under EA 2002, s.30 to make the statutory minimum procedures part of the contract of employment. This would have enabled employees to enforce them by civil proceedings independently of bringing another tribunal claim successfully. It has now been decided to wait and see what happens with the new procedures before venturing further.

9. Redundancy and Transfers of Undertakings

Redundancy

Compensation for redundancy was one of the first protective rights **9–001** introduced for employees by statute. Following closely on the Contracts of Employment Act 1963 (which gave employees the right to minimum periods of notice and a written statement of terms and conditions), the Redundancy Payments Act was passed in 1965.

Apart from amendments in 1975, the law on redundancy has remained in substantially the same form ever since, although it is now to be found as Part XI of the Employment Rights Act 1996. This is perhaps no longer appropriate given the other developments since then. The law of unfair dismissal has had a great impact, not least because levels of compensation for unfair dismissal are higher than for redundancy. The redundancy payment is the equivalent of the basic award alone. Thus whereas before 1972, cases involved employees arguing that they were redundant while the employer argued that they had been dismissed for some other reason, afterwards the position was reversed. Employers were more willing to make the lower redundancy payment (part of which they could claim back from the State by way of rebate), while employees sought to argue that they had been unfairly dismissed.

While the law on unfair dismissal was at least drawn up with an eye to its relationship with the law on redundancy, this can hardly be said of the other major development in this area, the Transfer of Undertakings (Protection of Employment) Regulations 1981 (TUPE). Introduced by a reluctant Government to comply with the Acquired Rights Directive (77/187/EEC), the regulations apply to all transfers of undertakings, whether or not a reduction of the workforce occurs. As a result, they overlap but are not coterminous with the rules on redundancy. However, the relationship between the two is opaque and at times inconsistent. An overhaul of the entire structure seems overdue.

A redundancy payment is not, and never has been, intended to be a kind of unemployment benefit, tiding the worker over until a new job is found. It

249

is more of a recognition of past service, of the worker's stake in and contribution to the enterprise. These points are illustrated by the fact that the amount of the payment depends on length of service, and that employees who qualify are entitled to their payment even if they have another job to go to the next day. Nevertheless, part of the rationale behind the scheme was to ease technological and other changes: it was hoped that employees receiving compensation would more easily adjust to the loss of their jobs and even consider moving to new work.

Qualification to claim redundancy

9-002 As with unfair dismissal, the worker has the burden of establishing that he is qualified to claim: he must be an employee, must not fall into one of the excluded categories and must have at least two years' continuous employment (see above, para. 8–016). Similarly, it is for the employee to prove that he was dismissed, if this is denied. The definition of dismissal in ERA, s.136 is generally the same as the definition of dismissal in relation to unfair dismissal, discussed above in Chapter 8.

A particular problem apt to arise in redundancy situations is shown by *Morton Sundour Fabrics v Shaw* (1967). The employer told the employee that they would be closing his department some time that year, but did not indicate exactly when. They helped the employee to find another job, so he gave notice and left. Because he was not actually under notice of dismissal at the time he left, it was held that he did not qualify for a redundancy payment (see also *Doble v Firestone* (1981)). The problem with this is that it is likely to encourage an employee to stay until the bitter end rather than to try and find another position as quickly as possible, quite the opposite of what was intended. Some palliation is provided by ERA, s.142, which allows an employee to leave early without jeopardising his entitlement, provided that during his statutory notice period he serves the employer with a counter-notice stating his intention to leave early. If accepted, the employee remains entitled to his redundancy payment. If the employer does not accept, she must serve a written counter-notice to the employee's counter-notice saying that he is required up to the last day. If the employee then leaves early, an employment tribunal must decide whether it is just and equitable for him to get all or part of his redundancy payment. However, section 142 would not help an employee in the circumstances of *Morton Sundour Fabrics v Shaw*, because he was not on notice at the time he left.

Once it is established that the employee has been dismissed, section 163(2) raises a presumption that the dismissal is by reason of redundancy, which means that the burden is on the employer to disprove it. While few cases turn on the burden of proof, the presumption proved vital in *Willcox v Hastings* (1987). W and L were employed by a small business owned by W's father. He sold it to a married couple, who both intended to work in the business and who therefore only needed one extra employee. Thus *prima facie* either W or L was redundant. However, the new owners planned that the third employee should be their son; so both W and L were dismissed, but only one of them for a redundancy reason. Not surprisingly, no one ever bothered to designate which of them was dismissed for what. It was held that both W and L were entitled to redundancy payments: the burden was on the employers to disprove redundancy in respect of each of them, and the employers could not do so.

The meaning of redundancy

Two situations are defined as redundancy under ERA, s.139. Broadly, the **9–003** first deals with the employer closing down the business, and the second, where the employee is surplus to requirements.

Cessation of business

Under section 139(1)(a) an employee is dismissed for redundancy if the **9–004** dismissal is wholly or mainly attributable to:

"the fact that his employer has ceased, or intends to cease—

(i) to carry on the business for the purposes of which the employee was employed by him; or
(ii) to carry on that business in the place where the employee was so employed . . ."

In general, redundancy on the ground of cessation of business is fairly straightforward as it involves a simple investigation of an objective fact – has the business ceased or not? The tribunal may not go behind the decision to inquire whether it was actually necessary to close down. In *Moon v Homeworthy Furniture* (1977) employees made redundant when a factory closed claimed that it had not been closed for economic reasons but as a retaliatory measure by the employer because it had a bad industrial relations record. Following the general principle adopted in company law, that it is for management to run the business, not the courts (*Re Smith & Fawcett* (1942)), the EAT declined to be drawn into a consideration of the reasons behind the company's decision.

One reason for shutdown may be that the employer is going out of business. If this is because the business is insolvent and is being wound up, it is often the case that the assets are insufficient to meet the claims for redundancy and pay in lieu of notice of employees. In this situation the payments will be met from State funds (ERA, s.166). Alternatively, when an employer ceases to trade the business may be sold to someone else. In these circumstances it is important to know whether there has been a transfer of an undertaking (in which case TUPE will apply). These issues will be considered below (para. 9–020).

The main area of difficulty which has arisen under the first limb of the definition of redundancy is where the business does not cease altogether but there is a shutdown at one particular place. For example, if a company with factories at Leeds and Sheffield shuts down its Leeds factory but has jobs available at its Sheffield premises, are the Leeds workers redundant or can they be required to relocate to Sheffield? The issue here is whether the test for deciding what is the place at which the employee is employed for the purposes of ERA, s.139(1)(a)(ii) should be *factual* (*i.e.* where has the employee actually been working?) or *contractual* (*i.e.* place of work means wherever the employee can be required to work according to her contract of employment). In the first case to reach the Court of Appeal on redundancy, *O'Brien v Associated Fire Alarms* (1968), it seemed that a contractual test was to be used. The employees were electricians whose work was directed from the Liverpool office. They were told that they would have to work in the Barrow area (some 120 miles away) when the Liverpool office closed for lack of work. While the Barrow area was within the region directed from the Liverpool office, they had always worked within the vicinity of Liverpool. As their work involved them in travelling to jobs, the court was prepared to accept that it was an implied term of their contracts that they should travel, but that it could only be implied that they would work at places within reasonable daily travelling distance of their homes. Since the employer had no right to require them to move to Barrow, the Court of Appeal held that they were dismissed on grounds of redundancy.

9–005   The contractual test has been criticised on the grounds that when the legislation was passed it was envisaged that relocation in these circumstances would constitute a redundancy situation. But in the more recent Court of Appeal decision, *High Table Ltd v Horst* (1997), the point was made that in *O'Brien v Associated Fire Alarms* the employer had purported to dismiss the employees for breach of contract and thus it was inevitable that the focus of the decision was on whether their refusal to move was a breach of contract or not. Once the employer's ground for dismissal was held not to operate, the statutory presumption of redundancy applied.

This explanation of *O'Brien v Associated Fire Alarms* (1968) enabled the court in *High Table Ltd v Horst* to use the factual approach without contravening the doctrine of precedent. The employer in this case provided catering services to firms in the City of London, and the employees had worked for a number of years as waitresses at Hill Samuel before being dismissed on grounds of redundancy following a reduction in the catering service required by Hill Samuel. They argued that they were not redundant because there was an express mobility clause in their contracts, so they could have been deployed elsewhere. In deciding what was the "place where the employee was so employed" the Court of Appeal was clear that a factual test should be used, saying that if an employee had always worked in one place it would be contrary to common sense to suggest that the place of work included other places because of a mobility clause. If, however, during the period of employment the nature of the work required the employee to go from place to place, then the contract might be of assistance in deciding what the place of work was. Here, the employees had always worked in the same place so they were redundant when work there ceased.

This case was the converse of *O'Brien v Associated Fire Alarms*, in that in *High Table Ltd v Horst* the employees wanted to move but the employer did not want to redeploy them elsewhere. It would seem, however, that if the employer had told them to move and they had refused, in this case they would have been in breach of contract because of the express mobility clause. It therefore seems likely that such a dismissal would not be for redundancy. This seems a little one-sided, with all the flexibility on the side of the employer. Note also that even if the employer does not have a contractual right to move the employee, she may still be denied a redundancy payment if the offer of employment elsewhere is seen as an offer of suitable alternative employment which she has unreasonably refused (see below, para. 9–010).

Surplus labour

The second situation where a dismissal will amount to a redundancy is **9–006** where it is wholly or mainly attributable to:

> "the fact that the requirements of that business—
>
> > (i) for employees to carry out work of a particular kind . . . have ceased or diminished or are expected to cease or diminish." (s.139(1)(b)).

This definition causes considerable problems in practice, since from the point of view of the employee, "work" is the job that she does: the whole package of the tasks performed and the terms and conditions under which they are performed. However, the statutory definition emphasises only the tasks performed, and it is unclear how far the "work of a particular kind" is linked to the employees who carry it out. While it is apt to cover the paradigm of a business whose work has fallen off so that it needs fewer people, many situations where labour is shed do not fit that pattern.

First, one situation which is increasingly common is where the amount of work remains the same, or may even have increased, but the employer decides that survival requires a cut in the salary bill – more must be done with less. In *Delanair v Mead* (1976) the company was in desperate straits and decided to cut the workforce by 10 per cent. The manager of Mead's department was told to cut his staff by one and selected Mead. The EAT remitted the case to the tribunal to consider whether the employer's true reason was that, having reappraised their needs, they did not need him (which would be redundancy) or whether they had merely decided to cut one salary – which would be a dismissal on grounds of economy, not redundancy. The decision has been criticised, for if management decides that it must make do with fewer people, for whatever reason, it must be the case that the requirements of the business have diminished. The wording of the Act does not empower the tribunal to go behind the decision to reduce the workforce to consider the motives for so doing.

This was recognised by a different EAT in *AUT v University of Newcastle* (1987) where a lecturer was dismissed when the funding for his course ceased and the tribunal considered that this was not a redundancy dismissal because the work still remained to be done, although the university could not afford to pay someone to do it. The EAT held that the requirements of the business are defined exclusively by the employer, and here it had been decided that the lecturer was not required. This was redundancy. However,

Delanair was distinguished rather than not followed, on the grounds that there was no operational review in that case, as there had been here. It is submitted that in most cases where the employer decides that fewer employees must do the same amount of work, those dismissed are redundant as surplus to requirements.

9–007 A second area of difficulty related to this is where there is a reorganisation of tasks among employees with the end result that someone's job disappears. In these circumstances, the employee may feel that he is not redundant but unfairly dismissed: his job is still there, but has been carved up among other people; there has been no diminution in the work. However, once more it seems clear that if such a reorganisation leads to management deciding that it needs fewer people, this is properly to be regarded as redundancy. An example is *Robinson v BI Airways* (1978). The employee had been employed as the flights operations manager, responsible to the general manager, operations and traffic. In the interests of economy and efficiency, tasks were reorganised and both these posts disappeared. A new post of operations manager was created and Robinson was dismissed. He claimed unfair dismissal, arguing that the new job was really his old job with a few added extras. It was held that the new job was sufficiently distinct from both the previous jobs that it could properly be said that his job had disappeared and that he was redundant. In these circumstances an employee may be able to claim unfair dismissal if not redeployed to the new position, but on the facts this was not the case here.

This is an illustration of the Act's emphasis on the tasks to be done rather than the employee as the holder of a job involving a package of tasks and terms and conditions. Another consequence of this is that if tasks are reorganised and the employee cannot cope with the new allocation, she may be held to be dismissed for incapability rather than because the "requirements . . . for employees to carry out work of a particular kind . . . have ceased or diminished". This in turn leads to difficult questions as to how different the package of tasks must be before it can be said that it is work of a different kind.

In *North Riding Garages v Butterwick* (1967) the respondent was the manager in charge of the repairs workshop and had been employed at the garage for 30 years. He had always been involved in doing a lot of repair work himself, but new owners of the garage put more emphasis on the managerial side. His job changed and the work was increased so that he spent less time on practical work and more on paperwork – which he did not do very well. Eight months later he was dismissed, and it was held that the reason was incompetence rather than redundancy. His argument was essentially that the employers now needed a different kind of employee and their need for employees to carry out work of the particular kind that he had done had diminished. But in effect it was more a reallocation of tasks, which the court felt did not actually make it a different kind of work. If new methods alter the way work is done, rather than altering the nature of the work itself, the employee can be expected to adapt, and the court evidently thought that this situation fell into the former category (see also *Hindle v Percival Boats* (1969)).

A comparatively rare example of a situation where a change in tasks was **9–008** held to amount to a change in the nature of the work is provided by *Murphy v Epsom College* (1985) where a school employed two plumbers, including the applicant, who worked mostly on the heating system. The school upgraded its heating system, introducing an electronic control system. Murphy was made redundant on the grounds that what was now needed was a heating technician – someone who could deal with the electrical as well as the plumbing work – rather than a general plumber like him. The Court of Appeal upheld the tribunal's decision that this was a change in the nature of the work, and thus a genuine redundancy. In assessing this decision, it must be borne in mind that whether there has been a change in the nature of the work is again a question of fact for tribunals, and so it is entirely possible that seemingly inconsistent decisions may be upheld on appeal; it is also relevant that the "hidden agenda" in this case was that Murphy was in dispute with the school over his hours and the scope of his duties, and it seems that he was reluctant to do the new work without some improvement. The governors responded by taking the view that if he said it was outside his duties, they needed a different kind of employee. His claim was for unfair dismissal, but the employer's contention that it was redundancy was accepted – a rather different situation from *North Riding Garages v Butterwick*.

In *North Riding Garages v Butterwick* (1967) the court referred to the fact that on his dismissal a new workshop manager had been employed as an indicator that he was not redundant. While this will not invariably prove that the reason was not redundancy (see, *e.g. Murphy v Epsom College*, above), where there is no reduction in the number of employees, as a rule of thumb there will usually be no redundancy. Thus in *Johnson v Notts Combined Police Authority* (1974) two civilian clerks had for more than 20 years been employed in normal office hours from Mondays to Fridays. Outside those times, essential clerical work was carried out by police officers. In order to release officers from this work, the police authority wished the clerks to work shifts (8am to 1pm and 1pm to 8pm) over a six-day week. They refused because of their domestic duties, and were dismissed. Replacements were taken on. It was held that they were not redundant. The work remained the same, there was just as much work to be done, and the fact that it was at different hours did not change its nature. Although such a change was a breach of contract, Lord Denning said, "It is settled . . . that an employer is entitled to reorganise his business so as to improve its efficiency and, in so doing, to propose to his staff a change in the terms and conditions of their employment: and to dispense with their services if they do not agree. Such a change does not automatically give the staff a right to redundancy payments". In *Macfisheries v Findlay* (1985) a change from night-shift to day-shift was held to constitute a change in the nature of the work done, the difference between day and night work being considered as of a different order of magnitude to the differences in daytime hours in *Johnson v Notts Combined Police Authority*. The clerks in that case did not claim unfair dismissal, but would probably have lost if they had, as the reorganisation would almost certainly have constituted "some other substantial reason" for dismissal.

Similarly in *Lesney Products v Nolan* (1977) machine setters had habitually worked a long day shift and a lot of overtime in the evenings. The employers reorganised to replace this with a double day shift to cut overtime costs. The employees could not claim to be redundant. In this case, the new arrangements meant that their weekly pay was reduced from £70 to £56 – a very substantial proportion. But this underlines again the fact that the definition of redundancy concentrates on the needs of the business and the functions performed, not the package of terms and conditions which constitute the employee's job (see also *Chapman v Goonvean & Rostowrack China* (1973)).

9–009   As noted already, today employees are more likely to claim that they are not redundant and that rather, their dismissal is unfair. If there is a flexibility clause in the contract, giving the employer the option of moving the employee to other work, can the employee argue that he is not redundant just because the usual job has disappeared? This is analogous to the argument about place of work, discussed above, and was the subject of conflicting authority until settled by the House of Lords decision in *Murray v Foyle Meats Ltd* (1999). Lord Irvine (who gave the main opinion) stated firmly that a tribunal considering redundancy only had to answer two simple questions of fact. First, did the requirements of the business for employees diminish, meaning that the employer needed fewer employees, for whatever reason? Secondly, did that cause the dismissal of this employee? If so, the employee is redundant.

In reaching this decision the House of Lords expressly endorsed the reasoning of the EAT in *Safeway v Burrell* (1997) and so it seems that it also deals with the problem of "bumping". This is the situation where, rather than dismiss a particular redundant worker, the employer decides to redeploy her to another post and make the holder of that post redundant. Is the person so "bumped out" redundant? While it is true that his job remains, it would seem that the dismissal of the bumped employee is wholly or mainly due to a reduction in the requirements of the business for employees, which is all that the statutory definition requires, and this was the view expressed by the EAT in *Safeway v Burrell*. It may be that the victim of the bumping may be able to claim it is also unfair dismissal: this will depend on the reason for the employer choosing to keep the one rather than the other (see above, para. 8–049).

Offer of suitable alternative employment

9–010 If the employer makes the employee an offer of a new contract of employment before the ending of his old contract, and the new contract is either the same work or suitable alternative employment, the employee will be disentitled to a redundancy payment if he unreasonably refuses it (ERA, s.141). While it is no longer necessary that the employer's offer should be in writing, it must be made before the ending of the old contract and sufficient details must be given to enable the employee to make an informed choice. If the new contract does not start immediately on the finishing of the old one, it must begin within four weeks thereafter.

Whether an offered contract is "suitable" and whether the refusal is "reasonable" would seem to involve two separate questions about different issues. Suitability seems naturally to refer to the objective characteristics of the job itself, while judging the reasonableness of the refusal seems to allow for subjective considerations relating to the employee's personal circumstances to be taken into account. That said, some factors may be relevant to both questions: if the new job involves extra travelling time, that may be relevant both to suitability and to whether it is reasonable to turn it down, for example. Perhaps for this reason, the Court of Appeal in *Spencer and Griffin v Gloucs CC* (1985) deprecated attempts to draw a rigid distinction between the two aspects. However, it is submitted that considering them separately is an aid to clarity of thought, and the wording of the Act suggests that they are separate and consecutive considerations.

As the question whether an offer of suitable employment has been **9–011** unreasonably turned down is a question of fact for a tribunal to consider, few cases are of much value as precedents. In general, anecdotal evidence seems to suggest that tribunals are reluctant to deprive employees who are *prima facie* redundant of their redundancy payments, and so may resolve doubtful situations in the employee's favour. Pay is a major factor to be considered, and it would be unusual for a contract on less pay to be regarded as suitable. Having said that, the fact that pay remains the same does not mean that the offer is suitable. In *Taylor v Kent CC* (1969) a redundant headmaster was offered alternative employment as one of a pool of mobile teachers, sent out to schools as required, with his pay maintained at its previous level. The drop in status and responsibility made it an unsuitable alternative.

The opportunity to exercise and maintain a level of skill may be relevant, although it should be borne in mind that an offer of an entirely different kind of work for which the employee would require retraining may be suitable. What would be relevant is whether the employee is likely to be able to complete the retraining successfully. An offer of less skilled assembly work was considered unsuitable for a skilled card wirer in *Standard Telephones & Cables v Yates* (1981).

Travelling time and cost is another major factor. Where the employer is prepared to pay travel expenses and for time spent travelling, this may help to indicate that the offer is suitable. However, for employees with domestic responsibilities in particular, it may be reasonable to refuse a job which will mean a greater time away from home. Analogously, a job which requires an employee to relocate to a different part of the country is more likely to be considered suitable if the employer is prepared to help financially and otherwise with the move; yet an employee with an employed spouse who cannot easily move, and/or children at a critical stage of schooling may reasonably refuse a generous relocation package.

A final example indicating some other factors which could be relevant to reasonable refusal is *Paton, Calvert & Co v Westerside* (1979). The company, in severe financial difficulties, sent redundancy notices to all staff. Before the notices expired, the company got a Temporary Employment Subsidy from the Government, so it wrote to all employees offering them their jobs back. Once given, of course, a notice of dismissal cannot be rescinded unilaterally, so technically this was a dismissal and an offer of alternative employment. Since the new jobs were the same as the old jobs, there was no suggestion that they were unsuitable. However, Westerside, who was aged 61, had already found a new permanent job. It was held reasonable for him to reject the offer: the company's financial prospects were still uncertain, and for someone of his age, within a few years of retirement and in an age group that usually has the greatest difficulty in finding new employment, permanence was extremely important.

Trial periods

9–012 If the alternative employment offered is very different from the employee's previous job, he is taking a bit of a shot in the dark by accepting. What if it does not work out? Until 1975, the employee had to take the risk. If he decided that he did not like the new job and left, he would have forfeited his right to a redundancy payment. For this reason the Employment Protection Act 1975 introduced the concept of a trial period, during which time neither side would be finally committed. It is now to be found in ERA, s.138.

Under section 138, if the terms of the new contract differ wholly or in part from the old contract, there will be a trial period of four weeks, or such longer period as the parties agree where retraining is required. If the trial period is to be longer than the statutory four weeks, it must be specified precisely in writing. If during the trial period the contract is terminated by either party, the employee is to be treated as having been dismissed as at the end of the original contract, for the original reason (usually, redundancy). This means that if the employer dismisses him for incompetence in the new job, the employee will be treated as dismissed for the original redundancy. If the employee resigns because he does not like the new job, it will be treated as a dismissal, but his entitlement to a redundancy payment will depend on whether the new job was suitable and whether his termination during the trial period was reasonable or not. Presumably the employee may have a stronger claim to say that a refusal is reasonable where he has actually tried the new work.

It has been held that in some circumstances the employee may be able to rely on the existence of a trial period at common law – which may not be for as limited a time as the statutory trial period. It all depends on how the employer handles the redeployment of the employee to new work. If the employer formally terminates the original contract, but offers a contract for different work before the old contract expires, then the only possibility is for a statutory trial period of four weeks. But if the employer instructs or requests the employee to move to different work, then assuming that there is no right to do this under the contract, the employer's instruction is in fundamental breach of contract or the request is an offer to vary the contract. By general contract principle, the innocent party faced with a fundamental breach has a reasonable time to decide whether or not to accept the breach as a termination of the contract (by resigning) or to affirm the contract. Similarly, he has a reasonable time to decide whether to accept a variation. This reasonable time in effect constitutes a trial period in the new job at common law.

Thus in *Turvey v Cheney* (1979), four employees in the polishing department were told that it was due to close because of lack of work and were offered work in different departments. They agreed to try the new work on trial. More than four weeks later, they left. The EAT pointed out that it was already well established that merely beginning to work under a new contract does not indicate acceptance of it: the employee has a reasonable time to make up his mind (see *Shields Furniture Ltd v Goff* (1973)). The statutory trial period was meant to add to an employee's rights, not to reduce them. The EAT's interpretation of this situation therefore was that if the employer had not formally given notice to terminate the employees' contracts and offer them new ones, then the request to move to different departments was not within the contract and they had a reasonable time to decide whether or not to accept this new or varied contract. At some point, whether or not they expressed their decision, it would be possible to say that a reasonable time had expired. At that stage, said the EAT, they would in theory be able to rely on the statutory four-week trial period, since by then the employment under the previous contract would have ended.

Reduction for misconduct

Under ERA, s.140(1), if the employee commits an act of misconduct which **9–013** at common law would entitle the employer to terminate the contract without notice, the employee will be disentitled to a redundancy payment, subject to the exceptions in s.140(2), (3). This is not a provision for a reduction in the redundancy payment but a total disqualification; however, there are exceptions. The oddity is that the exceptions seem to cover the entire ambit of the rule, leaving no situation where there would be a total disqualification.

There are two exceptions. Under section s.140(2), if the employee takes part in a strike or other industrial action while on notice for redundancy and is dismissed on that account, section 140(1) does not apply and the employee remains entitled to her redundancy payment. This takes account of the fact that the announcement of redundancies may well result in protest action by the workforce and it could be unfair for them to lose all compensation because of it. Also, under section 143, in these circumstances the employer can serve a notice of extension on the employees, requiring them to work the number of days lost through the action on top of their notice period. If the employees refuse, they will not get their redundancy payments.

The second exception, under section 140(3), refers to all cases of misconduct other than taking part in a strike or other industrial action, and provides that if the employee is dismissed for this misconduct while on notice for redundancy, the tribunal may award him such part of his redundancy payment as it considers to be just and equitable – which may be the whole sum.

The peculiarity of all this is that section 140(1) only applies to dismissals **9–014** for misconduct, yet the exceptions in section 140(2) and (3) seem to cover all cases of misconduct, and state that at worst in these cases the employee's payment will be reduced. However, there is a difference between the two sections. The exceptions are qualified by the requirement that the dismissals for misconduct or industrial action must have taken place while the employee was on notice for redundancy. This is not the case for section 140(1), which seems therefore to make the rather obvious point that if the employee is dismissed for misconduct she cannot get a redundancy payment. If this is all it means, one might wonder why it was stated at all. It was rescued from this abyss of meaninglessness by the EAT's decision in *Simmons v Hoover* (1977).

In *Simmons v Hoover* a strike of some months was causing a contraction in the employer's business. The employer therefore wrote to the employees who were on strike giving them notice that they were redundant. Simmons claimed a redundancy payment on the strength of section 140(2). The EAT held that section 140(2) applied only if the employees went on strike when they were already on notice for redundancy. Both exceptions in effect envisage two dismissals: an original dismissal for redundancy, which is then overtaken by a dismissal for misconduct or participation in industrial action. Here there was only one dismissal – said by the employer to be for redundancy, although it could have been for going on strike. The EAT held that where the employer dismisses for redundancy but could have dismissed at common law for misconduct, section 140(1) applies and the employee is disentitled to a redundancy payment.

9–015   While the decision gives meaning to section 140(1) it leaves two unanswered questions. Why should an employer who can dismiss for misconduct dismiss for redundancy instead? The answer to this may simply be ignorance of the law. But in that case, why should there be a special statutory provision to relieve an ignorant employer of the consequences of her mistake? Such a provision must be entirely unique.

So far as section 140(3) is concerned, it is clear that the issue is whether the employer is entitled at common law to dismiss for the misconduct. In *Bonner v Gilbert* (1989) an employee on notice for redundancy was dismissed for suspected dishonesty. On the basis that the employer honestly believed on reasonable grounds that the employee was guilty, an employment tribunal held that section 140(1) and (3) applied, and the employee should not get any part of his redundancy payment. The EAT reversed the decision, because the question must be whether the employee was actually guilty of the dishonesty (*i.e.*, whether there was an actual breach of contract) in order to satisfy the common law test.

Lay-off and short-time working

9–016   An employer may try to avoid or at least postpone redundancies by temporarily suspending operations, or reducing the number of hours worked. Unless the employer has the power under the contract to lay off employees without pay, or reduce their hours, it will be a fundamental breach of contract entitling the employees to leave and claim constructive dismissal (see Suspension, above, para. 8–007). Even where the employer has contractual power to do this, however, it is provided that in some circumstances the employee may leave and claim redundancy.

Under section 147, the employee is laid off in any week in which the employer does not provide him with work and he is therefore not entitled to remuneration. Short-time is defined as a diminution in work leading to the employee's remuneration being less than half a week's pay. If employees are laid off or put on short-time for four or more consecutive weeks, or for any six weeks within a 13-week period, they may give notice of an intention to claim a redundancy payment because of it. They must give the notice in writing, and must also give the proper period of contractual notice before leaving. The employer may contest the claim on the grounds that it is reasonably expected that there will be no further lay-off or short-time working in the next 13 weeks: this defence must be indicated in a counter-notice in writing served on the employee within seven days of her notice to claim (ss.149, 152).

The provisions as to notice and counter-notice, timing and supplementary provisions, of which only an outline is given above, are enormously complicated and have been described as the despair of all those concerned with the interpretation of industrial legislation (Lord McDonald in *Kenneth MacRae v Dawson* (1984)) and the chances of an employee navigating them successfully and qualifying for a redundancy payment are slight without good union or legal advice. It must be doubted whether such complexity can be justified.

Calculation of the redundancy payment

A statutory redundancy payment is calculated according to a strict arith- **9–017** metical formula which generally speaking is the same as for the calculation of the basic award for unfair dismissal (see above, para. 8–066), *i.e.* the amount of a week's gross pay (subject to a maximum of £260) multiplied by the number of complete years of service (subject to a maximum of 20) multiplied by ½, 1, or 1½ according to the age of the employee (ERA, s.162). Unlike the basic award, years below the age of 18 do not count (ERA, s.211(2)). In 2003 the maximum possible payment was therefore £7,800. Where the employee is within a year of her sixty-fifth birthday at the time of the redundancy, the payment is reduced by a twelfth for every complete month. Employees aged over 65 (or over their normal retiring age, if lower) are not entitled to a redundancy payment. It is likely that this will be altered when the new law on age discrimination comes into effect (above, para. 2–059). Where the employee has successfully claimed that his dismissal for redundancy was unfair, the amount of the redundancy payment is set off against the basic award to prevent double compensation (ERA, s.122(4)).

Insolvency of the employer

When the redundancy payments scheme was introduced, a Redundancy **9–018** Fund was set up to which all employers contributed via a top-slicing of their National Insurance contributions. The Fund served two purposes. First, it was government policy to spread some of the costs of redundancies across industry as a whole, and this was done by making all employers contribute and then allowing those who actually made people redundant to claim back a proportion of what they paid by way of rebate. Secondly, it provided a fall-back fund from which the employees of insolvent businesses could be paid.

The rebate, fixed at 50 per cent in 1969, was reduced to 41 per cent in 1977 and then to 35 per cent and only for employers with fewer than 10 employees in 1986. After these salami tactics, the rebate was finally abolished altogether by the Employment Act 1989. This reflected not so much a change of policy as a recognition that the Fund, which had been in surplus until 1979, had gone into deficit thereafter as a result of high unemployment and frequent business failure during the 1980s. The Redundancy Fund itself was wound up and merged with the general National Insurance Fund under the Employment Act 1990.

The function of providing a back-up where the employer's business is insolvent now falls therefore on the National Insurance Fund. The employee makes a claim to the Secretary of State for Trade and Industry under ERA, s.166. She must show that she was entitled to a payment and that she has taken reasonable steps to obtain payment from the employer. In practice the provisions work quite well and employees usually obtain their payments without difficulty. If the employee's claim is disputed, she will have to claim before an employment tribunal, where the Secretary of State will have *locus standi* to challenge her entitlement.

Time off to look for work

9–019 Under ERA, s.52 an employee who is given notice of dismissal for redundancy is entitled to reasonable time off work to look for new employment or to make arrangements for retraining. This applies only to employees with two or more years of continuous employment. If the employer unreasonably refuses to permit this, the employee may bring a claim to an employment tribunal, which can order the employer to pay compensation equal to the pay the employee would have got if allowed the time off – but subject to a maximum of two-fifths of a week's pay (usually therefore two days' pay). This does not mean that reasonable time off is limited to two days, only that the remedy is so limited.

It may be questioned whether this amounts to much more than a bit of window-dressing, given that increasingly employers do not require redundant employees to work out their notice, and the lack of an effective sanction for breach.

Transfers of Undertakings

9–020 It is now necessary to consider what happens to the employees when a business is sold. Can this count as a cessation of business (by the original owners) which entitles them to redundancy payments?

The first thing to know is how the business has been sold. In this country the vast majority of business operations are conducted through the medium of a company registered under the Companies Acts. A registered company is recognised in law as a legal person with pretty well the same capacities as a human person, but it is owned by human persons, the shareholders. If a company is being sold, the normal way of doing it is for a majority of the shares to be transferred from seller to buyer. So far as employees of the company are concerned, however, this kind of deal has no legal implications for their employment. The company itself is their employer, and the identity of their employer does not change because the share ownership changes. In practical terms, the change in the identity of the controllers may have a most important effect on employees: the new owners of the company may have radically different policies from the old. For this reason, some commentators criticise the fact that it is not treated as a change in employer. Under the Employment Relations Act 1999, s.38 the Secretary of State has power to make regulations to extend protection under TUPE to situations not presently covered, but there does not seem to be any present intention to extend them to share sales.

Assuming then a genuine change of employer, what are the implications **9–021** for employees? At common law a contract of employment is personal, so a change in employer would amount to a termination of the first contract and entering a new one. Such a change could not be forced on an employee against her will (*Nokes v Doncaster Amalgamated Collieries* (1940)) because it would offend the general principle we have already referred to against forced labour. At first sight then, this would suggest that the employees would be dismissed by reason of cessation of business and thus redundant. Redundancy law used to deal with this situation by providing that the employee would not be entitled to a redundancy payment if the new employer was prepared to keep her on. Thus, although the employee did not have to agree to a change in employer, there was a financial incentive for her to do so. The new owner of the business had a choice about whether to take on the employees; if they were not taken on, they could claim a redundancy payment from their former employer. However, this position was radically altered by the Transfer of Undertakings (Protection of Employment) Regulations 1981 (TUPE), which were passed in order to implement the Acquired Rights Directive (77/187/EEC) (see now the consolidation in 2001/23/EC). The idea behind the Acquired Rights Directive is that workers ought to be treated as having a right to their jobs. Therefore, if the business is transferred from one owner to another, workers should have the right to follow their jobs to the new owner. The Directive effects this by stating that in these circumstances, the workers' employment should transfer automatically from the old owner of the business (the transferor) to the new owner (the transferee) (Art.3(1)).

What is a transfer of an undertaking?

The TUPE Regulations apply where there is a "relevant transfer" of an **9–022** undertaking or part of an undertaking. Thus the two key concepts are "transfer" and "undertaking". These concepts have given rise to the greatest difficulty in the interpretation of TUPE and the Acquired Rights Directive. Originally the TUPE definition of "undertaking" (reg.2) excluded any business "not in the nature of a commercial venture". Many commentators argued that there was no warrant for this exclusion in the Acquired Rights Directive (77/187/EEC) and the EU Commission eventually took infraction proceedings against the United Kingdom for this and other shortcomings. So far as the Directive was concerned, the point was put beyond doubt by the ECJ's decision in *Dr Sophie Redmond Stichting v Bartol* (1992), holding that the Directive applied to a transfer involving a non-commercial organisation providing services to drug addicts. TURERA amended regulation 2 so that now the definition simply reads "undertaking includes any trade or business".

The leading authority at ECJ level on what constitutes the transfer of an undertaking is *Spijkers v Gebroeders Benedik Abattoir* (1986), where it was said that the decisive criterion is whether the business in question retains its identity on transfer. Given that the aim of the Directive is to ensure continuity of employment relationships within a business, what is being looked for is the business (or part of a business) being continued in other hands. The ECJ identified these factors as being relevant on that issue: the type of undertaking or business; whether or not the tangible assets of the business were transferred; the value of intangible assets at time of transfer; whether or not the majority of employees were taken over; whether or not customers were transferred; the degree of similarity between the activities carried on before and after the transfer; and the period, if any, for which those activities were suspended. It is also established that it must be a stable economic entity, implying some capability of permanence or continuity (*Rygaard v Strø Mølle* (1996)). An example of the application of this test is provided by *Merckx v Ford Motors* (1996). Merckx had been employed by Anfo who held a dealership in Ford cars for the Brussels area. Anfo proposed to discontinue its operations and Ford transferred the dealership to Novarobel, who operated out of their own premises, but covering the same geographical area. Novarobel thus took over no assets from Anfo, nor its business name nor any associated goodwill. It was, however, recommended by Anfo to its existing customers. Novarobel proposed to take over only 14 employees of the 64 employed by Anfo. The ECJ held that the dealership was an identifiable economic entity which was carried on as the same activity, on substantially the same conditions, without interruption, in the same area and with the same customer base: in consequence, although there was no transfer of tangible assets and only a small part of the workforce, it was a transfer of an undertaking within the meaning of the Directive.

Merckx also illustrates the point that the lack of a direct contractual link between the transferor and the transferee does not preclude the operation of the Directive: this point had already been established in *Daddy's Dance Hall* (1988) where the original employer held the lease of a restaurant bar. The ECJ held that the Directive applied where the lessor terminated the lease and awarded it to a new lessee (see also *Dr Sophie Redmond Stichting v Bartol* (1992)).

Contracting out

The decisions of the ECJ that there did not have to be a contractual link **9–023** between transferor and transferee for the Directive to apply set the stage for the next major development: the application of the Directive to the contracting out of services or parts of a business. The landmark case in this connection was *Rask v ISS Kantineservice* (1993). A company, Phillips, had a staff canteen at its factory in Denmark. Instead of running it themselves, through their own employees, they decided to contract it out to ISS, who were paid a fixed fee and were bound by conditions laid down by Phillips (*e.g.* as to price levels). ISS argued that this was not covered by the Directive because Phillips remained owner of the premises and ISS did not have the normal freedom of a typical business owner to fix prices freely to make profits; furthermore, it was not part of the core business of the company. They argued that it was in effect only a transfer of the management of an internal service. Nonetheless, the ECJ held that the Directive applied because there had been a transfer of responsibility for running a part of the business; and that was enough.

In *Schmidt v Spar-und Leihkasse* (1994) the ECJ went so far as to hold that the Directive applied when a bank transferred its cleaning services to an outside organisation even though only one employee was involved. This was the high point, where it seemed that there was hardly any situation of transfer, as opposed to shutdown, which would not come within the Directive. It is submitted that these decisions were right, given that the purpose of the Directive is to protect employees when there is a change of employer. Looked at from the point of view of the employee, in all these cases there is a change which is likely to affect their working arrangements and it is this situation that the Directive was designed to deal with.

The contracting-out decisions of the ECJ, coupled with the lifting of the unauthorised "commercial venture" restriction caused consternation to the Conservative Government, because of its potential to scupper its controversial policy of insisting on "market-testing" of public services. Under the Local Government Act 1988, local authorities were obliged to identify some services which would be put out to tender to see if private organisations could do them more cheaply than the authority itself. This is "compulsory competitive tendering" or CCT. Of course, the principal reason that private organisations can perform the services more cheaply is because they pay their employees a lot less; it is also the case that the services put up for tender have usually involved low-paid occupations anyway, also that they have frequently involved large numbers of women workers, but that should not come as any real surprise.

If what was transferred was an identifiable unit, which was often the case, **9–024** then it was fairly clear that it should come within the Directive and that TUPE should be interpreted so far as possible to give effect to this. And here was the rub: if it was a relevant transfer then the new provider automatically inherited all the existing employees on their existing terms and conditions of employment. Thus it became unlikely that the new provider could perform the service more cheaply.

After a period of uncertainty, the applicability of TUPE to the contracting out of public services was finally accepted by the Court of Appeal in *Dines v Initial Health Care Services* (1994), where a hospital changed the contractor providing its cleaning service. However, the previously understood position was thrown into doubt by the ECJ's decision in *Süzen v Zehnacker* (1997). In this case, eight employees were dismissed when a cleaning contract was transferred from one outside contractor to another. The German court referred two questions to the ECJ: whether, in the light of *Schmidt* and *Dr Sophie Redmond*, there was a transfer where a contract was switched from one outside contractor to another, and whether there was a transfer of an undertaking where no tangible or intangible assets were transferred. One might have been forgiven for thinking that these questions had already been answered in the affirmative, not least in the two cases cited by the German court in its reference. However, it was obviously worth asking again, because this time the ECJ gave a different answer. The critical point in the decision was the statement that "the mere loss of a service contract to a competitor cannot . . . by itself indicate the existence of a transfer" and it was the distinction between this situation and the genuine transfer of an economic entity which the Court seemed to be trying to make, although not with conspicuous success. While affirming the *Spijkers* test and casting no doubt on the decision in *Schmidt*, the ECJ nonetheless held there would be no transfer where one outside contractor was exchanged for another:

"if there is no concomitant transfer from one undertaking to the other of significant tangible or intangible assets or taking over by the new employer of a major part of the workforce, in terms, of their numbers and skills, assigned by his predecessor to the performance of the contract".

The Court of Appeal subsequently held in *Betts v Brintel Helicopters* (1997) that this meant at least a change in emphasis on the test for a transfer as previously understood. In that case, the defendant company had a contract with Shell to provide transport to some of their oil rigs. The company operated its own helicopters from its own airfield in Norfolk. The company lost the contract to KLM, who planned to use their own helicopters, based at Norwich airport, and who deliberately decided against taking on any of the Brintel employees, presumably in the hope that it would not be regarded as a transfer. Reversing the decision of the lower court, the Court of Appeal held that, in the light of *Süzen*, this could not be regarded as a transfer. The court was at pains to say that this was not just because of KLM's policy of not taking on any Brintel employees, but because this was an undertaking involving substantial assets, and there was no transfer of these. The court also indicated that the decision in *Dines v Initial Healthcare* was correct on its facts, as the new contractor had in fact taken on most of the previous contractor's workforce, but that the reasoning might not hold good any longer.

The regrettable result of all this seemed to be that in those industries **9–025** which were labour-intensive and used few assets (such as cleaning, catering, security and many other service industries), at least the second and subsequent generation of contractors would be able to avoid the operation of TUPE by the simple expedient of refusing to take on any of the workers of the previous contractor (although TUPE would apply to the initial, or "first generation", transfer). If so, far from being able to follow their work, these employees would actually be at increased risk of being made redundant than would have been the case had TUPE not applied. However, in *ECM (Vehicle Delivery Service) v Cox* (1999) the Court of Appeal upheld a tribunal's decision that a "second generation" transfer of a contract to deliver cars from the port of entry in the United Kingdom to dealerships in the north of England was a relevant transfer and suggested that the importance of *Süzen* had been exaggerated. The court noted that the ECJ had not only not overruled authorities such as *Spijkers* and *Schmidt* but also that it was still referring to the criteria in those cases in deciding whether the Acquired Rights Directive applied (see, *e.g. Sánchez Hidalgo v Aser* (1999)). Emphasising that the application of the tests is a question of fact for the tribunal, the Court of Appeal also held that the tribunal was entitled to treat as relevant the fact that the transferee in *ECM v Cox* had deliberately decided not to take on any of the former contractor's employees precisely in order to avoid the application of TUPE, on the basis that this had not been held to be an irrelevant factor in any of the ECJ decisions.

This seemed to leave a dilemma for tribunals as to whether they should follow the approach in *Betts v Brintel* or *ECM v Cox*. A consensus emerged that as *ECM v Cox* was the later decision of the Court of Appeal, and it was reached following a full consideration of *Betts v Brintel*, then it was the one to be followed (*cf. Cheesman v R Brewer Contracts Ltd* (2001)). Subsequent case law of the ECJ and British courts and tribunals has emphasised that the real issue in these cases is whether or not an economic entity can be said to have been transferred, as opposed to an identifiable activity. In deciding this, "the mere fact that the service provided by the old and the new awardees of the contract is similar does not support the conclusion that an economic entity has been transferred" (*per* Mummery L.J. in *ECM v Cox* (1999)). An economic entity presupposes an organised grouping of people and assets which enables the relevant activity to take place. Following a useful review of the authorities, in *Cheesman v R Brewer Contracts Ltd* (2001) Lindsay J. explained this as implying a degree of structure and autonomy, to be gathered from factors such as the identity of the workforce, the management structure, the way work was organised, the operating methods and the operational resources, where appropriate.

That said, it is still recognised, as the ECJ stated in *Temco Service* **9–026** *Industries v Imzilyen* (2002) that, "in certain labour-intensive sectors, a group of workers engaged in a joint activity on a permanent basis may constitute an economic entity", provided that they can be identified as an organised grouping who are specifically and permanently assigned to a common task.

This is probably as far as one can go with the law: its application is a matter of fact and degree for tribunals and as long as they direct themselves in accordance with the legal tests outlined above, it is unlikely that their decisions can be disturbed on appeal. Thus, in *RCO Support Services v Unison* (2002) the Court of Appeal upheld a tribunal's ruling that cleaning and catering services supplied to a hospital were capable of constituting economic entities and thus transferred from the first outside contractor to the second. The tribunal had correctly directed itself that it should be looking for an entity rather than simply an activity and the Court of Appeal denied that the only permissible conclusion on the facts was that this was the transfer of an activity.

Reform

9–027 In 1998 the EU agreed on Directive 98/50/EC to amend the Acquired Rights Directive (77/187/EEC), mainly by codifying the position reached in the jurisprudence of the ECJ. Thus Article 1 was expanded to explain that "transfer" means:

> "transfer of an economic entity which retains its identity, meaning an organised grouping of resources which has the objective of pursuing an economic activity, whether or not that activity is central or ancillary".

It further clarified that the Directive applies to public as well as private undertakings, whether or not they are operating for gain. These amendments were consolidated in 2001 (Directive 2001/23/EC).

The Government consulted on amendments to TUPE in 2001 which would extend coverage more clearly to labour-intensive service contracts. It was initially thought that Regulations would be in place by 2003, but by summer 2003 a draft was still awaited. However, the Government has issued two Codes of Practice on public sector transfers (the Cabinet Office Guidelines on Staff Transfers in the Public Sector (2000), and the Code of Practice on Workforce Matters in Local Authority Service Contracts (2003)), which provide, *inter alia*, that contractors should act in accordance with TUPE principles even where the Regulations do not strictly apply in legal terms.

Effect of transfers on contracts of employment

9–028 The central provision of TUPE is regulation 5, which provides that on transfer, the contracts of employment of employees of the transferor are automatically transferred to the transferee. The transferee takes over all the rights and liabilities under the contract except any provisions relating to an occupational pension scheme (reg.7). Originally this meant that the employee was deprived of her common law right to be transferred from one employer to another only with her agreement (*cf. Nokes v Doncaster Amalgamated Collieries* (1940), above, para. 9–021), but this was thought to be an inevitable side-effect of the Acquired Rights Directive. The only exception to this was if the transfer involved a substantial change in working conditions to her detriment: in this case the employee could leave and have the usual right to claim a redundancy payment (reg.5(5)). However, a change in the identity of employer alone would be unlikely to amount to such a change.

Following the ECJ decision in *Katsikas v Konstantinidis* (1993) it became clear that there had been a misunderstanding of what the Directive actually required and that it was not intended that employees should be transferred against their will. Hence TURERA amended regulation 5 to provide that there will be no automatic transfer where the employee informs either transferor or transferee that she objects to it (reg.5(4A)). However, in these circumstances regulation 5(4B) provides that the transfer will terminate the employee's contract without there being a dismissal in law. This means that the employee would not even be entitled to a redundancy payment, so it is unlikely that many employees will avail themselves of this option. In *University of Oxford v Humphreys* (2000) the Court of Appeal confirmed that regulation 5(4B) is subordinate to regulation 5(5), so that an employee whose terms would have been changed to his detriment if he had been transferred was able to pursue a claim for damages.

A related question arising in relation to regulation 5(5) is whether an **9–029** employee can resign and claim unfair dismissal where the transfer brings about a substantial change in her terms and conditions to her detriment, but is not actually a breach of contract. This would rarely be the case: normally a change in terms and conditions will constitute a fundamental breach of contract entitling the employee to resign and claim constructive dismissal (see above, para. 4–011). However, contracts of employment are sometimes drafted to give the employer quite a lot of flexibility to change employees' terms and conditions. If such a power exists in the contract, and the transferee exercises it to the employee's detriment, can the employee nonetheless rely on regulation 5(5) to claim that she has been dismissed in connection with a transfer?

In the joined appeals in *Rossiter v Pendragon* (2002) and *Air Foyle Ltd v Crosby-Clarke* (2002) the Court of Appeal held that they could not. In *Rossiter v Pendragon* the contract of a salesman allowed his employer to alter commission arrangements, which the new owner of the business did, making the employee £3,000 p.a. worse off, in his estimation. In *Air Foyle Ltd v Crosby-Clarke* an airline pilot was required to conform to current legal regulations on flying time. When his employer relocated from the United Kingdom to Belgium he found that he could be required to work for eleven days without a break, against a former maximum of four days. In both cases, as the changes were allowed by the contract, their resignations were not treated as dismissal. It is possible to sympathise with the court's wish to align TUPE with normal unfair dismissal principles, but it is unfortunate that employees have no protection in these circumstances, where the detrimental change was clearly because of the transfer.

It is necessary to consider in a little more detail exactly what is meant by **9–030** the statement in regulation 5(1) that the employee's contract "shall have effect after the transfer as if originally made between the person so named and the transferee". In *Morris Angel & Sons Ltd v Hollande* (1993) the employee, managing director of a theatrical costumier, was contractually bound to a restrictive covenant which prevented him soliciting his former employer's customers on leaving employment. His original employer transferred the business to the plaintiffs and the employee's contract was terminated. The issue was the meaning of the restrictive covenant: did it now apply to the customers of the transferee or did it still cover the customers of the transferor? The Court of Appeal held that it must still apply to the transferor's customers (who were the only ones the employee really knew). Otherwise, in a transfer situation, an employee could find herself subject to a much wider obligation than she originally agreed to, which would be contrary to the spirit of the Directive.

Regulation 5(2) goes on to state that "all the transferor's rights, powers, duties and liabilities" in connection with the contract are transferred to the transferee. In *DJM International v Nicholas* (1996) it was held that this included liability for sex discrimination by the transferor in forcing the employee to retire earlier than a man would have had to. As discrimination claims can result in unlimited compensation, this could be a significant risk for a transferee. On similar reasoning the Court of Appeal held in *Bernadone v Pall Mall Services* (2000) that the transferor's liability in negligence or for breach of statutory duty for an employee's accident at work also transferred to the new employer. The good news for the transferee in this case was that the court also held that it was entitled to the benefit of the transferor's indemnity under its employers' liability insurance. There are conflicting EAT decisions on whether liability for failure to consult as required by TUPE regulations 10 and 11 (below, para. 9–039) transfers, but in the most recent decision, *Tucker v Alamo Group (Europe)* (2003) the EAT held that it did. Because of the potential risks for unforeseen, expensive claims to emerge after the transfer has gone through it has become common for transfer contracts to require full disclosure by the transferor of any possible claims against it and indemnity against such liabilities. The amended version of the Acquired Rights Directive, Art.3 empowers Member States to require such disclosure, while stipulating that a failure to disclose should not affect an employee's rights in connection with the undisclosed matter.

9–031   According to TUPE, reg.7, occupational pension rights are not transferred under regulation 5. This is an enormously significant exception which produces a large gap in TUPE protection for employees. It is warranted by Article 3(4)(a) of the Acquired Rights Directive (2001/23/EC) which exempts supplementary company or inter-company pension schemes because it would be impractical for the transferor's occupational pension scheme actually to be transferred. However, Article 3(4)(b) goes on to state that Member States have an obligation to adopt measures to protect the interests of employees under such schemes. For employees it was argued that this meant the law should ensure that they receive equivalent pension rights from the new employer and that British law failed properly to implement the Directive in not providing this. The Government's view, however, was that the Directive merely requires the protection of accrued rights with the old employer. This was supported by the Court of Appeal in *Adams v Lancashire CC* (1997). The scope of this exception was narrowed by the ECJ's important ruling in *Beckmann v Dynamco Whicheloe Macfarlane Ltd* (2002), concerning a former NHS employee who was made redundant after being transferred to the private sector. As she was over 50, had she remained employed by the NHS she would have been entitled to very generous benefits: an immediate pension, early payment of a retirement lump sum, a compensatory annual allowance and a compensatory lump sum. She claimed equivalent benefits from the transferee and the High Court referred to the ECJ the question of whether these were old age, invalidity or survivors' benefits and thus within the scope of the exception in Article 3(4)(a). In a decision echoing its equal pay decisions (above, para. 7–024) the ECJ held that these were payments in connection with a form of dismissal and therefore liability did transfer to the new employer. The ECJ stated that only benefits paid from the time when an employee reaches the end of her normal working life could be classified as within the exception, even though the payments to the claimant were calculated in accordance with rules for pension benefits. The question of whether pension rights ought to transfer in some form is under consideration for possible reform. In the meantime, however, the Cabinet Office Guidelines on Staff Transfers in the Public Sector does require that transferees in the private sector should offer transferred employees benefits which are broadly comparable to those which they would have enjoyed had they remained in the public sector.

Apart from pension rights, however, employees are transferred on their **9–032** former terms and conditions. This is the key element in the employees' protection, but it can pose a problem for the transferee, who may wish to alter terms and conditions in the interests of efficiency or economy, or simply to harmonise contracts with those of the existing workforce. If the new employer either dismisses them and re-engages them on new terms, or else tries to insist on their accepting new terms with the result that they resign, there will be an actual or constructive dismissal of the transferred employees. Under regulation 8, such a dismissal is automatically unfair unless the employer has an economic, technical or organisational reason for it (see further, para. 9–037). But what happens if the transferee gets the new employees to agree to a change in their terms and conditions? Will such an agreement be valid?

This was the issue which it was hoped the House of Lords would decide in the joined appeals in *British Fuels v Baxendale* and *Wilson v St Helen's BC* (1998). The problem in both cases arose because at the time of the main events it was not appreciated that TUPE applied to the situation. In both cases the employees were made redundant by their former employers and then re-engaged on worse terms and conditions by the transferee, so that at that point they could have claimed that they were unfairly dismissed under regulation 8. However, it was not until 21 and 18 months later respectively that it was realised that TUPE applied to the transfers, by which time an unfair dismissal claim was out of time. The applicants therefore argued that their dismissals were void because they were in connection with the transfer and that they were entitled to the benefit of their previous terms and conditions of employment. If the dismissals were void, this raised the question of whether or not their agreement (however, reluctant) to the change in their terms and conditions was valid.

In the event the House of Lords held that the dismissals were not void, so that their only claim would have been for unfair dismissal within three months of the original terminations. This had the unfortunate result that it was not necessary for the House of Lords to decide the burning question of whether an agreement to vary because of the transfer would have been valid. Lord Slynn, giving the opinion of the House, did express the *obiter* view that a variation in terms and conditions could be regarded as being for an economic, technical or organisational reason rather than being because of the transfer even if it took place at the same time. Conversely, a variation some time after the transfer could yet be regarded as being connected with it and capable of giving rise to a constructive dismissal which would be unfair under regulation 8. These comments may be regarded as unsatisfactory for both employees and employers. The first point, recognising a possible justification for watering down terms and conditions at the time of the transfer, reduces the crucial protection which TUPE is meant to provide for employees. The second point disappoints those employers who desire a definite cut-off point after a transfer beyond which they may safely seek to alter employees' terms and conditions.

Dismissal connected with the transfer

9–033 The protection afforded by regulation 5 would be of little use if the transferee could simply dismiss the employees it did not want. Hence the importance of the associated provision in regulation 8 that dismissal of an employee either before or after a transfer will automatically be unfair if the transfer or a reason connected with the transfer is the principal reason for it. However, this apparently powerful protection is significantly watered down by the exception in regulation 8(2) that if the reason is also an "economic, technical or organisational reason" it will not be automatically unfair, but will count as "some other substantial reason" – which will mean that the dismissal is fair if the requirement of reasonableness is satisfied.

Which employer is liable?

9–034 Before considering the substance of regulation 8, it is first necessary to consider which employer will be liable if the dismissal is unfair. It will be noted that dismissal in connection with a transfer is unfair whether it occurs before or after the transfer (reg.8(1)). If the dismissal is before the transfer, then it might be expected that the transferor, or old employer, would be liable. If after, then it would be the new employer, the transferee.

However, this opens up the possibility of subverting the basic protection which is meant to be afforded by an automatic transfer of contracts under regulation 5. Suppose that the transferee company does not want to take on the new workforce. It simply makes it a condition of the purchase that the transferor company sacks the workforce before the transfer. That way their contracts will not be transferred. True, the transferor will be liable for unfair dismissal: but if the transferor company is insolvent, which is a very common reason for selling the business, it will not much matter.

In *Secretary of State v Spence* (1986) employees were dismissed for redundancy by the receivers of the business at 11.00 a.m., and three hours later the business was sold. The next day, the transferee re-engaged the workforce, who nonetheless claimed redundancy payments from their former (insolvent) employer. By way of defence, it was argued that their contracts were automatically transferred to the new employer by virtue of regulation 5. The Court of Appeal held that they were not. Regulation 5 applies only to those employed "immediately before" the transfer: this must mean the split second before the transfer takes place.

This question came before the House of Lords in *Litster v Forth Dry* **9–035** *Dock* (1989) in a different context. FDD was in receivership. A new company, Forth Estuary Engineering (FEE) was formed to take over the business. FEE had no wish to take on the employees of FDD because it planned to take on redundant workers from another shipyard who were willing to work for lower wages. The two companies therefore arranged that FDD's employees should be dismissed before the transfer. They were duly dismissed an hour before the transfer took place, and sued for unfair dismissal. FEE argued that because they were not employed immediately before the transfer, their contracts were not transferred and they could only claim against FDD. As this company was in receivership, the claim would have been worthless to a large extent.

The House of Lords upheld the Court of Appeal's interpretation of regulation 5 in *Secretary of State v Spence*. However, they noted that the ECJ in *P Bork International v Foreningen* (1989) made it clear that the Acquired Rights Directive was meant to prevent dismissals before the transfer. The House therefore adopted a purposive interpretation of the Regulations and held that the transferee was liable not only where employees were employed immediately before the transfer, but also where they would have been but for being unfairly dismissed under regulation 8. FEE was therefore liable to the employees for unfair dismissal.

Reason for dismissal

A dismissal is automatically unfair under regulation 8 "if the transfer or a **9–036** reason connected with it is the reason or principal reason" for the dismissal. What if the receiver of an insolvent business thinks there will be a better chance of selling it if there are no employees to be taken over and dismisses them for that reason although there is no prospective purchaser at that time? In *Ibex Trading v Walton* (1994) employees dismissed before any buyer had come forward for an insolvent business were held not to be dismissed in connection with a transfer, because they were not dismissed in connection with the actual transfer which eventually took place (which was nowhere near happening at the time when they were dismissed). But in *Harrison Bowden v Bowden* (1994) a different EAT held that a link with the particular transfer which actually occurred did not need to be shown. It is submitted that this is the better approach, and it was followed in the most recent EAT decision on the point, *Morris v John Grose Group Ltd* (1998).

The "ETO" defence

9–037 The employer has a defence if she can show that the dismissal was for an "economic, technical or organisational reason entailing changes in the workforce" (reg.8(2)). The phrase is lifted directly from the Directive (Art.4), which was plainly not drafted originally in English. None of these expressions has previously been used in British employment legislation and they are not defined in the Regulations. All that can safely be said about their interpretation is that they are potentially wide.

In *Wheeler v Patel* (1987) the transferor tried to argue that the fact that the transferee had made dismissal of the employee a condition of going through with the sale was an economic reason. This was rightly rejected, since it would have made a mockery of the protection. However, in *Whitehouse v Blatchford* (1999) the Court of Appeal held that the ETO defence could be used where the client who was switching a contract from one sub-contractor to another made it a condition that the transferee should cut costs by reducing the number of employees. The court denied that this was effectively the same as sacking people in order to achieve a better price for the business, holding that on the facts it was open to the tribunal to find that the client would have insisted on the reduction anyway, even if the contract had not been transferred.

In *Berriman v Delabole Slate* (1985) the employee left when the transferee reduced his pay in order to bring him into line with other employees in the transferee's business. The Court of Appeal held that it was not enough to show an economic, technical or organisational reason: it must also be shown that the reason entailed a change in the workforce as an objective rather than simply as a consequence of it. Furthermore, a change in terms and conditions of employment did not amount to a change in the workforce: this required either a change in numbers, or "possibly changes in the job descriptions of the constituent elements of the workforce which, though involving no overall reduction in number involves a change in the individual employees which together make up the workforce" (Browne-Wilkinson L.J.).

9–038 If the employer succeeds in showing that there is an economic, technical or organisational reason for the dismissal, this does not mean that it is automatically fair. Regulation 8 rather provides that it will count as a substantial reason for dismissal, and thus may be fair or unfair according to whether it was reasonable. This leaves a problem. Can it also be redundancy? This is, after all, a common reason for dismissal connected with a transfer. The fact that regulation 8 refers only to the possibility of it being a substantial reason is a glaring example of the sloppy drafting of the Regulations. After some hesitation, it was held by the EAT in *Gorictree v Jenkinson* (1985) that a fair dismissal under regulation 8 could nevertheless constitute a redundancy. This must be correct, for otherwise the effect of the Regulations would be to leave employees worse off than they would have been before their enactment. Because of regulation 5 and *Litster*, it will normally be the transferee who is liable to pay, however.

Consultation over Redundancies and Transfers

There are statutory obligations on employers to consult with workers over **9–039** redundancies and transfers of undertakings. In situations where there is a transfer which will involve redundancies, both obligations arise. The obligation to consult over redundancies was introduced as a result of the EU Directive on Collective Dismissals (75/129/EEC) (amended and replaced by the Collective Dismissals Directive (98/59/EC)) and is now contained in TULRCA, ss.188–198. For transfers of undertakings, the duty is found in Article 7 of the Acquired Rights Directive (2001/23/EC) and is implemented through TUPE, regs 10 and 11.

As originally formulated, these duties to inform and consult applied only where the employer recognised a trade union – something which used to be entirely at the employer's option. This limitation of consultation to recognised trade unions was clearly out of line with both directives, which require consultation with workers or their representatives. It was therefore no surprise when the ECJ upheld the Commission's complaint against the Government in this respect in *EC Commission v UK* (1994) in 1994. Remedial action was taken via the Collective Redundancies and Transfer of Undertakings (Protection of Employment) (Amendment) Regulations 1995, which amended TULRCA, s.188 and TUPE, reg.10, so that employers had a duty to inform and consult "appropriate representatives", who could either be employee representatives elected by affected employees or trade union representatives, where there was a recognised trade union.

The 1995 Regulations were criticised on three main grounds. Firstly, it **9–040** was open to an employer to bypass a recognised union and to consult with employee representatives instead. Secondly, in stark contrast to rules on trade union ballots, no framework for the election of employee representatives was stipulated. Thirdly, provided that the employer invited the workforce to elect representatives, if no election took place the employer was absolved of further duties.

These points were addressed by the Collective Redundancies and Transfer of Undertakings (Protection of Employment) (Amendment) Regulations 1999, which establish that if a union is recognised, it should be the conduit for information and consultation (TULRCA, s.188(1B); TUPE, reg.10(2A)). Broad standards for elections are stated: that the election is to be fair; in secret so far as possible; that sufficient numbers of representatives should be elected to ensure that the interests of different classes of employees are represented; and that no employee is unreasonably prevented from standing. Finally, if the employees fail to elect representatives, the employer now has a duty to provide the relevant information to each individual affected employee (TULRCA, s.188(7B); TUPE, reg.10(8A)). Complaints can be made to an employment tribunal where the employer fails to comply with any of these requirements. Trade union representatives receive protection from dismissal or action short of dismissal while involved in trade union duties (see below, Chapter 10). Non-union employee representatives are similarly provided with protection against dismissal or detriment for participating in the election process and for carrying out their duties (ERA, ss.47, 103). They are also entitled to reasonable time off to carry out their duties (ERA, s.61).

Consultation over redundancies

9-041 For the purposes of consultation only, the definition of redundancy is extended to include any dismissal for a reason which is not related to the individual concerned (TULRCA, s.195) and thus applies to some dismissals for "some other substantial reason". Originally, the duty to consult applied to all redundancies. However, when the Conservative Government amended TULRCA, s.188 in 1995 it took advantage for the first time of a derogation allowed by the Collective Dismissals Directive whereby there need not be consultation if fewer than 20 employees are dismissed in a 90-day period. In *R. v Secretary of State, ex p. Unison* (1996) it was argued that such changes required primary legislation, but this challenge was rejected by the Divisional Court.

Curiously, the unions did not attack a different aspect of timing in which the British legislation seems incompatible with the Collective Dismissals Directive. Under TULRCA, s.188 the duty to consult only arises when the employer is "proposing to dismiss" employees for redundancy. Consultation starts with the employer giving the representatives in writing the reasons for the proposals, the numbers and descriptions of employees to be made redundant, the total number of employees in the categories from which redundancies will be made, the proposed selection method, the proposed method for carrying out the dismissals (including the timescale) and how any non-statutory severance payment will be calculated. Thus while it is clear that the employer's duty arises as soon as there are proposals to dismiss, the provisions as to the information to be given seem to suggest that the proposals must have reached a fairly advanced stage before the duty arises. In *Hough v Leyland DAF* (1991) the EAT described it as a situation where, "matters have reached a stage where a specific proposal has been formulated and . . . this is a later stage than the diagnosis of a problem and the appreciation that at least one way of dealing with it would be by declaring redundancies". This seems out of line with the Collective Dismissals Directive, which refers to the obligation to consult arising as soon as the employer is contemplating redundancies. As Glidewell L.J. pointed out in *R. v British Coal ex p. Vardy* (1993), "The verb 'proposes' in its ordinary usage relates to a state of mind which is much more certain and further along the decision-making process than 'contemplate' ". It seems odd also that this did not feature either in the infraction proceedings taken by the Commission (*EC Commission v UK* (1994)). More recently the EAT has explicitly recognised that TULRCA, s.188 cannot be interpreted in such a way as to accord with the Directive (*MSF v Refuge Assurance plc* (2002)).

9-042 While declaring that consultation must begin in good time, section 188 also lays down some absolute minimum consultation periods for multiple redundancies. If between 20 and 99 employees are to be made redundant within a period of 30 days or less, the minimum consultation period is 30 days before the first dismissal takes effect; if 100 or more employees are to be made redundant within a period of 90 days or less, the minimum consultation period is 90 days before the first dismissal takes effect. In the case of multiple redundancies, there is a duty to provide advance information to the Department of Trade and Industry under TULRCA, s.193 which has some similarities to section 188. The purpose of this is to give the Department early warning where there is likely to be a sudden strain on its resources.

Having received the information, the representatives may make representations to the employer about any aspect of the redundancies. These representations must be considered by the employer, which must give reasons if they are rejected. This requirement seems designed to ensure that the employer does actually consider the representations rather than simply going through the motions. Since amendment by TURERA, consultation must also encompass ways of avoiding the dismissals, reducing the number of employees to be dismissed and mitigating the consequences of the dismissals, and must be undertaken with a view to reaching agreement with the representatives.

Consultation over transfers

The obligation to consult under TUPE is broader in many ways than the **9–043** obligation to consult over redundancies. Firstly, under regulation 10 both transferor and transferee have an obligation to give certain information to the appropriate representatives of any employees who will be affected. The representatives must receive information not only about the fact of the transfer but also about the "legal, economic and social implications" of it (reg.10(2)). Once again, this is a phrase lifted directly from the Directive whose actual meaning is unclear.

Secondly, where the transferor or transferee plan to take any measures which may affect their employees, they must actually consult with the employees' representatives about such measures, consider any representations made by them and give reasons if rejecting their ideas. Since amendment by TURERA, the employer has an obligation to undertake this consultation "with a view to seeking their agreement" to the measures. This sounds quite useful, but is limited by the fact that each party to the transfer need only consult with its own workforce, and the most likely eventuality is that the transferee will take action affecting the transferor's workforce, with whom it has no direct duty to consult.

Under TUPE no minimum period for consultation is specified, and the duty relates to the fact of the transfer, rather than a proposal to transfer. This suggests that the duty to consult arises rather later than it would if redundancies were proposed. As noted already, however, if what is proposed is a transfer resulting in redundancies, both sets of consultation requirements must be adhered to.

The special circumstances defence

9–044 An employer who fails to consult over redundancies has a defence if "there are special circumstances which render it not reasonably practicable for the employer to comply" (TULRCA, s.188(7)), although the employer must try so far as possible to do so even if making out the defence. An exactly similar defence is found in TUPE, reg.10(7), and presumably it will be interpreted in the same way.

In the leading decision, *Clarks of Hove Ltd v Bakers' Union* (1978), 368 of the 380 employees were summarily dismissed for redundancy on the same day that the company ceased to trade, with no prior consultation. It had been in severe financial difficulties for months, and that day the final hope of raising more capital had disappeared. The Court of Appeal held that something as common as financial difficulties and insolvency did not constitute special circumstances excusing the failure to consult; what mattered was the reason for the insolvency. If it had been some sudden disaster, such as the destruction of the plant, or a trading boycott, then the circumstances might be sufficiently out of the ordinary to be considered "special". But where, as here, it was simply the final manifestation of ongoing financial problems, there were no special circumstances.

This seems a realistic approach, especially given that part of the purpose of the consultation requirements is to allow the workforce time to prepare and to begin to look for other work. It is, as usual, a question of fact as to whether special circumstances are made out, and a contrast is afforded by *USDAW v Leancut Bacon* (1981) where the company spent the first half of 1979 attempting to negotiate its takeover by another company. In September, the suitor saw the company's half-yearly accounts and pulled out; this caused their bank to halt credit facilities and appoint a receiver. Two days later the workers were made redundant. The EAT considered that here the insolvency was the result of a sudden event – the bank's clampdown on credit and appointment of a receiver – and that the company could rely on the special circumstances defence. However, while the bank's final action may have been swift, it could hardly be described as unusual or unforeseeable!

Remedies for failure to consult

9–045 If the employer fails to consult, the wrong is actionable in the employment tribunal only by an elected employee representative or the trade union. However, the remedy granted is a protective award, which is payable to the employees in respect of whom the union should have been consulted (TULRCA, s.189). The award will be for the "protected period" – that is, a period beginning with the date on which the first dismissal complained of took effect and lasting so long as the tribunal decides is just and equitable. This is subject to a maximum period of 90 days. In *Spillers-French v USDAW* (1979) the EAT considered whether the aim of the protective award should be purely compensation to the employees for the consultation time lost, or whether a punitive element should be included. Since section 189(4) instructs the tribunal to have regard to the seriousness of the employer's default, the EAT considered that the award could be based on more than simply the question of loss to the employees, and the fact that they had suffered no loss did not mean that no award should be made.

The remedy under TUPE, reg.11 is very similar to this. Again it is for the trade union or employee representatives to apply to the employment tribunal, but the remedy is such award of pay to the affected employees as is considered to be just and equitable. It is subject to a maximum of 13 weeks' pay. Until 1993, a protective award under TUPE was set off against a protective award under TULRCA but, again because this was regarded as an infringement of the Directive, the set-off was abolished by TURERA.

10.   Freedom of Association

The freedom to form and belong to associations, whether trade unions, **10–001** religious sects or political parties, is regarded as an aspect of human rights, and is found stated as a right in the principal treaties on the subject: the Universal Declaration of Human Rights 1948 (Art.20), the International Covenant on Civil and Political Rights 1966 (Art.22), the International Covenant on Economic, Social and Cultural Rights 1966 (Art.8), and the European Convention on Human Rights (Art.11). Additionally the freedom is guaranteed by ILO Conventions Nos 87 and 98, the EU Social Charter (Art.14) and the Council of Europe's European Social Charter (Art.5).

What exactly is the effect of such guarantees? There are essentially three issues. Firstly, when these rather brief treaty statements are unpacked, what do they really mean? Secondly, is it possible to enforce them, or are they simply pious hopes? Thirdly, how far are they translated into English law? The first issue is connected with the second, since it is only really where there are enforcement procedures available that authoritative interpretation of treaty provisions is possible.

Freedom of Association and the State

International standards

If the freedom to associate is to mean anything at all, it must mean that the **10–002** State should not prevent citizens from forming and joining associations. However, exceptions are recognised in the treaties themselves. The International Covenant on Civil and Political Rights allows restrictions on grounds of national security or public safety, public order, the protection of public health or morals, or the protection of the rights of others – which would seem to allow a fairly wide scope for interference with the "right". ILO Convention No. 87 is narrower and more specific, permitting states to decide for themselves whether the police and armed forces should be given this freedom. In the United Kingdom they are not. The extent of both exemptions was examined in relation to civil servants employed at Government Communication Headquarters (GCHQ) at Cheltenham in the 1980s.

GCHQ was responsible for the constant monitoring of foreign signals to provide intelligence to the Government. Civil servants employed there had always belonged to the appropriate civil service unions. Between 1979 and 1981 the civil service unions, in dispute with the Conservative Government of the time, used the tactic of calling key personnel out on strike. On seven occasions this included GCHQ staff, and thus the round-the-clock monitoring operation was disrupted. As a result, in January 1984 the Secretary of State changed the contracts of employment of staff employed at GCHQ by removing their right to belong to an independent trade union.

The unions complained both to the ILO and to the European Commission of Human Rights. The ILO decided in 1984 that there was a violation of Convention 87 and urged the British Government to reach agreement with the unions. The Government took no steps in this direction, and in 1988 dismissed the remaining trade union members at GCHQ. This led the ILO Committee of Experts to look at the matter again, and to reiterate its recommendation. The case before the European Commission of Human Rights was lost. The ECHR exempts not only the police and armed forces but also those involved in the administration of the State, which was held to include the GCHQ workers (*Council of Civil Service Unions v UK* (1988)).

One of the very first acts of the new Labour administration elected in May 1997 was to restore the rights of civil servants at GCHQ to belong to trade unions. Those employees who had been dismissed for refusing to give up their membership were reinstated. However, the saga showed an unfortunate divergence between the different international standards.

Rights to join trade unions in the United Kingdom

10–003 In the United Kingdom, there is a general freedom to associate, with the exception of the police and the armed forces, in the sense that no other workers can be discriminated against for forming and joining trade unions. However, some are restricted in relation to taking industrial action.

Freedom of Association and the Employer

10–004 The freedom to associate is meant to be guaranteed as a positive right as against one's employer, through a combination of statutory employment protection rights and the law of unfair dismissal. Thus TULRCA, s.152 gives protection against dismissal on grounds of union membership and activities, section 146 covers detriment during employment on these grounds and section 137 makes refusal of employment on grounds, of union membership unlawful. While this may appear to provide a complete and coherent protection for unionists, in fact the law was developed in piecemeal fashion for different reasons. Protection against dismissal on union membership grounds has existed in some form since the introduction of unfair dismissal law in 1972. It is complemented by the protection from detriment during employment, which was introduced as one of a range of positive rights for employees under the Employment Protection Act 1975. However, protection from discrimination at the point of entry into employment was given only in 1990, for a very different reason. In general, the protection afforded by all these provisions applies not only to those victimised for belonging to a union, but also to people in the opposite situation: those who are victimised for refusing to belong to a trade union. When the Employment Act 1990 introduced protection at the point of job entry, its explicit aim was to outlaw the pre-entry closed shop (see below, para. 10–021). However, the policy of neutrality as between union members and those who are anti-union meant that the protection was given to union members also, although in a limited form. Most recently protection for unionists at the point of entry to employment was increased by provision in the Employment Relations Act 1999, s.3 for regulations to be made to outlaw the "blacklisting" of union members, although the Government stated in 2003 that it did not intend to exercise this power for the time being.

Dismissal and detriment on grounds of union membership

TULRCA, ss.152 and 146 are in largely parallel terms. Section 152 provides **10–005** that dismissal is automatically unfair if the reason or principal reason for it is that the employee was, or proposed to become, a member of an independent trade union or had taken part in, or proposed to take part in, the activities of an independent trade union at an appropriate time. Section 146, as amended by the Employment Relations Act 1999, provides that an employee has "a right not to be subjected to any detriment as an individual" by his employer for the purpose of preventing, deterring or penalising him for the same things.

Where employees are dismissed on this ground, the usual one-year qualifying period of employment does not apply (TULRCA, s.154). The burden of proof is therefore on the employee to show that the dismissal was related to union membership or activities. Dismissal will also be automatically unfair if the employee is selected for redundancy on union membership grounds, but only if employees in a comparable position are not made redundant (TULRCA, s.153). In *O'Dea v ISC Chemicals* (1995) the applicant's contract described him as a technical services operator, but as senior shop steward he spent 50 per cent of his time on union activities (with the employer's agreement) and had different working duties from the other two technical services operators to facilitate his time off. The Court of Appeal held that in comparing him with other employees, the time he spent on union activities was not to be taken into account; however, the tribunal was entitled to look at his actual working duties (rather than the contractual terms) and to conclude accordingly that there was no one in a comparable position so that section 153 did not apply. It is not clear why the protection should be limited in this way if it is established that the reason for selection was trade union activities.

If successful in an action for unfair dismissal on union membership **10–006** grounds, the applicant qualifies for a special regime of remedies. The basic award of compensation cannot be lower than £3,500 (TULRCA, s.156) and the employee may apply for interim relief in order to preserve his job until a full hearing. Such an application must be made to the tribunal within seven days of dismissal and must be supported by a certificate from the union stating that there appear to be reasonable grounds for the complaint.

Section 146 used to refer to "action short of dismissal" being taken against an individual rather than referring to "detriment". The wording was changed by the Employment Relations Act 1999 in order to reverse the effect of the House of Lords' decision in the joined appeals in *Associated Newspapers v Wilson* and *Associated British Ports v Palmer* (1995) that "action" in this context does not include omissions. In *Associated Newspapers Ltd v Wilson* the company derecognised the NUJ and entered individualised contracts with employees. Those who entered the new contracts got a pay increase but the others, those who wanted to retain collective bargaining, did not. Similarly, in *ABP v Palmer* employees who were prepared to enter individualised contracts got higher pay increases than those who stuck with collectively agreed terms. In both cases the Court of Appeal held that this contravened section 146: the employer's purpose was to end collective bargaining which was likely to lead to the withering away of union membership, as there would be little point in membership of a body which had no representation rights. Hence the court held that this was action taken to deter trade union membership.

The decision was appealed on two questions: whether the employer could be said to be acting to deter union membership if this was a likely result of its actions but not its main or only purpose, and whether protection for union membership covered things incidental to membership such as representation for collective bargaining and other purposes. These questions are returned to below, but were addressed only on an *obiter* basis by the Law Lords in *Wilson/Palmer*, because the House of Lords decided the appeal on a different and much more far-reaching issue. By a majority it held that "action short of dismissal" did not include an omission to act, such as an omission to give a pay increase, and it reversed the Court of Appeal's decisions on that ground (*Associated Newspapers v Wilson* and *ABP v Palmer* (1995)). This also had the effect of overruling the earlier Court of Appeal decision in *National Coal Board v Ridgway* (1987), where refusal to give a pay increase negotiated with the UDM to NUM members was held to be unlawful action short of dismissal because it discriminated against them on the basis of their membership of a particular trade union.

The effect of the House of Lords' decision in *Wilson/Palmer* was to undermine very substantially the protection that union members could expect during employment since it opened the door to all sorts of tactics designed to discourage membership provided only that they were framed as offering benefits for non-participation. The Employment Relations Act 1999 therefore amended TULRCA, s.146 to make it unlawful for the employer to subject an employee to a detriment "by any act, or any deliberate failure to act". Detriment by omission is now covered, although it is possible that proof of detriment by omission may be difficult to come by and there may be problems in measuring the three-month limitation period for claims, which runs from the date of the act or deliberate failure to act (s.147) (*cf. Southwark LBC v Whillier* (2001)).

This still left the other issues in the *Wilson/Palmer* litigation. The Court **10–007** of Appeal's decision in the two cases, that the employers' purpose of ending collective bargaining was a deterrent to union membership and thus contravened TULRCA, s.146, came out in 1993 just as the Trade Union Reform and Employment Rights Bill was going through Parliament. The Conservative Government saw this as a blow to its policy of encouraging individual contracting at the expense of collective bargaining. It therefore introduced an amendment to deal with the issue, but by then TURERA was having its third reading in the House of Lords, so there was little opportunity for a thorough consideration of its effects. TULRCA, s.148(3) now provides that even if the employer's purpose is discriminatory in terms of section 146, if it is also intended to further a change in the employer's relationship with any class of employees, the action is permissible unless it is something that no reasonable employer would do. "Class" of employees is widely defined to cover identification according to grade, category, description or geographical location.

While the purpose of this amendment was to reverse the effect of the Court of Appeal's decisions in *Wilson* and *Palmer*, it actually goes quite a lot further than that. Since there are no apparent limits on what kind of change of relationship the employer can be seeking, it seems possible that discrimination in favour of one union rather than another is permissible if it is aimed at rationalising bargaining arrangements, thus reversing *National Coal Board v Ridgway* (1987) on that point also. It also means that an employer having a main purpose of discouraging union membership yet escapes liability provided that he also has the purpose of "changing his relationship with all or any class of his employees", subject only to the qualification that if no reasonable employer would behave in this way with regard to that purpose the protection is lost. Section 148(3) does not even require that the latter should be the main purpose (contrast the position of trade unions taking industrial action for mixed purposes, below, para. 13–005). It is perhaps surprising that section 148(3) survived the Employment Relations Act 1999 intact. The only alteration was that a power was introduced to make regulations about cases where a worker is subjected to a detriment or dismissed for refusing to enter a contract which is different from the terms of an applicable collective agreement (ERelA, s.17).

Meanwhile, the applicants in *Associated Newspapers v Wilson* and *Associ-* **10–008** *ated British Ports v Palmer* took action against the United Kingdom Government in the European Court of Human Rights, arguing that the decision of the House of Lords indicated that British law was in breach of the right to freedom of association guaranteed by Article 11 of the European Convention on Human Rights. In 2002 the Court ruled that, "by permitting employers to use financial incentives to induce employees to surrender important union rights, the respondent State failed in its positive obligation to secure the enjoyment of rights under Article 11" (*Wilson v UK, Palmer v UK, Doolan v UK* (2002)). As a result, in its 2003 review of the operation of the Employment Relations Act 1999 the Government stated that it intended to repeal TULRCA, s.148(3) and also ERelA, s.17, which would therefore become redundant.

This will still leave the question, which already arises in cases where s.148(3) does not apply, as to what degree of intention is necessary for an employer to be liable under TULRCA, s.146. The approach of the House of Lords in *Wilson* and *Palmer* suggests it is only the overt purpose of the employer which will be scrutinised and that the employer will not be taken to have intended other consequences, even if they follow inevitably from its actions. In those cases the employers' purposes were described variously as being to bring about greater flexibility and efficiency and to persuade as many employees as possible to abandon union representation. Even if these purposes could be achieved only by discouraging union membership the House of Lords seemed to think that section 146 would not be infringed. This is evident also from *Gallacher v Department of Transport* (1994), where the applicant had spent the whole of his time on union activities over a five-year period. He was advised that he would not get promotion to a higher managerial grade unless he returned to normal duties so that he would be able to demonstrate his ability to manage people. While this would inevitably mean at least a substantial reduction in his union activities, the fact that this was an inevitable consequence did not, in the opinion of the Court of Appeal, mean that this was the employer's purpose (contrast *Southwark LBC v Whillier* (2001)).

Protection against detriment for union membership and activities is further limited by the requirement that the applicant must have been subjected to detriment "as an individual". Thus, as was pointed out in *Wilson* and *Palmer*, derecognition of the union could not be regarded as action taken against an individual member even though representation in collective bargaining is the main reason for union membership. In *Farnsworth v McCoid* (1999) the Court of Appeal explained that this restriction was included in order to prevent collective disputes coming within section 146, although the case illustrates that the boundary may sometimes be difficult to identify. In that case a collective agreement allowed the employer to withdraw recognition from individual shop stewards on grounds of misconduct. The employer had followed this procedure in respect of the claimant, who argued that this was a breach of section 146. The employer's defence was that this only affected his status as a shop steward, not as an employee, and therefore was not action against him "as an individual". The Court of Appeal held that this was not a collective dispute and the action could properly be regarded as directed at the claimant as an individual. The wording of the section did not warrant inclusion of a further requirement that it affected the individual in his capacity as an employee.

10–009 This leads to the final issue canvassed in *Associated Newspapers v Wilson* and *Associated British Ports v Palmer* (1995): does the protection of union membership safeguard only the bare freedom to associate, or does it also protect things incidental to membership? In *Wilson/Palmer* it was argued that collective bargaining and union representation were so closely connected to the fact of membership that action to deter or penalise them amounted to a deterrent to or penalisation of membership. This was in line with the EAT decision in *Discount Tobacco v Armitage* (1990) where an employee was dismissed after seeking help from a union official in resolving a disagreement with her employer about her terms and conditions of employment. In response to the employer's argument that there was a difference between union membership and seeking assistance from a union official, the EAT denied the distinction, describing the use of the official as "the outward and visible manifestation of trade union membership" and "an incident of union membership".

While not questioning the accuracy of this decision on its own facts, the House of Lords in *Wilson/Palmer* disagreed with this statement as a general proposition. Lord Bridge described it as "an unnecessary and imprecise gloss" on the language of the statute to suggest that union membership is to be equated with the use of its essential services, and Lord Lloyd went so far as to opine that protection under sections 146 and 152 is limited purely to the fact of membership. Such a narrow interpretation would substantially undermine the statutory protection, as very few employers are likely to object to the mere fact of membership, provided that it has no consequences. It puts a premium on the employee being able to argue instead that she has been penalised or dismissed for taking part in trade union activities (discussed below); however, that phrase is not very apt to describe the seeking of union advice or representation.

However, in a subsequent case on facts very similar to *Discount Tobacco v Armitage* the EAT salvaged some of that decision. In *Specialty Care v Pachela* (1996) the employee was also dismissed after seeking her union's assistance in a disagreement about changes to shift patterns. It was argued that, following *Wilson/Palmer*, this could not be regarded as within the statutory protection. The EAT pointed out that anything said in that case on the point was strictly *obiter*, as the decision had rested on the holding that "action" did not include "omission". Furthermore, there was a divergence of views among the Law Lords. Thus the EAT held that a tribunal was entitled to hold that the reason for dismissal related to union membership not only if she had been dismissed because she had joined but also if it was because she had introduced union representation into the employment relationship.

This should also be clarified as a result of the European Court of Human Rights' decision in *Wilson v United Kingdom* (2002). The Court stated that it was an essential part of freedom of association under Article 11 that employees should be free not only to join trade unions but also to instruct or permit the union to make representations on their behalf. This would include individual and collective representation. However, the Court stopped short of saying that freedom of association involved a right to collective bargaining so as to compel an employer to recognise a union for this purpose. The Government's response, in its 2003 review of the Employment Relations Act 1999, was to promise legislation stating a clear, positive right for union members to use their unions' services.

As well as membership, sections 146 and 152 protect union activities. **10–010** Union activities clearly include such things as the recruitment of members, representing members, holding union meetings and so on. In *Fitzpatrick v British Railways Board* (1990) it was held that dismissal of a union activist when it was discovered that her activities had been considered disruptive by a previous employer amounted to dismissal on grounds that she proposed to take part in union activities and came within the protection. However, in *Chant v Aquaboats* (1978) it was held that the protection did not extend to union-like activities, if not actually carried out by or on behalf of the union. The applicant was dismissed for organising a petition about an unsafe machine. Although a union member, he was not an official, nor was he acting at the union's request (*cf.* now ERA, s.100, above, para. 8–062). An even more technical restriction is found in *Carrington v Therm-A-Stor* (1983), where the employer instructed chargehands to dismiss any 20 workers in retaliation for the union having sought recognition. They were held by the Court of Appeal to be victims of the union's activities, but had not been dismissed on grounds of their own union activities – and so fell outside the protection.

These cases apart, the concept of union activities which attract the protection is generally broad; the important limitation on it is that protection is only given for activities undertaken at an appropriate time. "An appropriate time" is defined as a time which is either:

> "outside working hours, or is a time within his working hours at which, in accordance with arrangements agreed with, or consent given by his employer, it is permissible for him to take part in those activities" (TULRCA, s.146(2)).

In *Zucker v Astrid Jewels* (1978) the zealous applicant missed no opportunity of trying to persuade her fellow workers of the advantages of union membership. She talked about it at break time, at lunchtime and while standing working at her machine. It was held that all these were appropriate times, even while working, if the employers allowed conversation as they did, they could hardly stipulate that this was an impermissible topic. Similarly, in *Bass Taverns v Burgess* (1995), where a member of the management team was permitted to address trainees on an induction course in his capacity as the union shop steward, the Court of Appeal held that he should not have been demoted for making remarks critical of the company in the course of his presentation. Having consented to him carrying out this union activity during working time, the employer could not say that the consent was subject to a limitation that he would not use the opportunity to say anything disparaging about the company.

It is clear that an implied consent by the employer will suffice, and equally clear that such an implication will not be easily made. In *Marley Tile Co. Ltd v Shaw* (1980) it was held that no consent could be inferred where the employer was simply silent on being told that a meeting was to be called in working hours.

In order to claim under section 146 the employee must apply to the employment tribunal within three months of being subjected to the detriment. If it upholds the claim, the tribunal must make a declaration to that effect and may make an award of compensation. This is such amount as it considers to be just and equitable having regard both to the loss suffered by the employee and to the nature of the employer's infringement of the right (TULRCA, s.149). It was held in *Cleveland Ambulance NHS Trust v Blane* (1997) that the inclusion of the latter phrase justified including in the award a sum for injury to feelings.

Refusal of employment on grounds of union membership

In *City of Birmingham v Beyer* (1977) the appellant was a well-known union **10–011** activist who had been blacklisted on that account by the Council. He got a job on a council construction site by giving a false name: within an hour he was recognised and sacked. He claimed he had been dismissed on account of his union activities, which would have been unfair. The EAT held that he had been fairly dismissed because of his deceit when he applied for the job: it was true that he would have been discriminated against on grounds of his union membership and activities, but this, they pointed out, was not covered by the law.

This cut two ways: a refusal to employ a non-unionist (and thus to preserve a pre-entry closed shop) was lawful too. The Conservative Government of the 1980s was implacably opposed to the closed shop but was restrained from legislating against the pre-entry closed shop by the consideration that if non-unionists were protected from discrimination in recruitment, justice would demand that equal protection be given to unionists. However, following the promulgation of the European Social Charter, which recommended protection against discrimination on grounds of union membership and non-membership, both kinds of protection were granted by the Employment Act 1990 (now TULRCA, ss.137–143).

Under TULRCA, s.137 it is unlawful for an employer to refuse to **10–012** employ someone on grounds of their trade union membership, or on the grounds that they are not trade union members. The pre-entry closed shop is specifically prohibited and it is further provided that employment agencies may not discriminate on these grounds either (s.138). The remedy is to apply to an employment tribunal, which has the same powers to make declarations, recommendations and compensation orders as under the SDA and RRA.

The legislation has been criticised in that it applies only to direct discrimination (refusal to employ because of these grounds), not indirect, and because it extends only to a refusal to employ because of union membership, not union activities. On this basis, the applicant in *City of Birmingham v Beyer* would still be without a remedy. But as with the protection for dismissal and detriment on union grounds, this depends in large measure on whether section 137 is interpreted as applying only to the bare fact of membership or whether the incidents of membership can be included. In *Harrison v Kent CC* (1995) the applicant had been employed as a social worker by the council for 14 years, during which time he had been an active shop steward and one of the leaders in a long and bitter strike. He left for another job, but within two years he applied for a job back in Kent. He was rejected because of the "confrontational and anti-management approach" he had exhibited in the past. The EAT, citing *Discount Tobacco v Armitage*, held that it was open to a tribunal to find that this was contrary to section 137 on the basis that there was no rigid distinction between membership and activities. Following the House of Lords' decision in *Associated Newspapers v Wilson* (1995) and *Associated British Ports v Palmer* (1995) the correctness of the decision in *Harrison v Kent CC* was in doubt. While some stretching of the concept of membership may be possible, it could well be argued that section 137 cannot cover union activities, especially in view of the fact that membership and activities are separately treated in sections 146 and 152. On the other hand, if section 137 is interpreted restrictively, it would seem likely that it would be a breach of Article 11 of the European Convention on Human Rights, on the basis of the European Court of Human Rights' ruling in *Wilson v UK* (2002).

10–013   The Employment Relations Act 1999, s.3 gave the Secretary of State power to make regulations to make it unlawful to compile "blacklists" of union members or activists with a view to their being used by employers or employment agencies to discriminate against those who appear on them, especially in recruitment. Regulations may also be made to outlaw the supply and use of such lists and, perhaps surprisingly, the Secretary of State's powers even include power to create new criminal offences for these purposes. Such a measure might have assisted the applicant in *City of Birmingham v Beyer* (1977), but it has been suggested that the practice of blacklisting, undoubtedly used by a number of employers in the 1980s, has now largely ceased. The Government therefore indicated in its 2003 review of the Employment Relations Act 1999 that it did not intend to exercise this power, although draft regulations were prepared and could be activated if there were a resurgence of this practice. However, it is suggested that a far more valuable reform would have been simply to extend TULRCA, s.137 to cover discrimination in recruitment on grounds of union activities as well as union membership.

Contracts between employers

10–014   For the sake of completeness it should also be mentioned that if one employer were to insert a provision in a contract with another employer that the other should use only non-union labour in carrying out their contract, the term would be void and the employer would be liable to anyone adversely affected for the tort of breach of statutory duty. This is the effect of TULRCA, s.144, and it operates as a further guarantee of freedom to associate, at least in theory. It has never been invoked so far as is known, and was actually introduced as part of the protection of the freedom not to associate, as will become clear below (para. 10–019).

Freedom of Association and Trade Unions

10–015   So far we have considered protection for freedom of association against those who might wish people not to associate at all. Now we must look at a rather different problem. If you want to join an association, but they do not want to let you join, is your freedom to associate infringed? Is the freedom to associate only a freedom to associate with those who want to associate with you? The International Covenant on Economic, Social and Cultural Rights states that the right to join is subject to the rules of the organisation concerned (Art.8(a)). This is echoed in ILO Convention No. 87 (Art.2), which goes further and insists on the right of workers' organisations to draw up their own constitutions and rules without interference from the State. While the ECHR is silent on this, in *Cheall v UK* (1986) the European Commission on Human Rights held that Article 11 was not infringed by Cheall's expulsion from the union of his choice in order to comply with the Bridlington Principles. Thus it would seem that the right to associate is guaranteed by treaty only where the association is willing to accept the member.

Admission to trade unions

Until relatively recently, this was also the position under English law. It was **10–016** informed at common law not so much by consideration of basic principles of freedom of association or the nature of trade unions as voluntary organisations but by the prosaic fact that no recognised cause of action exists where you complain that other people refuse to enter a contract with you. Attempts to mitigate this rigorous application of the principle of freedom of contract were spearheaded single-handedly by Lord Denning in the Court of Appeal. In *Nagle v Feilden* (1966), where the Jockey Club refused a trainer's licence to Mrs Nagle solely on grounds of gender, he predicated a "right to work" which would be infringed if a body having a monopoly of the activity in question (as was the case there) refused admission without good reason. While other judges were not so enthusiastic, they were in general prepared to consider the point to be arguable; however, even if this reasoning were correct, it would apply only in monopoly situations (such as where a union maintained a closed shop in an industry).

A claim for breach of contract would be possible if a union's rules were written so as to constitute an offer of membership to anyone eligible to join. This would be entirely exceptional, however. Again, it has been suggested that if a non-returnable fee is payable on application there might be a sufficient nexus between the parties to give the applicant a right of recourse to the courts, but there is no authority to this effect.

In *McInnes v Onslow Fane* (1978), considering whether reasons should have been given for refusing an applicant a licence to be a boxing manager, Megarry V.C. denied any general duty to give reasons for rejection; however, he did consider that the board was under a duty to reach an honest conclusion without bias and without pursuing a capricious policy. If imported into trade union law, this dictum could afford grounds for relief at common law to someone refused membership.

These issues are unlikely to be clarified at common law, since inroads on the policy of abstention have been made by statute, and cases are now more likely to arise under statutory provisions. Originally, the main area where there was dissatisfaction with trade unions having an unfettered right to turn down would-be members was where union membership was necessary for a job – that is, where some form of the closed shop was in operation. Thus if union membership was denied, the worker was also deprived of an opportunity to earn a living in a particular field. To counter these criticisms, the TUC set up its own Independent Review Committee in 1976, consisting of three members who would hear complaints from people refused admission to or expelled from unions belonging to the TUC. While this body had no legal status or powers, and of course only had jurisdiction over TUC members, in practice this covered most unions operating closed shops, and the Committee dealt successfully with a number of complaints. It was not seen as sufficient, however, by the Conservative Government which came to power in 1979, and so the Employment Act 1980 introduced a statutory right to complain to an employment tribunal on grounds of unreasonable refusal of admission or unreasonable expulsion from a trade union where there was a closed shop. By the end of the 1980s closed shop agreements had become unenforceable in all circumstances, so the protection against exclusion or expulsion in a closed shop situation had little practical relevance. However, by this time the Conservative Government had the Bridlington Principles in its sights.

10–017   The Bridlington Principles were originally drawn up in 1939 at a TUC Conference held in Bridlington. They were amended over the years, but the basic purpose remained intact: to control the proliferation of trade unions and to avoid inter-union disputes in situations where more than one union was appropriate for a class of workers and they were competing for members. It is frequently the case in this country that more than one union is appropriate, because of the relatively piecemeal development of unionism in this country: unlike, say, Germany, where since the Second World War there have been industrial unions.

The Bridlington Principles dealt with two kinds of dispute: disputes between unions about who should organise a particular group of workers, and disputes over individual members changing unions. Disputes were referred to the TUC's own Disputes Committee and the ultimate sanction for a union refusing to comply with its ruling was suspension or expulsion from the TUC. Most TUC unions adopted a model rule permitting expulsion to comply with a decision of the Disputes Committee. The model rule was challenged on public policy grounds in *Cheall v APEX* (1983) where Cheall was expelled from APEX, which he had joined in preference to ACTSS, following a Disputes Committee ruling that APEX was guilty of poaching contrary to Bridlington. The House of Lords held that the Bridlington Principles, aimed at orderliness in industrial relations, were not contrary to public policy, and that freedom of association must be mutual: "there can be no right of an individual to associate with other individuals who are not willing to associate with him", said Lord Diplock, although he indicated that the matter might have been viewed differently if there had been a closed shop so that Cheall's job was at stake. As noted above, the European Commission on Human Rights took the same view when Cheall's case was taken there.

However, this was regarded by the Conservative Government as an unacceptable restriction on freedom of choice. TURERA substituted a new TULRCA, s.174 which provides that a union may only refuse admission to (or expel) someone on one of four grounds: that the applicant does not satisfy an enforceable membership requirement; that she does not come within the geographical area covered by the union; that she no longer works for the relevant employer in the case of a company-specific union or because of misconduct. Enforceable membership requirements are those which stipulate criteria like employment in a particular trade or occupational group or having particular qualifications. Misconduct is defined so as not to include things like having resigned from another union or being a member of a political party or unjustifiable discipline within the meaning of TULRCA, s.65 (discussed below, para. 11–021). Thus unions may no longer have rules barring members of the Communist Party or the National Front.

The effect of the new section 174 is virtually to abolish a trade union's **10–018** right to define its own identity through its membership rules. There is just one limited respect in which it is narrower than the previous law, namely that there is no reference to reasonableness. If a union refuses admission on the basis of an enforceable membership requirement, there can be no question of attacking its decision on the grounds that it is wholly unreasonable in the circumstances.

In that it is now possible for groups of disaffected members to leave one union and insist on joining another, this poses some threat to orderliness in industrial relations. It is also clear that TULRCA, s.174 constitutes a breach of ILO Convention No. 87, Art.3, guaranteeing unions the right to draw up their rules "in full freedom". In 1989 the Committee of Experts expressed its view that TULRCA, s.65 on unjustifiable discipline contravened Article 3 and the new provision goes much further. This cut little ice with the Conservative Government; however, it is surprising in these circumstances that revision of section 174 has not been addressed since the change of government in 1997.

There is probably quite a lot to be said for the view that a union's decision not to admit someone should be liable to review if it will have direct consequences for their employment. Since the closed shop is no longer legally enforceable (as will be seen below), it may be thought that this will rarely be the case in future. However, where a union is recognised for bargaining purposes, employees will rarely have any other opportunity to negotiate about their terms and conditions of employment. There would thus seem to be a good argument for saying that in these situations also, an individual should be entitled to review if a union refuses an application for membership; although this does not mean that acceptable reasons for refusal should be as limited as in TULRCA, s.174.

The Closed Shop

So far we have looked at the positive aspect of freedom of association – **10–019** how far the rights of people to associate together are protected. We must now consider whether the right to associate logically entails the opposite proposition, that people have a right not to associate; or at least whether the existence of a right to join means that in fairness there ought also to be a right not to join. That they are, to use a well-worn cliché, opposite sides of the same coin, is frequently asserted; the symmetry is apparently thought to be self-evident. It is notable that the Universal Declaration of Human Rights, Art.20 states the negative as well as the positive right, although the International Covenants on Economic, Social and Cultural Rights and on

Civil and Political Rights do not; nor does the ECHR, nor ILO Convention No. 87. However, in *Young, James and Webster v UK* (1981) the European Court of Human Rights held by a majority that Article 11 of the ECHR was contravened by English law which permitted the closed shop at that time, because employees risked dismissal if they did not join. The majority view was that compulsion to join one union restricted freedom of association because it prevented workers from forming or joining another; a concurring minority was prepared to go so far as to say that the positive freedom necessarily implied the negative.

10–020 Kahn-Freund, the pre-eminent theorist of British labour law in modern times, argued strongly that a right not to join is not simply the converse of a right to join. He drew an analogy between participation in the collective bargaining process through trade union membership and participation in democratic government through the franchise. The results of collective bargaining are as important in one's working life as the results of legislation are in one's life as a citizen. We believe that the State has a duty to let us take an indirect part in government by voting for our representatives; so the State should also let us take our indirect part in collective bargaining by guaranteeing our right to form and join trade unions. But in the same way that it is no function of the law to ensure that we do not have to exercise our rights as citizens, so (argued Kahn-Freund) it is no function of the law to ensure that we do not have to exercise our industrial rights. Hence freedom of association should be supported by the law, as an aspect of the worker's right and duty to participate in the bargaining process, but no similar considerations require legal support for the freedom not to associate.

Kahn-Freund's argument convincingly decouples the so-called positive and negative freedoms. It is not, nor was it claimed to be, a conclusive argument in favour of the closed shop. Kahn-Freund thought that this depended on essentially pragmatic and utilitarian considerations: do better or worse consequences flow from allowing the closed shop to exist?

Varieties of closed shop arrangement

10–021 It is necessary first to be more specific about what is being referred to when we talk about the closed shop. Essentially a closed shop is a workplace where belonging to a particular trade union (or one of a number of specified trade unions) is a condition of having a job. Access is "closed" to everyone else. While some closed shop arrangements were clear, written, and agreed by employers, others were informal arrangements, sometimes merely tolerated rather than specifically agreed to by management. There is an important distinction between pre-entry and post-entry closed shops: in a pre-entry closed shop, the worker must have joined the union before getting the job – union membership is in effect an essential qualification for applicants. In a post-entry closed shop, the requirement is that the worker should join within a short period after getting the job. Clearly the pre-entry closed shop gives most power to the union, since it means that the union controls the pool of applicants for a post; it may thus seem surprising that this manifestation of the closed shop only became unlawful under the Employment Act 1990.

Most closed shop agreements made provision for exceptional cases such as conscientious objectors or people who were already there before the agreement came into force. Some allowed employees not to join provided that they paid a sum equivalent to union dues to the union or to a charity – an arrangement known as the "agency shop" in the United States. The agency shop goes some way to counter the average union member's biggest objection to non-joiners, which is that they are taking a free ride on the backs of those who do pay subscriptions, because they get the benefits of negotiated improvements without paying for them.

Arguments for and against the closed shop

Trade unionists asked to justify a membership requirement refer most **10–022** frequently to the free rider argument. As noted already, this can be mitigated by payment of an equivalent sum to the union or to charity. But some have doubted the validity of the argument altogether: there are other organisations which people pay to belong to whose activities benefit non-members, like the National Trust or CAMRA. Kahn-Freund thought that the strongest argument in favour was that it was necessary for maintaining an equilibrium in industrial relations – thus if the organisation of workers and maintenance of decent wage levels is difficult or impossible without a requirement of union membership (as is the case in much of the entertainment industry), then insistence on the closed shop is justified. Others have argued that employers like the closed shop too, because it means that they can be sure that the union speaks for the whole workforce, and that resulting collective agreements will largely be policed by the union.

The freedom of the individual is the argument most often appealed to against the closed shop. It is a powerful, emotive concept, but really without meaning unless we know what it is we are free from or free to do. If it is simply asserted that we should be free not to join a trade union if we do not want to, it may be answered that we are already as free to do that as we are free not to work for a company if we disapprove of its activities or free not to work at all if we do not wish: that is, we have the freedom if we can afford to exercise it. In any case, it could be argued that the freedom of the individual can be adequately safeguarded by permitting conscientious objector clauses in closed shop agreements rather than by abolishing the closed shop altogether.

Stronger are the practical arguments against the closed shop. In the 1960s the Donovan Commission found that the industries where the closed shop was strongest were also those which were most strike-prone, and many considered the phenomena to be linked. Certainly the Conservative Government of the 1980s firmly believed that the closed shop was responsible for inefficient restrictive practices which significantly impeded Britain's international competitiveness, for overmanning and for the retention of outdated working methods, and its abolition was one of the main planks in their programme of labour law reform.

Present legal regulation of the closed shop

10–023   No law regulating the closed shop existed in the United Kingdom until the introduction of the law of unfair dismissal. Employers could not be legally compelled to enter closed shop arrangements, nor to continue them. In *Reynolds v Shipping Federation* (1924) it was held that a union seeking the dismissal of a non-member was not liable for the tort of conspiracy. However, once unfair dismissal was introduced, it was thought necessary to have special rules stipulating whether the dismissal of a worker for refusing to join a union was fair or unfair. This further necessitated defining what exactly counted as a closed shop (or "union membership agreement" as it was called in TULRA). The position under TULRA was that in principle dismissal for refusal to belong to a union was automatically fair – but there were certain limited exceptional circumstances where it was automatically unfair. The Employment Acts 1980–82 extended these exceptions considerably so that there was little left of the rule; but the complicated provisions were all rendered redundant by the Employment Act 1988 which finally made the dismissal of an employee for refusal to join or belong to a trade union automatically unfair whether or not there was a closed shop in operation (see now TULRCA, s.152). Furthermore, it is not possible to insist on the employee making payments in lieu of membership: dismissal for refusing to make such payments is treated as if it were dismissal for not being a member. Where unfair dismissal on this ground is made out, the employee will be entitled to enhanced rates of compensation, basically set at a high level to deter dismissals for this reason. Under TULRCA, s.146 an employee also has a right not to be subjected to a detriment on these grounds.

While the Employment Act 1988 meant that no post-entry closed shop arrangement could be enforced, it still left the possibility of a pre-entry closed shop, because it was still lawful to discriminate against a job candidate on grounds of non-membership of a union. This may seem odd, given that the pre-entry closed shop gives more power to a union than the post-entry closed shop, but the reason is soon explained. The general policy of the Conservative Government throughout the 1980s was formally to treat all "union membership reasons" in the same fashion. Thus if it was automatically unfair to dismiss someone for joining a union, it was automatically unfair to dismiss someone for not joining; if there was enhanced compensation for someone dismissed for not joining, then there was enhanced compensation for the unionist dismissed for being a member, and so on. It is the case that this formal equality was not maintained in all cases (see TULRCA, s.222), and that in practice the provisions were much more effective as a protection for the non-unionist than the unionist, but that is another matter. The policy of facial even-handedness was important as a matter of public relations. Now, if the Government wished to outlaw discrimination against non-unionists at the point of job entry (in order to outlaw the closed shop), formal equality would require that discrimination against unionists should be outlawed also. Such tactics as circulating "blacklists" among employers so that union activists could be kept out of the workplace would no longer be allowed. This was not necessarily on the Conservative Government's agenda at all.

Just when it looked as if the policy of even-handedness might be **10–024** dropped, and only discrimination against non-unionists made unlawful, the Community Charter of the Fundamental Social Rights of Workers was produced by the EU. It recommended member countries to prohibit discrimination on grounds of union membership and on grounds of non-membership. Delivered from its dilemma, the Government complied in 1990 (see now TULRCA, ss.137–143, discussed above, para. 10–012).

The Community Charter also got the Labour Party off the hook. It had remained committed to reintroducing the closed shop in some form, while recognising that this was something of an electoral liability. The Community Charter gave them a good reason to back down gracefully, so that reintroduction of protection for the closed shop was dropped as part of Labour Party policy by 1990.

It should be noted that the closed shop has not been rendered an unlawful institution by any of these measures. However, it has become impossible, or possible only on pain of very large compensation payments, to enforce any agreement between an employer and a union that all employees should be union members. As a result, even where they have not been officially terminated, closed shop agreements have largely fallen into disuse.

The Nature of Trade Unions

History in outline

Freedom of association may be a well-recognised principle today, but it **10–025** certainly was not at the beginning of the nineteenth century when the first unions were being formed. While guilds of craftsmen existed from the Middle Ages, it was not until the Industrial Revolution and the birth of an industrial working class that combinations of workers began to be created, both for the purpose of mutual support in case of sickness and unemployment and for the purpose of attempting to improve working conditions. The history of trade unionism cannot be dealt with in anything but the barest outline here; only some main themes will be identified in so far as they will aid understanding of the form of modern trade unionism.

At the beginning of the nineteenth century, trade unions were regarded by the law as illegal criminal organisations. Discovery was sure to lead to dismissal at the very least, so the early unions swore members to secrecy. However, the French Revolution was fresh in the minds of the ruling classes, who were therefore terrified of secret groups; the Unlawful Oaths Act 1797 imposed criminal penalties on any secret society which required its members to take an oath – the offence for which the Tolpuddle Martyrs were transported in 1834. Besides this, the Combination Acts 1799–1800 criminalised all agreements with the purpose of raising wages.

The Combination Acts 1824–25 reformed the law so that unions were not illegal in themselves, although most of their activities beyond the purely "friendly society" purposes of collecting and administering funds against misfortune were likely to be criminal. A strike was a criminal "molestation" of the employer, and if it involved a breach of the contract of employment, then that was a criminal offence on the part of the employee (although breach of contract by an employer was only a civil wrong). While no longer criminal organisations, unions were unlawful at civil law because their objects were in restraint of trade.

Following the extension of the franchise to a much wider class of working men in 1868, the Liberal Government accepted union lobbying and in 1871 passed the Trade Union Act and the Criminal Law Amendment Act, which removed unions from the ambit of the law of criminal conspiracy and provided that trade union purposes were not to be considered as in restraint of trade – a provision still necessary today and to be found in TULRCA, s.11. In 1875 the Conspiracy and Protection of Property Act defined an area of lawful industrial action. Thus unions had at last become fully recognised as lawful organisations; but the fact that they had to struggle so long without this recognition contributed to that general suspicion of the law which became deeply entrenched in British trade unionism. Also, the fact that unions had been organising themselves without the law for so long led to an antipathy to any sort of legal regulation of their internal affairs.

10–026 Despite the advances made in legislation, the courts remained hostile to trade unions. Throughout the nineteenth and twentieth centuries there was a discernible pattern: legislative protection granted to unions by statute; subsequently outflanked by case law; followed by amending legislation to reinstate the advance; followed by more restrictive case law – and so on. After 1875, the law of tort was extended in order to render union activities unlawful. However, this was subject to an important limitation. The law recognises two categories, and two categories only, of legal persons: natural persons (human beings) and corporations. Trade unions grew up as unincorporated associations – inevitably, given their history. That meant that in law a trade union had no existence of its own – the phrase "trade union" was simply a shorthand way of referring to all the members of the union. Legal opinion at the end of the nineteenth century considered that the technical difficulties in suing all the members in one action effectively precluded any action against the union in its own name. The practice developed of suing the principal officers of the union instead, and in general if an injunction was granted against an officer, the union accepted its terms too. However, this state of affairs meant that trade union funds were safe from damages awards.

The House of Lords decision in *Taff Vale v Amalgamated Society of Railway Servants* in 1901, that a trade union could be sued in its own name, therefore sent shock waves through the trade union movement, for it meant that a union's funds could be wiped out by a single damages award resulting from industrial action. It was also seen as the apogee of judges' hostility to trade unions. A Liberal Government was returned at the 1906 election with Labour support, committed to restoring the previous position. However, the Trade Disputes Act 1906 did not provide, as it might have done, that unions could not be sued in their own name; rather it gave them an almost complete immunity from liability in tort. This basic model, an unincorporated association with many of the characteristics of a corporation, with immunity (albeit much less) for certain kinds of action, remains in place today.

Nature and status of trade unions

We have seen that when unions started they were in the nature of clubs – **10–027** groups of people who unite for a common purpose. Like clubs, they were voluntary, unincorporated associations. Voluntary, in the sense that there was no legal or other compulsion to form unions; unincorporated, inevitably, given that for the first hundred years or so the law regarded them as illegal associations. When unions were legalised in the nineteenth century it was suggested that they should become corporate bodies like companies. It was suggested again by the Donovan Commission in 1968. On both occasions it was strongly resisted by the unions themselves. It has been argued that a corporate model would be inappropriate for trade unions because they are not "top-down" hierarchical organisations, as companies are. In a trade union, it is said, policy is decided by the members, and that drives the people at the top, who are ultimately accountable to and under the control of their members. This is only true up to a point: in most unions the officials are usually the people with the time and the information to initiate policy and, as in companies, they have the greatest control over communication with the members, and thus have considerable opportunities to persuade them to their point of view. However, a very good reason for resisting corporate status is that the internal affairs of companies are subject to a high degree of regulation and public scrutiny. Trade unions, as stated already, are suspicious of the law and do not wish to have it meddling in their internal affairs.

Trade union opposition to corporate status has been successful to date. The Industrial Relations Act 1971 forced corporate status on all unions who registered under the Act, but this was avoided by the vast majority of unions by the simple expedient of refusing to register, and the Act was repealed in 1974.

Trade unions are still defined according to their purposes and membership, and the definition of a trade union is wide. It is an:

> "organisation – whether temporary or permanent – which consists wholly or mainly of workers of one or more descriptions and whose principal purposes include the regulation of relations between workers . . . and employers or employers' associations" (TULRCA, s.1(a)).

An additional limb of the section widens the definition to include organisa- **10–028** tions of trade unions so that federations of unions such as the TUC or the International Transport Workers' Federation, which are made up of unions, are themselves to be regarded as trade unions. That the members must be workers led to the Law Society being held not to be a trade union (*Carter v Law Society* (1973)). The reference to a permanent or temporary organisation could be important. In *Midland Cold Storage v Turner* (1972) the company was blacked on the instructions of an ad hoc shop stewards' committee representing dockers. The committee had no official union status or powers. The Court of Appeal held that even though the committee had only come into being because of and for the duration of the dispute, it was properly to be considered a temporary organisation: it had a name, a basic structure, a convenor and a secretary. However, it was not a union because its purpose was to organise industrial action, not to regulate relations with employers. The case indicates that loose groupings, even in non-unionised workplaces, could be regarded as trade unions. As the limits of lawful industrial action became narrower, there was an incentive for more unofficial action to take place. The disruption of the London Underground in the summer of 1989 was a good example of this. In these cases it can be very difficult to identify the individuals against whom injunctive relief may be sought. The Employment Act 1990 sought to deal with this by extending the range of people for whom the union may be held liable (see below, para. 13–026); however, if the organisation could be identified, it would presumably qualify as a trade union, and the injunction could be granted against the body.

In *BAALPE v NUT* (1986) it was held that a union need not be capable of carrying out all the purposes of a trade union in order to come within the definition. Thus although the British Association of Advisers and Lecturers in Physical Education had only 402 members, its constitution stated that it was concerned with the professional interests of its members. In a dispute with the NUT over teachers' representation on a national negotiating committee, it was held to have the essential primary purpose of a union and was thus entitled to representation.

10–029   A definition in terms of purposes rather than structure is appropriate for an unincorporated association. As we have seen, before 1901, the unincorporated status of unions was thought to protect them from damages actions. In *Taff Vale v ASRS* (1901), the Law Lords had to explain how it was that an unincorporated association could be sued in its own name. Lord Halsbury said:

> "If the Legislature has created something which can own property, which can employ servants and which can inflict injury, it must be taken I think to have impliedly given the power to make it suable in a court of law for injuries purposely done by its power and procurement."

However, that is a policy reason rather than a legal reason. It demonstrates why the Law Lords were anxious to reach the decision. The means by which they did so are more opaque. In effect the decision hinged on the fact that the union was registered under the Trade Union Act 1871. This, they held, did not turn it into a corporation, but did bring it to a sort of halfway house between corporate and unincorporated status – and brought it far enough to be sued in its own name. The reasoning is dubious, but the effect was far-reaching. While the Trade Disputes Act 1906 limited its effect, it did not in any sense clarify or change the legal status of the union, which thus depended on their Lordships' opinions.

If a union had sufficient personality to be sued in tort, it must follow that it could also sue in its own name. This corollary was dramatically established in *NUGMW v Gillian* (1946), where the union successfully sued the General Secretary of another union for defaming it. In *Bonsor v Musicians' Union* (1956) the House of Lords decided that damages in contract (as opposed to simply an injunction) could be awarded against a union. Thus without satisfactorily explaining why, the courts had brought trade unions to a point where they were treated to all intents and purposes as if they had their own legal personality.

The Industrial Relations Act 1971 sought to formalise that position. The **10–030** name "trade union" was given only to those unions which registered under the Act, and they became corporations. The Industrial Relations Act was deeply unpopular with the trade union movement, and refusal to register became the rallying point of the campaign against it. Thus unions avoided corporate status – at the cost of being regarded in law as "organisations of workers" rather than "trade unions". This had little practical effect, but was regarded as insulting.

When the Industrial Relations Act was repealed by TULRA in 1974 the opportunity was taken to regularise the status of unions. TULRCA, s.10 now provides that a union is not, and is not to be treated as if it were a body corporate; but it is capable of making contracts; it can own property, the title of which must be vested in trustees on its behalf; it can sue and be sued in its own name; it can be prosecuted in its own name, and judgments can be enforced against it as if it were a corporation. A union is specifically prohibited from registering as a company.

This means that unions are now confirmed as unincorporated associations, but the technical inconveniences of that status are removed. This clarification does not merely restore the pre-1971 position. In *EEPTU v Times Newspapers* (1980) the union sued for defamation over an article which had appeared in the newspaper. O'Connor J. held that the law had changed since *NUGMW v Gillian* (1946) and a union could no longer maintain an action for defamation in its own name: the statutory injunction that a union is not and is not to be treated as a corporation meant that it should not be treated as having a personality capable of being damaged through defamation.

The effect of the present rules on the ownership of union property were considered in *News Group Newspapers v SOGAT '82* (1986), where the union's funds were subject to sequestration following for contempt. The union had about £5.25 million in its central general funds, but another £6 million was held by branches of the union. The sequestrators argued that since unions were unincorporated associations, and not charitable, a trust of branch funds would be void for perpetuity unless the funds were construed as belonging in reality to the central union (in which case they would be liable to sequestration). The Court of Appeal held that the property belonged to the branch, and that this did not infringe the rule against perpetuities. Drawing a distinction between branch funds and central funds in this way may be important in industrial disputes, since it effectively allows unions some leeway to arrange their property holdings so as to limit funds exposed to claims in the event of the industrial action being held to be unlawful.

Listing and Independence of Trade Unions

Listing

10–031 Many organisations regulated by law have to have their details recorded on a register open to public inspection. Companies are the most obvious example. When the existence of trade unions was recognised by law in the Trade Union Act 1871, a system of registration, conferring some slight advantages on those unions which registered, was introduced. Registration under the Industrial Relations Act 1971, which replaced this system, was quite another matter. It turned registered unions into corporations and exposed them to detailed regulation as to their internal affairs. By the time the Industrial Relations Act was repealed by TULRA in 1974, the whole concept of registration had attracted such opprobrium that the replacement system, which was similar to the 1871 notion, was called "listing" instead of registration.

Under TULRCA, s.2 the Certification Officer has responsibility for maintaining a list of trade unions. Any organisation believing itself to be within the definition of a trade union may apply to be put on the list on payment of a small fee. While there is no requirement that trade unions should be listed, there are advantages in becoming so. There are some tax advantages for listed unions; but more importantly, there are certain rights which are available to unions only if they can establish their status as independent or recognised unions, and listing is the first stage in establishing such status.

Independent trade unions

10–032 Under TULRCA, ss.6–9 the Certification Officer must decide whether a union is an independent trade union, and if so issue a certificate of independence. An appeal lies from his decision to the EAT. The reason for defining independent trade unions and giving them some legal support is to discourage "sweetheart unions" – which appear to represent the workforce but are in fact in the employer's pocket. An independent trade union is defined by TULRCA, s.5 as one which:

"(a) is not under the domination or control of an employer . . . and

(b) is not liable to interference by an employer . . . (arising out of the provision of financial or material support or by any other means whatsoever) tending towards such control."

In *Squibb UK Staff Association v Certification Officer* (1979) the Court of Appeal held that the words, "liable to interference" meant "vulnerable to interference" rather than "likely in fact to be interfered with". Thus in that case where the union was so dependent on the employer's support that it

302

could not have continued without it, it was held that it was not independent even though there was nothing to suggest that the employer was likely to abuse its power. The criteria used by the Certification Officer were set out in his Annual Report for 1976 and approved by the EAT in *Blue Circle Staff Association v Certification Officer* (1977), as follows:

(1) *Finance*. If the union receives any direct subsidy from the employer, it is ruled out.

(2) *Other assistance*. Employers may indirectly subsidise the union by providing free office and meeting accommodation, free mail and telephones, photocopying or check-off facilities. In the *Squibb* case, the union was dependent on all these things and the Certification Officer felt that the union would not have been able to survive without them. However, this should not be unduly weighted: provision of many of these facilities is generally regarded as good industrial relations practice. The Acas Code of Practice (No.3) on *Time Off for Trade Union Duties and Activities* states:

> "Employers should consider making available to officials the facilities necessary for them to perform their duties efficiently and communicate effectively with their members, fellow lay officials and full-time officers.
>
> Where resources permit the facilities could include:
>
> - accommodation for meetings
> - access to a telephone and other office equipment
> - the use of notice boards
> - where the volume of the official's work justifies it, the use of dedicated office space." (Para. 28.)

(3) *History*. Where the union was founded recently with the employer's assistance (as in the *Squibb* case), or where it is evolving from having been an employer-dominated organisation (as in the *Blue Circle* case), it may indicate that it is not yet truly independent.

(4) *Rules*. In the *Blue Circle* case, the committee of the staff association had originally included management representatives, who had the right to call meetings and see the minutes. When the rules were changed in the quest for independence, management helped draft the new rules. These facts tended against independence.

(5) *Membership base*. Where the potential membership of the union is restricted to one company or group of companies, it will clearly lack the strength of more open unions. In *Squibb*, membership was limited to workers in a particular grade at the company's two factories – a total of 291 people. However, the fact that it is a single company union is not an absolute bar to independence.

(6) *Attitude*. Finally, the Certification Officer considers whether the relationship is too cosy, or whether the union has demonstrated what is delicately described as a "robust attitude in negotiation". This is not meant to suggest that a record of militancy is the best means to a certificate of independence.

The consequences of a certificate of independence alone are less than they were, although it is only the members of independent trade unions who are protected against dismissal and detriment on grounds of their union activities (TULRCA, ss.146, 152). (Oddly, section 137 does not so limit its prohibition on discrimination in recruitment of union members.) However, there are a range of rights given to independent unions which are also recognised by their employer. Thus a union which has recognition will also desire a certificate of independence in order to claim these statutory rights. Recognition is discussed in Chapter 5 (above, para. 5–014).

11.   Trade Unions and their Members

Trade unions have always claimed that, as voluntary associations, they **11–001** should be left alone to run their internal affairs. In other voluntary associations, such as members' clubs, the members decide what rules they want, and how to run their affairs, and the law does not intervene. The same ought to be true of trade unions.

Against this view, it is often pointed out that a trade union is usually a much more important and powerful body than a members' club, often having power over the very livelihood of workers within its sphere of influence. A trade union is too important to be allowed to run itself in whatever way it thinks fit: the law should lay down minimum standards. This argument had particular force when closed shop arrangements were prevalent and expulsion from a union could indeed be a "sentence of industrial death" (as Younger L.J. once put it). However, even though closed shop arrangements can no longer be enforced, it could still be argued that the collective bargaining process is so important that workers ought to have a right to be represented, and thus there should be sufficient control over the rules of a union to ensure that they are not excluded from membership without good reason.

If accepted, this is an argument for control over rules on admission and expulsion in trade unions, but not for wholesale legal intervention. It must be balanced against the injunction in ILO Convention No.87 that unions should be free to draw up their own rules without interference. Furthermore, it could well be argued that membership of many other apparently voluntary organisations is in fact essential, yet the law does not govern their internal affairs in anything like the same way that unions are controlled. To which a riposte might be, then these other organisations should be brought into line with trade unions rather than the controls on unions relaxed!

In this chapter we will examine the ways in which the law has increasingly assumed control of the internal affairs of unions. Using a broadly chronological approach, we will look first at the political activities of unions, then at the constraints developed at common law, and finally at the ongoing legislative inroads on union autonomy.

Expenditure for Political Purposes

Common law

11–002 In the nineteenth century it was obvious to trade unions that they needed parliamentary representation if they were to gain the sort of legislative framework that they needed in order to achieve their aspirations. The Labour Party was born out of this wish, and trade unions were giving money to support candidates and for other political purposes from the 1880s. Provided that this was not contrary to the union's constitution, it was difficult to see what was wrong with this. Any organisation is allowed to use its property in lawful ways permitted by its constitution. Because of the political dimension, this was bound to be challenged. The Labour Party received over 90 per cent of its income from trade unions until the 1980s, although this fell to 50 per cent by the mid-1990s. In the first reported case, *Steele v South Wales Miners' Federation* (1907) the union's constitution specifically included financial support for MPs among its objects. Following a ballot in favour, the union began levying one shilling a year from members for this purpose. The union's objects were upheld as lawful, Darling J. saying:

"It seems to me that one of the ways of regulating the relations between workmen and masters . . . is to get laws passed by Parliament for their regulation and that one of the first steps towards getting those laws passed would be to send a representative to Parliament to promote a Bill for that purpose."

However, this view was swiftly overtaken by the House of Lords' decision in *Amalgamated Society of Railway Servants v Osborne* (1910). Osborne, a Liberal, objected to a levy payable to the Labour Party. Interestingly, the main ground for the House of Lords' decision that such expenditure was beyond the powers of a union appears to have been because of an analogy drawn with the position of companies. Apparently assuming that it would be *ultra vires* (outside the capacity of) a company to spend money on political purposes, their Lordships considered that trade unions should be similarly restricted.

The point is interesting because it is, of course, extremely common today for companies to give large amounts of money for political purposes, usually by way of direct donation to the Conservative Party. These amounts are greatly in excess of the income received by the Labour Party from trade unions (the Liberal Democrats do badly out of both sides of industry). Yet now it is hardly suggested that such payments by companies are *ultra vires*.

Osborne is another landmark case in trade union history, hardly less famous than *Taff Vale*. Again it was seen by many trade unionists (especially the railway workers!) to be an example of the system working against them. Again, it required legislation to restore the position as previously understood. However, the Trade Union Act 1913 did not reverse the effect of *Osborne* by giving unions *carte blanche* to spend money on political purposes. It required a union to set up a political fund, separate from its other funds, for such expenditure, and to allow every member the right to opt out of paying the political levy. These requirements stood unchanged for 70 years, but were made more stringent following amendment by the Trade Union Act 1984. They are now to be found in TULRCA, Ch.VI.

Statutory control

The first condition for political expenditure is that the members of the **11–003** union should be balloted to see whether they want a political fund. A simple majority of those voting is required. Under the 1913 Act this was a once and for all vote, but the 1984 Act introduced a requirement that there should be a ballot every 10 years. The justification for this was said to be union democracy: present members might have different views from their predecessors. However, it should be noted that members who do not wish to pay the political levy do not have to: it is thus not immediately apparent why there should be a ballot at all, since the result of a "no" vote is to deprive those members who do want to pay of the opportunity to do so. As most unions with political funds set them up soon after the 1913 Act, many had to hold a ballot within a year of the 1984 amendments. None lost the vote, having successfully persuaded their members that if they did not want to make political payments themselves, they should not prevent other people's freedom of choice.

The rules for the ballot must be approved in advance by the Certification Officer. Other than requiring that the ballot be secret and that every member should have a reasonable opportunity to vote, the 1913 Act did not lay down conditions as to the form of the ballot. The 1984 Act permitted workplace or postal ballots, but in line with the rules on the election of union officials the Employment Act 1988 tightened the rules further by requiring a fully postal ballot – *i.e.* the voting paper is sent out by post and returned by post in a prepaid envelope. Political fund ballots are also subject to similar provisions for independent scrutiny as ballots for the election of trade union officials (see below, para. 11–026).

At first public funds were available for re-ballots (on whether to continue a political fund), but not for an initial ballot. It is also worth noting that while a ballot is mandatory for setting up a political fund, the law does not require that members be balloted on a decision by the executive officers to close down the political fund. Such asymmetries in the post-1984 law have contributed to the generally held view that the purpose of the legislation was to make it harder for unions to make political contributions rather than to increase union democracy, which was the stated aim when the Trade Union Act 1984 was passed. Once it became mandatory for all ballots to be fully postal, there was no further need to offer inducements for unions to ballot in this way, so TURERA arranged for the phasing out of public funds to cover the cost by March 1996. At the same time TULRCA, s.116, giving recognised unions the right to use the employer's premises for workplace ballots, ceased to have effect.

11–004   Given the cost of holding ballots and the fact that no union member can ever be compelled to pay the political levy, the Better Regulation Task Force (set up in 1997 to advise the Government on the burdens of regulation and possible alternatives) questioned whether it was necessary to retain the requirement for repeat ballots on the political fund. However, in its 2003 review of the Employment Relations Act 1999 the Government stated that it intended to keep the present rule. A large number of unions will therefore need to reballot in 2004–2005.

Expenditure on political objects may only be made out of a political fund, not out of general funds. Political objects are defined by TULRCA, s.72 as expenditure of money:

"(a) on any contribution to the funds of, or on the payment of expenses incurred directly or indirectly by, a political party;

(b) on the provision of any service or property for use by or on behalf of any political party;

(c) in connection with the registration of electors, the candidature of any person, the selection of any candidate or the holding of any ballot by the union in connection with any election to a political office;

(d) on the maintenance of any holder of a political office;

(e) on the holding of any conference or meeting by or on behalf of a political party or of any other meeting the main purpose of which is the transaction of business in connection with a political party;

(f) on the production, publication or distribution of any literature, document, film, sound recording or advertisement the main purpose of which is to persuade people to vote for a political party or candidate or to persuade them not to vote for a political party or candidate."

The revised objects are wider than the 1913 formulation, thus requiring more kinds of payment to come out of the political fund. Some of the amendments simply updated the old law – *e.g.* the inclusion of film among publications and the inclusion of Members of the European Parliament. Some make explicit what was probably covered already: in *Parkin v ASTMS* (1983) the EAT held that the union's investment of £42,000 in the development of the Labour Party Headquarters on commercial terms, but on a "sympathetic basis", came within the political objects, as did political donations from companies wholly owned by the union. While it has been held that paying money to MPs as salary for services rendered (*e.g.* as parliamentary consultants) is not within the political objects, a gift of money or in kind will be. In *Parkin v ASTMS*, allowing the political fund to run into deficit was held to be lawful provided that the interest on the overdraft was also charged to the political fund; this is now embodied in TULRCA, s.83.

Most controversy has centred on the amendment to sub-paragraph (f), which, it was thought, could mean that any union literature critical of the Government would have to be paid for from a political fund, despite the limitation contained in the words "the main purpose". The fear was found to be justified to some extent in *Paul v NALGO* (1987) where a member complained about the NALGO "Make People Matter" campaign. Leaflets and posters highlighting cuts in public services, the damage caused by privatisation, and urging readers to "use your vote" were distributed near the time of local elections. Despite the inclusion of a disclaimer saying that NALGO was not affiliated to any political party and that it was not seeking or opposing the election of any particular candidate, it was held that overall its main purpose was to dissuade people from voting for Conservative candidates. Browne-Wilkinson V.C. stressed that such a campaign might have been paid for out of general funds if the timing had been different, but its closeness to the election clearly had a bearing on the decision about its main purpose. While not ruling out publicity critical of the Government as a lawful expenditure from general funds, this decision clearly made it a hazardous business. The result was that a number of unions representing public sector workers (whose employment conditions are therefore closely affected by government policy) took steps to establish political funds for the first time.

Is it justified to hedge the political expenditure of unions about with so **11–005** many restrictions? The usual argument is that individual members may not support the political party to which the union donates money. Of course, they need not themselves donate money; but equally it could be said that any member who does want to give money to the Labour Party can do so by joining it, or sending periodic donations. However, bearing in mind the reasoning behind the House of Lords' decision in *ASRS v Osborne* (1910), and the reality that unions give to the Labour Party and companies mostly give to the Conservative Party, it seems difficult to justify this elaborate control over union political donations when it is contrasted with the near absence of any control over political donations by companies. So far as companies are concerned, it seems accepted that political donations are in the interests of shareholders, and the only statutory control for many years was the requirement in the Companies Act 1985 (Sch.7, para.3) that any donation over £200 should be disclosed in the directors' report to the Annual General Meeting. This remains in force, but as a result of recommendations of the Neill Committee on Standards in Public Life, the Political Parties, Elections and Referendums Act 2000 amended the Companies Act 1985 so that companies may not make donations for political expenditure unless they have been approved by a resolution of the shareholders specifying the maximum amount which can be spent (Companies Act 1985 ss.347A–C).

Members' rights

Members have the right to opt out of paying the political levy. When the **11–006** union adopts political objects, members must be given notice of this right; it seems that they must give written notification to the union of their intention to opt out, but that it need not be in any particular form. When the 10-year review ballot comes up, members must be given a reminder of their right to opt out; however, the Trade Union Act 1984 stopped short of changing the position to one of opting in instead. The difference between opting out and opting in is significant in practice, since the most reliable human characteristic is inertia. When people must actually do something in order not to pay, the majority will not bother to do it. Thus opting out swells the political fund, and between 1927 and 1946 when opting in was necessary, the funds consequently dwindled.

11–006.1   Provided that the member gives notice within a month of being informed of the right to opt out when the fund is established, he or she has no liability to pay. However, if the member exercises the right at some other time, the exemption takes effect only from the following January. This simple rule is complicated by the fact that under TULRCA, s.86, where union dues are automatically deducted from a member's pay (the check-off system), the employer must immediately stop deducting the political contribution if informed that the member wishes to be exempt. Thus the money would not be paid automatically even though the member would remain contractually liable to the union for its payment.

Employers may not deduct union subscriptions (whether or not including political fund contributions) from wages without specific written authorisation from the member, which authorisation may be withdrawn in writing at any time (TULRCA, s.68). TURERA aimed to make the check-off system more difficult for employers to operate, no doubt with the aim of discouraging them from providing this facility, by stipulating that an initial authorisation would only be valid for three years and that any increase in the subscription during that time would require new written authorisation. Furthermore, it was the employer who had to give employees written notice of any changes and of their rights to cease payment. These rather petty complications were swept aside by the Deregulation (Deduction from Pay of Union Subscriptions) Order 1998 (SI 1998/1529) which restored the previous position. In the meantime, however, many unions had persuaded their members to pay their subscriptions by direct debit instead. This has the additional advantages that employers cannot readily identify union members and that the union will continue to get income even when members are not being paid (*e.g.* because they are on strike).

Finally, by TULRCA, s.82, there must be no discrimination against a member who has opted out of paying the political levy, and she must not be barred from holding any office on that account, except an office which involves the control or management of the political fund itself. In *Birch v NUR* (1950) the union's rules provided that the branch chairman should also manage the political fund. As Birch was a non-contributor, he was dismissed from his post as branch chairman, the union arguing that the post involved management of the political fund. The court held that a combination of duties in this way could have the effect of excluding non-contributors from wide areas of union activity and was therefore contrary to the Act.

Union Rules at Common Law

The rules of a trade union form a contract between the union and the **11–007** member. The rules are mostly express, and to be found in a rule-book; however, they may be derived from other sources. This was recognised by the House of Lords in *Heaton's Transport v TGWU* (1972) where it was pointed out that "union rule books are not drafted by parliamentary draftsmen" and should not be interpreted as if they were. In particular, it should be recognised that the rule-book might not be complete, and rules could be implied from, for example, custom and practice. On that basis, it was held that shop stewards had customary power under the union's constitution to call industrial action, although they had no express power to do so. This approach was applied in *McVitae v Unison* (1996), where the rules of the union, which had come into existence as a result of the amalgamation of three other unions, made no provision for the continuance of disciplinary proceedings begun by one of the constituent unions before amalgamation. A term to permit proceedings to be brought under the new union's rules was implied on the "officious bystander" test. In *AB v CD* (2001) the union rules required election of officials by single transferable vote, but did not state what should happen if two candidates tied for the top place. In the past such ties had been resolved by declaring elected the candidate who had scored most votes in an earlier round and it was argued that this rule should be implied on the basis of custom and practice. However, since there was no evidence that members would be aware of this, the court held that a customary rule could not be established. A term allowing the practice was implied instead on grounds that the contract was incomplete (*cf. Liverpool CC v Irwin* (1977) above, para. 4–016).

Since 1980 there has been increasing statutory regulation of union rules, including those governing the relationship of union and member. However, even before this, controls on the enforcement of the contract between union and member had been developed at common law, and these remain of residual importance. We shall look at this first in relation to the disciplining and expulsion of members.

Discipline and expulsion

Two points are worth noting at the outset. Firstly, unions have no wish to **11–008** reduce their membership, and so they are likely to use powers to expel sparingly. Similarly they must be circumspect in exercising disciplinary powers short of expulsion for fear that members will become disenchanted and leave. Where there were strong closed shops so that expulsion from the union meant loss of a job, these restraints on unions did not exist, and so unions having the most comprehensive and severe disciplinary codes tended to be those where the closed shop was strongest; correspondingly, weak unions have weak disciplinary rules. Secondly, it is instructive to compare the power of a union to expel a member with the power of an employer to dismiss an employee. There are differences, most notably that expulsion from a union does not mean that one loses one's livelihood and may thus be regarded as a less serious contingency than dismissal. However, as will be seen, the law places tighter controls on the union's power to expel than on an employer's power to dismiss. The courts have evolved two main grounds for their jurisdiction over the rules of trade unions: firstly, that the rules are contract terms to be interpreted by the court, and secondly, that the administrative law concept of natural justice applies.

Interpretation of the rules

11–009 Disciplinary rules are usually of two kinds: those which provide for specific offences and penalties (*e.g.* being in arrears with subscriptions); and open-ended, subjective rules which create vague offences such as "conduct prejudicial to the interests of the union", or even "conduct which, in the opinion of the branch (or national) committee, is detrimental to the union". The court's position as final arbiter on the interpretation of these rules was classically asserted in *Lee v Showmen's Guild of Great Britain* (1952), where the union had fined a member £100 for "unfair competition" contrary to the rules. The issue had been before an internal union tribunal, which had found against the member, and it was argued that their determination should not be disturbed. The Court of Appeal, led by Lord Denning, was prepared to accept that it should be bound by the findings of fact of the internal tribunal, provided that the court was satisfied that there was sufficient evidence to support their finding. Here, the Court of Appeal held that the conduct complained of was not capable of constituting unfair competition. This seems to come perilously close to the court substituting its opinion for the opinion of the internal tribunal – a tendency frequently castigated by the Court of Appeal in the EAT's handling of unfair dismissal appeals from employment tribunals, and indeed in tribunals' handling of employers' dismissal decisions.

It might be thought that subjective rules, especially those which incorporate reference to a committee's opinion, would be proof against such judicial incursions, for they seem to require only good faith on the part of the relevant committee. However, this is not the case. In *Esterman v NALGO* (1974), for example, a member refused to take part in a strike designed to disrupt local elections. She was expelled from the union for "conduct which, in the opinion of the branch committee, renders her unfit for membership". Templeman J. held that no reasonable tribunal could so have categorised her conduct: "I emphatically reject the submission that it was the duty of every member blindly to obey the orders of the national executive".

Thus where matters of discipline or expulsion are at issue, the court will intervene on behalf of a member if either the rules are not followed, or if the court considers that an internal union tribunal has not interpreted the union's rules correctly. In *McVitae v Unison* (1996) it was argued that the union could not discipline or expel a member unless it had an express power in the rules to do so. However, it was held that even such a penal power could be implied, although only in exceptional circumstances. In general, however, courts have leaned towards a construction of the rules which favours the member.

Can the court go further and strike down or treat as ineffective certain **11–010** rules? It is clear that on general principle a rule which attempted to exclude the jurisdiction of the courts altogether, for example, by stating that there was no appeal from a union decision, would be treated as void because contrary to public policy. However, if the rule states that all domestic procedures must be exhausted first, the effect would be to delay, rather than to remove, a right of recourse to the courts. In *Lawlor v UPOW* (1965) the member's claim was not barred by a failure to appeal internally first, but in that case there was no express rule that this should happen. However, in *Leigh v NUR* (1970) Goff J. held that, while not absolutely bound by such a rule, a court would normally require a good reason to be given for failure to exhaust internal remedies, and that it might expect a member to use internal remedies first even where there was not an express rule to that effect. One good reason for trying the court first might be the length of time that it takes to go through the union's own appeal machinery: in some unions the final right of appeal is to the annual conference, and could thus be a long way off, particularly if the disciplinary decision or expulsion is treated as effective in the meantime. Thus, TULRCA, s.63 provides members with a statutory right of recourse to the court if the union itself has not dealt with an application from a member within six months (see further below, para. 11–021).

This particular situation aside, there have been suggestions from time to time that rules which are unreasonable, or contrary to public policy, will be treated as ineffective. However, clear authority for this is lacking, and given present levels of legislative control over the rule-book, there would seem to be little scope for further common law development.

Natural justice

Natural justice is a public law concept stipulating certain minimum **11–011** procedural standards for decision-making bodies having quasi-judicial functions. Its requirements cannot be regarded as absolutely fixed, but basically embody two principles: firstly, that a person is entitled to a fair hearing before his or her case is decided, and secondly, that any decision must be taken by an unbiased tribunal. At least since *Lee v Showmen's Guild* (1952) it has been clear that trade unions must abide by the rules of natural justice when taking decisions affecting members.

The right to be heard involves being given adequate notice of the charge against you – adequate both in terms of length, so that there is time to prepare an answer, and in terms of detail, so that you know exactly what it is you are meant to have done. In *Annamunthodo v Oilfield Workers' Union* (1961) the appellant knew that he was charged with having made serious allegations of dishonesty against the union's president, for which he could be fined, but not that this was to be treated as conduct prejudicial to the union's interests for which he could be expelled. It was held that his expulsion was a breach of natural justice because insufficient notice had been given.

Most disciplinary procedures of whatever kind usually allow representation, but it seems from *Enderby FC v Football Association* (1971) that natural justice does not go so far as to require that legal representation should be allowed. Frequently it is specifically disallowed, because the presence of lawyers is sure to extend the length of the proceedings and without doubt the expense as well. On the other hand, it may be felt that the inarticulate will not get a fair hearing without a skilled advocate to speak for them.

The rule against bias must be interpreted with common sense when applied to internal tribunals, whether of trade unions or other bodies. There is a sense in which someone who has fallen out with the union is never going to believe that a tribunal composed of union people will give him a fair hearing. However, if the rule that there should not only be no actual bias but not even the appearance of bias were taken this far, then internal tribunals would become quite impracticable. It is clear that natural justice is not infringed just because union officials are involved in making the decision, but obviously anyone who has played a part in the dispute ought not to be involved in judging it. In *Roebuck v NUM (No.2)* (1978), the union president, Arthur Scargill, had successfully sued a newspaper for libel on behalf of the union. The two plaintiffs were members who had given evidence in that action on behalf of the newspaper; afterwards Mr Scargill reported that one had contradicted in court a statement that he had given to the union's solicitors and that the other had shown official correspondence to the newspaper's solicitors. This, he contended, was conduct detrimental to the union's interests. The area council (chaired by Mr Scargill) agreed and referred the matter to the area executive committee. The area executive committee (chaired by Mr Scargill) met four times, found the charges proved and recommended that the members be suspended from office. The decision was confirmed by the area council – chaired by Mr Scargill. Not surprisingly, this was held to be a breach of natural justice; in the words of the judge, the president had been "the complainant, the pleader, the prosecutor, the advocate and the chairman in the union proceedings".

11–012 Natural justice does not require that there be an appeal procedure, although again it is common for unions to provide internal appeal procedures. It should be noted that in *Leary v NUVB* (1971) it was held that a breach of natural justice at an initial hearing could not be cured by a proper appeal.

However, it would seem that natural justice does not apply to absolutely every case of discipline or expulsion. Often union members do not signify formally an intention to resign from the union, but simply stop paying their subscriptions. Unions thus frequently have rules which provide for a member's name being automatically removed from the register after a certain period of arrears. It would seem unnecessary, in this sort of case, to insist on the member having a right to notice first. Having said that, it should be noted that in *Edwards v SOGAT* (1971), such a rule was held to be contrary to natural justice. However, the circumstances in that case were rather special: it was the fault of a union official, not the member, that the subscriptions had not been paid, and the union, once aware of the mistake, far from apologising for their error, rather refused him re-admission on two occasions and ensured his dismissal from the printing shop where he worked on the grounds that it was a closed shop! In *Cheall v APEX* (1983), the House of Lords held that it was not a breach of natural justice for the union to expel the member without a hearing first in order to comply with a ruling of the TUC under the Bridlington Agreement.

Enforcing the rules

While it is the rules about discipline and expulsion that most directly affect **11–013** the member's relationship with the union, there are plenty of other rules which a member will be interested in seeing enforced. The contract of membership confers to some extent the right to have the business of the union run in accordance with the rules, but as with the enforcement of most contracts, this right is essentially negative: it is a right to restrain action in breach of contract or to sue for breach of contract rather than a right positively to insist on the conduct provided for in the rule being carried out. This is well illustrated in *Taylor v NUM (Yorkshire Area)* (1984) – one of many cases contributing to the jurisprudence of members' rights which arose out of the miners' strike of 1984–85. The National Union of Miners was a federation of Area unions. Under the national rules, no national strike action could be called unless there had been a ballot in which 55 per cent voted in favour of action. This rule, more stringent than the simple majority required by TULRCA, s.226, considerably pre-dated the statutory requirement, and was repeated also in the rules of most of the Area unions. Taylor challenged the strike on the grounds that there had been no ballot. In fact there had been a ballot in Yorkshire, where 85.6 per cent had voted in favour of action – but that was in 1981. Nicholls J. held that there was certainly an arguable case that this was national strike action (and there had been no national ballot) and that the ballot in Yorkshire was too remote in time to validate the Yorkshire action. However, he refused to grant an injunction either requiring the union to run a ballot or to call off the action – the only remedy to which a member was entitled was a declaration that the action was unofficial: "The member's right under the Rule is confined to being able to insist that a national strike cannot lawfully be held without a national ballot". There was no positive right to insist that the union should hold a ballot.

As we will see, members have now been given a statutory right to restrain action without a ballot, but the point remains valid that at common law action is possible to restrain breaches of the rule, not to enforce rule-observing behaviour.

The Rule in Foss v Harbottle

A further constraint, at least in theory, on the ability of a member to take **11–014** action where a breach of the rules is threatened is found in the rule in *Foss v Harbottle*, deriving from an 1843 company law case. In essence, the rule is that where certain non-serious breaches of the organisation's rules take place (non-serious breaches meaning those which are capable of ratification by a majority vote), then an individual member may not bring an action complaining of the irregularity. Notice that it is not essential that ratification should actually have taken place: only that the breach is capable of being ratified.

There is a theoretical and a practical justification for this rule. The theoretical justification is that a breach of the rule is really a wrong done to the organisation rather than to a particular member of it; thus it is the organisation which ought to be the plaintiff. If the wrong done is one which the organisation itself could put right if it wished by a majority vote, then there is no need to let an individual sue. The practical justification is to protect the organisation from costly and vexatious litigation: if the majority do not wish to take action, then it would be an unnecessary drain on the organisation's resources to allow an individual to do so.

The very formulation of the rule suggests the situations in which it will not apply. For example, in all the disciplinary and expulsion cases considered above, there is never any suggestion that a member cannot complain because of the rule in *Foss v Harbottle*: there the wrong is clearly done to the member, invading his or her personal rights, rather than to the union. Secondly, it only applies to non-serious breaches which are capable of ratification: so if what the member is complaining of is a serious breach, then an individual will have the right to take action. Unfortunately, the distinction between serious and non-serious breaches is not immediately obvious, at least in trade union cases. In *Cotter v NUS* (1929) (the case in which the rule was first applied to unions) a resolution to make an interest-free loan to the Miners' Non-Political Movement (in the wake of the General Strike) was passed at a Special General Meeting of the union against the advice of some officials. One official challenged it, claiming that the meeting had not been convened according to the union's rules, and that delegates had not been properly elected. The Court of Appeal held that even if the irregularities were proved, they were only minor breaches, capable of ratification, and the plaintiff was therefore barred from action by the rule in *Foss v Harbottle*.

11–015   If under the union's rules a special majority is required for a particular decision (*e.g.* the 55 per cent in favour of strike action required by NUM rules), then a breach of that rule is one which is not capable of ratification. For if ratification was allowed, it would effectively allow the union to do by a simple majority (in ratifying) what the rule said must be done by a special majority. This exception was established in *Edwards v Halliwell* (1950), where a delegates' meeting purported to raise subscriptions without getting the necessary two-thirds approval stipulated in the rules.

An action which is *ultra vires* the union (*i.e.* outside its objects and therefore its capacity) is clearly non-ratifiable. There can be no ratification of an *ultra vires* act, because this is not a situation where power has been misused, but a situation where there is no power to act in this way at all. In *Thomas v NUM (South Wales Area)* (1985) it was alleged that the conduct of the strike was bound to result in breaches of the criminal law (arising out of picketing activities) and the commission of torts, and was therefore *ultra vires* the union. Scott J. was of the view that it would be *ultra vires* for the union to organise activity which was definitely criminal, but he was "not clear" what the position would be if action was organised which was bound to result in a tort being committed. However, he did not feel obliged to decide either point, since he accepted that the action here carried only the usual risk of crimes and torts being committed; they were not inevitable. As the scope of trade union immunity for action in tort has now been substantially reduced, the point could become important in the future. However, this must be seen in the context of a contemporaneous first instance decision, *Taylor v NUM (Derbyshire Area) (No.3)* (1985). The energetic Taylor, having already established that the strike in Derbyshire was *ultra vires* for want of a ballot, here complained about payments from union funds to relieve hardship among strikers and their families and for pickets' expenses. He sought to stop future payments and to recover some £1.7 million paid out. Vinelott J. held that the payments, in connection with an *ultra vires* strike, were also *ultra vires*, and that an injunction should be granted. However, he declined to order the officials to repay the money spent. He was clearly influenced by the facts that the officials had acted in good faith, for no personal gain and that exhausting their own assets, while ruining them, would be a drop in the ocean against the sum claimed; furthermore, there was evidence that the majority of the members supported what had been done. Strictly, of course, these are not relevant considerations; in particular, if an action is *ultra vires*, then it cannot be ratified even if every single member wants it to be. However, Vinelott J., while restating that ratification was impossible, held that the majority could in good faith decide not to sue, and that that decision would bind the minority. It is difficult to see the difference between ratification and a decision not to sue, since both have the same practical effect of depriving a minority member of a right to sue, but if the decision is not a model of legal reasoning, it may perhaps be defended as a common-sense response in a highly charged atmosphere.

Wedderburn has attacked this decision more fundamentally on the **11–016** ground that the *ultra vires* doctrine is only applicable to corporations, which, as artificial persons, must have constitutions stating what they can and cannot do, and is inappropriate for trade unions, which are unincorporated associations. According to TULRCA, s.10, a union is not, and is not to be treated as if it were, a corporation. As decided in *EEPTU v Times Newspapers* (above, para. 10–030), this marks a break from past cases, such as *Cotter v NUS* (1929), where unions were treated more like corporate bodies and thought to be subject to the *ultra vires* doctrine. If this view is correct, it would mean that members would not be able to restrain action on grounds of its being outside the union's power to do it.

As *Taylor v NUM (Derbyshire Area) (No.3)* (1985) is a first instance decision, it is open to another court to take this view. However, by parity of reasoning, it might be considered that the rule in *Foss v Harbottle* is also a company law doctrine and inappropriate to unincorporated associations (although this was denied in *Cotter v NUS*), which would widen the possibilities for the union to be sued. The issue was not raised at all in the most recent case *Wise v USDAW* (1996), invoking the rule in *Foss v Harbottle*. The plaintiff, then president of the union, challenged decisions of the executive council in relation to the election of union officials, which, although they did not affect her personally, she argued were in breach of the rules. Chadwick J. held that the rule in *Foss v Harbottle* did not preclude her claim, essentially on the grounds that any member had a personal right to enforce adherence to the contract set out in the rule-book. This is a very broad concept of personal rights, since it does not require the member to show that her interests are particularly affected by the breach of the rules. If correct, it means that it is difficult to envisage any situation where the rule in *Foss v Harbottle* will stop a member bringing an action. Elias and Ewing pointed out that the rule in *Foss v Harbottle* has been relied on successfully in only five cases against trade unions, of which the most recent was as long ago as 1966 (*McNamee v Cooper*). Thus, even if still applicable in theory, it seems less and less likely in practice that it will inhibit a member who wishes to sue the union for a breach of its rules. In any case, common law rights have in many circumstances been overtaken by statutory controls over the union's rules.

Procedure

11–017 The usual route for an action for breach of contract, including the membership contract, would be the High Court. However, an important, if not widely publicised reform in the Employment Relations Act 1999 extended a parallel jurisdiction to the Certification Officer for certain kinds of breach of union rules, by inserting new sections 108A–108C into TULRCA.

Under new section 108A a member may complain to the Certification Officer instead of the High Court where she or he alleges a breach or threatened breach of union rules in relation to one of the following: appointment or election to a union office; discipline or expulsion of members (but not union employees); ballots (except industrial action ballots); constitution or proceedings of any executive committee or decision-making meeting; and anything else specified by order of the Secretary of State. The member has the choice of going to the Certification Officer or the court, but cannot apply to both. The advantages of proceedings in front of the Certification Officer are speed and cost: any claim is meant to be determined within six months.

To encourage local resolution of disputes as far as possible, the Certification Officer may refuse to entertain an application if the member has not taken all reasonable steps to use the union's internal complaints procedure first (TULRCA, s.108B). However, in such circumstances the member must keep a careful eye on limitation periods: application must normally be made to the Certification Officer within six months of the alleged breach. Where internal procedures have been invoked the limitation period becomes six months from the date of the conclusion of the internal proceedings or one year from the date of their commencement, whichever is earlier.

The Certification Officer may make or refuse a declaration that there has been a breach of the rules. If making such a declaration, he may also make an enforcement order. Declaration and enforcement orders made by the Certification Officer are enforceable as if made by a court. Appeals from the Certification Officer's decisions lie on a question of law only to the Employment Appeal Tribunal (TULRCA, s.108C).

Statutory Regulation of the Rule-book

Certain basic standards of efficient organisation are an unobjectionable **11–018** requirement, and so there is little criticism of the provisions contained in TULRCA that a member should always have the right to resign on giving reasonable notice (s.69) and that unions should keep proper accounts, to be filed annually with the Certification Officer and open to public inspection (ss.28–30). The former is in the nature of a tidying-up provision, as some unions did not have a procedure for resignation, and instead just inferred it from non-payment of subscriptions. The latter is a basic requirement for all kinds of organisation recognised by the law. However, since 1980, numerous other less neutral requirements have been introduced, many of which are fiercely resented by unions.

Financial affairs

In *Taylor v NUM (Derbyshire Area) (No.2)* (1985), the member sought to **11–019** inspect the union's accounts accompanied by an accountant. The court held that where, as here, the rules gave members the right to inspect the accounts, it impliedly gave them the right to do so with a professional agent. As a result the NUM altered its rules specifically to exclude the right to professional advice. This, coupled with the fact that in the miners' strike and certain other industrial disputes in the 1980s the whereabouts of union funds were difficult to discover, led to an amendment in 1988 to give members the right to inspect the accounts accompanied by an accountant and to oblige the union to supply them with copies if requested (TULRCA, s.30). Members may only see accounts relating to their own period of membership, and may be asked to pay a reasonable administrative charge, but they can see the records of any branch or section. The accountant, but not the member, may be required to give a reasonable undertaking of confidentiality. A member may apply to the Certification Officer or to the court for an order where inspection is refused, and a deliberate failure to maintain the relevant accounts is a criminal offence.

Controls on unions' financial affairs were taken further by TURERA. The Government based its case for further intervention yet again on events surrounding the miners' strike. Following allegations in the media in the spring of 1990, Gavin Lightman Q.C. was appointed by the NUM to investigate alleged irregularities in the conduct of union funds. The Lightman Report was critical of a number of matters, especially unauthorised dealings by senior officials of the union. The Report was commissioned by the union in response to the pressure of a media campaign: it had no obligation to look into the matter on behalf of members. Subsequently criminal proceedings were brought by the Certification Officer under what is now TULRCA, s.45, on grounds that the union had failed to keep proper accounting records and to submit true and fair accounts; however, the Lightman Report was judged to be inadmissible and the charges were ultimately dropped.

11–020   The TURERA reforms tackled this in three ways: firstly, by increasing the powers of the Certification Officer; secondly, by extending the range of criminal offences relating to the financial affairs of trade unions; and thirdly, by providing for increased disclosure to members to encourage them to challenge the union. Under TULRCA, s.37A the Certification Officer has power to require a union to produce any documents and to provide an explanation for them if he thinks that he has a good reason to do so. He is specifically enjoined to consider whether to exercise his new powers when a member complains of fraud or misconduct, or the auditor's report is critical of the accounts. In addition, TULRCA, s.37B gives the Certification Officer a power to appoint an inspector to investigate the financial affairs of the union whenever there are circumstances suggesting fraud, misfeasance or misconduct: it is specifically provided that any resulting report will be admissible in criminal proceedings (s.37C(8)).

These powers are similar to those afforded to the Serious Fraud Office in relation to the financial dealings of companies and provide expressly that refusal to make a statement is not justified on the grounds that it might incriminate the maker. However, in *Saunders v UK* (1994) (an attack on convictions resulting from the Guinness takeover scandal) the European Court of Human Rights criticised the use of information gained in this manner in subsequent criminal proceedings, suggesting that there may be a need to reform these powers.

In addition to the existing offences in TULRCA, s.45 of failure to keep proper accounts and failure in relation to audit arrangements or the annual return, TURERA introduced new offences: failure to produce documents to the Certification Officer; falsification or destruction of documents; and knowingly or recklessly making false statements. The sanction for most of these offences is imprisonment for up to six months and/or a fine at level 5; furthermore, under TULRCA, s.45B anyone convicted of such an offence will be banned from holding a position as a senior union officer for five or 10 years, depending on the seriousness of the offence.

The amended form of TULRCA, s.32 requires that the union's annual return to the Certification Officer must include details of the remuneration package payable to the president, general secretary and members of the executive committee of the union, and under section 32A every member of the union must be provided with a financial statement containing this information. This is clearly intended to encourage union members to complain about the conduct of the union's finances and gives union members rather more information than shareholders are entitled to about the directors of their companies.

Discipline and expulsion

11–021 In Chapter 10, dealing with admission to trade unions, reference was made to TULRCA, s.174, which prohibits exclusion or expulsion except on the grounds there specified. One of these is conduct; hence it remains possible to expel members for misconduct. However, this is subject to major qualification by virtue of TULRCA, s.64 which gives a member a right not to be unjustifiably disciplined.

Before this right was introduced by the Employment Act 1988 union members only received statutory protection against exclusion or expulsion where there was a closed shop in operation, on the grounds that in such situations the decision of the union actually affected a person's ability to work in a particular field. It seems justifiable to require adequate reasons in such situations, although it does not necessarily follow that a statutory procedure is necessary. The TUC attempted to deal with the issue by setting up its own Independent Review Committee, but this was not considered sufficient by the Government. Of course, the Independent Review Committee only dealt with unions which were members of the TUC.

Justification for such intervention might therefore be regarded as having disappeared when, with the Employment Act 1990, it became impossible for an employer to treat union membership as a prerequisite or a condition for employment. However, in the meantime the Employment Act 1988 had extended limits on discipline and expulsion, and this reform was fuelled by rather different considerations.

During the miners' strike attempts were made to expel members who **11–021** crossed picket lines. In *Taylor v NUM (Derbyshire Area) (No.1)* (1984), it was held that this expulsion was invalid because the strike itself had not been called in accordance with the rules. Further, when the National Union attempted to add an expulsion power, the rule change was declared void as being in contempt of an earlier court order (*Clarke v Chadburn (No.2)* (1984)). Many unions have traditionally had a power to expel for strike-breaking, which is seen as one of the most serious offences that a union member can commit, since it undermines the solidarity which is fundamental to successful action and thus successful unionism. In *Esterman v NALGO* (1974) (above, para. 11–009) we saw another example of a court's reluctance to uphold an expulsion on this ground. In the aftermath of the strikes of the 1980s, a number of unions exercised their lawful powers to discipline or expel members who had disobeyed strike calls. This led the Government to introduce the right not to be unjustifiably disciplined now found in TULRCA, ss.64–67. Any kind of disciplinary action is covered, and it is "unjustifiable" if the reason for it falls within the categories laid down in section 65: failure to take part in industrial action, or expressing opposition or lack of support for it; failure to break one's contract of employment in connection with any industrial action; claiming (in good faith) that the union has broken the law, or its own rules; encouraging anyone else to act similarly; seeking assistance from the Certification Officer; failing to comply with a union ruling that is itself a contravention of section 64 and proposing to do any of the above. To these, TURERA added refusal to participate in check-off arrangements for deduction of union subscriptions and a number of acts amounting to failing to behave in accordance with the Bridlington Agreement. While the list of reasons which are unjustifiable is long, it does not mean that unions can never take disciplinary action. In *Knowles v Fire Brigades Union* (1996) the union was absolutely opposed to full-time firefighters having "retained" contracts for standby duties in their free time. The plaintiff firefighter was expelled for accepting a retained contract in contravention of union policy. He argued that he had been expelled for refusing to take part in industrial action, contrary to section 64 but, as the Court of Appeal pointed out, although the union's policy was opposed to the wishes of the employers, the opposition had not in any sense taken the form of industrial action.

11–023 There is now such a large area of overlap between TULRCA, ss. 64 and 174 that it is difficult to see why two provisions have been retained. It made some sense when section 174 applied only to exclusions and expulsions in a closed shop situation, but now that it has been extended to all exclusions and expulsions except on the grounds there specified, which in substance cover the same issues as those in section 64, the duplication seems inelegant and unnecessary. There are differences, of course: most notably that section 174 only covers exclusion or expulsion; section 64 does not cover exclusion but it does cover all kinds of disciplinary action, including expulsion. In *NACODS v Gluchowski* (1996) it was held that suspension from membership did not amount to an exclusion or expulsion actionable under section 174 and the EAT also doubted that there could be a concept of "constructive expulsion" through the union committing a fundamental breach of its own rules. This would therefore be actionable only under section 64. Both sections provide that if an action is started under one of them, it cannot afterwards form the basis of a claim under the other; note, however, that any possible common law remedies are additional.

Remedies for breach of sections 64 and 174 are also similar. If a tribunal upholds the applicant's claim, it makes a declaration to that effect, after which the union has a period of grace in which to put matters right. If it does so, any claim for compensation goes to the employment tribunal, which awards such amount as is just and equitable subject to a maximum equivalent to the maximum of the basic and compensatory award for unfair dismissal (£61,300 in 2003). If the union fails to act on the declaration, a claim for compensation goes directly to the EAT, where compensation is awarded on the same basis and there is a minimum award (£5,700 in 2003). In *Bradley v NALGO* (1991), eight applicants who had been expelled for refusing to take part in a strike claimed compensation. The union did not contest the making of a declaration, nor did it revoke the expulsions. The EAT awarded each of them the minimum award only: there was no evidence that their job prospects would be in the least affected by their non-membership, nor that they were likely to be prejudiced if they applied to join another union. The EAT declined to import any kind of punitive element into the award, and limited itself purely to issues of compensation. The decision is interesting in a number of respects. The applicants had been subjected to an unpleasant bullying campaign after their expulsions but the EAT took the view that their injury to feelings arising from this was not an injury arising from the actual expulsions and was not therefore due to be compensated. Thus the decision is evidence of an apparent concern by the EAT to construe section 64 fairly narrowly; further, the interest in having at least an indirect say in collective bargaining which has been put forward as a justification for intervention in these matters was not argued nor raised of its own motion by the EAT. It will be interesting to see whether this point will ever be taken up, and if so how far it will be seen as of importance.

Election of trade union officials

Another plank in the policy of the Trade Union Act 1984 of increasing **11–024** democracy in trade unions was to require that certain officials should have to offer themselves periodically for re-election by the whole membership of the union. Before 1984, practice varied considerably, with at least some of the large unions (such as the NUM) providing that the president, once elected, had tenure until retirement. It was also very common for officials to be elected not directly by a ballot of all the members, but indirectly by a ballot among the representatives of the members. As union activists tend to be more radical than the membership as a whole, it is fairly clear that the Conservative Government of the 1980s believed that indirect elections led to candidates who were more left wing being elected, who would tend to favour confrontational tactics such as industrial action, and that this was an important element in making this reform.

The officials required by the Trade Union Act 1984 to offer themselves for re-election every five years were all the voting members of the principal executive committee of the union (whether called the National Executive, the National Council or whatever: the principal executive committee is that committee which is responsible for the day-to-day policy and management of the union). The requirement was restricted to voting members not just because the ones with the vote are the ones with the power, but to take account of the fact that most unions have a senior full-time official (usually designated as "General Secretary") who is an employee of the union and whose regular job is the general administration of the union; these career trade unionists, it was felt, should not have to put their jobs on the line every five years.

If the Trade Union Act 1984 was intended to make such officials as Arthur Scargill, at that time the life president of the NUM, offer themselves for re-election, it failed. For it could easily be circumvented if the official in question was prepared to give up his vote (as Mr Scargill did) and it may be doubted if this was much of a sacrifice, since decisions rarely turn on a single vote. Hence the Employment Act 1988 (in the so-called "Scargill clause") amended the Trade Union Act 1984 so that the president, general secretary, every member of the principal executive committee and even anyone entitled to attend and speak at executive committee meetings must offer themselves for re-election every five years (see now TULRCA, s.46). The selection of the five-year period was probably by analogy with the directors of public companies, who are also limited to a five-year period of office; however, the Companies Act 1985 allows numerous exceptions which are not available to trade unions.

In the calmer industrial relations atmosphere prevailing today, the Better **11–025** Regulation Task Force questioned whether it was necessary for union presidents to be separately elected by a postal ballot of the membership (at considerable cost) when they were almost certain to be elected members of the union's national executive. The Government agreed and has promised to remove this requirement for presidents who are directly elected members of the principal executive committee. Power is also to be given to the Secretary of State to change voting procedures to allow more flexibility, which could include introduction of internet voting and a return to workplace ballots.

In principle every member should be entitled to vote in the election, but two qualifications are allowed: some elections may be restricted to particular classes of members (*e.g.* by reference to a geographical or trade group), and some classes of member (*e.g.* unemployed members, new members) may be excluded. The mere fact that some members did not get a voting paper will not of itself invalidate the election, since the standard is reasonable practicability but unions now have a statutory obligation to maintain accurate membership lists (TULRCA, s.24), so errors should not occur on a grand scale. As with political fund ballots, the original legislation permitted workplace ballots, but was changed by the Employment Act 1988 so that the ballot should be fully postal. The member must be sent the ballot paper by post with a prepaid envelope for its return.

11–026 One advantage of the old indirect system of elections was that the candidates were usually known to the voters (although some regarded this as one of the disadvantages of the old system, arguing that it perpetuated an oligarchy and gave an outsider little chance of election). Under TULRCA, s.48, however, candidates may require the union to circulate an election address to all the members. The union is allowed to set a limit on this, but at least 100 words must be granted.

Since 1988, ballots for the election of officials and in relation to the political fund have been subject to independent scrutiny by a solicitor, accountant or a body such as the Electoral Reform Society. In January 1990 there were allegations of ballot-rigging in the elections for the Executive of the TGWU, which led to the ballot being re-run. The *Independent on Sunday* then revealed that the independent scrutineer, a solicitor, was a left-wing councillor, causing some furore, as the identity of the scrutineer was not widely known, and people had generally assumed that it was the Electoral Reform Society. This prompted an amendment in 1990 to the effect that the name of the scrutineer must now be notified in advance to the electorate (TULRCA, s.47). TURERA greatly extended the remit of the independent scrutineer. She is now required to inspect the membership register when appropriate but especially when requested to do so by a member in the run-up to an election, and her findings as to its accuracy should be included in her report on the election. In addition, TULRCA, s.51A requires that the election must actually be conducted, as opposed merely to being supervised, by an independent person, who will normally be the scrutineer. Similar scrutiny provisions apply also to political fund and industrial action ballots. The requirement to delegate the conduct of a ballot to an independent person has had some side effects which were probably not intended. For example, in *Veness v NUPE* (1992) members complained, *inter alia*, that only 100 out of 1,150 members at one branch and only 11 out of 2,200 at another had received ballot papers. But as the union had delegated the conduct of the ballot to the Electoral Reform Society, it was held that they had no claim against the union. Furthermore, in *Dundon v Graphical Paper and Media Union* (1995) it was doubted whether the union could cancel an election result (because of possible prejudice to one candidate) once the scrutineer had reported that the election had been conducted satisfactorily.

Candidates for union office

Until 1984, the only restrictions on union rules about who could run for **11–027** office in the union were that they should not discriminate against non-contributors to the political fund (Trade Union Act 1913), and, more recently, that they should not discriminate on grounds of gender or race (Sex Discrimination Act 1975, s.12; Race Relations Act 1976, s.11; under SDA, s.49 it is permissible to reserve a minimum number of seats on committees for women). Since 1984, no one may be unreasonably excluded from being a candidate, although the union is still permitted to exclude certain classes from standing (*e.g.* those who have not been members for a minimum period) (TULRCA, s.47). The major restriction on this is that no candidate can be required directly or indirectly to be a member of a political party (s.47(2)). Thus rules which exclude members of the Communist Party from being candidates (which are fairly common) are valid; but the other common rule requiring a candidate to be a member of the Labour Party (or to be qualified to attend the Labour Party Conference, which indirectly requires membership) is invalid. Section 47(3) provides that where a class of members is excluded from standing, that class may not be defined as those "whom the union chooses to exclude". This was held to have been infringed in *Ecclestone v NUJ* (1999) where the national executive committee refused to accept the claimant's candidature for General Secretary of the union, a post which he had previously held for 17 years but from which he had been dismissed following a serious dispute with the national executive committee. The committee's reason for refusing to accept him as a candidate was that it had lost confidence in him and therefore he was not qualified to stand for the office. The court held that this was tantamount to saying that those who the national executive committee did not want could not stand and therefore was in breach of s.47(3). It was also held to be an unreasonable exclusion in contravention of s.47(1) and a breach of the union's own rules.

Many unions in effect ensure continuity and executive experience among their senior lay officials by having a tiered system at the top: the Junior Vice-President automatically becomes the Senior Vice-President and then President and Immediate Past President. In *Paul v NALGO* (1987) the Certification Officer held that keeping the Immediate Past President on the executive committee without a further election did not infringe the rules; however, there was an infringement in not opening the office of Junior Vice-President to all the members. The case illustrates another interesting point: only members of the principal executive committee need to stand for election; here, the members of the important national committee on conditions of service were not subject to election. It was held that this did not contravene the law.

While the legislation requires a degree of even-handedness on the part of **11–028** the union towards candidates, it falls short of requiring completely equal treatment. It does not prevent the practice of designating some candidates as those having the support of the union's annual conference or of the national executive. Furthermore, in *Paul v NALGO* (1987) a practice of sending members a list of the branches expressing support for each candidate along with their voting papers was held by the Certification Officer not to constitute interference with the ballot.

TULRCA does not require unions to change their rules, nor does it invalidate anything done by officials appointed other than in accordance with its provisions. However, where there is non-compliance, any member has a right to complain either to the Certification Officer or to the High Court as outlined above (para. 11–017).

12. Industrial Action I

The law regulating industrial action is the most politically contentious area **12–001** of employment law, largely because of the propensity of industrial action to affect people who are not parties to the dispute. Where a strike affects the general public, there is likely to be a feeling that workers should not have total freedom to take industrial action because of its disruptive effect on the community. Many would argue that it is in any case a primitive method of dealing with disagreements, and would question whether a right to strike is really necessary in a modern state.

However, a number of reasons can be put forward in favour of a right to strike. The major one is related to the need to have trade unions in the first place – the equilibrium argument. That is, that workers need to be able to combine so that their aggregate power balances out the economic power of the employer. On this view, the possibility of strike action is a necessary weapon for the workers to have in their armoury, because it is only by the threat of collectively withdrawing their labour, or actually doing so, that they have any power. Can they not rely simply on the employer dealing with them fairly? In 1967 Grunfeld wrote:

> ". . . if one set of human beings is placed in a position of unchecked industrial authority over another set, to expect the former to keep the interests of the latter constantly in mind and, for example, to increase the latter's earnings as soon as the surplus income is available . . . is to place on human nature a strain it was never designed to bear."
> (C. Grunfeld, *Modern Trade Union Law,* Sweet & Maxwell 1966)

Human nature has not changed since 1967. So, according to the equilibrium argument, strikes or other forms of industrial action are an essential part of the collective bargaining process – the final stage if a negotiated agreement cannot be reached. However, while this argument supports a right of resort to industrial action, it does not presuppose an unlimited right: it would not be inconsistent with the equilibrium argument to insist on restraints, such as no action to be taken until all stages of the bargaining process have been completed and ended in deadlock, or until a specified "cooling-off" period has been exhausted. Some systems (for example, the United States) embody such restraints, and some version of them has either been tried or suggested in this country at different times.

Related to the equilibrium argument is what Kahn-Freund called the autonomy argument, based on that unusual feature of British labour law, the absence of the law from the collective bargaining process. Collective bargaining in Britain was traditionally a voluntary process – "voluntary" here meaning that it is not compelled by law, although it might have been practically compelled by other means and so be not truly voluntary. While collective bargaining was not compelled or regulated by law but by the autonomous arrangements agreed between employers and unions, then it was argued that sanctions in the collective bargaining process – including industrial action on the union's side – should also be none of the law's business. As long ago as 1942 Lord Wright said, ". . . the right of workmen to strike is an essential element in the principle of collective bargaining" (*Crofter Hand Woven Harris Tweed v Veitch* (1942)). This argument supports a free-for-all in industrial relations which would not be to the taste of many; it also loses force where the assistance of the law is enlisted to compel recognition and to support collective bargaining (on which see above, Chapter 5) or as employment protection laws establish minimum standards which would normally have had to be bargained for.

12–002   A different justification for industrial action was offered by nineteenth-century liberals such as Jeremy Bentham. Most people would support the notion that each of us should be free to dispose of our labour as we wish: the idea of "forced labour" is abhorrent in a free society. In that case, it is not possible to stop strikes, because that would be tantamount to forcing one person to work for another: a kind of slavery which cannot be tolerated in a society which places a high value on freedom. This is a strong argument, and probably accounts for the fact that the right to strike is seen in some countries as an aspect of human rights: it is enshrined in the International Covenant on Economic, Social and Cultural Rights 1966 (Art.8), in the Council of Europe's 1961 Social Charter (Art.6) and the EU Social Charter (Art.16). The same reasoning is behind the rule that an order to enforce a contract of employment will not be made against an employee, established at common law in the nineteenth century and now expressed in TULRCA, s.236. Only national security is seen as sufficiently important to override this right, hence the fact that the armed forces and the police may not strike.

While the liberal freedom argument is generally accepted, it will be noted that it only prohibits forcing people to return to work: rendering it economically desirable or effectively necessary for them to do so has not been seen as a contravention of this principle, even though for those at the sharp end there may seem to be little difference. Thus the argument is not terribly strong as a protection of the right to strike. It does, however, help to account for the shape of British law on industrial action, which never attempts directly to control those who are actually withdrawing their labour, but instead is aimed at those who organise the action. The freedom argument does not preclude ordering a union to call off industrial action, or imposing financial penalties if it declines to do so. While there is no guarantee that the strikers will obey the union's instructions, it can be expected that they will usually do so; for one thing, if union support is withdrawn, the facilities for organising the strike will be missing, so that in practical terms it becomes very difficult to continue. Thus we shall see that the way in which strikes and industrial action are regulated by the law is generally by the threat of unpleasant consequences for the organisers if the legal requirements are not complied with.

So far the term "right to strike" has been used rather loosely; what exactly is meant by this term? It is important to distinguish between a liberty to take strike action, and a right to do so. If you have a right to do something, not only are you legally able to do it, but others are under a duty not to interfere with your action. If you have only a liberty to do something, then all it means is that you are not under a duty to refrain from such action. It does not mean that other people are necessarily wrong in attempting to stop you: they have no duty to let you behave in this way. Thus a liberty is more precarious than a right would be. In the United Kingdom, the freedoms that are generally referred to as human rights, such as freedom of speech and freedom of association, are really only liberties. As we will see, this is the case also for the freedom to take industrial action.

Industrial Action and Individual Rights

Strikes and the contract of employment

Since being ready and willing to work is the main consideration given by **12–003** the employee under the contract, it would seem axiomatic that refusal to work is a fundamental breach of contract. Alternatively, it will be recollected that obedience to reasonable orders is a fundamental duty of employees (*Laws v London Chronicle* (1959)), so refusal to obey a reasonable order to work is also pretty clearly a fundamental breach. Hence the orthodox view has long been that a strike must be a fundamental breach of contract.

But it is comparatively unusual for employers to react to strikes by sacking the workforce. Firstly, that action would obviously escalate the dispute, and the employer's prime objective is to get it settled; secondly, handing out dismissal notices is a tactic which the employer may wish to hold in reserve in case the dispute cannot be settled quickly. Most importantly, both sides expect the strike to be a temporary disruption of their relationship, and each have their own reasons for wanting to revert to the status quo in the future.

In an attempt to accommodate the realities of the situation, some judges began to reach towards a concept of suspension rather than termination of the contract during a strike. Foremost is the judgment of Lord Denning in *Morgan v Fry* (1968), where he held that provided notice of the strike were given, of equal length to that required for a lawful resignation, then this could be interpreted as notice to suspend the contract for the duration of the strike. The Donovan Commission considered this concept, but felt that it was fraught with difficulties: what if the strike were not settled? At what point could the contract be said to have ended? Would the concept of suspension apply to all industrial action or just to official strikes? What if the employee committed some other breach of contract while on strike?

It is submitted that none of these difficulties was insuperable; however, the Donovan Commission did not recommend any change to the existing law along these lines. When the matter was considered by the EAT in *Simmons v Hoover* (1977), Lord Denning's approach was not followed. It is generally assumed that the orthodox view has prevailed.

12–004 However, even on the orthodox view, it must be the case that if employees collectively give adequate notice, not to suspend the contract, but to resign, then there would be no breach of contract. The fact that it is action undertaken collectively to put pressure on the employer could not turn it into a breach of contract. Thus it would be a completely lawful tactic. This was canvassed in *Boxfoldia v NGA* (1988). Here, the union gave two weeks' notice of a strike by its members, which happened to be the same as the notice period specified in their contracts. As there had been no ballot, the employer sued. The union argued that the strike notice was in fact notice of termination of employment by the workers, which it was handing on as agent for its members. Sadly, this ingenious interpretation of the events bore no relation to reality; however, if the members had invested the union with authority to give notice on their behalf, it seems that it would have been a successful argument – and a way for the union to avoid liability for inducing breach of contract. Interesting as this is to lawyers, it seems unlikely that it will catch on as a tactic, because although workers already risk losing their jobs without any compensation if they take industrial action, yet illogically that feels like less of a risk than tendering one's resignation.

Treating a strike as only a suspension of the contract could presumably be negotiated as an express term of workers' contracts of employment, although it is never done. In this case again, a strike would not be a breach of contract. Care would have to be taken in drafting such a term, to take account of the difficulties identified by the Donovan Commission, above.

Other forms of industrial action

12–005 So far, only indefinite strike action has been considered. Some commentators suggest that a one-day strike would be different: it might be a breach of contract, but not a fundamental breach, looking at the time lost in proportion to the length of the whole contract. If one looks at this argument from the point of view of the duty to be ready and willing to work, it has some strength: a one-day strike could be a fairly minor breach of this duty. But looked at from the angle of the duty to obey reasonable orders, it fails: one refusal is a fundamental breach. A go-slow, where workers deliberately work at less than their usual rate, would seem to be a fundamental breach of contract on similar reasoning (*General Engineering Services v Kingston & St Andrew Corp.* (1989)).

Blacking, where workers refuse to perform some part of their duties, or refuse to handle particular goods, equally involves refusal to obey reasonable orders. It would be possible to negotiate a term whereby, for example, workers are not bound to handle goods where the supply has been officially blacked by the union. Terms of this kind are called "hot cargo" clauses in the United States. In this case, the blacking would not be a breach of contracts of employment, though it would probably put the employer in breach of the supply contract.

Breach of the implied term requiring obedience to reasonable orders would also render a sit-in or work-in at the workplace a breach of contract. The additional tort of trespass would be committed by those who were on the employer's premises without permission. In the case of a work-in (sometimes used as a tactic to oppose closure of a factory), where the workers continue to perform their normal duties although the employer does not want them to, they may also commit the tort of conversion by using the employer's materials.

The work-to-rule presents more difficulty. The leading case is the Court **12–006** of Appeal decision in *Secretary of State v ASLEF (No.2)* (1972) where a work-to-rule by railway workers predictably brought chaos to the rail service. The union argued that the workers were simply carrying out the terms of their contract and so could not be faulted. The Court of Appeal found against them, but for a variety of reasons which are not all equally convincing. The first reason was that the rule-book which they followed did not actually contain the terms of the contract but only the employer's standing orders as to how they should carry out their duties (see above, para. 4–013). The significance of this was that standing orders, unlike contract terms, were susceptible to unilateral change by the employer. A second reason was that they were in breach of an implied term of the contract, variously claimed as an aspect of the duty of faithful service, or a duty not to interpret instructions in an unreasonable manner (see above, para. 4–027). Thirdly, it was said that by a course of dealing, one particular interpretation of the rules had been accepted, and they could not vary this unilaterally; but this seems inconsistent with the first reason. Fourthly, on the facts it seemed that the workers were in any case in breach of one rule, which required them to "prevent any avoidable delay". Finally, Lord Denning suggested that even if they were acting purely in accordance with the rules, their intention to disrupt could turn them into contract-breakers. This seems quite inconsistent with general contractual principle but, nonetheless, the theme was developed by a later Court of Appeal. In *Ticehurst v British Telecom* (1992) the Society of Telecom Executives instructed its members to withdraw goodwill in the course of a pay dispute, meaning that they should do nothing outside the terms of their contracts. They were also encouraged to swamp the administration with requests for written details about pension entitlements, applications for any jobs which they might possibly be qualified to do and requests for training courses. None of these acts would normally constitute a breach of contract. The claimant's pay was stopped when she refused to give an undertaking not to take part in the action in future.

The claimant was employed as a supervisor, and this seems to have been an important factor in the Court of Appeal's decision that her actions placed her in breach of the implied duty to give faithful service outlined by Buckley L.J. in *Secretary of State v ASLEF (No.2)* (1972). Having the intention to disrupt her employer's business was held to be enough for the breach to have occurred: there was no need for proof of actual disruption. Thus being in a state of dissent was in effect held to be a fundamental breach of the duty of good faith (although it was not a breach to refuse to sign the undertaking not to take part in action in future).

331

This decision has the potential to render every kind of industrial action a fundamental breach of employees' contracts, since in every case the employee must intend some kind of disruption to the employer's business. Hitherto the test for a breach of a contract has been objective, judging the act or omission against the terms rather than the motive of the actor. Also, it would undermine the assumption which has always informed the law that not all industrial action is a breach of contract (for example, the definition of industrial action in the Industrial Relations Act 1971 stipulated that it must involve a breach of contract, implying that some kinds did not, and the "health warning" which has to appear on ballot papers states only that industrial action may involve a breach of contract).

12–007   To hold that all kinds of industrial action entail a breach of the duty to give faithful service would also lead to absurd results. Take an overtime ban, for example. Whether or not a ban on overtime is a breach of contract depends on the terms of the contract itself. Only if it is obligatory under the contract for the employee to work overtime when required can it be a breach, as it was in *National Coal Board v Galley* (1958), for example. If the employee genuinely has an option whether to accept overtime or not, then surely refusal to work overtime cannot be a breach of contract, whatever the motivation.

This more rational view of the matter was adopted by the Privy Council in *Burgess v Stevedoring Services Ltd* (2002) where it was alleged that an overtime ban involved a breach of employees' contracts of employment. In fact the collective agreement between the employer and the union made it the union's responsibility to make up gangs for overtime and since the union refused to do so, the Privy Council held that the employees were not in breach of contract. Giving the advice of the Privy Council, Lord Hoffmann denied that motive alone would make otherwise lawful conduct unlawful. He suggested that Lord Denning's statement in *Secretary of State v ASLEF (No.2)* was limited to situations where employees would be justified in acting in a way which did not suit the employer if they had a bona fide reason for doing so, but would be in breach of contract if they so acted with the intention of disrupting the employer's business.

Remedies

12–008 The main importance of establishing whether industrial action is a breach of contract is in relation to the tortious liability of the organisers. However, it is of course true that the employer could, if so wishing, pursue the usual contractual remedies against the employees. Traditionally employers have not done this: they have been content either to dismiss striking workers or to let bygones be bygones once the dispute is over. From a managerial point of view, it will clearly not help to re-establish good industrial relations if the employer were to sue the workers for breach of contract after the strike was over. Another good reason for not suing is that very little may be recoverable by way of damages. In *National Coal Board v Galley* (1958), pit deputies refused to work overtime on Saturday mornings in breach of contract. As they were essential workers, it meant the whole shift output was lost, at a cost of £545, and the employer sued each worker for a share of the lost profit. It was held that the employer was only entitled to the cost of replacing each worker on the shift – that is, their wage of £3 18s 2d. Each worker was responsible only for the breach of his own contract – not the extra loss occasioned by the fact that they had acted in combination. It may be relevant that they were supervisory, not production workers: in one old case (*Ebbw Vale v Tew* (1935)) those actually engaged on production were held responsible for the loss of profit on what they would have produced.

In a number of disputes in the 1980s white collar workers adopted the tactic of refusing to do part of their duties as a way of pressurising their employers. The teachers' dispute in 1985–86 was a prime example of this, where teachers refused to cover for absent colleagues, to supervise children during breaks, to attend meetings or run clubs and sports outside hours. This is really an attempt to have it all ways: to take industrial action, yet to remain entitled to one's pay, for the usual amount of time is worked albeit not all duties covered. Some employers retaliated by withholding a part of the worker's pay to represent the unperformed duties. The legality of this was considered by the House of Lords in *Miles v Wakefield DC* (1987), where registrars of births, deaths and marriages refused to perform weddings on Saturday mornings. The Council deducted 3/37 of the registrar's pay, claiming that for 3 hours in his 37-hour week he was not working normally. The House of Lords held that an employee was entitled to pay only if he was ready and willing to work according to the terms of the contract. The employer was not bound to accept such a partial performance as was proffered here, and could refuse to accept it without terminating the contract. If, as here, the employer did accept the partial performance, then it was entitled to withhold an amount representing the work left undone. Presumably the employee could claim that the employer's quantification was wrong, but since the employer has the opportunity to withhold payment, and the employee would have to take expensive proceedings to challenge this, in practice it may not be a very attractive course of action. There is no recourse in these circumstances to an employment tribunal under the protection of wages provisions in ERA, Pt II (*Sunderland Polytechnic v Evans* (1993)), nor under the tribunals' contractual jurisdiction, since that is limited to termination of employment.

The implications of the decision in *Miles v Wakefield* were dramatically **12–009** illustrated in *Wiluszynski v Tower Hamlets* (1989). Here local government officers refused to answer queries from councillors as part of an industrial action campaign which lasted over a month. This was not a very time-consuming part of their duties – at the end of the campaign, the plaintiff answered in about three hours all the queries that had built up for him. At the outset the council stated that it would not accept partial performance. The officers were not physically prevented from entering the buildings where they worked, but each day they were told to leave unless they were prepared to work normally, and warned that if they refused to do so, any work they did would be treated as having been done on a purely voluntary basis. The employees came to regard this as a bit of a farce; they entered and worked as normal but for their refusal to answer councillors' queries. The Court of Appeal, applying *Miles*, held that they were not entitled to any pay at all for the duration of the action. The employer had made it clear that partial performance was not acceptable, and was not to be taken to have accepted it just because the employees were allowed to work. It would seem that this tactic is therefore unlikely to be very popular among unions in the future.

Strikes and unfair dismissal

12–010 When the action for unfair dismissal was introduced by the Industrial Relations Act 1971 it was obviously necessary to decide what stance to take where employees had been dismissed for taking part in industrial action. The general principle adopted at that time was that in the face of industrial action, the law's position should be neutral. It was felt that it would be disastrous if employment tribunals got drawn into adjudicating on the rights and wrongs of an industrial dispute.

The principle of neutrality may seem sensible; the way in which it was implemented is rather surprising. Provided that everyone who took part in the industrial action was dismissed, then none of them could claim unfair dismissal. The employment tribunal would have jurisdiction only if the employer dismissed some strikers but not others. Thus neutrality meant that, in most cases, employees could not bring unfair dismissal actions – a state of affairs that hardly looked like neutrality from their point of view. Nevertheless, this remained until recently the basic position, although there was considerable amendment over the years. The Conservative administration of 1979–97 revised the law to limit even further the situations where unfair dismissal could be claimed. But in the Employment Relations Act 1999, the new Labour Government introduced a novel category of dismissals in relation to industrial action which would be automatically unfair.

What activities are covered?

12–011 The rules on unfair dismissal and industrial action are now to be found in TULRCA, ss.237, 238 and 238A. They apply to dismissals in three situations: strikes, other industrial action and lock-outs. A "strike" is defined in TULRCA, s.246 as "any concerted stoppage of work". This definition was imported from the Trade Union Act 1984, where it was used only in relation to industrial action ballots. Although TULRCA was meant to be a purely consolidating measure, the draftsman extended this definition to the whole of Part V of TULRCA, meaning that it applies to all statutory regulation of industrial action. However, it came too late to prevent the bizarre decision in *Lewis v Mason* (1994) that there could be industrial action with just one worker taking part. In that case, an employee was dismissed when he was steadfast in his refusal to take an unheated lorry on an overnight trip from Wales to Scotland in December (his employer having refused to pay him £5 for bed and breakfast accommodation). Other employees threatened not to work unless he was reinstated, so they were dismissed too. An employment tribunal held that they were all taking part in industrial action at the time of their dismissals, even the original driver, although at the time of his dismissal he was acting alone. The EAT upheld the tribunal saying, amazingly, that the decision could not be described as perverse.

It has generally been thought that a strike meant action involving a complete cessation of work, but in *Connex South Eastern Ltd v RMT* (1999) the Court of Appeal held, rather surprisingly, that a ban on overtime and rest day working could be regarded as "strike action". However, as sections 237–238A cover "other industrial action" as well as strikes, the point is unlikely to be of any practical importance in the context of unfair dismissal, at any rate.

In *Power Packing Casemakers v Faust* (1983) three employees were dismissed for refusing to work overtime. Their contracts did not require them to work overtime, so this was not a breach on their part. However, the reason for their refusal was a dispute over a wage claim. In these circumstances, it was held that they were taking part in "other industrial action" at the time of their dismissal and that therefore the tribunal had no jurisdiction to entertain their claims for unfair dismissal. It is clear from this that motive plays a part in defining the activity as industrial action or not. To hold that there can be industrial action without a breach of contract can have some strange results. Presumably if Faust had acted alone and refused overtime because of a private dissatisfaction with wage levels, it would not have been industrial action because there would have been no element of combination. If he had been dismissed, he would have had a better than evens chance of winning an unfair dismissal claim. Why should the law be different because there were three workers involved? It is submitted that requiring proof of a breach of contract should be a minimum limitation on holding that an activity counts as industrial action, especially if it is going to be left as a question of fact for employment tribunals.

It may be surprising to find that the special regime for unfair dismissal and **12–012** industrial action also applies to self-help actions by employers in industrial disputes – *i.e.* to lock-outs. A lock-out is where the employer responds to an industrial dispute by refusing to let the employees work – they are "locked out". This means that employees can be precluded from claiming not only when they have instigated industrial action, but also where it is the employer's initiative. It is not apparent why this should be the case: if the employer precipitates a dispute through insisting that workers do more than is required by their contracts, why should this give the employer an immunity if it dismisses recalcitrant workers? It actually makes it advantageous for an employer to be confrontational in introducing change.

There is no definition of the term "lock-out" in TULRCA, although there is a definition in ERA, s.235(4), which deals with continuity of employment:

> ". . . 'lock-out' means—
>   (a) the closing of a place of employment,
>   (b) the suspension of work, or
>   (c) the refusal by an employer to continue to employ any number of persons employed by him in consequence of a dispute,
>
>   done with a view to compelling persons employed by the employer . . . to accept terms and conditions of or affecting employment."

In *Express & Star v Bunday* (1988) the Court of Appeal confirmed the widely-held view that this definition was not applicable to other parts of the legislation, although it could be used for guidance, as could dictionary definitions. The issue in *Express & Star v Bunday* was whether there could be a lock-out where the employer was not acting in breach of contract. The Court of Appeal held that it was not necessary that the employer's action should be a breach of contract, although it might be a relevant consideration. Their conclusion was reached by parity of reasoning with the line that had already been taken in interpreting the phrase "industrial action" in *Power Packing Casemakers v Faust* (1983).

12–013   There can be difficulties in distinguishing industrial action from trade union activities which, as we saw in Chapter 10, receive special protection provided that they are carried out at an appropriate time. While it is clear from *Power Packing Casemakers v Faust* (1983) and *Express & Star v Bunday* (1988) that there can be industrial action or a lock-out without a breach of contract, in *Rasool v Hepworth Pipe Co.* (1980), action in breach of contract was held to be a protected union activity! In this case there was a history of work at the factory being interrupted by unauthorised mass meetings of the workforce. The union convenor called a meeting although permission to do so had been refused. When the employees turned up, management representatives stood at the doors to tell them it was unauthorised. About half of the workers attended anyway, and they were all dismissed. In this case they were almost certainly acting in breach of contract yet the EAT held that it fell short of industrial action, saying rather that it was a union activity, for which time off was available under TULRCA, s.170. Thus the tribunal had jurisdiction to hear their claims, although it was ultimately held that they had been fairly dismissed because they had not been taking part in union activities "at an appropriate time" (see above, para. 10–010).

Finally, it should be noted that dismissals which are automatically unfair under ERA, ss.99, 100, 101A(d), 103, 103A and 104 are not to be taken as industrial action dismissals (TULRCA, s.237(1A)). This is particularly relevant for health and safety dismissals (ERA, s.100) where there might otherwise be a real risk that employees who refused to work in a dangerous situation could be regarded as taking industrial action (*cf. Lewis v Mason*).

Official and unofficial action

12–014   In its original meaning, official industrial action meant action which was called in accordance with the trade union's own rule-book. The rule-book would normally lay down who had authority to call strikes and other industrial action and whether any formalities had to be followed first. According to the House of Lords, the rule-book may be supplemented by custom and practice: in *Heaton's Transport (St Helens) Ltd v TGWU* (1972) there was a docks dispute over containerisation. Shop stewards at Liverpool and Hull formed unofficial committees which blacked firms who acted contrary to the union's policy on this. The issue was whether the union was liable. The union argued that the stewards were acting on their own initiative and did not have authority under the union's rule-book to organise this action. The House of Lords held that the rule-book had to be interpreted in the light of custom and practice in the union. According to long-standing practice, shop stewards had implied authority to act on behalf of their members with quite a high degree of discretion. In these circumstances, given that the shop stewards were acting in accordance with union policy, the House of Lords held that the union was liable for the stewards' actions, which were within the scope of their implied authority.

Whether or not industrial action was official or unofficial used to be irrelevant to the position of individual employees taking action. They were no better off if the action had been properly called by union officers in accordance with all the requirements of the law than if it was a wildcat strike provoked for wholly inadequate reasons. However, this changed in 1982, when the Conservative Government decided to make unions liable in their own name for unlawful industrial action. That meant that it was necessary to decide for whose actions the union would be liable, and a statutory definition was devised which is somewhat wider than the common law (TULRCA, s.20). Importantly, it also applies in relation to the law of unfair dismissal and industrial action, in that the law treats as "unofficial" any action which has not been authorised or endorsed by an official as defined by section 20 (regardless of what may be the position under the union's own rules).

Under TULRCA, s.237, an employee who is dismissed while taking part in unofficial industrial action in this sense has no right to claim unfair dismissal even if dismissed selectively. It is therefore very important to know whether the industrial action has been authorised or endorsed by a relevant officer or organ of the union. The categories stipulated in TULRCA, s.20 are: a person authorised by the union's rules for this purpose; the principal executive committee of the union; the president or general secretary of the union; any other committee of the union; and any other union official (whether or not employed by the union). In the case of the last two categories ("any other committee" and "any other official") the union may repudiate the authorisation or endorsement, provided that it acts in accordance with the procedure laid down in TULRCA, s.21 (see further below, para. 13–025). The employees have one day's grace before the action is then treated as unofficial.

While most industrial action is organised by trade unions and involves union members, it is possible for non-unionised workers to go on strike, or for non-members to join in action with unionists. If no one taking part in the industrial action is a union member then TULRCA, s.237 has no application. However, if there is unofficial action involving non-members and members, it is treated as unofficial in relation to them all. This may seem unfair on the non-members, but is to stop members trying to avoid the impact of s.237 by suddenly resigning their membership.

Protected official action

Assuming that employees are taking part in official action in the sense **12–015** discussed above it now becomes necessary to consider whether it is protected under section 238A, which was introduced by the Employment Relations Act 1999, Sch.5. The basic idea behind section 238A is that employees should be protected from dismissal if they are taking part in official, lawfully organised industrial action which has not been unduly protracted. The employer cannot actually be prevented from dismissing the employees, but if the conditions in section 238A are met, such dismissals will be automatically unfair.

There are two conditions for section 238A to apply. The first is that the employee should be taking part in "protected industrial action", meaning that the action is official and has been lawfully organised so that it will have immunity within the meaning of TULRCA, s.219 (considered below, para. 13–002) (s.238A(1)). The second condition is that the reason or principal reason for the dismissal is that the employee took part in the industrial action (s.238A(2)). This is a departure from TULRCA, ss.237 and 238 which concentrate on the *timing* of the dismissal rather than the reason for it. These sections apply only where the employee is dismissed *while* taking part in industrial action, and this wording was chosen so that tribunals would only have to establish an objective fact rather than the employer's subjective state of mind. Presumably the burden of proving the reason for the dismissal under section 238A will be on the employee, which may cause difficulties, although tribunals will probably be willing to draw appropriate inferences from the known facts about the industrial action.

Once these two conditions have been met, section 238A sets out three situations where the dismissal will be automatically unfair: firstly, where the dismissal occurs within eight weeks of the start of the industrial action (s.238A(3)); secondly, where the dismissal occurs after eight weeks, but the employee had stopped taking action within the eight-week period (s.238A(4)); thirdly, where the dismissal occurs after eight weeks and the employee was still participating in the action but the employer has not "taken such procedural steps as would have been reasonable for the purposes of resolving the dispute" (s.238A(5)). The sorts of procedural steps to which tribunals should have regard are set out in section 238A(6): whether relevant collective agreements have been complied with; whether either side has offered to take part in negotiations; and whether either side has unreasonably refused a request for conciliation or arbitration. The substantive merits of the dispute are *not* to be taken into account (s.238A(7)).

Section 238A marks an important step forward in employees' rights. It is astonishing to think that until this provision was passed an employee could always be dismissed without redress even if provoked into industrial action by the employer's intransigence and even if acting entirely lawfully. Indeed, workers found it particularly illogical that the organisation of industrial action was hedged about with detailed rules, but that compliance with them was of no benefit to individuals. The Government's hope was that the new section would provide an incentive for employers and unions to settle disputes within two months of the start, but by the time of its review of the Employment Relations Act 1999 in 2003 it was not obvious if this was the case. It is estimated that 90 per cent of disputes are settled within eight weeks, but this might be the case anyway. By summer 2003 only one case had reached a tribunal under the new law and the outcome of an appeal to the EAT was awaited. The case concerned a two-year dispute at a car parts manufacturer in Wales and led the TUC to argue that s.237A should be extended to provide indefinite protection for workers where the action was lawfully called. However, the Government stated that it intended no change for the time being.

Other dismissals

Where employees are dismissed for industrial action which is not "unoffi- **12–016** cial", so that TULRCA, s.237 does not apply, the next question must be whether section 238A applies. If it does not, perhaps because the industrial action is not protected within the meaning of TULRCA, s.219, or because it has lasted more than eight weeks and the proviso in section 238A(5) does not apply, then TULRCA, s.238 comes into play. This section retains the basic concept that employers will not be liable for unfair dismissal unless they have selectively dismissed or re-engaged employees taking part in the same action. It applies to an employee who, at the date of the dismissal, was taking part in a strike or other industrial action, or was "locked out" by the employer. Such an employee may only claim for unfair dismissal if other relevant employees have not been dismissed or, if they were dismissed, have been re-engaged.

Who are "relevant employees"?

Essentially the purpose of section 238 is to allow the fairness of the **12–017** dismissal to be reviewed if those taking part in the action are not treated in the same way. Thus "relevant employees" originally meant those employed by the same employer who had taken part in the industrial action. However, in the first case to reach the House of Lords, an anomaly was discovered.

In *Frank Jones (Tipton) Ltd v Stock* (1978) about 35 employees came out on strike. Two returned to work after two weeks, but the others remained out. Three months later all those still on strike were dismissed. Of course, the employer had not dismissed the two who had gone back. It was held that they were "relevant employees" because they had originally taken part in the action. Thus all the rest had the right to claim unfair dismissal.

As a result the law was amended so that in relation to strikes and other industrial action, "relevant employees" must still be taking part in the action at the time of the complainant's dismissal. This enables an employer to act on an ultimatum, by dismissing everyone not returning to work by a certain date, without facing unfair dismissal claims from those who do not return. In turn this provides a good reason for an employer not to react to industrial action by immediately dismissing all those taking part.

In relation to a lock-out the definition of relevant employees is wider: it includes all employees "directly interested" in the dispute. It is for this reason that it may be very important to know whether the action is a strike or a lock-out. In *Campey v Bellwood* (1987) the company was trying to insist on new working conditions. Faced with the threat of industrial action organised by the workers' union, the company suspended its operations altogether. A week later, all those who would not accept the new terms were dismissed. If they had been taking part in industrial action, they would not have been able to claim, for it was only the ones still holding out who were dismissed. However, it was held to be a lock-out, and "relevant employees" therefore meant all those who had been suspended, including those who had accepted the new terms and had been kept on. Thus the sacked workers could claim unfair dismissal.

It may be difficult to know whether a particular worker, alleged to be a "relevant employee", was taking part in the action or not. In *Coates v Modern Methods and Materials* (1982) L refused to cross a picket line on the first day of the strike because she was frightened of abuse. The following day she fortuitously went down with back trouble which put her out of action for the duration of the strike. Those who were dismissed claimed that she was a "relevant employee" who had not been dismissed. But had she taken part in the action? The Court of Appeal held that she had, by refusing to cross the picket line. Her motives were irrelevant: the test of taking part was objective, according to the actions of the employee rather than her private thoughts. This was applied in *Wood Group Engineering v Byrne* (1993), where an employee who originally joined a strike and sit-in on an offshore oil platform telephoned his employer and said he wanted to cease and come ashore. The employers instructed him to stay and act as an informant about what was going on aboard the platform. Ultimately the other employees taking part were dismissed. They lodged unfair dismissal claims alleging that the informant was a relevant employee who had not been dismissed. Using the objective test, that the employee's actions, not his private intentions, are to be considered, the EAT held that the informant was a "relevant employee".

In *McCormick v Horsepower* (1981) an employee who had initially refused to cross a picket line was claimed as a comparator by those strikers who had been dismissed. However, before the hearing he had been made redundant. The Court of Appeal held that because he had been dismissed too, there was no jurisdiction to hear the others' complaints. It did not matter that he had been dismissed for redundancy rather than for taking part in the action. This decision has led to another anomaly in the legislation, so far unaltered. In *P&O Ferries v Byrne* (1989) about a thousand seamen dismissed by the company following an extensive and bitter dispute claimed unfair dismissal. Although the company argued that it had dismissed everyone involved in the action, the seamen said that at least one person had been overlooked. The company asked for this person's name to be revealed to them before the hearing – a reasonable request, as it was crucial to their side of the case. The seamen refused for fear that the company would sack the man – and thus torpedo their one thousand claims! Recognising that the employer could do that, the Court of Appeal nonetheless ordered disclosure of the relevant employee's name.

12–018   Another amendment introduced in 1982 to make it easier for employers to avoid this kind of mishap limits "relevant employees" to those employed "at the same establishment" as the complainant. So if a company has a strike at both its Leeds and Manchester plants, and decides to use the opportunity to close down the Manchester plant, those employees cannot claim unfair dismissal on the grounds that the Leeds people are still employed. Note, however, *Bigham v GNK Kwikform Ltd* (1992), where a dismissed striker later obtained a job with another branch of the company. He had not concealed or lied about the earlier dismissal. When, four weeks later, the employers realised what had happened, they dismissed him – but the fact that he had been re-engaged, however, briefly, meant that the other strikers were entitled to claim.

Where employees dismissed for taking part in industrial action are able to bring claims under TURLCA, it does not follow that their dismissals are bound to be unfair. This will be judged according to all the circumstances, and thus involves the tribunal to some extent considering the merits of the dispute. Even where it is held to be unfair it may be argued that compensation should be reduced for contributory conduct. In *Crosville Wales Ltd v Tracey (No.2)* (1996) the Court of Appeal held that mere participation in a strike would not justify a reduction in compensation: there would have to be blameworthy conduct over and above just taking part. Nor would leading the strike amount to such blameworthy conduct, if the leader acted reasonably and not in an "over-hasty and inflammatory" manner.

Time limits

The usual limitation period requiring a claim to be made within three **12–019** months of dismissal has to be modified for section 238 dismissals, to cover the possibility that the employer might dismiss all the strikers, but then take some of them back. As originally worded, if the employer ever took back someone dismissed for industrial action, this immediately triggered a right for the others to claim, even if it was months or years later. In 1982 this was amended in two ways. Firstly, the complainant may only claim if the relevant employee was re-engaged within three months of having been dismissed, and secondly, the complainant may not in any case claim if it is more than six months since her own dismissal unless it was not reasonably practicable to do so (TULRCA, s.239).

Conclusion

The ILO Committee on Freedom of Association held in 1991 that United **12–020** Kingdom law on dismissals in connection with industrial action contravened ILO Conventions. Since then there has been a major step forward in the protection of individuals through the introduction of TULRCA, s.238A. However, it could be argued that the protection is still inadequate. Why should the individual's protection depend, for example, on whether her union has managed successfully to negotiate all the hurdles which are still necessary for industrial action to be lawful? How can she be sure whether this is the case or not? A good argument could be made for saying that individuals should be protected where they take action which they believe in good faith to have been officially organised by their trade union. Finally, the new law still has not removed the anomaly which permits an employee to be dismissed for industrial action even if she is not committing a breach of her contract of employment.

The Right to Organise Industrial Action

12–021 Since freedom of the individual precludes directly ordering strikers to return to work, direct control over industrial action has been exercised over those who organise it, by making them liable for the consequences. Strikes and other kinds of industrial action are pretty well bound to disrupt the commercial and social life of people not directly involved in the dispute. The first question about liability is therefore about remoteness – at what point do we regard the consequences as too far away from the action to hold the organisers responsible? It has been left to the common law to answer this question. The next question is one of policy: if we are persuaded that some level of industrial action must be permitted, it is necessary to relieve the organisers of strikes from liability which they would otherwise have. How far are we prepared to go in granting that relief? Or, to put it in more familiar terms, how far should unions and their members have immunity from liability for otherwise unlawful acts because they are taking part in industrial action?

The debate about industrial action in the United Kingdom has been cast in these terms since the beginning of this century. It may be noted that it is not the only way of dealing with this issue. In other common law jurisdictions, for example, the United States, the common law of contract and tort is largely irrelevant in industrial disputes: instead there is a statutory code enforced principally through a special body – the National Labor Relations Board – which reflects the current consensus on the limits of acceptable action in industrial disputes. There is a body of opinion which believes that something similar is required here too, and it may be that movement in this direction will be another long-term result of membership of the EU.

The pattern of immunity granted by statute from liability which would exist at common law was fixed in England following the famous case, *Taff Vale Railway v Amalgamated Society of Railway Servants* in 1901. The facts of the case were ordinary enough: a union official was dismissed by the company, as a result of which the workforce came out on strike, and picketed the company's railway station when replacement labour was being brought in. What made this case special was that the company sued the union, not its officials. Until that time it had been thought that a union could not be sued in its own name (see above, para. 10–026). Prior to *Taff Vale* therefore, the strategy of employers faced with strike action had been to sue named officials – the top people in the union – for an injunction requiring them to call off the action. As they were being sued as individuals there was little point in pursuing a damages claim against them because they would be likely to have only limited means. This state of affairs had worked reasonably well, for if an injunction was obtained against an official, although it could theoretically be ignored by other individuals, in practice the union played ball and acted in accordance with the order.

12–022 However, in *Taff Vale* the union was sued, and the House of Lords, albeit with less than total clarity, held that unions had a sufficient legal existence to be sued in their own right. This was a body blow to trade unions, for it meant that their funds were now exposed to damages claims from employers following a dispute, since, as already remarked, any strike action was very likely to cause breaches of contracts and other wrongs. The controversy caused by the decision ensured that it was one of the issues in the 1906 General Election. The Liberal Party came to power, with the assistance of a pact with the nascent Labour Party, committed to restoring the situation where unions could organise industrial action without risking bankruptcy each time. This could have been done by a statutory code giving unions a protected right to strike in defined circumstances: but it was not. Instead the Trade Disputes Act 1906 gave trade unions a complete immunity from all actions in tort, and gave individuals (officials, members and others) a partial immunity from actions in tort, provided that they were acting in contemplation or furtherance of a trade dispute. While the scope of the immunity has changed considerably over the years, this remains the basic pattern of the law today except for one major modification. In 1982 the total immunity from actions in tort enjoyed by trade unions was abolished. Today they are liable on the same basis as individuals, and so from that date on we see case references containing the names of unions as defendants rather than their presidents or general secretaries.

In 1971, a new Conservative Government, elected with a commitment to **12–023** reducing union power, attempted to break the mould by providing a new, entirely statutory code to deal with trade unions and industrial action: the Industrial Relations Act 1971. This was deeply unpopular with unions and contained technical defects which made it possible for unions to circumvent its provisions without acting illegally. It is generally accepted that it tried to do too much too soon. Its failure, and the consequent industrial unrest, were important factors in the defeat of that Government and its replacement by a Labour Government, whose first action was to repeal the Industrial Relations Act, and to replace it with the Trade Union and Labour Relations Act 1974 (TULRA).

TULRA was intended to put the law back into the pre-1971 position, although it differed from the 1906 Act in significant respects. The basic immunities contained in it were heavily amended and modified by the Employment Acts 1980–90, the Trade Union Act 1984 and the Trade Union Reform and Employment Rights Act 1993. Having learned from the mistakes of the Industrial Relations Act, the Conservative Government of the 1980s adopted different tactics in dealing with unions: the strategy was to introduce changes a bit at a time – a major Act at two-yearly intervals, each introducing new restrictions on industrial action. This proved more successful than the attempt at overnight wholesale revolution. The changes were consolidated in the Trade Union and Labour Relations (Consolidation) Act 1992, but almost immediately another wave of restrictive reforms was pushed through in TURERA, with the result that TULRCA was substantially amended almost before the ink was dry. The new Labour Government, elected in 1997, always made it clear that it had no intention of implementing a wholesale repeal of Conservative legislation, as many trade unionists wanted. In its White Paper, *Fairness at Work*, preceding the Employment Relations Act 1999, the Government made play of the fact that even after the reforms it did propose, the United Kingdom would still have tougher laws on industrial action than any of the other Member States of the EU. Thus the Employment Relations Act 1999 made minor rather than major modifications to the law on organising industrial action.

While the pattern of the law is understandable given its history, the result of this rather piecemeal development is that it is a complicated process to decide whether a particular campaign of industrial action is lawful or not. The question must be unpacked into a number of stages. First, you must ask whether or not the action involves any sort of wrong at common law. If it does, the next question is whether it is covered by the basic immunity contained in TULRCA, s.219. If not, there is liability. But if it is protected by section 219, the third question is whether the immunity has been lost for some other reason. There are numerous ways in which immunity can be lost: because the action involves unprotected secondary action, because there has not been a ballot, and so on. Balloting has assumed even greater importance in recent years in that if a ballot has not been held, union members or even unconnected third parties may be able to stop even industrial action which does not involve common law wrongs. In what follows, each stage will be looked at in turn. We will start by looking at whether industrial action involves any common law wrongs, and if so, whether TULRCA, s.219 gives immunity. The principal torts on which the employer is likely to rely are those which allege interference with contracts – and, as we will see, it will usually be necessary to show that the union has brought about breaches of contracts of employment by the workforce.

Liability in tort

12–024 The torts which are most likely to be committed in the course of an industrial dispute are usually called the "economic torts". Broadly speaking, they normally involve deliberate action designed to cause economic loss to the plaintiff. While economic loss has traditionally not been recoverable in tort for negligence, it is recoverable here because the action causing loss is intentional. During a campaign of industrial action it is quite possible for other torts to be committed as well as economic ones: picketing, in particular, may involve trespass and public nuisance at least, and also crimes such as obstruction of the highway. Picketing is therefore dealt with separately after the rest of the discussion of industrial action (see below, para. 13–029).

Inducement of breach of contract

12–025 We have already seen that a strike is usually a breach of contract by the workforce. Knowingly to induce someone to break a contract to the detriment of the other party to that contract was recognised as a tort actionable at the suit of the third party in *Lumley v Gye* (1853). L had engaged the opera singer, Johanna Wagner, to sing exclusively at his theatre in London. The defendant, G, offered her more money to sing at his theatre, causing her to break her contract with L. Naturally, Johanna Wagner was liable to L for breach of a contract for services, (*Lumley v Wagner* (1852), dealing with his remedy, is discussed at para. 8–011, above). The point is, however, that G was held liable to L in tort for bringing about that breach of contract.

This tort is very likely to occur in industrial disputes in this form in two main situations: first, where a union in dispute with an employer calls out the workforce, thus inducing them to break their contracts of employment with the employer. At common law, the union would be liable to the employer for this, in the same way that Gye was liable to Lumley. The second situation is where the union has a dispute with a worker (perhaps because the worker refuses to join the union) and the union persuades the employer to sack the worker in breach of contract. (Note that if the union persuades the employer to sack the worker without a breach of contract, this tort is not committed – see *Allen v Flood* (1898). However, it may instead be the tort of intimidation, para. 12–036, below.)

This may be called the direct form of the tort of inducement of breach of **12–026** contract. However, a breach of contract may be brought about indirectly as well. Instead of persuading one party to break the contract to the detriment of the other party, the tortfeasor may simply prevent the performance of the contract. For example, in *GWK v Dunlop* (1926) a car manufacturer contracted with X that all their cars appearing at an exhibition would be fitted with X's tyres. The night before the exhibition the defendant removed X's tyres and fitted the cars with its tyres instead. Thus the defendant had induced a breach of the car manufacturer's contract with X, not by direct persuasion, but by preventing its performance. This is also tortious – but only if performance of the contract is prevented by unlawful means. This qualification is necessary to keep the tort within bounds. After all, if A contracts to supply a commodity to B, and C prevents A's performance by buying up all the supplies of the commodity, then even if C does this with a view to damaging B, it would be unreasonable to make C liable to B in tort. What C has done is not unlawful, and since the nineteenth century it has been a fundamental principle of tort law that a wrongful motive should not make an otherwise lawful act unlawful. The distinction between direct and indirect inducement is thus very important, in that direct inducement is actionable even though the defendant has not used unlawful means. It is illustrated by *Middlebrook Mushrooms v TGWU* (1993). Employees dismissed by the company in a dispute over a pay cut picketed supermarkets supplied by the company in order to dissuade supermarket customers from buying Middlebrook mushrooms. The company argued that this would deter the supermarkets from performing contracts with them and that the pressure amounted to the direct form of the tort. The argument was rejected by the Court of Appeal because the persuasion was clearly aimed at the customers, not the supermarkets. At most, therefore, it could only have constituted an indirect inducement, and in these circumstances it was not tortious because no unlawful means had been used.

Translated to the industrial context, the most likely way that the indirect form of the tort will occur is where a union, wishing to put pressure on employer A, calls out the employees of employer B on strike in breach of their contracts of employment, so as to prevent employer B fulfilling a contract with employer A. This involves the union committing the direct form of the tort as against employer B, and the indirect form against employer A. In the indirect form, the contract breached is the commercial contract between A and B, and the unlawful means consist in inducing the breach of the contracts of employment of B's employees. The classic

345

statement of the elements of the tort is to be found in the judgment of Jenkins L.J. in *Thomson v Deakin* (1952). He stipulated four requirements:

(i) that the defendant knew of the existence of the contract and intended to procure its breach;

(ii) that the defendant persuaded or procured employees to break their contracts of employment with this intention;

(iii) that the employees did break their contracts of employment;

(iv) that the breach of the commercial contract which is complained of ensued as a necessary consequence of those breaches of employment contracts.

We will look at each of these requirements in turn.

(a) Knowledge of the contract

12–027 For either form of this tort to be committed, clearly the defendant must be aware of the contract between the person persuaded or prevented and the plaintiff. For example, suppose company A interviews B and offers her a job to start the next day, but unknown to A, B already has a job and is contractually obliged to give a month's notice. If B goes to work for A in breach of her other contract, it would be unreasonable to make A liable to the other employer. But what if A knows that B has another job, but not the terms about notice? In other words, what degree of knowledge of the broken contract will fix the defendant with liability?

From *Thomson v Deakin* it appeared that the union would have to have actual knowledge of the contract broken. However, a much lesser degree of knowledge was required in *Merkur Island Shipping v Laughton* (1983), where the union had blacked, and therefore effectively blockaded, a ship in Liverpool docks. The House of Lords held that the union must be deemed to know of the almost certain existence of commercial contracts which would be broken if a fully-laden ship could not leave port, and that this degree of knowledge was sufficient. This was quite a significant relaxation of the requirement. It is true that anyone would expect contracts to carry the goods on board the ship to be disrupted by the blockade. But that was not the kind of contract which the union was sued for disrupting. That contract was the charter contract between the shipowners (who brought the action) and the charterers of the vessel, who had themselves sub-chartered the vessel to the firm which was actually operating it at the time of the blacking. It is by no means obvious that a union would be aware of these rather complex arrangements. The result of this decision seems to be that knowledge that some contract will be disrupted will suffice for liability, even if the defendant is wholly unaware of the particular contract whose breach is alleged to have been procured. In fact, it is very difficult for unions to escape knowledge, since it is standard practice for employers to send copies of relevant contract provisions to trade unions at once. This did not happen in *TimePlan Education Group Ltd v NUT* (1997), where the NUT asked the New Zealand teaching union to consider whether it was appropriate to publish TimePlan's advertisements in the union journal, given that it was in dispute with the NUT over its rates of pay to supply teachers. The New Zealand union withdrew the advertisements in breach of its contract with TimePlan. The trial judge held that the NUT was liable for inducing the breach of contract as it must have realised that the advertisements were placed in pursuance of a contract. The Court of Appeal allowed the NUT's appeal: the union had not been expressly informed of the contract and would not necessarily have inferred that because advertisements had appeared, there was a contract in existence for future advertisements. Importantly, the Court of Appeal was not prepared to entertain an argument that the union was "put on notice" of the possibility of there being a contract and should have made further inquiries. However, in *Metropolitan Borough of Solihull v NUT* (1985) the honest belief of union officials that industrial action would not result in a breach of contract was not a defence when breaches actually occurred.

As noted in *Merkur Island Shipping v Laughton*, the first requirement really embodies two requirements: not only knowledge of the contract, but also an intention to disrupt it. It may seem difficult to intend to disrupt something of which you have no knowledge. In *Emerald Construction v Lowthian* (1966) it was pointed out that the contract whose breach the union was alleged to have procured could have been terminated lawfully, although it was in fact terminated unlawfully. The Court of Appeal held that the inducer is liable in these circumstances if he or she is reckless as to whether the person induced terminates the contract lawfully or not. A similar indifference as to what contracts might be disrupted by their action was regarded as a sufficient intention to break the charter contract in *Merkur*.

(b) Inducement

Is there a difference between communicating information to people that **12–028** causes them to break a contract, and persuading them to do so? Surely there must be; but the line is very difficult to draw. Suppose a union official tells the workforce the details of the employer's latest pay offer, without making any recommendation, and the workers decide to strike. Did the union official induce this? If the same information had been communicated by the works manager, or in a newspaper article, and the workers had decided to strike, we would not be likely to think either was liable for the tort of inducing breach of contract. "Induce" therefore seems to mean more than "cause". Probably the answer is that the question of inducement cannot be separated out from intention. If the information is communicated with the intention that it should bring about a breach, then it is an inducement; and the fact that it is described as advice, a friendly warning or simply transmission of information will not alter the situation.

Thus in the direct form of the tort the union will have to intend to bring about the breaches of contracts of employment; in the indirect form the union must intend that, and also intend thereby to disrupt the commercial contract.

(c) Causation

The third and fourth requirements for the tort are factual matters: did the **12–029** inducement actually lead to the workers breaking their contracts of employment? did that lead as a necessary consequence to the breach of the commercial contract? The answer will depend on the facts of each particular case, and is usually not in issue.

(d) Unlawful means

12–030 Where the indirect form of this tort is relied on, the defendant is only liable if unlawful means were used to prevent a party from performing the contract with the plaintiff. What counts as unlawful means? The answer to this question is not entirely clear, and as the use of unlawful means is an essential element in most of these torts, further discussion of this point is deferred until all have been examined (see below, para. 12–039).

(e) Who can sue?

12–031 Whenever a wrong is committed, the fall-out can affect a large number of people, some foreseeably and some not. In the law of negligence, rules which sometimes seem arbitrary are used to keep liability within bounds. It is not considered fair to make tortfeasors responsible for absolutely every consequence of their action, if negligent. Similarly, there are limits on who can sue as the result of an economic tort. It may be felt that the situation is morally different from negligence, because the damage results from deliberate actions: it could be answered that the loss caused is only economic (not injury to the person) and that these torts cannot be viewed in isolation from the industrial relations context in which they occur, where industrial action is part and parcel of the collective bargaining process.

Whatever the arguments, the limits of "remoteness" are not entirely clear. At first it seems to have been thought that employers could only claim for inducement of breaches of contracts of employment. So although a strike would be bound to disrupt the employer's commercial contracts with other parties, claims for inducing breaches of these contracts were not made, at least not until *Thomson v Deakin* (1952). The plaintiff publishing firm refused to employ trade union members and was consequently in dispute with the TGWU. The union called on its members employed by Bowaters, who supplied paper to the plaintiff, to black supplies for Thomson's. Since it was clear that the employees would comply with this instruction, Bowaters did not bother to try to get them to handle the supplies, but instead informed Thomson's that they would be unable to perform their contract with them. Thomson sought an injunction to get the union to call off the action. The Court of Appeal accepted that there could be tortious liability where the contract broken was a commercial contract rather than a contract of employment, although on the facts there was no liability, because unlawful means had not been used to prevent Bowaters fulfilling the contract. The workers had not actually broken their contracts of employment with Bowaters because Bowaters had not asked them to handle the blacked goods.

12–032 Once it was clear that there was liability for inducing the breach of commercial contracts, then the next question was, could all the parties to the commercial contracts sue? Suppose a union succeeded in temporarily closing down the operations of an employer with whom it had a dispute.

That employer could certainly sue (leaving aside any question of immunity for the time being); but could all the other businesses with whom the employer had contracts sue as well?

The first point to make here is that in the past the other businesses did not usually attempt to sue. One reason for this was that until 1982 it was not worth seeking damages because the union's funds were immune, and it was left to the employer in dispute to take any action to get the strike called off. Secondly, the other parties to the contract would not necessarily have suffered loss from its non-performance. A customer may, for example, be able to get supplies from elsewhere. Another reason may have been the desire simply to keep a low profile, grateful that the dispute was aimed at someone else. However, it was also thought that other businesses or people affected could not sue, because they were not the intended victims of the action. It was generally held to be an element of this tort that the defendant should have intended to harm the plaintiff. This does not mean a malicious intention, but more that the breach of contract was induced in order to affect the plaintiff in some way. This is now in some doubt as a result of two decisions. In *Falconer v ASLEF* (1986) a hero of the commuting classes successfully sued the railway unions when he was stranded overnight in London by a rail strike. The county court judge rejected the argument that British Rail was the intended victim, accurately pointing out that the unions did intend to inconvenience those holding tickets because that was their best way of putting pressure on the employer.

While this makes perfectly good sense, it should also be clear that, if correct, it makes industrial action extremely risky for unions in situations where there is doubt as to their immunity, for the possible plaintiffs are practically limitless. Some may think that this is no bad thing. However, if any of the arguments used at the beginning of this chapter in support of a right to strike seemed convincing to you, then you must recognise that the *Falconer v ASLEF* decision could render such a right nugatory. This may explain why the more traditional view of intention was taken in another first instance decision, *Barretts & Baird v IPCS* (1987). Here fatstock officers employed by the Meat and Livestock Commission were staging 24-hour strikes in support of a regrading claim. The plaintiff abattoir owners sued the trade union because they could not operate as a result. Henry J. considered it an essential element of the tort that the union's predominant purpose should have been to harm them. Since it was not, they had no claim. This case was not about inducing breach of contract, but the related tort of interference with trade – although the degree of intention required is thought to be the same for both torts. However, the intention requirement has now been circumvented to a large extent by the introduction of the so-called "Citizens' Charter" right which enables third parties who are not the intended victims of industrial action to sue to restrain it in some circumstances (see below, para. 13–011).

(f) Justification

There is some slight authority for the view that there may be a defence to **12–033** this tort if the defendant was justified in inducing the breach. Thus in *Brimelow v Casson* (1924) it was alleged that the manager of the King Wu

Tut Tut Revue chorus girls paid them such low wages that they were forced to resort to prostitution. The union which induced theatres to cancel their bookings with this rogue was held to have a defence of justification to his action for inducing breach of contract. However, the defence had not been accepted in the earlier, less exotic case, *South Wales Miners' Federation v Glamorgan Coal Co.* (1905) where the union pleaded entirely disinterested motives of safeguarding its members' interests in preventing a further reduction in their wages. "Therefore it seems that if the chorus girls in *Brimelow v Casson* had not been living in immorality, but had merely been living a life of chaste starvation, no defence of justification would have been available" (J. Riddall, *The Law of Industrial Relations,* Butterworths, 1982). In general it would appear that the defence has no practical relevance in industrial relations disputes.

(g) The statutory immunity

12–034 Unions or individuals who organise action which induces a breach of a contract, whether a contract of employment or a commercial contract, are protected by TULRCA, s.219(1)(a) provided that they act in contemplation or furtherance of a trade dispute.

Interference with contract

12–035 For there to be liability under the *Lumley v Gye* tort, there must actually be a breach of contract. However, the original tort has now been extended in a number of ways. First of all, it is no longer necessary that there be an actual breach of contract if there is substantial interference with its performance. This was established by *Torquay Hotel v Cousins* (1969). In this case the TGWU were in dispute with hotel owners who refused to recognise the union. The union informed Esso that a particular hotel was blacked and that fuel supplies to it should stop. Esso, most of whose drivers belonged to the TGWU, made no attempt to deliver oil to the hotel. There was a *force majeure* clause in their contract with the hotel, so they were not liable for this. The Court of Appeal was divided as to whether in this case there was a breach of contract which was excused, or whether the *force majeure* clause prevented there being a breach at all. However, they held that it did not matter either way, because it was tortious to induce a substantial interference with the contract.

It may seem reasonable to extend liability in such a situation as this, since if it was not a breach, it was as near as made no difference. However, the requirement of a breach focused on something definite and concrete. Interference with performance short of a breach is much vaguer: it postulates a notion of expected performance which *ex hypothesi* goes beyond what could be contractually required. So while it did not go much beyond a breach in *Torquay Hotel v Cousins*, it is capable of a much broader use in other cases. This development was also a staging post on the way to the development of the so-called super-tort, interference with trade or business by unlawful means, discussed para. 12–037.

Inducing interference with contract short of a breach has been recognised as a cause of action many times since *Torquay Hotel v Cousins*. It was actually interference rather than breach which was alleged in *Merkur Island Shipping v Laughton* (1983). In that case the House of Lords clearly took the view that the elements of the tort of interference with contract were exactly the same as for indirect inducement of breach of contract, save that it was not necessary to show that a breach had occurred.

Provided that it occurs in the context of a trade dispute, immunity is given by TULRCA, s.219(1)(a).

Intimidation

The tort of intimidation is committed where A threatens B that A will do **12–036** something unlawful to B unless B acts to the detriment of C, who is A's intended victim. A is here again using B as an instrument to get at C. Intimidation has existed for a long time as a tort and is exemplified by the early case, *Tarleton v M'Gawley* (1793), where plaintiff and defendant were both slave traders dealing off Africa. When a boat from the local community set out from the shore to deal with the plaintiff's ship, the defendant shot at them, which had the desired effect of deterring them from doing business with that ship and encouraging them to do business with the defendant's ship instead. Note that there is no requirement here that B's action be unlawful *vis-à-vis* C; it is enough that B acts to C's detriment because of A's unlawful threat to B.

As the name "intimidation" and the facts of *Tarleton v M'Gawley* suggest, it was generally thought that this tort was applicable in situations where one party was put in fear of violence. It was unknown in the sphere of industrial action until the House of Lords' decision in *Rookes v Barnard* (1964). R was employed by BOAC, and had resigned from his union, the AESD. The union had a closed shop at this workplace, and so it threatened BOAC with strike action if R was not dismissed. The company bowed to this pressure and dismissed R in accordance with the terms of his contract. Since BOAC committed no breach of contract by dismissing R, he could not sue the union for inducing a breach of contract. The House of Lords held that the union had, however, committed the tort of intimidation: they had threatened the employer, who had therefore acted to the plaintiff's detriment. What was the unlawful act? It was the threat that employees would break their contracts of employment. Lord Devlin said, "I find . . . nothing to differentiate a threat of breach of contract from a threat of physical violence . . .".

Thus the tort became established in the pantheon of economic torts which could be prayed in aid in case of industrial action. It may also be seen in some sense as an extension of inducement of breach of contract. Here the contract between R and BOAC was not broken, nor even interfered with. This tort goes further: the plaintiff had suffered a detriment and the defendants had threatened an unlawful act with the intention of bringing about that detriment, and so there was liability.

The introduction of intimidation to industrial disputes by the decision in *Rookes v Barnard* was highly significant in two ways: first, for unions, it was an example of the inadequacies of a system of immunities as a way of safeguarding the right to strike. A system of immunities only works if there

351

is a settled body of liability from which one is immune. But the economic torts were here shown, not for the first time, to be far from settled. Until 1964 there had been no immunity from liability for intimidation because it was not thought to be relevant in trade disputes. That is why it was used in *Rookes v Barnard*. The result was that the following year the Trade Disputes Act 1965 was passed to provide immunity in these circumstances (an immunity now contained in TULRCA, s.219(1)(b)). The other highly significant feature of the case was that it paved the way for the all-embracing tort of interference with trade or business by unlawful means.

Interference with trade or business by unlawful means

12–037   Until comparatively recently it was doubted that such a tort existed, although immunity against it was included in the Trade Disputes Act 1906 and repeated in TULRA, though repealed in 1982. If this sounds peculiar, it can be explained by reference to the well-known caution of lawyers. It has been pointed out already that the economic torts are not settled. At the beginning of the twentieth century they were even less settled. Hence there was genuine doubt as to whether there was tortious liability wherever one person acted to damage the business of another using unlawful means to do so. Even if there was not, there was certainly a possibility that it would be invented in the future – and so protection from liability for it was given.

The subsequent development shows that excessive caution can itself be dangerous. When the immunity from this liability was repealed by the Employment Act 1982 it began to be argued that there must be such a tort because there had been an immunity against it. It would not have made sense to repeal the immunity unless the immunity gave some sort of genuine protection. It does not take an expert in logic to see a flaw in this argument, but nobody drew attention to the emperor's lack of clothes. Perhaps this was because there was a better reason for supporting its existence. This was that after *Rookes v Barnard*, there was liability for threatening to use unlawful means to interfere with someone's trade or business, even if no breaches of contract were induced. If threatening to interfere was tortious, then surely actually interfering must be so too. The tort came to the fore particularly after 1982, because while there was immunity for the other torts discussed above, there was no immunity for this one. Also, wherever inducement or interference with contract, or intimidation, have been made out, then interference with trade or business by unlawful means must have been made out also. Thus there was never any harm in counsel adding it to the end of the claim, and it is fairly clear that this has become standard practice.

12–038   The existence of a tort of interference with trade or business by unlawful means was recognised by the House of Lords in *Hadmor v Hamilton* (1982), and that it might in time swallow up the others was foreseen by Lord Diplock in *Merkur Island Shipping v Laughton* (1983). In *Lonrho v Fayed* (1989) the Court of Appeal began to clarify the conditions necessary for its application, stating that it was not necessary that the defendant's predominant purpose should be to harm the plaintiff, but it must be shown that in some sense the defendant's unlawful act was directed against and intended to harm the plaintiff. It remains unclear what kind of interference with trade will found liability. In *Lonrho v Fayed* the plaintiff company alleged that it had been wrongfully deprived of an opportunity to bid to take over Harrods; the defendant moved to strike out the claim as disclosing no cause of action, alleging that this was insufficient to amount to an interference with trade even if proved. The Court of Appeal thought that the point was at least arguable and should go to a full trial.

Interference with trade or business by unlawful means is wide enough to embrace the three torts discussed above, and it is possible that in the end it will be recognised as a kind of super-tort of which the named torts of inducement, interference with contract and intimidation are just varieties. At present it is unclear what degree of knowledge of the business damaged and what degree of intention are required for commission of the tort, but there is a clear tendency to extrapolate from inducement of breach of contract and to apply the same principles. Most debate to date has centred on the issue of what amounts to unlawful means. As this is relevant to the other torts also, it is discussed in a separate section.

Unlawful means

It is settled law that inducing someone to break a contract will constitute **12–039** unlawful means for the purpose of other torts which have this requirement. It is also the case that since 1906 there has been immunity for inducing breaches of contract of employment in contemplation or furtherance of a trade dispute. If an inducement of breach is not actionable in its own right, can it yet count as unlawful means for the commission of some other tort?

The position on this was unclear during the 1960s, with the result that in 1974 a subsection was included in TULRA "for the avoidance of doubt" to indicate that a breach which was not itself actionable could not constitute unlawful means. This provision (TULRA, s.13(3)) was repealed by the Employment Act 1980, leading to a revival of the debate in *Hadmor Productions v Hamilton* (1982). The House of Lords decided in that case that section 13(3) had merely stated what was already the law, and that a wrong which was not actionable because of the immunity could not be used as unlawful means for the purposes of another tort.

With this proviso, it seems clear that otherwise commission of a tort will constitute unlawful means. In *Lonrho v Fayed* (1989) Lonrho alleged that the Fayed brothers had fraudulently deceived the Secretary of State for Trade into not referring their bid for the House of Fraser to the Monopolies and Mergers Commission, and that this had resulted in damage to Lonrho's business. It was argued for the Fayeds that the tort of deceit, which was the alleged unlawful means for the interference with Lonrho's trade, requires proof of damage, and since the Secretary of State had suffered no loss by reason of the deceit, it could not constitute unlawful means. This argument was rejected by the Court of Appeal.

In *Rookes v Barnard* (1964) it was held that a breach of contract, or **12–040** threat of breach, could constitute unlawful means. This was in the context of intimidation, and it is not clear whether it is true of the other torts as well (*per* Henry J. in *Barretts & Baird v IPCS* (1987)). Given that these civil wrongs constitute unlawful means, it may seem surprising to find that not all crimes do so. In *Lonrho v Shell* (1982) the plaintiff alleged that the defendant oil companies had conspired together to flout statutory provisions forbidding the supply of oil to Rhodesia following the illegal unilateral declaration of independence in that country. Breach of the statute was a crime, and Lonrho alleged that its business had suffered because of their actions. The House of Lords pointed out that it had long been the law that not every breach of statute would found a civil action. The tort of breach of statutory duty depends on whether the statute can be construed either as designed to benefit the class of people to whom the plaintiff belongs, or as creating a public right for the benefit of all citizens, and the plaintiff can show that he has suffered damage over and above the rest. This breach was not of either kind. Since Lonrho could not succeed in a claim for the tort of breach of statutory duty in its own right, the House of Lords held that the offence did not amount to unlawful means for the commission of the tort of interference with trade or business by unlawful means.

There remains one further complication. What if what is relied on for unlawful means is not the tort of breach of statutory duty but the separate tort of inducing breach of statutory duty? Must the plaintiffs be able to show that this tort would have been actionable at their suit before it can constitute unlawful means? The point was considered by the Court of Appeal in *Associated British Ports v TGWU* (1989). As these were only interlocutory proceedings the court had only to consider whether there was an arguable case on the point rather than reaching a final decision. They considered that it was at least arguable that inducing breach of statutory duty could be unlawful means even if the breach of statutory duty would not be actionable at the suit of the plaintiff.

Conspiracy

12–041 The source of union strength is the power to act in combination. Hence it is hardly surprising to find that conspiracy, a crime and a tort which also depends on combination, should be used against trade unions. In the early nineteenth century trade unions were by their very existence regarded as criminal conspiracies. This criminal liability was effectively removed by the Trade Union Act 1871, which legalised trade unions. The possibility of tortious liability, however, remained. There are two forms of this tort: conspiracy to injure, and conspiracy to use unlawful means.

Conspiracy to injure

12–042 Liability for conspiracy to injure is incurred where two or more combine with the intention of harming the plaintiff, even though they use lawful means to do so. Thus an action which would be lawful if done by one person becomes unlawful because done by more than one. This has been described as anomalous: if an action is all right for one person, how can it

354

be wrong just because it is done by more than one? The usual rationale is that there is strength in numbers. You may not be damaged if, say, your business is boycotted by one person; but if it is boycotted by many, you may be forced to close down.

> "But to suggest today that acts done by one street-corner grocer in concert with a second are more oppressive and dangerous to a competitor than the same acts done by a string of supermarkets under a single ownership . . . is to shut one's eyes to what has been happening in the business and industrial world since the turn of the century" (*per* Lord Diplock in *Lonrho v Shell* (1982)).

The force of numbers argument prevailed, however, in the case which established this liability, *Quinn v Leathem* (1901). The plaintiff butcher used non-union labour. The defendant union official told an important customer of the plaintiff that there would be a strike at his place of business if he continued to deal with the plaintiff. On the facts the threatened strikes would not have been breaches of contract, and of course, the customer committed no breach of contract by refusing to enter further contracts with the plaintiff. Although no unlawful means were used, the House of Lords held the defendants liable in tort, given that they had no justification for their actions. However, just three years earlier, in *Allen v Flood* (1898), the House of Lords had held that a malicious motive could not turn a lawful act into an unlawful one. The only way that *Quinn v Leathem* can be reconciled with this decision is because of the element of combination present, which serves to distinguish them. (The hidden agenda seems to be that Lord Halsbury would have liked to reverse *Allen v Flood*, but that is another story.)

However, a conspiracy to injure is not actionable unless the defendants' **12–043** predominant purpose is to injure the plaintiff. Rigorous pursuit of self-interest in the knowledge that the plaintiff is bound to suffer damage as a result does not amount to the requisite intention. This was decided by the House of Lords in *Crofter Hand Woven Harris Tweed v Veitch* (1942). On the island of Lewis were mills producing yarn and weaving Harris tweed. Cheaper yarn was produced on the mainland, so some manufacturers began to import yarn and simply have it woven on the island – thus undercutting the price at which cloth produced wholly on the island was sold. Officials of the TGWU to which the workers belonged had the incoming yarn blacked. On the facts, the dockers who did this were not in breach of their contracts, so the plaintiffs sued instead for a conspiracy to injure. The House of Lords held that the action was basically intended to protect the livelihoods of the union members, and that this was a justifiable motive; hence the union was not liable.

The result of this decision is that most kinds of industrial action do not attract liability for conspiracy to injure even at common law, because most of the time the action is intended to further the interests of the union and its members rather than to injure the plaintiff.

355

Conspiracy to use unlawful means

12–044 Unlike conspiracy to injure, if there is a conspiracy to use unlawful means to further the defendants' purpose, it is enough if damage to the plaintiff is likely to result, even if that is not the defendants' predominant purpose. This distinction between conspiracy to injure and conspiracy to use unlawful means was thrown into some doubt by the decision in *Lonrho v Shell* (1982) where the House of Lords, concerned to keep what was described as the anomalous tort of conspiracy within narrow bounds, seemed to indicate that there was no liability for a conspiracy to use unlawful means (sanctions-busting) unless the predominant purpose was to injure the plaintiff. This is how their decision was interpreted by the Court of Appeal in *Metall und Rohstoff AG v Donaldson Lufkin & Jenrette* (1989). However, in *Lonrho v Fayed* (1991) the House of Lords reaffirmed the traditional distinction, overruling *Metall und Rohstoff* on this point.

Conspiracy to injure is given immunity by TULRCA, s.219(2) where it is in contemplation or furtherance of a trade dispute. Conspiracy to use unlawful means is not so protected, although it will be recollected that actions which are the subject of immunity will not count as unlawful means.

Other torts

12–045 We have already seen that the impetus for the development of interference with trade or business by unlawful means was essentially the search for a cause of action which would be outside the immunities in the statute. For the same reason, other wrongs have been alleged in industrial disputes with more or less success.

Inducement of breach of statutory duty

12–046 The tort of breach of statutory duty committed in the course of a trade dispute would receive no protection; however, the tort would most likely be committed by the workers taking the action rather than the organisers. Thus it has been argued that there is also a tort of inducing breach of statutory duty, for which the union could be held liable. In *Associated British Ports v TGWU* (1989) it was alleged that by organising a dock strike, the union would be inducing a breach of the National Dock Labour Scheme set out in statutory regulations. The Court of Appeal regarded the existence of the tort as established, and by a majority held that it was not necessary for the plaintiffs to be able to show that the actual breach of the statutory duty would have been actionable in its own right. The point was not considered by the House of Lords, who reversed the decision on other grounds.

Inducement of breach of an equitable obligation

12–047 In *Prudential Assurance v Lorenz* (1971) an insurance company alleged that the union was inducing its agents to breach their equitable duty to account for money received on the company's behalf by urging them to withhold premiums as part of an industrial action campaign. Plowman J. thought the point sufficiently arguable to grant an interlocutory injunction against the union. However, in *Metall und Rohstoff AG v Donaldson Lufkin & Jenrette* (1989), the Court of Appeal denied the existence of any such tort, and considered it unnecessary, since the plaintiff could take action directly on the breach of the obligation. That case, of course, did not involve industrial action.

Economic duress

All industrial action is an attempt to influence an employer by means of **12–048** economic pressure. Where pressure amounts to duress, then in contract law a contract may be avoided and any money paid can be restored. It is recognised that economic pressure as well as physical can amount to duress. Usually this is not relevant to industrial action since unions do not usually enter contracts with employers. However, one tactic used by the International Transport Workers' Federation (ITF) in its campaign against flags of convenience has been to require employers to make financial contributions to the union's welfare fund as part of any agreement for the union to lift the blacking of a ship flying a flag of convenience. In *Universe Tankships of Monrovia v ITF* (1982) the employers claimed the money back after the blacking had been lifted. The House of Lords held that if the economic pressure was legitimated by being within the immunities, then an employer could not circumvent that protection by bringing an action for duress instead. But if it were unprotected, then an action for restitution would be an alternative to any action in tort. On these facts the House of Lords held by a majority that a dispute over welfare payments would not have been a trade dispute, and so this action was not protected. This was taken one stage further by *Dimskal Shipping v ITF* (1992), where the facts were similar, but the money was paid in Sweden, and the pressure was lawful under Swedish law. Because the contract by the shipowners to pay the money was governed by English law, the House of Lords held that they could get their money back.

13. Industrial Action II

In Chapter 12 we saw that where unions commit economic torts in the **13–001** course of industrial action, they are usually protected by the immunity given by TULRCA, s.219; although we also saw that increasingly employers seek to rely on the commission of other torts for which there is no such protection. In this chapter, we must first look more closely at the requirements for the application of TULRCA, s.219, and then, assuming that there is immunity, at the remaining question, which is, when is the immunity lost?

Immunity under TULRCA, s.219

TULRCA, s.219 gives immunity from action for the torts of inducing **13–002** breach of contract, interfering with contract by unlawful means, threatening to do either (intimidation), and conspiracy. But this immunity is applicable only when the tort is committed "in contemplation or furtherance of a trade dispute". This phrase, conveniently dubbed "the golden formula" by Wedderburn, has been hallowed by long usage, appearing first in the Conspiracy and Protection of Property Act 1875. However, the definition of the term "trade dispute", presently to be found in TULRCA, s.244, was subjected to extensive alterations in the 1980s, which meant that the phrase has become one of limitation rather than of explanation.

"Trade dispute" is defined in TULRCA, s.244(1) as,

> "... a dispute between workers and their employer which relates wholly or mainly to one or more of the following:
>
> (a) terms and conditions of employment, or the physical conditions in which any workers are required to work;
> (b) engagement or non-engagement, or termination or suspension of employment or the duties of employment, of one or more workers;
> (c) allocation of work or the duties of employment as between workers or groups of workers;
> (d) matters of discipline;
> (e) a worker's membership or non-membership of a trade union;

(f) facilities for officials of trade unions; and

(g) machinery for negotiation or consultation, and other procedures, relating to any of the above matters, including the recognition by employers or employers' associations of the right of a trade union to represent workers in such negotiation or consultation or in the carrying out of such procedures."

No existing dispute

13–003 Clearly there must be an actual dispute in existence before someone can be said to be acting in contemplation or furtherance of it. Thus in *Bent's Brewery v Hogan* (1945) the union had no immunity when it was sued for inducing breach of contract by asking its members for confidential information in order to frame a pay claim. If they had put in a pay claim and had it rejected, there would have been a dispute, but there was no dispute at this preliminary stage. A similar argument was used against the ITF in *Star Sea Transport v Slater* (1978), another of the cases arising from the ITF campaign against flags of convenience. The union had blacked a ship because the crew were being paid less than internationally agreed rates. However, the Indian crew members were quite happy with the pay they were receiving, which was good by their home standards. It was held that the action did not attract the immunity because there was no dispute in existence.

In *University College London Hospital NHS Trust v Unison* (1999), there was a dispute arising from the Trust's negotiations with a consortium of private companies to build and manage a new hospital using private finance. On completion of the project, some years into the future, it was envisaged that some of the Trust's employees would be transferred to private partners. The union and its members feared that if this came to pass, the workers would end up with terms and conditions of employment much inferior to those they enjoyed as public sector employees. One of the reasons for the Court of Appeal holding that this did not come within the trade dispute immunity was that it was not a dispute about existing terms and conditions of employment but about terms and conditions which employees might have with another employer at some point in the future (*cf.* also *London Underground v NUR* (1989)). This was relevant also to the next restriction.

"Workers and their employer"

13–004 Since 1982 the dispute must be between workers and their employer if there is to be immunity. Before the amendments of the Employment Act 1982, the dispute could be between any workers and any employer, or even between workers and workers. Thus in *University College London Hospital NHS Trust v Unison* (1999) the Court of Appeal held that the main thrust of the dispute was the union's attempt to gain binding guarantees about the terms that the private employers would offer to Trust employees who were transferred. This would amount to a dispute about the terms and conditions of an employer other than the employer at whom the strike action was to be aimed. It was not therefore a dispute between workers and their own employer.

Unison took this to the European Court of Human Rights arguing that this restriction on industrial action was a breach of the Article 11 right to "form and join trade unions for the protection of his interests" (*Unison v UK* (2002)). The court considered that the dispute did engage Article 11 because there could be some benefit, even if it was slight, to current members and so to that extent the union's proposed action could be seen as protecting the occupational interests of its members. However, the union's claim was rejected in the end on the basis that the restriction on the right to strike applied in the case was a reasonable balance between the competing rights of the parties and fell within the proviso in Article 11(2).

Does the removal of immunity from disputes between workers and workers mean that there would now be no protection for a demarcation dispute, where one group of workers claims that only its members should do a particular kind of work to the exclusion of another group?

In *Dimbleby v NUJ* (1984) journalists employed by the plaintiff refused to send printing work to TBF Printers rather than to their own associated printing house, where the printers were on strike. This was because TBF Printers was a subsidiary of T Bailey Forman, a company with which their union, the NUJ, was in dispute. They argued that this was a trade dispute under (c): allocation of work between groups of workers. While accepting that demarcation issues would normally be trade disputes, the House of Lords limited this to demarcation disputes where both parties worked for the same employer (*cf.* TULRCA, s.244(5)). Thus it seems that the usual kind of demarcation dispute would be within the definition of trade dispute; furthermore, if a dispute arose because an allocation of work to outside contractors was going to lead to job losses, there would surely be a trade dispute under (b) if not under (c).

The limitation of disputes to workers and their own employer does not mean that sympathy action is never immune. While the initial trade dispute must be between workers and their own employer, the sympathy strikers are acting in contemplation or furtherance of that dispute – and so their action is within the golden formula. However, it will almost certainly be secondary action and will now lose protection on that account.

Subject-matter of the dispute

Section 219 immunity will only apply if the dispute is "wholly or mainly" **13–005** about one of the items listed in section 244. This again represents a narrowing of the immunity as a result of amendment by the Employment Act 1982. Originally it was sufficient if a dispute was "connected with" one of the items. This was very wide: in effect, if the union was acting from mixed motives, it was sufficient if one of them was a trade dispute motive. A good example of the new test is provided by *Mercury Communications v Scott-Garner* (1984), where the POEU instructed its members working for the Post Office not to connect Mercury to the British Telecom network. At this time British Telecom was being privatised and also opened up to competition, with Mercury being the first competitor. The Court of Appeal considered that the union was acting partly out of concern for the job security of its members, but was also motivated to a large extent by ideological objections to privatisation. Therefore the dispute could not be said to be "wholly or mainly" for a trade dispute motive.

Cases such as *Mercury Communications v Scott-Garner* are often publicised as "political disputes" rather than trade disputes, and so it is claimed that they are outside the immunity. This is an argument that has been around a long time. In the only reported case arising from the General Strike in 1926, *NSFU v Reed* (1926), Astbury J. held that, "No trade dispute has been alleged or shown to exist in any of the unions affected, except in the miners' case, and no trade dispute can exist between the TUC on the one hand and the Government and the nation on the other". This prompted a famous article by Goodhart, sometime Professor of Jurisprudence at Oxford, who pointed out that much industrial action was designed to put pressure on a third party and argued that a dispute should not cease to be regarded as a trade dispute just because the third party was the Government.

13–006   Today the line between a trade dispute and a political dispute can be even harder to draw, first because of increasing government intervention in the collective bargaining process by legislation or other means, and secondly, because in the public sector (which employs nearly 20 per cent of the workforce) the Government controls policy and public expenditure and is thus the real decision-maker, not the nominal employing authority. In *Associated Newspapers v Flynn* (1970) a one-day strike against the Industrial Relations Bill (under banners proclaiming, "Demonstrate against the Bosses and the Blacklegs' Charter") was held to be political, even though it was argued that the Bill, if passed, would have a damaging effect on terms and conditions of employment. But in *Sherard v AUEW* (1973) it was accepted that a one-day strike protesting against an act which imposed a statutory wage freeze was about terms and conditions rather than being just political. Now, of course, there would be the added requirement that the purpose of the dispute was wholly or mainly trade rather than political. Unions may thus find themselves in some difficulty if their publicity attempts to galvanise members by placing their dispute in a wider national context: this makes it the more likely that they will be considered to be acting for a political motive. However, in *Wandsworth LBC v NAS/UWT* (1993), where the union had called on its members to boycott national tests for schoolchildren, the Court of Appeal showed itself sensitive to this issue. It finally rejected the council's claim that the boycott was motivated by ideological objections to the tests, accepting the teachers' argument that the main reason was the increased workload it would mean for them, which was clearly a trade dispute motive (*cf.* also *University College London Hospital NHS Trust v Unison* (1999) and *Westminster City Council v Unison* (2001)).

BBC v Hearn (1977) suggests a possible means whereby such disputes could clearly be established as trade disputes. Here the Association of Broadcasting Staff was planning to black the televised transmission of the Cup Final to South Africa because of the policy of apartheid in that country. The Court of Appeal granted an injunction because this was a political matter; however, Lord Denning at least drew attention to the fact that the staff had not asked for a term in their contracts to say that they should be allowed to act according to conscience in this matter. This carries the implication that if such a request were made and rejected, there would then be a bona fide dispute about terms and conditions of employment. Lord Cross *obiter* indicated disagreement with this view, saying:

> "A trade union cannot turn a dispute which in reality has no connection with terms and conditions of employment into a dispute connected with terms and conditions of employment by insisting that the employer inserts appropriate terms into the contract of employment . . . " (*Universe Tankships of Monrovia v ITF* (1982)).

However, it is difficult to see why not.

Location of the dispute

An alternative argument for the BBC staff could have been that they were **13–007** acting because of the bad terms and conditions of employment for black workers in South Africa. This would have been sympathy action if it could have been shown that there was a particular real dispute between those workers and their employer. But this avenue would no longer be open, because the effect of section 219(3), as amended in 1982, is that action in contemplation or furtherance of a dispute outside the United Kingdom is protected only if those taking the action are likely to be affected by it. This might be the case if, say, a car manufacturer was proposing to close a production plant in Sweden, causing an industrial dispute, and employees of the same company at an assembly plant in the United Kingdom feared that their jobs would also be lost if the closure went ahead. However, this action again could well be secondary action, and therefore unprotected.

Loss of Immunity

We now reach the third stage in deciding whether industrial action is **13–008** lawful. To recap, the first question is whether or not the action is tortious at common law. If it is, then the second question is whether or not it attracts *prima facie* protection under TULRCA, s.219. Not all torts are so protected, and even where they are covered, it is also necessary that the action was taken in contemplation or furtherance of a trade dispute. The third question, assuming that the action has immunity under section 219, is whether that immunity is to be forfeited. This is a question which divides into several parts, for there are now several grounds on which immunity can be lost, which will be considered in turn.

Secondary action

13–009 The winter of 1978–79 became known to the newspapers as the "winter of discontent" because of a number of serious industrial disputes which ultimately contributed in large measure to the defeat of the Labour Government in the subsequent general election. In order to increase the pressure and thus the effectiveness of their strikes, unions adopted the tactic of spreading disputes as widely as possible. The aim was usually to paralyse a whole branch of industry so that something had to be done to settle the dispute. Of course, a strike can only be spread if people not directly involved are prepared to help, either by taking strike action themselves or by refusing to cross picket lines or refusing to do the work of the strikers. In practice, in many industries, especially those with a long history of union activity, union solidarity was such that other members of the same union and members of other unions were prepared to support in this manner even if it meant losing pay and risking dismissal themselves. The use of another tactic, the "flying picket" (contingents of pickets prepared to move swiftly to different parts of the country to ensure that effective pickets were mounted even if local unionists were not eager to do it) helped to make sure that the spread took place. Their activities were seen variously as part of a brilliant strategy, stiffening the resolve of the less militant, interference in other people's business, or frankly intimidatory, according to one's point of view.

Very many people took the view that this was not really fair play, even if it was legal. The answer of some trade unionists would be that collective action and solidarity are the very nerve and life-blood of trade unions and that no restriction on voluntary collective action is justified. It will surprise no one that judges tended to be in the first camp. In a famous trilogy of cases arising out of the 1978–79 strikes (*NWL v Woods* (1979); *Express Newspapers v McShane* (1980) and *Duport Steels v Sirs* (1980)) the Court of Appeal, led by Lord Denning, attempted to develop a concept of "remoteness" and to remove section 219 protection from activities which they considered to be too far removed from the primary dispute.

One example will suffice. In *Express Newspapers v McShane* (1980) NUJ journalists working for provincial newspapers had a long-running dispute with their employers over pay. Dismissal of 105 journalists by the *Bolton Evening News* precipitated a national strike by provincial journalists. This did not have the hoped-for effect of shutting down the provincial papers because they could still pick up copy from the Press Association, an agency supplying news stories. Thus NUJ members working for the Press Association were instructed by the union not to supply copy to the provincial newspapers. Only about half complied; in consequence NUJ members working for national newspapers were told to boycott Press Association copy. Express Newspapers sued the General Secretary of the NUJ. The Court of Appeal took the view that the only trade dispute here was between the provincial papers and their employees. They were prepared to accept that the involvement of the Press Association journalists was in furtherance of that primary dispute, but not the action at the national newspapers. They considered that it was so remote from the primary dispute that it could not be said to be in furtherance of it, and it was very unlikely to have any effect on its outcome.

In this case, as in the other two, the decision of the Court of Appeal was reversed by the House of Lords, which held that acting in furtherance was to be judged subjectively: if the union officials honestly believed that they were acting in furtherance of the primary dispute, that was enough. This was clearly the correct interpretation of the law, and the House of Lords, while not enthusiastic about it, was mindful of the danger of judges appearing to act politically if they added extra requirements to those actually appearing in the legislation.

However, the new Conservative Government took up the Court of **13–010** Appeal's ideas, and the Employment Act 1980 introduced the concept of "secondary action". Secondary action is now defined by TULRCA, s.224, and consists in inducing breach of, or interfering with, a contract of employment, or threatening to do so, where the employer under the contract of employment is not a party to the trade dispute. Where secondary action occurs, the protection otherwise given for these torts by section 219 is removed, except in one situation. That is where there is lawful picketing by employees who are party to the dispute. The parameters of lawful picketing are discussed below (para. 13–029). Effectively this means that all sympathy action is now unprotected, as we can see if we look again at the facts of *Express Newspapers v McShane* (1980). Today, not only the blacking of Press Association copy by journalists employed by national papers but also the instruction to Press Association union members not to supply copy to the provincial newspapers would be unprotected secondary action. The union, by asking its members at the Press Association not to send copy to the provincial papers, would be asking them to break their contracts of employment. Since their employer, the Press Association, was not a party to the dispute with the provincial journalists, the action would be secondary.

You will remember that in *Express Newspapers v McShane* the Court of Appeal was prepared to countenance the action taken by Press Association journalists. It was the action by the national journalists which they considered to be too remote. As originally framed in 1980, this was also the position taken by the law. If the employer who was not a party to the dispute had a direct contractual nexus with the employer who was involved (*e.g.* to supply them with goods and services, or to buy something from them) then industrial action aimed at this "first supplier" or "first customer" was protected. Anything more remote, such as the action affecting the national newspapers which had no contract with the provincial papers in *Express Newspapers v McShane*, was unprotected secondary action.

Under this regime, therefore, a limited amount of sympathy action could be taken lawfully. However, the protection for limited secondary action was removed by the Employment Act 1990. Now the only type of sympathy action which retains immunity is that which occurs in the context of lawful picketing. If workers in dispute with their own employer picket the workplace, they will not only aim to discourage other employees from going to work but also to stop all deliveries in and out. If pickets induce a lorry driver who is meant to be delivering goods to turn back (and lots of workers are very reluctant to cross picket lines) they will probably have induced a breach of the driver's contract with his employer, who is not a party to the trade dispute. This, as we know, is secondary action. But it remains protected secondary action and the immunity in section 219 will still apply.

We saw in *Dimbleby v NUJ* (1984) that Dimbleby, in dispute with their own printers, decided to move their printing work to another firm, TBF Printers. In the United States strikers are allowed to "follow" struck work and it is legitimate for them to institute industrial action affecting the substitute employer in order to maintain the pressure caused by their original withdrawal of labour. The 1980 definition of protected secondary action also permitted this, although in a narrower form. The exception applied only if the substitute employer was a company belonging to the same group of companies as the employer in dispute. Since the Employment Act 1990, secondary action taken to follow switched production has no immunity.

Failure to hold a ballot

13–011 Prior to 1984 some unions, but by no means all, were required by their rules to ballot their members before industrial action (*cf. Taylor v NUM* (1984) above, para. 11–013). In the name of increased democracy within trade unions, the 1984 Trade Union Act indirectly imposed a requirement that all unions should hold a secret ballot before calling official strike action, by providing that immunity would be removed for the torts of inducing breach of contracts of employment or interfering with their performance unless a ballot in accordance with the statutory requirements had been held. Note that this only applies to official union action (in the sense described in Chapter 12, above, para. 12–014). Where unofficial action is taken by union members, or where non-unionists go on strike, there is no need to have a ballot to preserve immunity. However, if the union wishes to endorse unofficial action (thus protecting members' unfair dismissal rights) it needs to ballot the members first.

Since 1984 the law has been extended in three ways. Firstly, since 1988 every union member has a right to restrain the union from calling any industrial action (not just an all-out strike) without a ballot, whether or not the action involves a breach of members' contracts of employment (TULRCA, s.62). Secondly, the Employment Act 1990 extended the constituency of those to be balloted to self-employed workers working under a contract of personal service as well as employees (TULRCA, s.235). The third extension, carried out by TURERA, was the most significant. Introduced under the standard of the "Citizens' Charter", it is a right of a third party to get action called off whenever it is "unlawful" (TULRCA, s.235A). However, "unlawful" in this context has an extended meaning: it refers not only to action which is tortious and unprotected by immunity but also to any industrial action organised by a trade union where there has not been a ballot first. The third party need only show that the likely effect of the action would be to prevent or delay the supply of goods or services to him, or to reduce their quality; he need not show that he has any contractual right to them. *P v NAS/UWT* (2003) is one of the few examples of this right being invoked, in that case by a disruptive pupil whose schoolteachers were refusing to teach him.

Thus union members and third parties can now stop the union taking action without a ballot, although it remains the case that they cannot positively force the union to hold a ballot. It is worth noting that a non-corporate employer could also avail herself of the citizen's right to restrain action, although the reference in section 235A to an "individual" is thought to exclude companies. Otherwise, an employer would have no right to restrain action but would have to wait until the unsanctioned action has started and then sue in tort on the ground that the action has no immunity – although in *P & O Ferries v NUS* (1988) a court granted an injunction at the instance of the employer to stop the seamen's union balloting its members on strike action where it was clear that such strike action would be unprotected secondary action and thus have no immunity.

Balloting has thus moved to centre stage and compliance with the requirements for a valid ballot is of critical importance. As laid down in TULRCA, ss.226–234 and amended by TURERA, it seemed as if some of the highly technical requirements were aimed at least partly at making it extremely difficult for unions to call lawful action. The Employment Relations Act 1999 made minor amendments to deal with the worst excesses of technicality and managed to add some of its own, as will be seen. Reference should also be made to the Government's Code of Practice on Industrial Action Ballots and Notice to Employers (a revised version of which came into force in September 2000).

Requirements for a valid ballot

Who votes?

Only those who are to take part in the industrial action are entitled to vote **13–012** (TULRCA, s.227). This restriction is fair: it would not be right for some people to vote for other people to take action. Failure to allow votes to those entitled to vote, or allowing voting by those not entitled to vote, will invalidate the ballot (TULRCA, s.232A). Ballots must be postal and TULRCA, s.230 provides that "so far as is reasonably practicable" everyone entitled to vote must be sent a ballot paper by post. Again, failure to comply invalidates the ballot (TULRCA, s.232A).

In *P v NAS/UWT* (2003) school governors insisted on the reinstatement of a violent and disruptive pupil who had been expelled by the head teacher. The union balloted its members at the school on whether they should take industrial action in the form of refusing to teach the boy. Using the TULRCA, s.235A right for third parties, the boy sued to have the action called off on the basis that the ballot was defective because only 30 out of the 32 teachers at the school who were members of the union had been accorded their right to vote. The two left out were teachers who had only recently moved to the school and they had not informed the union of this. The vote in favour of action was 26–0, so their votes would have made no difference. However, it was argued that nonetheless there was a breach of the ballot requirements, so it was invalid according to s.232A.

The Employment Relations Act 1999 had introduced a new section 232B **13–013** into TULRCA to the effect that "small accidental failures" in complying with certain ballot requirements would not invalidate the ballot provided that the failures were not on such a scale as to be likely to affect the ballot result. However, curiously, the specific sections referred to in this exception did not include s.232A. Although inquiries when *P v NAS/UWT* was in the House of Lords revealed that the Parliamentary draftsman had indeed made a mistake and referred to the wrong section in s.232B, it further transpired that there had been no intention to excuse a breach of s.232A. The House of Lords managed to make sense of this mess by holding that the two teachers left out of the ballot had not been denied their entitlement to vote in these circumstances. As they had not informed the union of their move, it was held that it had not been reasonably practicable for the union to send them a ballot paper. This may have led to them being denied an opportunity to vote, but this was not the same as saying that they were denied entitlement to vote. The ballot was held to be valid.

An attempt to rely on the small accidental failures exception failed in *RMT v Midland Mainline Ltd* (2001) where the union failed to ballot 25 members for various reasons. The action was approved by only 25 votes to 17, with 49 others failing to record a vote.

In *London Underground v RMT* (1995) the union balloted its members in August over a series of one- and two-day strikes. By the time that the action was actually due to take place, active recruitment by the union had resulted in another 692 new members, who were called on to participate. The employer argued that the union should not be entitled to call out these new members, as they had not been balloted. The argument was rejected by the Court of Appeal. The Act specifically requires the union to ballot only those of its members who at the time of the ballot are reasonably expected to be called upon to participate in the industrial action. Provided that this is done, the action has the support of the ballot, which is all that the law requires. As Millett L.J. noted, the ballot provisions apply only to the union and its members. There is nothing to stop the union calling out non-members, and this will not affect its immunity.

One oddity thrown up by the ballot requirement was shown by *Shipping Company Uniform Inc. v ITF* (1985). The ITF is a federation of affiliated trade unions, with hardly any individual members. It argued that it was therefore exempt from the ballot requirement because it had no one to ballot. The argument was rejected by the court, with the result that a union in this position became quite unable to organise industrial action within the immunity. Such unions must change their rules so that individual members of affiliated unions are direct members also of the federation.

Notice to employers

13–014 Since 1993 it has become necessary for the union to give at least seven days' notice of the ballot to every single employer of employees who will be called on to vote (TULRCA, s.226A) and a further seven days' notice before the industrial action actually starts (s.234A). In addition to giving notice, the union must also send a sample voting paper to the affected employers at least three days before the ballot is due to start.

The most controversial aspect of this was that in both notices the union had to describe the relevant employees "so that he [the employer] can readily ascertain them". Despite a ministerial denial that this would entail naming names, that was precisely what was held to be necessary in the first case to reach the Court of Appeal, *Blackpool and the Fylde College v NATFHE* (1994). The union had stated that it would ballot all its members at the college. However, of the 872 staff, only 288 were union members. The employer claimed successfully that the union had not given enough information to ascertain the members and it was held that the union should disclose the names of the members to be balloted. This meant that members' rights to keep their membership private were infringed and it raised the risk of employers seeking to influence individuals as well as giving rise to fear of retaliation among union members.

The Employment Relations Act 1999 tried to deal with this by substituting a new wording in TULRCA, s.226A to the effect that the union must give the employer notice with such information "as would help the employer to make plans and bring information to the attention" of such employees. While information about numbers and categories of staff should be provided, it is specifically stated that failure to name the relevant employees will not mean that the notice is non-compliant. A similar change was made to section 234A (which requires the union to give seven days' notice of the start of any action). The new requirement was considered in yet another case involving rail workers, *RMT v London Underground Ltd* (2001), where the union gave notice that it would be calling out all its members who worked for the company, some 40 per cent of London Underground's total 17,000 employees. The union stated the approximate number of members involved and said that they were to be found in every workplace and in every category of staff. The employer argued that this did not give it sufficient information to be able to plan for the strike and asked for a list of names to check against its own records. The Court of Appeal held that the union's notice was insufficient to comply with TULRCA, s.226A and s.234A. The union ought to have provided a breakdown of the number of staff in each category at each workplace – no matter that this would be more onerous than the pre-1999 Act requirement of simply supplying a list of names. However, this does not mean that unions have a positive obligation to produce a breakdown of this kind if sufficient information is given without it (*Westminster City Council v Unison* (2001)).

It is perhaps surprising that the notice requirement was not removed entirely by the Employment Relations Act 1999. It is unclear why unions should have to give notice to employers that they intend to undertake the perfectly lawful activity of balloting their members.

Scrutiny

TURERA has in effect extended the rules relating to the independent **13–015** scrutiny of union election and political fund ballots, introduced in 1988, to industrial action ballots as well, unless fewer than 50 members are involved (TULRCA, ss.226B–C). The scrutineer, whose name must appear on the ballot paper, must be a qualified person within the meaning of the Trade Union Ballots and Elections (Independent Scrutineer Qualifications) Order 1993; *i.e.* solicitors, qualified trade union auditors and certain bodies like the Electoral Reform Society. The scrutineer is not charged with actually supervising the ballot, but has to report on it within four weeks stating whether or not he is satisfied that the requirements have been complied with and that there were satisfactory arrangements for the production, storage, distribution, return and counting of the ballot papers (s.231B). The union is obliged to comply with all reasonable requests from the scrutineer and must ensure that no one interferes with him in the performance of his functions. The union must make copies of the report available to any voting member or affected employer who asks for it within a six-month period.

Separate workplaces

13–016   Different regions, different groups of workers, even different plants may have quite different attitudes to taking industrial action. If a single result is returned for all those balloted, the fact that at plant A, say, 90 per cent opposed action may be submerged in an overall majority in favour. Unions could manipulate votes by making sure that well-known militant workplaces were always included in any ballot. Fear of this (rather than any evidence that it was actually happening) led to a limited requirement (in TULRCA, s.228) that there should be separate ballots and separate results returned. Unfortunately, section 228 was framed in an extremely convoluted fashion. The Employment Relations Act 1999 repealed and replaced section 228 with new sections 228 and 228A, aimed at clarifying rather than changing the law. Thus section 228 lays down a *prima facie* rule of separate ballots for separate workplaces. However, section 228A allows a single ballot for different workplaces in three situations: where there is at least one worker at the workplace affected by the dispute; where there is an occupational link between all the members balloted, whether or not they work at different workplaces or even have different employers and finally situations where all the workers of one or more employers in dispute are balloted. Allowing a single ballot of employees of different employers where there is an occupational link gives statutory force to the decision in *University of Central England v NALGO* (1993), where it was held that an aggregated ballot result could be given for staff working for different universities since they all had the same terms and conditions.

The Employment Relations Act 1999 also redefines "workplace" in TULRCA, s.228 as being the premises with which the worker's employment has the closest connection. This is to deal with the problems which arose in *Intercity West Coast Ltd v RMT* (1996) where it was argued that train conductors, all of whom worked at Manchester Piccadilly station (belonging to Railtrack) but who had separate employers, Intercity West Coast Ltd and North West Regional Railways, had separate workplaces. Under the new definition, the question of who owns or occupies the premises is no longer relevant.

The ballot paper

13–017   Since 1984 the ballot paper has had to contain the so-called health warning: "If you take part in a strike or other industrial action, you may be in breach of your contract of employment" (TULRCA, s.229(4)). As a result of the

Employment Relations Act 1999 amendments to unfair dismissal law, which mean that dismissals for taking part in lawful industrial action are automatically unfair in some circumstances, the health warning has had to be amended too, adding:

> "However, if you are dismissed for taking part in a strike or other industrial action which is called officially and is otherwise lawful, the dismissal will be unfair if it takes place fewer than eight weeks after you started taking part in the action, and depending on the circumstances may be unfair if it takes place later."

This falls into that category of legal statements which is completely accurate and utterly unhelpful. The reformers might as well have bitten the bullet and simply abolished the requirement to include any such statement.

Section 229(4) also stipulates that this statement may not be commented upon or qualified by anything else on the ballot paper, although presumably it may be accompanied by literature explaining the cryptic message. In *Newham LBC v NALGO* (1993) the employees were asked whether they were prepared to take strike action "on strike pay equivalent to full take-home pay", a formulation which passed without comment.

If industrial action short of a strike is contemplated as well as (or perhaps as a first stage before) a strike, then the two questions must be put separately on the ballot paper. Workers might be prepared to take part in an overtime ban (especially if this is not a breach of contract) but not an all-out strike. In *Post Office v UCW* (1990) the union asked members if they would be "willing to take industrial action up to and including strike action . . .". The Court of Appeal held that this rolled-up question did not comply with the requirements and rendered the ballot invalid.

There is no requirement that the union should state on the ballot paper what the dispute is about, although this is recommended by the Code of Practice. In *London Underground v NUR* (1989) the union balloted its members on four issues. The employer argued that this was invalid because three of the topics were no longer "live" issues between the parties, and that in any case the union should have asked the question separately in relation to each issue. The court held that the union was entitled to ask a single question in relation to separate issues, but only if the issues were all trade dispute issues within the meaning of TULRCA, s.244. This includes the requirement that they be matters of actual dispute.

Because of fears that shop stewards might jump the gun and use a "yes" vote to call instant industrial action before senior officials had decided if this was what they wanted to do, the ballot paper must now contain a statement of who is entitled to call industrial action in the event of a majority being in favour, and the action will not receive immunity unless that person calls the action (TULRCA, s.233). In the first case to reach the Court of Appeal on this provision, *Tanks & Drums Ltd v TGWU* (1991), the union had nominated its general secretary as having authority to call a strike. Negotiations with the employer had been led by the union's district organiser. Two weeks after a ballot in favour, the district official sought and obtained the general secretary's permission to implement action if a better offer was not forthcoming after a meeting with the employer the following day. As no further offer was made, the strike went ahead. The employer sued for an interim injunction claiming that the general secretary had in effect delegated his power to decide. The court held that this was not a blanket delegation, and that the permission of the general secretary was specific enough to the particular events to warrant holding that he was the person who had called the action, as required by the legislation. This seems sensible, particularly in a union as large as the TGWU, where the general secretary is unlikely to be personally involved in every dispute.

Conduct of the ballot

13–018 As a result of TURERA, ballots on industrial action must now be fully postal, with members enabled to vote at no cost to themselves (TULRCA, s.230). There is an exception for merchant seamen. The result must be reported to members as soon as possible (although individual notification is not necessary). More onerous is the requirement (s.231A) that notice of the result must also be given to all affected employers.

When the result is effective

13–019 The result must be promulgated to members as soon as reasonably practicable. For the action to attract trade dispute immunity, it is only necessary that there is a bare majority of those voting in favour (and a bare majority on each question if there are two: *West Midlands Travel v TGWU* (1994)). In practice the percentage turn-out and the size of the majority are most useful indicators to union officials as to what realistically they can hope to achieve, and most ballots tend to result in a vote in favour of action. The existence of a vote in favour can also be useful in convincing an employer that the union and the workers are serious about the issue, and can thus be a useful bargaining tool. These factors help to explain why the union movement largely dropped opposition to the principle of ballots before strikes, and why the Code of Practice exhorts unions to ballot only when they genuinely intend to call action.

Period of validity

13–020 Union officials cannot keep a mandate for industrial action in their back pocket indefinitely. Circumstances change, and it cannot be assumed that members will remain of the same mind for too long. Hence TULRCA, s.234 originally provided that action was only protected if it commenced within four weeks of the result being announced. The dispute over deregulation of the docks in 1989 revealed an anomaly in this limit. The TGWU got a vote in favour of industrial action but was prevented by interlocutory injunction from starting it. By the time the House of Lords set aside the injunction (*Associated British Ports v TGWU* (1989)) the four weeks had expired and a new ballot had to be held. By the time that was done, the deregulation had passed into law and the action was ineffective. The Employment Act 1990 therefore amended the law so that where action is held up because of legal proceedings the union may apply to the court for an order that the four-week limit be suspended for the duration. The court must consider whether the ballot still represents the views of the members or whether an event is likely to happen which would make members vote differently (*e.g.* a revised pay offer). The provision has been criticised because of the discretionary nature of the court's power, and because it is only applicable if the suspension would not take the start of the action beyond 12 weeks from the ballot. In keeping with the policy of encouraging the settlement of disputes, the Employment Relations Act 1999 removes the absolute necessity for unions to commence action within four weeks in order to retain validity even if negotiations with the employer are ongoing. TULRCA, s.234(1) now allows for the ballot to remain effective for up to eight weeks, if that is agreed between the employer and the union.

Under TURERA reforms, unions have to give employers seven days' notice of the date on which any action will commence (TULRCA, s.234A). If the action is to be discontinuous, such as a series of one-day strikes, there must be seven days' notice of each day on which action will take place, thus removing the element of surprise which has been a powerful weapon for trade unions. This has the effect of reducing by at least a week the "window" within which action can lawfully be called. If the recommendation in the Code of Practice were adopted, that unions should wait until they have received the scrutineer's report before implementing the action, unions would find themselves with almost no room to manoeuvre.

What happens if the employer offers to negotiate after the action has actually started, on condition that the action is suspended, but then talks break down? This is exactly what happened in *Monsanto plc v TGWU* (1987). The Court of Appeal considered that union officials should have the flexibility to be able to suspend action temporarily, and held that in these circumstances it was not necessary to re-ballot members. In that case the suspension was just under two weeks long. However, now it would be necessary to give seven days' notice to restart. In *Post Office v UCW* (1990) a ballot in September 1988 was followed by industrial action which lasted until December. No action took place between January and April; in May the union decided to restart the action and a strike took place in September 1989. While the dispute was over the same issue, the Court of Appeal held that it was a new and disconnected campaign and that a fresh ballot was needed. The question is not one of strict time limits but whether in fact the action can be regarded as part of the same campaign; clearly the more time that has passed, the harder it will be to convince a court that it is. In *Secretary of State for Scotland v Scottish Prison Officers' Association* (1991), the union called on members to hold meetings in working hours without permission one week after the ballot result. In fact, most officers sought and were granted permission by prison governors to hold the meetings. In the fifth week after the ballot, the union told members not to admit prisoners at the weekends. It was claimed that the first action was not a breach of contract, because permission had been given, and that the second action was outside the time limit. The Court of Session held that the union's instruction was an inducement to break contracts and it was not really relevant whether it was successful or not. Thus it was strongly arguable that the action had started within four weeks, and no interim injunction was awarded.

Action for prohibited reasons

13–021 The last method to be used to limit the ambit of lawful industrial action during the 1980s was the removal of immunity from disputes over particular issues – those which particularly exercised the Conservative Government at the time of their introduction. In the early part of the 1980s this was the closed shop. Later unofficial industrial action became the prime bugbear. The result of legislating on specific topics led to an odd asymmetry in the statutes, since some topics are included in the definition of trade dispute under TULRCA, s.244, but no longer attract immunity because of later amendments. However, no alteration has been made since the return of a Labour administration in 1997.

Pressure to impose union membership and union recognition requirements

13–022 At the beginning of the 1980s, as fast as the Conservative Government extended the situations in which individuals could opt out of unions despite a closed shop agreement, so Labour-controlled councils devised new ways of trying to ensure high levels of union membership among the firms they contracted with. In principle we are all free to make contracts or not with whoever we please. Many Labour-controlled councils used their freedom to decline to enter contracts with employers who did not recognise a trade union or who did not have a closed shop arrangement with a trade union. Given the enormous worth of public contracts, they could be very influential, so action was taken in the Employment Act 1982. Now TULRCA, ss.144–145 and 186–187 render void any terms in a contract which require the other party to recognise a union or to maintain a closed shop among its workers. More to the point for present purposes, sections 222(3) and 225 provide that there will be no immunity for industrial action designed to get such terms inserted into contracts between employers.

Pressure to maintain the closed shop

13–023 The process started with the above reforms in 1982 was taken a step further by the Employment Act 1988, which removed immunity from industrial action if the reason or one of the reasons for it was to pressurise the employer into discriminating against non-union members (now TULRCA, s.222). Oddly, section 244(1)(e) still states that "the membership or non-membership of a trade union on the part of a worker" can be the subject-matter of a trade dispute.

Reinstatement of strikers

13–024 As part of the campaign against unofficial industrial action, unfair dismissal claims by unofficial strikers were ruled out in 1990 (see above, para. 12–014). Under TULRCA, s.223, industrial action which is taken even partly because of the dismissal of unofficial strikers will have no immunity. This sits uneasily with the inclusion of "termination or suspension of employment" as one of the trade dispute topics in section 244(1)(b).

Liability of Unions in Tort

Before *Taff Vale v ASRS* (1901) union funds were effectively immune from **13–025**
action because the practical difficulties in suing the union were too great.
After the Trade Union Act 1906, designed to restore and clarify the
pre-1901 position, union funds were effectively immune because the Act
bestowed an almost complete immunity from liability in tort. The Donovan
Commission thought that unions should have complete immunity only
when acting in contemplation or furtherance of a trade dispute, but under
the Industrial Relations Act 1971 immunity was removed altogether. In
1974, TULRA repealed the Industrial Relations Act and restored in effect
the 1906 position with some minor alterations. This lasted until the
Employment Act 1982, which abolished the total immunity of trade unions
from actions in tort.

Was total immunity ever justified? The principal argument in favour is
that, without this immunity, a union is at risk of having its funds wiped out
in just one strike. Thus, if there ought to be a freedom to strike, then the
law ought to provide conditions under which the freedom can be enjoyed in
practice. Against this view, much play was made of the fact that by 1974 no
other body, not even the Crown, had such extensive immunity as trade
unions; and the image was presented of powerful bodies able to inflict
damage at will at no risk to themselves. The line adopted by the
Conservative Government was that there was nothing wrong with expecting
unions to play by the same rules as individuals, and their immunity should
be similarly limited.

Accordingly, the Employment Act 1982 took away the total immunity
and gave unions the same immunity as individuals (now TULRCA, s.20).
However, in a partial recognition of the argument in favour of total
immunity, section 22 lays down limits on the amount of damages which can
be awarded against a union in any one action. The maxima are related to
the size of the union: £10,000 if the union has fewer than 5,000 members;
£50,000 if the union has between 5,000 and 25,000 members; £125,000 if
there are between 25,000 and 100,000 members; and £250,000 if it has
100,000 members or more. Political funds and provident funds (*i.e.* those
used to pay benefits to members) are not available for satisfying awards of
damages, provided that the rules of the fund preclude it being used to
finance industrial action. According to *News Group Newspapers v SOGAT
'82* (1986), if rules are drafted appropriately, branch funds will not belong
to the union and thus will not be available for judgments against the union.
However, if more than one employer sues the union in respect of the same
industrial action, each will be entitled to damages up to the limit; also the
limits are not applicable to fines for contempt, which swiftly became
common when unions first responded to the change in the law. For
example, in the Stockport Messenger dispute in 1984, the NGA was
ordered to pay £100,000 damages, but was fined £675,000 for contempt.
Thus the limits have not been especially noticeable as a protective device,
which may account for the fact that it has never been felt necessary to
uprate them since 1982, although the Secretary of State has power to do so.

Of course, a trade union is a legal construct and cannot actually "do" anything in reality: a trade union can only be regarded as acting when certain human agents do things in its name or on its behalf. So once the immunity was removed, the question was immediately posed: whose acts would render the union liable in tort? When this question arose under the Industrial Relations Act, the courts answered it by applying the usual principles of vicarious liability. This was criticised on the grounds that trade unions are not "top-down" hierarchical organisations, with clear lines of command and control: the leaders govern by consent and follow as often as they lead. Thus in the leading case, *Heaton's Transport v TGWU* (1973) the House of Lords held that the custom and practice of the union gave shop stewards a general implied authority to institute blacking by their members. This may be seen as resulting from the non-hierarchical structure of the union and the fact that its rule-book was drawn up with the members rather than with lawyers in mind. But to hold the union liable vicariously for acts so far down the line (remembering that a union like the TGWU has hundreds if not thousands of shop stewards) was to make it extremely vulnerable to action in a situation where its real ability to control might be in doubt.

13–026 Nevertheless, once their immunity was again removed in 1982, this case was once more relevant authority on the vicarious liability of a union at common law. However, the position is more complicated than this. TULRCA, s.20 lays down a statutory test of vicarious liability where the union is sued for inducing breach of contract, interference with contract, intimidation and conspiracy, or for contempt of an order arising from such proceedings. However, where any other torts are involved, common law vicarious liability will apply, and may yield different results. Under TULRCA, s.20, the union is liable if the action complained of as constituting the tort was authorised or endorsed by the president or general secretary or the principal executive committee. This is entirely reasonable, for these are the people who carry out the day-to-day administration of the union. It makes sense also for the union to be liable, as it is, if the action is authorised or endorsed by someone specifically empowered by the rules to do so. In terms of those under their control, it was originally provided that the union would also be liable for any act done by an employed official, or any committee to whom that employed official reported, subject to a defence if the senior officials had repudiated the act in question. "Employed" in this context meant employed by the union. So if a union had a full-time regional official (an employee of the trade union) the union would be liable if that official called action. If, as is usually the case, the regional official reported to a regional committee, made up principally of lay union officials who were not employees of the union, a decision of that committee could still make the union liable, unless it was repudiated by the centre. But if a shop steward called out her members, the union would not usually have been liable under the law as originally framed. This is because a shop steward is not an employee of the union but a lay official, someone who has got involved with the union at her place of work and taken on union office. Also, a shop steward is not usually empowered by the union's rules to call industrial action (despite the decision in *Heaton's Transport*, above).

376

A main aim of the Employment Act 1990 was to reduce the incidence of unofficial industrial action, especially after an outbreak of unofficial action on the London Underground in the summer of 1989. While it is a defining characteristic of unofficial action that the union does not support it, the Government was evidently of the view that not all unofficial action was as unofficial as all that, and that with a little exertion, the union could do something about it. Hence TULRCA, s.20(2)(c) now provides that the union is liable for the actions of *any* official and of *any* committee of the union. Furthermore, an act is done by an official if it is done by any group of which he is a member – regardless of whether the group is recognised by the union or not. At the same time, the requirements for a valid repudiation were tightened: the union (via its president, general secretary or principal executive committee) must now give notice of its repudiation in writing as soon as reasonably practicable, not only to the delinquent officials, but also to every member of the union who is or might take part in the action, and to the employers of these members.

It goes without saying that subsequent conduct inconsistent with this statement will render the "repudiation" inoperative. In *Express & Star v NGA* (1986) the General Secretary of the union sent out three circulars stating that action should cease; but one branch official announced at a meeting in the presence of a national official that he had received a "nod and a wink" that they need not be distributed and another promised strike pay in the presence of a regional official. The case concerned common law vicarious liability, but affords an example of the kind of conduct that would presumably be considered inconsistent with repudiation. The end result is that unions may be vicariously liable for the actions of an enormous range of people, some of whom it cannot realistically be said to control.

Remedies

It used to be said that employers were not interested in suing for damages, **13–027** but in getting industrial action called off. That statement needs some qualification now. In the 1980s it became possible to sue unions instead of the individual officials, and industrial action became unlawful in many more situations. This statutory encouragement to sue for damages was taken up increasingly by employers throughout the decade. Nevertheless it remains the case that the primary remedy sought by an employer faced with industrial action is an injunction to stop the action. However, all legal proceedings take time: it is not at all uncommon to hear of cases coming on for trial years after a writ was first issued. This is not much use to a struck company: it needs an instant remedy; and the law provides it in the form of the interlocutory or interim injunction. This is designed as a holding operation: it is an order to preserve the status quo until there is a full trial of the action in situations where the plaintiffs can give sufficient evidence that if this does not happen they will not in the long run be adequately compensated by damages if they should win the final trial.

It should be noted that the employer will never be able to get an injunction to stop the employees breaking their contracts of employment, because there can be no specific performance of contracts of employment

(TULRCA, s.236; see above, para. 12–002). What will be sought is an injunction to stop the organisation of the industrial action, which will usually have the effect that everyone will return to work.

Most reported cases on trade disputes are in fact reports of interlocutory (interim) proceedings. This is unfortunate in some ways, because the time constraints do not permit the most thorough analysis of the law by either counsel or the court, yet full trials are so rare that reports of interlocutory proceedings are often the only available authorities.

An interlocutory injunction may be granted on an *ex parte* application as well as after *inter partes* proceedings. If it is an *ex parte* application, only the plaintiff is represented. Evidence is given by affidavit (sworn statement) only, and witnesses are not called for examination. While the plaintiff should disclose anything favourable to the other side, it is inevitable that the story the court gets is going to be rather one-sided. Thus an *ex parte* application should only be granted in cases of extreme urgency, and then only until there can be a hearing *inter partes* (between the parties).

At an *inter partes* hearing both parties will be represented, but may not have had much time for preparation – the defendant usually less than the plaintiff. The rules only require two days' notice to be given to the other side. Furthermore, while the court has a power to order cross-examination on the evidence, this happens comparatively rarely and most evidence is again likely to be given by affidavit.

13–028   What must the claimant prove to get an injunction? In *American Cyanamid v Ethicon* (1975), the House of Lords held that the claimant must show that the claim is not frivolous or vexatious and that there is indeed a serious case to be tried. Provided that this can be established, the court should then consider only the balance of convenience in deciding whether or not to make an order – and of course the balance of convenience is usually in favour of the status quo. This decision represented a relaxation of the law; previously the claimant had had to show at least a *prima facie* case which was likely to be successful at a full trial. It was feared that the new standard would work against trade unions, since the law is so complex that in any particular case it would be a poor lawyer who could not raise at least an arguable case that industrial action was likely to be unlawful, and the balance of convenience in a strike situation is practically bound to be on the side of the employer. An attempt to even up the odds was therefore made by TULRCA, s.221, so that the court is required specifically to consider the likely outcome at a full hearing, including whether the union will be able to establish a defence under section 219. Opinions differ as to whether this has redressed the balance sufficiently. The history of the litigation between the TGWU and Associated British Ports over the deregulation of the docks in 1989 affords a good example of weak claims being held sufficient for the grant of injunctions which had the desired effect of delaying action until it was futile (*Associated British Ports v TGWU* (1989)).

Having been used to a situation where they were rarely sued successfully, trade unions did not easily come to terms with the new legal requirements in the 1980s. Thus when employers were successful in gaining injunctions, as in the Stockport Messenger dispute in 1984, the Wapping dispute in 1986, the seamen's dispute in 1988 (or when members gained injunctions, as in the miners' strike of 1984–85), the reaction of the unions was to ignore the orders, or at least to hasten slowly to put them into effect. This led to several unions being held to be in contempt of court and to their having heavy fines levied against them. As noted already, these fines could be unlimited in amount, and some were enormous. Where there is any doubt as to whether the union can or will pay the fine, the assets of the union are liable to sequestration, as happened to the miners, seamen and others.

Contempt proceedings and sequestration orders should not be regarded as remedies for employers, since they are more to do with enforcing the orders of the court, and therefore to do with upholding the authority of the court. However, it seems that in the 1980s, the swift and severe punishment exacted for infraction of court orders taught unions a lesson the hard way. Today most senior union officers are anxious not to bankrupt their organisations by embarking on clearly unlawful action. However, the lesson was not at first understood among the members, who regarded the failure of the senior officials to back action as at best pusillanimous and at worst as disloyal and an indication of remoteness from ordinary members. The result was the increase of unofficial action which the Employment Act 1990 was meant to address, and the discomfort of many union officials who find themselves between a rock and a hard place.

Picketing

Picketing usually involves consideration of the criminal law as well as civil, **13–029** but the problems encountered in dealing with this difficult area do not stem from this cross-over. There are three main problems. Firstly, it is unclear whether or not the simple act of picketing (unaccompanied by violence, obstruction, large numbers, etc.) is unlawful or not. Secondly, there is no clear distinction between picketing and public demonstrations. Thirdly, while the law gives protection to pickets only for the purpose of "peacefully obtaining or communicating information, or peacefully persuading any person to work or abstain from working" (TULRCA, s.220), it is the case that pickets usually see their object as stopping people from working – by prevention if not by persuasion.

Why picket? From the trade union point of view, picketing is necessary to ensure the effectiveness of strike action. It is not enough to call the members out on strike; an effort must be made to see that the weaker brethren comply. Also, if the strike aims to shut down the employer's operation, it will work more quickly if the employer cannot get supplies in and out, and has no possibility of using alternative labour. On this view, if you accept the need for a freedom to strike, then you should accept the need for a freedom to picket as well. On the other hand, many would argue that no one should have the right to stop others going about their lawful business. It may be noted that the law does not in fact allow this. It could also be argued that picketing is a nineteenth-century tactic which has been out of date ever since motorised transport became common, and that it is time British unions started devising new tactics as has happened elsewhere.

Probably most people would say that people should be allowed to picket to put their point of view, but not to coerce other people. As with many liberal positions, this is actually quite difficult to translate into practice. For example, I may wish to break the strike because I am not in sympathy with the aims: but I do not want to have to walk past a line of people shouting abuse, or taking my name to display on a "roll of dishonour", or even staring at me sullenly. Assuming that there is not the slightest physical danger to me from the pickets, am I being coerced in any of these situations if I chicken out? Those who think that this does amount to coercion may care to reflect on the fact that it is still regarded as nothing out of the way for a woman to have to put up with stares and comments when she passes a building site. Is this really different?

Civil liability for picketing

13–030 If pickets are successful in their persuasion, they are certain to induce breaches of contracts of employment and commercial contracts. If they turn back employees of the employer in dispute, they induce breaches of their contracts of employment. If they turn back a lorry trying to make a delivery, the possibilities are greater. They will induce a breach of the lorry driver's contract of employment, and probably a breach of the commercial contract under which the supply was due. If the lorry driver is employed by a road haulage company which was contracted by the supplier to make the delivery, then the pickets will induce a breach of the contract of carriage as well as of the supply contract.

Thus at common law, pickets could be liable for the whole panoply of economic torts. However, the individual pickets, and the union which organises their activity will receive the basic protection of TULRCA, s.219, provided that they act within the terms of section 220. As noted already, this means that they must limit themselves to peaceful persuasion, and they must be acting in contemplation or furtherance of a trade dispute. The major restriction, however, introduced by a 1980 amendment, is that pickets will only have this immunity if they are either picketing at or near their own place of work (or where they used to work, if they have been sacked) or the picket is a union official accompanying members who she represents, who are picketing their own place of work. There is an exception for workers who do not have a single place of work (*e.g.* sales representatives), or who work at a place which it is not practicable to picket (*e.g.* an oil rig). They may picket the place from which their work is administered.

This provision suggests that there was an intention that everyone should have somewhere to picket: it has not, however, been so interpreted in practice. *News Group Newspapers v SOGAT '82* (1986) was one of the cases resulting from Rupert Murdoch's move from Fleet Street to Wapping. His company, the claimant in the action, published the *Sun*, the *News of the World*, *The Times* and the *Sunday Times*. When the unions refused to agree to the move, and began strike action, all those taking part (some 5,500 workers) were dismissed. They picketed Wapping – but of course they had been employed in central London. It would have been quite pointless for them to have picketed their former places of work, but the court held that

380

because they were not picketing at or near their own place of work they were not protected (*cf.* also *Union Traffic v TGWU* (1989)). However, there was a welcome recognition of realities in *Rayware Ltd v TGWU* (1989). The employer's premises were situated on a small industrial estate, which was all private property. The distance from the public highway to their premises was a little over two-thirds of a mile. The pickets would have been trespassing had they gone to the plant entrance, so they picketed at the entrance to the estate instead. It was held that this was "at or near" their place of work.

As indicated above, if picketing is successful, the contracts disrupted may well include contracts of employment with employers who are not parties to the dispute (the contracts of the supplier's or road haulier's employees) – which of course constitutes secondary action. But this is the one exceptional situation where secondary action is allowed. Under TULRCA, s.224(1), secondary action continues to be immune if it occurs as a result of lawful picketing.

So much for the economic torts. As we saw in relation to industrial **13–031** action in general, other torts may be committed in the course of the action for which no protection is given by section 219. This is particularly so in the case of picketing. Trespass is one which has already been mentioned. Pickets must take care to stay off property belonging to the employer. This means in practice gathering on the highway outside. Is this trespass to the highway? In *Hubbard v Pitt* (1975), a leading case on picketing which, however, involved a consumer rather than an industrial picket, Lord Denning expressed the view that pickets might well be trespassing on the highway, but as a civil matter, it would be for the highway authority to take action, which is a fairly unlikely contingency. However, trespass to the highway would only occur if there were an unreasonable use of the highway, and it seems clear that it is reasonable to use the highway other than for passage and re-passage. (See also *DPP v Jones* (1999), where the House of Lords held that a peaceful assembly on the highway was not trespassory.)

The issues were examined in relation to the Wapping dispute in *News Group Newspapers v SOGAT '82* (1986). At Wapping, the union stationed six official pickets identified with armbands at the outer gate of the premises for 24 hours a day. In addition, between, 50 and 200 demonstrators attended each day, usually at the times at which employees arrived for and left work. On Wednesday and Saturday nights, and sometimes at other times, from 700 to 7,000 people rallied at Tower Hill to march to Wapping, where they would be addressed in a square near the works. The rallies were organised by the union; the union denied organising the demonstrations but Stuart-Smith J. considered it at least arguable that it had done so. Evidence was given that pickets shouted abuse and used obscene language. Much was directed at individuals. The registration numbers of cars entering the works were noted. Employees complained of being followed home, of cars being vandalised, and of threats. On one occasion a coffin was suspended from a lamp post outside the works. There were reports of missiles being thrown, and that demonstrators sometimes rushed the outer gate to try and prevent lorries going through. The union condemned most of this behaviour.

The employer sought an injunction on grounds of nuisance, obstruction of the highway, interference with trade and business and intimidation. Stuart-Smith J. held that obstruction of the highway was capable of being a public nuisance, actionable in tort at the suit of a private claimant on proof of special damage beyond that suffered by the general public. But he considered that a march or a meeting would not necessarily amount to an unreasonable obstruction, although on the facts here the activities did. Private nuisance, that is, wrongful interference with enjoyment of property rights, was also established, because of extra costs of transport and security and staff turnover resulting from the campaign. As to intimidation, the judge held that swearing, abuse and even general threats such as "We'll get you!" did not amount to a threat of violence, but the serious threats that had occurred here were capable of amounting to intimidation. Interference with contract was also made out, and since the picketing went beyond the bounds of section 220 there was no immunity.

13–032   In *Thomas v NUM* (1986) Scott J. had suggested that there was a tort of harassment, which would be established where there was unreasonable interference with one's right to use the highway (as could occur if followed by abusive persons). In this case it was argued that no such tort existed: Stuart-Smith J. found it unnecessary to express an opinion on this. In subsequent cases not concerned with picketing there was a conflict of authority as to whether a common law tort of harassment existed and, if so, as to its ambit (*Khorasandjian v Bush* (1993), *Burris v Azadani* (1995), *Hunter v Canary Wharf* (1997)). This has largely been overtaken by the Protection from Harassment Act 1997, which created a statutory tort of harassment. The tort is committed by either pursuing a course of conduct which the defendant knows or ought to know amounts to harassment or which the defendant knows or ought to know causes fear of violence in another person. Conduct is defined so as to include speech, and a course of conduct means on more than one occasion. It seems clear that this tort could be committed in the course of picketing. In addition to compensation (which can include damages for anxiety and distress), claimants may seek injunctive relief.

News Group Newspapers v SOGAT '82 is also interesting in that the judge addressed the issue of the distinction if any between demonstrating and picketing. Having recourse to a dictionary definition as well as the terms of section 220, he was satisfied that the demonstrators in this case were properly to be regarded as pickets. This was not the case, however, for those involved in the rallies and marches – unless they turned to picketing after the rally had dispersed.

13–033   The final difficult issue in this case, as with similar cases arising out of the 1984–85 miners' strike, is whether or not the union is properly to be held responsible for everything which happens on the picket line. The Wapping dispute, because it was happening in central London at more social hours than the miners' dispute, attracted the attention of various political groups and wholly unaffiliated people who could hardly be said to be under the control of the union. This was recognised by the judge, who held that the union was not liable simply for organising activities in the course of which torts occurred, even if the commission of torts was entirely foreseeable. However, if, as here, the union continued to organise similar activities again and again, knowing the torts would be committed, and particularly if it had taken no steps to control the situation, then it must be taken to have authorised what happened. The judge noted that, although the print unions were well known for having some of the most severe disciplinary powers over their members, there was no evidence that pickets who had over-stepped the mark had been punished or even prevented from picketing again.

In *Thomas v NUM* (1985) Scott J. expressed the view that picketing outside the ambit of TULRCA, s.220, was not of itself tortious; that is, torts may be committed in the course of picketing, but the mere activity of picketing is not tortious so that it requires section 220 in order to make it lawful. This seems to be a correct statement of the law, and is a welcome clarification. However, the judge expressed the view that picketing at someone's home would constitute private nuisance, regardless of the numbers involved.

Does the presence of large numbers by itself (*i.e.* even if they are completely peaceful) constitute a tort? There are suggestions that this is so in *Thomas v NUM*, on the basis that large numbers are very likely to obstruct and to be intimidatory. But it is submitted that this should be treated with caution. Once, in the United States, I went to a gallery opening which was picketed by former employees of the industrialist who owned the pictures. By leaflet and placard, the pickets made it clear that they were not trying to dissuade us from attending, but wanted us to be aware of the facts about their former boss and to write letters about it, or perhaps to contribute to their campaign fund by post. Surely if there were large numbers of pickets engaged on such a purpose, the fact of large numbers would not render their conduct tortious?

The issue about numbers has been muddied because of the Code of Practice on Picketing originally issued by the Secretary of State in 1980. Like other Codes, it does not impose any legal obligations, but it is to be taken into account in any relevant proceedings. The Code recommends that,

> "the organisers should ensure that in general the number of pickets does not exceed six at any entrance to, or exit from, a workplace; frequently a smaller number will be appropriate" (para. 51).

Many have criticised the Code for in effect legislating by the back door. Certainly the figure of six has come to be treated as if it were a legal requirement, being used in court orders to unions on picketing, and being referred to by Scott J. in *Thomas v NUM* in support of his statement that a larger number was likely to be intimidatory. The Code on Picketing was revised in 1992. The revised version recommends that pickets at an entrance used also by other firms should not ask those employees to join the strike, that picketing should be as near to the workplace as possible, that pickets should not claim to be official unless organised and endorsed by the union, and that they should not jeopardise activities essential to the maintenance of important plant and machinery.

Criminal liability for picketing

13–034 When feelings run high and picket lines become violent, as happened in the Wapping dispute, clearly all sorts of criminal offences can be committed, ranging from insulting behaviour to grievous bodily harm. (During the miners' strike it was reported that police told pickets at one colliery that shouting "scabs" or "blacklegs" at working miners would be considered insulting behaviour. After negotiation, it was agreed that it would be all right for them to shout "bounders"!)

However, even if a picket line is entirely peaceful, it may still fall foul of the criminal law. The two most common offences with which pickets have been charged are obstruction of the highway and obstruction of a police officer in the execution of his duty. The two frequently go together: if a police officer considers that pickets are obstructing the highway and they refuse to obey an order to move, they will certainly be run in for obstructing the police officer. On the basis that using the highway for passage and re-passage is lawful, in *Tynan v Balmer* (1967) 40 men were led round in a circle in front of the factory gates. It had the effect of obstructing the entrance and they were told to stop by the police officer on duty. The court agreed that this was an improper use of the highway and that they were properly convicted of obstructing the police officer by refusing to desist.

The police are not infallible nor do they have unlimited powers. They must have reasonable grounds for their belief that an offence is being committed (*Piddington v Bates* (1960)). However, the courts have shown themselves very sensitive to the fact that they are judging with hindsight a situation that required a swift decision, and are fairly reluctant to gainsay the assessment of the acting officer. Since the Code of Practice, the police are apt to consider more than six pickets at an entrance as constituting obstruction.

In *Broome v DPP* (1974) a picket failed to persuade a lorry driver not to enter a site, so he stood in front of the lorry and refused to move when asked to do so by a police officer. He was then arrested and charged with obstructing the highway. There was no anger or violence and the whole incident lasted only about nine minutes. The magistrates therefore acquitted him, saying that this was not an unreasonable time to delay someone in exercise of the right to picket. The House of Lords pointed out that there is no such right, only a freedom to do so, and he should have been convicted. As noted already, there is no right to stop a person or vehicle if they are unwilling to stop. The Labour Government had plans to introduce a right to stop vehicles in the Employment Protection Act 1975, but finally dropped them, not least because of the difficulties such a right might give rise to in practice.

It should be clear from what has been said so far that relations with the police are in practice of the utmost importance. Sometimes the police will stop vehicles to allow pickets to talk to the drivers, provided the pickets agree that they will then not try to obstruct someone who still wants to enter. The question of what the police are prepared to permit in terms of obstruction of the highway is crucially important. Given the strong political and emotional overtones of some industrial action, it is worth considering whether it is right to put the police in this position, particularly since they are meant to be impartial.

Following the miners' strike and around the time of a number of bitter **13–035** disputes arising from the de-recognition of unions in some parts of the newspaper printing industry, the Public Order Act 1986 was passed. The Act replaced the old common law offences of riot, rout, unlawful assembly and affray; but of most direct relevance to picketing was the introduction of new general powers to control processions and public assemblies. Under sections 11–13, the police must be given advance notice of processions and can impose conditions if they think it necessary to avoid serious public disorder, serious damage to property or serious disruption to the life of the community. If the police believe that these powers are insufficient to prevent serious public disorder, they may apply to the council for the procession to be banned altogether. Under section 14, the senior police officer can impose conditions on the holding of any public assembly on similar grounds. A public assembly is defined as an assembly of 20 or more people in a public place which is wholly or partly open to the air. These provisions have attracted criticism on the grounds that civil liberties relating to freedom of speech should not be liable to restriction because of inconvenience to the public (which, it is feared, is what "serious disruption to the life of the community" may come to mean in practice). It is true that people should be able to live and go about their business in peace, but in a society that values freedom, it is argued that restrictions on such an important freedom as the right to demonstrate should only be countenanced if there are very compelling reasons for doing so.

Specific crimes relating to picketing were laid down in the Conspiracy and Protection of Property Act 1875. These are still in force (TULRCA, s.241) and were used fairly extensively in the miners' strike. The offences are committed by those who try to compel someone else to do, or not to do something (like working) without legal authority by means of:

(1) using violence towards that person, or his or her immediate family;
(2) persistently following the person around;
(3) hiding their tools, clothing or other property;
(4) "watching or besetting" their home or place of business;
(5) following the other person in the street with two or more persons in a disorderly manner.

The most common charge under this section is "watching and besetting". In plain English, watching seems to be enough for this, and since it can be committed at a place of business, its potential for wide application to picketing is obvious. Hence it becomes important to know whether it has been done "wrongfully and without legal authority", for only then is the criminal offence made out. It now seems clear that an action must be independently tortious or criminal before it will also constitute a criminal offence under section 241 (*Thomas v NUM* (1985)). Thus attendance that is lawful under section 220 is clearly not an offence, and attendance outside

385

section 220 would have to be shown to be tortious or criminal on other grounds before section 241 applied. The Protection from Harassment Act 1997, discussed above, makes the two forms of harassment into criminal offences as well as torts. In addition to the penalties of fine or imprisonment the court has power to make a restraining order under the Act.

Other criminal liability in trade disputes

13–036   Some groups of workers are subject to special rules making it a criminal offence for them to take industrial action. The police and the armed forces are obvious examples; it is true also of merchant seamen while at sea. Prison officers are the latest group for whom organising industrial action will be a criminal offence, by virtue of the Criminal Justice and Public Order Act 1994. Reflecting the privatisation of public services, the ban on industrial action applies to private sector as well as public sector prison officers. In some countries, strikes in essential services are forbidden, or at least subject to stringent control, but while this has been considered from time to time in the United Kingdom, it has not happened yet. One essential service, communications, is subject to special regulation: it is an offence under the Post Office Act 1953 deliberately to detain or delay the mail and under the Telecommunications Act 1984 to interfere with messages sent by a public telecommunications system.

There is a provision which could potentially be used in a great many public service disputes and some private ones, but in practice it is never used, though included in the latest consolidation (TULRCA, s.240). It was introduced by the Conspiracy and Protection of Property Act and states that it is a criminal offence deliberately to break your contract of employment when you know or have reasonable cause to believe that the probable consequences will be to endanger human life, or cause serious bodily injury, or even to expose valuable property to injury or destruction. Clearly industrial action by hospital workers, ambulance drivers or the fire service could endanger life; and numerous strikes in all sorts of areas could expose valuable property to injury. Curiously, there are no recorded instances of its having been used. It seems that no government has been ready to risk the opprobrium of using it, or of repealing it. There are always public-spirited persons who are prepared to try and force the authorities to take action even if they have decided not to, but as a result of *Gouriet v UPOW* (1978) they cannot bring prosecutions unless they can show an interest beyond that of the general public.

13–037   Finally, in terms of criminal offences which might be committed in a trade dispute, there are those arising out of the wrongful occupation of premises. Workers sometimes use the sit-in or work-in as a tactic, especially when they are trying to oppose the closure of a workplace. If they are present without permission, they commit the tort of trespass, and if they use materials they find there, they would commit the tort of conversion. These are civil matters for which the employer would have to take action. However, if violence is used to gain entry to premises where someone is present on the premises opposing entry, then an offence is committed under the Criminal Law Act 1977, s.6, and if any trespassers have a weapon of offence, they commit an offence under section 8 of the same Act. Thus breaking into a factory at night in order to occupy it is not an offence if there is no one there, but it is if there is a caretaker in residence. It will be an offence if anyone has a weapon, regardless of whether there is someone on the premises.

14.   Health and Safety at Work

The problem of accidents at work is still enormous and shows little sign of **14–001** decreasing. There are over 200 deaths and 29,000 serious injuries at work annually. In addition to the human costs, the economic costs of this are terrific.

The main aim of the law should be to contribute so far as possible to the prevention of accidents. This is done by statutory regulation of standards to be observed, enforced by criminal sanctions. The other aim of the law is to ensure adequate compensation for employees whose injury at work is attributable to the fault of the employer or someone for whom the employer is responsible. This is done through the employee's common law claim for damages. As an understanding of the common law is a necessary starting point for the legislation on health and safety, the common law claims will be examined first and then the Health and Safety at Work Act 1974 and European Community legislation will be considered.

Employers' Liability at Common Law

Basis for the claim

There is some doubt as to whether the employee's claim for damages **14–002** against the employer sounds in contract or in tort or in both. Traditionally the employer's duty of care has been treated as a branch of the law of torts, and many cases regularly referred to in elucidation of the law of negligence involve employees suing their employer. On the other hand, where an employee was injured abroad it was held that he could base his claim against his employer in contract in order to be able to sue in England (*Matthews v Kuwait Bechtel Corp.* (1959)). More recently in *Scally v Southern Health and Social Services Board* (1991) the House of Lords held that a claim that the employer was in breach of the duty of care could be based on an implied term in the contract of employment (*cf.* also *Johnstone v Bloomsbury HA* (1991)). However, this may be explicable more in terms of the particular circumstances of the claim, which was not for personal injury. In particular, their Lordships were anxious to establish that the claimant would not be better off by suing in tort rather than in contract.

There is thus some support for the proposition that a claim that the employer is in breach of the duty of care owed to the employee may be treated either as an implied term of the contract of employment or as a particular application of the general duty of care that each one of us owes our neighbour under the principle of *Donoghue v Stevenson* (1932), but that in either case the content of the duty is the same.

If the result is likely to be the same, then it may be thought that it does not much matter whether it is seen as a contract claim or a tort claim. However, in tort, unlike contract, it is generally impossible to claim for economic loss. In *Scally v Southern Health & Social Services Board* (1991) doctors employed by the board claimed that it had been negligent in failing to draw to their attention an opportunity to buy extra benefits under the applicable pension scheme, so that they did not find out about it until too late. Clearly the loss was economic, but as the House of Lords treated the employer's duty as arising in contract, the problem of recovery for economic loss did not arise.

The facts were unusual in that the right to buy the extra benefits was contractual, but the employees could be excused for not knowing about it because it was not a term negotiated with them individually but introduced by statutory regulation. In these circumstances the House of Lords considered it was necessary to imply a term that the employer should draw the right to the employees' attention. This comparatively generous approach to what could be expected of employer and employee respectively may be contrasted with the decision of the Court of Appeal in *Reid v Rush & Tompkins* (1989) where the employee had been sent to work on a project in Ethiopia. While there he was injured in a road accident through the negligence of an unknown third party. As Ethiopia did not require compulsory third party insurance, it transpired that he was not insured against the accident. He claimed his employers had been negligent in failing to insure him or at least in failing to advise him that he was not insured, so that he could make his own arrangements. On these facts the Court of Appeal held that necessity did not require imposition of an implied term. One wonders, however, what the parties would have said if the officious bystander had been at hand to ask the pertinent question.

14–003   A possible disadvantage of the contract approach would be that it would be possible for the employer to exclude liability for breach. This was at issue in *Johnstone v Bloomsbury HA* (1991) where a junior hospital doctor argued that his hours of work, sometimes as high as 100 per week, were endangering his health. The contract required him to work a 40-hour week and then be on call for an unlimited amount of overtime, although this was not to average more than 48 hours a week extra. The Court of Appeal held that the effect of the clause was to compel the employee to assume any risks associated with working these hours, and this was in substance an exclusion clause within the meaning of the Unfair Contract Terms Act 1977. Thus the employer could in theory exclude liability for breach of the duty, but under the Unfair Contract Terms Act such an exclusion would be void in so far as it related to excluding liability for death or personal injury (s.2), and otherwise, if contained in a standard form contract, it would be valid only if reasonable (s.3).

The employee may claim against the employer at common law in two ways: either on the basis of vicarious liability, where the employee is injured through the fault of another employee for whom the employer is responsible; or on the basis of a breach of the employer's own direct duty to take reasonable care for the safety of employees. There is obviously a high degree of overlap between these two claims, the reason for which is historical. In the nineteenth century the courts evolved the "doctrine of common employment", which meant that by taking a position with an employer you were taken to consent to the risk of negligent action by other employees (compare the defence of *volenti* below, para. 14–019). The doctrine soon came to be thought of as unfair to employees, but was not finally abolished until the Law Reform (Personal Injuries) Act 1948. In the meantime, a way round it was devised by the development of the concept of a non-delegable duty of care owed directly by the employer to the employee. Today either route may be relied on.

Under the Employers' Liability (Compulsory Insurance) Act 1969 all employers should be insured against potential liability to employees for negligence, and failure to have current insurance is a criminal offence. Unfortunately, however, if an employer is in breach, the employee may be left without means of redress. This is what happened in *Richardson v Pitt-Stanley* (1995). The plaintiff had been injured at work because of his employer's breach of statutory duty, but the company was not insured and was unable to pay the damages. It went into liquidation. He attempted instead to sue the directors of the company, who were guilty of a criminal offence under the Act for the failure to insure, but the Court of Appeal held that the Act had not been intended to create civil liability for the breach, only criminal liability.

The direct duty of care

The duty of care owed directly by the employer to the employee may be an **14–004** implied term of the contract of employment, but its content can best be understood as a specialised version of the duty of care each one of us owes our neighbour (the person who may foreseeably be affected by our actions) under the principle of *Donoghue v Stevenson* (1932). The leading case on its explication is *Wilsons & Clyde Coal Co. v English* (1938), where Lord Wright described it as a threefold duty: to provide competent fellow employees, adequate plant and a safe system of work. While each case must be tested against the general question, whether the employer took reasonable care for the employee's safety, it is convenient to consider the content of the duty under these heads.

Competent fellow-employees

"Upon principle it seems to me that if, in fact, a fellow workman is **14–005** not merely incompetent but, by his habitual conduct is likely to prove a source of danger to his fellow employees, a duty lies fairly and squarely on the employers to remove that source of danger" (Streatfield J., *Hudson v Ridge Manufacturing* (1957)).

The injured employee broke his wrist when wrestled to the ground by another employee engaging in horseplay. The practical joker had had a reputation for this sort of thing for four years before this incident and the employer's lack of care was in failing to maintain discipline and prevent potentially dangerous conduct. There should be no problem in establishing a fair dismissal should the employer dismiss the delinquent employee in these circumstances, provided as always that a fair procedure is followed and that the action taken is reasonable. Where the employer does not know of the employee's propensity to injure others, there would be no breach of the direct duty of care; however, the employer might be vicariously liable instead for the employee's action, if it could be seen to be in the course of his employment (*Harrison v Michelin Tyres* (1985); contrast *Aldred v Nacanco* (1987)).

Safe plant and equipment

14–006 The employer is responsible for ensuring that the workplace is not dangerous and that tools, machinery and other equipment used by the employees are suitable for the task and are safe. The employers may not themselves have the expertise or facilities for checking equipment: in such a situation the duty will be discharged if the equipment is bought from a reputable manufacturer and then kept in good repair (*Davie v New Merton Board Mills* (1959)). However, in *Taylor v Rover* (1966) the employer was held liable when the employee was injured by a chisel splintering in use, because although the manufacturers were responsible for over-hardening the chisel, the employer knew that someone else had been injured in the same way, but failed to withdraw the chisels or to check them.

If the employer is not liable because the equipment was obtained from a reputable source and the fault lies in the manufacturing process, the employee can sue the manufacturer for negligence. This has its drawbacks, in that the employee may find it difficult to establish who is the manufacturer, or the manufacturer may have gone out of business. For this reason, the Employers' Liability (Defective Equipment) Act 1969 provides that the employer will be held liable if the defect in the equipment is attributable to the fault of a third party. The employer may, of course, join the manufacturer as a defendant to the proceedings, but the idea is that the employee should be allowed to pursue the person easiest to identify. It is not, however, strict liability. The employer will only be held liable if fault on the part of the third party can be established. Also, the Act applies only to defective equipment, and thus does not include oils, powders and other similar items which are also capable of causing injury. However, in *Coltman v Bibby Tankers* (1988) the House of Lords held that the word "equipment" was wide enough to include a ship of whatever size provided by the employers for use in their business. It was there alleged that the design and construction of a bulk carrier had been defective with the result that the vessel was unseaworthy, causing it to sink with all hands. A claim under the Employer's Liability (Defective Equipment) Act 1969 was permissible.

Safe system of work

It is up to the employer to ensure that the methods used to undertake the **14–007** work, the system of supervision and general organisation add up to a safe system of work. That this duty lies squarely on the employer, even where the worker is knowledgeable and experienced, was stressed by the House of Lords in *General Cleaning Contractors v Christmas* (1953). The employee, a window cleaner, was balancing on a sill cleaning a window when the sash fell on his hand, causing him to let go and fall. The employers provided safety belts, but there were no hooks on this building to attach them to. The employer argued that the employees were skilled and experienced and as well able as the employer to devise adequate precautions. Nevertheless the employer was held liable; while it may be reasonable to leave quite a lot to the discretion of skilled employees who are sent out to different premises, this particular danger was common and it called for a system to meet it. It was the employer's responsibility to provide that system.

General Cleaning Contractors v Christmas illustrates the point that the employer's duty of care applies not only when the workers are on the employer's premises, but also on the premises of third party customers and others. The customers may also have the general liabilities of occupiers under the Occupiers' Liability Acts 1957 and 1984, although an occupier is not liable for a foreseeable risk related to the job to be done which the contractors themselves should appreciate and guard against. The case is also instructive on the relevance of trade practice. Part of the employer's defence was that this method of cleaning windows was in general use in the trade. This certainly counts in the employer's favour. As Lord Reid put it:

> "A plaintiff who seeks to have condemned as unsafe a system of work which has been generally used for a long time in an important trade undertakes a heavy onus: if he is right it means that all, or practically all, the numerous employers in the trade have been substantially neglecting their duty to their men."

However, it is clear that in some circumstances it may be held that a trade practice is unsafe. Forty years on from *General Cleaning Contractors v Christmas* the Court of Appeal held that employers should simply embargo customers who do not have anchor points for a safety harness unless the window can be cleaned from the inside (*King v Smith* (1994)). In *Thompson v Smiths Shiprepairers* (1984) the claimant's was one of a selection of test cases involving 20,000 similar claims for industrial deafness. While this was regarded as simply an occupational hazard in the industry until 1963, from then on expert advice and protective devices were available which were reasonably effective against this risk. The employees claimed that they got no protection until the early 1970s. The employers argued that it was common practice to continue to ignore this risk, but it was held that they were in breach of duty in respect of injury suffered after 1963. Conversely, where it is trade practice to take a particular precaution, the employer who fails to do so is almost certain to be found to have acted negligently.

14-008 Other examples of changing standards can be seen in the recognition of new injuries caused by increasingly stressful working practices. *Pickford v ICI* (1998) was the first reported case recognising claims for repetitive strain injury (RSI). The claimant was a secretary who spent an unusual proportion of her time typing. The advent of word processors meant that typists were more likely to be typing for long spells without any break in activity, and in 1983 the Health and Safety Executive distributed an advisory booklet on avoiding health risks. In 1987 the company had warned typists who spent substantially all their time typing of the need to take rest breaks before their hands and arms got tired, but this information had not been passed to secretaries, because it was thought that their work was only about 50 per cent typing, interspersed with other duties. The Court of Appeal upheld the secretary's claim because the same advice had not been given to her. The House of Lords reversed, but on the grounds that in this case, the Court of Appeal should not have interfered with the trial judge's findings of fact. The possibility of claims for RSI was established.

In *Walker v Northumberland CC* (1995) it was held that the duty of care extends to preventing psychiatric damage as well as physical injury. In that case, a social services manager suffered two nervous breakdowns brought on by the stress caused through overload of work and the failure of his superiors to do anything to alleviate it. Colman J. held that the first breakdown was not foreseeable, but the second was entirely likely unless the employer took steps to change the situation. Because it had not, the council was held to be in breach of its duty to provide a safe system of work. While this is a landmark in that it is the first reported case of an employer being held liable for stress at work, it should be noted that an employee pursuing this claim may have problems, first, in showing that the psychiatric damage was caused by work rather than other personal problems and secondly, that it was foreseeable. Note that the claimant in *Walker v Northumberland CC* failed to persuade the court that his original breakdown was reasonably foreseeable by his employer.

Nevertheless, in the wake of *Walker v Northumberland CC*, claims for psychiatric injury based on exposure to unacceptable levels of stress became prevalent. In *Sutherland v Hatton* (2002) the Court of Appeal, giving the decision in four joined appeals, stated some limiting guidelines. The Court held that an employer was entitled to assume that an employee was able to withstand the normal pressures of the job and to take what the employee said about her own health at face value. It was only if there were indications which would lead a reasonable employer to realise that there was a problem that a duty to take action would arise. In terms of whether injury to an employee was foreseeable, the Court held that this did not depend on whether a person of reasonable fortitude would have been able to cope, as the employer's duty is to each employee individually. Thus the question is what was foreseeable in relation to this employee. In considering foreseeability, factors such as whether the workload was abnormally heavy, whether the work was particularly intellectually and emotionally demanding for this employee and the level of demands made compared with other employees would all be relevant. In judging whether the employer was in breach of the duty of care, the question of what options were available should be considered. However, if the only way of making the employee safe was to dismiss him, the Court of Appeal did not consider that the employer would be in breach of duty by letting the employee continue if she was willing to do so.

In *Frost v Chief Constable of South Yorkshire* (1999) the Court of Appeal was prepared to extend the employer's liability for psychiatric injury to the situation of police officers who suffered post-traumatic stress syndrome as a result of being on duty at the Hillsborough football stadium disaster in 1989. Their decision was reversed by the House of Lords (*White v Chief Constable of South Yorkshire* (1998), who denied that employees were in any different position from any other secondary victim of an accident who suffers nervous shock.

Use of safety equipment

Clearly an important aspect of establishing a safe system of work is the **14–009** provision of appropriate safety equipment: helmets, gloves, goggles, overalls, safety harnesses and guards. Is it enough if employers simply provide the equipment, or do they have an affirmative obligation to make sure that the employees actually use it? Sometimes use of particular safety equipment will be required by statutory regulation, so that both employer and employee risk criminal penalties if it is not used. But where there is no statutory requirement, the picture is less clear.

"I deprecate any tendency to treat the relationship of employer and skilled workman as equivalent to that of a nurse and an imbecile child" declared Viscount Simonds in 1959 (*Smith v Austin Lifts*), arguing that provision of the equipment was enough. Those of us brought up in a more paternalistic society may feel that this is unduly robust. We do not always do those things that we know are good for us, especially if it is at all inconvenient to do so.

The high point of the rugged individualist view is found in *McWilliams v Arrol* (1962). A steel erector fell 70 feet to his death. At the time of the accident he was not wearing a safety belt, and indeed, none was actually provided at the site. However, they had been available up to a few days before the accident and the plaintiff had never worn one. The court concluded that he would certainly not have worn one had they been available on the day of the accident and that therefore the employer's default had not caused his death. But this is dependent on seeing the default as simple non-provision of the equipment. If there were an obligation to ensure use of safety equipment, the answer would have been different. It is submitted that to require the employer to ensure use of safety equipment would not be unduly onerous, for after all, the employer has supervision systems to make sure that work is being properly carried out, and this would only be one extra thing for a supervisor to check. Naturally it is impossible to guarantee that everyone will always do as they are told, but making non-use of safety equipment a disciplinary offence would be a simple step, and clearly employers who had taken such steps would not be held liable if an employee was injured while not using it.

The contrary view, expressed in *Smith v Scot Bowyers* (1986), is that such a duty would be too vague. While a duty to provide safety equipment has clear boundaries, a duty to encourage, exhort or instruct people to use safety equipment would be indeterminate. However, there have been cases where the employer has been held to be in breach of duty where the employees have not been adequately instructed in the need for and use of such equipment, or where the equipment was awkward to use or impeded work and was not used for that reason (*e.g. Bux v Slough Metals* (1974)). In *Crouch v British Rail Engineering* (1988) a fitter injured his eye when a piece of metal flew off as he was trying to loosen a nut with a hammer and chisel. Goggles were available in the storeroom, as he knew, but that was a five-minute walk away and he would have had to get down from his scaffolding, and the task was one of seconds. In these circumstances the Court of Appeal held that the employer's duty extended to the provision of goggles – an inexpensive and common piece of equipment – into the hand of each worker who might need them. It would have been easy to make it part of his general tool kit. However, the employee was held 50 per cent to blame, since he too could easily have made sure that he had some with him.

Standard of care

14–010 The employer's duty is only to take reasonable care for the safety of employees, not to make them safe at any cost. To trade safety in a cost-benefit analysis may seem distasteful, but it is something we accept in other areas such as road traffic regulation. In *Latimer v AEC* (1953) the factory was flooded in a storm. When the water subsided it left a greasy film over the surface. The employers had three tons of sawdust scattered over the floor to stop it being dangerously slippery, but the employee slipped on an untreated patch and was injured. The House of Lords held that the employers here had done what was reasonable: the only way to make people absolutely safe would have been to close down the factory completely until it had been properly cleaned. This would have been a very expensive course of action; while there remained a risk of injury, the employers had minimised the risk, and the kind of injury risked was not terribly serious. Slipping over is not usually life-threatening. The employers were entitled to balance the cost of a complete shutdown against the risks and keep the factory open. Where there are inherent dangers in the work, the employer may be justified in taking greater risks (*e.g. Watt v Herts C.C.* (1954); *King v Sussex Ambulance NHS Trust* (2002)).

On the other hand, the duty is a personal one, owed to each employee as an individual. It therefore varies according to the personal characteristics of the individual: the duty will be higher in relation to a young worker in her first job than it would be for a skilled worker with many years of experience. The best illustration of this is *Paris v Stepney BC* (1951). The employee, who was blind in one eye, was employed as a maintenance mechanic. He was rendered totally blind when a splinter of metal flew off while he was removing a bolt from a vehicle. It was not normal to provide goggles for this sort of work as the risk of such an accident was very small. However, goggles do not cost much, and the risk to him was much more serious than to an employee with normal sight, for to lose all sight is a greater disaster than to lose sight in one eye. The duty to this particular employee, therefore, was higher and he should have been provided with goggles.

It seems that the employer's obligation does not extend so far as to require dismissal of an employee, even if that is the only way that the particular employee can be made safe (*Withers v Perry Chain* (1961); *Jones v Lionite Specialities* (1961); *Hatton v Sutherland* (2002)). But in *Pape v Cumbria CC* (1991) it was held that a failure to warn employees of a danger which might not be obvious to them was a breach of the duty of care (*cf.* also *Coxall v Goodyear GB Ltd* (2003)). If the employer did dismiss an employee on grounds that his health would suffer if he continued to be employed, it would seem likely that the dismissal would be fair, if properly handled. Does this lead to an unacceptable level of paternalism? In *Page v Freight Hire* (1981) a woman worked as an HGV driver, delivering chemicals. The haulage firm was informed that the chemicals could be dangerous to an unborn child and that therefore a woman of child-bearing age should not be used on this work. The applicant, aged 23 and divorced, stated that she did not intend to have children and was willing to take the risk. It was held that the employer was entitled to remove her from this work in the interests of safety, the EAT saying:

> "We accept that the individual's wishes may be a factor to be looked at, although in our judgment, where the risk is to the woman, of sterility, or to the foetus, whether actually in existence or likely to come into existence in the future, those wishes cannot be a conclusive factor."

The principle of non-delegation

It is axiomatic that the employer may not escape liability for breach of the **14–011** duty of care by showing that someone else was responsible for performance of the duty, even if that person was carefully selected and properly qualified. This is what distinguishes the direct duty of care from the principle of vicarious liability. The clearest statement of this was made in *Wilsons & Clyde Coal Co. v English* (1938), where the employee was crushed when the haulage system in the mine was negligently put into operation as he was walking along a haulage road to get to the surface at the end of his shift. The employer's defence was that they had delegated operation of the haulage system to a qualified manager as they were required to do by statute. The House of Lords held that they retained a primary duty of care to the employee and were liable if it was not discharged, even if they were not themselves actually in charge at the time.

At that time the doctrine of common employment stopped the obvious claim, which would have been that the employers were vicariously liable for the actions of the manager of the haulage system. Today that would be an alternative cause of action for the employee. But the decision has two further implications: firstly, it means that the employer may in some circumstances be held liable for the actions of an independent contractor (compare vicarious liability, below para. 14–013) and secondly, there may well be situations where more than one employer is liable to the employee. Both points are well illustrated by the important decision of the House of Lords in *McDermid v Nash Dredging* (1987). The plaintiff was employed as a deckhand by the defendant company. They lent him to an associated company, Stevin, to work on a dredging contract being carried out off Sweden. The tugmaster, an employee of Stevin, negligently set the tug at full speed while the plaintiff was on deck with the ropes: he became entangled, was pulled overboard, and later had to have a leg amputated. Clearly Stevin was vicariously liable for the negligence of their employee; but there were practical difficulties in the way of suing a Dutch company (as Stevin was) in an English court in respect of an accident happening in Swedish waters. The House of Lords held that the defendant company, his permanent employer, was liable. The accident had happened because there was no safe system of work. The employer's duty to provide a safe system is non-delegable, and it was therefore liable for this failure. The theoretical basis for the employer's liability was the personal duty, not vicarious liability for the negligence of the independent contractor's employee – but the result looks very like vicarious liability for an independent contractor.

In view of the clear reaffirmation of the principle of non-delegation by the House of Lords in *McDermid v Nash Dredging* (1987) it is surprising to find it distinguished by the Court of Appeal in *Square D Ltd v Cook* (1992). In that case, an electronics engineer was sent by his employers to work on a contract in Saudi Arabia, 8,000 miles away. He was injured when he slipped into a hole in the floor made by the employees of a sub-contractor, and sued his own employer, the occupiers of the premises and the main contractor responsible for co-ordinating work on the premises. The Court of Appeal distinguished *McDermid* on the grounds that in that case "the hand of the employers still remained on the operation" in that they were joint contractors and it was only a small team. However, their attitude is indicated by the statement, "the suggestion that the home-based employer has any responsibility for the daily events of a site in Saudi Arabia has an air of unreality". The court seems to have been unduly impressed by the fact that in reality the employer was not in charge of what was going on. But it is clear from the decisions already looked at that this does not absolve the employer of responsibility.

Duty to independent contractors

14–012 In contrast to the relatively high duty of care owed to employees, the employer has no duty beyond the ordinary duty of any individual towards an independent contractor. If independent contractors come to work on the employer's premises, as an occupier the employer is entitled to expect that they will appreciate and guard against any risks relating to their work (Occupiers' Liability Act 1957, s.2(3)) and the only duty is to safeguard them from risks which are not obvious and of which they might otherwise be unaware. So far as the job itself is concerned, independent contractors are meant to take care for their own safety. This was precisely the issue in *Ferguson v Dawson* (1976). If the worker had the status of employee he could sue the employers for his injury, but if he had really been an independent contractor, he should have taken care for his own safety. The position under the Health and Safety at Work Act 1974 is different, as will be seen below, para. 14–022.

398

Vicarious liability

Liability for employees

The second route by which an employee can hold the employer liable for **14–013** injury suffered at work is where the employee alleges that the injury was caused by the negligence of another employee for whom the employer is responsible. Of course, not only employees but also third parties can hold the employer liable on the basis of vicarious liability. In theory, they can also claim against the actual tortfeasor; but in reality it is likely to be the employer rather than the employee who will be worth suing.

Not every action of every employee makes the employer liable. The limitation is that the employee must have been acting in the course of employment at the time of the negligent act. Discerning what is within the contract of employment and what is "a frolic of his own", in the quaint phrase, can be difficult. One way of expressing it is to say that the employer is liable when the employee is performing her duties, even if she is performing them badly, but not when she is doing something entirely outside the scope of the contract. In the old case, *Limpus v London General Omnibus Co.* (1862), bus drivers were specifically forbidden to race drivers from rival companies, but the employer was held liable when a driver engaged in a race caused an accident. He was doing what he was employed to do, but doing it badly. However, it seems that there comes a point where an employee can be performing so badly that it can be said that she is no longer in the course of employment. In *General Engineering Services v Kingston & St Andrew Corp.* (1989) firemen in Jamaica had instituted a go-slow in support of a pay claim. They made a point of not arriving at a fire until the building had substantially burned down. The Privy Council considered that this was action outside their course of employment rather than a defective performance of it. In *Lister v Hesley Hall* (2002) the House of Lords expressed the test in terms of whether or not the employee's tortious action had a "close connection" with what he was employed to do. On that basis, a children's home was held vicariously liable for a warden's sexual abuse of children in his care. In *Mattis v Pollock* (2003) the Court of Appeal went so far as to hold that a nightclub owner was liable for the actions of a bouncer who went home to get a knife before returning and stabbing outside the club a customer who had been part of a group which had earlier attacked the bouncer (*cf.* also *Fennelly v Connex South Eastern Ltd.* (2001)).

In *Rose v Plenty* (1976) a milk roundsman was specifically forbidden to allow children on the float to assist in delivering milk. He nonetheless employed a 13-year-old to help, who was injured while on the float. It was held that the employer was liable. The employee was doing what he was supposed to be doing, albeit the wrong way.

It may seem surprising that the employer was held liable even though the milkman was acting in contravention of a direct instruction. But if employers were not liable in these circumstances, it would be quite easy for them to escape liability by drawing up lengthy and specific codes of conduct for their employees, thus undermining the policy that the employer should absorb losses attributable to activities of the enterprise. Where an employee engages in criminal activity, the employer can be held liable if the employee was entrusted with performance of a duty in the course of which she commits the crime (*Lloyd v Grace, Smith & Co.* (1912)). But there is a distinction between this situation and one where the post merely affords an extra opportunity to commit a crime or tort. In *Heasmans v Clarity Cleaning* (1987) an employee of a company which provided office cleaning services ran up a telephone bill of over £14,000 telephoning the United States while ostensibly cleaning the plaintiff's offices. It was held that this was conduct outside his employment. His job had simply provided the opportunity for him to commit the crime by giving him access to the building. However, employers like this one usually insure against this kind of contingency, precisely because they might be expected to bear the responsibility.

14–014 One of the areas which has been most problematic in relation to vicarious liability has been the employee who gives someone a lift in the employer's vehicle although instructed not to, or who detours for her own purposes while on a journey on the employer's business. Some guidance was given by the House of Lords in *Smith v Stages* (1989), where Lord Goff said, "the fundamental principle is that an employee is acting in the course of his employment when he is doing what he is employed to do . . . or anything which is reasonably incidental to his employment . . .". In relation to travelling, the question is whether or not the employee can be regarded as being "on duty". Travelling to and from work is not usually included, although it could be if the employee is travelling to work in transport provided by the employer. Where the job involves travel, such as delivery drivers, sales representatives or those going out to provide services at the customer's premises, the employee will be in the course of employment. Deviations or interruptions to the journey, unless purely incidental, take the employee outside the course of employment for as long as they last, and no distinction is to be drawn between outward and return journeys. What was actually at issue in the case was whether payment for travelling time indicated that the employee was in the course of employment. The employees, who installed insulation materials, had been sent on an urgent job to Wales. They were paid for 16 hours' travelling time and the cost of a rail fare but it was left to them how they travelled. They went by car. At the end they worked 24 hours to finish the job and then set off immediately to drive back home. The driver, who was uninsured, went off the road. Because they were travelling from a place to which they had been sent especially and also bearing in mind that they were paid for the travelling time, the House of Lords held that they were in the course of employment.

So far as giving lifts is concerned, in *Rose v Plenty* (1976) the Court of Appeal accepted that if this was contrary to instructions it would be outside the course of employment. However, in that case they held that the milkman having the child on the float to assist him was rather a situation of the employee doing wrongly what he was employed to do properly, so the employer was liable. It would be different if a driver employed to make a delivery gave a lift to a hitch-hiker.

Liability for independent contractors

An employer is not usually liable for the actions of independent contrac- **14–015**
tors, which is one of the main reasons for needing to distinguish them from
employees (see above, para. 3–002). However, there are exceptions. If the
employer specifically instructs the contractor to perform the action which is
tortious, she will be liable. Where there is strict liability the employer can
be held responsible for things done by independent contractors. A good
example is *Rylands v Fletcher* (1866) which established the rule of strict
liability for damage done by things escaping from land where their
accumulation was a non-natural user of the land. The landowners had
employed independent contractors to build a reservoir on their land;
through the contractors' negligence the water escaped and flooded a mine
on neighbouring land. The landowners, as employers of the independent
contractors, were held liable. Finally, as seen in *McDermid v Nash Dredging*
(1987) (above, para. 14–011), the employer will remain personally responsible where independent contractors have charge of the safety of the
employer's employees, and in this way will be responsible for their
negligence in this regard.

Liability for breach of statutory duty

The difficulty for the employee who wants to sue her employer for breach **14–016**
of the duty of care is that it is necessary to prove negligence by the
employer or someone for whom the employer is responsible. However, if
the employee can show that the injury was caused by an action which was in
breach of statute or statutory regulation, she will have an alternative claim
for the tort of breach of statutory duty. In this situation all that the
employee has to show is that the breach was the cause of the injury. Thus in
Ferguson v Dawson (1976) the worker fell off a roof which was unfenced in
contravention of statutory regulation. He did not have to show that the
employer was careless in failing to fence the roof: it was enough that the
accident was caused by the breach. (Had Ferguson been an independent
contractor as was argued (see above, para. 3–007), it would have been his
duty to ensure that the roof was fenced, not the employer's.) In many cases
the employee will sue both for negligence and for breach of statutory duty.

The breach of statute or statutory regulation will normally attract some
sanction under the enactment itself – usually criminal liability. Civil liability
for the tort of breach of statute is additional, and is not available in every
case. Sometimes the statute itself will state whether or not a civil action is
possible. A good example is the Health and Safety at Work Act 1974, s.47
which states that breach of the general duties laid down in sections 2–8 of
the statute does not give rise to civil liability, but breach of any regulations
made under the statute will, unless it expressly states otherwise. In the
absence of an express provision it depends on the interpretation of the
statute. In *Lonrho v Shell* (1982) the House of Lords stipulated that for civil
liability it had to be shown either that the relevant provision was intended
for the benefit or protection of a particular class of person including the
plaintiff, or that it creates a public right and this particular plaintiff suffered

damage over and above that suffered by the general public because of its breach. Claims by employees are based on the first of these. In the landmark case, *Groves v Lord Wimborne* (1898), it was held that the precursor of the Factories Act was intended to protect workers and the employer was civilly liable for its breach.

However, not all parts of industrial safety legislation give rise to civil liability. In the interpretation of the Factories Act 1961 a distinction was drawn between the safety provisions (where there was civil liability for breach) and the health and welfare provisions (such as the requirements for washing facilities) where there was not. As the provisions in older legislation are replaced by newer regulations, any uncertainty should diminish, as the position will be clear under new regulations. Finally, the damage suffered by the employee must be caused by the danger to which the provision was addressed. This requirement led to the curious decision in *Close v Steel Co. of Wales* (1962) that the sections in the Factories Act stipulating that dangerous machinery should be fenced were aimed at keeping people out rather than at keeping materials in, and the employee injured by metal flying out did not have a cause of action for breach of statute.

Defences

14–017 There are two particular defences on which an employer faced with liability may seek to rely: contributory negligence and *volenti non fit iniuria*.

Contributory negligence

14–018 At common law, if a claimant claiming for negligence or breach of statutory duty was partly to blame for the accident, this was a complete defence to her claim. This severe rule was mitigated by the Law Reform (Contributory Negligence) Act 1945 which provided that in these circumstances the blame could be apportioned between the parties. Contributory negligence is thus a partial defence for the employer; the court will decide how far the claimant was also at fault and reduce damages by the percentage.

The court is not concerned solely with whether the claimant's conduct actually contributed to the accident but explicitly with how far this was the employee's fault.

> "What is all important is to adapt the standard of what is (contributory) negligence to the facts, and to give due regard to the actual conditions under which men work in a factory or mine, to the long hours and the fatigue, to the slackening of attention which naturally comes from constant repetition of the same operation, to the noise and confusion in which the man works, to his preoccupation in what he is actually doing, at the cost of some inattention to his own safety". (Lord Wright in *Caswell v Powell Duffryn* (1940)).

Consent

If you willingly consent to take a risk you cannot complain if the danger **14–019** materialises: this is the defence expressed in the maxim *volenti non fit iniuria*. It is generally a narrow defence. You do not consent to a risk just because you know about it (*Smith v Baker* (1891)), and even where you consent to a risk you do not consent to its being made worse through someone's negligence. Thus, being a lifeboat crew is more dangerous than being a teacher, and to that extent the crew consent to run a risk: but they would not be taken to have consented if their boat were lost because it had been negligently maintained.

In *Bowater v Rowley Regis Corp.* (1944) Goddard L.J. said that the defence is one which:

> "in the case of master and servant is to be applied with extreme caution. Indeed, I would say that it can hardly ever be applicable where the act to which the servant is said to be 'volens' arises out of his ordinary duty, unless the work for which he is engaged is one in which danger is necessarily involved."

However, one of the very few cases in which the defence has ever succeeded involved employees. In *ICI v Shatwell* (1965) a team of shotfirers were required by regulation only to carry out detonations from behind cover. On one occasion the wire was not long enough for them to get behind cover. One went to get more wire, but while he was away the other two decided to go ahead with the testing in the open. Both were injured in the subsequent explosion, but it was held that the employer was not liable, for with full knowledge of the danger, they had deliberately decided to run the risk.

Statutory Regulation of Health and Safety

In 1970 a Committee on Safety and Health at Work was set up chaired by **14–020** Lord Robens. Amazingly, it was the first time that any committee had been charged with the task of carrying out a comprehensive investigation of occupational health and safety in the United Kingdom. Until then committees or commissions had been instituted on an ad hoc basis, often in response to a disaster arousing public outcry, resulting legislation being entirely reactive in nature.

At the time the Robens Committee was established, there was much criticism of the existing position. Prosecutions for breach of existing legislation were rare, but even when successful, the fines were low. Plants could expect inspection no more frequently than every four years, given the staffing levels in the inspectorates, and in 1969 the Chief Factory Inspector reported that there was no longer a trend for injuries at work to decrease; they seemed to have reached a plateau.

The Robens Committee reported in 1972 (*Report of the Committee on Safety and Health at Work*, Cmnd.5034) and was severely critical of the existing state of affairs in two main respects. First, the fact that the law had evolved in a piecemeal fashion on an industry-by-industry basis meant that existing legislation was badly structured. As well as the main statutes – the Factories Act 1961, the Offices, Shops and Railway Premises Act 1963, the Mines and Quarries Act 1954 and the Agriculture (Safety, Health and Welfare Provisions) Act 1956 – there were another seven or eight major statutes and nearly 500 statutory instruments covering activities at work. Even so, it was estimated that a staggering seven to eight million workers were actually outside the statutory protection while at work. The Robens Committee concluded that the disorganised mass of legislation was counter-productive in that those faced with complying with it were liable to simply throw up the attempt in despair at ever working out exactly what they were meant to do. This led to the first main objective of the Robens Committee: that there should be a unified structure of law and enforcement systems covering everyone at work. But this would be difficult given the variety of needs in different industries. Therefore the Robens Committee decided that what was needed was an umbrella enabling Act, by whose authority specific provision could be made by statutory regulation for particular industries. An advantage over the old system, where requirements were stipulated in Acts of Parliament, is that it is a lot easier to amend statutory instruments than to amend statutes.

The second main problem identified by Robens was apathy. They noted that a large number of accidents each year were the result of stupid and entirely avoidable mistakes. But no one was really interested – not employers, not workers, not trade unions. Everyone was conditioned to thinking of health and safety as matters which were regulated by outside agencies who laid down the rules. They did not regard it as part of their own responsibility. Thus the second major objective for the Robens Committee was to involve everyone in safety issues; to convince all parties that it was their responsibility too. One of the most controversial aspects of the Robens Committee Report was the idea that some aspects of safety could best be dealt with by voluntary codes of practice agreed with industry rather than by detailed regulation.

14–021 The result of the Robens Committee Report was the Health and Safety at Work, etc., Act 1974 (HSWA). The only way in which the Robens objective of a unified structure could be achieved was by making it a general enabling statute, with power devolved to the Secretary of State for Employment to make regulations to flesh out the detail (HSWA, s.15). This meant that existing legislation was not repealed: it remained in place unless and until it was replaced by new regulations made under the authority of the HSWA. The same technique has been adopted at European Union level, with a Framework Directive on Health and Safety (89/391/EEC) followed by more specific directives, and their absorption into British law was easier because of this model.

The Health and Safety at Work, etc., Act begins with certain general duties relating to health and safety which apply not only to employers but also to workers. These establish a framework under which, as envisaged by the Robens Committee, three kinds of regulations can be drawn up: firstly, regulations about general matters, applicable to all kinds of employment (*e.g.* the Health and Safety (First-Aid) Regulations 1981); secondly, regulations about hazards which can occur in several industries (*e.g.* the Control of Substances Hazardous to Health Regulations 2002); thirdly, regulations dealing with hazards encountered in a particular kind of industry or activity.

The general duties

The general duties are set out in HSWA, ss.2–7 and, in so far as they relate **14–022** to employers, bear a striking resemblance to the threefold common law duty of care. There is no civil liability for breach of the regulations, however (s.47(1)); the sanction is criminal prosecution only (s.33).

Under section 2 an employer is enjoined to ensure "so far as is reasonably practicable" the health, safety and welfare of all employees. This specifically includes a safe system of work, safe equipment and a safe working environment. It also includes provision of information, training and supervision so far as necessary to ensure safety. Under section 3, employers and independent contractors have duties to make sure that they conduct their undertakings to ensure the safety also of third parties (who could be employees of another employer, independent contractors or the general public). Designers, manufacturers, importers and suppliers of articles for use at work have a general duty imposed on them by section 6 to ensure that the article will be safe, and section 7 imposes on employees themselves a general duty to take reasonable care of safety – both in relation to their own safety and to that of others who may be affected by their actions. All are subject to the qualification "so far as is reasonably practicable".

While framed in a similar way to the common law duty of care, important differences should be noted. In particular, it is clear that HSWA, s.3 imposes a much more extensive duty on employers in respect of independent contractors than is the case at common law. This was clearly stated by the House of Lords in *R. v Associated Octel* (1997). The company ran a large chemical plant, designated as a "major hazard site" by the HSE. The employee of an independent contractor taken on for specialist repair work was badly burned when fire broke out in a tank which he was inside repairing. He was working by the light of an electric bulb and had an open bucket full of acetone, giving off highly inflammable vapour. The light bulb broke and ignited the vapour. He could have had the acetone in a sealed container, the light unit could have been sealed and there could have been a ventilation system to prevent a build-up of vapour. The company was convicted under section 3, but appealed on the basis that the independent contractor was solely responsible for the conduct of the repair work.

The House of Lords stated that section 3 was not about common law vicarious liability, where the question of who had control of an employee can be crucial. The issue, in their view, was purely whether the activity in question could be regarded as part of the employer's undertaking. If so, it was within the employer's responsibility under section 3. This is essentially a question of fact for the trial court, but the House of Lords pointed out that the conduct of the undertaking included not only running it, but also cleaning, repairs and maintenance, at least when on the employer's premises. Thus the company was properly convicted.

Similarly, in *R. v Gateway Food Markets Ltd* (1997) the Court of Appeal held that the principle that a company should only be criminally liable for actions of someone who can be regarded as the "directing mind" of the company was not appropriate in deciding whether a company had committed an offence under HSWA, s.2 or s.3. The issue was only whether there had been a failure to ensure health and safety within the undertaking, so the company could be criminally liable for the actions of its store managers. However, the company may make out a defence that it has ensured safety "so far as is reasonably practicable" if it has proper control and safety systems and does everything possible to ensure that employees act in accordance with them (*R. v Nelson Group Services (Maintenance) Ltd* (1998)).

The Health and Safety Commission and Executive

14–023   From the seven or so inspectorates responsible for enforcing previous legislation, a single agency was created. The Health and Safety Commission consists of a chairperson appointed by the Secretary of State and six to nine members, who include employer and worker representatives (s.10). The HSC has general duties of promoting occupational health and safety, control of explosives, dangerous substances and emissions into the atmosphere, carrying out research and training, providing an advisory service, issuing and approving codes of practice and submitting proposals for regulations.

It may institute investigations whenever it thinks it necessary or expedient and has wide powers, including powers of entry and inspection, to enable it to exercise its rights. In effect, the HSC is charged with taking a proactive role to improve safety standards throughout industry. It may set up committees in order to have specialist advice on particular matters, and has in fact set up a number of advisory committees on things like Major Hazards and Dangerous Substances.

Enforcement is in the hands of the Health and Safety Executive. The HSE consists of a Director appointed by the Secretary of State, and two other members appointed by the Secretary of State after consultation with the Director. It controls the now unified inspectorate and is responsible for enforcing the legislation. The inspectorates operate through a regional structure with area offices. The Employment Medical Advisory Service, established in 1972, is now part of the Executive. Inevitably the effectiveness of enforcement depends to some extent on how likely it is that employers will get caught if they do not comply. During the 1970s and 1980s the number of inspectors dropped, until in 1982, when there were 742 inspectors, one study estimated that premises were likely to be inspected only once every seven years. In 2002 there were 1,625 inspectors.

Improvement notices and prohibition notices

Novel enforcement powers were granted to inspectors under HSWA, ss.21– **14–024**
24. An inspector has the power under section 21 to issue an improvement
notice where she believes that a person is contravening relevant statutory
provisions or has done so and is likely to repeat the contravention. The
notice must specify the violation, set out the reasons for the inspector's
belief and what must be done to remedy it within a stated period.

In effect this provision formalised what was the practice of many
inspectors already. While they have been criticised for not bringing more
prosecutions, one answer to that is that it takes up an awful lot of staff time
which could better be spent on prevention. Further, the deterrent effect of
the fear of prosecution and resulting bad publicity could be lost if every
violation were prosecuted. Seeing their ultimate aim as prevention of
accidents, inspectors would rather point out what is wrong and warn the
employer that prosecution will follow if it is not put right.

An employer served with an improvement notice has a right of appeal to
an employment tribunal. The notice is suspended until the appeal has been
dealt with.

A more powerful weapon still is the prohibition notice (s.22). Where the
inspector believes that the activity being carried on involves a risk of serious
personal injury, she may issue a prohibition notice which can have the
effect of stopping the activity at once. It is not actually required that there
should be a breach of any statutory provision. As with the improvement
notice, certain information must be provided in writing to the employer and
there is a right of appeal to the industrial tribunal. However, in this case,
the appeal does not suspend the notice, unless the tribunal is prepared to
make an order to that effect.

These enforcement powers have been regarded as successful, to the
extent that the strategy has been copied in other legislation (*e.g.* the
Consumer Protection Act 1987, ss.13–15).

Regulations and Codes of Practice

The Secretary of State has power to make regulations, either on the **14–025**
proposal of the Commission or after consultation with it (s.15). Relevant
bodies should also be consulted before regulations are made. Recently
important sets of regulations have been made which apply to all workplaces, thus bringing a welcome uniformity in line with the basic Robens
philosophy. The most important are the Control of Substances Hazardous
to Health Regulations 2002 (COSHH), but other examples include the
Health and Safety Information for Employees Regulations 1989 and the
Noise at Work Regulations 1989. Breach of regulations made under the
HSWA will attract civil liability for breach of statutory duty unless the
regulations specifically exclude it (s.47(2)).

Under section 16 the Commission has power to issue and approve codes
of practice "for the purpose of providing practical guidance" in relation to
the general duties in sections 2–7 or any other matters covered by the
legislation. The idea here was no doubt to try and involve employers and

407

workers in safety issues rather than reinforce the view that safety standards are imposed from outside. The criticism that the provision attracted was that codes of practice could lead to a lowering of standards as employers would not be too demanding of themselves. Further, breach of a code would not attract criminal sanctions in the way breach of regulations would. However, section 1(2) of the Act referred to codes and regulations being prepared in order to "maintain and improve" existing standards, which seems to offer a safeguard against a reduction in standards.

Safety representatives and safety committees

14–026 As part of the battle against apathy and in pursuit of the policy of involvement, employers have a duty to prepare a written statement of health and safety policy and to revise it as necessary (s.2(3)). Another major plank in this policy was the provision of a right for employees to have their own safety representatives who could consult with the employer. However, the initial provision, which would have permitted employees to elect non-union representatives in some circumstances, were scotched by trade unions, who were concerned that the use of any conduit for representing employees other than a trade union would be the thin end of the wedge undermining the role of the union. Hence the Act was amended in 1975 with the result that only recognised trade unions have the right to appoint safety representatives. Unfortunately, this meant that representation was denied to those employees whose need for it was arguably the greatest. Thus in the wake of the Piper Alpha disaster in 1988, when 167 people were killed as a result of an explosion on a North Sea oil platform, special regulations for safety representatives and safety committees had to be made (Offshore Installations (Safety Representatives and Safety Committees) Regulations 1989).

Following the decision in *EC Commission v UK* (1994), where it was held that consultation with recognised trade unions was not sufficient to discharge obligations to consult with employees under the Collective Dismissals and Acquired Rights Directives (above, para. 9–039) it became clear that the limitation of the rules on safety representatives to recognised trade unions must similarly be in breach of the Framework Health and Safety Directive (89/391/EEC) and so the Health and Safety (Consultation with Employees) Regulations 1996 were passed. Unlike the equivalent rules for consultation over transfers and redundancies, these do not replace the existing law, but introduce a new regime only for those employees where the Safety Representatives and Safety Committees Regulations 1977 do not apply: *i.e.* where there is no recognised trade union. This is because the requirements of the Framework Directive could be satisfied by granting lesser powers to representatives than those enjoyed under the 1977 Regulations, and the then Conservative Government was very anxious that there should be "no gold-plating" of European Union law requirements.

Under the Safety Representatives and Safety Committees Regulations 1977, safety representatives should investigate potential hazards and dangerous occurrences at the workplace; investigate complaints from employees relating to health and safety; and make representations on these matters to the employer and to the health and safety inspectors. They are entitled to carry out inspections of the workplace at a minimum of three-monthly intervals and on some other occasions also (reg.5) and they are entitled to inspect and take copies of relevant documents. If two safety representatives so request in writing, the employer must establish a safety committee which can keep policy and practice under review. Under the Health and Safety (Consultation with Employees) Regulations 1996, employers must consult either with employees directly or else with their elected representatives over: the introduction of any measure or any new technology which might affect health and safety; appointments under the Management of Health and Safety at Work Regulations 1999; information which it is required by law to provide; and health and safety training. The employer must make available to them such information as they need in order to participate fully and effectively in such consultation. The major differences from the Safety Representatives and Safety Committees Regulations are that there is no entitlement to a standing safety committee and no entitlement to carry out inspections.

Both kinds of safety representative are entitled to necessary time off with pay for the purposes of carrying out their functions or receiving training in relation to their functions. There are two Codes of Practice – Safety Representatives and Safety Committees (1978) and Time Off for the Training of Staff Representatives (1978) – which amplify these provisions, but only in relation to representatives appointed under the 1977 Regulations. Both kinds are protected from dismissal and detriment while carrying out their duties (ERA, ss.44, 100). The expansion of the law to all workplaces is to be welcomed, and it is hoped that the broader provisions in the 1977 Regulations will eventually be extended as well. In 2003, discussions were under way on combining and extending the consultation regulations into a single code.

Influence of the European Union

As the above indicates, directives and regulations from the EU covering **14–027** health and safety matters are increasingly important in this area. Article 137 of the Treaty of Rome states that:

> "the Community shall support and complement the activities of Member States in ... improvement in particular of the working environment to protect workers' health and safety".

Directives under Article 137 may be adopted according to the qualified majority voting procedure. In 1989 a Framework Directive on health and safety in the working environment was adopted (89/391/EEC), and a large number of other directives have been adopted under this. Six important sets of statutory regulations (dubbed "the six-pack") came into force at the beginning of 1993, designed to implement these. The most wide-ranging are the Management of Health and Safety at Work Regulations 1999, implementing the substantive provisions of the Framework Directive. The regulations require employers to carry out an assessment of the risks to health and safety arising out of the conduct of the undertaking, including risks to non-employees as well as employees. The employer is also obliged to make effective arrangements for the oversight of health and safety matters, including where necessary the appointment of a competent person to assist and in particular encompassing procedures for dealing with serious and imminent dangers. There is a duty to provide information to employees on all these matters. In effect, the regulations lay down general principles of good health and safety practice (amplified by a code of practice) and further the Robens philosophy of involving the consumers of health and safety in the devising of appropriate rules. Originally it was specifically provided that there would be no civil liability for breach of these regulations, but this was amended by the Management of Health and Safety at Work and Fire Precautions (Workplace) (Amendment) Regulations 2003 so that employees (but not third parties) may now bring civil claims based on a breach of the regulations.

Similarly, the Workplace (Health, Safety and Welfare) Regulations 1992 (implementing Directive 89/654/EEC), which lay down general principles about the safety, cleanliness, and maintenance of workplaces, including heating, lighting and ventilation, apply across the board to all workplaces, as do the Provision and Use of Work Equipment Regulations 1998 (implementing Directive 89/655/EEC). Breach of these will give rise to civil liability, as it is not specifically excluded, and have applied to existing workplaces since January 1996. The other sets of regulations in this group are the Manual Handling Operations Regulations 1992, the Personal Protective Equipment at Work Regulations 2002 and the Health and Safety (Display Screen Equipment) Regulations 1992 – the VDU regulations. All again carry the possibility of civil liability for their breach.

It seems likely that legislation from the European Union will continue to be a major source of developments in health and safety law in the twenty-first century.

Conclusions

14–028 A number of tragic disasters in recent years have put health and safety at the top of the agenda. The sinking of the *Herald of Free Enterprise*, the King's Cross fire, the Clapham rail crash, the sinking of the *Marchioness* on the Thames, the explosion on the Piper Alpha platform, the Paddington rail crash and the Potters Bar rail crash all led to calls for a re-examination of how safety matters should be dealt with. Inquiries following these disasters have often revealed systemic errors rather than a one-off mistake. There is always room for improvement in training and observance of safety standards. However, many commentators argue that in the absence of criminal prosecution of companies themselves and the senior people running those companies, there will be no real incentive to improve. This has been under consideration for some years. The arguments for and against corporate criminal responsibility are outside the scope of this work, but clearly safety at work is an issue which employers, trade unions and workers need to address with the utmost seriousness.

Index